ORWELL

ORWELL

The Authorised Biography

MICHAEL SHELDEN

POLITICO'S

1005019635

First published by William Heinemann 1991

Copyright © Michael Shelden 1991

Published 2006 by
Politico's Publishing, an imprint of
Methuen Publishing Limited
11–12 Buckingham Gate
London SW1E 6LB

Methuen Publishing Limited Reg. No. 3543167

A CIP catalogue record for this book is available from the British Library

10 9 8 7 6 5 4 3 2 1

ISBN 1 84275 173 5

Printed and bound in Great Britain by
St. Edmundsbury Press, Bury St. Edmunds, Suffolk

To the memory of
L. W. Mitchell,
my grandfather
(1898 – 1972)

Contents

A Note on Names

Writing this book would have been a little easier if Eric Blair had chosen to write his books under his own name. How should a biographer refer to him? Should one call him Blair or Orwell? He was nearly thirty when he decided to make George Orwell his pseudonym, but he never legally adopted it, and his family and oldest friends never stopped using his real name.

I call him by both names. In the early chapters I try to maintain a sharp distinction between the life of the young person named Eric Blair and the later reflections on that life by the writer known as George Orwell. But at the point in the story when Blair chooses his pseudonym, I close the gap and almost always refer to the man and the writer by one name only – Orwell.

Introduction

George Orwell did not expect to be so successful. In fact, he spent much of his life anticipating failure. In his long essay about his schooldays, 'Such, Such Were the Joys', he wrote, 'Until I was about thirty I always planned my life on the assumption . . . that any major undertaking was bound to fail.' He wanted success and worked diligently to achieve it, but he was never quite able to surrender the notion that his efforts would always come up short. At forty-six, when he was dying of tuberculosis, he confided in his private notebook that a deep sense of inadequacy had haunted him throughout his career. 'There has literally been not one day in which I did not feel that I was idling, that I was behind with the current job, & that my total output was miserably small.' Even in the first months after the tremendous success of *Animal Farm*, he was quick to discount his achievement, declaring in 'Why I Write' that his next book was 'bound to be a failure, every book is a failure'.

Of course, no conscientious author is ever completely satisfied with his work, but Orwell's doubts were so persistent that he often appeared more comfortable admitting defeat than acknowledging success. In 1940, shortly after the publication of his eighth book, he responded to an admiring letter from another writer by going out of his way to show the man why he was not worthy of his praise: 'It makes me laugh to see you referring to me as "famous" and "successful". I wonder if you know what my books sell – usually about 2000! My best book, the one about the Spanish war, sold less than 1000, but by that time people were fed up with Spanish war books, as well they might be.'[1] He seems here to be boasting about the dismal sales of his 'best book', as though he wants to wear his failure as a badge of honour. Certainly very few writers would admit so freely that even when they had tried to make a splash, they had barely produced a ripple. And few writers would volunteer the sales figures of their books if those numbers were as low as Orwell's.

In the same year an American biographical dictionary, *Twentieth Century Authors*, asked him for a short summary of his life, and he complied by contributing an eccentric document that mentions each of his major achievements and adventures, and then immediately undercuts them with some admission of failure or weakness. He was educated at Eton, he says, but quickly adds, 'I did no work there and learned very little.' He served with the Indian Imperial Police in Burma, but the climate had 'ruined' his health, and in any case there was no honour in having served the 'racket' of imperialism. He spent a year and a half writing fiction in Paris, but no publisher would accept any of his work. He fought in the Spanish Civil War, but the experience had given him 'a horror of politics'. Told in this way, his life seems to be full of disappointment and defeat, and he closes his account by implying that he is in semi-retreat from the world. Of his life in recent months, he remarks, 'I cannot honestly say that I have done anything except write books and raise hens and vegetables.'[2]

In part his self-portrait merely reflects Orwell's modesty and his fondness for understatement, but it also reveals more than a little fondness for playing the part of the enigmatic, failed writer. The photograph above his entry in *Twentieth Century Authors* is a gloomy one which Orwell himself recommended to the publishers. It is essentially a black box with a small pool of light at the centre exposing the rough features of an obscured face. Orwell is recognisable, but just barely. His eyes are cast downward, his neck is almost entirely hidden inside his shirt and his full head of hair is all but invisible.

Playing the loser was a form of revenge against the winners, a way of repudiating the corrupt nature of conventional success – the scheming, the greed, the sacrifice of principles. Yet it was also a form of self-rebuke, a way of keeping one's own pride and ambition in check. And Orwell did indeed have his pride and ambition. In the very year that he was presenting himself to *Twentieth Century Authors* as a gardener and chicken-farmer who also happened to write books from time to time, he was in fact maintaining a punishing pace of literary activity, turning out a total of eighty essays and reviews for a variety of London periodicals, including the *Adelphi*, *Horizon*, the *Listener*, the *New English Weekly*, the *New Statesman*, *Time and Tide* and *Tribune*. Some of this was done simply because he had needed the money, and some of it because he had felt a burning desire to speak his mind. But he was also doing what all ambitious writers – rich or poor – do: he was promoting his career by keeping his name in print in as many places as possible.

He drove himself relentlessly to make his mark as a writer, yet he was always doubting whether he had done enough to earn a respectable reputation, or even whether a respectable reputation was worth achieving. Of course, his behaviour is contradictory, but he thrived on contradiction. It is everywhere in his life and work. He called himself a socialist, yet he was always pointing out weaknesses in socialism. He devoted enormous effort to writing his novels, yet admitted near the end of his life, 'I am not a real novelist anyway.'[3] He was an intellectual who ran a small village shop and referred to himself as a 'grocer'; he was an ex-policeman who lived among tramps; he was an inveterate reviewer who complained that reviewing damaged a writer's soul. He liked to expose flaws in the works of great writers and to praise signs of greatness in the works of minor ones. He had a keen appetite for a literary contradiction which he called, borrowing the phrase from G. K. Chesterton, the 'good bad book'.

Whatever the subject, Orwell was always tempted to look at it from both sides. And when he considered another point of view, he did not usually do it half-heartedly. He became immersed in it and used all the powers of his imagination to identify with it. This ability allowed him to see what others ignored and to challenge comfortable assumptions. It is one of the sources of his greatness as a writer. But it also helps to explain why, whenever he turned a critical eye on his own work, he had no trouble finding faults and imagining the worst about his career.

He wrote in a style which seems 'plain' at first glance, but which is, in fact, the product of a highly sophisticated artistic process. Anyone who doubts this sophistication should try imitating his style for a page or two. At his best he makes writing look easy, but no one should underestimate his mastery of English prose. He loved the sound of 'mere words' and cultivated his style with devotion. Language was one of the things that made life worth living. 'So long as I remain alive and well,' he said in 'Why I Write', 'I shall continue to feel strongly about prose style, to love the surface of the earth, and to take pleasure in solid objects and scraps of useless information.'

Lionel Trilling was wrong when he praised Orwell's 'plainness' as an example of what ordinary writers could achieve if they tried to do their best. 'He is not a genius – what a relief!' Trilling said of Orwell.[4] It is true that Orwell was not a great novelist, but it is a mistake to deny his genius as a prose stylist. In his large body of work – thirteen books and hundreds of essays and reviews – he created a literary voice which is one of the most compelling in the history of English prose. He demands to be read. There is no one else like him.

The rich complexity of his character makes him a fascinating subject for a biography, but he was opposed to the idea and said so in his will. He gave no reason. His widow, Sonia, who had married him only three months before his death and who was fifteen years his junior, had her opinions, one of which was, 'He believed there is nothing about a writer's life that is relevant to a judgement of his work.'[5] He thought that a writer's aesthetic merits and his moral behaviour should be judged separately, as he explained in an essay on Salvador Dali: 'One ought to be able to hold in one's head simultaneously the two facts that Dali is a good draughtsman and a disgusting human being. The one does not invalidate or, in a sense, affect the other.'[6] But this does not mean that biography – even

4

when it reveals very intimate details of personal problems – is irrelevant to an understanding of a writer's work. In 1944, reviewing a new biography of Baudelaire, Orwell complained:

> What is one to think of a 'life' of Baudelaire which never once mentions that Baudelaire was syphilitic? ... This is not merely a piece of scandal: it is a point upon which any biographer of Baudelaire must make up his mind. For the nature of the disease has a bearing not only on the poet's mental condition during his last year but on his whole attitude to life.[7]

It is easy to make such an argument about another writer's biography, but one's own life is a different matter. Orwell was a private man and the thought of a biographer digging into his past would not have pleased him. He was probably convinced also that no biographer would understand him and would convey a misleading impression to readers. He knew how critical he could be of himself, and he could well imagine the extent to which an unsympathetic biographer might twist facts. Even a very sympathetic one would have some disturbing private details to reveal if the research were done honestly and thoroughly. In the 1940s Orwell told his young housekeeper, Susan Watson, that he was the only person who could do the story of his life properly, but that he would never attempt it because, as he explained it to her, 'in an autobiography you had to tell the whole truth'.[8] And the truth must sting. 'Autobiography is only to be trusted when it reveals something disgraceful,' Orwell wrote in his essay on Dali.

Whether certain facts sting or not, the story of his life deserves to be told with as much accuracy and fairness as possible. His life matters because his work matters, and there is no point in pretending that the two things are unconnected. Books are not written by machines in sealed compartments. The writer's character and personal history influence what he writes and how he writes it, and the more we know about him, the better we are able to appreciate his work. No biography of Orwell would be necessary if his worst fears of failure had been realised. Instead he succeeded beyond anything he could imagine, and the continuing growth of his fame is one justification for this book.

II

Others have come before me. Peter Stansky and William Abrahams wrote two short volumes of an Orwell biography in the 1970s, taking his life up to the period of the Spanish Civil War. They had the support of several of Orwell's friends and his one surviving sister, but Sonia Orwell was adamantly opposed and refused to allow them to quote from her late husband's works. Nevertheless, they produced a well-written, lively account of the early life and career, with good comments from a wide range of interviews. But nothing can compensate for the fact that the voice of the principal character is mostly mute. Only here and there can it be heard in tiny snatches quoted in defiance of Sonia's ban. As one reviewer pointed out, it was like *Hamlet* without the Prince of Denmark.

When the first volume appeared, Sonia went to the trouble of warning readers against it in the pages of the *Times Literary Supplement*, declaring that it was written against her approval and that it contained 'mistakes and misconceptions'. Because she did not want it to 'stand as the only existing biography', she decided to commission an 'official' life, and the man she chose for the job was Bernard Crick, a professor of politics at the University of London.[9] She knew nothing about him, but had been impressed by his review of a collection of essays on Orwell edited by her friend Miriam Gross. He was given access to Orwell's surviving papers and was allowed to quote as much as he wanted, but when Sonia read the biography, she was deeply disappointed by it. She condemned it as too political, too dry and too unsympathetic, and tried to stop it from being published. She wanted to break her legal agreement with him, but he held her to it and proceeded with his plans for publication. 'She wasn't in a good position,' Crick later wrote. 'She had actually lost the contract, her agent had never seen it, and she had had to ring me up to get a copy to take advice on how to break it; so the threat wasn't as seriously [*sic*] as it sounded. And my small solicitor . . . had done his work well. It withstood the scrutiny of the big boys.'[10] Though Sonia continued to complain bitterly about the biography to anyone who would listen, there was little she could do to prevent it coming out. By the time it was being printed, she was very ill with cancer, and she died near the date of its publication, at the end of 1980.

Crick's biography is a large collection of facts which relies heavily on the notion that facts speak for themselves if presented in enough detail. He keeps a safe distance between himself and his subject, reporting Orwell's actions without commenting much on the motives and feelings behind them. It is impossible to understand another person's inner life, he argues in his introduction, so it is best to avoid discussions of personal character and to focus instead on 'a subject's public life'. He believes that 'the main tale' in Orwell's case 'must be of how his books and essays came to be written and of how they were published'. If this sounds like a dull tale, Crick has no apologies for creating that effect. 'An honest biographer must be more dull than he could be,' he says.

In practice his method results in a large number of facts being given attention for their own sake, as in his list of the number of hangings which took place in Burma while Orwell was a policeman there. Orwell says that he saw a hanging, so which one was it? 'It could have been any one of the 116 hangings in 1923, the 145 in 1924, the 162 in 1925, or the 191 in 1927.' There seems to be no purpose to this list except to highlight the extent of Crick's research. Although it is certainly true that a great many executions took place in Burma, a detailed list for each year sheds no light on the hanging which Orwell witnessed.[11]

Some facts are indispensable, but so are some matters of character and spirit, which cannot be weighed and measured. To pretend that Orwell's inner life is secondary to events in his public life is to reduce him to the level of a dry functionary. He was not a bloodless writer of dreary social tracts, and his life was anything but dull. Although he was quiet and reserved, he was motivated by strong passions, and no biography can do justice to his story by deliberately downplaying the importance of those passions.

A biography is not a textbook. It must have a strong narrative, and it must provide some sense of the human character behind the public face. That character must come to life on the page, not through some literary trickery, but by the biographer's willingness to look at the world through his subject's eyes, and to convey that experience to the reader. It requires an extension of sympathy and imagination, but that does not mean inventing information or withholding criticism. At its most basic level, it is simply the act of one person trying to understand another person's life. Doing that means keeping an open mind. There is nothing to be gained from imposing rigid methods of interpretation, looking for certain patterns where none exists. Every life is full of pieces that do not fit.

My book is an authorised biography, but the views expressed are entirely my own, and no one attempted to steer me in a special direction or to discourage me from following a particular line of thought. Orwell's current literary executor is the London agent Mark Hamilton, and I am happy to say that he allowed me to pursue the story of Orwell's life with complete independence. I was able to see all the available documents and to ask any questions I considered appropriate, even when they touched on delicate subjects.

Readers of the previous biographies will find a great deal of new information in this book. In fact, there is something new on practically every phase of Orwell's life. I interviewed nearly seventy people, many of whom were not contacted by other biographers or scholars. Almost everyone on my list was able to provide some fresh details or helpful insights. The list includes two close friends from his childhood; former pupils at his preparatory school; Old Etonians who were in College with him; two men who served with him in Burma; a girlfriend who knew him in his tramping days; an old pupil from the small school outside London where he taught in the early Thirties; a former assistant at the Hampstead bookshop where he worked; friends and relatives of his first wife, Eileen; old comrades from the Spanish Civil War, including the captain of his unit; a former patient at a tuberculosis sanatorium where he spent six months in 1938; literary friends such as Anthony Powell and

Stephen Spender; one of his secretaries at the BBC; his adopted son; a woman who rejected a marriage proposal from him in the Forties; and various friends and relatives of Sonia.

Some previously unknown documents have come to light. They include a number of important records from his preparatory school, which provide a fresh background for understanding 'Such, Such Were the Joys'; a very candid letter giving evidence of his romantic attachments to other boys at Eton; records in the India Office Library that alter the conventional view of his service in Burma; a copy of *Down and Out in Paris and London* with handwritten annotations by Orwell indicating how much of the book is based on real events; a detailed set of his medical records which provides insight into his early struggles with tuberculosis and other illnesses; evidence of a possible affair between his first wife and one of his commanders in the Spanish Civil War; a security police report from archives in Madrid confirming his fears that he was in grave danger of being arrested during his final weeks in Spain; and the first detailed information about the secret list of Communist sympathisers which Orwell compiled in the last years of his life.

This book also draws on many previously unpublished letters from Orwell, his first wife and other friends and family members. In previous accounts of their marriage, Eileen has seemed a faceless, dull character, but she was an exceptionally bright, vibrant woman and the evidence of her letters will help to bear this out. Another important collection is Orwell's extensive correspondence with his literary agent, Leonard Moore, a large portion of which was missing until only a few years ago. There are nearly a hundred 'new' letters to Moore, all of which can be found in the Lilly Library at Indiana University. The letters provide a vital source of information about the author's career, especially with regard to his often difficult relations with the publisher Victor Gollancz, and they shed light on many aspects of Orwell's personal life. Recent discoveries of numerous letters and documents in the BBC Written Archives Centre are also an interesting source, providing some new details about his two years of frustrating employment as a radio talks producer.

It should be clear that there is no lack of new material to justify another biography. As the notes at the back of the book will show, the abundance is much greater than I have been able to indicate here. But an entire train load of documents is not enough to make a good biography if they serve only to bury the subject beneath mounds of facts. A little space has to be cleared from time to time for another glimpse of Orwell's elusive figure.

CHAPTER ONE

First Impressions

I

In the early summer of 1939, Richard Walmesley Blair, aged eighty-two, was slowly dying from cancer at his home in Southwold, on the Suffolk coast. His family was at his side, including his only son, Eric, with whom his relations had long been strained. His son had disappointed him some years earlier by abandoning a well-paid position in the Indian Imperial Police for an uncertain career as a writer. The old man was himself a retired colonial official – a veteran of more than thirty-five years of service in British India – and he was never able to understand why Eric had decided to turn his back on the Empire. As one who seldom read anything more substantial than the daily newspaper, he did not appreciate his son's love of literature and saw no future in a life devoted to writing books. He gave him no encouragement and showed little enthusiasm when the first book – *Down and Out in Paris and London* – was published in 1933. There is no evidence that he cared one way or the other that it came out under the pen-name of George Orwell, though in the case of the second book – *Burmese Days* – he must have been relieved not to have the family name associated with its harsh criticism of imperialism.

In the last months of his life, however, his opinion of his son's career changed for the better. It was difficult not to respect the young man's uncompromising dedication to his work and his extraordinary productivity – by 1939 he had seven books to his credit. Moreover, his father could not ignore the growing number of critics in the national press who had given the books high praise. A few days before his death Mr Blair was told that his son's latest novel – *Coming Up for Air* – had been favourably reviewed in the *Sunday Times*. Indeed, it was called 'brilliant', and the headline proclaimed 'MR GEORGE ORWELL'S SUCCESS'. He asked to hear the review, and the words were read aloud to him. They were the last the dying man would hear. Orwell recalled the scene in a letter written shortly afterwards: 'Curiously enough his last moment of consciousness was hearing that review I had in the Sunday Times. He heard about it and wanted to see it, and my sister took it in and read it to him, and a little later he lost consciousness for the last time.' It was some comfort to know that his father had finally shown a little interest in his chosen career. As he remarked in his letter, 'I am very glad that latterly he had not been so disappointed in me as before.'[1]

Eric Blair had always desired his father's good opinion, but he had never been able to establish a close relationship with him, in large part because they had spent so little time together during Eric's childhood. Until he was eight he barely saw his father, who was away in India. By the time Mr Blair returned home to enjoy his retirement, his son was away at boarding school, and their subsequent time together during school holidays was short and generally uncomfortable. Looking back on this period, Orwell wrote that his father had appeared to him 'simply as a gruff-voiced elderly man forever saying "Don't" '.[2]

It did not help that the father was so much older than the son. He was very much a Victorian figure, and the age difference between them amounted to almost half a century. He was born on 7 January 1857. George Gissing, the Victorian novelist whose work would later be a source of so much fascination for Orwell, was born in the same year. The Crimean War had recently ended, Lord Palmerston was Prime Minister and Queen Victoria was preparing to give birth to the last of her nine children. Charles Dickens was writing *Little Dorrit*, Thomas Hardy was still in his teens and George Bernard Shaw was only six months old. Like Shaw, Richard Blair would lead a life so long that it would take him from the dawn of the railway age to the dawn of the nuclear age.

Yet he was hardly the kind of person who welcomed change. He was a reserved, cautious, deeply conservative man who liked to keep his life within the confines of an undemanding routine. His abilities were modest, his habits moderate, his opinions conventional. Driven by no strong ambitions or passions, he took few risks and avoided confrontation. Throughout his adult life he maintained the carefully composed exterior of a faithful bureaucrat. His appearance was immaculate. He wore crisp, well-tailored clothes, and had a sturdy build, a firm jaw and a pair of deep-set blue eyes. His favourite pastimes were golf and bridge. In old age he kept a reserved seat at his local cinema and dutifully sat through each new film, regardless of its quality. In the words of one family member, he was a 'superbly unadventurous' man.[3]

He came from a large family. The youngest of ten children, he was born in Milborne St Andrew, Dorset, where his father was the vicar. In the eighteenth century the Blairs had been a prosperous family with aristocratic connections. Richard's great-grandfather had married a daughter of the Earl of Westmorland, and had enjoyed the income from several lucrative properties in Jamaica. But little of this wealth had trickled down to Richard's father, who led a simple, quiet life in his country parish. He died when Richard was ten, leaving only a small income for his family's support. At eighteen Richard had to make his own way in the world, and he chose to do it in the service of the Empire.

Many imperial paths were open to him. The Army was perhaps the most obvious choice, but if he had been really ambitious, he might have tried to enter the exalted ranks of the Indian Civil Service, which was limited to about one thousand carefully selected men. They held the top administrative posts in the various provinces of the sub-continent, and were widely admired for their efficiency and integrity. Below them were the specialised services – the police, the civil engineers, the forest service, etc. It was at this second tier of the bureaucracy that young Richard found a place. With a little help from a family friend in London, he managed to secure a position in the least distinguished, most obscure branch of the specialised services – the Opium Department.

In one brief autobiographical note from 1947, Orwell refers vaguely to his father's years as 'an official in the English administration' of India.[4] Orwell never wrote anything more specific about the job, but it was not something which he could have described with pride. Other writers have given the impression that his father was a sort of policeman engaged in a benign supervision of the native drug trade. But the truth is that Mr Blair spent his entire working life helping to perpetuate one of the worst evils of the British colonial system.

Although the high-minded Victorian defenders of imperialism were reluctant to admit it, British India profited enormously from the sale of opium. It was legally available in India, but the real money came from exports to China. When Richard Blair began his new job in 1875, the government opium monopoly in Bengal was producing 4000 tons of the narcotic annually, and nearly every ounce was destined for China's cramped slums where millions of addicts smoked it. They prized Indian opium because of its exceptional purity, and the job of the Opium Department was to keep it that way. English agents like Blair carefully supervised every step of production to ensure quality. Too much money was at stake to do otherwise. The trade produced a staggering profit of £6.5 million, or roughly one-sixth of the government's total revenue for India. There was no way to justify the trade morally, but giving it up was not easy when the benefit to the treasury was so handsome. As one historian put it, 'Politically, the British Raj was as addicted to opium as any twenty-pipe-a-day coolie.'[5]

Mr Blair was a loyal, efficient servant of this trade, and there is no sign that he ever had any serious doubts or regrets about the nature of his work. It was a secure job, the pay was good and the skills required were few. One can only speculate about his reasons for joining this particular service, but once he was in it, he stayed until retirement. It was the same for so many men who devoted their lives to the work of the Empire. Confident that its ultimate goals were just, they did what was expected of them and asked few questions. It was a way of life which Eric Blair would later come to know only too well in Burma. But as George Orwell he would devote considerable effort to repudiating it, repeatedly asking the hard questions about colonialism which his father's generation had evaded.

Burdened with the awkward title of Assistant Sub-Deputy Opium Agent, 3rd grade, Richard Blair spent his first year of service in the far north of the sprawling province of Bengal. As he slowly worked his way through the department's lower ranks, he was posted to a variety of stations scattered over Bengal and the United Provinces. At each place his duties required him to spend nearly half his time travelling round his district. He was expected to keep a close eye on the poppy growers in his area, making sure that each was employing proper methods of cultivation, advancing loans to those who needed them and making estimates of production. It was a lonely existence, with few recreations or diversions. Nights were spent in tents or in the ubiquitous *dak* bungalows, which were reserved for touring officials. The great cities of India were hundreds of miles away, and extended leaves from service were infrequent. During the hottest months – from April to October – the insects, rain and scorching temperatures made life miserable. When he was not travelling, much of his time was spent on paperwork.

As a bachelor, he braved twenty years of this life without complaint, and then one day in 1896 – when he was thirty-nine – he married an attractive young woman who was nearly half his age. Her name was Ida Mabel Limouzin. She had been a governess in India, and had been engaged to marry another man, but was jilted, and accepted Blair on the rebound. A slender woman with large eyes and thick wavy hair, she had a dark, faintly exotic appearance. Her family background was itself somewhat exotic. The daughter of a French father and an English mother, she was born on 18 May 1875 in the small suburb of Penge in South London. She grew up, however, thousands of miles away in Moulmein, a busy port in Lower Burma, where her father's family was established in the teak trade, and in boat building. There was even a street named after them in the town. At the height of their prosperity they lived very well indeed. One of Ida's sisters would later boast that their father, Frank, had lived 'the life of a prince' in Burma, employing at one point a staff of thirty servants.[6] This may have been the case for a short period, but the fact is that he was a reckless man who wasted his fortune. His taste for grand living led him to risk a large part of his capital on a speculative venture in the rice trade. He lost most of this investment, and his other businesses went into decline. Ida's mother, Theresa Catherine, was a stalwart Victorian lady who endured not only her husband's thriftless ways but also the pains of bearing their nine children, and of bringing them up in an arduous tropical climate. She was still leading an active life in Moulmein in the early 1920s when her grandson Eric arrived in Burma as a young colonial policeman.

After her wedding Ida lived with Richard Blair in Bengal for eight years. A proud, independent woman, she had a lively mind and was not in the least intimidated by her older husband. Indeed, she wasted little time establishing herself as the dominant partner. She made a good home for Mr Blair, but it was on her terms, and he was not one to raise objections. She always called him 'Dick', and took a slightly condescending attitude towards him. In later years they kept separate bedrooms, and though there was never any ill-will between them, Ida always made it clear that she was in charge of the home. 'Poor old Dick,' one relative recalled, 'if he was heard poking the fire it was "Dick, put that poker down".'[7]

Having grown up in Moulmein, Mrs Blair was more prepared for life in the hinterlands of Bengal than were most English wives of the period. She knew how difficult the climate could be, and she was used to living among people whose language, food and customs were different from her own. All the same, the dangers and hardships were formidable. Choleia and other diseases were a constant threat, and childbirth was often fatal for young women so far away from qualified doctors and hospitals. But Mrs Blair was fortunate. She gave birth to two children in India, and there were no complications. Her first was a girl. Born in April 1898; the child was named Marjorie Frances Blair.

Five years passed before the arrival of the second baby. A few months before its birth, the family settled in one of the more remote stations in Bengal. It was a small town near the border with Nepal, some four hundred miles northwest of Calcutta. Located on the bank of a lake, Motihari was a typical outpost of the Empire, with its small railway station on a branch line, its Protestant mission (called the 'Regions Beyond Mission'), its large jail and its colourful troop of Indian cavalry. There were not many Europeans, and only a few minor industries. But there was no lack of work for Mr Blair. The town lay in the middle of a district which produced three hundred tons of opium a year. He arrived there at a busy time, just before the big March harvest in the poppy fields. By June, when the first of the heavy rains arrived, most of his travelling for the season was behind him, and he was able to stay closer to home. On 25 June 1903 Ida Blair gave birth to a son at the family's bungalow in Motihari. The couple named him Eric Arthur Blair.

The first photograph of the new baby was taken only six weeks later. Dressed in a long white gown, he was carried from the house to the garden and held up to the camera by his smiling mother. In the photograph a tuft of fair hair sticks out from the top of his large round face, and a chubby arm is curled round his mother's grip. His eyes are bright and his complexion clear. It is the face of a contented, well-nourished baby, with no hint of the poor health which would trouble him in later life.

Less than a year after this photograph was taken, Mr Blair took up a new post at a much larger town, Monghyr, on the Ganges. It was decided, however, that the rest of the family would not resettle there. Marjorie was six, and the custom was to send English children of that age back home to be educated. Sometimes the mothers remained in India with their husbands, but many chose to stay in England until their husbands retired, or at least until the youngest child had reached adolescence. Ida Blair preferred to be with her children in England. At some point in 1904 she left India with Marjorie and Eric. Mr Blair stayed behind to serve out the seven years that remained before his retirement. In all that time he was able to spend only one leave in England – a short three months in 1907.

II

Mrs Blair and her 'chicks', as she liked to call her children, made their new home in the Oxfordshire market town of Henley-on-Thames. They lived at its southern end in a quiet neighbourhood with wide streets, neat gardens, and attractive villas of recent construction. Their first real home was called Ermadale, and was in Vicarage Road. The house was spacious, and there was a servant to help with the cooking and cleaning. As Orwell later remembered fondly, his mother had given the house its name, creating it from the first two letters in each child's name – *Er*ic and *Ma*rjorie.[8] She was a loving, attentive mother who was determined to give her children a comfortable middle-class life.

The river lay less than a mile away, bordered on one side by a long stretch of lush meadow, and on the other by densely wooded hills. A short distance downstream, the wide stone arches of the town bridge spanned the river, with the turreted church tower sitting picturesquely behind it. At the foot of the bridge stood the old coaching inn, the Red Lion, where Dr Johnson and James Boswell had once spent a night. Several boathouses lined the banks, and the river traffic included everything from barges and steam launches to punts and canoes.

Orwell's memories of his childhood in Henley were bright and detailed. He drew heavily upon them for his fourth novel, *Coming Up for Air*, vividly evoking the unspoiled countryside of his youth, 'the great green juicy meadows round the town . . . And the dust in the lane, and the warm greeny light coming through the hazel boughs'. In the novel he describes the crowded market days when 'chaps with round red faces like pumpkins' drove their animals through the streets in the early morning hours. Above all, he recalls life along the river and the simple enjoyment of an hour's fishing. 'Summer days, and the flat water-meadows and the blue hills in the distance, and the willows up the backwater and the pools underneath like a kind of deep green glass.'

In his memories of that river-valley landscape, 'it was summer all the year round'. He liked to think that 'the skies were bluer and seas greener' in his youth.[9] As an adult, he was increasingly tempted to idealise this period as 'a very good time to be alive', claiming in 1943 that 'a carefree attitude towards life was more possible then than it has been since'.[10] Whatever the realities of Edwardian life may have been, he preferred to judge it according to his experience of the stable, prosperous environment in Henley. The more complicated his adult life became, the more he yearned for the simple pleasures of this lost, golden world of childhood. He remembered the seemingly endless days devoted to such innocent pursuits as swimming, climbing trees, playing with tin soldiers, strolling along the towpath, bird-nesting and picking blackberries in narrow lanes. He had especially strong memories of the local sweet shop, where a penny bought a large handful of sticky sweets, all the names of which he could recall thirty years later.

As a small child, he spent a great deal of time with Marjorie, who had many friends and often let her little brother accompany her when she went out. He did not make friends easily and seems to have had few who were his own age in Henley. His first real playmates were a group of plumber's children who lived on the outskirts of his middle-class neighbourhood. He went bird-nesting with them, and also enjoyed other, less innocent pleasures. 'We used sometimes to play games of a vaguely erotic kind. One was called "playing at doctors", and I remember getting a faint but definitely pleasant thrill from holding a toy trumpet, which was supposed to be a stethoscope, against a little girl's belly.' It did not take long for the games to become more advanced. 'Playing at doctors' was followed by 'mothers and fathers', which Eric was a little slow to comprehend. 'Coming from a more crowded home the plumber's children were more precocious in this.' In no time they were all 'inspect[ing] each other's sexual organs with great interest'. The day soon came when he was forbidden to play with these children, perhaps because his mother had discovered the nature of their 'games', but in later life Orwell suspected that his mother's class prejudice was the true cause. 'They were "common" and I was told to keep away from them.'[11]

Playing with the plumber's children was certainly more fun than going to polite little parties for middle-class boys and girls. He never forgot how much he disliked obeying one of the formalities of these occasions. 'As a child I was taught to say "Thank you for having me" after a party, and it seemed to me such an awful phrase.'[12] It is not surprising that he invented an imaginary friend with whom he could play freely. For some unknown reason he called him 'Fronky'.

One local boy who helped to spark Eric's interest in fishing was an older youth named Humphrey Dakin. He was a doctor's son and the leader of a small group of middle-class boys who played together on the river or in the woods near the edge of the town, building wigwams and pretending to be Red Indians or bold explorers. They went fishing regularly, and Eric was occasionally allowed to come along. In *Coming Up for Air* George Bowling recalls a childhood adventure with an older 'gang' of boys who had reluctantly included him on a fishing trip to a local pond. The boys kept him at a distance, and forced him to fish in 'a rotten part of the pool', but he found enjoyment nevertheless:

> I was sitting on the grass bank with the rod in my hands, with the flies buzzing round and the smell of wild peppermint fit to knock you down, watching the red float on the green water, and I was happy as a tinker . . . I felt the rod tighten in my hand. Christ, that feeling! The line jerking and straining and a fish on the other end of it!

Like young George Bowling, Eric was not really a welcome companion among the older boys. Humphrey Dakin was much taken with Marjorie's good looks, and tolerated her little brother's company in order to please her. This early infatuation resulted, a decade later, in his marriage to Marjorie, but he never had much respect for her brother. He thought that Eric was too sensitive and weak. He dismissed him contemptuously as 'stinking little Eric', an annoying child 'full of "nobody loves me" and torrents of tears'.[13]

Without a father at home, or an older brother, Eric was ill-prepared for the rowdy world of bigger boys like Dakin. He was, in his own words, 'a chubby boy', with few physical talents. And he was indeed a sensitive child. He was introspective, imaginative and probably a little spoiled. He learned to read at an early age and spent many hours alone with books. He could not get enough of them and raced through new acquisitions. On the day before his eighth birthday he discovered a copy of *Gulliver's Travels* among his presents, and could not wait until the next day to look through it. He began at once to 'furtively read' it. It became one of his favourite books. 'Its fascination seems inexhaustible,' he wrote in the 1940s, proudly noting that 'a year has never passed without my re-reading at least part of it'.[14]

His mother was the first to recognise his talent for words, and she encouraged it. Orwell liked to claim that the urge to write had been with him since early childhood. In his forties he recalled composing a poem when he was only four or five. It was about a tiger with 'chair-like teeth', and his mother had proudly written it down while he recited it to her. His first published poem appeared in a local newspaper when he was eleven. Orwell believed that his early literary activity was partly the result of a lonely boyhood. 'I had the lonely child's habit of making up stories and holding conversations with imaginary persons, and I think from the very start my literary ambitions were mixed up with the feeling of being isolated and undervalued.'[15]

Nothing is known of his reaction to his father's brief appearance in Henley during the summer of 1907, but it must have been a very curious experience to have him at home on a three-month's leave. Suddenly there was a man living in the house, and then just as suddenly he disappeared, not to be seen again for four years. Eric was barely four at the time, and probably did not remember much about it later. There is no comment upon it anywhere in Orwell's writings, though he does make it clear in the essay 'Why I Write' that his sense of loneliness in childhood was partly related to his father's long years of separation from the family. He definitely regretted not having his father at home during those crucial early years, but it is unlikely that Mr Blair would ever have been capable of giving him the strong affection and guidance he craved. The old gentleman was not the type to establish a close bond with anyone, least of all with children, whose activities interested him hardly at all.

Ida Blair managed remarkably well while her husband was away in India. There is no indication that money was a serious problem for the family, at least not in the early years at Henley. The only significant source of income was Mr Blair's pay, which was approximately £650 a year during this period. It was hardly a princely sum, but it was six times greater than the average working-class family's yearly income. Mr Blair's needs were modest, and it is likely that he was sending two-thirds of his money home. On an annual allowance of about £400, Mrs Blair would have been able to live quite comfortably in a small town such as Henley, particularly when her children were still young. She may also have been helped, in minor ways, by her brother Charles Limouzin, who had some money in various investments, and who lived near Bournemouth.

Mrs Blair was not a dull Edwardian housewife. She had an artistic temperament and liked to surround herself with fanciful objects – rainbow silky curtains, embroidered cushions and stools, ivory figurines and small hand-carved boxes full of sequins and beads. She was an amateur photographer and developed her own negatives. Though not a great reader, she appreciated good books and was curious about new ideas. Several of her friends were active in the suffragist movement, and her sister Nellie enjoyed a brief career on the stage.

Ida's diary for her first complete year in Henley has survived, and the entries reveal that this young mother of two led an active social life. She seems to have thoroughly enjoyed herself. She played bridge, croquet, tennis, and golf, and took long walks in Henley Park or along the river. She entertained friends at home, and gave small parties for Marjorie. She made several trips to London, where Nellie Limouzin had a flat. The journey took little more than an hour on the Great Western Railway. In one week in June she visited Kew Gardens, saw Sarah Bernhardt on the stage, attended a lecture at the Mansion House, and went to a dog show. In July she spent three full days on the river enjoying the Henley Regatta, and just a few days later she was at Wimbledon to watch the tennis finals. 'I saw Miss Sutton win the ladies' and Mr Doherty the gentlemen's singles. Glorious day.'[16] The next month she and the children had a long holiday in Essex, at Frinton-on-Sea.

Mrs Blair's youthful energy and independent ways did not escape the attention of the opposite sex in Henley. Dr Dakin, Humphrey's father, was unhappily married, and had a wandering eye. He and Ida spent time together at the local golf club, and eventually he fell in love with her. There was a brief but very embarrassing scandal. According to his son, the doctor received no encouragement from Ida, and after a time he stopped trying to win her affection, but not before Mrs Dakin had become 'jealous and spread stories'.[17]

There is, indeed, no evidence to suggest that Ida was ever unfaithful to Mr Blair, despite their long separation and the great difference in their ages. All the same, living apart from her husband for so long cannot have been an easy arrangement, and there must have been times when she had regrets. The only indisputable fact is that she learned to get along without him. His name is completely missing from her one surviving diary, for 1905; there are no observations about him, no mention of news from him, no comment on any letters sent or received.

Near the very end of his life, Orwell recalled occasions in his childhood when he had overhead his mother and her friends talking about the opposite sex. From these conversations his child's mind had formed the 'impression that women *did not like* men, that they looked upon them as a sort of large, ugly, smelly and ridiculous animal who maltreated women in every way, above all by forcing their attentions upon them'. Nothing seems to have been said against his father, or even against Dr Dakin, but there is no way of knowing because he picked up only bits and pieces of conversations. The significance of the comments may have been exaggerated in his mind, but he was an intelligent and observant child, and such things made a strong impression on him. The overheard remarks rang in his ears – 'It just shows what beasts men are'; 'My dear, I think she's behaving like a perfect fool, the way she gives in to him'; 'Of course, she's far too good for him.'

These were words which he only dimly understood, but the general implication seemed clear enough to him at the time. 'Somehow, by the mere tone of these conversations – the hatefulness – above all the physical unattractiveness – of men in women's eyes seemed to be established.' The immediate effect of this was to make him wonder whether his mother's apparently low opinion of males had undermined her love for him, her only son. As he later confessed in one of his notebooks, he was thirty before he finally realised that he had 'in fact' been his mother's 'favourite child'.[18] But the doubts in the early years contributed to his image of himself as someone isolated and undervalued, and that image was slow to fade, lingering in his mind long after maturity had brought with it greater confidence.

After 1907 Eric and Marjorie were no longer Ida's only children. Although little is known of Mr Blair's summer visit, he seems to have been quick to renew his acquaintance with his wife. She became pregnant soon after his arrival in Henley, and in the following spring – after he had returned to India – she gave birth to her third and last child, a girl. The baby was named Avril. She was born at home, but at this point the family was no longer living at Ermadale. They had moved to another place in the same neighbourhood, a house called The Nutshell.

Mr Blair did not see his new daughter until she was three. At the beginning of 1912 he finally left the Opium Department, having spent a lifetime working his way up to the grand rank of Sub-Deputy Opium Agent, 1st grade. Ironically, after all his years of service, the opium trade with China was on the verge of being wiped out. Under pressure at home and abroad, the government had been gradually reducing exports of the drug, and in 1913 a formal treaty with China banned further shipments. Blair's work was finished, in more ways than one, but his pension was secure, and would give him slightly more than £400 a year. It was a sum which would seem increasingly inadequate as the years went by.

The greatest financial burden facing the family was the cost of educating the three children. While they were very young, the two girls and Eric attended a small day school in Henley; but when

Marjorie was eleven or twelve, she went away to boarding school, and when Eric turned eight, it was decided that he also was ready to leave home. Recognising her son's intellectual potential, Mrs Blair was anxious to place him in a preparatory school with a good record of sending boys on to Eton or to one of the other prestigious public schools. Her brother Charles found such a place in Sussex, on the outskirts of Eastbourne, sixty miles south of London. It was called St Cyprian's. The school accepted Eric in the summer of 1911, and he began his first term in September. He would spend a little more than five years there, and come away with a deep and enduring hatred of the place.

CHAPTER TWO

Cold Lessons

I

As Orwell portrays it in 'Such, Such Were the Joys', St Cyprian's appears to have been a prison camp cunningly disguised as a top-notch, expensive preparatory school. To make his case against it, he strips away its respectable exterior and reveals a cold, miserable environment where fear and humiliation held sway. He argues that underfeeding was routine, punishments severe, overcrowding common and filth pervasive. He depicts the headmaster and his domineering wife as sadistic, greedy snobs who held a cynical view of education as nothing more than a mechanical process of cramming facts into young minds. He contends that they seized every opportunity to increase their profits from the school, and that they ruthlessly bullied anyone who challenged their authority. So thorough was their control, he says, that they seemed able to read their pupils' minds and to know which ones were truly obedient and which were merely feigning obedience.

What he resented most was being made to feel a special obligation to them because they had chosen not to charge his family the full cost of his education. Ordinarily, his school fees would have been £180 a year, but this was beyond what his family could afford, amounting to more than a third of his father's pension. Recognising that he was a bright boy who might bring credit to them, the headmaster and his wife had accepted him at half-fees, but, according to him, he was made to suffer for this ostensible act of charity. He was an investment, and his benefactors expected a good return. If he worked hard and won a scholarship to a prominent public school, then the evidence of his success could be used to attract more pupils. If he slacked off, he would be cheating not only himself and his family but also his benefactors. For the first two or three years they did not tell him about his reduced fees, but he claims that at the age of eleven he was told, and that the couple then began to pressure him with a vengeance. They 'began throwing the fact in my teeth', he says.[1]

Completed in the last years of Orwell's life, and published posthumously, 'Such, Such Were the Joys' has been viewed by some readers as the product of a dying man's perverse determination to open old wounds and to blame old enemies for his misfortunes. But the idea of writing an account of his schooldays had been in his mind for many years, and it was never a subject which he was inclined to treat charitably. In 1938 his friend and old schoolfellow Cyril Connolly had included a long reminiscence of St Cyprian's in *Enemies of Promise*, and Orwell had remarked to him at that time, 'I'm always meaning one of these days to write a book about St Cyprian's . . . People are wrecked by those filthy private schools long before they get to public school age.'[2] The need to avoid the risk of libel was one reason why Orwell did not write about the school earlier. The risk was real. When *Enemies of Promise* first appeared, Connolly had been surprised to learn that the headmaster's wife, Mrs L. C. Vaughan Wilkes, was still very much alive. Although his book's criticism of the school was relatively mild, she was outraged by it and had sent him a stinging letter of rebuke, saying that his negative comments had upset her so much that she could hardly bear to think about them, and that the book had caused her 'serious psychological damage'.[3] Fortunately, she let the matter end there, but it was clear that, even in old age, she was not someone to be trifled with.

A few years later, when Connolly was editing *Horizon* magazine, he rashly suggested that Orwell should write an essay for him about St Cyprian's. 'Such, Such Were the Joys' is the result of that suggestion, but it never appeared in *Horizon* because, when it was finished, Orwell himself judged it 'too libellous to print'.[4] As long as Mrs Wilkes remained alive, there was really no chance of its publication in England, and in fact she went on living for many more years. One version was published in America in the 1950s, with the name of the school altered to 'Crossgates', but British publication did not occur until 1968, several months after Mrs Wilkes's death at the age of ninety-one.[5]

Various old St Cyprianites have come forward to defend Mrs Wilkes and her husband against Orwell's charges, and oddly enough this group eventually included Cyril Connolly. In the 1960s he took time to reflect on his schooldays from the vantage point of old age and concluded that he had misjudged the couple. They were not so bad after all. Indeed, he decided that they had been 'true friends' who had tried to do their best for him from the start. He even went so far as to describe Mrs Wilkes as 'warm-hearted and an inspired teacher'.[6] Yet this was the same woman whom Orwell condemns so vehemently as the great oppressor of his boyhood, the woman who tried to crush his spirit by repeatedly humiliating him, in public and in private.

Was Orwell exaggerating? Some new clues may help to answer that question. In the early 1980s one of his contemporaries at the school – W. H. J. Christie – donated to the Eastbourne public library the only surviving photographs of young Eric Blair at St Cyprian's. The most interesting of these is a full portrait of the assembled pupils and staff taken in the summer of 1913. If Eric's chubby face was not unmistakably present in the second row, it would be difficult to accept that this innocent-looking group had anything in common with the joyless inmates depicted in Orwell's essay. After reading Orwell, one would expect many of the boys to look sickly, stunted and frightened. Instead the photograph reveals a large group of seemingly robust, attractive boys, many of whom appear quite relaxed and even cheerful. The younger masters are ruggedly handsome and bear little resemblance to the weak, timid types who are vaguely present in Orwell's descriptions.

At the centre, looking very maternal and affectionate, is a small, stout woman with a young boy on her lap and several others nestled comfortably around her. She hardly seems to merit comparison with the fierce, cold-hearted woman in the essay, but this is Mrs Wilkes, whose first name, incidentally, was Cicely – not a very convincing name for a bully. A few feet away sits Mr Wilkes, a dull-looking man slumped down in his seat with a slightly dazed expression on his face and small, squinty eyes. He looks like a lethargic, absent-minded clerk. At his feet sits a boy casually petting a small dog, and next to him is a distinguished-looking old gentleman – the deputy headmaster – striking an avuncular pose with his hand on a boy's shoulder. A little farther along in the same row is ten-year-old Eric, his face partially obscured by the matron's big hat. He at least does look as unhappy as he later claimed he felt. But this photograph does help to explain why some old boys have had trouble understanding how Orwell could criticise their school so harshly. Obviously for many of them the place was not bad at all, and it is little wonder that they have seen no connection between their experiences and his essay's portrait of pale, cringing boys suffering under the arbitrary rule of a pair of unforgiving despots.

In the archives of the Eastbourne library are a few photographs and illustrations of St Cyprian's and the surrounding area as it was in Eric's time. Far from seeming dreary and run-down, the main building is an impressive, large redbrick structure with numerous gables, tall chimneys and dozens of high windows. It was built only six years before Eric first arrived, and contained several classrooms and dormitories, a dining hall, and a library. There was a gymnasium attached to one wing, and a small chapel at the back. The windows of the upstairs dormitories looked down on a wide playing field, at the far end of which was a cricket pavilion. The school occupied about five acres and was bounded on two sides by low brick walls. On either side were the grounds of rival boys' schools. A third side was bounded by a road which ran next to the Royal Eastbourne Golf Club, and in the distance lay the Downs.[7]

One of the more ardent defenders of St Cyprian's was Walter Christie, who, in addition to preserving his photographs of the school, also preserved some of his memories of it in a little-known essay published by *Blackwood's Magazine*. In part he used the essay to make specific replies to Orwell's charges, and his remarks are worth considering because their basic positions at the school were similar. He was a pupil during the last three years of Eric Blair's time, and, like him, he later went on to Eton as a King's Scholar. From there he went to King's College, Cambridge, and subsequently enjoyed a distinguished career in the Indian Civil Service. In 1947 he was Joint Private Secretary to the Viceroy. He died in 1983, but a decade earlier – during his long retirement – he wrote his essay 'St Cyprian's Days'. In it he claims that Blair 'had a chip on his shoulder', and that St Cyprian's was in fact 'an excellent school . . . where many boys were for the most part happy'. Like Blair, he was there on reduced fees because his middle-class family had not been able to afford the full amount. But he insists that this caused him no problems:

> I knew nothing of it until, years later, my mother told me of this act of generosity. There was no mention of it while I was at St Cyprian's, although it must have happened when I was about eight years old, and long before anyone could think of me in terms of advertisement. Then and later I was often in trouble at school, and in disfavour with the authorities. There was no conceivable reason why I should have been treated differently from Blair.[8]

In Orwell's account, the pressure on scholarship boys was so great that Mr Wilkes regularly beat them as one way of making them work harder. Orwell says that he received beatings for such things as failing to translate a Latin sentence properly in class. He often heard Mr Wilkes castigate him with the words, 'You are living on my bounty', and at least once he listened to these words 'between blows of a cane'. The headmaster also had a nasty habit of using a big silver pencil to rap the heads of slow pupils.

But Christie takes exception to the notion that Mr Wilkes was a brutal man. He describes him as a 'shy character, non-aggressive by inclination. If he had to cane a boy it was usually a token performance.' He does admit the detail about the pencil, however. 'An odd exception to his apparent distaste for violence was his use of a heavy-ended silver pencil on the skulls of some of us, to drive home points over which he thought we were being stupid.' Almost as an afterthought he acknowledges that 'this could be annoying and painful'. He concludes that Orwell's attack on the school must have been 'subconsciously misdirected, that St Cyprian's is only the whipping-post for some more deeply seated object of his hate. It reminded me of a cobra discharging its self-generated venom by spitting at a harmless tree whose roots had sheltered it.'

It is easy to say that the school was not nearly as bad as Orwell's essay claims, but it would be wrong to go the next step and conclude that Mr and Mrs Wilkes were 'harmless'. They may look that way in the old photograph, and in the memories of certain old boys reflecting on the lost days of youth, but the angry view of them in 'Such, Such Were the Joys' is not built on some eccentric fantasy. From the viewpoint of young Eric Blair their capacity to do harm was quite real, and there were good reasons for him to turn against them.

Mrs Wilkes, who exercised the real power at the school, was a tricky personality. In some ways she was an admirable woman, full of great charm, ambition and energy. She enjoyed literature and could recite long passages from the English poets and the Bible. She played the piano and the organ, and taught several subjects at the school, including French and history. She was also the mother of five children – two boys and three girls – but somehow she always managed to combine family responsibilities with active involvement in almost all aspects of life at the school. It is fair to say that no major decisions were reached at the school without her approval. She was so attached to her second family – the boys of St Cyprian's – that she insisted they address her as simply 'Mum'. Behind her back, they called her 'Flip' and her husband 'Sambo'. It was the ample shape of her breasts which inspired the boys' choice of her nickname. The word would go round the classroom or dormitory, 'Here comes Flip ... flapping nicely, eighty to the minute, everything in clockwork order.'[9]

She cultivated the devotion of certain boys, and warmly rewarded those in her favour. She would pick out three or four boys who had pleased her in some way and take them on a special outing. A popular treat was a visit to Hyde's cake shop in Eastbourne, where she would buy her entourage pink-iced gingerbread. Her birthdays were always occasions for great celebration at the school because the boys were allowed a free day in her honour. At her best, she could be not only generous but also sympathetic and even a little playful.

Some boys worshipped her and continued to show their respect by coming back for visits long after their schooling had ended. Even in her nineties she was still receiving such visits, addressing her grey-haired guests by their school nicknames and still insisting that they call her Mum. She was proud of her long list of admirers who had made names for themselves in the world. Among Blair's contemporaries there was Charles Rivett-Carnac, who was appointed Commissioner of the Royal Canadian Mounted Police in 1959. In his autobiography, *Pursuit in the Wilderness*, he praised her for helping to give him a strong sense of self-discipline ('[She] taught me much which stood me in good stead in later years, when, despite risks and consequences, I had always to go on.')[10] Another admirer was Henry Robert Foote, who won the Victoria Cross as a tank commander in North Africa during the Second World War, and who eventually rose to the rank of major-general in the Army. He had entered St Cyprian's in 1909, when he was only four years old. His mother had died and his father was away in India, so Mrs Wilkes had agreed to board him at the school. He stayed for the next nine years. When he was interviewed in the 1980s, he spoke warmly of her. 'I owe a great deal to her,' he said. 'She was a mother to me.'[11]

But as even her fondest admirers admit, she had a less appealing side to her. Her moods were unpredictable and could change without warning. One could easily, and inexplicably, lose favour with her. 'She was frankly capricious,' Orwell wrote. 'An act which might get you a caning one day might next day be laughed off as a boyish prank.' There were days when nothing seemed to please her, and then 'there were days when she was like a flirtatious queen surrounded by courtier-lovers, laughing and joking, scattering largesse'. Although Walter Christie's essay is highly sympathetic towards Mrs Wilkes, it does not deny that her changeable nature could make life difficult for everyone around her. Christie wrote that her face was one which could glow with good humour or suddenly 'cloud over and tremble with rage'. He expanded on this point by offering a striking image almost worthy of Orwell: 'No primitive farmers ever scanned the omens of the sky more anxiously, to divine the mood of the Earth Mother, than we watched for changes in the climate of Flip's grace and geniality.' For him, the warmth of her good moments made the rage of her bad ones endurable, but Blair was not so accepting. 'Whether one laughed or snivelled or went into frenzies of gratitude for small favours . . . one's only true feeling was hatred.'

At least one former pupil condemned Mrs Wilkes even more strongly than Orwell did. David Ogilvy, the successful advertising executive, hated her so much that he called her 'satanic' in his autobiography. According to him, she 'carried the art of castration to extraordinary perfection. Like a chess master playing simultaneous games against several opponents, Mrs Wilkes played games of emotional cat-and-mouse against every boy in the school.' He also says that she saved a small fortune over the years by deliberately underfeeding the boys, and that she once grabbed him by the cheek and threw him to the ground after he had mispronounced a word in a play rehearsal.[12]

If Mrs Wilkes's mood of the moment happened to be foul, she could indeed seem a fearful bully, especially in the eyes of an impressionable boy who – for one reason or another – was not among her favourites. She could make life extremely miserable for those who were out of favour. When she was sufficiently provoked, she did not hesitate to slap a boy's face or pull his hair. One contemporary said that Blair had his hair pulled so often by Mrs Wilkes that he began keeping it greasy so that she could not pull it so hard. But she preferred to use her eyes and her firm voice to reprimand those who had offended her. Orwell could not forget the 'anxious, accusing' looks which she gave him: 'It was difficult to look her in the face without feeling guilty, even at moments when one was not guilty of anything in particular.' Her favourite phrases of reproach had powerful effects on the minds of small boys. As Orwell recalls, 'There was "Don't *be* such a fool!" (or, "It's path*etic*, isn't it?") which made one feel a born idiot; and there was "It isn't very straight of you, is it?", which always brought one to the brink of tears.' When such words were not enough, she gave the dread command, 'Report yourself to the headmaster,' which invariably resulted in the offender receiving a beating. One old boy – the golfing correspondent Henry Longhurst – succinctly described life under Mrs Wilkes's rule: 'If you were in favour, life could be bliss: if you weren't, it was hell.'[13]

Although Cyril Connolly was reluctant to admit it until many years after leaving school, he was frequently 'in favour' with Mrs Wilkes, receiving more than a fair share of her 'largesse'. One reason why he eventually softened his view of her was that he had taken a second look at various documents from his schooldays and had found that he had enjoyed a better life at St Cyprian's than he had realised at the time. In his last book, *The Evening Colonnade*, he wrote that these old letters and school reports 'revealed a considerable distortion between my picture of the proprietors and their own unremitting care to bring me on'. Perhaps realising how stiff and forced this sounds, Connolly immediately thought of how his old friend Orwell would have responded to such a change of heart. 'At this point I hear Orwell's wheezy chuckle. "Of course, they knew they were on to a good thing. What do you think was our propaganda value to them as winners of Eton scholarships – almost as good as being an Hon." '[14]

It is impossible to say that Orwell's 'Flip' reflects the true character of Cicely Vaughan Wilkes. She may have been a better woman than he believed. But he does not claim to be giving an objective portrait of her in his essay. His aim is to portray her through the eyes of a child, to show the reader what he saw and heard then. Again and again in the essay, he speaks of his desire to recapture the perspective which he had developed as a child – 'my own childhood outlook' – and to present that view as faithfully as he can. He readily admits that this approach may lead to exaggeration, since anything seen from a child's view must, by the standards of an adult mind, appear distorted. From an adult standpoint, he is willing to admit that Mr and Mrs Wilkes were probably not such bad creatures. 'How would St Cyprian's appear to me now, if I could go back, at my present age, and see it as it was in 1915? What should I think of Sambo and Flip, those terrible, all-powerful monsters? I should see them as a couple of silly, shallow, ineffectual people, eagerly climbing up a social ladder which any thinking person could see to be on the point of collapse.' Old men can claim that their memories of St Cyprian's are warm and golden, but Orwell is not writing a version to satisfy them. His account of childhood terrors is so compelling not because every word of it is literally true, but because – from beginning to end – it strives to be true to the one thing which matters most to its author: the impressions and feelings of his boyhood, a time when he lacked the articulate voice to speak up for himself. Throughout his work, Orwell uses his power over words to provide an eloquent voice for others whose voices have been silenced or ignored – political prisoners in Spain, tramps in London, miners in Wigan. In 'Such, Such Were the Joys' he is an impassioned advocate for himself, for the boy he once was.

II

Orwell took the title of his essay from one of William Blake's *Songs of Innocence*:

> Such, such were the joys,
> When we all, girls & boys,
> In our youth-time were seen
> On the Echoing Green.

The painful irony in his title is obvious in the contrast between Blake's pleasant image of childhood and the cold lessons of life at St Cyprian's. But in the back of his mind he may also have been thinking of a similar quotation which had a specific connection with St Cyprian's. It appears in the school magazine, which was largely the work of Mr and Mrs Wilkes. At the top of the first page in each issue, just below the title of the magazines, there is an inscription from Virgil printed in bold type: **'Forsan et haec olim meminisse juvabit.'** ['Perhaps one day even these things will be pleasant to remember.'] It is an absurd but unforgettable motto. 'You may dislike the place now,' it seems to say, 'but maybe time will erase the pain and soften your view.'[15] One can almost hear Mrs Wilkes adding, 'So *buck* up, old chap,' which was another of her favourite remarks.

In the 1960s, when she was in her nineties, Mrs Wilkes was asked to describe her memories of the little boy whom she had known as Eric Blair. She clearly recalled his first day when she had noticed him standing alone with a sad expression on his face. She had tried to comfort him, but he had resisted her soft words and friendly embrace. He had even refused to perk up when she had taken him on one of her special outings a day later. In her memory there was no fault on her part. She saw herself as the beloved Mum who had tried her best to reach him. The fault was all his. 'There was no warmth in him,' she insisted.[16]

As he recalled it, his predominant emotions during that first year were fear and confusion. He was a little boy of eight away from home for the first time, and his new environment was a demanding one. He had no privacy. There were three to five beds in a dormitory with no partitions and few furnishings. The doors on the lavatories did not fasten. At night the matron put on soft slippers and quietly patrolled the corridors listening for the sound of talking. Anyone caught in the act was reported to the headmaster. The day began at a quarter past seven with a plunge into the icy cold water of the school swimming bath, which was about five yards long. Mr Wilkes stood at the side scolding anyone who hung back ('Go on, Marsden, you stink like a polecat').[17] One by one the boys swam the length of the slimy pool and climbed out shivering, reaching for damp towels hanging from the walls. After they had put on their school uniforms, which included a green cap displaying a light blue Maltese Cross, they assembled on the asphalt in front of the gymnasium for a short spell of physical training, which was followed by chapel, and then – finally – breakfast. They were usually given bread and margarine, and porridge served in cold pewter bowls. Sitting at the head of one table, Mrs Wilkes began teaching scripture to the boys even before they had finished breakfast.

During the day they endured long hours in the classroom studying mainly languages, history, and mathematics. Geography and drawing were also taught, but little importance was attached to them because they were not relevant to the scholarship examinations. The process of education at St Cyprian's was, in Orwell's words, 'a preparation for a sort of confidence trick. Your job was to learn exactly those things that would give an examiner the impression that you knew more than you did know.' Everything was reduced to its 'examination-value'. In history, the things which mattered were not ideas but names, places and dates. 'I recall positive orgies of dates, with the keener boys leaping up and down in their places in their eagerness to shout out the right answers, and at the same time not feeling the faintest interest in the meaning of the mysterious events they were naming.'

Such methods did produce results. The pages of the school magazine – the *St Cyprian's Chronicle* – overflowed with success stories. In the summer of 1914, for example, the magazine proudly announced: 'During the past fourteen months the whole of the top-form have now been elected to scholarships at public schools.' The boys' names were prominently listed at the front of the magazine, along with the grand names of their new schools: 'G. Bailey, Rugby' ... 'J. K. Graham, Marlborough' ... 'J. Carlton-Holmes, Eton' ... 'P. Mitchell-Innes, Harrow' ... 'A. Trench, Charterhouse', and so on down the page. Such a list was the school's best advertisement, and its future prosperity was secure as long as it could continue to produce these impressive results.

Every effort was made to cultivate strong ties with influential housemasters at the public schools. There was an especially good friend at Harrow. Between 1906 and 1916 nearly thirty boys from St Cyprian's became members of George Townsend Warner's house at Harrow. Every year Townsend Warner came down to St Cyprian's to present a school prize named in his honour, and every year he was an examiner for the prestigious Harrow History Prize, which was awarded to boys from St Cyprian's with uncommon frequency. When he died in 1916, the *St Cyprian's Chronicle* sadly noted his passing. 'We have had an intimate connection with his house at Harrow, and we have lost in him a true and valued friend ... He examined each year for the Harrow History Prize, and he used laughingly to say that he was tired of always awarding it to St Cyprian's and that *caeteris paribus* he should give it to a boy from some other school!'

Eric Blair went along with St Cyprian's' educational 'confidence trick' and learned to play the game as well as anyone, though each year he hated it more and more. Academically, his first year was a success. He received high marks for his work, especially in Latin. But there was trouble outside the classroom, and it came within two weeks of his arrival. One morning he awoke to find that he had wet his bed. It was not an isolated incident. It happened again and again. There was no way to hide it, and no one showed any sympathy for his problem. He was made to feel that he was doing it on purpose, and was warned that a beating would follow if he did not stop it.

One day Mrs Wilkes called him to her table in the dining room where she was entertaining a woman visitor. 'Here is a little boy,' she said to her guest, 'who wets his bed every night.' With her eyes on Eric, she added, 'Do you know what I'm going to do if you wet your bed again? I am going to get the Sixth Form to beat you.'

The visitor appeared shocked and exclaimed, 'I should think so!' She was dressed in what looked like a riding-habit, and she seemed, in the boy's eyes, 'an intimidating, masculine-looking person'. Her expression of disapproval left him 'almost swooning with shame'. He was so unnerved by this humiliating encounter that he 'misheard the phrase "the Sixth Form" as "Mrs Form" ', and came away bewildered by the thought that this woman might be given the job of punishing him.

When he wet his bed again, he was indeed beaten, but not by so bizarre a figure as 'Mrs Form'. Naturally, the job fell to Mr Wilkes. When the evidence of his 'crime' was discovered, he heard those terrible words, 'Report yourself to the headmaster', and trudged downstairs to receive his punishment. He had tried to do what was expected of him, even fervently praying at night, 'Please God, do not let me wet my bed!' But nothing had worked. After the beating was over, the physical pain quickly subsided, but 'a deeper grief' remained, 'a sense of desolate loneliness and helplessness.' He had learned a powerful lesson, though it had nothing to do with controlling his bed-wetting. 'I was in a world where it was *not possible* for me to be good . . . Life was more terrible, and I was more wicked, than I had imagined.'

He wet his bed once more, was beaten again, and then suddenly the problem went away. Looking back on the whole episode, Orwell observed coolly, 'So perhaps this barbarous remedy does work, though at a heavy price, I have no doubt.'

Although he may have believed that it was not possible to be 'good' in Flip's world, the fact is that for most of his schooldays he worked very hard to win her regard. As the years went by, there were periodic indications that his value as an 'investment' was good. Twice each year C. Grant Robertson ('Fellow of All Souls and Senior Tutor at Magdalen College, Oxford') came down to examine the school, and his reports speak highly of Eric's work in almost all subjects. At the end of the summer term of 1915, when Eric was twelve, he was praised by Robertson for doing 'very promising work' in Mr Wilkes's scholarship class. According to the report, there was 'a good prospect' that he would win 'distinction' for himself and St Cyprian's. His hard work that year also earned him the school's English prize.[18]

Despite such encouraging developments, he could not relax. The pressure to succeed appeared to be constant, and none of his accomplishments received unqualified approval. 'Looking back, I realise that I then worked harder than I have ever done since, and yet at the time it never seemed possible to make quite the effort that was demanded of one.' Even as he made steady progress towards the goals set for him, he could not escape the feeling that he was always on the verge of failure. All the 'canings, reproaches and humiliations' had frightened him into working harder, but they had also planted in him a nagging sense of inadequacy. He hated his 'benefactors' for making him feel so unworthy, and then he hated himself for hating them.

Long before he was informed that he was living on 'Sambo's bounty', he was keenly aware of the financial gap which separated his family from the families of so many of the other boys. A few hundred pounds a year was adequate for a small middle-class family in Henley, but he was now in the company of many boys whose fathers made a thousand pounds or more a year, and there was no way that he could ignore this fact, especially when some of them taunted him with questions about his background. 'How much a year has your pater got? . . . How many servants do your people keep? . . . Have your people got a car?' As the son of a retired sub-deputy opium agent, he could scarcely provide satisfactory responses to such an inquisition. Indeed, it was probably best for him to say as little as possible, which is apparently what he did. At the age when boys enjoy boasting about how rich or famous or strong their fathers are, he had little to boast about. In the 1930s Orwell observed, 'Perhaps the greatest cruelty one can inflict on a child is to send it to school among children richer than itself. A child conscious of poverty will suffer snobbish agonies such as a grown-up person can scarcely even imagine.'19

At another kind of school the question of money might not have mattered very much, but it entered into life at St Cyprian's on many levels. The richer boys always had more money to spend on 'extras' – such as toys and sweets – and they were able to afford additional lessons in riding and shooting. They usually spent their holidays in fashionable places, and, inevitably, many of the boys were arrogant about it. Mrs Wilkes never let Eric forget that his parents lacked the money that other boys' parents had. When he wanted to buy a new cricket bat or a shiny model aeroplane, she was quick to ask, 'Do you think that's the sort of thing a boy like you should buy?' More humiliating was her refusal to allow him the luxury of a birthday cake. 'It was usual for each boy to have a large iced cake with candles, which was shared out at tea between the whole school. It was provided as a matter of routine and went on his parents' bill.' But Mrs Wilkes decided on her own that Mr Blair did not need to waste his money on such a frivolous item. 'I never had such a cake, though my parents would have paid for it readily enough.' This may seem like a minor disappointment, but at the school these occasions were treated as major events. The cake was brought out with great fanfare, and as soon as the candles were extinguished, the boy was allowed to make a ceremony of going among his friends and presenting a candle to each one. 'Year after year, never daring to ask, I would miserably hope that this year a cake would appear. Once or twice I even rashly pretended to my companions that this time I *was* going to have a cake. Then came tea-time, and no cake, which did not make me more popular.'

Most of the boys at the school were children of 'the ordinary suburban rich', as Orwell called them. The rest could be divided into two small groups. One was made up of boys who were 'scholarship fodder', like Eric, and the other consisted of a few boys whose families were at the very top of the social scale. Among other things, the rigorous life at St Cyprian's was supposed to build character, so occasionally a millionaire or an aristocrat would send his son there for some intense character-building. During Eric's time, this group of boys included Lord Charles Cavendish (the second son of the 9th Duke of Devonshire), Lord Malden (the future 9th Earl of Essex) and Lord Pollington (the future 7th Earl of Mexborough). At one point, there was even a Siamese prince, whose name was grandly displayed in the school magazine as 'H. H. Prince P. Chira'. The names were impressive, but the personalities did not appeal to Eric. In 'Such, Such Were the Joys', Orwell speaks contemptuously of these boys, describing one as 'a wretched, drivelling little creature, almost an albino, peering upwards out of weak eyes, with a long nose at the end of which a dewdrop always seemed to be trembling'. (Cyril Connolly later said this was a reference to Lord Pollington.) Orwell also makes it clear that the school placed a high value on their snob appeal. 'Sambo always gave these boys their titles when mentioning them to a third person . . . Needless to say he found ways of drawing attention to them when any visitor was being shown round the school.'

Snobbishness at St Cyprian's took various forms. Mrs Wilkes

had traced her family's origins back to some fierce clan in Scotland and was so proud of this connection that she had become a snob about all things Scottish. There were several Scottish boys at the school, and they were encouraged to wear kilts on Sundays. As a place where the rich spent their summers, Scotland had a strong appeal, but Mrs Wilkes preferred to praise it as a land where character-building occurred as a matter of course. Occupying a place of honour on a wall inside the school was a large steel engraving of the charge of the Scots Greys at Waterloo. It was meant to serve as an emblem of Scottish greatness. The boys were taught to admire the Scots as exemplary figures of courage, fortitude and resourcefulness. As Orwell wrote, it was 'all somehow mixed up with the invigorating effects of porridge, Protestantism, and a cold climate'.

Not surprisingly, there was a great deal of importance attached to games – especially football. By playing hard and fearlessly, a boy could prove that he really did have 'character'. Eric saw no point in football and hated playing it. ('The cold, the mud, the hideous greasy ball that came whizzing at one's face, the gouging knees and trampling boots of the bigger boys.') He preferred cricket, and showed some talent for it. In the summer of 1914 the school magazine gave this account of him in the 'Characters of the 1st XI': 'BLAIR – Has improved very much of late . . . should with care bat very well. He catches well but must learn to move more quickly. Can bowl a little.' As a swimmer, he had a few moments of glory, nearly winning a diving competition during his final year. But this kind of success did not mean much: 'What counted was football . . . The lovers of football are large, boisterous, nobbly boys who are good at knocking down and trampling on slightly smaller boys. That was the pattern of school life – a continuous triumph of the strong over the weak.'

Appropriately, boxing was also popular at the school. The boys received instruction from a colourful character named Sergeant Barnes, who had once been middle-weight champion of the Army. He liked to tease them by boxing with three boys at one time. He amazed them with his skill, and entertained them with jokes and tricks. But he was not hired simply to teach boxing. His principal job was to serve as drill-sergeant for the Cadet Corps of St Cyprian's, which was officially part of the 2nd Home Counties Brigade, Royal Field Artillery.

The Corps was supposed to help build character, but most of its activities were routine and mindless. Regular parades and drill took place on Tuesday and Thursday afternoons. The boys marched up and down the playing field with dummy carbines, and once or twice in every term they would be inspected by some visiting colonel or major. On field days they roamed the Downs engaging in mock battles with other schools or with the grey-uniformed veterans of the Volunteer Reserve. On one occasion Mr Wilkes arranged for a small contingent of boys to disguise themselves as Zulu warriors and ambush the main body of the Corps. The 'Zulus' were soundly defeated. The only real weapons available to the boys were bayonets and the small calibre rifles which they used on the school's miniature range. There were quite a few expert marksmen among them. Every year St Cyprian's proudly took home various shooting prizes in national competitions against other preparatory schools.

Eric's name does not figure in the lists of cadets who distinguished themselves on the rifle range, and – strangely enough – 'Such, Such Were the Joys' makes no mention of his participation in the corps. But a surviving photograph from 1913–1914 does reveal that he was a bugler in the Cadet Corps band. He looks rather forlorn and ill at ease standing in the back row with his instrument held at his side. His face is smooth, round and babyish. Another photograph from roughly the same period shows him with a slight grin in a group portrait of the entire Corps. Various boys are holding up the shields and cups which the school's shooting teams had won, and Mr Wilkes is sitting in the centre wearing the uniform of a captain. To the casual observer, Eric looks no different from the rest of the company, but Walter Christie, who preserved the photograph for posterity, attached an indignant note to it pointing out that cadet Blair's cap badge is 'askew and the top button of his tunic is undone'.[20] All the other boys appear to have dressed properly for the occasion. It is the kind of trivial thing that

Mr or Mrs Wilkes may have seized upon afterwards as another sign of Eric's unworthiness. There is no way to know whether he was just being careless or was inviting a beating by indulging in a bit of rebelliousness. His grin seems to weigh in favour of the latter possibility.

After the First World War began in the late summer of 1914, the boys were constantly reminded that military training was serious business. Old boys visited the school on leave from the front and reported on the perils and hardships which they had endured. One of the younger masters, Charles Loseby, had joined the Army in September 1914, and had gone off to France in January. Before the war he had been the school lieutenant in the Cadet Corps, second only to Mr Wilkes, and had led the boys in the mock battles fought on the Downs. But in less than a year he was back among them recuperating from injuries suffered in a real battle. He had been gassed at Ypres in May 1915. He shared his experiences with the boys when he visited the school after his discharge from hospital in June. Then, like a good soldier, he rejoined his regiment at the front.[21]

The war made it easier for Mr and Mrs Wilkes to drive home the message of 'Character, character, character'. When old boys fell in battle, they were celebrated in the pages of the school magazine as perfect embodiments of the values which St Cyprian's preached. One was remembered for 'his pluck . . . and his fearless tackling on the football field. We hear he died a gallant death leading his men in a charge at Givenchy.' In just the first two years of the war nineteen old boys were reported killed or missing in action – a very large number for a small school whose history was relatively short. 'They have died the most glorious death,' the magazine declared, 'but they will live for ever in the memories of St Cyprian's boys – a perpetual example of duty nobly done.'[22]

The boys were asked to contribute to the war effort. They grew vegetables for victory, sacrificed pocket money to send parcels out to the front and devoted long hours in the evenings to knitting socks and mufflers for the troops. They also paid visits to convalescent soldiers at a camp in Summerdown Road, bringing them sweets and

Woodbine cigarettes, and inviting them to attend theatricals in the school gymnasium. On one cold, rainy November afternoon the King and Queen visited the camp, and the boys formed a guard of honour. They stood at attention in the rain for over an hour, and then marched back to the school soaking wet. 'This duty was thoroughly appreciated by the cadets,' the school magazine confidently declared.[23]

In *Coming Up for Air* Orwell looks at the camp from a different perspective, describing it as it might have appeared to one of the soldiers. This approach results in a fascinating mixture of childhood memories and adult imagination. 'Do you remember those war-time hospital camps?' George Bowling asks. 'The long rows of wooden huts like chicken-houses stuck right on top of those beastly icy downs – the "south coast", people used to call it, which made me wonder what the north coast could be like – where the wind seems to blow at you from all directions at once.' Bowling is sent to such a camp in Eastbourne after he is slightly injured at the front, and among his visitors are groups of local schoolboys. 'Sometimes the kids from the slap-up boys' schools in Eastbourne used to be led round in crocodiles to hand out fags and peppermint creams to the "wounded Tommies", as they called us. A pink-faced kid of about eight would walk up to a knot of wounded men sitting on the grass, split open a packet of Woodbines and solemnly hand one fag to each man, just like feeding the monkeys at the zoo.'

It was not easy for a young boy to resist the patriotic fever of the times. Shortly after the war began Eric wrote twelve lines of verse calling for the young men of England to rally to the country's defence. It is a bad poem, but its straightforward patriotism made it suitable for publication in his family's local newspaper, *The Henley and South Oxfordshire Standard*, which printed it at the bottom of page eight on 2 October 1914. It is titled 'Awake! Young Men of England' and the young poet is identified as 'Master Eric Blair, the eleven-year-old son of Mr R. W. Blair'. The last stanza gives some notion of its quality:

Awake! oh you young men of England,
For if, when your country's in need
You do not enlist by the thousand,
You truly are cowards indeed.

This is the sort of thing which Mr and Mrs Wilkes liked to hear, and indeed it won him a short period of favour at the school. Mrs Wilkes thought it was such a promising piece of work that she had him read it aloud to an assembly of all the boys. As much as he hated her methods, a part of him could not help wanting to please her, and he was 'tremendously proud' whenever she gave him some sign of approval. 'At the first smile one's hatred turned into a sort of cringing love.' But such moments never lasted very long. Inevitably, her smiles faded, and his guilty resentment returned.

CHAPTER THREE

Consolation Prizes

I

Not all of the adults at St Cyprian's were as difficult as Mr and Mrs Wilkes. But in 'Such, Such Were the Joys' Orwell mentions only two 'whom I did not either dislike, or fear'.[1] They were Mr Knowles and Mr Sillar (the names have been changed to Mr Batchelor and Mr Brown in the essay). Mr Knowles was a 'very hairy man who wore shaggy suits and lived in a typical bachelor's "den" – book-lined walls, overwhelming stench of tobacco.' He taught some of the boys Latin and Greek, but was not a full-time master at the school. He was a specialist who gave extra tuition to bright boys at several schools in Eastbourne, so Eric saw him only one or two evenings a week. Walter Christie remembered that poor Mr Knowles was so overworked that 'even his tea had to be swallowed between mouthfuls of syntax, and bits of egg sandwich, caught in his moustache'.[2] His style of teaching was unimaginative, but he was not severe or intolerant and Eric found him 'likable'.

Robert L. Sillar was his best teacher at St Cyprian's. He taught geography and drawing, and made both subjects exciting by illustrating his lectures with magic-lantern slides. He had a good voice and loved to read aloud to the boys. Dickens was his favourite author. Every December he went before the whole school and gave a dramatic reading from *A Christmas Carol*. On his birthday he read from *A Tale of Two Cities*, heightening the drama by using graphic slides of 'blood-stained aristocrats'.[3] He had been with the school from the beginning and was universally admired by the boys. He was patient, sympathetic and generous. He seems to have been the only adult at the school who liked doing things for the boys just for the fun of it. On Guy Fawkes Day he always delighted them with a colourful display of fireworks.

A handsome, white-haired gentleman, he had a boyish enthusiasm for natural history. His collection of butterflies and moths was enormous, and he was constantly prowling the Downs – a large green net in hand – searching for new specimens. He encouraged the boys to assemble their own collections, and avidly reported the latest finds: 'Specimens of Dark Green Fritillary have been taken on the cricket field for the first time, as also Ligniperdi, the goat moth, Sambrucaria and the Ghost Swift . . . The White Admiral has been plentiful in Abbotts Wood, but restricted train service has made it impossible for anyone to go there without a bicycle.'[4] Every year he organised an exhibition of the boys' insect collections, and gave out prizes. He inspired a love of nature in many of his pupils, gently telling them in his deep voice, 'No one can understand difficult things like their own lives and other people unless they understand simpler things like animals and birds first.'[5]

What was such a sensitive, intelligent soul doing at St Cyprian's? No one knows why he came in the first place, or why he stayed, but he seems to have enjoyed a considerable degree of freedom at the school and was rarely troubled by Mr and Mrs Wilkes. On the few occasions when the headmaster and his wife were both absent from the school, he acted as the deputy headmaster, and in that capacity he managed to make things a little easier for the boys. At morning chapel he would ignore the appointed lesson and read one of the lively stories from the Apocrypha.

He was allowed his independence partly because of his age and experience, but also because he was, in the words of one old St Cyprianite, the 'high-priest of the shooting trophies'.[6] He had some mysterious talent – perhaps unique among serious butterfly collectors – for teaching boys to shoot at paper targets with pinpoint accuracy. Everyone acknowledged that he was primarily responsible for the school's perennially high standing in the Private School

Rifle Association. In an organisation representing nearly 300 schools, the St Cyprian's team was almost always among the top ten.

Although Eric was apparently not one of the better marksmen at the school, he did like shooting and showed enough interest in it for Mr Sillar to give him a look at a treasured firearm. 'Once he took me into his room and showed me in confidence a plated, pearl-handled revolver – his "six-shooter", he called it – which he kept in a box under his bed.' But what really drew him to Mr Sillar was their shared love of nature. One of the few times that Orwell actually uses the word 'joy' in 'Such, Such Were the Joys' occurs in his description of butterfly-hunting trips with Mr Sillar. Though Mrs Wilkes did nothing to stop boys from going on these trips, she made it clear that she did not approve, taunting them on their return in a 'babyish' voice, 'And have you been catching *little butterflies*?' She thought that such pursuits were childish and unworthy of a strong boy with real character, but Eric found the trips irresistible, not least because they allowed him to escape from the school for a few hours.

> The ride of two or three miles on a lonely little branch line, the afternoon of charging to and fro with large green nets, the beauty of the enormous dragonflies which hovered over the grasses, the sinister killing-bottle with its sickly smell, and then tea in the parlour of a pub with large slices of pale-coloured cake! The essence of it was in the railway journey, which seemed to put magic distances between yourself and school.

One boy who sometimes accompanied Eric and Mr Sillar on these outings was an odd-looking little fellow with a pug nose, small blue eyes and a thick brow. He was three months younger than Eric and came from a family which was only slightly better off than the Blairs. His father was a retired Army major, and since he was the only child, the family was just able to pay his full fees at St Cyprian's. His name was Cyril Vernon Connolly, and he was Eric's best friend at the school.

Books had brought them together. Both were passionate about the pleasures of reading, and each was delighted to share that passion with the other. They read everything from boys' weeklies and Sherlock Holmes stories to Carlyle and Shakespeare. They had a particular liking for H. G. Wells. When a copy of Wells's *The Country of the Blind* fell into their hands, they were so taken with it that they kept 'stealing' it from each other. Orwell never forgot its powerful appeal, writing more than thirty years later, 'I can still remember at 4 o'clock on a midsummer morning, with the school fast asleep and the sun slanting through the window, creeping down a passage to Connolly's dormitory where I knew the book would be beside his bed.' (Eric often rose early during midsummer mornings so that he could enjoy 'an hour's undisturbed reading . . . in the sunlit, sleeping dormitory'.) Their devotion to books eventually got them into trouble. Mrs Wilkes severely reprimanded them when she discovered that they had been reading a copy of Compton Mackenzie's *Sinister Street*, a popular novel whose title alone was probably sufficient to earn her displeasure. It was a daring piece of work in its day, and the boys must have been thrilled by its exaggerated descriptions of sexual passion in such sentences as, 'The sensuousness of her abandonment drugged all but the sweet present and the poignant ecstasy of possession.'[7]

The two friends also showed each other poems which they had written. They would meet and compare their latest efforts. 'I would . . . be critical of his,' Connolly remembered, 'while he was polite about mine, then we would separate feeling ashamed of each other.'[8] One small sample of Eric's 'polite' criticism has survived. In June 1916 Mrs Wilkes asked the boys to compose some verses in memory of Lord Kitchener, who had died in the first week of the month. (He had gone down in a ship hit by a mine in the North Sea.) Connolly completed a short tribute in his notebook and showed it to Eric, who wrote on the other side of the page: '*Dashed* good. Slight repetition. Scansion excellent. Meaning a little ambiguous in places. Epithets for the most part well selected. The whole thing is neat, elegant and polished. E. A. Blair.'

Connolly was thrilled. Above '*Dashed* good' he wrote, 'My dear Blair!! I am both surprised and shocked.' He even sent the poem home for his mother to admire, boasting that it had been praised by 'the best poet' in the school.[9] Eric was certainly one of its few published poets. His own tribute to Kitchener was good enough to earn him a second appearance in the pages of the *Henley and South Oxfordshire Standard*, which published the poem on 21 July. The first stanza is the best:

> No stone is set to mark his nation's loss
> No stately tomb enshrines his noble breast;
> Not e'en the tribute of a wooden cross
> Can mark his hero's rest.

When Connolly later wrote about St Cyprian's in *Enemies of Promise*, he praised his old friend as the only boy at the school who 'was an intellectual'. Young Eric 'saw through' St Cyprian's and 'was one of those boys who seem born old'. But there was a less serious side to him, and Connolly was perhaps the only person at the school who saw that his friend's sense of humour was sharp and vibrant. He wrote of him, 'His eyes were made to glitter with amusement, his mouth for teasing.'[10] His jokes were understated and usually sardonic. He seemed to enjoy them without caring too much whether anyone else did. During his boyhood Eric answered an advertisement one day from a woman named Winifred Grace Hartland who claimed to have a cure for obesity. He did this purely for his own amusement, and was highly pleased when she wrote back urging him to visit her establishment in London at once. The best part was that she had assumed that E. A. Blair was a woman, and had replied, 'Do come before ordering your summer frocks, as after taking my course your figure will have altered out of recognition.' She continued sending him letters until he finally grew weary of the joke and wrote back to say that his 'obesity' had been cured 'by a rival firm'.[11]

A good sense of humour was a necessity for anyone who was Cyril Connolly's friend. Connolly was a born comedian and was constantly joking about one thing or another. As he freely admitted, he made a 'career' in school of 'trying to be funny'. At his best, he could be very funny indeed, as in this memorable description of St

Cyprian's: 'Though Spartan, the death-rate was low . . .'[12] As a boy, he enjoyed making fun of Mr and Mrs Wilkes; in one daring letter which he sent home from the school he ridiculed Sambo as 'fat ass Sammy'.[13] (Connolly suffered from a lifelong habit of writing dangerously indiscreet letters.) In chapel he mocked 'the end-of-term hymn "Lord dismiss us with thy blessing" by joking under his breath, "Thanks for canings past received".'[14]

In his essay Orwell makes no mention of his friendship with Connolly or with anyone else. More significantly, there is hardly any mention of home or family. Like most boys, he suffered periodic bouts of homesickness, but there was not much that he could do about it. St Cyprian's was supposed to be good for him, and his parents expected him to stay there and to do his best to succeed. Why should they have felt otherwise? They assumed that he was fortunate to be at such a 'successful' school with boys from good families, and they owed a debt of gratitude to Mr and Mrs Wilkes for making it all possible by reducing his fees. School life was not supposed to be easy, and it would have taken a great deal to persuade any parent of the time that St Cyprian's was a terrible place. In any case Eric had neither the words nor the will to make a convincing argument against it. Asking his parents to remove him from the school was simply out of the question. 'To do so would have been to admit yourself unhappy and unpopular, which a boy will never do.' Moreover, he always doubted that his parents could have done much to help him, even if they had understood his real feelings. 'Even before I understood about the reduced fees, I grasped that they [Mr and Mrs Blair] were in some way under an obligation to Sambo, and therefore could not protect me against him.'

Accordingly, the few letters which have survived from his days at St Cyprian's do not show any evidence of his discontent. His letters home are simple and direct. He asks predictable questions about family life and dutifully reports his academic progress. He talks about the weather, his stamp collection, special events at the school, and he thanks his parents for sending presents. In one of his better efforts he writes to his mother about a pleasant outing with an unnamed master (probably Mr Sillar): 'It was ripping on the picnic we went today, – I've never drunk water from a bucket drawn straight up from a well before. We did this at a farm where six of us went with a master to buy milk. By the way, I have 3 catterpillars now, as my partner made over his stock to me. They're called Savonarola, Paul, and Barnabas.'[15]

An adult hand made spelling corrections in the early letters; presumably this was the work of Mrs Wilkes. She made a habit of inspecting the letters which the boys – especially the younger ones – sent home, ostensibly because she wanted to keep an eye on their spelling and handwriting. But in practical terms this meant that the boys could not feel free to say what they wanted to say. There was no point in telling your parents how miserable you were if Mrs Wilkes was going to read your comments first.

He quickly learned to keep his thoughts to himself. Children are good at doing this, Orwell observes in his essay. 'Not to expose your true feelings to an adult seems to be instinctive from the age of seven or eight onwards.' When he went home for the holidays, he enjoyed himself and gladly put aside his thoughts about school. He was quiet, but in most respects he appeared to be content. Speaking of his childhood, his younger sister Avril later declared, 'He always seemed perfectly happy.'[16] There was not much to complain about in his home life. Comparing it with life at St Cyprian's, Orwell wrote, 'Your home might be far from perfect, but at least it was a place ruled by love rather than fear, where you did not have to be perpetually on your guard against the people surrounding you.' His father's retirement in England, after so many years away in India, does not seem to have made much difference to Eric's view of life at home. His father was little more than a vague presence in the house. For attention and affection, he relied on his mother and his sisters. Mr Blair spent his time pottering around the garden and playing golf. (Shortly after returning from India, he had become the secretary at the Henley Golf Club.)

From 1912 to 1915 – between the time that Eric was nine and twelve – the family lived in the small village of Shiplake, which occupied a peaceful spot along the Thames some two miles south of

Henley. A railway station stood near the river, so it was relatively easy to go back and forth to Henley. Up to that time, the village's chief claim to fame was that the poet Tennyson had been married in Shiplake church. The Blairs' house, Rose Lawn, was more attractive than any of their previous residences. It was in Station Road, near the top of a gently rising hill overlooking the Thames. A large two-storied house, Rose Lawn was surrounded by almost an acre of garden. The house was not grand, but it must have been expensive to maintain on the family's limited income. Certainly, they would never again occupy as large a place.

Eric loved Shiplake. There were beautiful fields and woods almost at his door, and the banks of the river could be reached on foot in only a few minutes. But when Orwell came to write *The Road to Wigan Pier* in the 1930s, he criticised middle-class families like his for their pretentiousness, and he may well have been thinking particularly of the days at Rose Lawn.

> Before the war you were either a gentleman or not a gentleman, and if you were a gentleman you struggled to behave as such, whatever your income might be. Between those with £400 a year and those with £2000 or even £1000 a year there was a great gulf fixed, but it was a gulf which those with £400 a year did their best to ignore ... Practically the whole family income [was spent] in keeping up appearances.

This does indeed seem to have been the practice in his own family, but one could not expect his father to have done otherwise. Mr Blair was a conventional man, and after spending more than thirty years in India he was no doubt determined to enjoy his retirement in the best manner possible. But it was a futile effort. After the war began, keeping up Rose Lawn became much more difficult, and in 1915 the Blairs went back to Henley, moving into a smaller place at 36 St Mark's Road. It was a semi-detached house with a tiny front garden.

During the holidays Eric spent much of his time playing alone, though he did spend some time entertaining his younger sister, going for walks with her or playing simple games. Before the war the family would sometimes go down to Polperro in Cornwall for part of the summer. An old family friend – a Mrs Perrycoste – lived there, and her two children provided some companionship for the Blair children, playing with them at the seaside or accompanying them on walks down long country lanes. Orwell had good memories of these holidays. Many years later he wrote about his childhood visits to a farm in Cornwall where the farm hands 'used to let me ride on the drill when they were sowing turnips and would sometimes catch the ewes and milk them to give me a drink'.[17]

There is no evidence that any boys from school visited him at home, or that he went for visits to their homes. There was not even a visit from Cyril Connolly. As Orwell admitted in a typical understatement, 'It is true that I am by nature not gregarious . . .' In fact, his family was in Shiplake for at least a couple of years before he made any close friends there. He met them on a hot day in the summer of 1914. He was out walking when he came upon three children playing French cricket in a field near his house. He did not approach them or call out to them. He merely stood on his head and waited for them to notice him.

'Why are you standing on your head?' he was asked.

His reply was perfectly reasonable. 'You are noticed more if you stand on your head than if you are right way up.'[18]

This amused the children and they soon made friends with him. The oldest of the group was Jacintha Buddicom, a tall young girl with long dark hair. She was thirteen at the time. With her was her brother, Prosper – a small fair-haired boy one year younger than Eric – and their sister, Guinever, a thin little seven-year-old in pigtails. They lived in a large house directly behind Rose Lawn, and for the rest of that summer they and their friend Eric played together nearly every day. He would remain a close friend of theirs until the end of his teens.

They spent much of their time in the Buddicoms' enormous garden, which was a bit overgrown and wild in parts. It was obviously the most interesting place to play, but they did not stay there entirely by choice. Mr Blair discouraged them from playing at Rose Lawn. He did not lose his temper with them or say anything unkind; he simply made it clear that he did not want a group of noisy children playing anywhere close to him. Jacintha remembered him as a stiff, unsmiling old gentleman who rarely said anything to her. By contrast, she thought Mrs Blair was 'vivacious' and 'spirited'.[19]

Prosper Buddicom was a good companion for Eric. He liked fishing. The two of them would dig up worms in Prosper's garden and then walk with their rods resting on their shoulders to a favourite spot above Shiplake where the water was so clear that one could easily see fish swimming in the shallows along the bank. They also had a fondness for wild experiments with chemicals and fireworks. On one occasion they tried to construct a whisky-still, but it blew up when they put it on top of the kitchen stove at Prosper's house. They also ran into trouble when they started a bonfire in the garden and threw some gunpowder into the blaze. Eric's eyebrows were singed by the explosion and both boys came· away with black faces and clothes. Otherwise they were unhurt, though they did suffer strong reprimands from their families afterwards.

One of Eric's favourite toys was a small brass cannon mounted on a wooden gun-carriage. It was barely six inches long and cost only ten shillings, but it used real gunpowder and 'went off with a noise like the Day of Judgment'.[20] One may find it difficult to believe that any parent would allow a boy of eleven or twelve to have a 'toy' such as this, but apparently it was not uncommon at the time. Moreover, guns and rifles were easy to obtain. Orwell remembered that 'before the [First World War] you could walk into any bicycle shop and buy a revolver, and even when the authorities began to take an interest in revolvers, you could still buy for 7s.6d. a fairly lethal weapon known as a Saloon rifle. I bought my first Saloon rifle at the age of 10, with no questions asked.'[21] Whenever he had trouble buying gunpowder, he made his own. As he later boasted, 'A resourceful boy could make gunpowder for himself if he took the precaution of buying the ingredients from three different chemists.'[22] The word 'resourceful' is the key term here. Orwell always enjoyed making things from scratch, even if the results were not entirely satisfactory. He liked feeling independent and self-reliant, and as an adult he would devote a great deal of energy to such activities as growing his own vegetables, keeping a goat and chickens, and making his own furniture.

With Jacintha Buddicom, he enjoyed more refined pleasures. They read poetry together, played card games, and told each other ghost stories. Eric was enthusiastic on the subject of ghosts. He liked to speculate about them and once informed Jacintha that ghosts probably made up half the population in the towns. 'In towns so many [people] would be strangers anyway that we wouldn't know whether they were ghosts or not, if they walked about like anyone else.'[23] During the evenings Eric and Avril would play a form of hide-and-seek with the Buddicom children, and Eric would tease Jacintha about the darkness of their hiding places. 'How can you be sure I'm *me*? It's dark in the corners, and I might have been *got into* by the shadow of a shadow.'[24]

Besides his own family and the Buddicom family, Eric appears to have spent little time with anyone else in Shiplake. Even when the Blairs moved back to Henley, he did not make new friends in the town, continuing instead to spend time with Prosper, Jacintha and Guinever. He would travel the two miles to Shiplake by train or ride down on his bicycle. When Jacintha came up to Henley to see him, he would often take her past his family's old home in Vicarage Road and would stop and touch the name on the gatepost. 'Eric seemed very fond of Ermadale,' Jacintha recalled.[25]

He was briefly involved with the children of a very prominent family in Henley. At the Golf Club Mr Blair had become acquainted with Lord Rathcreeden, whose house – Bellehatch – stood very near the course. During the Christmas holidays of 1915–1916 Lady Rathcreeden decided to put on a pantomime for friends and family in the drawing-room of the house, and she asked the Blair children to take part in her production of *Cinderella*. They agreed and rehearsals began. Her son Peter, who played one of the ugly sisters, later observed that twelve-year-old Eric was not an impressive addition to the cast. 'I remember he was a terrible actor and he was the shyest of all of us – he was very shy. My mother, who produced the pantomime, had great difficulty in getting him to act at all. He had to kneel down and sing a song. He was very gauche.'[26] It must have been an exceedingly painful experience for Eric, but we can only speculate about that. He never made any mention of it in print. We do know that the production as a whole was well received, and that Lady Rathcreeden arranged for her young troupe to put on two more performances. One was given at Harpsden Village Hall as a treat for Sunday School pupils, and another took place on the stage of the Henley Town Hall as an entertainment for convalescent soldiers. (The building had been converted into a Red Cross hospital, and many of the soldiers watched the performance from their beds.) On each occasion Marjorie Blair played the cruel stepmother, and Avril had a small part as a page. Lady Rathcreeden's daughter Sylvia, aged thirteen, played Cinderella. And Eric's part? He was Prince Charming.

II

Several days after he finished his short theatrical career in Henley, Eric returned to St Cyprian's, where only one more year of work awaited him. Academically, this period proved to be a brilliant conclusion to his time at the school. In February 1916 Mr Wilkes took him to Wellington College to sit the scholarship examination. The *St Cyprian's Chronicle* announced the happy result: 'Our best congratulations to E. A. Blair on being elected to the First Open Scholarship for Classics at Wellington College.'[27] But even this triumph was not enough. There was still something grander to strive for. In the spring Mr Wilkes took Eric to Eton to sit their examination, a gruelling affair which lasted two and a half days. If all went well, he would be awarded a place as a King's Scholar. Only seventy boys are entitled to this honour at any one time, which means that the number of annual openings is usually no more than twelve or thirteen. As it happened, Eric was placed fourteenth among the boys who sat the exam. He was out of the running in the short term, but if there were additional openings in the coming months, a spot might still be found for him. In the meantime his scholarship at Wellington was secure, and he planned to take his place there when the year was out.

More honours were to come before he left St Cyprian's. He won the school's Classics Prize, and in June 1916 the news arrived that he was the first runner-up in the Harrow History Prize, Mrs Wilkes's favourite competition. The first-place winner was also from St Cyprian's – Cyril Connolly. They were at the top of a group of sixty-one candidates representing fifteen preparatory schools. Connolly's favour with Mrs Wilkes soared, but he was not especially thrilled with the prize itself. 'The Harrow History Prize came yesterday,' he wrote to his mother. 'I got three rather dry books but they were very well-bound.'[28]

In 'Such, Such Were the Joys' Orwell heaps scorn on the competition, calling it 'a piece of nonsense'. He condemns it for turning history into meaningless lists of things to be memorised:

> It was a tradition for St Cyprian's to win it every year, as well we might, for we had mugged up every paper that had been set since the competition started, and the supply of possible questions was not inexhaustible. They were the kind of stupid question that is answered by rapping out a name or a quotation. Who plundered the Begans? Who was beheaded in an open boat? Who caught the Whigs bathing and ran away with their clothes?

In this matter his memory is remarkably accurate. A copy of Connolly's examination questions has survived, and they are indeed as simple-minded as Orwell claims. 'On what charge were the Seven Bishops tried?'; 'Under what statute was Wolsey condemned?'; 'Who was killed at Tewkesbury?'; 'Name a battle in the War of the Roses in Yorkshire?'[29] To make certain that their boys excelled at answering such questions, Mr and Mrs Wilkes 'crammed' them 'with learning', Orwell says, 'as cynically as a goose is crammed for Christmas'. Some absurd ways were devised to help the boys remember everything which had been 'crammed' into them. 'Did you know,' Orwell asks, 'that the initial letters of "A black Negress was my aunt: there's her house behind the barn" are also the initial letters of the battles in the Wars of the Roses?'

There is no question that Eric had been sufficiently 'crammed'. The school's outside examiner, Mr Robertson, gave him a glowing report in December 1916, at the end of his final term. Interestingly, his name and Connolly's are paired again and again. They were clearly the star pupils.

GREEK. Form VI. – Blair and Connolly both did well; about equal in translation, but Blair was distinctly better in grammar . . .
LATIN. Scholarship Class. – There was little to choose between Blair and Connolly in grammar, but in composition Blair was distinctly superior . . .
FRENCH. Form VI. – The four top boys, Blair, Kirkpatrick, Connolly, Gregson, were very close together. Blair was best in translation and composition . . .
ENGLISH ESSAY. Form VI [Subject: 'What is a national hero?'] – I place the boys in the following order: Maximum marks 50. – Connolly, 48; Blair, 43; Thomas, 42; Colver, Kirkpatrick, Gregson, 41; Wright, 40; Brown, 39; [Walter] Christie, 38; . . . Northcote, 36.

Unfortunately, Eric's English Essay has not survived, but one hopes that his work was partly responsible for this mild criticism from Mr Robertson: 'In the subject "What is a national hero" some paid more attention to heroism than to the qualities of national heroism.'[30] Perhaps it is this 'fault' which cost Eric seven points.

In his last few weeks at St Cyprian's he took to the stage again. A rather elaborate 'dramatic entertainment' was performed twice in the 'School theatre – the gymnasium of normal days', and was repeated three more times for large audiences of wounded soldiers. The cast was memorable. Eric and Connolly played together in a scene adapted from *Pickwick Papers*. Connolly was given the part of the 'undesirable mature spinster' Miss Wardle, and Eric played her father, Mr Wardle. In another skit a new boy – Cecil Beaton – made his stage début playing, appropriately enough, a 'little buttercup'. To these amusing pieces, Mrs Wilkes added a dramatic moment dear to her heart. Her daughter Rosemary and four boys in kilts (her 'admiring Scottish attendants') sang 'I Love a Lassie' and danced up and down the stage.[31]

The term ended a week before Christmas. On the morning of his last day Eric put on his Old Boys' silk tie and went down to say goodbye to Mrs Wilkes. She was polite. She shook hands and called him by his first name. But he felt certain that 'there was a sort of patronage, almost a sneer, in her face and in her voice'. The tone of her 'goodbye' was too much like the mocking tone which she had used to deride his interest in 'little butterflies'. He had won a scholarship and some prizes, but he had never been able to hide his resentment of her or his determination to think for himself. He tried to interpret her 'parting smile'; it seemed to say, 'We know you disbelieve in everything we've taught you, and we know you aren't in the least grateful for all we've done for you. But there's no use in bringing it all up now.' He left St Cyprian's and never returned. 'How happy I was, that winter morning, as the train bore me away with the gleaming new silk tie (dark green, pale blue and black, if I remember rightly) round my neck! The world was open before me, just a little, like a grey sky which exhibits a narrow crack of blue.'

But escaping the influence of Mrs Wilkes would not be so easy. She had occupied an important place in his life for too long a time. In fact, he saw a great deal more of 'Mum' Wilkes than he did of his own mother during those important years between his eighth and thirteenth birthday. Except in the holidays, Mrs Wilkes was a constant presence, and she could never have been far from his thoughts even during the holidays. She helped to shape his character, and he never entirely outgrew her influence, no matter how much he may have wanted to blot it out. There is ample evidence of it in his adult life – his incredible drive, his acute sense of guilt, and his great fear of 'wasting time' must surely have owed something to her influence. She also forced him to develop a certain toughness. To survive five years at St Cyprian's, he had found it necessary to acquire 'a power of facing unpleasant facts', a quality which he claims for himself in his essay 'Why I Write'. One cannot overlook the possibility that her methods may even have helped him to develop as a writer of English prose. Several of her former pupils have said that English was her favourite subject, and that she taught it with greater sensitivity than she showed in her French instruction or her Scripture lessons. She preached the virtues of a simple, straightforward style, and one of her favourite techniques was to use simple passages from the Authorised Version of the Bible as models. She would then 'translate' them into bad oratory or journalese in order to illustrate the virtues of the original model. Of course, this is the same method which Orwell employs so effectively in his most important essay on style, 'Politics and the English Language'.[32]

The importance of Mr Sillar's influence must also be acknowledged. Eric had an instinctive fondness for the natural world, but Mr Sillar helped him to understand that world better, and he showed him that seemingly insignificant things like 'little butterflies' did indeed matter. His boyish fascination for such things never faded. A friend from the 1930s remembered an occasion in London when Orwell proudly displayed a Hawk Moth caterpillar during a visit to the office of the *Adelphi*.[33] A few years later, when Orwell was staying at a tuberculosis sanatorium in Kent, a patient was startled to find him one day sitting cross-legged in a field happily balancing two caterpillars on a stick.[34]

In the last years of his life he thought that one day he might go back and have another look at his old school, but he was not even sure that it still existed. He hated the school so much that for years he avoided going anywhere near Eastbourne. He had heard a 'rumour' that it had been destroyed in a fire. One might suspect that he was merely indulging in a bit of wishful thinking, but this was indeed the fate of St Cyprian's. One Sunday morning in May 1939 an enormous fire broke out and the school burned to the ground. There was nothing left except a small part of the gymnasium and the cricket pavilion at the far end of the playing field. All the boys were rescued, but a sixteen-year-old servant named Winifred Higgs died in the blaze. Mrs Wilkes went into retirement, and the school was never rebuilt.[35]

CHAPTER FOUR

King's Scholar

I

Eric Blair did not care for Wellington College. He went there after the Christmas holidays of 1916–1917, but he stayed for only nine weeks. In March the news came that he had finally received his scholarship at Eton, and he wasted no time in accepting it. He packed his belongings, left Wellington and went home for the Easter holidays. At the beginning of May he went down to Windsor by train, crossed the Thames into Eton and began his new life as a King's Scholar. He was one month away from his fourteenth birthday.

It could be said that he was once again living on someone else's 'bounty', to use Mr Wilkes's term. But this time the benefactor would not be tormenting him. He was safely dead. He was King Henry VI, who had founded the College at Eton in 1440 with the declared intention that it was for the benefit of seventy scholars. By 1917 there were more than a thousand boys at the school, but as one of the seventy King's Scholars, Blair was required to pay only token fees. In return he and the other Collegers, as they were also called, prayed once each week for King Henry's soul, in Latin, as the original charter instructed them to do. It was a fair bargain.

The boys lived according to a set of arcane rules and customs which helped to preserve their distinct identity within the school. They lived together in the ancient buildings of the College itself, whereas the other boys in the school – the Oppidans – lived in various houses in the town. They wore gowns over the customary black and white uniform of the school, they used the initials K. S. after their names, their head boy was always the Captain of the School, and they were the guardians of the mysteries of the Wall Game, one of the oddest inventions in the history of sport.

They tended not to form close friendships with Oppidans, and there was a touch of ill-feeling in the relations between the two groups. Oppidans were sometimes caricatured as rich snobs with weak brains and strong backs, and Collegers were portrayed as middle-class bookworms with few social graces. These generalities were meaningless, but they did have an influence on each group's perception of the other. Among the Oppidans, the favourite term for Collegers was 'Tug', probably a derivation of *togati*, 'gowned'. It was usually employed in a joking, casual way, but sometimes the jokes could turn cruel. Blair appears to have been taunted with it. Sir Richard Rees, reminiscing about Eton, brought up the word in a conversation with Orwell in 1948, and was surprised to see him wince 'as if I had trodden on his tenderest corn'.[1]

For a new 'Tug', the occasional gibes from Oppidans were nothing in comparison with the daily hardships of life in College. In his first year Blair lived in a long, barn-like room known as Chamber which he shared with the thirteen other boys in his Election (a term denoting all those who had been 'elected' to receive scholarships in the same year). Each boy was assigned a wooden stall which rose half way to the ceiling. He had a few simple pieces of furniture – a desk, chair, bookcase and fold-up bed. It was a cold, clammy room with no carpets and only one fireplace. On the infrequent occasions when a boy took a bath, he had to use a tin hip-bath on the floor of the room. Discipline was maintained by the ten boys of Sixth Form, the senior leadership of College. They had the authority to decide who would be beaten, and they – not the masters – administered the punishment. A junior boy could be beaten for almost any mistake, and sometimes no specific reason would be given. He could be punished merely for being 'generally uppish'.

Beatings were fairly common in a boy's first year, and there is evidence that Blair felt the sting of the cane on more than one occasion. The ritual which preceded the punishment was a terror in itself. From the common-room in Sixth Form Passage a runner would be dispatched to Chamber with the name of the boy or boys wanted for punishment. 'You're wanted' the victim was informed. This was the beginning of his ordeal. He had to put on his gown and go to the Sixth Form to answer their summons. If a chair was positioned in the centre of their room, he knew that he would receive a beating. He was lectured, his punishment was announced and then he was told, 'Take off your gown.' The cane was brought out and the boy was ordered to kneel on the chair. Leaning over it with both hands gripping the back, the unfortunate boy waited anxiously, and then suddenly the waiting was over. The beating began. When the deed was done, a member of Sixth Form would politely say 'Good night', and the boy would return to Chamber, rubbing his bottom.

As bad as this was, Blair actually considered life in Chamber to be an improvement over life at St Cyprian's. The canes used by the Sixth Form hurt no less than the one used by Mr Wilkes, but the punishment was easier to accept. For one thing, his position was not as helpless as it had been at St Cyprian's. He was older and tougher, and his adversaries were not adults but other boys in their final year of school. They would be leaving in due time, and a new group of boys – perhaps ones more charitable in spirit – would take their places. In any case the likelihood of receiving a beating decreased considerably after the first year in College, and of course a boy could always take some satisfaction from the thought that he would one day be a member of Sixth Form himself. By contrast, a boy at St Cyprian's was always at the mercy of Mrs Wilkes's changing moods. Her power had the aura of omnipresence and permanence.

Blair learned to look out for himself at Eton, though at one point he asserted his will in a rather unorthodox form. A slightly older boy in College had irritated him in some minor way, so he decided to use a little black magic against the boy. He carved an image of him in soap and stuck pins in it. (Clearly, he had read one too many adventure stories in boys' weeklies.) But, apparently, the curse worked. The boy experienced a string of bad luck, and received two beatings from Sixth Form in one week. Satisfied with these results, Blair dropped the soapen image in some hot water and let it dissolve.[2]

At the end of their year in chamber, his Election moved out of their primitive stalls and each boy took up residence in a room of his own. For the first time in his schooldays Blair had some real privacy. And he finally had a good amount of time to spend as he wanted. As a King's Scholar, he was expected to work hard, but the masters tended to let boys develop in their own ways, and did not subject them to the kind of bullying and scolding practised at places like St Cyprian's. He had seen enough of that and had decided to 'slack off and cram no longer'.[3] He was true to that resolve. From the very first year, his academic work was undistinguished. At the end of the Michaelmas half of 1917 (with supreme indifference to logic, Eton calls its three terms halves) he was at the very bottom of his Election in their Latin division (class). At the top was Roger Mynors (later Sir Roger Mynors, Professor of Latin at Oxford). He had accumulated 520 points from a possible total of 600. Blair's number was 301.[4]

He was determined to relax and enjoy himself. The typical week was a full one, but Tuesday, Thursday, and Saturday afternoons were half-holidays. Boys were expected to spend some of that time in athletic pursuits of one kind of another, especially in the autumn months. But it was also possible to spend part of the afternoon on one's own, and this was Blair's preference.

He chose to spend as much time as possible reading books simply for the pleasure of it. Greek and Latin bored him, but he devoured the works of modern writers whose controversial ideas interested him. He read everything he could find by Jack London, George Bernard Shaw and H. G. Wells. He liked London's emphasis on the raw forces of nature in *The Call of the Wild*, and he admired his first-hand account of poverty in *People of the Abyss*. With Wells, the great attraction was the immense vitality of the novelist's imagination. During one of the darker years of the Second World War, Orwell remembered his boyhood encounters with Wells's books and described the bursts of excitement which they had aroused in him. 'There you were, in a world of pedants, clergymen and golfers . . . and your dull-witted schoolmasters sniggering over their Latin tags; and here was this wonderful man who could tell you about the inhabitants of the planets and the bottom of the sea, and who *knew* that the future was not going to be what respectable people imagined.'[5]

Shaw was appealing because he was so good at 'debunking' the cherished ideals of the establishment. As Orwell wrote in 1940, Shaw was at his best when he was attacking 'the humbug of a puritanical monied society. It was something solid to kick against, and he kicked memorably.'[6] Blair responded to Shaw's scepticism, but he was not an uncritical reader. He was well aware that the playwright's work included not a few half-baked ideas and bombastic pronouncements. In his copy of Shaw's *Plays, Pleasant and Unpleasant*, he scribbled various retorts in the margins, turning his own developing sense of scepticism against the master himself. To this statement in the volume, 'We should all get along much better and faster', he provided the annotation, 'Where to?'

The boy who had 'seen through' Mrs Wilkes was discovering that the world was full of people and events which could not be taken at face value. He was learning that everything was open to question, even the views of fellow sceptics who were asking some of the best questions about society's values. Indeed, the boy who loved Wells would soon grow up and make an enemy of him by turning his critical eye against him. In 'Wells, Hitler and the World State' (1941) Orwell wrote that his old hero was too old to understand the evils of the modern world. 'A lifelong habit of thought stands between him and an understanding of Hitler's power,' the essay declared. Wells, who was then seventy-five, did not appreciate the criticism. He responded by rebuking Orwell in a letter, referring to him as 'you shit'.[7]

Books had helped to awaken this spirit of scepticism, but an equally important factor in its development was the feeling of disillusionment which had spread so widely in the last months of the 'Great War'. The number of old St Cyprianites killed in the war was large for a school of its size, but the figures from such schools paled in comparison with the staggering losses suffered among Old Etonians. By the time the slaughter ended in 1918, the number of OE's killed was 1,157, which was the equivalent of some terrible plague wiping out the entire population of the school. Among the dead were sixty-seven Old Collegers. One of them was a legendary player of the Wall Game who reportedly 'went into action for the last time wearing his College Wall colours'.[8]

Too many young men had marched off to war in a jolly spirit of patriotism, responding to sentiments not unlike those displayed in 1914 in the poem 'Awake! Young Men of England' by 'Master Eric Blair', aged eleven, of Shiplake. But by the time Master Eric had arrived at Eton in 1917, the patriotic fever had passed and the war was merely a series of pointless movements back and forth over ravaged, muddy fields. It no longer exerted an immediate influence on the lives of boys like Blair, except in the matter of food rationing. He never forgot the bad food – the oily margarine or the servings of such things as 'Miss Martin's pudding', which consisted mostly of cold suet and bacon fat.[9] 'It is an instance of the horrible selfishness of children that by 1917 the war had almost ceased to affect us, except through our stomachs. In the school library a huge map of the Western Front was pinned on an easel, with a red silk thread running across on a zigzag of drawing pins. Occasionally the thread moved half an inch this way or that, each movement meaning a pyramid of corpses. I paid no attention.'[10] Even when young officers came back from the front to visit the school, he showed no enthusiasm for their stories of rugged military life. He had heard such stories many times before.

Like most boys at Eton, he served in the school's Officer Training Corps, but his attitude towards the spit-and-polish side of military life had not improved since his days in the Cadet Corps at St Cyprian's. He later wrote, 'To be as slack as you dared on O.T.C. parades, and to take no interest in the war, was considered a mark of enlightenment.'[11] He had no patience for the drudgery of drills, inspections and field days, but he did enjoy the activities which he could perform by himself or in small groups – such things as compass work, map-reading, and rifle practice. He joined the signalling section, which gave him more freedom to be on his own. Instead of running up and down the countryside on field days, he could idle away the hours under a tree with a field telephone at his side. The military objectives which were created for these exercises were hardly inspiring. One November day the Corps was instructed 'to fight a delaying action on the line of the Basingstoke Canal'.[12] He spent part of one field day sitting under a haystack with half a dozen boys from his section. He kept them entertained by reading out loud – in a comic way – passages from *Eric, or Little by Little*, a popular novel of school life which he ridiculed. (The book helped to make the name Eric less appealing to Blair, K. S.) One boy who was there remembered the humorous effect of Eric reading the novel's earnest prose in 'a flat, disillusioned voice'.[13] His general mood in this period has been described as 'sardonically cheerful'.[14]

In quieter moments, when he was alone, he indulged a taste for romantic fatalism in the works of such poets as Ernest Dowson, A. E. Housman and Shelley. By the time he was seventeen he had memorised all of Housman's *A Shropshire Lad*. These poems produced a kind of mesmerising effect on him. He would read them out loud and savour the sound of each word. He appreciated the simple music of such lyrics as 'With rue my heart is laden', and in later life spoke admiringly of the poet's 'charming fragile verse . . . composed almost entirely of words of one syllable'. Orwell also indicated that his early interest in Housman had been fuelled by 'self pity – the "nobody loves me" feeling'. He had been fascinated by the poet's general view of life, his 'bitter, defiant paganism, a conviction that life is short and the gods are against you . . .' And he had been intrigued by the poet's 'unvarying sexual pessimism (the girl always dies or marries somebody else) . . . [This] seemed like wisdom to boys who were herded together in public schools and were half-inclined to think of women as something unattainable.'[15]

After his early, revealing encounters with the free-spirited plumber's children in Henley, his knowledge of sex had developed slowly. At St Cyprian's the boys had received the usual warnings against masturbation, and most of them had developed the usual guilt about it, anxiously checking their eyes for black rings, the 'dreaded stigma, the confession which the secret sinner writes upon his own face'. And they had been warned against homosexual acts, though the warnings had been difficult to decipher. The subject had been discussed with absurd vagueness in a general lecture on the 'Temple of the Body'. Orwell wrote that he was 'almost sexless' at St Cyprian's.[16] That may be, but before he left he did develop a strong interest in penny postcards which featured sexual jokes with illustrations of big-breasted women in tight dresses. These cards were easy to find in a big resort town such as Eastbourne, and he collected as many as he could. During his teens he kept them in a small album. By the time he was in his forties, he had collected hundreds of them and kept them in a large drawer. Orwell wrote about them in 'The Art of Donald McGill' and gave this typical example of a caption:

'I like seeing experienced girls home.'
'But I'm not experienced!'
'You're not home yet!'

His sexual education was a jumble of misinformation, low jokes and noble laments for lost love. A boy of his time and social class could not have expected much else.

II

He sought romantic attachments. One object of his desire was his old playmate Jacintha Buddicom. As she and Eric grew older, her fresh country looks increasingly interested him, and their animated discussions of favourite poems and stories aroused romantic feelings in him. She was two years older and was not inclined to take him seriously as a boyfriend, but he did what he could to bridge the age gap. In October 1918 the fifteen-year-old Etonian sent his seventeen-year-old friend a love poem, with the suggestive title, 'The Pagan'. It has some of Housman's favourite images and imitates his monosyllabic simplicity, but there is none of his pessimism. Eric was hoping for better things.

So here are you, and here am I,
Where we may thank our gods to be;
Above the earth, beneath the sky,
Naked souls alive and free.
The autumn wind goes rustling by
And stirs the stubble at our feet;
Out of the west it whispering blows,
Stops to caress and onward goes,
Bringing its earthly odours sweet.
See with what pride the setting sun
Kinglike in gold and purple dies,
And like a robe of rainbow spun
Tinges the earth with shades divine.
That mystic light is in your eyes
And ever in your heart will shine.[7]

This was pretty serious stuff for a boy of his age, and a little daring for the times. The image of the 'naked souls' was more than Jacintha thought proper, and she later asked him to change it to 'unarmoured souls'. It was a bad substitute and not at all in keeping with the simple diction of the poem, but he dutifully crossed out the offending word and added Jacintha's term.

There was a specific context for the poem. In the previous month, at the end of the summer holidays, he and Jacintha had gone together to a field on the side of a hill overlooking Shiplake and had spent a long lazy afternoon picking mushrooms and talking about books. It was a warm, sunny day and there was a good breeze blowing across the hillside. Jacintha liked to think of herself as 'a natural Pantheist', and she enjoyed telling Eric about her attempts to question Christian practices at her school. She was a bright, independent young woman, and she had natural charm. With her quick laughter and long flowing hair, she made a very attractive 'pagan' in Eric's eyes. They remained on the hillside and talked until the sun began to set. They paused and watched it go down. Jacintha recalled that it was a magnificent sunset. They were up high and the light was golden. 'We both said we would never forget it.'

Matters might have progressed swiftly from this point, but Eric was too shy to do anything more than declare his admiration in his poem 'The Pagan', which he apparently composed after he returned to Eton. He enclosed it in a letter and sent it to her from the school. They were writing to each other almost every week. Unfortunately, their correspondence has not survived, but in Jacintha's memories of that time, their friendship never went beyond the stage of innocent flirtation. 'I never had a kiss from him, and I didn't try to give him one. It was all a kind of mental romantic feeling on his part, and I think I was goodnatured about it, but we were not in love.'[18] The only solid evidence of his feelings is the poetry he composed for her, which includes not only 'The Pagan' but also a sonnet written two months later. Being older, Jacintha may have been in control of her emotions, but he seems to have let his run free, at least on paper. The first eight lines of the sonnet are bold:

> Our minds are married, but we are too young
> For wedlock by the customs of this age
> When parent homes pen each in separate cage
> And only supper-earning songs are sung.
>
> Times past, when medieval woods were green,
> Babes were betrothed, and that betrothal brief.
> Remember Romeo in love and grief —
> Those star-crossed lovers – Juliet was fourteen . . . [19]

He was doing his best to appeal to the 'pagan' streak in her, protesting at the stifling 'customs of this age' and suggesting that romantic matters were handled better 'when medieval woods were green'. The mention of Juliet's age acts as a reminder that Eric, at fifteen, was not too young for real romance. But it is difficult to believe that he meant her to take this kind of talk seriously. She was probably in no danger of receiving an actual marriage proposal from him. All the same, the poem is not a trivial thing and cannot be lightly dismissed. It shows some skill and appears to flow from sincere emotions. He may have been out of his depth, but it must have taken some courage to present this sonnet to his older friend.

In his awkward, adolescent way he was trying to establish a more intimate relationship with his 'pagan'. But it did not work.

It was perhaps inevitable that he would develop strong feelings for Jacintha because he was on especially close terms with her family during the last two years of the war. In August 1917 he spent a long enjoyable holiday with Prosper and Guinever at their grandfather's house in Shropshire. Ticklerton Court had ten bedrooms and was part of a small estate with half-a-dozen farms. Every day the boys went out to hunt or fish, with Guinever sometimes accompanying them. Photographs taken during this stay reveal that Eric was finally beginning to grow out of his pudgy child's body. His face is still round and fleshy, but his legs are long and his shoulders broad. Standing beside Prosper, who was only a year younger, he appears considerably taller than his friend, whose head barely rises above the level of Eric's shoulders.

During the Christmas holidays of 1917 Eric and Avril stayed with the Buddicom family in Shiplake. This was arranged at the request of Mrs Blair, who paid Mrs Buddicom for having the children as guests. It may seem like an odd arrangement, but it was made necessary by some major changes in the Blair family. In September of that year Mr Blair had decided to do his part for the war effort and had taken a commission as a second lieutenant in the Army. He was sixty at the time and was supposedly the oldest man in his rank. What prompted him to take this action is not known. It may have been a delayed outburst of patriotic feeling. But at his age there was not much chance that he would be sent to the trenches. He was, in fact, posted to the 51st Indian Labour Company in Marseilles, where his chief responsibility was to supervise the care and feeding of Army mules.[20]

With her husband away, Mrs Blair decided to take a wartime job in London. She moved into a flat at 23 Cromwell Crescent, Earls Court, and began working at the Ministry of Pensions. Her daughter Marjorie joined the Women's Legion as a dispatch-rider. In November Mrs Blair wrote to Mrs Buddicom requesting that she take Eric and Avril for the Christmas holidays. 'I am very awkwardly placed; as you know, my husband is in France, I am working up

here, & our house [in Henley] is let till the end of January! ...
These are such extraordinary times that one is forced to do out-of-
the-way things, & as you have children of your own and have always
been so kind to mind, I felt I *could* ask you.'[21]

Eric and Avril were delighted with the arrangement, so much so
that they 'implored' their mother to let them do the same thing in
the Christmas holidays of 1918. Their wishes were granted and it
was during this second Christmas with the Buddicoms that Eric
wrote his 'marriage' sonnet to Jacintha. He wrote it in the large
dining-room of the Buddicoms' house. Jacintha remembered the
scene vividly. There was a warm fire, the younger children were
playing card games at the dining-table, Jacintha was reading a book,
and Eric was supposedly writing letters to his parents. Instead he
was composing his love poem. When the younger ones left, he
walked over to Jacintha and proudly handed her the sonnet. It was
written out on lined paper in an old exercise book. Since this
romantic youth was temporarily living under the same roof with her,
Jacintha was probably wise not to give him much encouragement.

But Jacintha was not his only romantic interest. There is
evidence of others at Eton. A close friendship between two boys at a
public school used to be called a 'romantic friendship'. Some of
these were sexual, some were more platonic. Cyril Connolly, who
became a Colleger one year after Blair, enjoyed several close
friendships with boys above and below his Election. Although he
was aggressively heterosexual in later life, the great love of his youth
was a boy in Blair's Election, Robert 'Bobbie' Longden.

He did not spend much time with Blair at Eton. In *Enemies of
Promise* his old friend is described as 'aloof', a self-contained boy
'perpetually sneering at "They" – a Marxist-Shavian concept
which included Masters, Old Collegers, the Church, and Senior
reactionaries'. He and Blair were still friends, but they tended to go
their separate ways. On at least one occasion, however, their
friendship was threatened by a conflict over the affections of
another boy. Connolly was inordinately fond of making romantic
conquests and he did not like competition. When Blair developed
an interest in a boy from Connolly's Election, he immediately began

to fear that Connolly might be tempted to interfere. He wrote to him asking that he not do anything to ruin his chances. The letter itself has not survived, but Connolly had a habit of quoting from his correspondence when he wrote letters to friends, and he quoted a large part of Blair's letter when he wrote to another Etonian during the holidays.

The surviving document provides an intriguing glimpse into the immensely complicated network of romantic alliances which Connolly exploited so skilfully, but it also offers a rare insight into Blair's adolescent sexuality, about which very little has been written. In fact, most accounts of his youth leave the impression that he had only a slight interest in the opposite sex, and absolutely no interest in other boys. This portrait of a rather passionless young intellectual is contradicted by his letter to Connolly, which he wrote towards the end of his time at Eton. In quoting from this letter for the benefit of another friend, Connolly could not resist adding his own comments parenthetically.

I got this curious communication from Blair this hols. I will only quote part of it.
    'I am afraid I am gone on Eastwood (naughty Eric). This may surprise you but it is not imagination I assure you (not with shame & remorse). The point is that I think you are too (to the pure all things are pure) at any rate you were at the end of last half. I am not jealous of you (noble Eric). But you, though you aren't jealous, are apt to be what one might call "proprietary". In the case of Maud and Caroe you were quite right (you remember the episode of the lascivious Dane Watson) but what I want you to do is not to regard me as another Caroe, whatever points of resemblance there may be. Don't suspect me of any ill intentions either. If I had not written to you [until] 3 weeks into next half you would notice how things stood, your proprietary instincts would have been aroused, and having a lot of influence over Eastwood you would probably have put him against me somehow, perhaps even warned him off me. Please don't do this I implore you. Of course I don't ask you to resign your share in him only don't say spiteful things.'

Rather a revelation, of course. I have been much too busy with . . .
NHB to look on Eastwood as anything more than an exploitable side
line who might perhaps gratify some of my peculiarly sensual moods
. . . Of course I like him very much and shall steal him from Blair
who deserves no commiseration. When gone on someone you do not
ask for a half share from the person who owns the mine . . . Anyhow
Eastwood has noticed it and is full of suspicion as he hates Blair.[22]

Connolly was in his element plotting strategies in these wars over
schoolboy attachments, and Blair knew it. That is why he wrote to
him asking for a little consideration. It was a game to Connolly and
he played it to win. The subject of this fuss, Christopher Eastwood,
was a boy two years younger than Blair. In later years he was a
government bureaucrat who eventually became Commissioner of
Crown Lands. Whether Blair ever managed to win his affections is
uncertain. Shortly before he died in 1983, he spoke about Blair to the
Canadian Broadcasting Corporation, but did not claim to have been a
close friend. He remembered him as one who liked 'standing aside
from things a bit, observing – always observing'.[23] From the evidence
of Blair's letter, it would appear that Eastwood himself was being
observed, and perhaps more closely than he might have imagined.

The references in the letter to other boys – F. G. Caroe and John
Maud (later Lord Redcliffe-Maud) – would suggest that the
Eastwood affair was not an isolated incident. He had been 'gone on'
boys before, and from these previous experiences he had learned to
be wary of Connolly's machinations. Though the emotions aroused
by these affairs were no doubt deeply felt at the time, the attraction
to his own sex was only a passing phase in his life, and there are
indications that he felt a deep sense of guilt about it later on. That
sense of guilt may help to explain his later hostility towards 'Nancy
boys', a term which he used on several occasions, particularly in the
1930s, to make uncharitable references to homosexuals.[24] In any
event, it would be unwise to assume that his adolescent affections
for other boys ever reached an advanced stage of sexual contact. He
may well have been as chaste in his relationships with boys as he was
in his relationship with Jacintha. As his letter to Connolly reveals,
he was awkward in romantic matters and was slow to assert himself.

No one who was at Eton with him has ever claimed that they knew him well. Almost everyone remembered him as a quiet boy who did not make friends easily. Richard Steele, a Colleger who was three years his junior, recalls that 'he had a habit of speaking with his mouth almost closed, which gave him the appearance of being unemotional or detached'.[25] He found small ways to show his independence. He smoked cigarettes when he was beyond the watchful eyes of authority, and enjoyed making fun of visiting parents behind their backs. His own were not exempt from this ridicule, and some boys were shocked by his willingness to find fault with his elders. Denys King-Farlow, who was a member of his Election, was one of those who was taken aback by Blair's 'jeering comments' about parents: 'For my generation the precept of honouring your mother and father at least in public was very much ingrained in everyone.' He believed that Blair 'always enjoyed playing the lone wolf'.[26]

But King-Farlow did become a friend, and together the two enjoyed some memorable summer afternoons swimming at a place called Athens, which was a pleasant spot on the Thames half a mile upstream from Windsor. They were usually joined by a few other Collegers, including Connolly's great friend Bobbie Longden (who later became headmaster of Wellington College). According to King-Farlow, 'Blair loved swimming . . . but never bothered about swimming or diving with any style.' He was also fond of 'fishing for pike in Jordan (a small tributary of the Thames) – at Eton then not at all an approved pastime.'[27]

He and King-Farlow worked together on two literary magazines, one of them a very primitive, handwritten thing called *Election Times*, which other Collegers were allowed to read for a penny, with the provision that it had to be returned when they were finished with it. The other magazine was a much more ambitious, and even lucrative, undertaking. It was called *College Days* and Blair contributed material to at least two issues, both of which came out in 1920. The most successful issue was the second of these, which was published to coincide with the Eton *v.* Harrow Cricket Match at Lord's in the summer of 1920. It was commercially printed, sold for a shilling and carried advertisements for national brand names, including Pears Soap and Eno's Fruit Salts. The companies were happy to exploit the snob appeal of advertising in a magazine produced by Etonians, and must have paid handsomely for the opportunity because King-Farlow later claimed that he and Blair made a profit of about one hundred pounds on the issue.

The stories and poems which Blair contributed to the two magazines are ordinary adolescent creations, none of them as good as his 'Pagan' poem for Jacintha. A typical contribution is his short 'Ode to Field Days', from *College Days*, 1 April 1920. It is an amusing satire on the drudgery of service in the Officer Training Corps, recalling 'those blessed field-days' when boys stumbled over rocks, struggled up hillsides, crouched in bogs, and shivered in the damp air of mid-December.

This satiric approach went a bit too far in another one of his contributions to the issue of 1 April. The Master in College, J. F. Crace, was a bachelor and, according to King-Farlow, he had 'a tendency to be overfond of some boys'. Blair and King-Farlow devised a cryptic entry for the personal column in the magazine which read simply. 'A.R.D. – After rooms – Janney'. Few Collegers would have had trouble deciphering the meaning of this fake invitation from 'Janney' Crace to his current favourite among the boys. Crace was furious, King-Farlow recalled, but the master was unable to do anything effective about it because he had been compromised.[28]

This was risky business, but Blair did not seem to care much about the opinions of his schoolmasters. He made little effort to improve his academic standing in the school. He tried specialising in science for one year, but he seems not to have taken the work seriously. He did like dissecting things, however, and used to make trips with another boy to a butcher in Windsor who sold them various animal parts for dissection. Once he used a catapult to bring down a jackdaw which was perched on the top of a building, and then he carried it to the biology lab for dissection. He and his friend slit the gall bladder and made a great mess in the lab.[29]

His academic weaknesses were quite plainly revealed in his

Trials (exams) of Summer half, 1920. On a list of 140 boys, both Collegers and Oppidans, his poor results earned him a spot at 117. No one else from his Election was below him.

III

He spent the final week of that Summer half at an OTC camp on Salisbury Plain. When it was over, he took a train to Cornwall, where his family was enjoying the holidays at Looe. Mr Blair had left the Army and its mules, and was settled into retirement again. Mrs Blair had also given up her job in London. Avril was with her parents, having come down from her boarding school in Ealing, but Marjorie was married and living in London. In July she had married her old friend from Henley, Humphrey Dakin.

On the way down from Salisbury to Cornwall, Eric missed a rail connection and had to spend the night alone in Plymouth. He was still wearing his military uniform, and as he wandered through the town after dark he was mistaken at least once for a real soldier who had been demobilised. It was an adventure to be so completely on his own, and there was a part of him which relished it. Another part of him was cold, frightened and hungry. He had only seven pence in his pocket and no place to sleep. He was able to buy some buns, but had no money left for a bed, so he sneaked into a farmer's field and went to sleep on the ground behind some bushes. He had no blanket, and when he awoke his teeth were chattering. He managed to catch a train and was able to reach his family later that day. Afterwards he wrote to a Colleger friend, Steven Runciman, boasting about his 'first adventure as an amateur tramp'. It was the beginning of a long fascination with tramping, but after this first experience he was happy to have a family to go home to. 'I am very proud of this adventure, but I would not repeat it.'[30]

Part of the attraction of tramping was the opportunity which it gave for an escape from the life of E. A. Blair, K. S., the boy who was expected to make something of his advantages and not to squander them in idleness. As a tramp, even an 'amateur' one for a single night, he could imagine himself free, with no masters to obey, no parents to please, and no expectations to live up to. But it was still merely an illusion. He would never be anything more than a 'temporary' tramp. There would always be a roof and a meal waiting for him somewhere if he needed it.

He was also drawn to tramping for the simple reason that he liked amateur experiments. What would it feel like to sleep all night in a farmer's field? How would you spend your last seven pence? In *Down and Out in Paris and London* Orwell describes the effects of going without food for three days, and seems to be observing it all with the detachment of a scientist in a lab. He writes about his spittle as though he were back at Eton dissecting a jackdaw and trying to describe its parts. On the third day his spittle was 'curiously white and flocculent, like cuckoo-spit. I do not know the reason for this, but everyone who has gone hungry several days has noticed it.'

There was always a spirit of boyish recklessness behind his curiosity. Boys test themselves in absurd ways just for the sake of the experience, and this tendency is apparent in Eric Blair's life at almost every stage. One week after his first tramping experiment, he was back in Henley and was eagerly engaged in a different experiment, one which was ridiculously dangerous. Prosper Buddicom was his assistant and the experiment is documented in Prosper's diary for August 1920.

18 Wednesday   Eric came over for the day but it was too wet to shoot. Made chemical experiments instead.

24 Tuesday   Eric came over. We made nitro-glycerin & gun cotton but the nitro-glycerin would not precipitate.[31]

There is no telling what would have happened to these two boys if their experiment had succeeded. A few months later Eric wrote to Prosper about a much safer experiment. 'I have got an idea of buying Turkish tobacco & making cigarettes of it, but it's awfully hard to get.'[32] In adult life he was never content merely to smoke a cigarette. He always needed to buy the tobacco and paper separately and roll his own. It was a form of daily experimentation.

The shape and consistency of each cigarette was always a little different from the one before it. It was a nasty habit, and in time it helped to ruin his health, but the whole process of making and smoking the cigarettes gave him great pleasure.

Tobacco was an especially bad habit for him to take up because his lungs were never very good. The diary which his mother kept during their first year in Henley contains references to Baby's [Eric's] 'bronchitis', and in 'Such, Such Were the Joys' Orwell says that one reason for his failure to do well at games was that he had 'defective bronchial tubes and a lesion in one lung which was not discovered till many years later'. He says that even as a boy he suffered from a chronic cough. One of the aunts in the Buddicom family took note of this when he visited Grandfather Buddicom's house in 1917. 'Eric has a bit of a cough,' the aunt remarked in a letter to Mrs Buddicom. 'He says it is chronic.'[33] In fact, in the very next year he went down with a serious case of pneumonia, and three years later he was afflicted with a second case of it. Ignorance of lung diseases was profound in those days, and he never received the proper attention his condition called for. Orwell recalled that Mr Wilkes was one whose response was less than enlightened. ' "You wheeze like a concertina," Sambo would say disapprovingly as he stood behind my chair; "You're perpetually stuffing yourself with food, that's why." '

Despite his chest problems, he grew a good deal taller during his last two years at Eton, almost reaching his full adult height of six feet three inches. His face became leaner and longer. His build set him apart and suddenly he was more in demand for College athletic teams. With his bad lungs, he could not contribute much to the field game, Eton's unique combination of soccer and rugby, though he did play it and enjoyed a few moments of success. But his great size made him very useful in the Wall Game. He learned to play it, and in the autumn of 1921 he earned his Wall colour. It was a rough game. In a typical contest, the two opposing teams spend much of their time jammed together against a high brick wall trying to get control of a muddy ball. One side tries to get the ball down to its opponents' end of the wall (the two ends are called good calx and bad calx), and then when the ball is positioned in just the right way, a goal can be scored by kicking the ball at a garden door at one end and an old elm tree at the other. But goals are hardly ever scored.

Getting muddy and bruised seems to be the main purpose, though the intricate rules of the game suggest other possibilities. Simply trying to understand the rules, which are unintentionally hilarious, requires considerable effort. One summary of the game includes these bewildering details. 'When the ball gets into calx, that is, within striking distance for one team or another, a new form of bully is constituted, composed of a getter, a second, and a getting furker on the offensive side, and a stopper, a second, and a stopping furker on the defensive side.'[34] In the *Eton College Chronicle* an account of one match praises Blair for 'making a fine kick more than half the length of the wall well into bad calx'.[35] The annual match on St Andrew's Day is the highlight of the Wall season, and Blair was a member of the College team on that day in 1921 when College played against the Oppidan team. The College team was photographed before the match, and Blair looks impressively tough with his cap pulled down almost over his eyes and a look of grim determination on his face.

When the photograph was taken, he was in the middle of his best term, or 'half', at Eton. He was a member of Sixth Form and the College Debating Society ('College Pop'). He had special privileges and was entitled to live in one of the comfortable rooms in Sixth Form Passage. He was finally at the top of the hierarchy. But his Election was more liberal than the ones before it, and did not rule over College with harsh discipline. They avoided using the cane and, as far as anyone can remember, Eric Blair never gave any beatings.

Boys in Sixth Form were required to memorise a long passage of poetry or other writing and recite it at a formal occasion called 'Speeches'. They chose the works themselves. This event was usually held on the Fourth of June, Eton's grand day of celebration when parents come down for picnics, a traditional procession of boats on the Thames and other festivities. But Blair did not become a member of Sixth Form until after the Fourth of June, and he was set to leave school at Christmas. So he gave his recitation in early October, with five other boys joining him on the occasion. One recited Tennyson's 'Ulysses', another Matthew Arnold's 'The Scholar Gypsy', and a third chose John Bright's 'On Trade Unions'. Blair's was the most imaginative choice. He recited a long passage from Robert Louis Stevenson's 'The Suicide Club', the story of a London club for people who wish to die. Richard Steele believed that Blair chose this story about people who were tired of life because 'he always pretended to feel that way'. In any event the *Eton College Chronicle* was impressed: 'Blair's speech was skilfully chosen . . . It might have been told dramatically, or melodramatically, with abundant expression of the emotions belonging to the scene; but the even and unmoved coolness with which Blair let the story make its own effect was certainly very successful.'[36]

He finished his last half at Eton on 20 December 1921. He left only a few traces behind – a small collection of scattered facts in College records and in the pages of the school magazine. But there was one odd relic unearthed many years later. One day in 1972 a boy discovered in College Reading Room an old book with a long title – *Misalliance, The Dark Lady of the Sonnets, and Fanny's First Play, With a Treatise on Parents and Children*, by Bernard Shaw. Inside the book, written in ink, were the words 'Presented to College Reading Room, June 1920, by E. A. Blair.' The book had been sitting on the shelves for fifty years, more or less neglected. Realising that Blair was the famous writer Orwell, the boy proudly added to the page the words 'discovered in 1972'. But the inscription is not the important thing. It is the contents of the book that matter. Blair was leaving behind a message for future Collegers, a message conveyed in the long opening section of the book, Shaw's essay on 'Parents and Children'. It is a seditious document for a public-school reading room, and Blair must have taken some pleasure from the thought that it would sit there like a landmine waiting to explode, filling another Colleger's head with some of the 'unconventional' thoughts which had filled his.

Shaw's section on 'School' is the most relevant one. It begins with an unforgettable tirade against the school-as-prison, which is a conventional image, but Shaw adds his own twist to it, arguing that schools are worse than prisons.

> In a prison, for instance, you are not forced to read books written by the warders and the governor ... You are not forced to listen to turnkeys discoursing without charm or interest on subjects that they don't understand and don't care about ... In a prison they may torture your body; but they do not torture your brains; and they protect you against violence and outrage from your fellow prisoners. In a school you have none of these advantages.

It is a long essay and no doubt contains some points which would not have met with Blair's approval, but in the main Shaw's criticisms sound very much in tune with Blair's attitudes after five years at St Cyprian's and five more at Eton.

It is important to emphasise, however, that he did not hate Eton. There were too many good things about it – the beauty of the ancient buildings, the Thames nearby, and the great romantic towers of Windsor Castle looking down on the entire scene. But best of all was the fact that, as school-prisons go, Eton allowed its inmates – especially the older ones – an uncommon degree of freedom. In later years Orwell liked to attribute this to the 'medieval chaos' of Eton's educational system. Characteristically, what he admired about the system was its lack of efficiency. As one of his contemporaries in College explained, 'If it is true that his interests even during his schooldays were not bounded by the world of Eton, Eton, I think deserves some credit for this. The general freedom of Eton life combined fortuitously with the special freedom which the regime of College allowed him. There was a kind of insolent carelessness about what was taught at Eton, arising from a confidence that the pupils would not attend to it very much anyway.'[37] Writing in 1948, Orwell praised this relaxed attitude as the factor most responsible for the school's 'one great virtue ... and that is a tolerant and civilised atmosphere which gives each boy a fair chance of developing his individuality.'[38] He would not have been so generous in 1921, but at that time he was too busy 'developing his individuality' to recognise any debt to the school-prison from which he was at last escaping.

CHAPTER FIVE

Lost in Mandalay

I

After Eton, the next logical step for a Colleger was to go up to Oxford or Cambridge. 'It was the done thing to do,' one of his contemporaries observed.[1] But Eric Blair's academic record was a dismal one, and he had no reasonable hope of winning a university scholarship. His family could not be expected to bear the expense themselves, since they had already spent a significant sum on his education over the past ten years, and he had not done much at Eton to justify their sacrifice. His classical tutor at Eton, Andrew Gow, later wrote that Richard Blair had ruled out any question of his son going to a university 'unless he got a scholarship and . . . there was not the faintest hope of his getting one'.[2] Some of his friends believed that he had never been interested in obtaining a university degree, but Jacintha Buddicom was convinced that his heart had been set on Oxford for years, and that he would have done well there if only his parents had been willing to send him.

As Jacintha remembered it, Mrs Blair supported Eric's desire to continue his education, but Mr Blair was 'adamant' in his opposition to it. He thought that his son should follow in his footsteps and serve the Empire in some capacity. It is difficult to imagine Mr Blair, who was normally so unassuming, being 'adamant' about anything. But it is perfectly reasonable that he would want to stop spending his limited income on educating a son who was old enough to begin a suitable career. Other family friends have claimed that he was not the driving force behind the idea, that it was really Mrs Blair who wanted their son to find a place in the Empire, encouraging him to go to Burma where her mother and other relatives still lived. A friend at Eton, Steven Runciman, thought that the idea came from Eric himself: 'He used to talk about the East a great deal, and I always had the impression that he was longing to go back there . . . It was a sort of romantic idea.'[3]

There is probably an element of truth in each of these versions. All that can be said for certain is that young Blair did have a taste for adventure, and a colonial job in Burma was a logical option. But at his age he could not have understood the full implications of accepting this option. His father knew what it meant to work in isolated parts of the Empire for years on end, cut off from family and friends in a punishing climate. Although Mr Blair must have occasionally talked about it, his son was too young and in-experienced to appreciate the difficulties of such a life. A young man could only vaguely imagine the vast stretch of time involved in a colonial career lasting twenty-five or thirty years. In the service which Eric applied to, the Indian Imperial Police, the usual retirement age was between fifty and fifty-five, and the average time between visits home was five years.

But of all things, why the police service? Why not something less dangerous or more lucrative? Mr Blair would have known enough about the job to make the case that it was not as dangerous or as unremunerative as it might sound. In terms of prestige, it was the most respected of the specialised services in the several provinces of India, of which Burma was one. Its entrance standards were demanding, its reputation for integrity was high and the pay was excellent. At nineteen or twenty, a young officer began his career at a salary close to £400 a year, and in a few years he could be earning twice that amount. In other words, Eric would begin his police career earning a sum roughly equal to his father's pension, and would soon be making far more than that. For a young bachelor living in a distant province of the East, such a salary could go a long way.

Obviously, the job had its dangers, but in most provinces they tended to be few. The British officers of the Indian Imperial Police were essentially administrators, and were rarely called upon to fight crime on their own. They were not like Canadian Mounties enforcing the law on the frontier with only their wits and a few weapons. Most of their time was spent filing reports and supervising the work of the local police forces serving under them. Like many other expressions used by the colonial rulers, the name 'Indian Imperial Police' is misleading. It was rare to find an Indian who belonged to it. Its ranks were limited to only a few hundred men, the great majority of whom were recruited in England. They were scattered over the enormous area of the sub-continent, and would have been powerless without the loyal help of thousands of native-born constables in each province. There was an official policy in the 1920s to admit more Indian officers to the ranks of the Indian Imperial Police, but this policy was slow to take effect, and another decade would pass before a significant number were admitted.

Each year in London the India Office held a competitive examination for admission to the Imperial Police. It was administered by the Civil Service Commission in its imposing building near the Royal Academy of Arts, and to this place Eric came in June 1922 to spend an arduous week writing a series of papers on a variety of academic subjects. Few of the questions had anything to do with the practical side of police work in the East. In history, for example, the prospective police officer was expected to answer such questions as, 'Who was the greatest Prime Minister since Pitt?' Surprisingly, Blair's performance was weak in history, and only average in English and French. In Greek and Latin, however, his work was superior, which was perhaps predictable for a King's Scholar. Overall, he accumulated enough points to be ranked seventh in the group of twenty-six finalists, but a few weeks later his position fell by more than a dozen places after he received the poor results of his compulsory riding test. His experience with horses was slight, but he had bravely attempted the required routines, which included jumping hurdles. Tall and ungainly, he was lucky to have come through this part of the test in one piece. Despite his low marks he remained on the qualifying list, and in October received his appointment as a probationary Assistant District Superintendent of Police.

When asked to rank the Indian provinces according to his preference for service, he listed the province of his birth – Bengal –at the very bottom, and put Burma at the top ('Have had relatives there') and the United Provinces second ('My father was there for some years').[4] Both these choices clearly show the influence of his parents, but in terms of comfort and security Burma was a bad choice and was at the bottom of most candidates' lists. Not only was it regarded among many officials as the 'backwater of India', but it was also the one province in which a policeman was most likely to find trouble. It was infamous for having the highest crime rate in the Empire, and murder in particular was a widespread problem, the number of cases having more than doubled in the previous ten years. As one scholar has pointed out, the murder rate in some parts of the country was six times higher than Chicago's during the days of Al Capone. If a young man was actively looking for opportunities to fight serious crime, Burma was the place for him to go.

A large part of the problem was the lawlessness of 'dacoit' gangs, small groups of men who roamed the country, mostly at night, looking for homes to rob. Their thievery was frequently accompanied by murder, which they committed with long knives called 'dahs', or with home-made guns. Although most of the work of tracking down the dacoits and capturing them was done by ordinary constables, British officers were occasionally involved in terrifying pursuits of the gangs. The annual editions of the Report of the Police Administration of Burma are filled with gruesome details of dacoit crimes. Among the cases described in the edition of 1925 are a few random examples from districts in which Blair served:

In Hanthawaddy District, a Coringhee fisherman was brutally hacked to death by a band of five hooligans merely because his daily catch of fish was coveted by the daughter of a village headman. In a case from Insein District the dacoits before leaving a house with their booty covered the complainant's wife with a blanket soaked in kerosene oil and set fire to it ... A most brutal case, in which twelve dacoits armed with guns were concerned, occurred in Amherst District. The house-owner was shot dead and his little daughter was raped by the leader of the gang.[5]

The high rate of crime was partly related to the country's political instability. There was widespread animosity towards British rule, and many young Burmese had lost respect for law and order under the system imposed upon them by the foreign power. The British defeat of the last of the Kings of Burma had taken place as late as 1885, and the conquest was still a source of bitter resentment among the people. Young Buddhist monks were at the forefront of protests against the colonial government, organising boycotts of British goods and encouraging a strike by students at the University of Rangoon. There was a constant threat that open rebellion might break out, and as a precaution the authorities maintained a sizeable contingent of British and Indian troops, and a special force of military police numbering twelve thousand, most of whom were Indians.

The appeal of Burma among the colonial services was so low that men who chose to serve there were given a 'sort of consolation prize', as one officer put it, in the form of a 'Burma Allowance' which added several pounds to their pay each month. Blair must have had some idea of Burma's problems, but he may have been feeling too adventurous to take them seriously, or his mother and her family may have helped to convey a false image of Burma's reality. As he later noted, his grandmother was so out of touch with ordinary life in Burma that she never bothered to learn a word of Burmese during her forty years there.

Whatever reservations he may have had, there was little time to think about them in the short period which elapsed between his acceptance and his voyage to Burma. In an effort to make the change to a tropical climate as easy as possible, the India Office had arranged for new recruits to arrive in the East in November, at the beginning of the cool season, so Blair had only a few weeks to prepare for the voyage. The journey would last three weeks and would begin in Liverpool on a ship of the Bibby Line, the MV *Herefordshire*. Though he would not be returning for at least several years, he seems to have had no farewell party with friends, and he showed no outward sign that he was unhappy to be going away.

Years later, neither Jacintha nor her sister Guinever could remember their last meeting with him before he sailed to Burma, but there is evidence that he was deeply concerned about having to leave Jacintha behind. Near the end of his life, after having lost contact with her for many years, he wrote to her, 'You were such a tender-hearted girl . . . But you were not so tender-hearted to me when you abandoned me to Burma with all hope denied.'[6] Jacintha never seems to have understood how much she meant to him, and he was not one to make a show of his feelings, except in poems and letters. She recalled receiving three letters from him after he had arrived in Burma, and in each of them he complained bitterly about the place. 'You could never understand how awful it is if you hadn't been here,' he said in his first letter, and the other two continued in a similar vein of disappointment. She responded to the first, but never replied to the last two. It was not because she had wanted to snub him, she recalled, 'It just *happened*, without being deliberate . . . Before I got round to writing, the letters were lost and I couldn't remember the address.'[7]

Regardless of the reason, he must have been hurt by her silence and must have interpreted it in the worst way, seeing it as the final rejection. He had never made his intentions clear, and it is difficult to say what he had planned for their future. When he left England, he may have thought that they would continue their friendship by correspondence, and if all went well, he would propose to her when he returned on his first leave, which was at least four or five years away. If this was his idea, it was unrealistic, but it was something to hope for, a fantasy to keep him going during a long period away in a remote part of the world. When she failed to keep in touch, that hope was 'denied'. In one of his last poems for her, which was composed during the summer before he went to Burma, he lamented the fact that his friendship was accepted, but not his love:

Friendship and love are closely intertwined,
My heart belongs to your befriending mind:
But chilling sunlit fields, cloud-shadows fall —
My love can't reach your heedless heart at all.[8]

II

His long voyage from Liverpool to Rangoon began on 27 October
1922. He was nineteen, and this was his first trip outside England
since he had arrived from India with his mother and older sister
eighteen years before. During this return to the East he lived in
grand style on the liner, travelling first-class at government
expense. He later wrote that he spent almost the entire journey
sleeping, eating, drinking and playing deck games. After sailing
across the Mediterranean, the ship called at Port Said where it was
the custom for new recruits to purchase their first topi, or pith
helmet, at the store of Simon Arzt. It was thought that a European
would inevitably succumb to sunstroke if he did not have his helmet
to protect him from the dangerous Indian sun, and Blair later
listened to long lectures from old Burma hands explaining why, rain
or shine, the helmet was a vital necessity. As he was solemnly
informed, the natives did not require one because they had 'thicker
skulls', but the white man could not do without it even when the sun
was covered by clouds. 'The deadly rays filter through the envelope
of cloud just the same,' he was told, 'and on a dull day you are in
danger of forgetting it. Take your topi off in the open for one
moment, even for one moment, and you may be a dead man.'[9] After
years of loyally wearing his topi, the veteran official could give it a
decent burial at retirement by observing the custom of casting it into
the sea on the last voyage home.

From Port Said the ship moved through the Suez Canal, sailed
into the Red Sea and finally entered the enormous expanse of the
Indian Ocean. Blair's first view of life in Asia came when the ship
reached Ceylon. Its exotic atmosphere is neatly captured in a brief
passage from *Burmese Days*. 'They sailed into Colombo through
green glassy waters, where turtles and black snakes floated basking.

A fleet of sampans came racing out to meet the ship, propelled by coal-black men with lips stained redder than blood by betel juice. They yelled and struggled round the gangway while the passengers descended.' As Orwell recalled in a short article written much later, there was a disturbing side to this spectacle. While he had been observing the busy scene on the ship, he had noticed a coolie struggling to unload a large piece of luggage. It was a long tin uniform-case and the size of it was more than the man could manage properly. As the coolie moved along the deck trying to balance it, passengers and crew had to duck to avoid being hit in the head. A white police sergeant, who had been supervising some of the unloading, quickly came over and gave him a violent kick in the behind which sent the poor man staggering across the deck. This was bad enough, but what was most disturbing about the incident was that none of the passengers seemed shocked by the brutality. 'The most selfish millionaire in England, if he saw a fellow-Englishman kicked in that manner, would feel at least a momentary resentment. And yet here were ordinary, decent, middling people ... watching the scene with no emotion whatever except a mild approval. They were white, and the coolie was black. In other words he was sub-human, a different kind of animal.'[10] He would see a great deal more of this kind of behaviour in the next five years, and would himself be guilty of lashing out at servants and coolies. But he would come to hate himself for it, and to hate the system which encouraged it.

In the last week of November, as the ship approached the coast of Burma, the ocean turned brown. A kind of stain spread over the water, the result of tons of mud flowing down from the delta of the Irrawaddy, the country's principal river. This was hardly an inspiring sight and may have given Blair his first real moments of doubt about the wisdom of coming to such a place. The ship sailed into the wide river and slowly worked its way to the landing at Rangoon, where treacherous currents made it necessary for liners to anchor in the stream while small boats ferried passengers to the docks. As soon as he was ashore, he reported his arrival to the office of the Inspector-General of Police in an enormous building called the Secretariat, which was the administrative centre of the capital. Within twenty-four hours, he was on a slow-moving train bound for a destination four hundred miles to the north – Mandalay, the site of the Provincial Police Training School.

When young officers such as Blair arrived in the provinces of India, they usually had no experience or knowledge of police work and no understanding of the native languages. All that mattered was that they were British and had passed their examinations back in London. These were their only real qualifications. The aim of the training school was to transform the young, rather innocent recruits into real police officers capable of functioning in a foreign land. The normal probationary period was two years, nearly half of which was spent at the school, where the recruits were expected to make an extensive study of criminal law and police procedure, using a long list of books with such titles as the *Indian Penal Code*, the *Criminal Procedure Code*, the *Evidence Act*, the *Manual of Medical Jurisprudence*, the *Indian Manual of First Aid* and the *Police Drill Manual*. It was a tedious business of memorising dry explanations of sometimes ridiculously complex rules.

But by far the most difficult part of the training was the language instruction in Burmese and Hindustani. Recruits needed to pass examinations in both languages, demonstrating the ability to read, write and speak them. Burmese was especially difficult for the young Englishmen because of its complex arrangement of sounds – a single syllable can have three or four different meanings depending on the manner of pronunciation. The men were fortunate, however, to have an excellent teacher, an amiable, middle-aged police inspector named Po Thit, who was fond of boasting that none of his pupils had ever failed to meet the language requirement. Part of the secret of his success was his own lack of proficiency in English. As one former pupil explained, Po Thit 'was obliged to interject, right from the start of his teaching, Burmese words between his English ones. This involuntary dual language teaching seemed to make it easier for us to memorise the strange words and their meanings. We reached an understandable collo-quial knowledge in an astonishingly short time.'[11]

The superintendent of the school was a tall, rugged Scotsman named Clyne Stewart. He was responsible for teaching some of the classes in police procedure, but almost everyone else on the staff was Burmese or Indian, and most of the men in training were Burmese constables preparing to move up to the rank of sub-inspector. About seventy of these pupils were at the school. Blair and two other Englishmen were the only assistant superintendents receiving instruction. The fact that just three men were being trained at this level is not unusual because in all of Burma the total number of officers in the Indian Imperial Police was only ninety. It is extraordinary to consider that Burma was a land of thirteen million people with a large native-born police force of thirteen thousand men, yet almost all police operations were controlled by a tiny contingent of foreigners, some of them barely old enough to shave. With a few exceptions, the British officers occupied all the top ranks – from Inspector-General to Superintendent and Assistant Superintendent.

As one of the privileged few, Blair was not required to live in the compound of the training school. Instead, he and his two colleagues – Roger Beadon and Alfred Jones – lived a short distance away in the Indian Police Mess, a two-storied building of brick and wood with a large dining-room, a billiard room and an expensively furnished living-room on the ground floor, and several bedrooms with private baths on the floor above. The three recruits had this large place more or less to themselves, sharing it only when officers from other districts were visiting Mandalay. According to William Tydd, who lived at the officers' mess later in the 1920s, and who eventually became assistant commissioner of the Rangoon Town Police, the building had one peculiar feature. One of the bedrooms was always kept unoccupied. In his memoirs Tydd recalled the story behind this custom:

> Although many young men had passed through the mess over the years, only one tragedy had been recorded. A young probationer, unable to bear the homesickness which assailed us all at times, shot himself after his first four months. He stretched out on the

rug beside his bed, placed the barrel of his shot-gun in his mouth and then pulled the trigger; he had occupied one of the two end bedrooms. We occupants of course knew the story and followed, by tacit agreement, the age-old custom of a succession of mess members, in leaving the fateful bedroom unoccupied.[12]

If Orwell knew this story, and it is very likely that he did, the image of the suicide's empty bedroom would have been difficult to forget. It may have been in his thoughts when he wrote the dramatic ending of *Burmese Days*, in which the protagonist, John Flory, goes to the bedroom of his bungalow, closes the door and puts a bullet through his heart.

According to Roger Beadon, Eric Blair spent a good part of his time at the training school alone in his room. While Beadon and Jones were enjoying themselves at the Upper Burma Club in Mandalay, Blair would stay behind and read in his room. As Beadon later remarked, 'He was not what I would call a socialite in any way. In fact I don't think Blair went to the club very much.' He also noticed how awkward Blair's height made him seem. Clothes never seemed to fit him properly, and he always appeared uneasy with the formalities of police life. Beadon was impressed, however, with his colleague's performance in their classes. Beadon was able to learn Burmese and Hindustani only with considerable effort, and he was stunned to see how easily the languages came to Blair. 'I'm told that before he left Burma, he was able to go into a *pongyi kyaung* which is one of these Burmese [monasteries], and converse in very high-flown Burmese with the *pongyis*, or priests.'[13]

Beadon did make an effort to be friends, and the two went on a few brief excursions together. They went hunting, played golf and visited the principal hill-station of the province, Maymyo, which was less than two hours away by train. Later in the year, they returned to this pleasant retreat for one month of training with a regiment of British soldiers, but their initial visit was solely for pleasure. Beadon recalled that they both enjoyed the trip but that his companion had stayed rather aloof the whole time and had limited his conversation to commonplace remarks. 'I don't suppose we really had very intelligent conversations beyond what was going on and why . . . I don't think we ever got on to a very high-flown level. I mean, I certainly wouldn't have thought that he was a person who was going to write or anything like that, at least not in those days.' Blair may not have revealed much to his friend, but he was quietly taking everything in with a sharp eye for detail, storing up colourful images which would later emerge in a most unlikely context. In the late 1930s he used his memory of the journey to draw an analogy in *Homage to Catalonia*, explaining that the pleasure of returning to Barcelona after being away at the front for three and a half months reminded him of the 'same abrupt and startling change in atmosphere' which he had experienced at the end of the train journey to Maymyo.

> It is rather a queer experience. You start off in the typical atmosphere of an eastern city – the scorching sunlight, the dusty palms, the smells of fish and spices and garlic, the squashy tropical fruits, the swarming dark-faced human beings – and because you are so used to it you carry this atmosphere intact, so to speak, in your railway carriage. Mentally you are still in Mandalay when the train stops at Maymyo, four thousand feet above sea-level. But in stepping out of the carriage you step into a different hemisphere. Suddenly you are breathing cool sweet air that might be that of England, and all round you are green grass, bracken fir-trees, and hill-women with pink cheeks selling baskets of strawberries.

Back in Mandalay, Blair and Beadon sometimes went for short outings together on motor cycles. Their mode of transport was something of a novelty in those days. The young men were encouraged to travel everywhere on horseback because all recruits were expected to improve their riding skills – an advanced test was given at the end of the school year – and each man was allowed a certain sum for the purchase of a horse. But 'as a sop to modernity', the authorities had decided that a recruit could also use this allowance to buy a motor cycle.[14] Even so, it was not so easy to find good machines in Burma, and Blair's was an odd American contraption with four cylinders mounted on a very low frame. It was so low to the ground, and he was so tall, that his knees almost reached his face.

He tried valiantly to make the best of this uncomfortable arrangement, but on one occasion it nearly caused him injury in a crash. He and Beadon were exploring the grounds of Fort Dufferin, which had once been the main fortress of the Kings of Burma. Enclosing the grounds was a high brick wall with teak watchtowers, and as Beadon and Blair approached one of the gates they realised too late that it was closed. Beadon managed to stop, but Blair was flustered and would have hit the wall if he had not stood up at the last minute, letting the machine move ahead without him. There was no major damage, except for Blair's bruised pride.

Even with all its exotic charms, Mandalay did not win his heart. It was a bustling centre of trade, attracting buyers and sellers from hundreds of miles in all directions, including traders from China and Siam. Yet in *Burmese Days* the city is contemptuously dismissed: 'Mandalay is rather a disagreeable town – it is dusty and intolerably hot, and it is said to have five main products all beginning with P, namely pagodas, pariahs, pigs, priests and prostitutes.' If anything attracted his interest in the city, it was in fact the seamy side, not the relatively genteel world of Beadon and the regulars at the Upper Burma Club. He made a point of getting to know the most disreputable Englishman in Mandalay, a former Army captain who had been dismissed from the military police and was leading the life of an opium addict. The man, whose name was Captain H. R. Robinson, would tell anyone who would listen that he had discovered the secret of the universe. It was all contained in a single sentence, but he could never remember it after his opium trances were over. During a long crazy night of dreaming about this secret, he managed to write down the pearl of wisdom, but when he looked at it in the morning, all it said was, 'The banana is great, but the skin is greater.'

Captain Robinson did try to break his drug addiction, but eventually he succumbed to depression and tried to 'blow his brains out'. He botched the attempt, damaging his eyes with the gunshot, which doomed him to a life of blindness. All the same, he was later able to write a book about his experiences, calling it *A Modern De Quincey*, and when it appeared in England in 1942, Orwell gave it a kind review in the *Observer*.[15]

This was the sort of man – the outcast, the failure, the unhappy dreamer – who interested Blair. The dry routine of social life in Mandalay's polite society bored him, especially the tiresome ceremony which he had been obliged to perform shortly after his arrival. Armed with a stack of calling cards, each engraved with his name and rank, he had moved through the European district dropping his card into the slots of small brown boxes outside the houses of the local officials and businessmen. It was simply a way of alerting residents to the presence of a newcomer, so that they could send social invitations later, but Blair thought it an incredibly silly thing to do. It was not considered proper merely to introduce oneself on the street, or to go up to a house and ring the bell. One was supposed to leave the cards and pretend that the inhabitants were all away visiting someone else. For that reason each box had the words 'Not at Home' painted in white on the front. The caller had to repeat this routine every time he moved to a new post, and if he failed to carry it out, the local hostesses would take great offence.[16]

Although Burma was an enormous country, the European community had managed to turn it into a very small one, living so completely among themselves and ignoring much of the life outside their closed circle. Each person had an assigned place in this world, the hierarchy of which was spelled out in the Civil List. This tome was the 'Debrett of Burma', as Orwell called it in *Burmese Days*, a 'Who's Who' of all the officials which gave their salaries, titles, honours and service histories. There was no way of disguising who you were or who you were not, because one look in the Civil List would reveal all. The stifling atmosphere of this social world may have led Blair to think that he was much better off staying put in the largely empty officers' mess.

If this life was so uncongenial, then why did he stay in the Imperial Police for five years? It was largely a matter of pride. After all the preparation and expense of going out to Burma, it would have been too humiliating to give up immediately and return home. Moreover, as a source of secure employment – with a generous salary and pension – it was not a profession which a young man of the middle class would have been quick to abandon. Blair had to stick it out and try his best to wait patiently until his first leave came up. At that point he would be allowed a free passage home, and would have several months of free time to think things over.

In the meantime, he did what was expected of him. By the end of his first year in Burma, he had satisfied all the requirements of the training school, and had received approval to spend his second probationary year acquiring practical police experience at a district headquarters. His superiors showed no lack of confidence in his progress. With his reserved manner and apparent fondness for solitude, he was doubtless a disappointment socially, but these things would not have been held against him professionally, at least not at this early stage in his career. If his superiors had entertained any serious doubts about him, he would have been held back for more training at the school, or – in the worst case – he would have been discharged and sent back to England. But, in fact, he was an excellent candidate for advancement because his linguistic skills gave him such a great advantage in Burma, where so much of a young officer's success was measured according to his progress with Burmese and Hindustani. A great deal of the paperwork which passed through the typical district headquarters was written in Burmese, so a young officer who could use the language well had an obvious advantage over colleagues who were still struggling with it.

Though he could not hide his talents, he was careful to keep his thoughts to himself. With each passing year in Burma, he became more convinced that he was in the wrong profession, and that the entire system of imperial rule was wrong, but he could not bring himself to say such things openly. Several years after leaving Burma, he wrote, 'Every Anglo-Indian is haunted by a sense of guilt which he usually conceals as best he can, because there is no freedom of speech, and merely to be overheard making a seditious remark may damage his career. All over India there are Englishmen who secretly loathe the system of which they are part.'[7]

Occasionally, young Blair was unable to contain his anger and dared to voice his true feelings, but only to sympathetic listeners. In *The Road to Wigan Pier* he recalls confiding his 'secret' thoughts to a stranger in Burma – an official in the Educational Service – who was sharing a compartment with him on a rail journey at night. 'It was too hot to sleep and we spent the night in talking. Half an hour's cautious questioning decided each of us that the other was "safe"; and then for hours, while the train jolted slowly through the pitch-black night ... we damned the British Empire.' But such uninhibited conversations were rare indeed, and offered small relief from the essential loneliness of his life in Burma, the pattern of which was not unlike Flory's in *Burmese Days*. 'He had learned to live inwardly, secretly, in books and secret thoughts that could not be uttered ... But it is a corrupting thing to live one's real life in secret. One should live with the stream of life, not against it.'

CHAPTER SIX

Servant of the Empire

I

Previous accounts of Eric Blair's years in Burma have described his police career as a dismal failure from beginning to end. He has been portrayed as a basically incompetent, unpopular officer who was given 'poor and lonely postings', and who was frequently bullied by dim-witted, bigoted superiors.[1] But no one has clearly indicated who these bullies were, and no specific reasons have been established for their supposed hostility to Blair. It is an argument based largely on speculation and hearsay. Nevertheless, it has been widely accepted because information about the period has been so difficult to come by. No personal letters have survived, and many of the relevant police files were destroyed during the Second World War, when Burma was under Japanese occupation.

But not all the records were in the East. Some important documents can be found in London, in the vast archives of the India Office Library, and they reveal a few surprises. As an assistant superintendent, Blair was posted to five different districts in Burma, and in three of these places, he was directly under the supervision of men who were far removed from the stereotype of the whisky-swilling, 'damn-the-natives' English officer. In fact, they were Burmese. U Ba Thin, U Ba and U Maung Maung were among the first men in their country to be admitted into the ranks of the Imperial Police, receiving their appointments in the early 1920s as a result of the government's determination to begin gradually adding more native-born officers. They were all middle-aged men who had spent many years in the Provincial Police before winning their promotions to the more prestigious service. If the case is to be made that Blair suffered under arrogant, abusive superiors, these three names will have to be eliminated from the list of suspects. As veterans of the local forces, they were in the habit of showing deference to young English officers, and the relative insecurity of their new positions would have prevented them from indulging any temptation to bully their nominal subordinate Blair. They also understood that because the system of advancement favoured officers from Britain, young Blair might eventually be their superior. They had nothing to gain from mistreating him.[2]

One possible 'bully' has been vaguely identified. In the 1970s an American who had once worked for the Burmah Oil Company recalled meeting Blair and another police officer in 1924 near the large refineries at Syriam, which was about ten miles from Rangoon. The American described the second man as 'Blair's superior' and gave the officer's name as simply 'De Vine'. His chief memory of this man was that he had joked about his subordinate's public-school education. 'De Vine . . . introduced Blair to us as "a highly educated sort of chap, ha, yes, Blair was eaten and brought up – ha, sorry, brought up at Eton".' From this tiny scrap of information, one writer on Orwell has constructed a menacing character for this mysterious figure named 'De Vine', saying that he was 'a difficult and probably bullying superior, one who sneered at him for having been to Eton'.[3] But this is false. The officer was James Chancellor de Vine, and he was neither Blair's superior nor a bully.

When he was interviewed for this book in 1989, De Vine was ninety and was living comfortably in retirement at his home in Leicestershire. A jovial man with a ruddy complexion, he laughed at the news that he had bullied a man whom he had barely known. He had joined the Imperial Police only one year before Blair, and in 1924 they were both assistant superintendents serving in the Hanthawaddy District, which included Syriam. 'We met for the first time in December 1924 when our district superintendent asked me to accompany Blair to his new post at Syriam, where the big oil outfit was. I introduced him to some of the men there and helped him settle in, and then I left. I don't think we saw much of each other after that.'

De Vine confessed that he had made the joke about Eton to the American at Syriam. 'But there was no sneering. It was a joke that Blair and I had shared earlier. He told it to me. It was something that he had brought from the training school – where the joke began, you see – and we had laughed about it together, on our way to Syriam.'

Blair did have trouble with one of his superiors, De Vine said. It was their superintendent in the Hanthawaddy District, a man named Henry Lanktree. 'He was a bad fellow, not one of us, if you know what I mean. He was ex-Army, but he was not a good officer. He didn't know how to handle men, and I gathered that Blair did not like him, but, fortunately, we didn't have to see much of Lanktree because his office was in Rangoon.'[4]

How much bullying took place is impossible to determine, but Lanktree could not have been entirely unhappy with Blair. The young man's two-year probation period came to an end while he was serving under Lanktree, and if the older officer had really wanted to punish him, he could have made trouble by advising his superiors to reject or postpone final approval of Blair's appointment. But this approval came without delay, and he was then given another post under Lanktree – the job of overseeing security at the Syriam refineries. This may not sound like an impressive position until one understands that these refineries and the enormous storage tanks nearby were the most important industrial complex in the country. British India was almost entirely dependent on Burma for its oil supply, and most of it was refined in one place – Syriam. Though he was only twenty-one at the time, Blair was placed in charge of a local force of nearly two hundred men who were responsible for guarding the industrial area and enforcing the law in the adjoining town. Such a job would not have been given to one so young unless his superiors had been confident of his ability to manage it.

The notion that Blair was given 'bad' postings does not stand up to scrutiny. It is true that he served in some remote areas of the province, but Burma was a large, undeveloped part of the Empire – it was roughly the size of Texas – and any one of its forty districts, with the exception of Rangoon, could be reasonably described as remote. A young officer could not have expected to spend all his time in the relative comfort of the capital. If he wanted to assume higher positions of authority, he needed to know how the police forces functioned in various parts of Burma.

It has been said that one indication of Blair's difficulties is that he never stayed long in any one place, but this was not uncommon for assistant superintendents at that time. During his three and a half years of service after Mandalay, his record of postings is not much different from those of the two Englishmen who had received their training with him. Roger Beadon was sent to five different places – spending only four months at one – and Alfred Jones had four postings, one lasting only seven months. These three were not being moved from place to place because their performance was unsatisfactory. Working under a number of superintendents, each man was acquiring a wide range of experience to help prepare him for the day when he would command his own district headquarters.

His first posting after Mandalay was to Myaungmya – a district headquarters in the Irrawaddy Delta, some eighty miles west of Rangoon. Blair's superintendent there was one of the most experienced men in the police. Peter Burke had entered the service in 1889, and was only a few months away from retirement when Blair joined him in January 1924. Burke introduced him to the basic duties demanded of an assistant – showing him how to prepare cases for prosecution, how to compile crime reports from local police stations, how to manage the payroll and how to supervise the distribution of police supplies. Blair was also expected to make at least one inspection tour of the district. This involved travelling by launch with Burke from one delta village to the next, spending only a little time at each stop to talk with constables and village leaders. When Burke was away on an extended tour of the district, Blair's job was to take charge of the headquarters.

The Myaungmya district covered almost three thousand square miles, and was largely made up of flat islands divided from each other by numerous branches of the Irrawaddy. There were long stretches of tidal forest in the south and endless fields of rice in the north. Like so many other districts in Lower Burma, it was hot, wet and primitive. Leopards and tigers roamed freely in certain parts, and monkeys and crocodiles were plentiful in the southern forests. Since the railway did not extend into the district, the only reliable method of travel to and from Rangoon was by the large river steamers of the Irrawaddy Flotilla Company.

This was a difficult environment, by anyone's standards, but Blair performed well during the short period of his stay. So well, in fact, that he was left in complete charge of the headquarters for nearly a month. Burke took his retirement leave at the beginning of April and a new superintendent did not arrive until early May. This new man was U Ba Thin. Blair stayed for three weeks to help the Burmese officer become acquainted with the headquarters operations, and then he went to his next posting, which was Twante, one of two sub-divisional headquarters in the Hanthawaddy district. This was not a demotion or an indication that he had somehow incurred the disapproval of Superintendent Burke or U Ba Thin. On the contrary, what awaited him was the next important step in the career of a promising young officer – a six-month period supervising his own sub-division, which was about half the size of a normal district.

If he had been interested only in the advancement of his career, Blair would have had little reason to complain about Burma. At a very young age he had reached a position of considerable authority. There were two hundred thousand people living in the Twante sub-division, and he was the head of their police force. While some of his old friends from Eton were still struggling to complete their university degrees, he was overseeing life-and-death matters for a population which was equal to that of a medium-sized European city. Whenever a major crime was reported, he was called to the scene to supervise the investigation. Whenever a dangerous criminal was at large, he directed the effort to capture the man. He settled quarrels between village leaders, disciplined errant constables, observed interrogations of prisoners and testified at important trials and inquests. It is also interesting to note that the author of *Nineteen Eighty-Four* was once in charge of an extensive surveillance operation. As the Police Manual reveals, one of the major responsibilities of sub-divisional officers was to make certain 'that the police of the subdivision are acquainted with the residence and movements of all bad characters, and that efficient and intelligent supervision is exercised over them as well as over conditionally released prisoners'.

He was fortunate to be posted to Twante. Compared with other areas in Burma, its rate of violent crime was modest. And the place was not isolated. Rangoon was only a dozen miles away, and it was not difficult to make frequent visits there. He had a large staff to help him with his police duties, and servants to do all his cooking and cleaning. One servant took care of his clothing and made his bed, another kept the floors clean and emptied the chamber pot, and a third prepared his meals.

In many ways it was not a bad life. He became accustomed to being waited upon at every step. 'When you have a lot of servants,' he wrote later, 'you soon get into lazy habits, and I habitually allowed myself, for instance, to be dressed and undressed by my Burmese boy.'[5] He also developed the habit of flicking cigarette ashes on the floor, confident that his sweeper would clean them up. (When he stayed at his parents' home after returning from Burma, they were shocked to see him absent-mindedly dropping ashes on the carpets, as though he still expected servants to take care of such things.)

Reading continued to dominate whatever spare time was available to him, and with Rangoon so close, he had a good range of books to choose from, both at the Rangoon Library and at Smart & Mookerdum's, the capital's best bookshop. In later years he recalled, at various times, certain books which he had read in Burma, including *War and Peace*, Lawrence's *Women in Love* and Samuel Butler's *Notebooks*. Some of these books went home with him when he left Burma, though he joked that they were 'none the better for having gone through several rainy seasons'.[6]

English newspapers and magazines were nearly a month old when they arrived in Rangoon, but Blair did make an effort to keep up with events back home, and he is known to have subscribed to at least one 'highbrow' monthly – John Middleton Murry's *Adelphi*. In the 1930s he became a frequent contributor to it, but in Burma he was more than a little annoyed by the often eccentric nature of the magazine's intellectual debates. He had a novel way of expressing his dissatisfaction. On at least one occasion, he marched out of his bungalow, propped the magazine against a tree, aimed his police carbine and fired at it for target practice. He was always an aggressive critic.

But he was not annoyed merely with the magazine. He was also frustrated by the thought that he was so far away from the literary world which the *Adelphi* represented. He wanted to be part of that world, but he was reluctant to admit it to himself. Ever since his last year at Eton he had been trying to persuade himself that his early literary ambitions were unrealistic. As Orwell explains in 'Why I Write', 'From a very early age . . . I knew that when I grew up I should be a writer. Between the ages of about seventeen and twenty-four I tried to abandon this idea, but I did so with the consciousness that I was outraging my true nature and that sooner or later I should have to settle down and write books.' His decision to come out to Burma must have made him feel that he had in fact abandoned any hope of becoming a writer. How could a busy police officer find time to write books? And who would publish anything written by an unknown young man in an obscure part of the Empire?

Yet the urge to write was so strong that he did try to produce a few short pieces while he was in Burma, and may have even made a tentative effort to write a novel. Some poems and a few sketches have survived which appear to have been written towards the end of his time in the Imperial Police – indeed, much of this material is written on official stationery. The quality of the work is not good, though some of the sketches represent rough attempts to describe characters and incidents which would later find their way into *Burmese Days*. The one small gem of the collection is a delightfully cynical poem called 'Romance':

When I was young and had no sense,
In far off Mandalay,
I lost my heart to a Burmese girl
As lovely as the day.

Her skin was gold, her hair was jet,
Her teeth were ivory;
I said, 'For twenty silver pieces,
Maiden, sleep with me.'

She looked at me, so pure, so sad,
The loveliest thing alive,
And in her lisping, virgin voice,
Stood out for twenty-five.

Perhaps the most striking thing about this early material is that so much of it is concerned with prostitutes. A poem called 'The Lesser Evil' describes a 'house of sin ... with dying flowers round the door'. An untitled sketch features an unnerving encounter with a young prostitute whose 'hard mercenary expression' gives her the appearance of 'an evil-minded doll'. A brief fragment of another sketch decribes an older Englishman's attempt to persuade his young English subordinate not to lower himself by marrying a Eurasian woman. 'Women, out here, are a big problem,' he says. 'It's hard, I know.' He implies that having sex with 'native & half-caste' women is acceptable only if there is no possibility of marriage. 'Well, of course, young fellows will be young fellows; & some of these women, native & half-caste, are very charming. When I was your age, – well, no nonsense, that's all. No marrying. You understand that?'

Writing such pieces – however weak and incomplete they may be – was one way for him to resurrect his literary ambitions, but they also provided him with the chance to address the problems of loneliness and sexual frustration which inevitably confronted young single men in Burma. Only a tiny fraction of the population was of European origin – fewer than twenty thousand – so the challenge of finding a suitable female companion within such a small group was extremely difficult, especially since some districts had no single

European women at all. Because this same small community objected so strongly to inter-racial marriage, young officials who were not content to be celibate for several years had little choice but to take a Burmese or Eurasian mistress, or to visit prostitutes. There is no conclusive evidence that Blair kept a mistress like John Flory's Ma Hla May in *Burmese Days*, or that he had relations with prostitutes, but it seems unlikely that he would not have slept with any native-born women during his five years in Burma. One interesting piece of evidence in this regard is Harold Acton's claim that during a conversation with him in Paris in 1945, Orwell confided that he had enjoyed having sexual relations with Burmese women. 'I prompted him to reminisce about his life in Burma, and his sad earnest eyes lit up with pleasure when he spoke of the sweetness of Burmese women.'[7]

There is, of course, the possibility that he fell in love with a European woman, as Flory does with Elizabeth Lackersteen, and that perhaps he even contemplated marriage. The only clue in this matter is an intriguing letter written by a woman named Elisa-Maria Langford-Rae. The circumstances which prompted her to write her letter are as fascinating as the letter itself. Curiously enough, they involve Walter Christie, Blair's contemporary at St Cyprian's. During the 1950s, when Christie was living in India, he read an Indian newspaper article which commented on Orwell's schooldays, and he wrote a letter to the editor in response, giving details of his positive memories of St Cyprian's. This drew a reply from a woman who claimed that she had been a friend of Blair's in Burma.

> I knew Eric Blair very well when he was stationed in Insein, and later, in Moulmein, Burma. We used to have long talks on every conceivable subject, but the one impression I carried away with me was his profound gratitude to the schools that had trained him.
>
> I once remarked to him on the minute care with which he sifted each case, his passion for justice, his dislike of prejudiced remarks about anyone, however lowly, and his sense of utter fairness in his minutest dealings. He replied: 'This was the most

important part of the education I received at Eton – this and the capacity to think for myself.'[8]

This solemn praise for his schools is hardly what one would expect to hear from Blair. On the other hand, there is reason to believe that Elisa-Maria Langford-Rae's claim of friendship is genuine. After retiring to England, Christie lost track of her, and subsequent efforts to trace her have failed. But the fact that she mentions knowing Blair at Insein is one indication that she was indeed a friend because, in the 1950s, very few people outside Burma were aware that this had been one of his postings. And even fewer knew that this posting had *preceded* the one at Moulmein. If one accepts that her letter is sincere, the most likely explanation for the comments she attributes to him is that he made such commonplace remarks because he thought they were the very things which she wanted to hear. As he candidly admits in *The Road to Wigan Pier*, he spent most of his time in Burma hiding his true feelings from others and saying things which he did not really believe.

It is impossible to determine how close the two friends were. Nothing is known of the woman beyond the information given above. But if they did indeed 'have long talks on every conceivable subject', they must have known each other quite well. Apparently she saw enough of him to gain a clear impression of his work as a police officer, and it is worth noting that she considered him not only fair but efficient.

By the time she met him in Insein, he had completed not only his six-month stay at Twante but also a nine-month period at Syriam. At Insein he was once again in close proximity to Rangoon. A popular residential suburb, it was located on a rail line only ten miles north of the capital. It was an excellent posting, yet it is also one of the places in which he was supposedly bullied by his superior – a devious tyrant, presumably English. But again this is without foundation. Blair served at Insein from 26 September 1925 to 18 April 1926, and throughout that time his superintendent was a Burmese officer named U Ba, who had joined the Provincial Police in 1906, and who had patiently worked his way up the ranks to the heights of the Imperial Service. His district was an important one, in part because it was the home of the second largest jail in the province – an enormous place housing more than twenty-five hundred prisoners.

Blair seems to have lived more or less as he pleased in Insein. He was the headquarters assistant and occupied a large, modern bungalow, but he made little effort to keep his home in neat order. Roger Beadon visited him there and was taken aback by the casual way in which his fellow officer was living. 'I went there and as far as I can remember he had goats, geese, ducks and all sorts of things floating about downstairs, whereas I'd kept rather a nice house. It rather shattered me, but apparently he liked that . . . it didn't worry him what the house looked like.'

Although there may have been some romance in Blair's life at the time, Beadon saw no sign of it. Nothing was said about any women friends – European or Burmese. 'As for female company, I don't honestly think I ever saw him with a woman; he certainly was not like me – I had an eye for anything that was going.'⁹

There can be no doubt that Blair had little in common with such a conventional young man as Beadon, and if Elisa-Maria was his friend at this time, it was probably just as well that he did not introduce her to a man who 'had an eye for anything that was going'. In any case Blair had a lifelong habit of not speaking openly to one friend about the existence of another. In later life he was silent about so many aspects of his past that friends were often surprised by some abrupt revelation concerning other people he had known or places he had seen. For example, almost nothing would have been known about his reaction to meeting his maternal grand-mother in Moulmein if he had not happened to remark – at the very end of a letter written to a stranger twenty years later – that he was disappointed in his grandmother's refusal to learn Burmese.¹⁰ Similarly, his mysterious friendship with Elisa-Maria would have remained completely in the dark if she had not responded to Walter Christie's letter thirty years after her friend had left Burma.

II

Because of its large jail, one might be tempted to think that Insein is the real setting for 'A Hanging', which was first published in the *Adelphi*, under Blair's own name, only four years after his return from Burma. Many executions took place at Insein, but it is also true that executions were carried out from time to time at other jails in districts where Blair had served – for example, at the Mandalay Jail and the Myaungmya Jail. Sadly, any official who wished to witness an execution could do so in almost any part of Burma. Practically every district had a large jail, and most of these had a scaffold and a hangman. In the ordinary course of his duties, a police officer would not have been required to attend an execution; he might be asked to serve as a witness, but no regulations compelled him to agree to such a request. If Blair witnessed a hanging, he did so voluntarily.

The overburdened jails in Burma were not notable for humane treatment of prisoners. In the largest jail, at Rangoon, 'incorrigible' inmates were made to wear metal collars and were confined to small cells where their days were filled with drudgery. In each cell was a large crank which turned a mill for grinding raw peanuts, and the convict's job was to keep this crank going for a good part of each day. Discipline was maintained by flogging and by a bizarre form of punishment called 'cannon-ball drill', which involved having a convict perform – at the sound of a gong – various lifting exercises with a cannon ball weighing thirty-two pounds. As an American visitor to the jail noted in 1924, 'This exhausting exercise goes on for hours at a time, and I am told that the fatigue soon becomes so terrible that the men will welcome any other punishment rather than be assigned to a cannon-ball drill.'[11]

Of course, the ultimate punishment of the gallows awaited those who had been convicted of the most serious crimes, and in *Burmese Days* Orwell implies that the system was not always so careful about who it condemned. After one of the English characters in the novel – Maxwell – is killed, the district superintendent of police searches for the culprits and soon returns with two 'murderers under arrest', but Orwell cannot resist adding cynically – 'or at any rate . . . people who would presently be hanged for Maxwell's murder'.

Everything about the sketch 'A Hanging' suggests that it is based on a real experience. It is a riveting piece of work whose emotional power comes from a slow but steady accumulation of details. The whole point of the piece is to bring home the horrific reality of an act which is so much easier to sanction in the abstract if one never has to witness it in the flesh. No detail is too insignificant because each one helps to convey a sense of what is lost when a life is destroyed. As he and a party of jailers and officials escort the Hindu convict across the prison yard to the gallows, Blair studies the man's 'bare brown back', his clumsy walk as he tries to march with his arms bound and his footprints in the wet gravel. And then one detail illuminates all the others when the man takes one small step to avoid a puddle. 'Till that moment I had never realised what it means to destroy a healthy, conscious man . . . His brain still remembered, foresaw, reasoned – reasoned even about puddles. He and we were a party of men walking together, seeing, hearing, feeling, under-standing the same world; and in two minutes, with a sudden snap, one of us would be gone – one mind less, one world less.'

One authority on Blair's career in Burma – Maung Htin Aung, the first Burmese to hold the Chair of English at the University of Rangoon – believed that the description of the jail in 'A Hanging' was derived not from Insein, but from Blair's next posting, Moulmein – the third largest town in Burma. It was the most important of all his postings, and was the one place where he would have had a good reason to attend an execution. As he says in 'Shooting an Elephant', he was the 'sub-divisional police officer of the town', and as such, he was in charge of all police activities, just as he had been in the less-important sub-division of Twante, which did not have its own prison. 'Insein jail was too large and complex to fit the description given by [Blair]', Htin Aung wrote in the early 1970s. 'It would have been more logical for Blair to be present at a hanging in Moulmein jail; the law required only the District Medical Officer (who was also the ex-officio superintendent of the jail) and a magistrate to be present, but Blair had the right to be there, for as the murder took place in his sub-division he would have supervised the investigation, arrest and prosecution of the accused.'[12]

Htin Aung's interest in Blair was not merely literary. As a very young student at the University of Rangoon, he had encountered Blair on one occasion, but the experience had not been a pleasant one for either of them. It occurred during Blair's stay in Twante. He had come up to Rangoon for the day, dressed in civilian clothes, and was walking down the stairs of a suburban railway station when a playful schoolboy accidentally bumped into him and caused him to fall. Losing his temper, Blair quickly stood up and used his walking stick to hit the boy once across the back. Htin Aung and some of his university friends observed this incident and angrily ran up to Blair to protest at his treatment of the schoolboy. It was a tense moment for everyone concerned. When Blair's train arrived, he walked through the crowd which had gathered round him and boarded it, but Htin Aung and his friends followed. They boldly entered his carriage and continued their argument with him until the train reached the next station, at which point tempers had cooled a little, and they parted from him peacefully. A policeman on the platform later informed them that the tall Englishman was an officer of the Imperial Police.

Looking back on this episode fifty years later, Htin Aung had lost all his anger towards Blair, and was willing to give him credit for preventing a bad situation from becoming something much worse. 'He never overplayed the part of an Imperial policeman as has been suggested by some writers, and he handled a group of angry and arrogant Burmese freshmen, including myself, with patience and courage, and without revealing that he was a police officer. If he had said that he was a policeman he would have made us more furious.' No doubt because of this memorable encounter, Htin Aung developed a strong curiosity about Orwell's career, and read his early works when they first appeared, beginning with *Burmese Days*. He gave lectures on Orwell, and at one point he even travelled to Moulmein to gather information about him from older residents. He was not able to discover much, except for a few details about some football matches in which Blair had proven himself to be 'a sporting and skilful centre-forward' for the Moulmein police team. One person recalled seeing him arrive at 'the football ground on a powerful motorbike, looking impressive in the red jersey of the Police First Eleven'.

Orwell recalls one of these matches in 'Shooting an Elephant', but his memories of them are not happy. What remained uppermost in his mind was the kind of petty harassment which he and other officials of the Empire frequently suffered when they came into close contact with 'the natives'. 'As a police officer I was an obvious target and was baited whenever it seemed safe to do so. When a nimble Burman tripped me up on the football field and the referee (another Burman) looked the other way, the crowd yelled with hideous laughter. This happened more than once.' Taken individually, such minor incidents were tolerable, but they mounted up, and Orwell's simmering resentment is evident in the terse comment, 'This happened more than once.'

On one level, his reaction was simply to return the hatred shown to him, to strike back violently against any sign of insolence, whether it was real or imagined. By the time he was sent to Moulmein his anger and frustration were becoming increasingly difficult to contain. 'The sneering yellow faces of young men that met me everywhere, the insults hooted after me when I was at a safe distance, got badly on my nerves. The young Buddhist priests were the worst of all. There were several thousands of them in the town and none of them seemed to have anything to do except stand on street corners and jeer at Europeans.'

It is easy enough to see how imperialism enslaves its subjects, but the great lesson which Orwell learned in Burma is that the system also has endless ways of enslaving its masters. In Moulmein he exercised great power, with nearly three hundred men under his command. The area over which he had authority was a vital part of the Empire – it was a major administrative centre of the provincial government and an important commercial port. To be in his position at twenty-three, which was his age when he first arrived in the town, was remarkable. Yet, as far as he was concerned, what was the chief result of wielding so much power? He sums it up in the first sentence of 'Shooting an Elephant': 'In Moulmein, in Lower Burma, I was hated by large numbers of people – the only time in my life that I have been important enough for this to happen to me.' He was one of the young gods of the Empire, but he was also one of its prisoners, a man encircled by an unyielding wall of prejudice and resentment which both the rulers and the ruled had helped to build. He began to hate both sides with an almost equal passion, and this planted some dark, irrational thoughts in his brain. 'With one part of my mind I thought of the British Raj as an unbreakable tyranny ... with another part I thought that the greatest joy in the world would be to drive a bayonet into a Buddhist priest's guts.'

The system was threatening to turn him into a brute – or so it seemed to him – and his own growing awareness of this corrosive influence was his strongest reason for deserting the Empire. He had done his job well, and had advanced his career; but as a policeman, he was doing 'the dirty work of the Empire', as he put it, and that work made him feel less human, less free, less alive. He was haunted by all the misery he had seen – the frightened looks in the eyes of men who had been condemned to suffer execution, the ugly scars on the backs of men who had been flogged in prison, the pathetic cries of women whose husbands had been taken away from their homes in handcuffs. He would have seen some of the same painful things if he had been a policeman in any other country, but he was not merely a policeman; he was an outsider – an agent of a foreign power – charged with maintaining order in a conquered land. As he recalled later, 'The thief whom we put in prison did not think of himself as a criminal justly punished, he thought of himself as the victim of a foreign conqueror. The thing that was done to him was merely a wanton meaningless cruelty. His face, behind the stout teak bars of the lock-up and the iron bars of the jail, said so clearly.'[13]

He never forgot a humiliating incident which took place during one of his inspection tours of a police station. While he watched one of his men trying to intimidate a suspect into making a confession, he saw an American missionary, whom he knew, enter the building and come towards him. The man stood nearby for a few minutes, watching the interrogation, and then, dispassionately, he remarked to Blair, 'I wouldn't care to have your job.'[4] It was not meant as an insult, but it stung all the same. It was a sharp reminder of the 'dirtiness' of his work, and of the demeaning position in which this brutal business placed both the criminals and the police.

Any attempt to improve the system was hampered by the pressure placed upon all white men in the East to maintain the pretence of superiority. In one of the fragmentary sketches which Blair appears to have written in Burma, a veteran servant of the Empire spouts the traditional wisdom on the subject of the white man's burden: 'A white man . . . is always on his best behaviour before the native. Esprit de corps! Prestige! Once lower that, & it's all up with you. We white men have to hang together.' The effect of such words, of course, was to double the guilt suffered by any wavering imperialist. Give an inch to the Burmese and you betray your white brothers, turn your back on the just claims of the Burmese and you lose your sense of moral integrity.

'Shooting an Elephant', which was first published in 1936, offers the definitive portrayal of this dilemma. On one level, it is a rather plain tale of the Raj. In the Moulmein teak yards dozens of trained elephants were used to move the heavy logs, picking them up with their tusks and keeping them balanced there as they walked. Normally, they were docile, but now and then one would stray into the town, and in rare cases go on a rampage. Htin Aung recalled that it was customary in those days for the local police officer to shoot any dangerous elephant, and he remembered watching such a shooting when he was a boy in the timber town of Pakokku. These incidents inevitably attracted crowds, but few people attached any special significance to the destruction of the beasts – except, of course, the owners, and any unfortunate victims of the rampage.

In 'Shooting an Elephant' the killing of the beast assumes enormous significance because the decision to shoot it has nothing to do with any threat from it. Orwell's runaway elephant is peacefully standing in a paddy field stuffing grass into his mouth when he is finally tracked down. It is only necessary to wait for his handler to come and lead him home. But a large crowd has gathered and expects more dramatic action, and Orwell treats this mood of expectation as the real danger in the situation because it reflects the worst tendencies of the system under which the people live. He must shoot the elephant because he must live up to the image which the system has imposed upon him. 'A sahib has got to act like a sahib; he has got to appear resolute, to know his own mind and do definite things.' But under such circumstances he really has no mind of his own, no will that can be exercised independently; he can act only as a sahib would act. He was 'an absurd puppet', Orwell says, 'pushed to and fro by the will of those yellow faces behind . . . When the white man turns tyrant it is his own freedom that he destroys.' In the end he kills the elephant 'solely to avoid looking a fool'.

III

Shortly before Christmas 1926, Blair left Moulmein and took up a new posting. He was sent to a place in Upper Burma called Katha, which was two hundred miles north of Mandalay. It was located on the banks of the Irrawaddy, and was the headquarters of a district which covered a hilly area of several thousand square miles, most of it thick with jungle and thinly populated. In Moulmein there was a significant European community, but in Katha there were no more than twenty Europeans in the entire district. Blair's position was headquarters assistant, which was an important job in such a big district because his superior would need to be away on tour a great deal of the time, leaving him in charge of the headquarters.

Katha was the most remote of all the places in which he served, but in many ways it was also the most beautiful, with clear streams and waterfalls, a wide variety of exotic plants and an abundant population of wildlife. One of its drawbacks, however, was its 'bad reputation for malarial and other fevers', to quote the description in the *Imperial Gazetteer*. 'In the hot months,' the *Gazetteer* explains, 'the heat all over the district is great, and the absence of wind at this season and in the rains adds to the discomfort of the residents, while

even the cold season is made unhealthy by fogs near the Irrawaddy.'
Of course, almost every place in Burma was plagued by tropical
fevers, but apparently it was in Katha that Blair contracted an odd
malady called dengue fever. When he compiled his medical history
for the English sanatorium where he stayed in 1938, he listed
dengue fever as his only major illness during the period 1922–1927,
but he did not specify exactly when or where the sickness struck him
in Burma.[15] Dengue fever is spread by mosquitoes, and, though it is
rarely fatal, it can cause a very painful and prolonged illness.
Usually, the first attack of the fever lasts three or four days, and then
– after a brief respite – a second attack follows which is slightly less
severe than the first. The fevers are often accompanied by a dark-
red rash on the neck and shoulders. No drug can treat it effectively,
and patients sometimes take weeks to recover fully from its
debilitating effects. 'During convalescence the patient is much
depressed,' a contemporary Indian handbook noted.[16]

It seems most likely that Blair was stricken by this illness not long
after he went to Katha because only a few months after his arrival
he applied for a long leave, citing health problems. He never
publicly mentioned the cause of these problems, except to assert
vaguely that the climate had 'ruined' his health.[17] There is no sign
that he suffered lasting damage from the fever, but he was
sufficiently weakened by it to win permission to return to England
for eight months of sick leave.

When he fell ill in Katha, he would have been placed under the
care of the district's Civil Surgeon, an Indian by the name of Dr
Krishnasawmy. This man was almost certainly the model for the
character of Dr Veraswami, the Civil Surgeon in *Burmese Days*,
which is set in an Upper Burma district very much like Katha. Little
is known about the background of the real doctor, but he was
certainly the best educated man in the district, and probably the one
whose conversation Blair would have enjoyed above all others.
There were no English officials to speak to. Blair was the only
Englishman of any importance in the district. His superintendent
was Burmese – U Maung Maung, a veteran policeman who was
nearly twice as old as Blair – and there were also Burmese men

occupying the senior positions of Sessions Judge and Deputy Commissioner (the chief magistrate of the district). As the chief medical officer in the district, Dr Krishnasawmy was responsible not only for health matters but also for Katha's small jail.

It was exceedingly rare to have so much of the authority in a district concentrated in the hands of men who were not English. But in such circumstances there may have been some rivalry between the three Burmese officials and the one Indian, just as there is between Dr Veraswami and the minor official U Po Kyin in *Burmese Days*. Educated Indians in Burma tended to suffer a double-dose of prejudice, suffering from the superior attitudes of Europeans, and from the resentment and envy of Burmese who considered them 'favourites' of the English authorities. Even if Blair's illness had not brought him into close contact with the Indian doctor in Katha, they would probably have been drawn to each other, since both were out of place in this most Burmese of Burmese districts.

The conversations between Flory and Veraswami in *Burmese Days* provide Orwell with a way of dramatising some of the contradictions in the imperial system, and a good part of their talk may reflect the things which Blair and Dr Krishnasawmy discussed in Katha. The irony behind their friendly arguments about the Empire is that every comment in its favour comes from the Indian and every remark against it is made by the Englishman. The Indian repeats, with sincere conviction, all the empty promises of Imperialism, all the false hopes raised by countless works of propaganda. The British are 'torchbearers on the path of progress'. They have rough exteriors, but 'hearts of gold', and have graciously bestowed upon the backward colonies the blessings of 'unswerving British Justice and the Pax Britannica'. No, says the Englishman, a better name for it would be 'Pox Britannica . . . Of course, we keep the peace in India, in our own interest, but what does all this law and order business boil down to? More banks and more prisons – that's all it means . . . We should chuck it quickly enough if it didn't pay.'

Of course, the real empire-builders were men like the good doctor. Without such men to staff the hospitals, the schools, the police, the law courts, the prisons, there would not have been an empire. The whole system continued to spin along because they were willing to keep it oiled, even though so little of it belonged to them. His English friend obviously admires the doctor's unselfish devotion, yet is amazed that this 'victim' of the system is so determined to serve it. 'His faith in British justice was so great that even when, at the jail, he had to superintend a flogging or a hanging, and would come home with his black face faded grey and dose himself with whisky, his zeal did not falter.'

Dr Veraswami is eventually disgraced by the false accusations of his enemy U Po Kyin, and is sent away to serve out the rest of his career at a lower rank in the medical service, but this was not the fate of the doctor in Katha, who was posted to an even better district not long before Blair left Burma. There is no reason to believe that the Burmese officials in Katha were as devious and as corrupt as U Po Kyin. The novel is not based merely on that one place and time in Upper Burma, but brings together and transforms a vast range of experiences from all his postings. He could have encountered men like U Po Kyin anywhere from Mandalay to Moulmein.[18]

Similarly, the most repulsive white man in the book – Ellis, the district manager of a timber firm – embodies the very worst characteristics of all the bad Europeans in the East, whether businessmen or officials. In Katha, Blair would not have witnessed anything like Ellis's nasty tirades against admitting Burmese and Indians to the local European Club because at least a few had already joined it. (There was no way that the chief official of the district, the Burmese deputy commissioner, would have been excluded from it.) But he had heard such sentiments in other parts of the province, and had grown weary of listening to the same words and phrases repeated over and over: 'If we aren't going to rule, why the devil don't we clear out . . . Instead of ruling them in the only way they understand, we go and treat them as equals . . . We've got to hang together and say, "We are the masters, and you beggars keep your place," ' etc.

During his recovery from the attack of dengue fever, Blair had time to consider his future in Burma, and to ponder the consequences of resigning from the police when his medical leave was over. There was no point in trying to keep up the pretence that he belonged in the service, but giving it up would mean walking away from five years' worth of effort building his career, and there was no definite job waiting for him in England. He wanted to write books, but how could he explain to his parents that he was abandoning the Indian Imperial Police for the uncertain life of a working writer? They would surely think that the fever had damaged his brain.

At the end of June 1927 he boarded a train in Katha for the long ride down to Rangoon, and on 14 July he sailed for home on a brand-new ship of the Bibby Line – the MV *Shropshire*.[19] A dozen years later he would refer to his life in Burma as 'five boring years within the sound of bugles', but that was a typical understatement.[20] The boredom was frequently punctuated by intense, unforgettable images and incidents which would continue to haunt him until the end of his life. The landscapes, especially in Upper Burma, exercised such a potent hold on his imagination that they took on 'the qualities of a nightmare', he said later, adding that they 'stayed so hauntingly in my mind that I was obliged to write [*Burmese Days*] . . . to get rid of them'.[21] Only a few months before he died he was trying to write another book about Burma – a short novel called 'A Smoking-Room Story'. Throughout his career, stray images and thoughts from that period kept finding their way into his writing. Some were even comical, such as his dry comment on the Burmese film industry: 'About 1925 the Burmese . . . began producing their own films, and their first products were imitation Westerns, with five-gallon hats, fringed trousers, Mexican spurs and other paraphernalia as far away from their own experience as the costumes of Tibetan lamas would be from a Cotswold villager.'[22]

But most of his recollections were made in passionately serious contexts, as in his criticism of W. H. Auden for using the phrase 'necessary murder' in the poem 'Spain'. 'Personally,' he wrote in 1940, 'I would not speak so lightly of murder. It so happens that I have seen the bodies of numbers of murdered men – I don't mean killed in battle, I mean murdered . . . I have some conception of what murder means – the terror, the hatred, the howling relatives, the post-mortems, the blood, the smells.'[23] He could also never forget the execution which he had witnessed, saying in *The Road to Wigan Pier* that even the horror of criminal murder could not begin to compare with the brutality of an 'official' one. 'I watched a man hanged once; it seemed to me worse than a thousand murders.'

Above all, he could not forget the faces of the many men whom he had watched the system punish, and who had regarded him with sullen defiance. 'Innumerable remembered faces,' he called them later. More than anything else – more than any abstract political notions or theories of moral justice – the accusing looks on those faces had made his work in the police unbearable. He had been well-trained and had worked hard to satisfy his superiors, but his professionalism could not prevent him from being unnerved by those looks. 'Unfortunately I had not trained myself to be indifferent to the expression of the human face.'[24]

CHAPTER SEVEN

London and Paris

I

On the return voyage from Burma, Blair decided to leave the ship when it reached the South of France, in early August 1927. It was not uncommon for English passengers to save a few days of travel time by disembarking at Marseilles and going home by way of Paris. But he seems to have been in no particular hurry to get back to England, choosing instead to spend the extra time relaxing in the sunny Mediterranean climate. He was still in Marseilles in the latter half of the month, idly wandering the streets and making casual conversation with strangers. One day he was standing on the steps of an English bank in the town, talking to some of the clerks, when he suddenly found the street filled with a large crowd of working people. They were taking part in a march to protest at the imminent execution in America of the anarchists Sacco and Vanzetti. As the marchers moved down the street waving banners, one of the English bank clerks remarked to Blair, 'Oh, well, you've got to hang these blasted anarchists.' The clerk could not have known that he was addressing a policeman who had seen more than a few examples of official injustice, and was 'half-shocked' when Blair coolly raised the possibility that Sacco and Vanzetti might be innocent of the crime for which they had been condemned.

The remarkable thing about this encounter is the simple fact that, after five years of hiding his true thoughts, he felt that he could speak his mind to a stranger on the street. He was able to shock a fellow Englishman with unconventional talk and not worry about any repercussions. It must have been an enormous relief. There was no one to reprimand him for letting down the side, for daring to question the established order. There was no longer any need to maintain a pretence of superiority or to mouth acceptable phrases. He clearly relished the moment, and the details remained fresh in his mind long afterwards. In 1932 he went out of his way to insert a lengthy description of the incident in a book review for the *Adelphi*.[1]

Shortly after witnessing the protest march, he travelled to Paris and then crossed the Channel for the final leg of his long journey home. He arrived in England at the end of August. 'When I came home on leave in 1927,' he wrote later, 'I was already half determined to throw up my job, and one sniff of English air decided me.'[2] In Burma, thousands of miles away from home, he had almost forgotten how different life could be in a world where free expression was taken for granted. But as soon as Burma was behind him, he was amazed to think that he had sacrificed so much of his freedom in the service of Imperialism. As he said of the Empire in *Burmese Days*, 'It is a stifling, stultifying world in which to live . . . In England it is hard even to imagine such an atmosphere. Everyone is free in England; we sell our souls in public and buy them back in private, among our friends. But even friendship can hardly exist when every white man is a cog in the wheels of despotism. Free speech is unthinkable.' No matter what it required of him, he was determined that he would never again allow himself to suppress his desire to think and act freely. He could not return to his old job and face another long term of silent misery in a world plagued by heat, hyprocrisy, loneliness and guilt.

The immediate problem was to face his parents and tell them of his decision. Back in 1922, when he had been preparing to enter the Imperial Police, his parents had moved from Henley to Southwold – a sedate, uncrowded resort town on the Suffolk coast – and it was to their house at 3 Queen Street that he came after he left France. His sister Avril, who was still living at home, remembered how surprised the family was when they saw him for the first time in five years. 'His appearance had changed quite considerably. He had become very like my father to look at, and he had grown a moustache.' He was also thinner, and his body had not yet fully recovered its strength after his illness in Burma. 'The first thing that he did when he came back,' his sister recalled, 'was to say that he wanted to go down to Cornwall for the month.' They all went down to Polperro for a long holiday which lasted until the end of September, and it was during this period that Eric announced his plans for the future. 'He told my mother that he wasn't going back to Burma; that he'd resigned his commission. Of course, she was rather horrified, but he was quite determined that what he wanted to do was to write, and he wasn't going to be any kind of charge on the family. He was determined to make his way, but he was going to do it in his own way.'[3]

Mabel Fierz, a close friend of Eric's in the 1930s, who was also well-acquainted with his family in Southwold, remarked in 1970, 'When he left the Burma post, his father was very disappointed. And looked upon him as a sort of failure . . . His mother and I were very good friends, and she said to me, "You know, Eric loves his father far more than he loves me". And I said, "No, I don't think he does – he wants his father to acknowledge him as a successful son". The son who couldn't make money in old Mr Blair's concept was not the right sort of son.'[4] No matter what Mr Blair may have initially thought of Eric's decision to join the Imperial Police, he could not appreciate any reasons for abandoning such an important job. He may have had his doubts about the value of his own humble service in the Opium Department, but he had devoted more than thirty-five years of his life to it, and his loyalty to the Empire had enabled him to give his family a comfortable middle-class life in England. Eric was rejecting not merely a job but a tradition of selfless service which men such as Mr Blair had proudly upheld. His decision went against everything that his father stood for, and to make matters worse, he was giving it all up for a vague plan to write books. To practical Mr Blair, the idea was outrageous, especially in view of the fact that Eric was walking away from a salary which had reached £660 a year in 1927. Yet what could Mr Blair say to his grown son that would make him reconsider this plan? He was not the type to argue or to make a scene, and it was clear that Eric had made up his mind. In the end he could do no more than shrug his shoulders and resign himself to the fact that his son intended to follow a path different from his. But there was no doubt that he was deeply disappointed, and his son felt that disappointment keenly. One comment from Mr Blair was especially stinging. He said that Eric's plan was that of a 'dilettante'.[5] The old man could not have been more mistaken, but at the time there was no way to make him believe otherwise.

One measure of Eric's determination to make a quick break with his old life in Burma is the fact that he planned to have his resignation take effect on 1 January 1928, which was only five and a half months after he had left Burma. The timing is important because it was his right to receive full pay for the entire eight-month period of sick leave, which was not due to expire until mid-March 1928. At the rate of £55 a month, he was sacrificing almost £140 in order to gain his freedom as soon as possible. It would not have been easy to arrange an earlier date. At some point in September or October he sent his letter of resignation – which has not survived – to the Inspector-General of Police in Rangoon. Knowing that it would take perhaps as long as a month for the letter to arrive – as well as another month for a decision to be reached – he wisely decided that the first of the year was the best date possible for an early resignation. To his relief, he learned in early December that his request had been accepted. At the end of November the India Office had received this brief telegram from the Home Department of the Government of India: 'E. A. Blair, India Police, Burma, who joined on 27 November 1922, and is on leave in England up to 12 March 1928, has applied for permission to resign from 1st January next. Government of Burma recommends acceptance. We agree.'[6]

His decision to surrender the pay he was owed is not an insignificant fact. He had no job to fall back on and no clear prospect of earning money as a writer, and since he had no intention of asking his parents for financial help, he needed to make the best of every available penny if he wanted to be free to write. In 1927 the additional pay of £140 was quite a substantial amount to refuse. To appreciate the overall financial sacrifice involved in leaving the police, consider what Blair told his Southwold friend, Brenda Salkeld, a few years later. 'He said that through writing he'd made a hundred pounds, and through teaching or tutoring, he'd made two-hundred pounds, and dish-washing twenty pounds; other jobs, twenty.' To this list, he added a rough figure for his earnings in Burma, which was so much greater than the pay from his other jobs that he could not resist making a joke about the absurdity of it. 'In the Indian Police he'd made two thousand, but he hated it, and he thought perhaps if he could find something he really loathed still more, he might become quite rich.'[7] In fact, he had to wait fourteen years before he found a job in England which paid as much as he had earned during his final year in Burma, and again it was work which – in his view – threatened his independence and integrity. The position was Talks Assistant at the BBC, and at the time of his appointment in 1941, the annual pay was £640.[8]

Relying mainly on funds which he had managed to put aside during his time in Burma, he was able to support himself for many months while he struggled to launch his literary career. He was prepared to live very meagrely, and not merely because his money would last longer that way. His refusal to collect all of his sick pay was just the beginning of a long, complicated process of renouncing material advantages. Feeling tainted by his 'success' as a young officer in the East, he wanted to shun anything that reminded him of the unjust system which he had served. 'I felt that I had got to escape not merely from imperialism but from every form of man's dominion over man,' he explained later. 'Failure seemed to me to be the only virtue. Every suspicion of self-advancement, even to "succeed" in life to the extent of making a few hundreds a year, seemed to me spiritually ugly, a species of bullying.'[9]

Like Gordon Comstock, the protagonist in his *Keep the Aspidistra Flying*, he wanted to 'make it his especial purpose *not* to "succeed" '. But it is too simple to say that this was the direct result of his experience in Burma. The idea had planted itself in his mind long before he became a police officer. St Cyprian's had prejudiced him against success very early in life because it had given him such a corrupt view of merit. He had discovered that winning was the only thing which mattered at the school, and one became a winner by 'being bigger, stronger, handsomer, richer, more popular, more elegant, more unscrupulous than other people' – in short, by 'getting the better of them in every way'. As a boy, he could not have put such thoughts into words, but as a man he knew exactly how to summarise his impression of the school's ethos: 'Life was hierarchical and whatever happened was right. There were the strong, who deserved to win and always did win, and there were the weak, who deserved to lose and always did lose, everlastingly.' At the school, he had been made to feel that he was one of the weak, and that no matter what he did, he would never be a winner. The one consolation for him was the knowledge that there was honour in losing. One could take pride in rejecting the wrong view of success. If he judged his life on the basis of his own values, he could see himself as a winner for not being seduced by false values. 'I could accept my failure and make the best of it. I could resign myself to being what I was, and then endeavour to survive on those terms . . . The weak have the right to make a different set of rules for themselves.'[10]

Yet there was another element in his character which worked against this feeling, and which had helped him to emerge from his five years at St Cyprian's as the winner of an Eton scholarship. As he put it in 'Such, Such Were the Joys', the 'sense of guilt and inevitable failure was balanced by something else: that is, the instinct to survive'. One part of him wanted to accept the idea that he was doomed to be a failure, and that success was, in any case, not worth the effort. But another part of him wanted to fight back, and to show the world that he could succeed, regardless of the obstacles placed in his way.

This had caused him to make a great mistake in Burma. At the innocent age of nineteen, he had chosen the wrong career, and had found himself allied with the strong against the weak. But in order to avoid failure – the disgrace of having to go home prematurely as a quitter or as one unfit for service – he had played along with the system, inwardly despising it but nevertheless serving it well. As he admitted later, this had left him with 'an immense weight of guilt that I had got to expiate. I suppose that sounds exaggerated; but if you do for five years a job that you thoroughly disapprove of, you will probably feel the same.'[11] Failure was the price which he felt compelled to pay for his 'success' in Burma. Regardless of the cost, he wanted to live by his own rules, scorning traditional ideas of comfort and advancement. But of course he was too bright and too independent to remain a failure for long. The urge to fail pulled him one way, but the urge to succeed was always there to pull him in the opposite direction. He could not stop himself from pursuing success, though he would always insist that if it came his way, it would have to be on his terms. In the end, success obliged him.

II

After staying with his parents for a few months, Blair decided to look for an inexpensive place in London where he could live quietly and write. For help, he turned first to Ruth Pitter, a poet and artisan whom his sister Marjorie had known in London just after the war. The young woman was employed by an arts and crafts firm in Notting Hill Gate, helping to make and decorate furniture and other household goods, but she also had a modest reputation as a poet, with two books to her credit in 1927. On one previous occasion, back in 1920, she had met Eric while visiting Marjorie. He was then only seventeen, and she was five years older, but his appearance had interested her, and many years later she could still vividly recall her first impression of him. 'I saw a tall youth, with hair the colour of hay and a brown tweed suit, standing at a table by the window, cleaning a sporting gun. There was something arresting in the way he looked up. His eyes were blue and rather formidable, and an exact pair.' Seven years passed before she saw him again, but her appearance had also stayed in his memory, and he later told her – partly in a spirit of jest – that his first thought had been, 'I wonder if that girl would be hard to get.'[12]

One day in the late autumn of 1927, she was surprised to receive a letter from him asking whether she would help him find 'a cheap lodging' in London. As it happened, there was a small room available in a house next door to her employer's workshop in the Portobello Road. It was a cramped, unheated room, but he took it, and for the next several months it was his home. She recalled that he seemed 'far from well' when he came to the Portobello Road at the beginning of winter, but he did not complain about his health, and quietly endured the cold conditions in his room, using a candle to warm his hands while he tried to write. Eventually, Ruth and her close friend Kathleen O'Hara realised how much he must have been suffering, especially after his many months in the hot climate of Burma, and were able to find an old oil-stove to lend him for the remainder of what proved to be a very cold season.

He showed them some of the things he was writing, but they were not impressed. 'We tried not to be discouraging, but we used to laugh till we cried at some of the bits which he showed us. You must remember that we were hard-working women, older than he. To us, at that time, he was a wrong-headed young man who had thrown away a good career, and was vain enough to think he could be an author.' Occasionally, they invited him to dinner, but for the most part he went his way and they went theirs. Although she was glad to have his friendship, Ruth found that he was not an easy person to know. She was frustrated by his stubborn refusal to take better care of himself. He would go out into frigid weather without a proper overcoat, gloves or hat, and would ignore any suggestion that he should wear warmer clothing. At one point she became so upset that she 'made an open attack on him, trying to get him to take proper advice and attend to his health'. But she discovered that this was 'all in vain', and concluded that 'he would never face the facts'.[13]

His landlady, a Mrs Craig, had once been in the employ of a noblewoman and thought she was too good for the Portobello Road. She paid little attention to her lodger until one day something went wrong with the front door, leaving her, her husband and Blair locked out. When Blair suggested borrowing a ladder from a man next door so that they could open an upper window, Mrs Craig objected. 'I wouldn't like to do that,' she told him. 'We've been here fourteen years, and we've always taken care not to know the people on either side of us. It *wouldn't do*, not in a neighbourhood like this. If you once begin talking to them they get familiar, you see.' In the end Mr Craig borrowed a ladder from a relative who lived almost a mile away, and Blair dutifully helped him carry it to the Portobello Road.[14]

Given his landlady's absurd social pretensions, it is just as well that she was ignorant of his activities elsewhere in London. She would have been appalled to know that her polite young lodger was making secret expeditions to the East End, spending time in the company of tramps and beggars. He began this unusual activity not long after moving to London. He wanted to learn about the living conditions of the poorest of the poor, and his plan was to go among them disguised as a tramp. Worried that his educated accent would raise suspicions that he was spying for the police, he planned his first trip with some trepidation. He took great care to make himself look like a real tramp, acquiring a shabby coat, black dungaree trousers, faded scarf and rumpled cap. Walking to a seedy area near the West India Docks, he began his investigations surrounded by rough characters – stevedores, sailors and unemployed labourers. But, much to his surprise, his effort to pass himself off as a tramp worked perfectly, and he was delighted to discover that he was treated no differently from anyone else. Clothes did indeed make the man. He stayed in the district for two or three days, sleeping at a common lodging-house in Limehouse Causeway, and paying ninepence a day for the privilege. This experience encouraged him to go 'on the road' for a short period. Looking ragged and dirty, he wandered through the outskirts of London, spending his nights in crowded 'spikes' – the casual wards of local workhouses.[15]

By the early 1930s, he had made quite a few of these tramping expeditions, and some of his experiences eventually found their way into the pages of *Down and Out in Paris and London*, which came out in 1933. It is doubtful that there was a clear literary purpose in his mind during his early trips to the East End. He seems to have had only a vague desire to collect information for a book, without really knowing whether he would put it to use in a novel, a book of short stories, a series of essays or a long autobiographical report. One definite source of inspiration was Jack London's *The People of the Abyss*, which is based on the American writer's close observation of life in the East End at the beginning of the century. Blair knew the book and was following its example when he chose to assume a disguise before entering the unfamiliar world of the slums. Jack London began his exploration of that world by changing into some old clothes which he had purchased at a rag shop in Stepney, and in this disguise he had lived among the poor for most of one summer. 'What I wish to do,' he declares in his first chapter, 'is to go down into the East End and see things for myself. I wish to know how these people are living there, and why they are living there, and what they are living for.' He wrote his book with lightning speed, finishing it in less than a year, but Blair – who was too inexperienced and unsure of himself – needed much more time to find his voice as a writer, and to discover the best form for his work.[16] Like many good writers, Blair discovered a subject worthy of his talent long before he found an appropriate style.

In any event, it was not merely for literary reasons that he wanted to spend time among the lowest classes of society. Quite apart from his desire to collect material for his writing, he had a genuine desire to understand how the poor lived, and to experience something of their suffering. It was not enough to view such things from a distance or to think about poverty and class as abstract problems. He needed to see the poor at close quarters, talking directly with them about their lives, sharing meals with them, sleeping in the same rooms. Having rejected 'every form of man's dominion over man', he wanted 'to get right down among the oppressed, to be one of them and on their side against their tyrants'.[17]

Pretending to be a tramp was also a quick way of satisfying his urge to fail, without costing him any permanent sacrifice. Simply by changing his clothes and dirtying his face, this former officer of the Indian Imperial Police could sink to the lowest level of society and subject himself to a brief but intense spell of misery. The misery was certainly real, but when he had experienced enough of it, he could always retreat to his other, more respectable life and resume his struggle to establish a literary career for himself. He was never truly down and out. There was always a way out of the abyss. The truth is that his tramping was something of a game, one which reflected his profound ambivalence towards his own background, his ambitions and his future. But it is important to remember that the game had its serious uses. It was never frivolous, never anything so pointless as slumming. He cared about the destitute people whose sufferings he shared, and he wanted to help them, but he could not ignore the fact that he was not one of them. He had talent, an education and parents and other relatives willing to help him. The best that he could do for those who were less fortunate was to speak out for them, to remind the rest of the world that they existed, that they were human beings who deserved better and that their pain was real. And this he did, again and again.

III

He soon grew weary of the hollow respectability of Mrs Craig's house, and began to think of moving to a place which would do more to inspire his literary efforts. When the spring arrived, he made a dramatic decision. Like so many other aspiring writers in the 1920s, he concluded that the best place for him to write was Paris. Without any sign of hesitation, he packed a few belongings and headed for France. He took a small room at a run-down hotel in the rue du Pot de Fer, a dingy, cobbled street in the Latin Quarter. The walls of his room were thin, dirt was everywhere in the building and bugs were a constant nuisance. The immediate area was full of similar hotels – most of them with rooms to rent by the week for fifty francs, which was quite a bit less than a pound in those days. There were brighter, more prosperous streets nearby. Only a short walk away was the Ecole Normale Supérieure, where Jean-Paul Sartre was a student at the time, and where Samuel Beckett was just beginning a two-year appointment as the English *lecteur*. (It is tempting to think that Blair might have encountered one of these two, but they moved in a different world, and there is no evidence of any contact.) There were quite a few prominent places which could easily be reached on foot. To the north, towards the river, was the

Sorbonne and the imposing Panthéon – where Voltaire, Rousseau, Hugo and Zola were buried. To the east were the botanic garden, menagerie and natural history museum of the Jardin des Plantes. The Jardin du Luxembourg lay about a mile to the west, and to the southwest were the huge Montparnasse cafés.

It was the perfect area for Blair. He could live as seedily as he wished in his obscure little street, but could quickly escape it, taking long walks through some of the more attractive parts of the city. Even the narrow streets which adjoined his own were not without their charms. On one side was the rue Mouffetard, a busy market street with a great variety of vegetables, fruits and meats on display. This led into the Place de la Contrescarpe, which Hemingway describes fondly in a nostalgic passage in 'The Snows of Kilimanjaro', evoking its crazy mixture of humanity – the drunks, the prostitutes, the unwashed children, the respectable working people. (In 1922 Hemingway and his first wife lived in an apartment just off the Place de la Contrescarpe.)

Orwell overplays the shabbiness of this area in *Down and Out in Paris and London* (he gives his street the fictional name of rue du Coq d'Or), and it is easy for readers of the book to assume that everything about his life in Paris was gloomy and difficult. But Orwell was careful to inform readers of the French edition that his general impression of Paris had been good during his stay. 'I want to emphasise this point particularly for my French readers because I would be distressed if they thought I have the least animosity towards a city of which I have very happy memories.'[18] In saying this, he was not merely being polite. He did have some happy memories, though they were not quite the kind that most visitors to the city take away with them. Near the end of his life, he wrote to Celia Paget – an English friend who was temporarily living in Paris – and included in his letter a brief reminiscence about his life in the late 1920s. In his comments he cheerfully combines beautiful and sordid memories from that period:

How I wish I were with you in Paris, now that spring is here. Do you ever go to the Jardin des Plantes? I used to love it, though there was really nothing of interest except the rats, which at one time overran it & were so tame that they would almost eat out of your hand. In the end they got to be such a nuisance that they introduced cats & more or less wiped them out. The plane trees are so beautiful in Paris, because the bark isn't blackened by smoke the way it is in London.[19]

The image of Blair wandering though the magnificent Jardin des Plantes playfully trying to coax a rat into eating something from his hand is at odds with the generally solemn mood of *Down and Out*, but it is a reminder that his eighteen-month stay in the city had its less serious moments.

The literary and artistic life of Paris in the Twenties has often been portrayed as one long, extravagant celebration, but Blair had nothing to do with this legendary social world. He met none of the famous people who were associated with it, and he had nothing but contempt for the many charlatans who inhabited its edges. 'During the boom years,' he wrote in 1940, 'when dollars were plentiful and the exchange-value of the franc was low, Paris was invaded by such a swarm of artists, writers, students, dilettanti, sight-seers, debauchees and plain idlers as the world has probably never seen. In some quarters of the town the so-called artists must actually have outnumbered the working population.'[20] Blair saw very little of the fashionable cafés and did not attend any important literary gatherings. He was a nobody who very much felt the part, and was too modest to introduce himself to the big names of the day. On one occasion in 1928 he thought he recognised James Joyce sitting at a table at the Deux Magots, but he could not be certain, and did not dare to approach the man.

But he was not a complete loner in Paris. For one thing, he had a strong family connection in the city. Nellie Limouzin, his aunt, had left England in the early 1920s and moved to Paris, where she lived with her companion, a Frenchman named Eugene Adam. He was a socialist and noted Esperantist who, in the early 1920s, founded the *Sennacieca Asocio Tutmonda*, which in Esperanto means the 'World Association of Non-Nationalists'. Its purpose was to promote Esperanto as a tool for achieving world peace, on the assumption that nationalism would disappear once the whole world was speaking one language. But by the time Blair came to Paris, this organisation could claim a membership of only six thousand, and Adam was immersed in almost constant ideological debates with rival advocates of a universal language. ('For sheer dirtiness of fighting,' Orwell wrote later, 'the feud between the inventors of various of the international languages would take a lot of beating.')[21] Adam, who also wrote under the pseudonym of 'Lanti', was so fanatical in his devotion to Esperanto that it was the only language he would use at home. Eventually, he married Aunt Nellie, who was devoted to him and to his cause, but he later abandoned her after going on a world tour, and ended his days in Mexico, where he committed suicide in 1947.[22]

Blair had little sympathy for Adam's movement, arguing later in life that 'if any language is ever adopted as a world-wide "second" language, it is immensely unlikely that it will be a manufactured one'.[23] But despite the eccentric character of her companion, Aunt Nellie was always a great favourite of Eric's, and she in turn was 'very fond' of him, according to Avril.[24] She was a lively, inquisitive woman who admired her nephew's independence and intelligence. They had serious discussions about literature and politics, and were open and honest with each other. She was more like a close friend than a relative. After he left Paris, they wrote long letters to each other, but only one has apparently survived. It is a typed letter from Nellie addressed to 'My dear Eric' and dated 3 June 1933. A few excerpts from it will give some idea of why Eric found his aunt's character so engaging.

Comparing the merits of two London suburbs, she remarked, 'I rather fancy from my experience of an afternoon's trip to Uxbridge, that it is about as stinking a hole as Hayes.' On the subject of French preparations for a major war, she noted cynically, 'While attending the Disarmament conferences, [the French authorities] are at the same time preparing for war pretty thoroughly, including the building of subterranean passages. But how on earth can they construct enough to hold the millions of inhabitants? Then they are beginning "practice" with those hideous gas masks.' The range of her curiosity was wide, and she enthusiastically shared her thoughts about some of her recent reading:

> I have begun the *Chartreuse de Parme*, but have read only a few pages as yet, for I saw a reference in some work to *The Prince* and, as I have never read it, I have begun that also and am about half way through it ... There is a very long Introduction in the edition I have ... which annoyed me when I looked at it, but I found it quite enlightening in the end. I don't know whether you dislike introductions; to me they are irritating as a rule, because they hold one from the real text and yet one doesn't like to miss them.[25]

Aunt Nellie had no children, and was happy to give her nephew not only her affection but also a little financial assistance when he needed it. She did not have much money, but she was able to give him small gifts of cash on occasion. In fact, her one surviving letter to him included a small amount of money, part of which she wanted him to spend on a vegetable garden he was tending. But she had her own ideas about the best way to acquire gardening tools. 'Of course seeds must have cost something, perhaps some manure and also perhaps tools, although I hope you were able to borrow or steal those.' According to Humphrey Dakin, there was always a touch of madness in Aunt Nellie's high spirits, and indeed, her mood turned black when Eugene Adam abandoned her. In the wake of his suicide, she suffered from bouts of mental illness. In 1950, only a few months after her nephew's death, she died in hospital in England.[26]

The fact that Eric's relationship with his aunt was so close is important because of the light it sheds on *Down and Out*. Nothing in that book is more painful to read than the passages describing his period of starvation. A mysterious young Italian 'with side whiskers' had stolen money from him, Orwell says in the book, having gained entry to his room by the use of a duplicate key. The theft left him almost penniless. He lived as frugally as he could for a few weeks, and looked for work, but he found nothing and his remaining money 'oozed away'. He was soon destitute and had nothing to eat for three days. 'Hunger reduces one to an utterly spineless, brainless condition, more like the after-effects of influenza than anything else. It is as though one had been turned into a jellyfish, or as though all one's blood had been pumped out and lukewarm water substituted.' There is little doubt that he did endure such an experience, but it was by choice, not by necessity. Aunt Nellie was living in Paris throughout this period, though there is no mention of this fact in the book. Given the nature of their relationship, it is inconceivable that she would have refused him assistance if he had gone to her after he lost his money. Of course, it is possible that he did not want to admit that he needed help, but Nellie Limouzin was not a prim moralist who would have scolded him for his failure, or have been shocked by it. After all, this was a woman with Bohemian habits who read Machiavelli and Stendhal for pleasure.

She would probably have been fascinated by the story about his stolen money if he had told her the truth, which apparently had nothing to do with a mysterious Italian. Several years later he told Mabel Fierz, who was instrumental in helping him find a publisher for *Down and Out*, that his money had actually been taken by a girlfriend named Suzanne – 'a little trollop' whom he had 'picked up in a cafe in Paris. She was beautiful, and had a figure like a boy, an Eton crop, and was in every way desirable.' At some point it seems that she moved in with him, but Suzanne also had another boyfriend elsewhere in the city – an Arab man – and one day there was some kind of violent altercation between him and Blair. A few days later Blair returned to his room to discover that Suzanne had disappeared with all his luggage and money. This story may have been another invention, but it seems more plausible than the one put forward in *Down and Out*.[27]

The book focuses on the last three months of Blair's time in Paris, and says little about his life before the theft. There were some successes in that earlier period, and for a few months his literary career had looked promising. In the autumn of 1928 his first article as a professional writer appeared in print. It was a piece called '*La Censure en Angleterre*' and was published in Henri Barbusse's paper, *Monde*, on 6 October. Eugene Adam had received some support from Barbusse in the fight for Esperanto, and it may be that Aunt Nellie or Adam himself had put Blair in touch with the editor. Someone must have spoken up for the young Englishman because his article does not seem worthy of publication. It is dull and awkward, but this may have something to do with the fact that another writer translated it into French from Blair's English original, which has been lost. Nevertheless, it must have boosted his confidence to see his work in print, and he had more good fortune over the next four or five months.

On 29 December 1928 his first article to appear in England, 'A Farthing Newspaper', was published by G. K. Chesterton in *G. K.'s Weekly*, and on the same day in Paris, the radical paper *Le Progrès Civique* brought out an article he had written on unemployment. This paper published two more of his articles in January – one on tramps, one on beggars. He was keeping very busy, writing not only articles but also stories and at least one novel, though no publisher seemed to want his fiction. But in February he received some encouraging news from England. L. I. Bailey, a literary agent in London, wrote to say that he wanted to see some of Blair's work. He was employed by a large firm in Fleet Street, the McClure Newspaper Syndicate, which also had offices in New York and Sydney. Earlier in the month, Nellie had written to him about her nephew, and Blair had followed this up with a letter of his own, giving the agent a general description of some stories he had written, and mentioning that he might also have a 'Tramps and Beggars book' to send him at some future date. Bailey showed little interest in this second project, and nothing more was said about it, but Blair did send him the stories. At the end of March, Bailey acknowledged that he had received them, and added: 'As I am terribly anxious to come to Paris for the holiday, I may have the pleasure of looking Miss Limouzin and you up sometime, assuming, of course, you will be in Paris.'[28]

The two men did meet in early April, and on the 23rd Bailey wrote to say how much he had enjoyed their 'little chat'. But this letter also contained his first detailed evaluation of Blair's stories, and some of his comments were sharply critical. He called one story 'immature and unsatisfactory', and said that another was 'tedious'. One problem was that there were too many long passages of poetic description. 'Stories of action,' he advised, 'will much more readily find a market than slow-moving descriptive (no matter how beautiful) ones will.' He also informed him, 'You deal with sex too much in your writings.' Obviously, he was looking for stories that would satisfy the mass-market tastes of the time, and only one of Blair's stories seemed to have good commercial potential. ' "The Man in Kid Gloves" impressed me very much, and I consider it an extremely clever story. It holds the attention of the reader and strikes a crisp note.' Whether he was right or wrong will never be known because, unfortunately, none of these stories was published, and the typescripts have not survived. The agent spent two months trying to sell 'The Man in Kid Gloves' to editors, but he had no luck and soon lost interest in Blair.

Blair's 'little chat' with Bailey, before the stories had been read and evaluated, marked the high point of his literary expectations during his stay in Paris. For a brief period it must have seemed that he had taken a major step forward in his career. Bailey was friendly and encouraging, and there was talk of finding a publisher to bring out a book of his short stories. With an agent in Fleet Street on his side, he may have imagined that it would only be a matter of weeks before a publisher's contract was in his hand. But such things were not to be, and the lost hopes simply helped to reinforce that side of his character which expected failure. It is not surprising that his stories disappeared. Apparently, he threw them away, convinced that they showed no promise. In the late 1940s he wrote, 'In 1928–9 I lived in Paris and wrote short stories and novels that nobody would print (I have since destroyed them all).' In the last year of his life he recalled how, in his early days as a writer, he used 'to destroy a dozen pages for one that was worth keeping. I tore up a whole novel once & wish now I hadn't been so ruthless.'[29]

There was another major setback at this time. On 7 March he coughed up some blood following a bad attack of bronchitis and went for help to the Hôpital Cochin, which was a mile away from his hotel. He was suffering from a temperature of 103°, and was later diagnosed as having pneumonia, but when he arrived at the reception desk, he was forced to spend twenty minutes answering questions before the clerks would admit him. By that time he was barely able to stand up. He was placed in a public ward where sixty men were crowded into three long rows of beds, and he remained there for the next three weeks.[30]

In the 1940s he recalled the experience in his essay 'How the Poor Die', which depicts the hospital as a dark, filthy place of nightmarish suffering. The care was harsh and backward, as he quickly discovered when he received his first treatment from one of the doctors. A cupping glass – heated inside to exhaust the air – was popped on to his chest and the vacuum drew up a large blister, which was then cut. The glass was applied again and a 'dessert-spoonful of dark-coloured blood' was drawn out. This procedure was repeated several times, and then a mustard poultice was placed on his chest for fifteen minutes. 'For the first five minutes the pain is severe, but you believe you can bear it. During the second five minutes this belief evaporates.'

He felt as though he had stepped back in time and was trapped in an early Victorian hospital from which patients rarely escaped alive. But, eventually, his illness attracted some reasonable attention. Every day a tall, bearded doctor made his rounds with a large group of medical students, and Blair's case aroused their curiosity. 'If you had some disease with which the students wanted to familiarise themselves you got plenty of attention of a kind. I myself, with an exceptionally fine specimen of a bronchial rattle, sometimes had as many as a dozen students queueing up to listen to my chest.' Although he does not mention it in the essay, someone at the hospital finally decided to check him for signs of tuberculosis. A sputum test was performed, but no evidence of the tubercle bacillus was found. He did not give much thought to this at the time, and did not seek another opinion when his hospital stay ended. Later, in the 1930s, he was repeatedly tested for tuberculosis, but these tests also produced negative results. It was not until the end of 1947 that he was finally diagnosed as having the disease, and by then his lungs were in such bad condition that he was able to survive for only twenty-five months.

He always knew his lungs were weak, but as friends such as Ruth Pitter realised, nothing could persuade him to take better care of his health. Whenever he fell ill, he resisted admitting it, and always tried to avoid doctors and hospitals if he could. He had an instinctive dread of hospitals, and his painful experience in the public ward in Paris only served to confirm his worst fears. What he objected to most was the powerlessness of the patients, the way in which they were treated like objects with no will of their own. 'I had never been in the public ward of a hospital before, and it was my first experience of doctors who handle you without speaking to you, or, in a human sense, taking any notice of you.' By the time Orwell wrote his essay, he had acquired enough experience of hospitals to know that even in the best of them, there was always a touch of the cold, impersonal atmosphere which had pervaded the Hôpital Cochin. He was not afraid of dying, but he did not want it to happen in a hospital bed. 'It is a great thing to die in your own bed, though it is better still to die in your boots. However great the kindness and the efficiency, in every hospital death there will be some cruel, squalid detail, something perhaps too small to be told but leaving terribly painful memories behind, arising out of the haste, the crowding, the impersonality of a place where every day people are dying among strangers.'[31] He did not get his wish. When his time came to die, he was alone in his room in the private patients' wing of a London hospital.

IV

On the day Blair left the Hôpital Cochin, an editor at *Le Progrès Civique* wrote to give him the good news that the paper was going to publish another of his articles, a piece on Burma which he had submitted before his illness. It is a straightforward attack on British Imperialism, with some interesting background information on the organisation of the provincial government, but much of it reads like a school report. It begins with the dull statement, 'Burma lies between India and China.' It makes a good case against the economic exploitation of the country, and exposes some of the false promises of the empire-builders, but there is no personality in the piece, no sense that it was written by someone with an intimate knowledge of the way the colonial system works. But it must have given him great satisfaction to see some of his 'seditious' thoughts openly disseminated, with his name prominently given at the top of the piece as 'E. A. Blair'.[32]

The article appeared in May, but it was not followed by more contributions from him, and he did not succeed in finding other outlets for his work during the rest of his time in Paris. By the end of the summer his career was at a standstill. A terse letter written near the end of September gives some idea of the frustration he was feeling. It was sent to Max Plowman at the *Adelphi* in London and concerned an article about life among tramps in a spike, or casual ward. After reminding Plowman that he had sent him the typescript in August, Blair wrote: 'As a month has now gone by, I should be glad to hear from you about it. I have no other copy of the article, & I want to submit it elsewhere if it is no use to you.'[33] A mere month of silence from the *Adelphi* did not merit a letter of this kind, but Blair was clearly in no mood to be patient. One way or the other, he wanted to move his career forward, and he was tired of waiting for someone to give him his next break.

It was not long after he wrote this letter that the ordeal described in the Paris section of *Down and Out* began. After having endured his three days of starvation, Orwell says that he managed to have a proper meal when he and his Russian friend, Boris, pawned their overcoats. A former waiter, Boris eventually helps him to find a job as a dishwasher and kitchen porter at one of the finest hotels in the city (the book calls it the 'Hotel X'). It is miserable work and Orwell spares none of the ugly details when he describes the hot, filthy conditions in the service quarters, unseen by its wealthy guests. 'Dirtiness is inherent in hotels and restaurants, because sound food is sacrificed to punctuality and smartness. The hotel employee is too busy getting food ready to remember that it is meant to be eaten.' His labours last only a few weeks before he and Boris take jobs at a small restaurant employing mostly Russians. The conditions in this place are so bad that Orwell writes to a friend in

London – identified only as 'B.' – and asks that he help him find a job in England. A few days later 'B.' replies with an offer of a position caring for a 'congenital idiot', and Orwell accepts right away, adding that such work will 'be a splendid rest cure' after the seventeen-hour days which he has been spending at the restaurant. 'B. sent me a fiver to pay my passage and get my clothes out of pawn, and as soon as the money arrived I gave one day's notice and left the restaurant.'

Many of Orwell's works occupy a border zone between fact and fiction, which makes them more interesting as literature, but which makes his biography harder to write. Biographies must try to sort fact from fiction, but previous accounts of his life have had great difficulty ascertaining how much of the Paris section of *Down a·d Out* comes from his own experience. The handful of surviving documents from his Paris years does nothing to illuminate the story, and his few public statements about it are inconclusive. But new evidence came to light in 1989 with the discovery of a first edition of *Down and Out* annotated in the margins by Orwell for his Southwold friend Brenda Salkeld. It was a presentation copy, and his comments were provided in confidence, with no thought that they would one day be published. As far as can be determined, it is the only one of his books which he marked in this way.[34]

One of the early annotations concerns Boris. Many readers of *Down and Out* have wondered whether this colourful character was based on a friend whom Orwell had met in hospital, as he claims in the narrative. He seems almost too colourful to be true. A Russian refugee, he is absurdly proud of the fact that he was once a captain in the Czar's Second Siberian Rifles, and he confronts the miseries of poverty as though he were waging a military campaign, telling Orwell: 'We shan't starve ... It's only a question of persisting. Remember Foch's maxim: "Attaquez! Attaquez! Attaquez!" ' He has some of the best lines in the book, the most memorable of which are contained in this advice to Orwell: 'Writing is bosh. There is only one way to make money at writing, and that is to marry a publisher's daughter. But you would make a good waiter if you shaved that moustache off.' In the margin beside the paragraph which introduces Boris to the story, Orwell wrote in Brenda's copy: 'This is a fairly accurate portrait except for the name.' And at the point where he first visits Boris in his tiny attic room, the annotation reads: 'All this fairly exact description of actual happenings.' Of their encounter with the 'Communist secret society' (which turns out to be merely a clever bunch of swindlers preying on Russian refugees), Orwell's handwritten comment is, 'This happened very much as described.'

The annotations confirm that Orwell went without food for three days. 'This all happened,' he writes at the top of the seventh chapter, which begins with the words, 'My money oozed away.' The comments also confirm the factual accuracy of Orwell's employment at the place which he calls the 'Hotel X'. 'All as exact as I could make it,' he writes at the top of the chapter which describes his first day of work. ('We will give you a permanent job if you like,' the *chef du personnel* tells him at the end of the chapter. 'The head waiter says he would enjoy calling an Englishman names.')[35] A similar annotation appears at the top of the chapter which describes the beginning of his employment at the Russian restaurant (the one in which he finds 'two large rats sitting on the kitchen table, eating from a ham'): 'All the following is an entirely accurate description of the restaurant.'

There are sixteen marginal comments in all, but they follow no logical plan. They are random remarks hastily written down for a friend's pleasure. Some major points receive no comment at all, such as the identity of his benefactor, the shadowy character named 'B.' But in an early annotation Orwell makes it clear that, in writing the book, he had given himself the freedom to rearrange events and to add and subtract certain details. At the beginning of the third chapter, which includes his story about a young Italian stealing his money, he says, 'Succeeding chapters not actually autobiography, but drawn from what I have seen.' In other words the book cannot be read as literal autobiography, but all the events reflect something of the world in which he had immersed himself. He was robbed and he did starve, but how he was robbed (by a young Italian? by a French 'trollope'?), and why he starved (by necessity? by choice?) are matters which he felt free to alter for the sake of his story.[36]

Whether his 'fiver' came from 'B.' or from Aunt Nellie, it did come and he did return to England, just before Christmas 1929. But his reason for going home may not have been because of a job offer, but because of a letter he had received in late November or early December. It was a response to the rather abrupt letter he had sent to Max Plowman at the *Adelphi*. He was probably expecting a rejection when he opened the envelope, but his luck had turned. The magazine which he had blasted to pieces at target practice in Burma had decided to publish his article on tramps. In mid-December he sent a quick response on a postcard.[37]

> 6 Rue de Pot de Fer, Paris 5
>
> Dear Sir
> Please excuse the delay in answering your letter. You may have the article on the terms mentioned by you. If there are any further communications, will you address [them] to
>> 3 Queen St
>> Southwold
>> Suffolk.
>
> which is my permanent address.
>
>> Yours faithfully
>> E A Blair

CHAPTER EIGHT

A Provincial Life

I

Blair's first acceptance at the *Adelphi* marked the beginning of a long association with the magazine, and he was always grateful to Max Plowman for showing faith in his talent at such an early stage. Plowman was twenty years his senior, and in later years they had strong differences of opinion on many issues, especially on the subject of pacifism, to which Plowman was deeply committed. But the two men respected each other's sincerity, and their disagreements did not prevent them from becoming good friends. Blair liked the fact that Plowman was not a typical intellectual. He once described him as a man 'of strong physique and simple tastes, a lover of cricket and gardening'. When Plowman died in 1941, Orwell told his widow, 'I always felt that with Max the most fundamental disagreement didn't alter one's personal relationship in any way, not only because he was incapable of any pettiness but also because one never seems able to feel any resentment against an opinion which is sincerely held . . . I was very fond of him, and he was always very good to me.'[1]

By the time that Blair became a regular contributor, John Middleton Murry had relinquished editorial control – though not ownership – to Max Plowman, and to Sir Richard Rees. A young baronet with a comfortable private income, Rees used his own money to help pay the magazine's bills. Initially, Rees was not as impressed with Blair's work as his co-editor was, finding him 'intelligent and able' but not 'especially original or gifted'. But after they met in London in 1930, they became friends, and their friendship continued for the rest of Blair's life, growing stronger in his last years. What Rees found so appealing in the young writer was his modesty. He had none of 'the jealous, pushful, intriguing, self-centred mentality which is so common among young ambitious literary men'.[2]

He made a third friend at the *Adelphi*, a young working-class writer named Jack Common who was an assistant employed by the magazine to sell subscriptions. One afternoon in 1930 Common walked into the office in Bloomsbury Street and found a visitor sitting with Rees and Plowman. The editors introduced their guest as Eric Blair, and as he rose to shake hands with Common he displayed an easy grace which surprised the assistant. His appearance had at first suggested a rough character. With his 'scrub of hair and curiously ravaged face', Common recalled, 'he looked the real thing: outcast, gifted pauper, kicker against authority, perhaps near-criminal'. But his manners revealed something more refined. 'A sheep in wolf's clothing, I thought, taking in the height and stance, accent and cool built-in superiority, the public school presence.' Common was slow to warm to this odd character, not knowing quite what to make of him. Was he a rebel pretending to be a gentleman? or vice versa? In time, he realised that any attempt to place a label on Blair was pointless, and he came to expect, and appreciate, the contradictions in his friend's character. He learned to enjoy the peculiar process of debating ideas with him. 'We got on almost merrily by regularly turning over one another's statements to look for the bug beneath, an intellectual equivalent of the turn-and-turn-about grooming and de-lousing of the great apes.'[3]

Blair wrote mostly reviews for the *Adelphi*, but he also contributed some poems to it, as well as two of his best documentary sketches, 'The Spike' and 'A Hanging'. The typescript which he had submitted from Paris was a longer, less polished version of 'The Spike'. After the initial acceptance of this piece, Plowman had asked for revisions, and partly for that reason publication was delayed for more than a year. In the meantime he was given various books to review, and his first appearance in the magazine came in the spring of 1930 when he reviewed a new biography of Herman Melville. Although he had not yet adopted his pseudonym, this is the first published piece in which the distinctive voice of Orwell emerges. It is confident, insightful and direct. At last – after all the struggles in Paris – he sounds like a real writer. Discussing Melville's poetry, he uses a sharp, simple image to repudiate literary criticism which is too intent on extracting a 'meaning' from individual poems. It 'is like eating an apple for the pips', he says. Quoting an example of one critic's convoluted literary analysis, he observes, 'Very ingenious . . . but how much better not to have said it.' Sweeping aside the pedantic approach of such critics, he creates an arresting phrase to capture the essence of Melville's character: 'He was a kind of ascetic voluptuary, disciplined . . . and yet amorous of delightful things wherever he found them.'[4] Perhaps not by coincidence, it is also a description appropriate to Blair's own character.

He fully justified Plowman's faith in him when he submitted his revision of 'The Spike'. It is based on one of his early tramping experiences outside London, and shows the same economy of style and precise attention to detail which distinguish all of Orwell's best work. Like 'A Hanging' and 'Shooting an Elephant', its narrative merges the techniques of journalism and fiction – using the dramatic powers of dialogue, setting and character to strengthen the powers of factual observation and commentary. It does more than simply recount one day in the life of a 'tramp'. It undertakes the difficult feat of conveying two perspectives simultaneously. Convincingly disguised as a tramp, Blair is a character playing a part in the action of the piece, enduring the same misery as the other tramps who spend the night in the spike. But he is also the narrator, and as such he stands outside the action, describing it in a sophisticated, very articulate voice for his largely middle-class readership. He is with 'us', acting as a guide to an alien world, and he is one of the tramps – one of the outcasts, one of 'them'.

The two perspectives are brilliantly managed. When the tramps are forced to strip to the waist for a medical inspection inside the large bathroom of the spike, the narrator's voice invites the reader to consider the pathetic sight of the shivering, half-naked men with their sagging muscles, hollow chests, haggard faces and unruly hair. At the same time, of course, as the reader surveys the scene painted by the narrator, Blair is standing there with the rest of the tramps, his tall, bony figure exposed to the same 'filtered light, bluish and cold' which 'lighted us up with unmerciful clarity'.

This double vision deliberately blurs the line between 'them' and 'us', compelling readers to feel, if only for a moment, what life is like in that largely hidden world of the spike, and to understand – in a palpable way – how dehumanising that world is. When the tramps enter the spike on a Saturday, they are forced to remain locked up in cramped quarters until Monday morning, with little to occupy their time between meals which typically consist of bread, margarine and 'so-called tea'. This is the grudging relief provided them by society, and it is unnecessarily severe. 'It is a silly piece of cruelty to confine an ignorant man all day with nothing to do; it is like chaining a dog in a barrel.'

But they live like dogs because they are habitually perceived from the outside as being something less than human, and so strong is this view that even one of the tramps expresses it to Blair. A young, unemployed carpenter tells him, 'You don't want to have any pity on these tramps – scum, they are.' Blair, as narrator, is scathing in his condemnation of this man's absurd refusal to recognise any connection to the human beings sharing the spike with him. 'It was interesting to see how subtly he disassociated himself from his fellow tramps. He had been on the road six months, but in the sight of God, he seemed to imply, he was not a tramp. His body might be in the spike, but his spirit soared far away, in the pure aether of the middle classes.' Like society in general, the young man seems to think that the tramps – the 'scum' – will disappear if he only pretends they are not there. As Orwell observed much later in his career, 'To see what is in front of one's nose needs a constant struggle.'[5]

Parts of 'The Spike' reappear in *Down and Out in Paris and London*, which became the principal object of Blair's literary labours in 1930–1932. His progress with the book was slow, but for most of this period he was relatively free to focus his attention on his writing. He did not have a full-time job until the spring of 1932. He lived primarily at his parents' home in Southwold – in Queen Street and later at 36 High Street – and he earned a little money from his contributions to the *Adelphi*, and from a few temporary jobs. His parents did not make him feel unwelcome, but they were discouraged by their son's stubborn desire to pursue a literary career at all costs. He had little to show for his efforts, and there was no reason for them to believe that another two years of effort would bring better results. But by this stage in his life they had stopped expecting him to act like other middle-class men of his age. Eric was 'different', and nothing was going to change that.

His parents led a comfortable life in Southwold. Mr Blair, who was in his early seventies, was a familiar figure in the town, and was well-thought-of. Ida Blair gave their home a cheery, inviting atmosphere, and was fond of having friends over for bridge. And Avril owned a small tea shop in the town called the Copper Kettle, which served real ice cream and fresh cakes, as well as coffees and teas – all prepared by Avril and one assistant. There were only a few tables, but it was a popular gathering place, and Avril made a respectable living from it until she closed it at the beginning of the Second World War. Occasionally, her brother was one of her customers, but he was not very comfortable in the genteel atmosphere of the place. A few years later he subjected it to some mild ridicule in his novel *A Clergyman's Daughter*, calling it 'Ye Olde Tea Shoppe' and describing it as 'the principal rendezvous' of the ladies in his fictional town of Knype Hill, Suffolk. He gives an amusing sample of the conversation during 'morning coffee':

> What, my dear, you don't mean to say you're paying for my coffee *again*? Oh, but, my dear, it is simply *too* sweet of you! Now tomorrow I shall simply *insist* on paying for yours. And just *look* at dear little Toto sitting up and looking such a *clever* little man with his little black nose wiggling, and he would, would he, the darling duck, he would, he would, and his mother would give him a lump of sugar, she would ... *There*, Toto!

It is not known what Avril thought of this, but it may have taught her that friends and relatives of novelists can never rest easy. Their lives are always tempting sources of material.

Avril was certainly in no doubt about her brother's attitude towards Southwold. 'Eric loathed Southwold,' she told an interviewer in the early 1960s.[6] It is true that Blair never cared much for the town, whose population in his day included a good many retired officials from British India, but he enjoyed the beach and the surrounding countryside, particularly the fields and marshes which spread out from the banks of the River Blyth, between Southwold and the little town of Walberswick. He was fascinated by the half-abandoned Church of St Andrew's in Walberswick, which stands on a prominent spot overlooking the river, and he liked to go there on fine summer days to explore the large churchyard and to sit in a shady place with a book. Most of the church was built in the fifteenth century, when the town was larger and much more prosperous, but half of it was dismantled in the seventeenth century when the population declined. All that remains of that part are the ivy-covered ruins of its high walls.

During one of his visits to the church, he thought he saw a ghost walking among the ruins. It was in late afternoon on a day in July, and he was sitting under one of the ruined arches. Suddenly, he caught a glimpse of a small, stooped figure in brown walking through the ruins towards the churchyard. Thinking that it was probably a workman, he looked away and then realised that the man had passed him without making the slightest noise. He stood up and walked into the churchyard, but the figure had vanished. He was so intrigued by what he had witnessed that he took the trouble to draw a diagram of the scene and to write down an account of the incident for one of his friends in Southwold. He had been fond of ghost stories as a boy, and it is conceivable that he invented this story as way of creating an adventure for himself, but he gave no indication of that, and did not try to exaggerate its significance.[7]

He often went over to Walberswick during his first year at home because he had found a job there tutoring a boy who suffered from both mental and physical handicaps. It is not clear how severe these handicaps were – he is described in one letter as being 'very backward' and 'a cripple'. The unfortunate phrase used in *Down and Out* – 'congenital imbecile' – may have been technically correct. In any case, it seems likely that Blair found this job not through 'B.', but through family friends after his return from Paris. Almost nothing is known about his work with the boy. Only a brief glimpse of their time together has survived, and it is found in a rather strange story recalled by Orwell ten years later. It seems that the boy was able to go for walks, and during one outing on Walberswick Common, he and Blair discovered a neatly tied-up parcel hidden under a gorse bush. It was a cardboard box lined with cloth and it contained some tiny pieces of handmade furniture arranged to look like a room in a doll's house. There were also 'some tiny female garments including underclothes'. And one other item – a simple message neatly written on a scrap of paper. It said, 'This is not bad, is it?' Blair had no idea how the box had come to be there, but he could only conclude that they had stumbled upon some weird private joke. Although it is possible to see it as an innocent joke, he seized upon a more sinister explanation. His suspicions were aroused by the evidence of the underclothes, and by his impression that the handwriting belonged to a woman:

What chiefly impressed me was that anyone should go to the trouble of making this thing, which would have meant some hours' work, then carefully tie it up in a parcel and thrust it under a bush, and in a rather remote spot at that. For what such 'intuitive' feelings are worth, I may say that I felt convinced (a) that it had been put there with the intention that someone should find it, and (b) that it had been made by someone suffering from some kind of sexual aberration. Walberswick has a very small population and one could probably have deduced who was responsible with a little trouble. I may add that the boy I was with could have had nothing to do with it. He was not only very backward but was a cripple and so clumsy with his hands as to have been quite incapable of anything of the kind. The strange thing is that I do not remember what finally happened to the box. To the best of my recollection we put it back under the bush and

on coming back some days later found it was gone. At any rate I
didn't keep it, which would seem the natural thing to do. I have often
puzzled over the incident since, and always with the feeling that
there was something vaguely unwholesome in the appearance of the
little room and the clothes.[8]

What is most interesting about this account is not the theory it
puts forward, but the insight it provides into the mind of the once
successful officer of the Imperial Police. In some ways his account
reads like a police report, perhaps very much like the reports he was
responsible for writing in Burma. There is a careful sorting of
evidence, a methodical consideration of motives and the implication that a suspect can be found. The ex-policeman's voice is most
apparent in the line, 'One could probably have deduced who was
responsible with a little trouble.' It is almost possible to imagine
Superintendent Blair going from door to door 'making inquiries',
and obtaining a quick confession from some unfortunate woman
living nearby.

Blair worked with the 'backward boy' for several months, and
then he had another brief spell of employment tutoring three
brothers whose mother was a friend of Mrs Blair. By coincidence,
the father – C. R. Peters – was an officer in the Imperial Police.
Blair's job was not demanding – he tutored the boys during three
school holidays in 1930 and 1931, and he seems to have spent a
great part of that time playing games with them and leading them on
long expeditions into the countryside. One of the boys, Richard
Peters, later wrote a delightful account of this period, recalling the
various unconventional methods of education employed by their
tutor. His memoir is especially interesting because he wrote it at a
time when he was Professor of the Philosophy of Education,
University of London.

The qualities which Peters appreciated in Blair were his
boundless sense of curiosity, his unpretentious way of sharing his
knowledge and his genuine love of nature. He remembered that
Blair 'had a slow disarming sort of smile which made us feel that he
was interested in us yet amused by us in a detached sort of way'. He
taught them how to fish in a mill-pool by using bent pins and bread

pellets; they investigated an old Roman barrow; they went down to the marshes and listened to him lecture on the properties of marsh gas; they visited a heronry and they staged mock battles in the sand-dunes at Walberswick. And in defiance of all reason, they made bombs, exploding them in Mrs Peters's garden. 'He had a patent firing mechanism which involved tipping a test-tube of sulphuric acid from a distance by means of cotton on to a fuse composed, as far as I can remember, of chlorate of potash and sugar.' The boys loved it, of course, and Blair was careful to keep them out of danger, but all the same, this could not have been what their mother had imagined for them in the way of tutoring. 'My poor mother would look anxiously out of the window to see which part of the garden was going to disappear next.' Even at the age of twenty-eight, Blair still had a wide streak of boyish foolishness in his character, and in looking back on that period, Richard Peters was particularly impressed with the way that this eccentric adult had so easily become a part of a child's world, entering it 'unobtrusively'. When they played games on the sand-dunes, Blair 'was merely the boy who played the game with his head'.[9]

He did not function so easily in the adult world of Southwold. He had only a few close friends. One was a young man two years his junior – Dennis Collings – whose father was the Blair family's doctor. They met in 1921, very soon after the Blairs came to Southwold, but did not become firm friends until after Eric's return from Burma. Dennis had also seen something of the world, having spent the mid-1920s in Mozambique, where he grew sisal. Later he read anthropology at Cambridge, and eventually joined the Colonial Service, becoming an assistant curator of the Raffles Museum in Singapore. He and Blair held different views of the Empire, and of social conditions in England, but they discussed their differences openly, and in a friendly spirit. 'The great thing about Eric,' Collings recalled, 'was that he could disagree with you very strongly, yet not allow it to affect his feelings towards you. He wanted you to see things his way, but if you didn't, there was no resentment. You were still his friend.'[10]

At the beginning of the 1930s Blair's closest friend was Brenda

Salkeld, an intelligent, handsome woman who was then in her early thirties. A vicar's daughter, she had grown up in Bedfordshire, and had come to Southwold to work at St Felix's School for Girls where she was the gym mistress. She and Blair saw a great deal of each other after he came home from Paris. They went for walks on Southwold Common, and occasionally went riding together on the heath near Walberswick. 'We would hire the horses for the day,' Brenda remembered, 'and then in the evening we liked to stop at the Harbour Inn for a drink. We always arranged to have a small room to ourselves where we could talk. We loved books and would spend hours talking about the things we had read. He was always trying to shock me with some strange fact or observation, and you could see the delight in his face whenever he succeeded.'[11]

It was not only with words that he tried to shock her. Sometimes he would meet her for a date dressed flamboyantly, with a large colourful French scarf round his neck, and at other times he would look scruffy, wearing an old coat or a dirty shirt. 'He was just waiting for my reaction. I remember one afternoon I had been playing golf, and was wearing a very nice tweed skirt when I went to meet him, but then he came up wearing a shirt which was obviously dirty, and gave me a defiant look, as though daring me to say something. But I just ignored it, and that was that.' At another time, when she was staying with her family in Bedfordshire, he stopped at the house during one of his tramping expeditions. He came to the door and asked for breakfast. 'He looked perfectly awful, and my mother was not amused, but he came in and I said, "You must have a bath." He did as I told him, and I think one of my sisters was laughing and said later, "I hope he's not using my loofah." All that business about being a tramp was just ludicrous. He had a home, he had a nice family.'

Brenda knew his family well and liked them. She met old Mr Blair from time to time at the Southwold Golf Club, and she was one of Avril's customers at the Copper Kettle. Mrs Blair invited her to the house in Queen Street to play bridge, which she enjoyed except that it was always so difficult to get Eric to come down and join them. 'He was writing up there and didn't want to stop. His writing always came first with him. There was no doubt about that.' He would occasionally show her a draft of something he had just written and ask her for her comments. He respected her literary views and wanted her good opinion, which is one reason why he later went to the trouble of annotating her presentation copy of *Down and Out*.

Brenda had many other friends, and liked going to parties, but Eric avoided them. 'I always liked the dances at the Constitutional Club, but you would never have found Eric there. After a Saturday night dance in summer, my friends and I liked to go down to the beach the next morning and make a huge Sunday breakfast, cooking eggs and bacon on gas burners, and I think Eric would sometimes join us. But would he come to the dances? No, never. I can't imagine him dancing with anyone.'

They made an unlikely pair for romance, and according to Brenda, she was never in love with him. But at some point in 1930 Eric decided that he was in love with her and proposed marriage. She said no, but he continued to bring up the subject for several months before finally accepting her decision. 'I suppose you could say that I liked my independence too much. I did not want to marry anyone, though there were others besides Eric who had shown an interest. Eric and I began as friends, then he fell in love, but marriage was not for us. I'm sure he would have been impossible to live with.' There can be no doubt that he was deeply fond of Brenda and thought that she might make a good wife. But he probably understood very well that she would never accept him as a husband, and his proposals may simply have been another way of teasing her. He found various ways of adding something to each proposal which would draw a shocked response from her, telling her one day, 'Of course, when we are married, I wouldn't want you to have anything more to do with your brothers.' And, of course, she gave him the indignant reaction which he expected, saying that she was devoted to her brothers and his idea was absurd.

It takes two to play this game, and if Brenda had not derived some enjoyment from it, she would have quickly put an end to their friendship. But the truth is that they remained good friends for the rest of his life. Although she had no intention of marrying him, and was often exasperated by his impractical behaviour, she developed a sisterly feeling towards him. His own feelings are apparent in the affectionate and confiding letters he wrote to her in the mid-1930s, long after she had refused his first proposal of marriage. Although 'Dearest Brenda' is his usual salutation, the emphasis in these letters is on their shared love of ideas, not romance. In one letter he writes to her at great length about his enthusiasm for James Joyce's *Ulysses*, clearly hoping to stir up the same enthusiasm in her, and in another he turns against one of the model figures of his youth, Bernard Shaw, urging her to tell her friends who admire the playwright that he is merely 'Carlyle & water'.[12] He filled his letters with so many random opinions and observations that Brenda could not have been able to respond to them all, but she knew that he did not expect that. He was thinking out loud and she was his audience.

One random idea which he shared in a letter may not have seemed very significant to Brenda when she first encountered it, but the passage of time has made it stand out. He wrote to her that he had been thinking about how a song can take on a life of its own after it has been composed. Over a period of time the words may change, the composer may be forgotten and the tune may be used to celebrate different things in different cultures, but one way or another it continues to live. This led him to say, 'It struck me that an *idea* is very like a tune in this way, that it goes through the ages remaining the same in itself but getting into such very different company.'[13] Of course, it is precisely this process which has overtaken some of Orwell's ideas. Political groups of almost all persuasions have tried to lay claim to them and to insist that if Orwell were still alive he would be on their side. But a slightly different point can be made in relation to such famous words and phrases as 'Big Brother', 'Thought Police', '1984', 'Newspeak', 'Orwellian'. They too are like tunes which have taken on a life of their own, acquiring endless variations of meaning, appearing in a wide range of contexts, and becoming familiar terms to millions of people who never heard of Eric Blair.

II

One of Blair's favourite pastimes in Southwold was painting. He enjoyed doing landscapes and seascapes, and though he had no serious ambitions for this work, it is interesting to note that he sometimes identified himself as an indigent painter when he was tramping. Describing a day at a spike in *Down and Out*, he says, 'I gave my trade as "painter"; I had painted watercolours – who has not?' In the summer of 1930 he felt sufficient interest in this hobby to make regular trips to a favourite spot on the beach at Southwold where he liked to spend mornings sketching or painting. It was here, one day in August, that he met Francis and Mabel Fierz, who had taken a cottage nearby for a month's holiday. They were a middle-aged couple from London, where Francis made a comfortable living as an executive in a steel manufacturing firm. Mabel was a plainspoken woman who loved literature, and who had a soft spot in her heart for unconventional causes and odd characters. She and Blair were drawn to each other right away. He came to think of her in the same way that he thought of Aunt Nellie. She opened her home to him, treating him like a member of her own family, and she encouraged him to share his thoughts with her. In the early 1930s he was a frequent guest at 1b Oakwood Road, the Fierzes' house in Hampstead Garden Suburb. 'He felt entirely at ease with us,' Mabel remembered, 'and he would tell us anything. He knew that we liked him and were tolerant, and he felt entirely at home in our house.'[14]

Mabel introduced him to other young writers of her acquaintance, and urged him to spend more time in London so that he could establish the right contacts in the literary world. It was an obvious piece of advice, but he was reluctant to follow it because he did not want to appear to be chasing success. She tried to give him a gentle push. In Southwold she told him, 'As a literary man it won't help you much to live down here. You must meet literary people who will help with your work.'[15] Mabel did him a great service by helping him to become better acquainted with Max Plowman, who – as luck would have it – also lived in Oakwood Road. And in late

1931 she persuaded him to contact a literary agent, a man named Leonard Moore whose agency – Christy & Moore – was located in the Strand, and who knew Mr Fierz from various encounters at their tennis club. Blair's decision to write to Moore would turn out to be one of smartest moves of his career. Despite the fact that Mabel and Francis Fierz were so willing to assist him, Blair rarely asked them for help. It usually had to be forced upon him. There were a few minor exceptions. Mabel remembered him asking her husband one day, 'Francis, have you an old pair of trousers? Are they pretty bad? Do you mind if I dirty them still more?'[16] He was preparing for another tramping experience, of course, and though Francis complied with the request, the respectable businessman must have had mixed feelings about it when he saw Blair take the trousers into the garden and tread on them.

According to Mabel, this incident occurred in the summer of 1931 when Blair was getting ready to go hop-picking in Kent. Indeed, a letter from him to Dennis Collings, explaining his plan for beginning this trip in a week or two, gives 1b Oakwood Road as his return address. He rather casually informed Collings, 'They say hop-picking disables your hands for weeks after – however, I'll describe that to you when I've done it.'[17] He was determined to make a careful record of this experience, so he planned not only to describe it in a detailed diary but also to jot down impressions in letters which he would send to Collings whenever possible. Earlier in the summer he wrote to Brenda, telling her of his trip, and teasing her by inviting her to come along. 'I will promise to have no lice . . . What fun if we could both go hopping together. But I suppose your exaggerated fear of dirt would deter you.'[18]

His adventure began in London where he stayed for two nights in cheap lodging houses, with a third night spent roughing it at Trafalgar Square, keeping out the cold by using newspaper posters for blankets. (Another tramp sharing this 'blanket' with him remarked, ''Ere y'are, mate, tuck in the fucking eiderdown.')[19] The next morning he shaved in the fountains, and then spent the rest of the day sitting with the tramps reading a Balzac novel in a French edition. It was not exactly the most inconspicuous choice of reading matter for an Old Etonian in disguise, but by this stage in his tramping career, he was not so fearful of being exposed as an impostor. He had learned that few disguises are more convincing than old clothes and dirt. Five years later he wrote, 'Even a bishop could be at home among tramps if he wore the right clothes; and even if they knew he was a bishop it might not make any difference, provided that they also knew or believed that he was genuinely destitute. Once you are in that world and seemingly *of* it, it hardly matters what you have been in the past.'[20] In fact, the only reaction to Blair's book was a matey one. The tramps were approving because they assumed that since he had a French book he must be reading pornography. As one tramp said, 'Ah, French? That'll be something pretty warm, eh?'[21]

When at last he began his journey to the hop fields in Kent, he was accompanied by three other tramps, one of whom – Ginger – was a young thief who, according to Blair's reckoning, had 'probably broken the law every day for the last five years'.[22] Travelling mostly on foot, they had numerous chances to support themselves by stealing, and they did. They took everything, from knives and forks at Woolworth's to apples and cigarettes from a grocer's shop. Ginger even wanted to rob a church, but was talked out of it by Blair. With such a fellow as his 'mate', Blair ran a very good risk of being arrested, but he was aware of this before they left London, and seemed almost to expect it. Writing to Collings at the outset of the journey, he said, 'If you don't hear [from me] within a fortnight it probably will mean I've been pinched for begging, as the mates I'm going with are hardened "tappers" [beggars] & not above petty theft.'[23]

He worked in the hop fields for eighteen days – at a farm in Mereworth – but was paid so poorly that his honest labour earned him only sixteen shillings after expenses were deducted. It is no wonder that thievery seemed such an attractive option to Ginger. Putting aside the fact that he was an habitual criminal, Ginger was 'really a very likeable fellow', Blair wrote to Collings.[24] The average working day was nine or ten hours, and after the first day Blair's hands were stained dark black by the hop-juice. In a day or two they began to crack and 'were cut to bits by the stems of the vines, which are spiny. In the mornings, before the cuts had reopened, my hands used to give me perfect agony.'[25] Yet he confessed to Collings that despite such pains there was something appealing about the work, and that in the short term it was 'rather fun'. He also spoke of wanting 'to make a saleable newspaper article out of it'.[26]

When he returned to London, he moved into another common lodging house, this time in Bermondsey. Making use of the reading room in the local library, he did indeed manage to produce a 'saleable' article, and he wrote it very quickly. He left the fields on 18 September, according to his diary, and in less than a month – on 17 October – 'Hop-picking', by Eric Blair, appeared in the *New Statesman*. It is essentially an informal report on conditions in the fields, and though it is skilfully written, it is a pale piece of work in comparison with his diary account of life among the hop-pickers, many of whom were gypsy families and East-Enders on 'holiday'. Unfortunately for Blair, a great deal of his material was unusable because by the standards of the day it was improper. He could tell the readers of the *New Statesman* that he and three other workers were forced to share a tin hut with no furniture except a heap of straw, but he could not tell him about the old deaf tramp who was one of the men living with him. Deafie, as he was known, was an amiable fellow. But when the hop-picking was done, and the workers headed back to their homes, Blair discovered that Deafie had a nasty habit. 'When we got to Wateringbury station,' he recorded in his diary, 'about fifty hoppers were waiting for the train, and the first person we saw was old Deafie, sitting on the grass with a newspaper in front of him. He lifted it aside, and we saw that he had his trousers undone and was exhibiting his penis to the women and children as they passed. I was surprised – such a decent old man, really.'[27]

None of the material from his hop-picking days was used in *Down and Out*. He had been working on the book since the beginning of 1930, but by the time he went hop-picking he had finished it. During July or early August of 1931 he had submitted the typescript to the publishing house of Jonathan Cape. It was not his first submission to the firm. A much shorter version of *Down and Out*, in the form of a diary, was sent to Cape in the autumn of 1930, but was rejected because 'it was too short and fragmentary'.[28] At that point he had been led to believe that his chances of acceptance would improve if he expanded the book and dropped the diary technique. He followed the suggestion, creating a work which was almost identical to the version eventually published, and gave it to Cape. But it was rejected again. The bad news came in September, just after he had returned from hop-picking.

Dejected, he went to Sir Richard Rees for advice and was told not to give up on the book. Rees promised to recommend it to one of the editorial directors at Faber & Faber – T. S. Eliot. Encouraged, but still wary of encountering another rejection, Blair decided to take a cautious approach. He wrote to Eliot, mentioning Rees's name, but he made no mention of the book. Instead he offered to do a translation of a French novel *A la Belle de Nuit*, by Jacques Roberti, which he described as 'the story of a prostitute, quite true to life so far as one can judge, & most ruthlessly told'. He meant well, but it was an eccentric proposal, and nothing came of it except a polite letter from Eliot, who asked to see a copy of Roberti's novel. Anything which was not an actual rejection was worth something, however, and Blair replied that he was 'anxious to get hold of some work of this kind', modestly adding, 'I think I could do it as well as the average translator'.[29] But in a letter to Brenda, he acknowledged that his plan was unpromising, telling her, 'I'm afraid they'll junk it (it is the life history of a prostitute & extremely realistic; I should think reading it would put any girl off the primrose path) but it is worth trying.' In any event, the experience enabled him to offer Brenda a small gift: 'By the way, did you say you collected signatures? I have T. S. Eliot's signature if you want it.'[30]

He did not submit his own book to Eliot until December. In the meantime he made his first contact with the literary agent Leonard Moore. He did not want Moore's help and wrote to him only because Mabel Fierz had insisted that he do so. In late autumn he curtly informed the agent: 'I doubt whether I have anything in hand at the moment which will be of the smallest use to you, but I am sending two short stories which you *might* be able to use. There is also the ms. of a book, about which I think Mrs Fierz spoke to you, but I am sending that to Faber & Faber.'[31] After his disappointing experience with L. I. Bailey, of the McClure Newspaper Syndicate, he was not inclined to place any faith in the efforts of literary agents, and he felt that Rees had already done more for his book than any agent could, since he had brought it to the attention of no less a figure than T. S. Eliot. Nothing is known about the two stories which he sent to Moore except that one was called 'An Idiot', and that both had been written 'a long time' ago. Not surprisingly, Moore was uninterested in them, but Blair began to have second thoughts about using an agent and wrote again to Moore in early January. At that point his book was under consideration at Faber, but he was growing increasingly anxious about its fate. 'If they *do* accept it,' he told Moore, 'which I am afraid is unlikely, I will put them in touch with you. But if they won't have it I doubt whether anyone else would, as it was sent to T. S. Eliot with a personal recommendation from a friend of his.'[32]

He was expecting the worst, partly because he was already in a depressed state over another problem with his career. He had been looking forward to earning a little money by contributing short stories to a new magazine called *Modern Youth*, and had given them two stories when the word came that the magazine had gone bankrupt. The first issue was scheduled to appear at the end of October 1931, but the magazine did not pay its printing bills for a sample issue, and the printer seized all the copy, including Blair's stories. Apparently he never recovered them. This was a great blow, not merely because the stories were lost, but also because he had been hoping to receive regular commissions from the magazine. He had stayed on in London after finishing his article for the *New Statesman*, taking a modest room in Paddington at 2 Windsor Street, and had been expecting that his work for *Modern Youth* would help to support him until he received better offers. In October he wrote to Brenda, 'I have been doing a good deal of work, & hope to do a greal deal more for the new paper "Modern Youth", tho' I'm afraid they won't give me a regular job. It is to appear on the

29th, & from the advance copy I have seen looks a pretty poisonous rag – something for the young business man who is not yet tired, but will be later in life. They only commission me to do stupid things, but we must live, of course.'[33]

Having lost his stories – as well as the anticipated income from *Modern Youth* – he was in a mood to think that more misfortune was headed his way. While he waited for Eliot's decision, he decided to invite misfortune by undertaking his most extreme experiment as a tramp. His aim was to spend Christmas in prison by going to the East End in his usual disguise and becoming so drunk that the police would have to arrest him. He began the experiment on a Saturday, about a week before Christmas. Downing four or five pints of beer and a quarter bottle of whisky on an empty stomach, he soon became – according to the understated description which he wrote later – 'tolerably drunk'. He was arrested as he staggered down the Mile End Road, but was held in custody for only two days. He seemed to have expected a harsher sentence for public drunkenness, and was disappointed that he had been released so soon, especially since Christmas was still a few days away. He tried another form of the experiment the next day, presenting himself in a drunken state at the entrance to a spike, hoping that he would be charged with violating a provision against drunkenness in the Vagrancy Act. When this failed even to get him arrested, he resorted to simple begging on the streets in plain view of the police, but no one paid any attention to him, and he gave up his efforts, admitting to himself that his trip had been 'more or less a failure'. The worst thing he had seen during his two days in custody was the WC in the small cell he had shared with five other men. It 'was disgusting in so small a cell, especially as the plug did not work'.[34]

He may have learned to play the part of a tramp well enough, but the former policeman could not manage the more demanding role of social offender. He did not have it in him to commit a really serious offence, one which would have guaranteed a longer period behind bars. In any case he could not afford for his experiment to be too successful. There was always the chance that the right letter from T. S. Eliot would improve his view of the world in a flash. But waiting for it proved to be a trial. All of January went by without so much as a postcard from the poet. By mid-February Blair could not stand the silence any longer. He telephoned Eliot at his office and politely asked whether a decision had been reached. He was told that the typescript had not yet been read, but that Eliot 'would have a look at it shortly'.[35] Two days later the suspense ended. Employing the stiff phrases typical of so many rejection letters, Eliot wrote, 'We did find it of very great interest, but I regret to say that it does not appear to me possible as a publishing venture.'[36] After all the weeks of waiting, after all the hopes, this was the way it ended. Blair's response may have been something like Gordon's in *Keep the Aspidistra Flying*, after his poems are rejected: ' "The Editor regrets!" Why be so bloody mealy-mouthed about it? Why not say outright, "We don't want your bloody poems." '

There is no question that Blair was bitterly disappointed by this decision. He may have been expecting it, but that did not make it any easier to bear. Overwhelmed by a sense of futility, he decided that he could no longer face the book. On a visit to Oakwood Road he handed the chapters to Mabel Fierz. 'Throw them away,' he said, 'but keep the paper-clips.'[37]

CHAPTER NINE

Writer and Teacher

I

Mabel Fierz read the chapters of 'Days in London and Paris', as the book was then called, and was astute enough to see that her friend was wrong to abandon it. She knew that persuading him to reconsider his decision would be difficult, so she decided to make her own effort to place it with a publisher. One day in April 1932 she took it to Leonard Moore's office in the Strand and asked whether he would try to sell it. The cool tone of Blair's early letters to Moore had made a poor impression, and the agent was reluctant to give any more time to an obscure writer who seemed so unwilling to promote himself. He informed Mabel that he was not interested. 'Oh no, nobody knows your friend,' he told her. 'I'm afraid there's no hope.'[1] But she was a persistent woman, and did not leave the office until she had received Moore's promise that he would keep the typescript and look at it when he had time.

Blair knew nothing of this effort on his behalf until late April when a letter arrived from Moore. After reading the book, the agent had concluded that there was some promise in it after all, and wrote to Blair offering to find a publisher for it. This reprieve was welcome, but Blair was careful to keep his hopes in check. 'I should of course be very pleased if you could sell it, and it is very kind of you to take the trouble of trying ... If by any chance you *do* get it accepted, will you please see that it is published pseudonymously, as I am not proud of it.'[2] Although there was no mention of a specific pseudonym in his reply to Moore, it was this simple request which would lead, in a few months' time, to the creation of 'George Orwell'. At this early stage the idea was appealing because it was essentially a quick, convenient way to resolve his ambivalence towards literary success. Using a pseudonym would make it possible for him to have things both ways. If the book was a failure, it would not be Eric Blair's failure. And if success was the result, it would not be Eric Blair's success.

For the time being, he was content to leave the choice of a pseudonym open, but he did take the important step of entering into a formal agreement with Moore. He was careful to insist, however, that he would not go through the agent to sell any short stories or articles, declaring proudly, 'I get the commissions for these myself.' Making a great deal of money on Blair's commissions must have seemed a most unlikely prospect at that time, and Moore could not have been encouraged by some of his new client's impractical ideas for earning extra money. Blair suggested – among several things – that Moore keep him in mind if any books in Old French came his way. 'I [can] translate old French, at least anything since 1400 A.D.'[3]

After the agreement with Moore was made, another period of waiting began, though this one was less anxious than earlier ones because he had fewer hopes. He doubted whether any publisher would make his agent an offer, so there was no point in worrying about it. But there were other problems to distract him. He was overwhelmed with work in a new job. Money had become such a problem that he had finally been forced to seek steady employment, and in April he had taken a teaching position at a small school in Hayes, on the western outskirts of London. The Hawthorns High School for Boys was a day school with only fourteen or fifteen pupils, and two masters – Blair and a Mr Grey. Most of the boys were sons of shopkeepers and small businessmen in the area, and the school itself was operated as a profit-making venture by Derek Eunson, a man whose primary place of employment was the nearby gramophone factory of His Master's Voice. Normally, he did not teach any of the classes, but he did try to act as a substitute whenever one of his two employees was ill. The school was housed in two rooms on the ground floor of a former rectory, and above it lived the proprietor, his wife, their son Denis, and also their lodger–schoolmaster, Eric Blair.

In *A Clergyman's Daughter* Dorothy Hare teaches at a girls' school which resembles The Hawthorns, and the novel includes a scathing attack on the proprietors of such schools. Very little is known about Derek Eunson, but Orwell has nothing good to say about the hundreds of unqualified men who, like Eunson, had decided to go into the education 'business'. The novel presents a typical conversation between an aspiring 'educator' and his wife as they contemplate the prospect of 'us two keeping school': 'We'll do it in style. Get in one of these Oxford and Cambridge chaps as is out of a job and'll come cheap, and dress 'im up in a gown and – what do they call them little square 'ats with tassles on top? That 'ud fetch the parents, eh? You just keep your eyes open and see if you can't pick on a good district where there's not too many on the same game already.'

After barely two months at The Hawthorns, Blair began ridiculing it to friends as a 'foul place', adding that Hayes itself was 'one of the most godforsaken places I have ever struck'.[4] Unlike the East End, the problem had nothing to do with poverty and grime. What made Hayes seem so unpleasant to him was its dreary uniformity. Since the end of the nineteenth century it had been developing rapidly from a sleepy little place into a busy suburb with several large factories in the general area and seemingly endless rows of identical suburban dwellings. 'You know how these streets fester all over the inner-outer suburbs,' George Bowling says of his London suburb, 'West Bletchley', in *Coming Up for Air*. 'Always the same. Long, long rows of little semi-detached houses ... The stucco front, the creosoted gate, the privet hedge, the green front door ... At perhaps one house in fifty some anti-social type who'll probably end in the workhouse has painted his front door blue instead of green.'

For some relief from this dull scene, Blair liked to retreat to the parish church, St Mary's, parts of which had been built in the thirteenth century. The rugged ancient architecture appealed to him, as did the spacious churchyard, and he soon became a friend of the curate, whom he once described as 'High Anglican but not a creeping Jesus & a very good fellow'. The only drawback to such a friendship was that he felt obliged to attend the church service, which was too elaborate for him. He did not know how to keep up with 'everyone bowing and crossing themselves'. As an adult, he was always immensely fond of old churches and country church-yards, but he did not want to take part in religious ceremonies, particularly ones which seemed 'popish'. He did his best to tolerate the rituals at St Mary's, observing them quietly while trying not to laugh at such things as 'the poor old vicar . . . dressed up in cope & biretta & led round in procession with candles etc., looking like a bullock garlanded for sacrifice'. As a contribution to the main-tenance of the church, Blair volunteered to repaint a small statue of the Virgin Mary, but secretly resolved to have some fun with the job by making her look 'as much like one of the illustrations in *La Vie Parisienne* as possible'.[5]

There was little opportunity for amusement in his new job. As a schoolmaster, he was not as free and easy in his methods as he had been with the Peters brothers in Southwold. Officially, he was the headmaster of The Hawthorns, and Mr Grey was the junior master, but he was forced to follow Derek Eunson's rules, and also had to take into consideration the wishes of the rather conservative parents, who wanted to make certain that they received 'good value' for the money they paid the school. Most of them did not care for any 'fancy' methods of teaching; and they tended to favour instruction in 'practical' subjects, such as arithmetic, spelling, grammar, handwriting – and for its snob appeal, French. The aim of the school was not to prepare a boy for further education but for a place in a family business.

A typical pupil was Geoffrey Stevens. He came to The Hawthorns when he was eleven, in 1931, and left five years later to take his place in his father's joinery business. He remembered Blair as a teacher who could be unnecessarily strict in the classroom, but who was usually relaxed and generous outside it. 'There was no formal instruction in art at the school, and not much in natural history, but he was very keen on these subjects and seemed to enjoy sharing his knowledge of them after school hours. I had never done any oil painting until he took the time to give me a few lessons. I also went with him on some of his walks. We used to go to the marshes at Cranford, south of [Hayes], and he taught me how to stir up the gas with a long stick so that we could trap it in jars, cork it and then put a match to it. We thought that was great fun.' In the classroom Blair was at his best teaching French, using the approach to language instruction which he had learned from his Burmese teacher, Po Thit. According to Stevens, Blair 'insisted on conducting all our French lessons in French, with absolutely no questions allowed in English.'[6]

As a teacher, his most ambitious undertaking involved staging a school play at St Mary's church hall. He spent a good part of one term labouring on the project – writing the script for the performance, making costumes and scenery and rehearsing the boys in their parts. His play was called 'King Charles II', and is a silly piece of work in which characters say things like 'ten thousand curses' and 'Hark!'. But it was an exciting drama for young boys to perform, with lots of exaggerated speeches and noisy action. Geoffrey Stevens had a small part to play, but enjoyed the experience so much that he held on to his copy of the script for more than fifty years. 'The performance lasted only half an hour, but we spent hours and hours in preparation, finding props, constructing the scenery, etc., all of which he supervised closely. It was ambitious. Some of the boys wore fake armour, and there was a very large set depicting a village inn. He arranged for plywood doors on either side to have saw cuts made in them so that Cromwell's men could break them open with their pikes. It worked perfectly and made a great crashing noise coming down.'[7] Blair's assessment of the performance was rather less enthusiastic. In tortuous prose he informed Leonard Moore, 'The miserable school play over which I had wasted so much time went off not badly.'[8]

Towards the end of his first term at The Hawthorns, he received some surprising news from his agent. A publisher wanted his book.

Moore had sent the typescript to the relatively new publishing house of Victor Gollancz in Covent Garden, and in late June the firm decided to accept it, with the provision that certain changes be made to avoid the risk of libel and to tone down anything which might be considered obscene. Blair met the publisher and agreed to make the necessary changes; after all his previous work on the book, this seemed a small price to pay for its publication. But it was difficult for him to believe that someone was actually going to pay him for it. Reporting the news of his meeting to Moore, he wrote, 'I did not say anything about the book having no commercial value as he seemed to think fairly well of it, so perhaps you will be able to get good terms from him.'[9] He need not have worried too much about his publisher's understanding of 'commercial value'. Victor Gollancz was a shrewd businessman and was in no danger of overpaying his new author. When a contract was offered in August, it provided a paltry advance of £40, but Blair raised no objections.

Gollancz had launched his business only four years earlier, but his devotion to hard work and hard bargaining had helped to make the firm a great success from the beginning. He did not believe in wasting time, and spent long hours at his office overseeing every aspect of the business. In a *News Chronicle* profile of 1932, he was portrayed as an unstoppable force speeding through the normally placid world of publishing: 'Gets through work like a destroyer through sea (his is virtually a one-man business), guts a 75,000 words MS in 45 minutes, sleeps five hours every night and 20 minutes in office armchair every afternoon, often works from 9.15 a.m. to 1 a.m. next day, but believes he could do four times as much work quite easily.' Yet this superhuman worker was a very plain-looking little man. 'Thirty-nine, but looks forty-nine,' the *News Chronicle* reported, 'burly head dominated by its bald dome, eyes brown, rather small, humorous, shrewd. Likes to smoke a pipe and pace about while he talks.'[10]

He had a special talent for promoting books, especially ones directed towards a middle-brow audience. Although he was normally a frugal businessman, he was not afraid to spend large sums on bold advertisements when he thought a book had strong commercial potential. He sometimes bought a full page of space in papers like the *Observer* to call attention to his biggest titles. Other publishers criticised his aggressive promotional campaigns as 'undignified' and angrily challenged the exaggerated claims which he routinely made for his books. He was determined to do things his own way, and this attitude frequently put him in conflict not only with business rivals but also with agents, authors and his own staff. He never wanted to admit that he was wrong. Once when an agent tried to correct him, he shouted, 'How dare you, I am incapable of error!'[11]

He made a healthy profit selling a mixture of popular fiction, biographies and anthologies, but politics was his passion, and in the early 1930s he became firmly committed to socialism. In 1932 he declared that his ambition was 'to help one day in the building, nationally and internationally, of a more decent economic system'.[12] His list began to reflect his growing enthusiasm for socialism, and though Blair's book was only vaguely political, it appealed to Gollancz as a powerful statement against social injustice. He wanted to be known for publishing such books, and was not concerned that his author was a relative unknown who wanted to write under a pseudonym. He set a publication date for the beginning of 1933, and gave the book a new title of his own choosing. He thought it should be called 'Confessions of a Down and Out in London and Paris', and he informed the author that a pseudonym had also been found for him. Gollancz may have been a tough entrepreneur, but he had no talent for making up names. He wanted to call his author 'X'.

II

When the time came for his summer holiday, Blair was relieved to put Hayes behind him and go home to Southwold for a few weeks of relaxation near the sea. An important change had taken place since his last visit. His parents had given up their rented place in Queen Street and had acquired a larger home at 36 High Street, also known by the more dignified address of 'Montague House'. It was a pleasant old place of red brick, with a slate roof covering its two storeys. He was fortunate to have the house more or less to himself during much of his holiday. Avril's job at the Copper Kettle kept her away from home until late in the evening on most days, and his parents spent a good part of the summer with Marjorie and her husband in the North of England. Avril remembered that her brother took advantage of their parents' absence by conducting an ambitious experiment in the house. One day she discovered 'yards and yards of rubber tubing' stretched across the kitchen in every direction, all of it leading back to a boiling kettle full of black treacle and water. For some reason he had decided that he wanted to make rum, but the final product fell considerably short of commercial quality. 'Eventually the stuff did come out distilled at the other end as pure alcohol,' Avril recalled. 'When we tasted it, it had the most frightful taste of rubber tubing.'[13] For Eric, it did not really matter that the rum was bad. He was amusing himself, and would probably have been disappointed if his experiment had worked well.

Very little of his time was spent in the company of his friend Brenda Salkeld. She had gone to her family's home in Bedfordshire to spend the school holiday, so she saw him only once or twice that summer. But there was another reason why they did not meet more often. He was busy pursuing a new romantic interest. The object of this pursuit was Eleanor Jaques, an attractive dark-haired woman of Huguenot descent who was a few years younger than Eric. Her parents had retired to Southwold when she was in her teens, and she had been acquainted with the Blair family in a casual way for several years. In early 1932 she and Eric had begun to pay more attention to each other, and they had made a few attempts to meet in London. For various reasons, such a meeting proved impossible, but this did not cause Eric to lose interest. In his letters he playfully hinted that his feelings for her had been aroused. Writing to her in June, he suggested that she might be too much of a temptation to him if he spent his holiday in Southwold. Knowing that she was there might prevent him from doing any writing at all. 'I think perhaps it would be best for me to go to some quiet place in France, where I can live cheaply & have less temptation from the World, the

Flesh & the Devil than at S'wold. (You can decide which of these categories you belong to.)'[14]

He might well have gone to France if Eleanor had not been in Southwold, but when he realised that she was indeed willing to tempt him away from his work, he did not hesitate to forgo a trip abroad. From August to early September, he and Eleanor were often together, spending long days in the countryside or sunny afternoons at the beach in Walberswick, where they liked to have picnics. They grew increasingly closer. One day during a walk in a wooded area near the River Blyth, they made love. Eric recalled the moment in a letter written shortly after their summer had ended. 'We had excellent weather at S'wold, & I cannot remember when I have ever enjoyed any expeditions so much as I did those with you. Especially that day in the wood ... where the deep beds of moss were. I shall always remember that, & your nice white body in the dark green moss.'[15]

None of Eleanor's letters to him has survived, but it would appear that she enjoyed their summer as much as he did. 'Dearest Eleanor,' he wrote to her later that year, 'it was so nice of you to say that you looked back to your days with me with pleasure.'[16] He was eager to repeat the experience, but he always had serious doubts about his attractiveness to women, and was uncertain whether Eleanor had really wanted to have sex with him or had simply given in to his desire: 'I hope you will let me make love to you again some time, but if you don't it doesn't matter, I shall always be grateful to you for your kindness to me.'[17]

There was good reason for him to worry about their future together. For several years she and Dennis Collings had been involved with each other, and though this relationship had not always been smooth, Eric was reluctant to complicate matters for Dennis by appearing to be his rival. He was willing to accept the possibility that he might have to remain in the background indefinitely or give up Eleanor altogether. He had been able to spend so much time with her during the summer because Dennis had been away in Cambridge working as an assistant at the University Museum. He did not hold out much hope for his relationship with Eleanor unless she chose to move away from Southwold. From his room at The Hawthorns he wrote to her in the autumn: 'How I wish you were here. Whatever happens you must get some kind of job in London so that we can meet from time to time. I shall be a little less penniless next term, I hope . . . When we were together you didn't say whether you were going to let me be your lover again. Of course you can't if Dennis is in S'wold, but otherwise? You mustn't if you don't want to, but I hope you will.'[18]

He did manage to see her at least a couple of times during the term, escorting her on one occasion to a Saturday matinee performance of *Macbeth* at the Old Vic. ('I so adore *Macbeth*,' he told her.)[19] It was a successful outing, but the focus of their relationship was not a shared devotion to things cultural. His letters to her – unlike those to Brenda – rarely mention serious literary ideas and contain only a few brief references to the books which he was reading. Most of the things he talks about are the everyday events of his life and his plans for arranging meetings with her. His longing for some physical contact with her dominates his letters. In one he declares, 'We simply must meet if it can be managed,' and in another he pleads, 'Do please try & come out somewhere with me when you are up in town again.'[20]

The constraints of his job and his pocketbook made it difficult for him to entertain her in a proper fashion, and he did not try to hide the degree to which this upset him. Museums, parks, pub meals and inexpensive matinees were the best he could offer her. 'How would it be to go out some Sunday into the country, where we could go for a long walk & then have lunch at a pub? London is depressing when one has no money.'[21] Even if a little more money had been available, they would not have been able to afford much in the way of privacy for their lovemaking. A good hotel would have been too expensive, and taking her to his room at The Hawthorns was not allowed. A country walk in good weather was the simplest solution to the problem, though certainly not the most comfortable. He did his best to work out the logistics for a day trip. Passion made him an eager student of timetables and Ordnance survey maps. 'For instance if you could take a ticket to Uxbridge from Paddington & let me know the time, I could get in at Hayes & we could go on to Uxbridge & have a good long walk, & get lunch at Denham or somewhere – I hardly know the country but could consult a map.'²²

Such complicated trips were both frustrating and thrilling. There was the inevitable discomfort outdoors, as well as the fear of being discovered, but Blair was also attracted to the sense of adventure and the pleasure of doing something which was unconventional and slightly risky. The erotically charged atmosphere of such adventures is captured on two different occasions in Orwell's fiction. In *Keep the Aspidistra Flying* Gordon and Rosemary try to make love in a wooded area outside London because there is nowhere else for them to go. 'There are so many pairs of lovers in London with "nowhere to go",' Orwell writes, 'only the streets and the parks, where there is no privacy and it is always cold. It is not easy to make love in a cold climate when you have no money.' Like Blair with Eleanor, Gordon Comstock takes particular pleasure in the sight of Rosemary lying nude on a bed of mossy grass. 'They spread her clothes out and made a sort of bed for her to lie on. Naked, she lay back, her hands behind her head, her eyes shut, smiling slightly, as though she had considered everything and were at peace in her mind. For a long time he knelt and gazed at her body. Its beauty startled him.' But the spell is broken when Rosemary refuses to have unprotected sex with him, and her criticism makes him ashamed of his plan. 'It had seemed so right, so natural only a minute ago; now it seemed merely squalid and ugly.'

The same situation is presented with a twist in *Nineteen Eighty-Four*. Because of Big Brother's restrictions on sex, Winston Smith's decision to make love to Julia in her wooded hideout is not merely adventurous but potentially fatal. However, this added element of danger only increases the pleasure of the experience for both of them. For Winston it is a dream come true. 'She stood looking at him for an instant, then felt at the zipper of her overalls. And, yes! It was almost as in his dream. Almost as swiftly as he had imagined it, she had torn her clothes off . . . Her body gleamed white in the sun.'

A few years before he wrote this scene, Orwell was having a

conversation with his friend Anthony Powell and suddenly asked, without any apparent reason, 'Have you ever had a woman in the park?'

'No – never,' Powell responded.

'I have.'

'How did you find it?'

'I was forced to.'

'Why?'

'Nowhere else to go.'

If he had been even more forthcoming, he might have admitted that this was a necessity which he had learned to appreciate. But when Orwell told this little tale in the 1940s, Powell knew him well enough to understand that what lay behind this unprompted confession was an odd mixture of pride and guilt. 'He spoke defensively, as if he feared I might blame him for this urban pastoral. It was a Victorian guilt, and in many ways Orwell was a Victorian figure, for, like most people "in rebellion", he was more than half in love with what he was rebelling against.'[23]

III

At the same time that Blair was trying to arrange meetings with Eleanor in London, he was overwhelmed with work in Hayes. His teaching duties were demanding, but he was faced with an extra burden in November when the proofs of his book came to him for final correction. Since the book was scheduled for publication in early January, he did not have much time to make his corrections. In addition, Gollancz had requested some last-minute changes which needed special attention. Although Blair had dutifully made several revisions at his publisher's request when the book was still in typescript, Gollancz was so nervous about facing any potential legal problems that he had uncovered more sentences where the language was a little too daring for comfort. Blair strained to comply under the pressure of an early deadline, but he was not always successful at finding a convincing substitute for the offending word or phrase. It is unfortunate that he had to waste his time altering a line such as, 'he farted loudly, a favourite Italian insult', to the more polite but ridiculous expression, 'he delivered a final insult in the same manner as Squire Western in *Tom Jones*'.[24]

There was also the problem of the book's title. He did not care for Gollancz's choice, and had suggested other possibilities. He had favoured 'In Praise of Poverty', telling his agent that it was 'the best title' he could think of.[25] But when the proofs arrived, he found that Gollancz had disregarded that suggestion and had used instead 'Confessions of a Down and Out in London and Paris'. As a first-time author, Blair was understandably reluctant to challenge his publisher's decision, but he did not like the title and tried gently to make his disapproval known. It was the 'down-and-out' phrase that bothered him. 'Would "The Confessions of a Dishwasher" do as well?' he asked Leonard Moore. 'I would *rather* answer to "dishwasher" than "down & out".' At the last minute Gollancz shortened the title to *Down and Out in Paris and London*, and Blair accepted the decision in the belief that 'Mr G.', as he called him, understood what was 'best for selling purposes'.[26]

The final problem was to select a pseudonym. He was tempted to accept Gollancz's choice of 'X', though he knew very well that it sounded silly, and would not do anything to further his career. If he had truly believed that success was unimportant, then 'X' would have served his purposes as well as any other name. But in the end he could not resist creating a real pseudonym for himself, one that would serve him well for as long as he wanted to keep it. Whatever he did, however, he did not want to appear to be taking the problem too seriously. 'I suppose the thing is to have an easily memorable [pseudonym],' he casually remarked to Moore, 'which I could stick to if this book had any success.'[27] On 19 November – only seven weeks before his book was published – he produced a list of possible names. There was 'P. S. Burton' – an alias which he had used on tramping expeditions – and then there were three recent inventions: 'Kenneth Miles', 'George Orwell', and 'H. Lewis Allways'. Although the tramping alias would have been the most logical choice for this book, he declared that 'Orwell' was his favourite.

Why 'Miles' and 'Allways' were on his list is anyone's guess, but he attached a great deal of importance to names, and must have had some special reason for suggesting them. 'How important names are,' he once told Brenda. 'If I have the choice of going through two streets, other things being equal I always go by the one with the nicer name.'[28] He did not like the sound of his own first name, telling a friend in 1940, 'It took me nearly thirty years to work off the effects of being called Eric.'[29] Presumably, he thought that 'George' was a solid, quintessentially English name. He did not have to look far to find the second half of his pseudonym. Snaking along the southern boundary of Suffolk, the River Orwell reaches the sea at a spot only thirty-five miles down the coast from Southwold. Unlike the Thames and the River Blythe – or the Irrawaddy, for that matter – the Orwell was not a river which he knew intimately, but its name was well-suited to his purposes – it was simple yet distinctive, and thus 'easily memorable'.

When he arrived at his parents' house in Southwold for his Christmas holiday, George Orwell found that a parcel containing his first copies of *Down and Out in Paris and London* was waiting for him. He gave all of them away to friends and family. On 28 December he travelled to Bedfordshire to present Brenda with her copy. Along with its annotations in pencil, the book carried a formal signature in dark ink, 'Eric A. Blair'. To his family and old friends he never pretended to be 'Orwell', not even for the purpose of autographing a presentation copy. But with the appearance of these early copies of his first book, George Orwell's career was launched, and the brief history of publications by Eric Blair was almost at an end. One must say 'almost' because he continued to write magazine articles under his real name until 1934. Initially, he was prepared for the pseudonym to be only a temporary thing, but *Down and Out* was not the 'flop' that he had feared it might be, and afterwards it was difficult to abandon the name which was attached to the book's success. In effect, the writer 'Eric Blair' died with the first good review of *Down and Out*.

There was no shortage of good reviews. The publication date was 9 January 1933, and by the end of the book's first week in print, Orwell's mood had changed from pessimism to cautious optimism.

The reviews 'were very much better than I had expected', he told Moore, 'particularly those in the Evening Standard and the Daily Mail. I believe there was a good one in the Morning Post, but I didn't see that one. No libel actions hitherto, I hope? The book was listed in this week's Sunday Express among "best sellers of the week". Does that mean anything definite?'[30] The bestseller lists must have been much easier to enter in those days because sales of the book did not exceed three thousand copies. That was a respectable performance for an unknown author, but the modest figures were not nearly as important to the young writer as the encouraging confirmations of his talent in the literary pages of the national newspapers and magazines. There was strong praise from Compton Mackenzie in the *Daily Mail*, and in the *Adelphi* C. Day Lewis commended the book for its 'clarity and good sense'. The *Times Literary Supplement* made a favourable comparison between the book's odd characters and some of the eccentric types in Dickens's novels; and the *New Statesman* recommended it as a work 'packed with unique and strange information'. Perhaps the most perceptive comment came from *Time and Tide*: 'It is not only George Orwell's experiences that are interesting; George Orwell himself is of interest.'[31]

Of course, as a first book, it was bound to have its flaws, and the most serious of these is the fragmented nature of the work. It is not a coherent narrative but a series of sketches, some much better than others. This circumstance is further complicated by the fact that the Paris sketches have little in common with the London sketches. They are both concerned with life on the fringes of society, but the French and English societies are too dissimilar for comparison. Certainly an older, more experienced writer would have chosen to focus on a dishwasher's life in Paris or a tramp's life in London, and would not have tried to crowd the two lives into one short book, as Orwell did.

The transition which takes the book from Paris to the slums of London hangs on a fragile thread. Orwell says in the book that when the job of looking after the 'imbecile' was delayed for a month, he had no choice but to 'exist in some hole-and-corner way' until the month ended. This is an unconvincing method of introducing his tramping expedition, and he admitted privately to Brenda that he had made the story up. 'This incident is invented to explain trip,' he wrote in her annotated copy. It is the only one of the annotations which confirms that an event had been created to further the narrative. But he could not have given a plausible reason for the progression from dishwashing to tramping since he had taken part of his London material from much earlier adventures in the East End, adventures which occurred before he went to Paris. Without his invention of the job delay, the framework of the book would have collapsed. This difficulty with structure was a perennial problem for him, and he was well aware of it. As he later complained to Brenda, 'I don't know how it is, I can write decent passages but I can't put them together.'[32]

In *Down and Out* there are more than enough 'decent' passages to compensate for the narrative's shaky structure. One of the most important is Orwell's description of the pavement artist whom he meets on the Embankment, near Waterloo Bridge. He is a largely self-educated man who loves books and who cultivates an amateur interest in astronomy, surprising Orwell by eagerly searching the sky at odd moments to note the appearance of one constellation or another. He tries not to allow his poverty to control his life, and at one point he taps his forehead and declares proudly, 'I'm a free man in *here*.' But in some ways this noble figure is the saddest character in the book. His life has been one disaster after another. As a young man, he earned a decent living as a house-painter, but one day he slipped and fell forty feet, smashing his right foot to 'pulp'. At one time he was engaged to a young French woman, but she died a terrible death, crushed under the wheels of a bus. Unable to work at his chosen trade, he has become a 'screever', or pavement artist, and barely manages to live on the little money given him by tourists and other passers-by. The future awaiting him is bleak. 'His damaged leg was getting worse and would probably have to be amputated, and his knees, from kneeling on the stones, had pads of skin on them as thick as boot-soles. There was clearly no future for him but beggary and a death in the workhouse.'

But what is most striking about this poor screever, who goes by the unappealing name of Bozo, is his determination not to succumb to self-pity or self-reproach. He makes no excuses for his life and is not ashamed of his poverty or the fact that he must live on the charity of those who admire his drawings. 'He had faced his position, and made a philosophy for himself. Being a beggar, he said, was not his fault, and he refused either to have any compunction about it or let it trouble him.' He may never escape from poverty, but he has freed himself from the guilt which burdens the lives of so many of the poor in *Down and Out*. Though society may look down on him, he does not think less of himself because he is poor, nor does he accept the notion that he should be grateful for charity. He regards the loss of self-respect as a fate worse than poverty. In his eyes beggars are contemptible only if they come to share society's contempt for them. When they beg, they must always have 'the decency to be ungrateful'.

Down and Out does not offer a plan for the redemption of tramps and beggars. The book has been criticised for its lack of specific proposals for reform, but its purpose is not to offer a 'solution'. Rather, it strives to alter the common perception of the problem so that future efforts to improve it will have a better chance of success. No plan will work as long as poverty is generally regarded as a kind of shameful disease which infects people who are incapable of helping themselves. From his experience in the spikes, the Salvation Army shelters, and in various churches which provide free food, Orwell recognises that efforts to help the tramps are continually undermined by conditions which make acceptance of charity humiliating. He admits that the Salvation Army shelters are neat and efficient, but the 'semi-military discipline' enforced among the tramps is degrading, and the rooms are 'oppressively clean and bare'. They 'stink of charity'. Even more depressing are the smaller charitable groups who mean well but who always expect some show of contrition, as though poverty signified a sinful soul. In one tin-roofed chapel a lady wearing a crucifix with a blue silk dress dispenses tea to the tramps on the condition that they pray. 'Bareheaded, we knelt down among the dirty teacups and began to mumble that we had left undone those things that we ought to have done, and done those things that we ought not to have done, and there was no health in us. The lady prayed very fervently, but her eyes roved over us all the time, making sure that we were attending.'

In contrast to this dismal scene is the simple conduct of the anonymous young clergyman who regularly distributes meal tickets to the tramps on the Embankment. He is shy and moves quickly among the men without making a show of his charity, pausing only to say good evening as he gives each man a ticket. He expects nothing in return, not even a word of thanks. He respects their right to be ungrateful, which is another way of saying that he refuses to take from them the dignity of freedom. Naturally, the tramps admire him. 'Well, *he'll* never be a f—— bishop!' one tramp shouts when the clergyman leaves. As Orwell explains, this remark was 'intended as a warm compliment'.

CHAPTER TEN

George Orwell, Novelist

I

Mr and Mrs Blair did not know what to make of George Orwell. Immediately after the publication of *Down and Out in Paris and London*, they read the book 'with great interest', according to Avril, but they found it hard to believe that their Eric had produced such a work. The general elements of the story did not surprise them. They knew that the last months of his life in Paris had been difficult, and they were aware that he had lived among tramps in England. But they were not at all prepared for the book's frank comments on sex, some of which appear as early as the second chapter when the loquacious Charlie relates the tale of his brutal attack on a young prostitute ('I pulled her off the bed and threw her onto the floor. And then I fell upon her like a tiger!') Although Mr and Mrs Blair professed not to be shocked by such behaviour, they were 'rather surprised' to find their normally bashful son describing it so openly. 'In his relations with his family,' Avril wrote later, 'my brother had always been detached and one almost might say impersonal. There was never any discussion of sex or his love affairs or anything of that nature at all. So, when all those matters came out in his book, it almost seemed as if it had been written by a different person.'[1] There was a great deal that his family did not know about him, but in typical fashion they did not press him for more information, nor make a fuss about the seamy side of his adventures.

The book and its good reviews at least demonstrated to his family that his literary ambitions had some substance to them, but, unfortunately, the royalties were not large enough to prove that he could make a career out of authorship. Despite all the excitement of seeing his book praised in various papers, he was still faced with the reality of having to earn his livelihood teaching in Hayes. Only ten days after the publication of his book, he was back at work in the classroom at The Hawthorns, carrying out the same burdensome duties of earlier terms. These burdens were occasionally lightened by the appearance of another review of his book. There was a favourable one, for example, in the February 1933 issue of J. C. Squire's *London Mercury*, which called *Down and Out* 'exceptionally good'.

The strangest response to the book came at the end of January, in the form of a letter to *The Times* from one Humbert Possenti, of the Hotel Splendide in Piccadilly. When Mr Possenti was not busy managing this immodestly named establishment, he apparently enjoyed – among other things – reading the *Times Literary Supplement*, and one day he had been dismayed to see, in a review of *Down and Out*, that Orwell's book complained of unsanitary conditions in the kitchen of a Paris luxury hotel. This could not go unchallenged, Possenti declared in his letter, since it was inconceivable that such kitchens could be anything but clean and orderly. Any word to the contrary could damage public confidence in hotels everywhere because Paris set the standard for the rest of the world as 'the nursery of hotel management'. As a '*restaurateur* and *hotelier* of forty years', he could say with confidence that luxury hotel kitchens were 'cleaner than those of most private homes'. If people were seduced into believing the book's baseless charges, 'infinite harm would be done to the London and Paris restaurant trade'.

The pompous Humbert Possenti and his Hotel Splendide should have made Orwell laugh, and when he had finished laughing, he should have derived some satisfaction from the thought that anyone would consider his book a threat to the entire restaurant trade in two capital cities. But Orwell took the charge seriously, as though it were an attack from some leading literary critic. He immediately wrote a reply and sent it not only to *The Times* but also to his agent. For Leonard Moore's benefit, he enclosed a copy of Possenti's 'rather snooty letter' and confided earnestly, 'It would have been most damaging to let it go unanswered.'² Orwell's response, which *The Times* printed on 11 February, was itself a bit 'snooty', but its overly formal style does work to his advantage in one delightfully precise sentence: 'I do know that in our hotel there were places which no customer could possibly have been allowed to see with any hope of retaining his custom.' Fortunately, he chose not to reply to a later attack on him in something called the *Licensed Victuallers Gazette*, deciding wisely that 'they are beneath answering'.³

While Orwell was defending his honour in the pages of *The Times*, his agent was trying to find an American publisher for the book. By the end of February he had made a deal with Harper and Brothers, and when he gave his author the good news, Orwell replied that he was 'very pleased'.⁴ He was not so pleased, however, when Harper's sent him a standard request for a short biographical statement and a photograph. 'I don't think I care for that idea of giving biographical details,' he told Moore, 'after the way I have seen American publishers use them. As to photographs, I am not certain whether my photograph would be a very good advert.'⁵ Though he was reluctant to admit it, he could not go on giving his words to 'George Orwell' while keeping his life to himself. The pseudonym needed a face and a history to go with it, and those things would have to come from him. If he wanted to continue using the name, he would have to play the part all the way.

He did provide Harper's with a few details, and though his publishers seemed to have used them judiciously, the same cannot be said for at least one American magazine which reviewed the book when it was published in New York later in the year. In a vulgar oversimplification the *Nation*'s anonymous reviewer described Orwell as 'an old Eton boy and ex-civil servant who became a dishwasher in Paris and a bum in his own country'.⁶ Most of the American reviews were, however, discerning and approving, especially one from James T. Farrell, in the *New Republic*. He praised the book as 'genuine, unexaggerated and intelligent', and closed his review with a straightforward statement of the book's purpose. 'Orwell has escaped from the depths. There are thousands to whom no door of escape is opened. *Down and Out in Paris and London* will give readers a sense of what life means to these thousands.'[7]

With his first book behind him, Orwell wasted no time moving ahead with his second book. In January he completed the first hundred pages of *Burmese Days*, the novel which he had been trying to write – in one form or another – since his last months in the Indian Imperial Police. His agent's success at finding a publisher for *Down and Out* must have given him the extra incentive to work harder on the novel, but he was still deeply in doubt about its prospects when he sent the typescript of the early chapters to Moore for his opinion. Orwell had little confidence in the literary quality of his draft, and before he went any further with it, he wanted Moore to tell him that it was worth completing. In February he wrote to his agent, 'I know that as it stands it is fearful from a literary point of view, but I wanted to know whether given a proper polishing up, excision of prolixities & general tightening up, it was at all the sort of thing people want to read about.' In the case of *Down and Out*, he had shown practically no interest in whether poverty was 'the sort of thing people want to read about', but after seeing that book listed – if only briefly – as one of the *Sunday Express* 'best sellers of the week', he was beginning to give more thought to the market-place. Even if *Burmese Days* failed to meet his own expectations, he might push on with it in the hope that readers would find its exotic subject matter appealing. As he explained to Moore, 'I should think that [the] fact that it is about Burma, and there are so few novels with that setting, might offset the lack of action in the story – it is mostly description, I am afraid; there are to be a murder and a suicide later, but they play rather a subsidiary part.'[8]

Despite his author's misgivings, Moore was confident that the story had potential. 'The agent was very pleased with the 100 pp. of my novel I sent him,' Orwell told Eleanor Jaques in mid-February, 'and harries me to get on with it.'[9] This was just the boost he needed. A few days later he announced to Moore, 'I think I can promise you a further 100 pp. of the novel about as near completion as the last, by the end of this term (i.e. in April).'[10] Although the first hundred pages had cost him many months of effort, Moore's encouragement was enough to make him think that he could write the next hundred in less than two months. Given the fact that his teaching duties did not leave much time for writing, he was setting quite a rigorous pace for himself. And the process of putting so many words on paper was complicated by his need to revise extensively. 'With me almost any piece of writing has to be done over and over again,' he confided to Brenda a few months later. 'I wish I were one of those people who can sit down and fling off a novel in about four days.'[11] Of course, he was not writing the kind of novel that a hack could 'fling off' so quickly, but he proved equal to the promise he had given Moore. On 7 April he wrote to him, 'I wonder whether you will be in your office on the 15th . . . I would like to see you, if possible, & I will bring the second 100 pp. of my novel at the same time.'

With so much of his attention focused on his novel, he had time for only two diversions. One was a small vegetable garden which he had begun digging behind the school in late February. It was a simple way to relax, but he tended to work hard even when he was supposedly relaxing, and not surprisingly, his garden turned into a fairly ambitious undertaking, with a great variety of vegetables planted, including broad beans, shallots, peas, potatoes, and even a pumpkin. The other diversion was Eleanor. Arranging meetings with her remained a complicated business, but he was always ready to put aside his work for a day with her. When spring came, he could barely contain his urge to take her on another of their leisurely walks in the country. 'It is such lovely weather,' he wrote to her in May, 'and it would be so delightful to go for a long walk in the country somewhere. If you can't manage a Saturday or Sunday, I can always make an excuse & get away. Or at worst we could meet in town for an afternoon.'[12]

This particular request brought a positive response, which made him so happy that he began searching bus and railway timetables to devise not one but three possible outings for them. In his letter of reply he listed the plans by number as though they were part of a story outline. If she wanted to spend the day walking along the canal bank outside Uxbridge, then she could take a Green Line bus to, appropriately enough, the Adam & Eve pub, where he could meet her. Or she could take a train to Hayes from Paddington Station at 10.26, though this plan caused him a little anxiety – 'Don't forget it is Hayes, Middlesex: don't get carried away into Kent or somewhere.' But neither of these plans interested him as much as his third one: 'I think it would be nicest if we went somewhere where there are *woods*, seeing what the weather is like; e.g. to Burnham Beeches. So perhaps the best thing of all would be for me to come up to town & meet you any time & place you like, but preferably at Paddington, because I suppose we should take the train from there.' When he made a date, he did not want to leave anything to chance. He even advised Eleanor to 'pray for good weather'.[13]

Which of these options she chose is not known. When presented with similar choices in *Keep the Aspidistra Flying*, Rosemary enthusiastically endorses Burnham Beeches. 'It's so lovely at this time of year . . . you can walk all day and hardly meet a soul. We'll walk for miles and miles and have dinner at a pub. It would be such fun.' Her outing with Gordon ends unhappily, but there is no way to know for certain what happened with Eleanor and Orwell on their trip. The only indication that they did indeed go out together is Orwell's opening sentence from a letter written in early July: 'It seems so long since that day I went out with you – actually, I suppose, abt a month.' The tone of this letter is warm, and Orwell makes it clear that he is looking forward to seeing more of her when he comes home to Southwold for his summer holiday. 'Perhaps we can go & picnic as we did last year. I am so pining to see the sea again . . . keep some days free for me during the first fortnight in August.'[14]

But a second letter written towards the end of July provides a hint of trouble. Eleanor had not responded to his earlier letter, and he was concerned that he might not see her at all in August. His tone is still affectionate, but it is tinged with anxiety. 'Do write & tell me if you will be in S'wold during the summer holidays . . . If you are to be there, try & keep some days free for me, & it would be so nice if we could go & bathe & make our tea like we used to do last year along the W'wick shore. Let me know.'[15] Even at this stage he may have realised that those pleasurable times in the previous summer were not to be repeated. Something was obviously wrong, but it would not have taken much work on his part to guess what it was. In any case, he soon discovered the truth. Eleanor had decided that she wanted marriage, and Orwell did not strike her as the 'marrying kind', at least not at that time in his life, when he was so burdened by the demands of his writing and his teaching. Her old relationship with Dennis Collings seemed more promising.

Collings was preparing to enter the Colonial Service, and there was every reason to believe that he had a good, solid career ahead of him. The fact that he was going to be leaving the country soon made it necessary for her to come to some decision. She chose her old love over Orwell, and they were married in Cambridge a little more than a year later. Near the end of 1934 they went out to Singapore, and Orwell never saw them again except for one brief visit in 1939, when they returned home for a short leave.

'I knew that he was fond of her,' Collings recalled, 'but I don't think it was marriage he had in mind. And I know he didn't hold anything against me for marrying her. He never said a word about it.'[16] What he said to Eleanor will never be known. Among his surviving letters to her, none was written later than the one he sent in late July 1933. According to Collings, there were others, but they were lost several years later when his wife was evacuated from Singapore before the Japanese occupied it. Collings was captured by the invading army and spent four years in a prison camp. Eleanor, who never spoke publicly about her relationship with Orwell, died in 1962. It was purely by chance that some of his letters to her were kept. Before she and her husband went to Singapore, she happened to leave the letters with some other belongings at her mother's home near Southwold, and it was only after Eleanor's death that they were discovered.

II

In the last two of his surviving letters to Eleanor, Orwell complained bitterly about the burdens imposed upon him by his job, declaring, 'God send I'll be able to drop this foul teaching after next year.'[17] He was hoping that when he had finished his novel, Gollancz would pay him a proper advance, and that he would then be able to live for a while on his earnings as a novelist and literary journalist. He had the potential to be a very good teacher, but the job consumed far too much of his energy. He needed more time for his writing and was frustrated by the constant pressure of having to divert his attention to the demands of the classroom. But for the time being he needed the steady income, and his only hope for improving the conditions of his work was to find another, less demanding position. In the late spring he was offered a job at another school, and though he accepted this offer, he had his doubts about the place. 'Please [God] I get a little spare time in my next job,' he told Eleanor. 'I went over to see the prize-giving at the school & it looked pretty bloody – the girls' section of the school (which I shall have nothing to do with – perhaps it is for the best) sang the female version of Kipling's "If".'[18]

His new school was called Frays College, and it was located only a few miles northwest of Hayes, in Uxbridge. It was a much larger establishment than The Hawthorns, with nearly two hundred pupils and a staff of sixteen. The headmaster and proprietor, John Bennett, was a decent man who considered himself an educational reformer. Impressed with Orwell's French, he had given him the job of teaching the language at Frays, bringing him in as a replacement for a Frenchman who had recently returned to his own country. Although there is no question that the school was an improvement over The Hawthorns, Orwell did not gain any additional free time in the new job, and was hard pressed to continue turning out more pages of *Burmese Days*.

After a month at Frays, he complained to Moore that he was 'submerged with work in this place', but he was determined to finish his novel and declared that he would have the final typescript ready by the end of November.[19] He pushed himself as hard as he could, typing late into the night in his small room at the school. He spent almost no time among the other masters, and made only a slight impression on the pupils as an odd character whose sole recreation seemed to be riding a motorcycle in the country. He had acquired a used model and was in the habit of riding it in all kinds of weather, wearing nothing heavier than a sports coat as he went off to explore the sights along some country lane. Perhaps the inspiration for this activity had come from the intense process of writing *Burmese Days*, which may have brought back vivid memories of similar rides on the narrow roads in Burma.

One day in early December, Orwell finished writing the last page of *Burmese Days* and gave the typescript of almost four hundred pages to Moore. He had told his agent a week earlier that the best way for him to deliver the novel was to bring it out to Moore's house in Gerrards Cross, which was four miles down the road from Uxbridge. It was difficult for him to get away from school during the week, so it made more sense for him to go to his agent's home on a weekend, making the journey on his motorcycle. It is not clear that he stuck to this plan, but it is easy to imagine him driving off to Gerrards Cross, crouched over his machine in the cold December wind, a heavy parcel strapped to the back and a look of resolve on his face.

Although he had finally proven to himself that he could write a novel, he was unhappy with it, and was quick to tell Moore how bad it was. He thought it was too long and would need cutting, but he did not want to face up to the task. 'I am sick of the sight of it,' he declared. 'Let's hope the next one will be better.'[20] He was not specific about its faults at the time, but much later in his career he looked back on this period and was able to summarise perfectly what his aims had been. 'I wanted to write enormous naturalistic novels with unhappy endings, full of detailed descriptions and arresting similes, and also full of purple passages in which words were used partly for the sake of their sound. And in fact my first complete novel, *Burmese Days* . . . is rather that kind of book.'[21]

In other words, it is a work infused with a spirit of romantic fatalism, the same spirit which had exerted such a strong hold over him in his teens, when he was reading A. E. Housman's poetry over and over, and writing lovesick verse to Jacintha Buddicom. Joseph Conrad, Somerset Maugham and E. M. Forster have been suggested as possible influences on Orwell's novel, but it is also important to recognise that the ghost of Housman hangs heavily over the book. As Orwell noted in 'Inside the Whale' (1940), his early enthusiasm for Housman was based on the poet's celebration of rural landscapes, the use of sound for its own sake, the 'exquisite self-pity' underlying the poetry, and the use of dramatic themes – 'murder, suicide, unhappy love, early death'. All of these themes and literary devices are prominent in *Burmese Days*. To a great extent, it is Housman's world – as Orwell perceived it – transported to the exotic setting of Upper Burma.

Against a background of extraordinary natural beauty, John Flory is tormented by self-pity because he thinks no one loves him. Housman's line, 'with rue my heart is laden', sums up Flory's general mood as he struggles with his deep sense of loneliness. Some of Orwell's descriptions of that struggle are prose versions of typical laments found in Housman's poetry, complete with melodramatic expressions: 'A pang went through Flory. Alone, the bitterness of being alone! So often like this, in lonely places in the forest, he would come upon something – bird, flower, tree – beautiful beyond all words, if there had been a soul with whom to share it.'

When young Elizabeth Lackersteen comes into his life he is tempted to think that fate has sent her as the cure for his loneliness, but she turns out to be heartless, raising his hopes and then slowly destroying them. Her rejection is one of the reasons he commits suicide. The thought of living without her, enduring more years of solitude at his small outpost, is unbearable. Orwell's cold portrait of Elizabeth is part of his effort to create a prose melodrama in the manner of a Housman poem. As he notes in 'Inside the Whale', the typical woman in Housman's poetry is the fantasy figure 'who leads you a little distance and then gives you the slip'.

But, as Orwell gradually came to realise, his weakness for

romantic fatalism was 'adolescent', and represented a dead end for his talent. Its hold on his imagination would never be lost completely, but its influence is especially potent in his early novels and is largely the cause of the major flaws in those works. The elements of *Burmese Days* which are least appealing are those which are closest to the spirit of romantic fatalism – the doomed love affair, Flory's morbid self-pity, the strained attempts at poetic prose. These elements give the novel an extravagant sentimentality which is so conspicuously at odds with the impressive sense of cool restraint in most of Orwell's non-fiction. It is no wonder that when he helped to prepare a new edition of the novel near the end of his life, he was amazed at how little it had in common with his more mature work. 'I just corrected the proofs of [*Burmese Days*],' he wrote to Julian Symons in 1948, 'which I wrote more than 15 years ago & probably hadn't looked at for 10 years. It was a queer experience – almost like reading a book by somebody else.'[22]

Orwell always believed that one of the strengths of his first novel was its treatment of the lush landscape in Upper Burma. The setting did cause some 'purple passages' to flow from his pen, but there are also some unforgettable descriptions written in prose of simple elegance. On the night that Flory nearly succeeds in proposing to Elizabeth, there is a full moon which is so extra-ordinarily bright that it looks like a 'white-hot coin' in the sky, its brilliance making the stars invisible. Flory says that the night is 'brighter than an English winter day', and even Elizabeth, who is normally 'indifferent to such things', is stunned by the spectacle. 'Elizabeth looked up into the branches of the frangipani tree, which the moon seemed to have changed into rods of silver. The light lay thick, as though palpable, on everything, crusting the earth and the rough bark of trees like some dazzling salt, and every leaf seemed to bear a freight of solid light, like snow.'

The most successful aspect of the novel is its portrayal of the damaging effects of imperialism on both the rulers and the ruled. Other writers have made sharper attacks on the evils of the system, but few have been able to match Orwell's ability to show how those evils poison every aspect of daily life. He is most effective at exposing the ordinary ways in which the system forces people to behave irrationally. The scheming Burmese magistrate U Po Kyin and the good Dr Veraswami are at odds with each other over the most trivial of prizes – membership in the run-down European Club, where the few whites in the town waste their time drinking and arguing over even more trivial things. Race and social status have assumed so much importance in the place that almost every point of dispute touches upon one or the other of these factors.

Orwell exposes the absurdity of this situation in scene after scene, but perhaps the most telling incident occurs when the spiteful bigot Ellis starts an argument with Lieutenant Verrall, the aristocratic officer who is briefly posted at the town. When Ellis learns that Verrall, who is not a regular member of the club, has kicked the Indian butler for failing to put ice in a whisky and soda, he is outraged and rebukes the young officer. His outrage has nothing to do with the butler's welfare, of course, but with Verrall's lack of respect for the subtleties of the social order among the Europeans.

> 'Who are *you* to come kicking our servants?'
> 'Bosh, my good chap. Needed kicking. You've let your servants get out of hand here.'
> 'You damned, insolent young tick, what's it got to do with *you* if he needed kicking? You're not even a member of this Club. It's our job to kick the servants, not yours.'

Orwell manages this scene perfectly, allowing the characters to damn themselves with their own absurd comments. One cannot help laughing at the twisted logic, but it also reveals how impossible the system has become. It is clearly past any hope of reform when the empire-builders are reduced to fighting over who has the right to kick the butler – completely ignoring the question of whether anyone should have that right in the first place.

Within a few days of completing the typescript of *Burmese Days*, Orwell wrote a long, rambling letter on the subject of fiction in general, and Joyce's *Ulysses* in particular. It was addressed to Brenda Salkeld, who had recently read *Ulysses*, largely because

Orwell had encouraged her to do so. In recommending it to her, he had said that 'it sums up better than any book I know the fearful despair that is almost normal in modern times'. After finishing his first novel, he had a much better understanding of the difficulties of writing fiction, and he wanted to share some of his thoughts on the subject with Brenda, using Joyce's work as a touchstone. His comments reveal how anxious he was to improve his skills, and to make his reputation as a novelist. At this stage in his career, it was not politics or journalism which commanded his attention but the art of fiction, and in taking Joyce as his model, he was obviously setting his sights high.

Everything about *Ulysses* fascinated him, and he found that the words flowed easily when he began describing the novel to Brenda. 'The fact is Joyce interests me so much that I can't stop talking about him once I start.' He was amazed by Joyce's ambitious experiments with style and structure, and he envied the writer's ability to create a character as convincing as Molly Bloom. He enjoyed the sexual frankness of the novel, and admired Joyce's way of combining earthy realism with high intellectual concerns. Most intellectuals, he told Brenda, are cut off from the ordinary life of the man in the street and would not dare to look into the mind of a common man like Leopold Bloom, much less attempt to capture his point of view as completely as Joyce does. 'If you read the words of almost any writer of the intellectual type, you would never guess that he is also a being capable of getting drunk, picking girls up in the street, trying to swindle somebody out of half a crown, etc. I think the interest of Bloom is that he is an ordinary uncultivated man described from within by someone who can also stand outside him and see him from another angle.'[23]

What Orwell is describing here is the very talent which can be found in his own work – the use of a dual perspective to bring into intimate contact two normally separate worlds. This talent is at work not only in 'The Spike' and *Down and Out in Paris and London* – which show Orwell observing the world of the social outcasts from both within and without – but also in most of his important non-fiction, from his experiences alongside miners in *The Road to Wigan*

Pier, and alongside Spanish soldiers in *Homage to Catalonia*, to his effort at recovering the perspective of his boyhood in 'Such, Such Were the Joys'. It is even present in his fiction, particularly in *Coming Up for Air* (though his attempt to see George Bowling's life from within and without is not very successful). Joyce's example helped to inspire Orwell, but the inspiration proved far less effective in his novels than in his 'documentary' works.

Orwell felt free to speculate at length on the appeal of *Ulysses* because, with *Burmese Days* behind him, he was finally able to use his spare time for something besides the grinding work of typing out page after page of his novel. In this slightly more relaxed mood, he went for a long ride on his motorcycle one day in mid-December. As usual he was dressed in light clothing. At some point, rain began to fall and he was soaked to the skin. How long he was out in this cold downpour is unclear, but soon after he arrived back at the school, he began to suffer the first signs of what would become his fourth bout of pneumonia. Unfortunately, this case turned out to be the most severe of them all.

A few days before Christmas 1933 he was admitted to Uxbridge Cottage Hospital. His condition was so bad that it was feared he would not survive. His mother was sent for, and she came down by car with Avril from Southwold, both of them probably expecting the worst since they had been told that he was 'desperately ill'. But their Eric was lucky this time. Avril recalled that when they arrived they found him 'very ill indeed, but the crisis had passed then, and he was recovering'. They learned from the nurse that he had been 'delirious' earlier, and in that state of mind he had done nothing but talk about money. 'We reassured him that everything was all right, and he needn't worry about money. It turned out that it wasn't actually his situation in life as regards money that he was worrying about, but it was actual cash: he felt that he wanted cash sort of under his pillow.'[24]

Evidently, he was in such a state of delirium that he believed he was tramping again, and that he was not in hospital but in some cheap lodging house where he was forced to hide his cash under his pillow to keep it safe. His last tramping expedition was many months behind him, but the old precautions remained sharp in his memory. There had been trouble before. During one night in a lodging house where the beds had been only two feet apart, he had been awakened about midnight by a hand slipping under his pillow to take his money. As he recalls in *Down and Out*, the man next to him 'was pretending to be asleep while he did it, sliding his hand under the pillow as gently as a rat'.

Orwell was allowed to go home on 8 January 1934. The illness had caused his mother such concern that she prevailed upon him to give up teaching and to come back to Southwold for a long rest. He was happy 'to chuck teaching', as he put it, but he was not prepared to spend much time resting.[25] Another idea for a novel was simmering in his imagination even while he was slowly regaining his strength in Uxbridge Cottage Hospital. He agreed to his mother's plan primarily because he saw it as an opportunity to write his next novel very quickly. He speculated that he could finish it in six months instead of the year or two it would take if he were forced to continue teaching. 'Every book is a failure,' he remarked in later years, but as soon as one 'failure' was complete, he could not wait to go on to write the next, always unsatisfied, always in doubt about his talent but always intent on doing his work better and faster than the time before.[26]

In the meantime he waited for his agent to sell *Burmese Days*. But shortly after he left Uxbridge, he learned the bad news that Gollancz did not want to publish it. The decision had little to do with the novel's artistic merits. The literary weaknesses which troubled Orwell were not nearly as important to Gollancz as the book's potential for attracting lawsuits. He feared that Orwell's old acquaintances in the colonial administration of Burma would believe that they were the objects of the book's criticisms and would seek redress in the courts, at great expense to Victor Gollancz, Ltd. This was a reasonable fear, but he also had his own reasons for being especially wary of such risks. His attitude towards the whole question of libel had been soured by an unfortunate episode three years earlier. He had published a first novel set in a girls' school – *Children Be Happy*, by Rosalind Wade – and almost immediately after its appearance, he had been besieged by old girls claiming that the author had maligned them in thinly disguised portraits of their lives. The book had to be withdrawn, and damages were paid out to some of the women. The expense was substantial, though by no means crippling. It was enough, however, to make Gollancz think very carefully before publishing any book which might expose him to libel actions. 'He spoke of the episode in terms of horror,' the official historian of the firm has stated, adding that for a long time afterwards 'it coloured Victor's relations with authors. Every book was read for libel by Harold Rubinstein, the firm's solicitor (which had only happened before in very special cases), and Victor demanded enormous libel reports which, at least for some years, he took very seriously indeed.'[27]

Harold Rubinstein's report on *Burmese Days* was not good, and Gollancz felt that the only choice open to him was to reject the novel. At first Orwell was led to believe that the decision was partly based on a fear that the India Office might somehow try to keep the book from the public. 'My publisher was afraid the India Office might take steps to have it suppressed,' he wrote to Henry Miller a few years later.[28] But this fear was unjustified, and Orwell knew it. In 1946 he explained the real circumstances in a letter to a reader who had written him with questions about the novel.

Mr Gollancz, or his lawyer, feared that if the book were
published the India Office might intervene and get it suppressed,
or on the other hand that there might be libel actions by
individuals who believed themselves to have been caricatured . . .
In fact, the India Office would not have had the power to
suppress it in any direct way, even if it had wanted to . . . The
danger of libel actions was a real one, because the whole top-rank
official community in Burma, British and Oriental alike, only
amounted to a few thousand persons and it would be natural to
look for caricatures. There was also the complicating fact that
there are very few Burmese names, innumerable people bearing
the same name. Thus if you had as a character a Burmese
magistrate bearing a genuine Burmese name, such as 'Maung
Ba', there would inevitably be scores of hundreds of magistrates

bearing this name, and any one of them might claim he had been libelled.[29]

Writing so many years after the fact, Orwell was able to make a cool assessment of the reasons for Gollancz's rejection, but in 1934 it came as a great blow. He had assumed that the good notices for *Down and Out* would make Gollancz eager to have his next book, and that if there were any problems with the typescript, revisions could be made to satisfy the publisher. But he was not even given the chance to make changes. Gollancz viewed the whole book as one big risk, and did not want to take a chance on it – at least not for the time being. Eventually, he would change his mind, but only after Orwell's American publisher had taken the risk of bringing the book out first.

Fortunately, Harper's was willing to work with Orwell, suggesting alterations to the book which would reduce the libel danger. The firm's editor-in-chief, Eugene Saxton, was visiting London, and Moore arranged for him to meet Orwell at the end of January. One week after this meeting took place, Saxton wrote to Moore that Harper's would publish the book provided certain changes were made. 'Harper's asked me to make some small alterations,' Orwell recalled in 1946. 'I don't remember very clearly what these were, but I think the chief one was to change a few characters from government servants into businessmen so as to make the book less directly an attack on British imperialism.'[30] He agreed to make all the changes except for one suggested revision which had nothing to do with libel. Apparently, Saxton was not impressed with the last few pages of the novel, in which Orwell explains what the future held for Elizabeth, Veraswami, U Po Kyin and the other characters who live on after Flory's death. These pages are, in fact, some of the best in the novel, describing the workings of fate with a kind of cheerful cynicism, and Orwell successfully fought to keep them. He told Moore, 'With regard to Mr Saxton's remarks about the last two or three pp. of the novel, I am sorry to say I don't agree with him at all. I will cut these out if it is absolutely insisted upon, but not otherwise. I hate a novel in which the principal characters are not disposed of at the end. I will, however, cut out the offending words "it now remains to tell" etc.'[31]

In mid-March he signed a contract with Harper's for *Burmese Days*, though the deal did not become final until several months later, when the firm's legal advisers gave their approval for publication. All the talk about libel had made even Orwell think twice about the danger, and he went so far as to ask Harper's 'to insert at the beginning of the book a note to the effect that "all the characters in this story are entirely imaginary" etc.'[32] He had good reason to know that the libel danger might be worse than Harper's expected. It would seem that he never bothered to mention to them that the first words of the novel – 'U Po Kyin' – gave a name which was not only genuinely Burmese but also one personally known to him. In his early days in the Imperial Police he had known a fellow officer named U Po Kyin, whose service to the Empire was as virtuous as the fictional U Po Kyin's is corrupt. Perhaps he believed that no one in Burma would confuse the real man with the fictional creation, or that it could not be easily proved in an English court that he actually knew someone by that name. How could he have known then that the only photograph of him in Burma which would survive was one showing him standing a few feet to the left of U Po Kyin in a group portrait at the Police Training School?[33] But, as it happened he had nothing to fear. The novel was never involved in any libel action, from Burma or elsewhere. The only report of any dissatisfaction among the governing officials came years later from Roger Beadon, who remembered the reaction of Clyne Stewart, the Principal of the Police Training School. 'I'm told that when he read [*Burmese Days*] he went livid and said that if he ever met that young man he was going to horse-whip him.'[34] Perhaps it is just as well that Orwell never went back to Burma.

III

Orwell's health quickly improved after his return to Southwold, so much so that he began to think of more literary projects to give his energies to. When he had talked with Eugene Saxton in London, he had caught the editor off guard by suddenly suggesting that Harper's commission him to write a short life of Mark Twain. He seemed to have no awareness of how unrealistic such a proposal might sound to Saxton. He was asking a major American publishing house to commission him to write a biography of a major American writer even though he was an obscure English writer who had never attempted a biography and had never written anything of significance about Twain. But, of course, if Saxton had been rash enough to agree to the idea, the result might well have been a small masterpiece. There can be no doubt that, despite his apparent lack of 'qualifications', he was capable of doing the job. Only five years later he would produce a 25,000-word essay on Dickens which effortlessly blends biography and criticism, and which is widely regarded as one of his best pieces, and a model of practical criticism. Yet he was not, strictly speaking, qualified to write such a long essay on the most famous Victorian novelist. He was not an 'expert' on Dickens or the Victorian age. He was not even a university graduate. His only real qualifications were his good taste, his common sense, his sympathetic understanding of another writer's work, and his lively prose – all of which make his piece much more interesting than the vast majority of articles by Dickens 'experts'.

Sadly, Harper's editor-in-chief was not so unconventional a man that he could imagine publishing a biography of Twain by George Orwell. He politely recommended that Orwell present the idea to an English publishing house. He suggested Chatto and Windus. 'I don't know whether it is really worth asking Chatto's,' Orwell wrote to Moore in February, 'but there is this, that if they do intend to publish anything about Mark Twain for his centenary next year, they might not find it so easy to get anyone who knew anything about Mark Twain.'[35] There was at least a better chance of selling his idea in England, where authorities on Twain were harder to find. But it does not appear that anyone was willing to give him that chance, and the idea was soon abandoned.

By the beginning of spring, Orwell was working steadily on his next novel, *A Clergyman's Daughter*. The phrase was one which he associated with Brenda, though it cannot be said with confidence that the resemblance between the heroine of the novel – Dorothy Hare – and Brenda is anything other than circumstantial. After it was published he did say to her, 'You will see if you read *A Clergyman's Daughter* that I have employed you as a collaborator in two places,' but he gave no more specifics, and when she was interviewed more than fifty years later, Brenda claimed that she could not recall what he was referring to.[36] What is certain is that he liked to use the phrase given in his title as a way of teasing her about her religious heritage as a vicar's daughter. Just before *Burmese Days* was published in New York, he wrote to her, 'Please pray for its success, by which I mean not less than 4000 copies. I understand that the prayers of clergymen's daughters get special attention in Heaven, at any rate in the Protestant quarter.'[37]

With Eleanor no longer an object of his passion, he began spending more time with Brenda again, and since they were both in Southwold for most of 1934, they saw each other frequently. His feelings for her were still strong, but according to her recollections, she continued to resist any suggestion of a closer relationship. All the same, the language of his letters to her in the period of 1934–1935 is unusually warm. One ends, 'With much love and many kisses,' and another letter – which was written to her while she was on holiday in Ireland – pleads strongly for her return: 'Do come back soon, dearest one. Can't you come & stay with somebody [in Southwold] before the term begins?'[38]

Whenever Brenda was away from Southwold, he complained to her of the loneliness he felt in the town, where he had no close friends left except for her. He tried to spend more time with his father, sometimes accompanying the old gentleman on weekly visits to the local cinema, but as he reported to Brenda, his father could be annoying at times. 'I went to the pictures last week and saw Jack Hulbert in *Jack Ahoy* which I thought very amusing, & a week or two before that there was quite a good crook film, which however, my father ruined for me by insisting on telling me the plot beforehand.' He still liked to go for long walks on the beach or along the River Blythe, but in the summer – when Brenda was away from her job at St Felix's Girls' School – he did not have anyone to accompany him. One morning, during one of his solitary walks on a deserted stretch of beach, he was seized with the desire to go for a quick swim. 'I had walked out to Easton Broad not intending to bathe, & then the water looked so nice that I took off my clothes & went in, & then about 50 people came up & rooted themselves to the spot. I wouldn't have minded that, but among them was a coastguard who could have had me up for bathing naked, so I had to swim up & down for the best part of half an hour, pretending to like it.'[39]

That summer he worked furiously on his novel, completing large sections of it with great speed, but as usual he was unhappy with the quality of his work. Even the appearance of the proofs of *Burmese Days*, which arrived from America at the beginning of August, failed to build his confidence. Quite to the contrary, they only increased his doubts. 'Everything is going badly,' he complained to Brenda. 'My novel about Burma made me spew when I saw it in print, & I would have rewritten large chunks of it, only that costs money and means delay as well. As for the novel I am now completing, it makes me spew even worse, & yet there *are* some decent passages in it.'[40]

His complaints were so strong that Brenda felt it necessary to make a complaint of her own. His letters, she told him, were too gloomy. 'I suppose I must try and put on what Mr Micawber called the hollow mask of mirth,' he replied, 'but I assure you it is not easy, with the life I have been leading lately.' Part of the problem was that while he was trying to finish *A Clergyman's Daughter*, he was reading *Ulysses* again, and he could not help disliking his own work more after observing Joyce's masterful handling of the elements of fiction. 'It gives me an inferiority complex. When I read a book like that and then come back to my own work, I feel like a eunuch who has taken a course in voice production and can pass himself off fairly well as a bass or baritone, but if you listen closely you can hear the good old squeak just the same as ever.'[41] This amusing image is itself proof that he was no 'eunuch'. He had talent, but it was useless for him to compare it to Joyce's. It is not simply that Joyce was a better novelist, but that their talents had equipped them for different tasks. Orwell had it within his power to write great prose, but it would not be in the form or style of a novel like *Ulysses*, and it was a mistake to judge himself by that standard. Any time spent imitating Joyce was merely wasted time.

Unfortunately, that was partly what he was trying to do in *A Clergyman's Daughter*. Dorothy Hare is his pale attempt to create a fictional character whose basic position in life is different from his, but whose existence he can attempt to describe from within and without, as Joyce does with Bloom and Molly. But Dorothy is a muddle – she is partly Orwell and partly a mixture of characteristics belonging to women whom Orwell had known. He was simply unable to describe a completely fictional character with the sharp perception which he brought to his non-fiction, and a female character was especially difficult for him to capture in words. His understanding of women was too limited, and the view he provides of Dorothy is clearly that of an outsider who is unable to look at the world through her eyes.

The novel opens with a long chapter which imitates the structure of *Ulysses* by tracing the flow of events in a single day. Dorothy leads a sad existence devoted to 'good works' in the small town of Knype Hill, where her dull, ungenerous father is Rector of St Athelstan's. Reverend Hare is inclined to do as little as possible for his congregation, and accordingly, he has imposed upon his daughter the 'dirty work' of parish visiting and other tedious jobs. Her average day is spent consoling the sick and aged, giving advice to young housewives and playing games with 'sour-smelling' children of poor families. She is captain of the Girl Guides and honorary secretary of the Mothers' Union. But she herself has never married and vows that she never will, though over the years she has attracted 'rather more than her share of casual attention from men'. A quiet woman in her late twenties, she has 'a thin, blonde, unremarkable kind of face, with pale eyes'. Partly because of her pious upbringing, she has an aversion to sex, referring to it as '*all that*'. She likes men as friends, but she cannot bear their physical advances. 'Why couldn't they leave you *alone*? Why did they always have to kiss you and maul you about? They were dreadful when they kissed you –

dreadful and a little disgusting, like some large, furry beast that rubs itself against you, all too friendly and yet liable to turn dangerous at any moment.'

The one man in town who shows a strong interest in her is a bald-headed, middle-aged philanderer named Warburton. By turns amusing and annoying, he is the most interesting character in the novel, and there is more than a slight touch of Orwell in him. Warburton – whose name resembles Orwell's old tramping alias, P. S. Burton – is a man of independent income who occupies some of his leisure time producing 'mediocre' paintings of Suffolk landscapes. He has outrageous opinions and behaves indecently in Dorothy's company, but there is something appealing about his free-spirited wickedness, and it is a matter of pride with him to uphold his reputation as 'a proper old rascal'. He embodies that side of Orwell which loved nothing better than to shock respectable people by saying and doing unconventional things. At his best, Warburton is affectionately playful with Dorothy, in a manner not unlike Orwell's towards Brenda:

> A sort of friendship had grown up between the two, even to the extent of Dorothy being 'talked about' in connection with Mr Warburton . . . Dorothy, born into the twentieth century, made a point of listening to Mr Warburton's blasphemies as calmly as possible; it is fatal to flatter the wicked by letting them see that you are shocked by them. Besides, she was genuinely fond of him. He teased her and distressed her, and yet she got from him, without being fully aware of it, a species of sympathy and understanding which she could not get elsewhere. For all his vices he was distinctly likeable, and the shoddy brilliance of his conversation – Oscar Wilde seven times watered – which she was too inexperienced to see through, fascinated while it shocked her.

The long first chapter ends when Dorothy's day comes to a disturbing conclusion after a late-night visit to Warburton's house, where he makes advances and is rebuffed. It is at this point that Orwell loses direction completely and allows the structure to break down into a series of fragmentary episodes loosely strung together.

Improbably, Dorothy suffers an attack of amnesia, wanders away from Knype Hill and finds herself in London, where she is befriended by two Cockney youths and a young woman who take her to Kent to work with them in the hopfields. This is followed by other incredible adventures, including a cold night spent among tramps in Trafalgar Square (presented as an experimental scene consisting mostly of dialogue, in the manner of Joyce's 'nighttown' section in *Ulysses*), and a dismal period of teaching in a fourth-rate girls' day school in the fictional town of Southbridge – 'a repellent suburb ten or a dozen miles from London'.

It is clear that Orwell did not know where to take the story of Dorothy Hare after the day-in-the-life chapter, and ended up extending the novel by giving his heroine various experiences drawn from his own past. One of the problems is that these experiences are vividly described, but Dorothy is not. It is impossible to believe that *she* is living through any of these things – they seem merely to be happening to her with no sense that she has a will of her own with which to confront them. It does not help that Orwell occasionally comments on these experiences by unexpectedly inserting passages which more properly belong in separate essays. Such passages are especially troublesome in his chapter on Dorothy's life as a teacher. At times he seems to forget completely that he is writing a novel: 'There are, by the way, vast numbers of private schools in England ... At any given moment there are somewhere in the neighbourhood of ten thousand of them, of which less than a thousand are subject to Government inspection.' For a moment, at least, the novel seems on the verge of becoming a pamphlet on education.

It would have been so much better for Orwell if he had simply written directly about his experiences instead of forcing them to play a part in the implausible story of Dorothy Hare. 'One difficulty I have never solved,' he confessed to Julian Symons in 1948, 'is that one has masses of experience which one passionately wants to write about ... and no way of using them up except by disguising them as a novel.'[42] The unfortunate truth is that Orwell was not free to do what he did best. If he had written an honest, detailed account of his life in Southwold, or of his lonely existence as the headmaster of

The Hawthorns, no one – least of all Victor Gollancz – would have dared to publish them because of the strict libel laws of the day. Yet these would have been, in all probability, excellent works. The case of 'Such, Such Were the Joys' is a perfect illustration of the problem. This long piece represents his talent at its very best, but after he wrote it, he knew that it was unpublishable because it was, in his own words, 'too libellous to print'.[43] One solution, of course, was to write honestly about experiences which involved people who were not likely to initiate lawsuits (i.e., understanding friends, residents of faraway countries, or the lower classes) or people who could be described so vaguely as to be unidentifiable. In fact, these conditions apply in almost all of the literary non-fiction published in his lifetime. There was not much reason to fear lawsuits from Boris or Bozo in *Down and Out*, or from the faceless crowd of Burmese in 'Shooting an Elephant'.

On 3 October 1934 Orwell completed *A Clergyman's Daughter* and sent it to Moore, telling him, 'It was a good idea, but I am afraid I have made a muck of it – however, it is as good as I can do for the present.' He was even more negative in a letter to Brenda: 'I don't believe anyone will publish it or if they do it won't sell.'[44] It had taken a little more than six months of hard work to finish the book, and at the end of this period he was ready to put Southwold behind him and return to living in London, though he did not have any desire to go back to teaching. His plans for supporting himself were vague, but he was not penniless. For one thing, he had an advance coming from Harper's for *Burmese Days*. They were due to pay him £50 on the date of publication, which was set for 25 October. With that money, and perhaps another advance for *A Clergyman's Daughter*, he would have enough money to keep him for at least a few months in London. As he explained to Brenda, he did not require much money to support his way of living: 'When I said that I was going to stay in a slummy part of London I did not mean that I am going to live in a common lodging house or anything like that. I only mean that I didn't want to live in a respectable quarter, because they make me sick, besides being more expensive. I dare say I shall stay in Islington.'[45]

He had written to his Aunt Nellie in Paris to tell her of his plans for the autumn, and she had decided that there was a way she could help him. She told him that she had some friends in London who ran a small bookshop, and that they might be able to give him a job. The friends were a couple named Francis and Myfanwy Westrope, and their shop was located in Hampstead, on South End Green. It was called Booklovers' Corner. Nellie knew them because they were followers of the Esperanto movement. Near the end of September, she wrote to Mrs Westrope:

> I had a letter from Eric yesterday, saying that [*Burmese Days*] was scheduled to come out in New York [soon]. He is pretty sick that it can be sold only over there and hopes that 'two or three thousand' will go off. He intends finishing his third [book] before the end of this month and will then go up to London and 'stay some months'. I shall give him your address and hope you will be able to see him. I shall advise him to write to you first, for no doubt you are both pretty busy.[46]

He did contact them, and they offered him a part-time job and a place to live in a room above the bookshop. He accepted, and by 20 October he was established in his new position, selling books in the afternoons, and trying to write during the remainder of each day.[47]

CHAPTER ELEVEN

Booklovers' Corner

I

Orwell's lodgings above Booklovers' Corner were plain and dark, but he could not have asked for a better landlady than Mrs Westrope, who was uncommonly considerate. When her new lodger arrived, she showed him to his room and kindly enquired whether there was anything he 'particularly wanted'. He replied, 'The thing I most want is freedom.' Interpreting this to mean a particular kind of freedom, she asked, 'Do you want to have women up here all night?' He quickly tried to reassure her on that point, giving her a firm, 'No.' But he need not have feared her response. 'I only meant,' she explained, 'that I didn't mind whether you do or not.'[1]

Jon Kimche, a young assistant in the bookshop, remembered Mr and Mrs Westrope as 'a refined, middle-aged couple' who were 'almost too nice to be true'. Kimche, who later became an editor at *Tribune*, thought that the couple behaved more like friends or family than employers: 'I would say that Orwell and I were treated in a kind, parental manner. They took an interest in us, and were always very sincere and understanding.' Mr Westrope was a tall, gentle man with a special fondness for books on natural history. Mrs Westrope was a vigorous woman with a strong interest in women's rights. She and her husband were also supporters of the Independent Labour Party, as was Kimche, who met them as a result of his ILP connections. ('Marxism from a moral angle' was the phrase Kimche later used to describe the ILP philosophy.)[2]

According to Kimche, his fellow worker introduced himself as 'George Orwell', but also used his real name at the shop. (He was simply 'Eric Blair' to others who met him in this period, but he may well have enjoyed creating a little confusion for some people by using both names.) He and Kimche got along reasonably well, but they did not see a great deal of each other because they usually worked at different times of the day. It was Orwell's job to come down in the morning and open the shop at eight-forty-five. He would stay for about an hour, and then Kimche would take over until two p.m., at which time Orwell's four-hour shift would begin. Mrs Westrope helped out at various times, but her husband did most of the work, routinely spending seventy hours a week in the shop. The stock was mostly second-hand books, so this meant that Mr Westrope had the additional burden of making constant expeditions after hours to buy books.

Booklovers' Corner occupied two rooms – a large one filled with the second-hand books, and a small one containing a lending library of novels. There were several minor sidelines, including a small stock of used typewriters, and some calendars. The shop also sold stamps to collectors, but this business held little interest for Orwell. 'Stamp-collectors are a strange, silent, fish-like breed,' he commented later, adding that the oddest aspect of the breed was its sex – as far as he could tell, they were all male. 'Women, apparently, fail to see the peculiar charm of gumming bits of coloured paper into albums.'[3] Interestingly, the image of Orwell which remained most vivid in Kimche's memory from these days was that of a tall, imposing figure standing in the centre of the shop looking down at a small boy buying stamps.

All types of customers frequented the place, 'from baronets to bus-conductors', to quote Orwell's description in his essay 'Bookshop Memories', which appeared in November 1936. By all accounts he did his job well, but he was more than a little annoyed by some of the customers, especially the ones who came in looking for a book whose cover they could remember as being a certain colour but whose title and author they had completely forgotten. 'Many of the people who came to us,' he wrote, 'were of the kind who would be a nuisance anywhere but have special opportunities in a bookshop.' He was astonished at the number of people who would order special books or ask for certain volumes to be put aside for them, and then never return. He speculated that half the people who made such requests never came back to pick up the books. He was bothered not only by the fact that they caused him unnecessary trouble, but that so many of them apparently never intended to return. He concluded that merely ordering the books was satisfaction enough for them because 'it gave them . . . the illusion that they were spending real money'.

But dealing with a wide range of customers taught him some sobering things about the book market. It gave him real insights into readers' tastes, and reminded him that publishing was a business, not a philanthropic endeavour. Books were a commodity, a manufactured item consumed by people with diverse tastes, and though he wanted to think of books as something precious and profound, he saw how easily they could be reduced to serving the particular appetites of certain consumers, produced in quantity and devoured rapidly, like so many sausages. He saw this plainly in the insatiable appetite for detective fiction. One subscriber to the shop's lending library read at least four or five detective novels each week, and appeared never to take out the same book twice. 'Apparently the whole of that frightful torrent of trash (the pages read every year would, I calculated, cover nearly three quarters of an acre) was stored for ever in his memory. He took no notice of titles or authors' names, but he could tell by merely glancing into a book whether he had "had it already".' All authors like to imagine that their work will be treasured by their readers, but clearly some books are merely 'had', tasted once and tossed aside.

Orwell claimed that working in a bookshop caused him to lose his enthusiasm for books as special objects. He saw them too often as things which had to be searched for in a dim light or carted from one spot to another, and after a time this depressed him and took away the fascination with which he had previously regarded such things as the look of the binding or the smell of the paper. Standing in the shop day after day, he grew weary of the sight of so many books.

'Seen in the mass, five or ten thousand at a time, books were boring and even slightly sickening.' But this was an exaggeration. No doubt there were moments when he felt overwhelmed by the sense that books were merely things which piled up and collected dust, but he was also at home among them and took delight at uncovering curious or long-forgotten titles. He had a keen interest in bound volumes of old magazines, and he collected odd volumes of the *Gentleman's Magazine*, Thackeray's *Cornhill*, and the *Strand*. (The last of which afforded him the pleasure of reading the Sherlock Holmes stories as they had originally appeared when published in the *Strand* during the 1890s.) 'The great fascination of these old magazines,' he wrote in the 1940s, 'is the completeness with which they "date". Absorbed in the affairs of the moment, they tell one about political fashions and tendencies which are hardly mentioned in the more general history books.'[4]

One of his favourite discoveries from his days at Booklovers' Corner was a collection of the *Girl's Own Paper* from the 1880s. He was intrigued by the mixture of sincerity and ignorance which pervaded such popular works, and could spend hours leafing through them, chuckling to himself over the absurdities which he encountered in their pages. 'I have been deriving a lot of pleasure from some numbers of the *Girl's Own Paper*,' he wrote to Brenda. 'In the answers to correspondents two questions crop up over and over again. One, whether it is ladylike to ride a tricycle. The other, whether Adam's immediate descendants did not have to commit incest in order to carry on the human species. The question of whether Adam had a navel does not seem to have been agitated, however.'[5] These burning issues help to explain why Orwell heartily recommended the magazine to the readers of his 'Bookshop Memories', declaring that 'for casual reading – in your bath, for instance, or late at night when you are too tired to go to bed, or in the odd quarter of an hour before lunch – there is nothing to touch a back number of the *Girl's Own Paper*.'

Besides being attracted to odd titles, he also enjoyed finding books by authors with unusual names. This harmless diversion led him to contemplate a possible comic pseudonym for himself. As he joked to Brenda, 'I think it would be rather amusing, as so many women writers have chosen male pseudonyms, to choose a female one. Miss Barbara Bedworthy or something like that. With portrait of the author on the jacket.'[6] This joke appealed to him so much that he found a way to bring it to a larger audience. He went to the trouble of inventing a career for Ms Bedworthy, and used the information not on the back of a book jacket but in a satiric passage of his next novel, *Keep the Aspidistra Flying*. The passage occurs in a scene set in Gordon Comstock's place of employment, a second-hand bookshop embodying all the worst aspects of Orwell's work at Booklovers' Corner. When a plain but immodest woman named Miss Weeks enters the shop in search of 'a good hot-stuff love-story. You know – something *modern*,' Gordon leads her to the lending library and tries to be of some assistance, putting on 'his homey library manner':

> 'Something modern? Something by Barbara Bedworthy, for instance? Have you read *Almost a Virgin*?'
> 'Oh no, not her. She's too Deep. I can't bear Deep books. But I want something – well, *you* know – *modern*. Sex-problems and divorce and all that. *You* know.'
> 'Modern, but not Deep,' said Gordon, as lowbrow to lowbrow.
> He ranged among the hot-stuff modern love-stories. There were not less than three hundred of them in the library.

When Orwell began working for the Westropes, he had imagined that his job would bring him into contact with many congenial spirits – lovers of good books whose questions and comments would make his work stimulating. But one of his first disappointments came when he realised that 'really bookish people' were something of a 'rarity' in the shop, even though it featured a large selection of 'exceptionally interesting' second-hand volumes.[7] Nevertheless, a few 'bookish' people attracted his notice and received special attention. One was Kay Welton (later Kay Ekevall), a young woman with literary ambitions who lived near the bookshop. She had published a few poems in the *Listener*, but she made her living from her own small secretarial agency which was located in Hampstead.

Because of his height Orwell interested her from the very first moment she saw him. 'I saw this new assistant and thought he was a great asset because he was so tall he could reach all the shelves nobody else could without hauling a ladder out!'[8]

He showed an interest in her choice of books, and they began talking about what they had read recently, comparing opinions and exchanging information about their favourite authors. Similar discussions occurred on future visits to the shop, and soon they were going out together for coffee, or for walks on Hampstead Heath. On these rambles she was frequently impressed by his sharp observation of nature, and found that he was a storehouse of information about trees and plants. She also discovered that he knew a great deal about birds and was 'passionately fond' of them. To her amusement, she later learned that he was equally fond of cats, but that he could 'never square the fact that cats killed birds'.[9]

They enjoyed a close relationship for several months in 1934–1935, but neither of them gave any serious thought to a long-time romance. Kay even made a point of telling him – as she had told previous boyfriends – that she would not hold it against him if he stopped seeing her because he had found someone else. She asked only that he declare his true intentions. She was a confident, independent woman, and Orwell appreciated her openness. When he did fall in love with another woman, later in 1935, he told Kay what his feelings were, and they parted on good terms. Many years later, she recalled that, among all her former boyfriends, he was the only one who had been honest about his intention to leave her. The others had simply 'faded out'.

One of the common bonds between Kay and Orwell was their love of poetry. At the time that she knew him, he was reading a great deal of verse, from Chaucer to T. S. Eliot, and was writing some poems of his own. One of his ambitions, he told Kay, was to write an epic poem about English history, and it appears that he composed at least a short section of it, which has since been lost, before he abandoned the idea. A few of his poems had appeared in the *Adelphi*, and one of these was reprinted in a volume called *The Best Poems of 1934*, which Jonathan Cape published. Despite this honour, it must be said that the poem is painfully weak – beginning with its awkward title, 'On a Ruined Farm near the His Master's Voice Gramophone Factory'. Poetry brought out the weakest elements of his literary talent, encouraging him to use an inflated style which he normally avoided. He loved lyrical poetry, and took pleasure in the 'joy of mere words', as he once put it, but this 'joy' caused him to rely too much on traditional 'poetic' diction, and resulted in such stiff phrases as these from his anthologised poem of 1934: 'a sharper pang'; 'my mortal sickness'; 'the winged soul'; 'so alien still'.[10]

Eventually he realised that his prospects as a poet were not bright, though the anthology from Cape briefly encouraged him to think otherwise. He regarded the honour with pride until one day he learned that his triumph was not as sweeping as he had imagined. A letter arrived from his old friend Ruth Pitter, which included the news that there were 'several dozen of these anthologies of the so-called best poems of the year', and that Ruth's work was represented in no less than four, including a poem in something called *Twenty Deathless Poems*.[11] This immediately caused him to doubt whether the term 'best poems' meant anything at all.

But Orwell's efforts as a poet did produce at least a few enduring lines. They are found in a poem which he wrote in the late 1930s, after he had returned from the Spanish Civil War. They celebrate the nameless Italian militiaman whose strong face symbolised for Orwell the common man's determination to be free of tyranny. The famous last stanza has a simple poignancy:

> But the thing that I saw in your face
> No power can disinherit:
> No bomb that ever burst
> Shatters the crystal spirit.[12]

II

Orwell's disappointment over *Best Poems of 1934* was followed by discouraging news of the response to *Burmese Days* in America. Harper's published the novel on 25 October 1934, but as late as mid-November only one review had reached Orwell, and it was a negative one. The title alone was bad enough: 'Burmese "Natives" and White Folks' the headline read in the *New York Herald Tribune* review of 28 October. The reviewer – one Margaret Carson Hubbard – makes the novel sound like a cheap guidebook: 'You'll see the jungle, the dances, the native mistress, the fat yellow Buddha of a villain.' For some odd reason Orwell is criticised for showing too much sympathy towards his Indian and Burmese characters, and the anti-imperialism theme is dismissed as uninteresting. 'The trouble with this novel is that the ax Mr Orwell is grinding is so vastly important to him that it has chopped to pieces all interest in the very situation he most wants to expose.' After reading Margaret Carson Hubbard's dreary prose, Orwell found only one good thing to say about her review. At least the headline was large, he told Moore on 14 November, 'which I suppose is what counts'.

But matters were not as bad as they first seemed. Although he did not know it when he wrote to Moore, a very good review had appeared in the *New York Times* on the same day as the *Herald Tribune*'s piece. 'This is a superior novel,' wrote F. T. Marsh, 'not less because it tells an absorbing story. Orwell has made his people and his background vividly real. And he knows of what he writes.' More good reviews followed, and sales were better than Orwell expected. He guessed that it would sell no more than fifteen hundred copies, but in fact the novel went into a second printing and sold somewhere between two thousand five hundred and three thousand copies. By the standards of the day, it was a modest success.[13] He regretted that there was still no interest in the novel from any British publisher, but he did have the satisfaction of seeing the American edition on the shelves in at least one English bookshop – Francis Westrope kindly purchased a copy for the lending library of Booklovers' Corner.

In the meantime Victor Gollancz was trying to decide whether to accept Orwell's second novel. Once again the publisher was greatly worried about those aspects of Orwell's work which were potentially libellous. In November he informed Moore that a number of changes would have to be made before the firm could agree to publish *A Clergyman's Daughter*. Orwell was not surprised when the news was relayed to him. 'I knew there would be trouble over that novel,' he told his agent. But he was prepared to do his best to satisfy Gollancz and was of the opinion that 'the points about libel, swearwords etc. . . . could be put right by a few strokes of the pen'.[14]

At a meeting between author and publisher on 19 November, he agreed to make a number of small but widespread changes and to revise extensively the long chapter describing Dorothy's life as a teacher at the Ringwood House Academy for Girls. Gollancz and his solicitor, Harold Rubinstein, were worried that Orwell's attacks on 'fourth-rate' private schools were too strong and asked that they be toned down. It took Orwell almost a month to make all the necessary alterations. Some of his work involved merely the excision of certain names – such as a reference to the *Sunday Express* – but much of the rewriting was done in order to make it difficult for anyone to claim that the girls' school was based on a real establishment, or that the novel defamed schools of its kind. On 17 December, when he sent back the revised typescript, Orwell wrote to Gollancz, 'In general, throughout this school part I have toned down, but not cut out altogether, the suggestion that private schools of this type are apt to be more or less of a swindle, existing only to make money and not giving much more than a pretence of education.'

Rubinstein, who was a playwright as well as a lawyer, considered himself something of a literary critic, and had suggested to Orwell that the relationship between good-hearted Dorothy and the irresponsible Mr Warburton was 'incredible' because it was 'unlikely' that the man 'would take any interest in her'.[15] Orwell was willing to admit that the novel had many flaws, but he did not think this was one of them. The implausibility of their relationship 'had not struck me', he said, but the suggestion did prompt him to add this wonderful explanation to the first scene between Dorothy and Warburton:

People wondered sometimes how such a girl as Dorothy could

consort, even occasionally, with such a man as Mr Warburton; but the hold that he had over her was the hold that the blasphemer and evil-liver always has over the pious. It is a fact – you have only to look about you to verify it – that the pious and the immoral drift naturally together. The best brothel-scenes in literature have been written, without exception, by pious believers or pious unbelievers.

This was probably a much more explicit explanation than Rubinstein had wanted, but it was allowed to stand.

After putting a good deal of effort into making these changes, Orwell was not inclined to do any more work on the book, and decided that if the changes were not enough to satisfy Gollancz, he would withdraw the book from consideration. He thought that the *Adelphi* might publish separately his favourite chapter – the one showing Dorothy in a dramatic scene set among the tramps of Trafalgar Square – but as for the rest of the novel, it seems that he intended either to shelve it indefinitely or throw it away, as he had tried to do with *Down and Out*. As a matter of fact, Gollancz and his lawyer did require him to make a few more changes, but he was patient and managed to provide satisfactory alterations. When Moore wrote to him that the novel had finally passed inspection, and that a contract had been offered, Orwell was relieved but seemed to take some satisfaction from the thought that Gollancz would find the book difficult to sell. 'I am afraid he is going to lose money this time, all right.'[16]

Having tried his best to please his publisher, he had one special favour to ask of him. When *A Clergyman's Daughter* was published, he wanted *Burmese Days* to be listed on the page titled 'Books by the Same Author'. This seems a simple request, but he thought Gollancz might not want to comply with it since *Burmese Days* was not one of the firm's titles. The request was important to Orwell. The good reviews from America had helped to improve his view of the book's merit, and he wanted to see its existence advertised in some way at home. 'I want that book, if possible, not to be altogether lost sight of.'[17]

Only ten days after he wrote those words, Orwell received a surprise request from Gollancz. His publisher wanted to have another look at *Burmese Days*. The libel points still troubled him, but his willingness to reconsider it may have been tied to Orwell's strong effort to make *A Clergyman's Daughter* 'safe'. Perhaps they could perform the same successful operation on the earlier novel. Of course, he was also influenced by the fact that no one had tried to sue Harper's over its edition. But he was in for a small surprise of his own when Orwell replied to his request for the typescript. It had been destroyed, he was told, and Orwell did not have his own copy of the Harper's edition. He had given some of his copies away, and had sold the rest. But he hastened to assure Gollancz that a copy would be found for him. He thought that his agent had one, but if that proved not to be the case, there was another possibility. 'I will send you the one that is in our lending library as soon as I can get it back from the person who has it now.'[18]

One way or the other, a copy was found for Gollancz, and on 22 February he and Rubinstein met with Orwell to sort out the libel problems. It was a polite meeting and agreement was soon reached on the extent to which changes were needed. Orwell referred to them at the time as 'trifling alterations' which he could make in a week.[19] They were not exactly 'trifling', but he did complete them in only six days, and Gollancz responded by agreeing to bring out this revised edition in June, with only three months separating it from the March publication date set for *A Clergyman's Daughter*. His publisher was quickly making amends for their past difficulties.

Several names in *Burmese Days* had caused Rubinstein particular concern, but Orwell found good substitutes for all of these. U Po Kyin, for example, was altered to U Po Sing. 'This is not a possible Burmese name,' Orwell explained when he submitted his revision, 'but I fancy it will sound sufficiently like one to pass muster with the majority of readers.' To find a safe substitute for the name of Veraswami, he went to a specialist in Oriental languages at the British Museum and received help in finding 'a good Sanskrit name which *sounds* all right but which could not actually belong to any real individual'. The alternative which they devised was Murkhaswami. Finally, to reassure Gollancz that the English names posed no dangers, he consulted a copy of the Burma Civil List. 'I have been through this,' he declared, 'and cannot find any of the names I have used.'[20]

The letter accompanying Orwell's revisions bears a new address – 77 Parliament Hill. He was still working at the bookshop, but in mid-February he had agreed to leave his lodgings above it because, as he explained to Brenda, he had been given it on one condition – 'that I should have to give it up if somebody offered to take it & another room that are beside it together, & now somebody has done so.'[21] Mabel Fierz, who was always willing to give Orwell whatever help she could, came to the rescue by finding him a room in a large flat belonging to her friend Rosalind Obermeyer. The flat, which overlooked Hampstead Heath, was spacious and airy, with three bedrooms. Mabel was convinced that it was a healthy spot which would prove beneficial to Orwell's troublesome lungs. She brought her two friends together at her home in Oakwood Road, and arrangements were made for Orwell to move into the flat as soon as possible.

Rosalind was South African and had come to England in the 1920s. She was eight years older than Orwell and had already been married and divorced. When Orwell met her, she was taking an advanced course in psychology at University College, London, and was sharing her flat with another woman, a medical student named Janet Gimson. The two women and one man lived in the same flat for about six months, and maintained good relations throughout that time, each respecting the privacy of the other two. Orwell was friendly, but he led his own life and did not attempt to establish a close relationship with the women. Of the two, Rosalind came to know him better, though she later spoke of him as being rather aloof and not easy to warm to. She felt that 'something hadn't blossomed in him'.[22]

Although he may have seemed distant to her, his social life was, in fact, much more active than it had been for many years. He was making new friends and strengthening his ties with old ones. In this period his friendship with Sir Richard Rees deepened. One of the best things in *Keep the Aspidistra Flying* is its portrait of a character who has much in common with Rees – Ravelston, a wealthy socialist editor of a 'middle to high brow monthly'. Ravelston is acutely self-conscious of his upper-class background and defensive about his unearned income. Gordon speculates that Ravelston receives nearly two thousand pounds a year after tax – a very comfortable sum in those days – but this has instilled so much guilt in him that he is constantly trying 'to escape from his own class and become, as it were, an honorary member of the proletariat'. In a volume of autobiography published in 1963, Richard Rees took great care to present himself as an average man, while at the same time making it clear that he was fully aware of the position which his wealth had created for him among his less fortunate friends. 'I have never had the spending of much less than £1,000 a year of unearned income, and sometimes considerably more, even after deducting tax and allowances to relatives. Before the war this was wealth, especially for an unmarried man. Many of my socialist and intellectual friends were paupers compared to me.'[23]

One of those 'paupers' – at least in 1935 – was Orwell, who was lucky if he made £200 that year, from both his literary and bookshop incomes. He appreciated Rees's editorial support at the *Adelphi*, and he sincerely enjoyed having him as a friend, but he could not have avoided feeling some degree of resentment towards a man who had no real job but who enjoyed an income four or five times greater than his. As long as there was such an enormous difference in their material circumstances, they could never be completely at ease with each other. Appropriately, their friendship reached its best stage in the last years of Orwell's life, when his literary success eliminated the gap between their incomes, making the question of money seem much less important. (The remaining difference, of course, was that Orwell had to work for his money.)

Rees must be given credit, however, not only for encouraging Orwell's literary ambitions in the early years, but also for introducing him to other writers in London. One such introduction took place on an evening in early 1935 when he and Orwell were at Bertorelli's in Charlotte Street. Joining them for dinner that night were two young writers whose careers had received Rees's support – Dylan Thomas and Rayner Heppenstall. As usual, Thomas was more than a little drunk and did not seem to remember anything of the meeting, but Heppenstall did, and he soon became one of Orwell's friends. At that time Heppenstall had published only poetry and reviews, and was still a few years away from finishing his first novel (he wrote seven in his long career). What he chiefly recalled of their first encounter was not anything Orwell had said, but simply his striking appearance – and the odd sound of his laughter. He was 'a tall, big-headed man, with pale-blue, defensively humorous eyes, a little moustache and a painfully snickering laugh'.[24]

Theirs was a curious relationship because they appeared to have little in common. Orwell was eight years older, and he seemed to Heppenstall a rather old-fashioned, circumspect fellow with a strange taste for useless bits of information on obscure subjects. He had peculiar prejudices and would expound on them at length in Heppenstall's company, rambling on about the faults of 'Scotchmen', as he liked to call them, or English Roman Catholics, never making it very clear why such groups had earned his disfavour. Heppenstall concluded that Orwell was a 'nice man, but confused'. Talking at any length with him was frustrating, because he often found that once Orwell began '*his* conversation', the flow of ideas was so strong that interrupting him was not easy.

Heppenstall had little enthusiasm for his friend's satiric humour, which he regarded as overdone. Orwell liked to joke about the letters he received from women readers in America, saying that they tended to be very earnest, and that they usually included a question such as, 'What do you consider the most worthwhile thing in life?' It amused him to write in reply, 'The love of a good woman.' This gentle mockery was typical of his comic remarks, which were aimed at himself more often than not, but the innocent fun was lost on Heppenstall. He could not resist analysing the remark, dulling its effect by questioning how many letters had been sent from America, and how many of the women had posed questions about 'the most worthwhile thing in life'. Probably there was only one letter, but Orwell was merely making a joke, and would not have expected anyone to take his remark so seriously.

He tried to make a good impression on his new friend, inviting him to the flat in Parliament Hill for a steak dinner which he cooked, with evident pride, on a newly purchased Bachelor Griller (a small gas-stove). One evening the two friends spent several hours drinking together at a pub, and afterwards Heppenstall stayed the night at Orwell's place. The next morning Orwell received a letter from Brenda which included some negative comments about a review of a new book by Professor C. E. M. Joad – the review had been written by Heppenstall, but Brenda had not realised that he was someone Orwell knew. He took pleasure in explaining the strange coincidence to her:

> It was curious that you should mention that review of Joad's book, because Heppenstall, the man who wrote it, stayed at my place the night before last – in fact he was having breakfast with me when I was reading your letter. I did *not* tell him what you said about 'second-rate highbrows'. As a matter of fact, he is very nice – a Yorkshireman, very young, twenty-four or five I should say, and passionately interested in the ballet . . . As to people having no 'sympathy', I should think that anyone who had sympathy with a person like Joad would have something seriously wrong with them.[25]

In this same letter Orwell mentioned that *A Clergyman's Daughter* was to be published in four days' time – on 11 March. He hastened to add that the novel was 'tripe', but that thought did not seem to weigh on his mind. He was hard at work on his next book – *Keep the Aspidistra Flying* – which he hoped would be far superior to the other two novels. He was prepared to take greater pains with it. 'I want this one to be a work of art,' he confided to Brenda, 'and that can't be done without much bloody sweat.'[26] In the meantime he was not willing to abandon all hope for *A Clergyman's Daughter*, despite his disparaging remarks about it. A little success would not hurt, and he had in mind a plan to guarantee that the novel received at least one good review. He explained his idea to Moore: 'I was talking last night with a friend named Rayner Heppenstall who writes a good deal for the Adelphi. He tells me that he does reviews for the Yorkshire Post, and that if they would send him A CLERGYMAN'S DAUGHTER, he would give it a boost. I wonder if one could arrange this?' These are hardly the words of a man resigned to failure, nor one who was unaware of ways to play the review 'game'. As he cleverly suggested, 'Perhaps one could send a copy to the Yorkshire Post with the remark "This might interest Mr Heppenstall", or words to that effect?'[27]

The reviewers were not as unsympathetic towards the novel as Orwell feared, but most of the praise it received was qualified. In the *Spectator* V. S. Pritchett was impressed with Orwell's satiric powers, declaring in a memorable sentence, 'He is out to make the flesh of vicars' daughters creep and to show the sheltered middle-class women that only a small turn of the wheel of fortune is needed for them to be thrown helpless among the dregs of society.' But this was followed by the complaint that the novel too often resorts 'to the glib cruelties of caricature'.[28] In the *New Statesman* Peter Quennell gave a succinct verdict: '*A Clergyman's Daughter* is ambitious yet not entirely successful.'[29] And in the *Observer* L. P. Hartley declared that even though the novel's thesis was 'neither new nor convincing', the treatment was 'sure and bold', and the dialogue was 'often brilliant'.[30]

There was nothing to be ashamed of in these reviews, and though his own opinion of the novel would always be low – he called it a 'silly potboiler' in 1945 – he was able to continue working on his next book without feeling that his previous effort had been a complete disappointment.[31] He must have been feeling somewhat more confident about the future because in the spring he took a bold step – at least it was bold for him. He decided to give a party, and he asked his landlady, Rosalind, to join him in the fun by inviting some of her friends from University College. She agreed. It was not a large party – perhaps no more than a dozen people. Rees and Heppenstall were among Orwell's guests, and there were about five or six of Rosalind's friends, all of whom were either students or teachers in the Psychology Department of the College.

One of these guests was a slender woman with broad shoulders and dark brown hair. She was nearly thirty and was a graduate student working on a Master's degree in educational psychology. Her name was Eileen Maud O'Shaughnessy, and Orwell was attracted to her from the moment she walked into the room. They spent much of the evening talking, and at the end of the party he walked her to the bus stop. When he came back to the flat, he went to Rosalind's room and announced to her that Eileen was 'the sort of girl I'd like to marry'.[32]

This woman, who would indeed become George Orwell's wife, was an exceptional person. She came from a proud Irish family who had come to England in the early nineteenth century and had settled on the Tyneside. The daughter of a Collector of Customs, she was born on 25 September 1905 in South Shields. There was only one other child in the family, her older brother Laurence, and she was devoted to him. Both children received excellent educations. He studied medicine at the University of Durham and in Berlin, and was the winner of four scholarships. At the age of twenty-six he was elected a Fellow of the Royal College of Surgeons. She was educated at Sunderland High School, and then won a scholarship to one of the women's colleges at Oxford – St Hugh's – from which she received her degree in English Letters in 1927.

Because she earned only a Second Class Honours degree, she did not attempt an academic career, but chose instead to accept the first job which was offered to her – a teaching position in a private boarding school for girls. She did not find the job to her liking, however, and left after only one term. Over the next three years she worked at a succession of temporary jobs, which reportedly included doing social work among London prostitutes. Then, in 1931, she assumed the ownership of a small secretarial agency in London – Murrells Typewriting Bureau – which was located in a basement office at 49 Victoria Street.

One of her assistants in the office was a girl of only fifteen, Edna Bussey, who had joined the business just before it was sold to Eileen. The relationship between Edna and her new employer was exceedingly warm, with Eileen developing a sisterly affection for her young assistant. 'We got along so very well,' Edna recalled, 'we seemed to know each other's thoughts and sometimes even the next moves. She wanted me to go and live with her and her mother and ... [study] English. She thought I had potential and took a great interest. Her idea was for me eventually to try to enter a university. However, my mother had very different ideas – I feel she was very jealous of my friendship with Eileen.' When her parents moved to the country in late 1933, Edna reluctantly left her job in London, but she corresponded with Eileen for several years afterwards, and retained fond memories of her time at the agency:

> She was a very happy person and had a very vivid personality. I don't think she ever made very much money as she was too generous and I fear most unbusinesslike. She was untiring in her efforts to help people. I well remember a [Russian academic] who was writing a thesis for his professorship, being taken under her wing. She literally re-wrote his thesis for him, and I have always felt that it was she who earned the professorship.[33]

Eileen gave up the typing bureau when she decided to pursue a degree in psychology. She was encouraged in this ambition by her brother, whom she assisted in her spare time by editing and typing his scientific papers. If Laurence O'Shaughnessy is mentioned at all in accounts of Orwell's life, he is usually described vaguely as a 'dedicated medical scientist' or as a 'surgeon and chest specialist', but he was a far more important figure than these common terms suggest. From 1933 to 1935 he was Hunterian Professor at the Royal College of Surgeons and was at the forefront of research on heart disease and tuberculosis. In 1936 he founded a clinic at Lambeth Hospital for the treatment of cardiovascular disease, and also became the consultant surgeon to the Preston Hall tuberculosis sanatorium – which was an advanced centre of research and treatment operated by the British Legion. He gave lectures on his work to scientists in France, Germany and the United States, and he was co-author of two influential textbooks – *Thoracic Surgery* (1937) and *Pulmonary Tuberculosis: Pathology, Diagnosis, Management and Prevention* (1938). The astonishing thing about all this work is that it was done before he was forty. Of course, the fact that Eileen's brother was one of Britain's leading experts on tuberculosis was of no small interest to Orwell, and, as future chapters will show, Dr O'Shaughnessy had an important part to play in Orwell's life.[34]

At the time she met her future husband, Eileen was living at 24 Croom's Hill, which borders Greenwich Park. The house belonged to her brother and his wife, Gwen, who was also a doctor. It was a Georgian house with elegant bay windows on two of its three floors, and was originally the home of an astronomer at the Royal Observatory. Eileen was happy there, and enjoyed playing at least a small part in her brother's brilliant career, but she was also looking forward to having a career of her own as an educational psychologist. And then Orwell came into her life. He took her out to dinner not long after the party at Rosalind's flat, and, as Eileen later reported to her friend Lydia Jackson, he proposed to her. Lydia was stunned: 'What! already? . . . What are you going to do about it?' To which, Eileen responded, 'I don't know . . . You see, I told myself that when I was thirty, I would accept the first man who asked me to marry him.' Eileen would turn thirty in September, so time was running out. But Lydia did not take the comment too seriously. It was a 'typical' thing for Eileen to say, she recalled. 'One could never be certain whether she was being serious or facetious.'[35]

It was this slightly mischievous sense of humour which attracted Orwell to her in the first place. She could appreciate his dry wit, and she was capable of matching it with her own quips. She was not intimidated by him, and she was not the kind of woman whom he could easily shock with his unconventional remarks. She was also one of the most intelligent women he would ever meet, and he was well aware of it. Having read widely in English literature, she could hold her own with him in discussions about poetry or fiction. And as her surviving letters show, she was an excellent writer, with a strong sense of style. Her friends thought that Orwell's marriage to Eileen was, among other things, beneficial to his writing. They believed that she was a perceptive critic and influenced the development of his style by reading his works while he was in the process of writing them, and giving him her honest opinions.

She certainly felt free to speak her mind in his presence, and knew how to contradict some of his wild generalisations in a tactful way. Lydia Jackson remembered a good illustration of Eileen's manner of handling George's exaggerated claims. She was having breakfast with them one day when Orwell suddenly remarked that every villager in England should be able to keep a pig and cure bacon at home, but that bacon manufacturers had conspired against this by encouraging strict sanitary regulations to control the practice.

> Eileen gave me a quick glance and a smile. 'Now what made you say this?' she exclaimed. 'Isn't it rather a sweeping statement to make?' The look in George's face showed that he was both amused and a little embarrassed but he stuck to his guns.
> 'It is in the interests of bacon manufacturers . . .' he began.
> 'Yes, I know, but have you any evidence to show that they were responsible for the sanitary regulations?' He had not, and she added: 'That's the kind of statement an irresponsible journalist would make.' George had enough sense of humour not to mind this kind of challenge, and Eileen often challenged him in these ways.[36]

During the summer of 1935 Orwell and Eileen spent many weekends together, staying in Greenwich or making excursions into the countryside. He repeated his proposal, but she put him off for the time being, explaining that she did not want to marry until she had completed all the work for her degree, which would take another year. Orwell could not promise her an easy life if she accepted him; he did not have much money, and his literary prospects were uncertain. But he felt certain that Eileen was the right woman to be his wife, and wanted to marry her as soon as the time was right for both of them. He was so serious about marrying her that he wanted them to become formally engaged, but even that had to wait for a little longer. 'You are right about Eileen,' he wrote to Rayner Heppenstall during this period. 'She is the nicest person I have met for a long time. However, at present, alas! I can't afford a ring, except perhaps a Woolworth's one.'[37]

He made good progress that summer on his new novel, and was hoping to finish it by the end of the year. Gollancz was eager to see it. *A Clergyman's Daughter* and *Burmese Days* did not produce large sales, but they did make a little money for the firm, and much to Gollancz's relief, there was no mention of a libel action from any quarter. He brought out his edition of *Burmese Days* on 24 June, and after the first two thousand five hundred copies were sold, a small second printing was ordered. The novel was not as widely, or as favourably, reviewed as *Down and Out* had been, but one review in particular caught Orwell's attention. It appeared in the *New Statesman* on 6 July, and its opening comment was strongly favourable. '*Burmese Days* is an admirable novel. It is a crisp, fierce, and almost boisterous attack on the Anglo-Indian. The author loves Burma, he goes to great lengths to describe the vices of the Burmese and the horror of the climate, but he loves it, and nothing can palliate, for him, the presence of a handful of inefficient, complacent public school types who make their living there.' But as good as this was, the last sentence was guaranteed to please Orwell: 'I hope a copy finds its way to the club at Kyauktada.' This was precisely the kind of humorous remark which Orwell enjoyed, but he must have been especially pleased when he looked at the foot of the review and saw that it was the work of Cyril Connolly.[38]

III

Orwell had not been in touch with Connolly since they were at Eton together. After he returned from Burma, he did see a few old friends from his schooldays, but he had not kept up with them. Connolly had no idea what had become of his old friend, but then in the early spring of 1935 he happened to learn from one Old Colleger that Eric Blair was writing books under the name of Orwell. As a regular contributor to the *New Statesman* in the 1930s, Connolly asked the literary editor of the paper to let him review the next book by Orwell. He made the request more out of curiosity than anything else – he wanted to see what the book was like – but he also hoped that the review would bring him back into contact with his friend. If he had wanted to find out right away where Orwell was living, he could have managed it easily enough by writing to Gollancz, but he preferred to see what response his review would bring. It was more fun that way. And, indeed, the plan worked. A short time after the review came out, he received a letter of thanks from Orwell and an invitation to visit him some time in Hampstead.

Connolly took up the offer and Orwell asked him to dinner at Rosalind's flat. He cooked the meal on his Bachelor Griller, and Connolly later wrote that the food was 'excellent', which was a high compliment coming from him. Since leaving Eton, he had refined his tastes for the good life at Oxford, and in the South of France with his wealthy American wife Jean, and he considered himself a very discriminating gourmet. When Orwell greeted Connolly upon his arrival at the flat, both men were immediately struck by the great changes which had taken place in their appearances during the past fourteen years. 'His greeting was typical, a long but not unfriendly stare and his characteristic wheezy laugh, "Well, Connolly, I can see that you've worn a good deal better than I have." I could say nothing for I was appalled by the ravaged grooves that ran down from cheek to chin. My fat cigar-smoking persona must have been a surprise to him.'[39] Written some twenty-five years after the event, this description of Orwell's face is exaggerated, but it is true that illness and rough living had left its mark on him, making him look older than his age, which was only thirty-two at the time of this meeting.

Connolly and Orwell would see a good deal more of each other over the next few years, especially at the beginning of the Second World War, when Connolly was busy recruiting contributors for his new magazine, *Horizon*. But why, after Eton, did it take so many years for them to re-establish contact with each other? Orwell was a fairly regular reader of the *New Statesman* from the time he left Burma in 1927, which was the same year that Connolly's reviews began appearing in the paper. He would have had abundant opportunities to see Connolly's name in its literary pages, and could have made some attempt to reach him at any time. But he kept to himself.

One explanation for this is that facing Connolly would not have been easy before 1935. After Eton, Connolly had been a Brackenbury Scholar at Balliol College, Oxford, and by 1927 he had been given his own review column in the *New Statesman*. Having returned from Burma a 'failure', with only vague hopes of becoming a writer, Orwell would surely have found it humiliating to reveal his 'failure' to his old friend and occasional rival. But in 1935 he could meet him without any need to feel apologetic about his career. He still wanted to believe that he did not need success, and that he did not need to prove anything to anyone, but when their meeting took place, he had the satisfaction of knowing that he had experienced far more success than Connolly, who had yet to publish his first book. He was a novelist, and Connolly was still only a reviewer of novels. That fact mattered enormously, and both men knew it.

One incident from the early autumn of 1935 illustrates very dramatically how confident Orwell was becoming. On 16 October he gave a lecture titled 'Confessions of a Down and Out' to the South Woodford Literary Society in Essex. This may sound like a minor event, and conjure up images of a tiny gathering of dilettantes listening to Orwell speak on tramps for half an hour, but that would be far from the truth. As Orwell happily reported to his friends afterwards, he spoke before 'an audience of 400 or 500 people'. He had never done any public speaking on this scale before, and it is difficult to believe that a man who was normally rather shy in public was able to stand up before such a large crowd and talk for over an hour on his experiences among tramps. But he did it, and by all accounts it was a success. A few days later the local newspaper ran a story about it, and gave a good many details of his talk, which Orwell appears to have drawn almost verbatim from certain passages in his book. Nevertheless, it is interesting to read that he concluded his mostly anecdotal talk with a strong, straightforward plea to his largely middle-class audience: 'Mr Orwell ... said that many people were apt to regard a destitute man as a rogue who needed discouraging as much as possible, and he did not think much could be done in the way of improvement until people realised that they were human beings like the rest of the community, driven by force of circumstances to lead this wretched life.'[40]

Orwell came away feeling not only that he had done a good job, but that he would also like to give more lectures. 'Lecture on Wed. went over *big*,' he wrote to Heppenstall. 'Was surprised to find how easy it is.'[41] In another letter, to Moore, he reported that the audience 'seemed quite interested, & the secretary asked me to come again next year. This suggested to me that we might perhaps try to get some more lecture engagements . . . and perhaps it would be a useful sideline.'[42]

One other fact about this talk is significant. To give it, he had to interrupt his work on *Keep the Aspidistra Flying*. In the past, when he was nearing the completion of a book, he was always in such throes of agony that he would never have been able to put aside his work to deliver a lecture, especially to such a large crowd. Clearly, he was having an easier time with the new novel, but it was also the case that he felt a little more relaxed and confident about his ability to finish it, to get it published, and to survive the reviews – whatever their verdicts might be. And he was under some pressure to complete it quickly. Only two weeks before he faced the crowd in South Woodford, he told Moore, 'I had a letter from Gollancz, harrying me about my novel. He says he must have it by the end of the year, to come out at the end of February [1936].' But he was prepared to handle this pressure, declaring, 'I think I can just about manage that.'[43]

As usual, he did meet his deadline, maintaining a fairly steady pace of work throughout the autumn. He was able to do this despite the fact that he had moved to a new place, and was sharing it with flatmates who were not as quiet and respectful as Rosalind Obermeyer and Janet Gimson. In the late summer he had moved from Parliament Hill and taken up residence at 50 Lawford Road, sharing the rent with Heppenstall and a third friend, Michael Sayers – a young Irishman who wrote stories and drama criticism for the *New English Weekly*. They were all friends of Mabel Fierz, and it had been her idea that they should try living together. Their flat was at the top of a yellow-brick house on a plain street near

Camden Road. Each man had his own bedroom, the largest one – which was at the back – going to Orwell because he paid the largest share of the rent.

Problems soon arose when Heppenstall fell behind in his rent, and Orwell had to make up the difference out of his own pocket – the flat had been let in Orwell's name, so he had the responsibility of paying the rent on time. Then late one night real trouble broke out. Heppenstall came home 'exceedingly drunk', as he admitted later, and made a lot of noise coming up to the flat. He woke Orwell, who began giving him an angry lecture about his behaviour. Heppenstall was feeling sick and tried to cut the lecture short, telling him first to shut up, and then swinging a fist at him. Orwell responded with a firm punch to Heppenstall's nose, which brought forth a stream of blood.

When the bleeding stopped, and he stumbled off to bed, Heppenstall suddenly heard a key turning in the bedroom door. Realising that he was being locked in, he lost his temper completely and began kicking out the panels of the door, yelling for Orwell to unlock it. As his foot went through one of the panels, he heard the key rattle in the lock, and the next minute Orwell was standing before him holding a shooting-stick, which was used to push him back into the room. When he tried to fight back, he was hit across the legs with the stick, and as he went down, he looked up to see another blow on its way. He managed to block it with a chair, and Orwell retreated.

When he recounted this incident in the 1950s, he recalled that he had caught a glimpse of Orwell's face just before the last blow had come down. 'Through my private mist I saw in it a curious blend of fear and sadistic exaltation.' This story has sometimes been used to demonstrate that Orwell was a repressed sadist whose fame as a 'decent man' is unfounded. There is no lack of evidence that he was a flawed human being – he was not 'a kind of saint', as V. S. Pritchett called him in an obituary notice. But it is odd to think that anyone would attach so much importance to a drunken man's impression of a face glimpsed through a 'private mist'. He may have seen a sadistic expression, but he may also have been simply a drunk misinterpreting a look of genuine outrage from someone whom he had awakened in the middle of the night, and against whom he had attempted to strike the first blow, without justification. He was a much younger man, and, as he admits elsewhere in his account, a much stronger man than Orwell. Given his irrational behaviour that night, it was a sensible precaution to lock him in his room, and it is difficult to blame Orwell for overreacting when Heppenstall began tearing down the door.

When Mabel Fierz was interviewed in the 1960s, she confirmed that the so-called 'shooting-stick incident' had indeed taken place, but she also pointed out a few things which are missing from Heppenstall's account. According to her, the young man 'was always at odds with everyone and very difficult', and she said that he had been 'incredibly difficult' on the day of the incident. She could attest to this because he had spent the day at her house, where he had made a scene by climbing onto the roof and refusing to come down. When he came to her again the next day, his face bruised, she had no 'sympathy for him'.[44]

Earlier that morning, Heppenstall had been standing in the kitchen of the flat, and had suddenly encountered Orwell again. But this time there had been no violence. Determined to put an end to the business in a manner befitting a former police officer, Orwell had interrogated Heppenstall 'like a district commissioner', and had then ordered him to pack his bags and leave. Perhaps that should have been the last chapter in their relationship, but it was not. They met a year later, patched up their differences and became friends again, remaining on reasonably good terms for the rest of Orwell's life, without any discussion between them of the 'incident'. But Orwell was never given the chance to write a response to his friend's account of that night. Heppenstall waited until Orwell had been dead for five years, and only then did he offer his version of the event, describing it in an article with the dramatic title, 'The Shooting Stick'.

CHAPTER TWELVE

A Window on Wigan

I

On an early autumn day in 1935 Orwell went to Greenwich to see Eileen, and while he was there he paused to watch the ships going up and down the Thames. In exactly five years' time the vast docks in the distance would be on fire, the targets of Hitler's bombers, but Orwell was already contemplating such a fate as he gazed at the river on that day in 1935: 'I thought what wonders a few bombs would work among the shipping.'[1] The growing threat from Germany was clear enough to anyone willing to recognise it, and Orwell observed its development with an odd mixture of dread and satisfaction. He knew the coming war would be terrible, but part of him could not help thinking that a world corrupted by money and power invited destruction, and deserved whatever it got. In late 1934 he declared, 'This age makes me so sick that sometimes I am almost impelled to stop at a corner and start calling down curses from Heaven.'[2] By the beginning of 1935, when he was writing the early chapters of *Keep the Aspidistra Flying*, he was able to imagine – with uncanny accuracy – one form of destruction which would rain down on Britain in a few short years: in the novel Gordon Comstock thinks he hears 'the humming of the aeroplanes and the crash of the bombs'. When he looks up 'at the leaden sky', he sees nothing, but he feels certain that 'those aeroplanes are coming. In imagination he saw them coming now; squadron after squadron, innumerable, darkening the sky like clouds of gnats.'

Even though all of Orwell's books have social themes, the focus of his attention during the first half of the 1930s was on literature, not on politics and world events. It is interesting to note that the Nazis came to power in the very month that he published his first book, but the news does not seem to have provoked any comment from him at that time. It was not until the danger of fascism became obvious to him that he began to show a greater concern for political matters. At the end of the decade, he looked back on its tumultuous events and found a turning point. 'In the world of 1935,' he wrote in 'Inside the Whale,' 'it was hardly possible to remain politically indifferent.'

But the increased attention which he gave to politics in 1935 did not immediately prompt him to support a specific cause. It took another year for that to happen. The deciding factor was his recognition that there was only one way to oppose fascism effectively. 'Socialism,' he wrote in 1936, 'is the only real enemy that Fascism has to face.'[3] He concluded that the 'capitalist-imperialist governments' would not have the heart to stand up to Hitler and Mussolini, that they would try appeasement for as long as possible. Eventually, these governments would pay dearly for that policy, but he thought that nothing would keep them from pursuing it. They were not serious about stopping the fascists because, he believed, they had too much in common with them. 'Fascism after all is only a development of capitalism,' he wrote in 1937, 'and the mildest democracy, so-called, is liable to turn into Fascism when the pinch comes. We like to think of England as a democratic country, but our rule in India, for instance is just as bad as German Fascism, though outwardly it may be less irritating.'[4]

After his experience in Burma, he was naturally sceptical of the motives of 'capitalist-imperialists', but he did not endorse the socialist cause until its appeal was enhanced by the danger of fascism's rise. Although many of his friends were socialists, and his opinions often reflected the influence of socialist thinking, he had been reluctant to identify himself with the movement. Indeed, he was not inclined to identify himself with any formal ideology. In a conversation with Jack Common in the early 1930s, he 'airily described himself over a cup of tea as a Tory Anarchist', and of course, part of his pleasure in making this pronouncement was to leave the contradictory term unexplained.[5]

Even in 1935 he was still keeping his distance from the socialist cause. One Saturday in May of that year he went to Richard Rees's flat to borrow some money, but was told that his friend was attending a socialist meeting nearby. Orwell wandered into the meeting, and almost immediately found himself involved in a long debate with some of the people there. 'I spent three hours,' he recalled a few days later, 'with seven or eight Socialists harrying me, including a South Wales miner who told me – quite good-naturedly, however – that if he were a dictator he would have me shot immediately.'[6] That was one debate Orwell could not win, but he never tired of arguing with socialists, especially after he decided to join their movement. Fighting with them against fascism made sense, but it was considerably more difficult to find agreement on what socialism stood *for*, and how it should be put into effect. He would be engaged in the debate on those two crucial questions for the rest of his life.

Orwell did not abandon his interest in literary values when his attention shifted to political ones. As he makes very clear in 'Why I Write', he wanted to combine the two elements. Written in 1946, the essay explains the change which occurred in his career between the writing of *Keep the Aspidistra Flying* (a self-conscious attempt to create 'a work of art') and *The Road to Wigan Pier*, a 'documentary' written in 1936.

> What I have most wanted to do throughout the past ten years is to make political writing into an art. My starting point is always a feeling of partisanship, a sense of injustice. When I sit down to write a book, I do not say to myself, 'I am going to produce a work of art.' I write it because there is some lie that I want to expose, some fact to which I want to draw attention, and my initial concern is to get a hearing.

In 1935 Orwell was trying to work out the position which is so clearly defined above. He realised that it was time to move his career in a different direction, that he could no longer continue simply turning out one novel after the other, each with its own vague artistic aims and eclectic social commentary. He was keenly aware that his artistic aims had been misdirected, leading him into purple prose and weak imitations of other writers, and he was equally aware of the need to write with a strong sense of political purpose. Yet he was uncertain of the next step. He knew what was wrong, but he was still searching for a way to put it right.

This mood of uncertainty is present in *Keep the Aspidistra Flying.* Gordon's plight is, in many ways, the same as Orwell's. He abandons a 'good', steady job in order to pursue a literary career, and while he waits to write his masterpiece, he works in a bookshop. His friends resemble Orwell's, as do some of his adventures, and he is preoccupied with ideas about art and society which are similar to those favoured by his creator. He rages against the corruption in a society obsessed with money and power, and he takes refuge in a private world where high art is his god. Much of his spare time is spent in painstaking efforts to write his long poem 'London Pleasures' ('two thousand lines or so, in rhyme royal, describing a day in London'). It is a sort of miniature *Ulysses* in verse.

What makes this novel fascinating, despite a weak plot, is the highly critical portrait of Gordon which emerges from the narrative. Orwell turns on himself, so to speak, and satirises the self-defeating aspects of his life in the early 1930s – his lack of self-confidence, his sometimes bitter cynicism, his romantic fatalism, and his unrealistic literary ideals. Gordon is defeated by these things, giving up on his poem after writing only one-fifth of it, and returning to his previous career in advertising, a trade which is described in an early chapter as 'the rattling of a stick inside a swill-bucket'. He gives up on art because he cannot satisfy his own impossibly high standards, and because he loses faith in its importance against the menacing background of world events. 'Poetry! *Poetry*, indeed! In 1935.'

He cannot place his faith in any political movement. Socialism, to him, is a dismal creed: 'Four hours a day in a model factory, tightening up bolt number 6003. Rations served out in greaseproof paper at the communal kitchen.' This is not unlike some of Orwell's own criticisms of socialism, but the vital difference is that Gordon simply gives up in the face of uncertainty and despair. Orwell must have been tempted to do the same. Faced with a future inimical to art, and filled with doubts about the possibility of any effective political response, one could end all the doubts by committing a kind of spiritual suicide. Of Gordon's decision, the narrative comments, 'He would sell his soul so utterly that he would forget it had ever been his.' Why argue with socialists who want to shoot you, why write books which always disappoint you, when you can just quit and lose yourself in an ordinary, undemanding life? Make a bit of money, put an aspidistra in the front window and enjoy a little cosy domesticity before the bombs begin to fall. Gordon even has a rationalisation for this move: 'Everyone rebels against the money-code, and everyone sooner or later surrenders. He had kept up his rebellion a little longer than most, that was all.'

Just before Gordon throws his manuscript away, he scans its pages briefly and is almost tempted to keep it. He hesitates, reading a line of it. 'Momentary regret stabbed him. After all, parts of it weren't half bad!' But he refuses to give it another chance and reminds himself that he really has only two choices. 'Either surrender or don't surrender.' Those were the appropriate terms for 1935, for free individuals as well as for free nations. In Gordon's case the price of surrender is high. His talent is placed at the service of the New Albion advertising agency, and he prospers there by helping to launch a campaign for a new foot deodorant. He turns out a steady stream of copy describing the shame of smelly feet and consoles himself with the thought that he writes 'with the economy that is only learned by years of effort'.

Orwell would never have succumbed to such a fate, but he did have his moments in 1935–1936 when he wanted to surrender. His genius as a writer of political literature – after 1935 – is so impressive that it is difficult to believe he once wanted to avoid such work. In 'Why I Write' he openly acknowledged the existence of another impulse in his career: 'In a peaceful age I might have written ornate or merely descriptive books, and might have remained almost unaware of my political loyalties.' The

circumstances of his time made it necessary for him to choose
between a life devoted to those 'ornate' books or one devoted to
political literature. He made the right choice, but the moody,
idealistic world of the early Orwell, the man who wanted to be a poet
and who wanted to write novels like *Ulysses*, was not so easy for him
to leave behind. While he was trying to make up his mind about the
direction of his career, he wrote a poem which expressed his
'dilemma', to use his word. Written at the end of 1935, the first two
stanzas describe the comfortable 'aspidistra' world which might
have been his:

> A happy vicar I might have been
> Two hundred years ago,
> To preach upon eternal doom
> And watch my walnuts grow;
>
> But born, alas, in an evil time,
> I missed that pleasant haven,
> For the hair has grown on my upper lip
> And the clergy are all clean-shaven.[7]

It is convenient to think that the calm, determined voice of his
famous essays on politics and society was always his voice as a
writer, but he created that voice by an act of will, suppressing other
urges. Despite serious reservations, he became involved in the
political life of his time, and won fame on a level far above anything
he could have imagined for himself in the early 1930s. When he
considered the consequences of his choice in 'Why I Write', he
concluded that he had enabled his best self to emerge: 'And looking
back through my work, I see that it is invariably where I lacked a
political purpose that I wrote lifeless books and was betrayed into
purple passages, sentences without meaning, decorative adjectives
and humbug generally.'

II

Orwell submitted the typescript of *Keep the Aspidistra Flying* to
Gollancz in person on 15 January 1936. At some point in the next

few days his publisher asked him to consider accepting a new project – writing a book about unemployment and general living conditions in the North of England. Earlier in the previous autumn an editor at the *News Chronicle* in London had asked Orwell to write an article – perhaps even a series of articles – on the subject of unemployment, but he had turned down the offer, saying, 'For the moment I am rather tired of that subject.'[8] But by January, with his novel completed, he was ready to consider a book-length treatment of the idea, and a deal was struck with Gollancz for publication of a trade edition in about a year's time. He quit his job at Booklovers' Corner, gave up his flat in Lawford Road, said goodbye to Eileen, and then set off on his long journey north.

If he had not been so deeply involved with Eileen, he might have devoted several months to the research for his book. But as he told Cyril Connolly, he did not like the idea of spending so much time away from 'my girl', as he called her.[9] Instead of making it a long stay he planned to return to the South in about two months. The first leg of his trip – which began only a fortnight after he submitted his novel – took him to Coventry by rail. He arrived there in the afternoon on the last day in January. He was still a hundred miles from Manchester – where he planned to begin his research – but he wanted to see something of the towns and countryside along the way, so for the second part of his trip he travelled on buses and on foot.

Richard Rees and John Middleton Murry had given him names of *Adelphi* contacts in the North, and some letters of introduction. With these, he was able to meet people who could find him a place to stay and who could take him to visit slum neighbourhoods, coal mines, and workers' meetings. His first important contact was Frank Meade, a trades-union official in Manchester, who was his host for a few days. It was Meade who suggested that he visit Wigan, and who put him in touch with an electrician who worked there in the mines, a man named Joe 'Jerry' Kennan. On 8 February he made the short trip to Wigan and found Kennan's house. 'There was a knock at the door one Saturday afternoon,' Kennan remembered. 'We were just having tea. I opened the door and there was this tall fella with a pair of flannel bags on, a fawn jacket, and a mac.' He invited him in for tea and Orwell explained that his purpose in coming to the area was to find out what life was like for ordinary working people and to write about it. Kennan helped him to find lodgings in the town at the home of an unemployed miner in Warrington Lane, but a few days later Orwell moved to a different place at 22 Darlington Street, the address of the tripe-shop and lodging house which he later described in the opening chapter of *The Road to Wigan Pier*. According to Kennan, Orwell took a room there because 'he wanted to see things . . . at their worst'.[10]

As Orwell's diary of the trip confirms, this was indeed a dreadful place. There was no sign that anyone had bothered to clean or dust in ages, and he was told by other lodgers that the supplies of tripe in the cellar were covered with black beetles. After six days in the house, Orwell noted in his diary, 'The squalor of this place is beginning to get on my nerves.'[11] It was on this same day that he was disconcerted to find a full chamberpot under the table at breakfast.

Despite this unwelcome discovery, he kept these lodgings until the end of the month. Fortunately, there were a great many things to occupy his attention elsewhere in Wigan. He spent his days touring the town and the surrounding area, examining housing conditions and interviewing workers. He also spent a substantial amount of time at the Wigan Public Library compiling facts and figures on the coal industry and local unemployment. One fact which he quickly determined was that Wigan Pier – the butt of music-hall jokes for many years – had been demolished, but the story behind it gave some indication of the forlorn condition of the town. As he explained a few years later in a radio broadcast:

Well, I am afraid I must tell you that Wigan Pier doesn't exist. I made a journey specially to see it in 1936, and I couldn't find it. It did exist once . . . At one time, on one of the little muddy canals that run round the town, there used to be a tumble-down wooden jetty; and by way of a joke someone nicknamed this Wigan Pier. The joke caught on locally, and then the music-hall comedians got hold of it, and they are the ones who have succeeded in keeping Wigan Pier alive as a byword, long after the place itself had been demolished.[12]

In the middle of his stay in Wigan he was forced to give valuable time to an unexpected, and irritating, request from Gollancz's very young (aged twenty-nine) Deputy Chairman, Norman Collins. It had nothing to do with his book project in Wigan, but concerned the usual fuss over libel alterations, this time involving the page proofs of *Keep the Aspidistra Flying*. He had made a number of changes in the typescript, at the firm's request, before leaving London, but on 17 February he received a letter from Collins telling him that more were needed. There were some possibly libellous parodies of advertising slogans which required alteration, and there were names of well-known people and companies which needed to be replaced with less recognisable terms. But some of Collins's requests were ridiculously petty: 'Your frequent use of the word "sod". Though this sounds utterly grotesque, I believe that it will chop off a sale of several hundreds to let this word remain, and I would suggest that you change it in every instance to "swine".'[13]

More serious was Collins's fear that Gordon's employer at the bookshop – Mr McKechnie – might resemble too closely Orwell's employer at Booklovers' Corner – Mr Westrope. What particularly concerned Collins was a suggestion in the novel that McKechnie might have a secret drinking problem. In his reply Orwell pointed out that Mr Westrope had been shown the passages describing the fictional bookshop proprietor and had raised no objections.

As I had been working in a bookshop I thought the idea might cross Mr Gollancz's mind that I intended a portrait of my late employer, & for that reason alone I said it might be better if my employer O.K.'d the passages referring to the bookshop. It was not because any portrait was intended, but merely to set Mr Gollancz's mind at rest. In the book 'Mr McKechnie' is described as an old man with white hair & beard who is a teetotaller & takes snuff. My late employer . . . is a middle-aged clean shaven man who is not a teetotaller & never takes snuff. In any case I know him far too well to suppose he would take any action even if he imagined himself to be caricatured. If you really wish I will get him to furnish a written undertaking not to bring a libel action.[14]

Orwell's phrase 'if you really wish' gives a hint of the exasperation which he felt at this last-minute effort to make the book 'safe for both of us', as Collins put it. He refused to cut 'sod', explaining, 'I have used it in all my books before', and he dismissed the objection that it would hurt sales by noting that the word appeared freely in Robert Graves's *Goodbye to All That*, 'which was a best-seller'. He made most of the requested changes, however, even though this put him to considerable trouble. To avoid the expense of resetting type, Collins wanted Orwell to invent new advertising slogans containing the same number of letters as the ones he replaced. This was a nuisance, of course, especially since he was trying to work with the proofs in the less than salubrious atmosphere of his lodgings above the tripe shop. But, more important, he felt that he was being pressured into tampering with his novel in a way that destroyed the delicate balance of his carefully worded prose. In a letter written to Moore on 24 February, he complained bitterly about the process:

> It seems to me to have utterly ruined the book, but if they think it worth publishing in that state, well and good. Why I was annoyed was because they had not demanded these alterations earlier. The book was looked over and O.K.'d by the solicitor as usual, and had they *then* told me that no reminiscence (it was in most cases only a reminiscence, not a quotation) of actual advertisements was allowable, I would have entirely rewritten the first chapter and modified several others. But they asked me to make the alterations when the book was in type and asked me to equalise the letters, which of course could not be done without spoiling whole passages and in one case a whole chapter . . . I would like to get this point clear because I imagine the same trouble is likely to occur again. In general a passage of prose or even a whole chapter revolves round one or two key phrases, and to remove these, as was done in this case, knocks the whole thing to pieces.

Given Orwell's acute appreciation of stylistic matters, it was inevitable that he would object so strongly to this hastily arranged revision. He also resented having to take instructions from Collins, whose youthful arrogance offended him. 'What particularly stuck in my gizzard,' he wrote to Jack Common, 'was that the person who dictated the alterations to me was that squirt Norman Collins.'[15] Gollancz, however, saw nothing wrong with the revisions and went ahead with publication, satisfied that the changes had given him the protection he wanted. Orwell instructed Moore to make certain that any American edition used the unrevised proofs. 'I should like there to be one unmutilated version of it in existence.'[16] Unfortunately, he never had the satisfaction of seeing such an edition. Moore was unable to interest any American publisher in the book, primarily because it was perceived as being 'too British'. Harper's published *A Clergyman's Daughter* in the summer of 1936, but they sold fewer than a thousand copies, and showed no interest in acquiring the rights to *Keep the Aspidistra Flying*. An American edition of the novel would not appear until 1956, six years after his death.

The day that Orwell sent his complaint to Moore was not a good one, and the angry tone of his letter may partly reflect the fact that he was suffering physically. He was in bed trying to recover from the ordeal of inspecting the conditions at the Crippen's coal mine in Wigan. Joe Kennan had taken him on a tour of it. 'It was for me a pretty devastating experience,' he reported to Richard Rees, 'and it is a fearful thought that the labour of crawling as far as the coal face (about a mile in this case but as much as 3 miles in some mines), which was enough to put my legs out of action for four days, is only the beginning and ending of a miner's day's work, and his real work comes in between.'[17] When he had agreed to go down into the mine, he had not realised that he would have to walk such a long way down a tunnel whose roof was only four feet high. 'I had vaguely imagined wandering about in places rather like the tunnels of the Underground,' he wrote in his diary, 'but as a matter of fact there were very few places where you could stand upright.'[18]

It would be difficult to exaggerate the pain this excursion caused him. Because of his great height, he had to walk with his body doubled up as he tried to make his way along the cramped tunnel. The coal dust took its toll on his weak chest, and his head was banged repeatedly by the supporting beams. It is no wonder that he offered such great praise for the miners' sturdy helmets in *The Road to Wigan Pier*, calling them 'a godsend'. After about an hour of walking, he made it to the coal face and was able to observe the huge cutting machines used in the mining operation. But he was just barely able to make the long trip back to the entrance. 'The periodical effort of bending and raising oneself at each successive beam was fearful, and the relief when one could stand upright, usually owing to a hole in the roof, was enormous. At times my knees simply refused to lift me after I had knelt down.'[19] It was in this weary state that he arrived back at the tripe shop to face the task of correcting his page proofs.

He visited a total of three mines during his period in the North, and by the end of his stay he had developed a keen understanding of the dangers which faced the miners in their daily work. There were so many ways to suffer a fatal or crippling accident. Explosions and loose rocks were the common killers, but Orwell seems to have reacted most strongly to the stories he heard concerning cage accidents. Occasionally, as a cage carried a group of men down into a mine, it malfunctioned, and its unfortunate passengers plummeted to their deaths at the bottom of the shaft. One woman told Orwell about a relative who fell twelve hundred feet: 'They wouldn't never have collected t'pieces only he were wearing a new suit of oilskins.'[20]

His research in the public library revealed that miners were suffering a phenomenally high rate of accidents. He learned that nearly eight thousand had died in the mines in the period from 1927 to 1934. He calculated that 'every year one miner in about nine hundred is killed and one in about six is injured'. His research notes have survived, and they include a quotation from one book which pointed out that 'more men are killed and injured in our mines every year than the whole of the casualties sustained by the Gallipoli Expeditionary Force'.[21] To be sure, many of the non-fatal injuries reported by the miners were insignificant compared with the wounds inflicted on the troops in the disastrous Gallipoli campaign. Nevertheless, this reference helped Orwell to see that there was a kind of war being waged in the North – and that only one side was taking casualties.

This impression was reinforced by a small but revealing notation which he found on one miner's pay-checks. A shilling was deducted from the man's pay whenever a fellow miner was killed – the money was contributed to a fund for the widow – but this deduction, or 'stoppage', occurred with such grim regularity that the company used a rubber stamp marked 'Death stoppage' to make the notation on the pay-checks. 'The significant detail here is the *rubber stamp*,' Orwell wrote in *The Road to Wigan Pier*. 'The rate of accidents is so high, compared with that in other trades, that casualties are taken for granted almost as they would be in a minor war.' There is certainly the sense in the book that there are quite a few 'walking wounded' among the men who worked in the mines – the ones, for example, whose lungs and eyes have been damaged by years of exposure to the coal dust. Orwell gives a touching description of a miner whose sight has been destroyed by the dust and whose disability pension is in danger of being cut in half by the coal company.

Of course, the casualties of this 'war' were not only the workers but also their families, who suffered when the fathers were hurt or unemployed. Indeed, Orwell found that some of the families in Wigan were living in conditions as bad as those in a refugee camp. There was an acute housing shortage in the town, and he was shown a 'caravan-colony' on the banks of the 'miry canal' which reminded him of some of the worst slums in Burma. 'But, as a matter of fact, nothing in the East could ever be quite as bad, for in the East you haven't our clammy, penetrating cold to contend with, and the sun is a disinfectant.'[22] The appalling conditions in these tiny caravans are detailed extensively in his research notes: 'Conditions inside these places have to be seen to be grasped. It is almost literally impossible to turn round . . . In one caravan there were a mother, a father, a son and a daughter, the last two round about 18 years old. The mother slept with the daughter and the son with the father –

they were plainly afraid of incest. A question I would have liked to ask, but had not the nerve, was what happens in these places when anyone dies.'[23]

Near the end of February he paid a brief visit to Liverpool, touring the docks and inspecting some poor neighbourhoods, and then in March he spent most of his time in South Yorkshire, staying in Sheffield and Barnsley. He took notes on a communist meeting which he observed in the Market Place of Barnsley, but he dismissed it as 'disappointing' in his diary. The speakers were dull and the small crowd listened quietly with 'expressionless faces'.[24] This was in sharp contrast to a clamorous meeting which he had witnessed a week earlier at the Public Hall. It had drawn a crowd of seven hundred, and had given Orwell the chance to see the dangerous tactics of fascism at work. Oswald Mosley was the principal speaker. He was protected by no fewer than a hundred of the Blackshirts in his British Union of Fascists, who periodically attacked and ejected hecklers in the crowd. In large numbers they were a daunting presence, but Orwell thought that, individually, they were 'weedy-looking specimens'. The speech was initially greeted with a lot of booing. One by one the dissenters were dealt with by the Blackshirts, and by the end of the speech, which lasted an hour and a half, Orwell was dismayed to see that the crowd's mood had shifted in Mosley's favour. He thought that the audience – which was mostly working class – had been 'bamboozled by M speaking from as it were a Socialist angle, condemning the treachery of successive governments towards the workers. The blame for everything was put upon mysterious international gangs of Jews who are said to be financing among other things, the British Labour Party.'[25]

Although he regarded the speech as utter nonsense, he later told a young miner – Tommy Degnan – that he thought the heckling was wrong. He had made Degnan's acquaintance through a contact in Wigan, and had a beer with him after the speech. The young man had been one of those ejected from the hall, and he defended the necessity of disrupting the meeting as the only effective way of undermining Mosley's influence. But Orwell did not like the idea of using tactics which were too much like those of the fascists. According to Degnan, he said, 'You ought to be British, fair play and all that sort of thing.'[26]

Orwell had his own way of dealing with the threat from the Blackshirts. His contemptuous phrase for them in *The Road to Wigan Pier* – 'Mosley and his pimpled followers' – is more damaging than any amount of heckling because it so neatly strips them of their air of invincibility. He hoped that the English people would never be intimidated by such ridiculous troublemakers, and described Mosley as 'a Gilbert and Sullivan heavy dragoon'. But he was also aware that it was too easy to say that the British fascists were a bad joke. 'Mosley will bear watching, for experience shows (*vide* the careers of Hitler, Napoleon III) that to a political climber it is sometimes an advantage not to be taken too seriously at the beginning of his career.'

III

Orwell's two months in the North pushed him closer to socialism. He felt that something urgently needed to be done to even the odds in the economic war which was bringing so much misery to the working people in towns like Wigan. And it was vital that the false appeal of fascism be exposed, before it became stronger and attracted more followers. Whatever he decided to say about his trip, it was obvious that he would have to grapple with these larger issues. He could not simply 'report' on what he had seen, though he had conscientiously accumulated enough 'hard' information to produce the kind of socialist writing which Storm Jameson advocated in *Fact* magazine (July 1937):

> The narrative must be sharp, compressed, concrete ... The emotion should spring directly from the fact. It must not be squeezed from it by the writer, running forward with a, 'When I saw this, I felt, I suffered, I rejoiced ...' His job is not to tell us what he felt, but to be coldly and industriously presenting, arranging, selecting, discarding from the mass of his material to

get the significant detail, which leaves no more to be said, and implies everything.[27]

When Orwell's book came out, various writers on the Left criticised it for failing to let the facts speak for themselves. They charged that he was at fault for putting too much of himself in the narrative, and that the heavily autobiographical Part II was a travesty which tried to shift the reader's attention from the really important social problems to the insignificant life of 'a disillusioned little middle-class boy . . . and late imperialist policeman', as Harry Pollitt called him in the *Daily Worker*.[28] But even his critics could not help admitting that Part I was a powerful piece of work which graphically exposed the plight of the industrial poor. 'The first part of his book is, I think, admirable propaganda for our ideas,' Harold Laski acknowledged in the *Left News*.[29]

It was convenient for his critics to see what they wanted to see, and over the years the book has frequently been portrayed as a misshapen creature with one 'good' section (Part I – a cool, realistic presentation of the facts) and one 'bad' section (Part II – a vague, idiosyncratic discussion of political ideas). Gollancz even took the precaution of issuing Part I as a separate edition, so that the Left could use it for 'propaganda distribution', without having to explain the embarrassing personal comments in the second part. But this distinction between the two sections is simplistic. Orwell's individualism is reflected in every page. And in any case, Part I is not lacking in personal, 'irrelevant' information. A great deal about the author is revealed. It is clear, for example, that he has a deep nostalgia for his pre-war childhood and has a sentimental attachment to the military glory of Britain's past. He likes to think that soldiers were bigger and stronger in his youth. What is the earnest student of socialism to make of his question in Part I, 'Where are the monstrous men with chests like barrels and moustaches like the wings of eagles who strode across my childhood's gaze twenty or thirty years ago?'

Also in Part I, the reader learns that Orwell is haunted by the landscapes of Burma and wrote a novel to exorcise his memories of them. He is prejudiced against the appearance of Sheffield, condemning it with the sweeping description – 'the ugliest town in the Old World'. He thinks that the English 'are exceptionally ignorant' about food and says that a common French labourer's tastes in food are 'civilised' compared with the average Englishman's. The *Manchester Guardian* gave one of his books a bad review, and he has not forgotten it. He hopes that he will produce thirty novels by the time he reaches sixty. He is tall but lacks physical stamina. He likes to garden. He is not afraid to crawl through small tunnels hundreds of feet underground even though he knows that almost a thousand men a year are killed in such places. He prefers not to eat at a table with a full chamberpot under it. And he does not like strangers poking their noses into his private life, and is amazed that people in the North answered his questions with so much patience: 'If any unauthorised person walked into *my* house and began asking me whether the roof leaked and whether I was much troubled by bugs and what I thought of my landlord, I should probably tell him to go to hell.'

Such is the colourful portrait of the author as it is sketched within the supposedly impersonal Part I. It is there to be savoured by readers whose minds are receptive to it. And it is not irrelevant to the larger social concerns. Bare facts and stark passages of description cannot make readers care about the lives of the miners and their families. Their plight moves the reader – an outsider – because it moves another outsider named Orwell. He makes their world come alive. He cares enough about their lives to go among them and find out who they are – as he did with the tramps in London – and his compassion draws out the reader's. As our guide to that world, his personality is important. Everything is seen through his eyes, and for that reason the first priority is to establish a bond with his readers.

He analysed this intimate connection between writer and reader in 'Inside the Whale'. There he explains that the effect of such a connection 'is to break down, at any rate momentarily, the solitude in which the human being dwells'. He felt this effect in his reading of Joyce, and he found it also in the novels of Henry Miller. He had many reservations about Miller's work, but when he discovered it in the early 1930s, he felt an immediate attraction to the writer's voice: 'It is as though you could hear a voice speaking to you, a friendly American voice, with no humbug in it, no moral purpose, merely an implicit assumption that we are all alike. For the moment you have got away from the lies and the simplifications, the stylised marionette-like quality of ordinary fiction . . . and are dealing with recognisable experiences of human beings.' With a few slight changes, this passage might be used to describe the experience of reading Orwell's best work.

The individual sound of Orwell's voice – its character – is crucial to its appeal. It works because it is so recognisable, which is no easy thing to achieve. Open any page of *The Road to Wigan Pier*, and there it is speaking directly to you: 'The earth is so vast and still so empty that even in the filthy heart of civilisation you find fields where the grass is green instead of grey; perhaps if you looked for them you might even find streams with live fish in them instead of salmon tins.' It is very much an educated voice, but there is a common touch to it. It moves easily between two worlds – forging a connection between the busy world of the street and the sedate world of the reader's study.

The trick for the writer is to maintain the right balance between the two worlds. To remain 'inside' and 'outside', he cannot shift very far in either direction. He will embarrass himself and his readers if he becomes too intimate. He will seem cold if he becomes too detached. Orwell found the perfect analogy for his position when he said, in 'Why I Write': 'Good prose is like a window pane.' His voice shapes that window and gives the reader a clear field of view, whether the scene is a Burmese prison yard, the Embankment, Wigan, Barcelona, Manor Farm or Airstrip One.

There is no better illustration of his method than a passage in the first chapter of *The Road to Wigan Pier*. It describes a young woman who is standing at the back of her house trying to unblock a lead waste-pipe with a stick. In his diary he records that he passed her while he was walking along 'a horrible squalid side-alley'.[30] But in his book he makes a subtle alteration to the scene. He frames it in the window of a train which is taking him away from Wigan. The clarity of his prose is stunning, and the 'implicit assumption' of a common bond of humanity is unmistakable:

> She looked up as the train passed, and I was almost near enough to catch her eye. She had a round pale face, the usual exhausted face of the slum girl who is twenty-five and looks forty, thanks to miscarriages and drudgery; and it wore, for the second in which I saw it, the most desolate, hopeless expression I have ever seen. It struck me then that we are mistaken when we say that 'It isn't the same for them as it would be for us,' and that people bred in the slums can imagine nothing but the slums . . . She knew well enough what was happening to her – understood as well as I did how dreadful a destiny it was to be kneeling there in the bitter cold, on the slimy stones of a slum backyard, poking a stick up a foul drain-pipe.

This woman's world is not his, and he cannot pretend to be a part of it. 'Though I was among them,' he says of the coal miners, 'and I hope and trust they did not find me a nuisance, I was not one of them, and they knew it even better than I did.'[31] But it is not necessary to be *like* them in order to be on their side. 'It is a question of sticking to essentials,' he states in Part II of *The Road to Wigan Pier*, 'and the essential point here is that all people with small, insecure incomes are in the same boat and ought to be fighting on the same side. Probably we could do with a little less talk about "capitalist" and "proletarian" and a little more about the robbers and the robbed.' Socialism offers a way for the robbed to protect themselves from the robbers, but it can work only if its base of support is broad. The miner and the London typist may live in different worlds, but they have certain interests in common, and when they recognise their bond, then there is a chance for change to occur. 'The people who have got to act together are all those who cringe to the boss and all those who shudder when they think of the rent. This means that the small-holder has got to ally himself with the factory-hand, the typist with the coal-miner, the schoolmaster with the garage mechanic. There is some hope of getting them to do so if they can be made to understand where their interest lies.'

Like everything else in his book, Orwell's approach to socialism is individualistic. He wants to be part of a collective effort, but he always wants to be free to speak his mind, to disagree with colleagues, to read what he wants, to go where he wants to go. He does not want to be a statistic in someone else's master plan. He advocates a classless society, yet he fears losing his own distinct identity as a son of the middle-class. He wants to be part of a new social order, but not if it means that he will become faceless, voiceless. 'I cannot proletarianise my accent or certain of my tastes and beliefs, and I would not if I could. Why should I? I don't ask anybody else to speak my dialect; why should anybody else ask me to speak his?'

Almost all of his doubts about established socialist thinking are related to what he perceived to be its tendency to encourage conformity, and its preoccupation with centralised planning. He mocks those socialists whose 'desire, basically, is to reduce the world to something resembling a chess board'. He dreads the thought of poverty being 'abolished *from above*', and worries that the powerful, 'clever' few in the movement will covet power for its own sake and construct a rigid, self-serving ideology. And this is where he gets into trouble. By refusing to spell out a narrow set of socialist principles – making instead a plea for a broad-based movement which encourages dissent – he opens himself to the charge that he is hopelessly vague and unrealistic. Gollancz himself criticised his author for advocating an '*emotional* Socialism' when what was clearly needed was a workable 'scientific Socialism' (the phrases are Gollancz's).[32]

But Orwell could not accept the notion that the messy business of human life could be managed so neatly, and he saw little hope for socialism's future if its supporters were burdened with a weighty load of ideological baggage. The situation was too urgent for that. 'The Socialist movement has not time to be a league of dialectical materialists, it has got to be a league of the oppressed against the oppressors.' If anything was unrealistic, it was the ideologue's intransigence: 'Sometimes, when I listen to these people talking, and still more when I read their books, I get the impression that, to them, the whole Socialist movement is no more than a kind of exciting heresy-hunt – a leaping to and fro of frenzied witch-doctors to the beat of tom-toms and the tune of "Fee, fi, fo, fum, I smell the blood of a right-wing deviationist!" '

Right-wing he may not have been, but 'deviationist' certainly fits him. Though they are a troublesome lot, every movement needs its deviationists. The trouble is that they are forever raising questions for which there are no easy answers. They can be irritating characters, and their doubts may often be exaggerated or unfounded. There is no denying that some of Orwell's remarks are vague and inconsistent, and that some are unfair. He does nothing to help his cause when he launches into an intemperate attack on the people whom he considers socialist 'cranks' – 'all that dreary tribe of high-minded women and sandal-wearers and bearded fruit-juice drinkers who come flocking towards the smell of "progress" like bluebottles to a dead cat'. Yet there is also a great deal which is relevant and just in Part II, and which deserves to be taken seriously. In any case, what good is a movement which cannot abide such criticisms as he offers? During his five years in Burma, Orwell lived under a system in which he had been made to feel that any dissent was equivalent to an act of betrayal. He did not want to be in that position again. As he said in the 1940s, 'If liberty means anything at all it means the right to tell people what they do not want to hear.'[33]

In terms of Orwell's career, what is so extraordinary about *The Road to Wigan Pier* is its startling revelation of the author's intense engagement with complex political questions. If *A Clergyman's Daughter* and *Keep the Aspidistra Flying* were all that one knew of his work, it would be difficult to believe that he wrote *The Road to Wigan Pier* immediately after these two self-conscious literary efforts. Even *Down and Out in Paris and London* and *Burmese Days* do not prepare one for the high level of achievement which he attains in his first major attempt 'to make political writing into an art'. It was a revelation even to some of his closest friends. Richard Rees remembered how much the achievement amazed him when he read the book for the first time. 'This book, *The Road to Wigan Pier*, was something of a sensation . . . Up till then he had been groping, and it would have been possible to read *Keep the Aspidistra* as a sign that he was in a cul-de-sac. But in *The Road to Wigan Pier*, besides revealing what he had seen in the mining towns of the north, he began to reveal his true self.'[34]

IV

Orwell was not a complete alien in the North. His sister Marjorie, her husband Humphrey Dakin, and their three children lived in Leeds, and he stayed at their home for almost a week in early March 1936 between his visits to Sheffield and Barnsley. He had spent some time with them in the early Thirties, so this was not his first trip to the area. Although he never got along well with Humphrey, he and Marjorie were still close, and her children liked him, though they regarded him as a curious, mostly silent character who seemed never to be without a book in his hand. His niece Jane recalled one family expedition in their father's small car with Orwell squeezed into the back seat, his knees high in the air, and a book of French poetry propped near his face. Absorbed in the book, he was oblivious to the noise and squirming of the children as the car rattled along the road.

The family home in Leeds was a comfortable middle-class house and Orwell had a room to himself. When he stayed there in 1936, he was reminded that one of the disadvantages of life in a crowded slum dwelling was the lack of 'elbow-room'. If he wanted privacy, he could easily have it in the Dakin home. But as he noted in his diary, it was impossible for many poor families to enjoy such a basic privilege. During this visit Marjorie and Humphrey took him on a short outing to see the Brontë home at Haworth (what fascinated Orwell most was a display of Charlotte Brontë's cloth-topped boots, which seemed tiny to him), and there was also another short trip the next day to the Dakins' small rented cottage at Middlesmoor, 'high up on the edge of the moors', as Orwell later described it. Afterwards, he noted in his diary that even this relatively isolated spot seemed tainted by factory pollution.

'Perhaps it is only the time of year, but even up there, miles from any industrial towns, the smoky look peculiar to this part of the country seems to hang about anything. Grass dull-coloured, streams muddy, houses all blackened as though by smoke.'[35]

On 30 March Orwell finished his work in the North and returned to London, but he did not go back to his old job at Booklovers' Corner nor did he look for another flat. He took one day to gather his belongings, and to pay Eileen a visit, and then he left on another journey. But this was a short one. His destination was a small village thirty-five miles north of London. He had been hoping for some months to find a place in the country where he could live cheaply, have a bit of garden, and perhaps keep a few chickens and goats. He had also been hoping that, if he found such a place, he would soon be sharing it with Eileen. She was planning to finish her degree at University College in the summer. They were still talking about marriage, but nothing had been settled. In February, however, some friends had told him of a seventeenth-century cottage in Hertfordshire which was available at the extraordinarily low rent of 7s 6d a week (less than two pounds a month). Without even bothering to inspect the place, he had made the necessary arrangements to rent it, and on 1 April he moved in. The address was 'The Stores, Wallington'.

The cottage belonged to a Mr Dearman who had purchased it a few years earlier from a firm called Agrar Ltd., which had operated a general store and Post Office in the front room. The shop had been closed for a year when Orwell arrived, but part of the attraction of the place was the idea that he would revive the business. There was no other shop in Wallington – it had only thirty-four houses, two pubs, and a church – but Orwell liked the notion of becoming the village grocer, and thought that the business might produce a modest profit. His plan was to keep a schedule similar to his bookshop hours – he would open the shop in the afternoons only, and leave his mornings free for writing. At the same time that he was making preparations to launch his new enterprise, he began writing *The Road to Wigan Pier*, intending to finish it by the end of the year.

Besides the front room, the ground floor included a sitting-room – which he used as a study – and a small kitchen with a little oil oven. Two bedrooms were upstairs, and were reached by a dark, twisting stairway made of elm. The front door was quaint, but uncomfortably low. It was just under four feet high. When the landlord bought the place, its thatched roof was badly in need of repair, but he had cut costs by replacing it with corrugated iron sheeting. In addition to its ugliness, the new roof produced an awful racket in thunderstorms. The chimney was also defective and smoked badly, but nothing had been done to fix it.

The surrounding countryside was pleasant, with gently rolling hills. There was a small pond not more than a hundred yards from his door, and near it was the farm to which his cottage had once belonged. Agrar had been forced to sell both The Stores and the farm after going bankrupt in the 1920s. As Orwell knew, the firm had tried to run the place as a 'model farm', but hard economic times had doomed the effort and the losses were so great that they had been forced to abandon their idealistic project. The name of the farm at which this failed experiment in advanced agricultural methods took place was Manor Farm.[36]

Life at the cottage was not easy. He had a bicycle but no car, and the nearest town was Baldock, almost three miles away. The cottage had no electricity, no hot tap-water, and no indoor lavatory. The primitive contraption in the back garden was so temperamental that unless the proper paper was used the cesspool backed up 'with disastrous results', Orwell discovered. When Jack Common was looking after the place in his friend's absence during the late 1930s, he was advised to avoid thick paper. Only one brand could be relied on, Orwell confided. 'The best to use is Jeyes paper which is 6d. a packet. The difference of price is negligible, and on the other hand a choked cesspool is a misery.'[37]

Orwell did his best to make the front room presentable, and on 11 May he opened his shop. There was not much to it – a counter, a bacon slicer, some scales, a few shelves, and some containers for sugar, flour and other staples. His best customers were the village children who came in regularly to buy sweets. By the end of his first month in business, he was satisfied to be selling about thirty shillings of merchandise a week. His profit from that was just enough to cover his rent. When no one was in the shop, he retired to his study and read or wrote letters. There was no bell at the entrance, but he could see whether anyone had come in by looking through four squint holes which he had cut in the door of his study. He did not mind the interruptions. 'It is very little trouble & no hanging about like in a bookshop,' he remarked in the first month of business. 'In a grocer's shop people come in to buy something, in a bookshop they come in to make a nuisance of themselves.'[38] When Cyril Connolly paid him a visit later in the year, he pointed out another advantage of the business: whereas selling books had made him more anxious about writing them, selling groceries posed no such threat. As Connolly recalled, 'He didn't have that same ambivalent feeling that he ought to be creating the groceries, not selling them.'[39]

During the early part of that spring, booksellers were able to offer a new product from George Orwell's pen. On 20 April Gollancz published *Keep the Aspidistra Flying* with a first printing of three thousand copies. It did not do well. Only 2,194 were sold, and some of the reviews were quite bad. William Plomer called it 'crude' in the *Spectator*, and even Cyril Connolly felt compelled to make some unfavourable comments about it in the *New Statesman*. He thought that in comparison with *Burmese Days*, it was distinctly inferior: 'The writer of *Burmese Days* was ... fond of Burma and included many beautiful descriptions of it, while the writer of *Keep the Aspidistra Flying* hates London and everything there. Hence the realism of one book was redeemed by an operating sense of beauty, that of the other is not.'[40]

It did not please Connolly to make this criticism of the novel, and he wrote Orwell a conciliatory letter soon after the review appeared. 'I hope you weren't disappointed with my review of the Aspidistra; I felt that it needed more colour to relieve the total gloom of the hero's circumstances & self-hatred – there must be jam if people are to swallow the pill because otherwise they choke.' Connolly had already arranged for a copy of his novel – *The Rock Pool* – to be sent to Orwell for review, and he more or less invited him to attack it. 'You can have your innings. I think [*The Rock Pool!* is] lousy myself.'[41] In response to this, Orwell produced one of his most memorable reviews, giving his old friend some odd compliments, as well as some rather stringent criticism.

He wrote the review for Philip Mairet's *New English Weekly*, and it came out later that summer. The opening sentence is a gem of overstatement. 'As Mr Cyril Connolly is almost the only novel reviewer in England who does not make me sick, I opened this, his first novel, with a lively interest.' More common praise followed this ('the treatment is mature and skilful'), but then the attack came, and its brief intensity suggests that Orwell was aiming at something besides Connolly's little novel about a group of decadent expatriates in the South of France. 'The awful thraldom of money is upon everyone and there are only three immediately obvious escapes. One is religion, another is unending work, the third is the kind of sluttish antinomianism – lying in bed till four in the afternoon, drinking Pernod – that Mr Connolly seems to admire. The third is certainly the worst, but in any case the essential evil is to think in terms of *escape.*'[42] This is another version of the simple choice given to Gordon Comstock – 'Either surrender or don't surrender.' Orwell had made his choice, and was defending it, using Connolly's novel about a world devoted to pleasure as one way to denounce any effort to escape from social responsibility.

As for his friendship with Connolly, it survived this attack easily. Connolly knew that Orwell was sincere, and he knew that the shots aimed in his direction were meant for bigger targets. He also understood that political concerns had become an obsession with Orwell, and he knew – perhaps as well as anyone – how strong Orwell's obsessions could be. In the 1960s he wrote, 'Orwell was a political animal ... His line may have been unpopular or unfashionable, but he followed it unhesitatingly; in fact it was an obsession. He could not blow his nose without moralising on conditions in the handkerchief industry.'[43]

The poor reception given *Keep the Aspidistra Flying* did not surprise Orwell. Despite his high hopes for the novel when he began writing it, he quickly came to regard it as a book which belonged in the same category as *A Clergyman's Daughter* – 'a silly potboiler'.[44] This was unfair, but it was clearly not the kind of novel which he wanted to write in the future, and he thought it best to put it out of his mind. It will always have a certain appeal both as an autobiographical work, and as a perceptive portrait of 'a man at the end of his tether' – to use a phrase applied to Gordon by one of the book's admirers, Anthony Powell. In fact, when he first read the novel in 1936, Powell liked it so much that he wrote its author 'a fan letter'. Later, in the early 1940s, they became friends, but Orwell's reply to that 'fan letter' is worth noting at this stage in his career because of his comment on reviewers: 'I prefer the ones who lose their temper & call me names to the silly asses who mean so well & never bother to discover what you are writing about.'[45]

CHAPTER THIRTEEN

Foreign and Domestic

I

Orwell's American publishers, Harper & Brothers, rarely wrote to him. They usually got in touch when they wanted some publicity material. 'Dear Mr Orwell,' one of their letters began, 'We are aware that requests for publicity notes and new photographs for use in connection with books published in America may prove an annoyance, but the custom of the American literary pages run so much in this direction that we venture to urge you to send us all such material so that we may give your work as much help as possible.'[1] Such a long-winded sentence should have elicited a short reply, but when the letter arrived in April 1936, Orwell was in a mood to be forthcoming about his life. He was even prepared to present himself as a modestly happy, slightly offbeat English author whose manner of living might strike Americans as 'picturesque'. He consulted his agent about the wisdom of this approach: 'Would it be considered a picturesque detail to say that George Orwell is just setting up a village "general" shop in Hertfordshire?' Of course, such an image would indeed work well with American readers, who could sit back in Milwaukee or Denver and imagine the author waiting on the gentle village folk in a neat little shop with a slate roof and a bow window framed in ivy. But there was one more detail which he wanted to add – namely, that the grocer was 'thinking very seriously about getting married'.[2]

He did not have to think about it for very long. His reply to

Harper's was made in early May; a month later he and Eileen were married. On 9 June they walked the short distance to the parish church of Wallington, where the Rev. J. H. Woods married them 'according to the Rites and Ceremonies of the Church of England'. Although he joked earlier in the day that he was 'steeling' himself 'against the obscenities of the wedding service', this was precisely the service he wanted.[3] To be married in a village church satisfied his desire to honour traditional English values. His parents and Avril came over from Southwold for the ceremony, and Eileen was accompanied by her mother, and by Laurence O'Shaughnessy and his wife. Interestingly, in the column marked 'Rank or Profession' on the marriage certificate, Eric Arthur Blair ('33, bachelor') proudly identified himself as 'Author', whereas Eileen Maud O'Shaughnessy ('30, spinster') merely drew a line through the space.

Eileen had left University College without finishing the MA degree which she had worked on for the past two years. All of the requirements had been met except for the writing of her thesis. She had chosen the subject for it – 'the use of imagination in school essays' – but in order to do the research she needed to spend time interviewing a fair number of schoolchildren. This would have been simple enough in London, but there were problems in Wallington. The nearest school was three miles away, and she had no car. Buses came through the village, but only on two days of the week. When she accepted Orwell's proposal, she may have told herself that she would find some way to finish her studies, but after she moved to the village, she stopped working on the thesis and never completed her degree.

Her ambitious, hard-working brother must have wondered why she was throwing away a chance at a good career in order to live in a primitive cottage, far from any major towns, with an 'author' who wanted to be a shopkeeper and whose literary earnings were modest and insecure. In fact, Orwell had been worried about the reactions to their marriage from both their families, and had feared at one point that they might 'combine against us in some way & prevent it'. He knew that their decision might appear 'rash', but he and Eileen had reached the conclusion that if they waited for the perfect time to marry, they might wait for ever.[4] Some of Eileen's friends certainly thought that she was making a mistake, but her decision did not surprise them. 'Eileen was a dreamer,' her friend Margaret Branch recalled. 'To marry Orwell and share his curious lifestyle at Wallington, she had to have a streak of mystical dream.'[5] Even Orwell's own mother thought that Eileen might have acted rashly. At the wedding Mrs Blair took her aside and said, 'You *are* taking on something!'[6]

The wedding made Orwell happy. His lighthearted mood at the time can be seen in a letter he wrote a few hours before the ceremony. By coincidence, he had received that day a letter from his old schoolfriend Denys King-Farlow. Like Connolly, King-Farlow had not seen Orwell since they had been at Eton together, and he was curious about his friend's decision to adopt a pseudonym. In his reply Orwell agreed that they should meet soon, but he took obvious delight in explaining why he was not free to pay anyone a visit right away: 'Like the chap in the *NT* I have married a wife and therefore I cannot come. Curiously enough I am getting married this very morning – in fact I am writing this with one eye on the clock and the other on the Prayer Book.'[7]

King-Farlow waited for a few weeks before he contacted Orwell again, and was pleased to receive in response an invitation to visit The Stores. He drove to the village one Sunday and Orwell greeted him warmly when he arrived. King-Farlow's first impression, after fifteen years apart, was similar to Connolly's. He thought Orwell had aged a lot, and he was surprised to see how thin he had become. When they had known each other at school, Orwell's cheeks had been full, 'something like a hamster's', but on that Sunday in 1936 he looked more like a 'scarecrow' – very tall and almost painfully thin. But the one thing which had not changed was Orwell's 'pale, china-blue eyes'. They still had a mischievous, amused look.

King-Farlow was impressed with Eileen, whom he found attractive and friendly. She served their lunch and proudly offered some pickles which she and Orwell had made together. After their meal, he went for a long walk with Orwell, who at one point confided that he had recently tried an unusual activity – prison visiting. Having served in the Imperial Police, he found it easy to secure official permission for such visits, and it may be that he was planning to write a book on the subject (a sort of 'Road to Newgate'). But the results of his first visit dampened his enthusiasm for inside views of prisoners' lives. He had been taken to the cell of a mild-mannered, middle-aged man, and had spent some uncomfortable minutes trying to draw the prisoner into conversation. He tried to begin with innocent topics, commenting on such things as football and the weather, but the man said little in return. Exasperated, he took a direct approach, asking the man why he had been sent to prison. The reply was prompt, 'Oh, for having carnal knowledge of my three infant daughters.' This answer left Orwell so flustered that he quickly put an end to the visit. 'Really, what was there that I could say after that?' he remarked to King-Farlow.[8]

If he had really wanted to continue his research, nothing would have stopped him. But there were more promising ideas in his head. Of course, the job of writing *The Road to Wigan Pier* was his main concern, and he made excellent progress on it that summer. He did find time, however, to do one of his 'sketches' and to send it to *New Writing*, John Lehmann's excellent magazine. He appears to have written the piece in a period of only two weeks, finishing the typescript just three days after his wedding day. Lehmann had written to him in May inviting him to submit some of his work to the magazine. He replied that he was busy trying to finish his book, but he said that there was something else which he might be able to finish in the near future. 'I have in mind . . . a sketch, (it would be abt 2000–3000 words), describing the shooting of an elephant. It all came back to me very vividly the other day & I would like to write it, but it may be that it is quite out of your line. I mean it might be too low brow for your paper & I doubt whether there is anything anti-Fascist in the shooting of an elephant.'

If Orwell had written a plain tale of the Raj, it would indeed have been out of place in Lehmann's magazine, which was publishing the latest works of the 'Auden generation'. But Lehmann knew enough about Orwell to understand that the sketch might be an uncommon piece of work, and he asked to see the piece. If he had said no, it might never have been written. 'Of course you can't say in advance that you would like it,' Orwell wrote to him, 'but perhaps you could say tentatively whether it is at all likely to be in your line or not. If not, then I won't write it.'[9] Although it was apparently done very quickly, and with little forethought, 'Shooting an Elephant' is not unconnected to the work he was doing in *The Road to Wigan Pier*. Part II of that work includes a long passage on his life in Burma, providing a context for his interest in the struggle between the oppressed and their oppressors. As he explains in the book, the road to Wigan began for him in Mandalay. So the sudden appearance of his brilliant sketch – long after he had written 'A Hanging' and *Burmese Days* – is not as surprising as it might seem. Lehmann had no doubts about accepting it, and published it in the autumn issue of his magazine.

When Eileen married George, she knew how important his writing was to him, so she was probably not surprised to see him rushing to finish 'Shooting an Elephant' in the first few days of their marriage. In fact, she may have helped to type it. She wanted to help him with his work, just as she had helped her brother with his. But she did not have to look for things to keep her busy. Much of her time was occupied by her work in the shop, and by her efforts to make the cottage more comfortable and to impose some order on its unruly garden. When Orwell first arrived at The Stores, he began digging away in the garden, saying that it was in an 'unspeakable state'. It was cluttered with all kinds of junk, including a great many tin cans and no fewer than twelve boots. What these boots were doing there is anyone's guess. With Eileen's help, conditions soon improved.

He was always proud of the flower bushes and fruit trees which they planted at the cottage that year. They put in some apple and plum trees, some gooseberry bushes and some rose bushes. The prize of the lot was a rambler rose which cost him only sixpence at Woolworth's, but which grew rapidly and produced 'a beautiful little white rose with a yellow heart'. When Orwell came back to the cottage after a long absence in the 1940s, he saw that the rambler 'had grown into a huge vigorous bush', and was so satisfied with the result that he wrote about it in his 'As I Please' column in *Tribune*. Some anonymous ideological purist of the Left wrote him an 'indignant letter' complaining 'that roses are bourgeois'. Orwell was unrepentant, telling *Tribune* readers, 'I still think that my sixpence was better spent than if it had gone on cigarettes or even on one of the excellent Fabian Research Pamphlets.'[10]

Orwell and Eileen were not the most efficient shopkeepers in England, but they never actually lost money, and both of them seemed to have enjoyed the thought that they were providing a service to the villagers, who otherwise would not have had any shop at all. Even in slow periods when the weekly sales dipped precariously low, Eileen took comfort from the fact that there was usually some sort of profit for them. When one of her friends expressed doubts about the venture, she had a quick response, 'But we get our groceries at wholesale prices.' The village children developed a special fondness for her, partly because she always gave them generous bargains when they came in to buy sweets. But she showed her generosity in other ways as well. When she discovered that a village boy of ten was unable to read, she took upon herself the job of teaching him and was successful. She prepared him so well that he was soon accepted by a local grammar school. According to Lydia Jackson, this made her 'as proud . . . as if he were her own son'.[11]

In August Orwell made a brief excursion to Essex, where he attended the *Adelphi* summer school held at John Middleton Murry's retreat in Langham. He had been invited to give a talk, and he had decided, reasonably enough, to speak on his recent investigations of life in the North. The text of his speech has been lost, but a programme leaflet has survived and reveals that his title emphasised his position as an observer trying to understand a world to which he did not belong. Presented on 4 August 1936, his talk was called 'An Outsider Sees the Depressed Areas'.[12] Richard Rees recalled that Orwell also participated in some of the political discussions at the school, and was impressive in a debate with some Marxists. 'Without any parade of learning he produced breathtaking Marxist paradoxes and epigrams, in such a way as to make the sacred mysteries seem almost too obvious and simple.'[3]

In early October he managed to finish a draft of his book, and was tentatively calling it 'On the Road to Wigan Pier'. He was confident that he would complete his revisions by December. But in this instance he was not merely trying to meet a publishing deadline. There was something more important urging him on. Earlier that summer he had been excited by the news that Spanish workers had taken up arms to oppose General Franco's revolt against the nation's elected government. The conflict seemed to hold out the hope that the fascist movement in Europe might finally suffer a serious set-back. Up to this point the fascist powers had been enjoying a long string of fairly easy successes, including Mussolini's conquest of Abyssinia and Hitler's reoccupation of the Rhineland. 'When the fighting broke out on 18 July,' Orwell later wrote of the Spanish Civil War, 'it is probable that every anti-Fascist in Europe felt a thrill of hope.'[4] Orwell decided that he would finish *The Road to Wigan Pier* as soon as possible, and then go to Spain to witness the fighting, and possibly to take part in it.

There is no indication that Eileen tried to dissuade him. On the contrary, she shared his strong feelings about the war and wanted to go with him. As it happened, she stayed behind for only two months before making the journey to Spain. He was ready to go in mid-December. On the fifteenth he sent the typescript of his book to his agent and announced that he was leaving England just before Christmas. He was not certain what reaction Gollancz might have to the book, but he was so anxious to reach Spain that he did not want to waste time waiting for his publisher to go through the usual agonies over libel and obscenity questions. He gave Eileen complete authority to deal with any problems which might arise in his absence, and asked Moore to see whether Gollancz could give some response to the book before Christmas.

A meeting between publisher and author did take place on 21 December, and Gollancz agreed to publish the book in a normal trade edition, but he did not say whether it would appear as a monthly selection in his increasingly popular Left Book Club. This was not a minor point. A first printing of the trade edition might run to two or three thousand copies, but if the Left Book Club issued it, the printing would be in the tens of thousands. Gollancz had launched the club in May 1936, advertising it as a 'service' to readers 'who desire to play an intelligent part in the struggle *for* World Peace and a better social and economic order, and *against* Fascism'. One new book in limp orange covers was sent to members each month at the very modest price of 2s. 6d. The membership stood at twelve thousand after the first month of its existence, but this figure had soared to forty-four thousand by the time Orwell completed his book.[15]

Gollancz had never made any commitment to publish Orwell's book as a club selection, and when it was submitted, the author himself admitted that 'the chances of Gollancz choosing it as a Left Book Club selection are small, as it is too fragmentary and, on the surface, not very left-wing'.[16] Strictly speaking, the final approval for any selection was made by the three people who formed the club's editorial committee – Gollancz, Harold Laski, and John Strachey – so Gollancz could not make a firm commitment until his colleagues had seen the book.

When Orwell left England on 23 December, he was still in doubt about the club's decision, and the final word did not reach him for many weeks. It was not until early February that Moore was able to get a definite answer. He passed it along to Eileen, who replied excitedly, 'The news that the book is definitely chosen for the Left Book Club is splendid.'[17] Because of this one decision, *The Road to Wigan Pier* enjoyed better sales than all of Orwell's previous books combined. It was published in March 1937, and sold forty-four thousand copies in the Left Book Club edition, two thousand in the trade edition, and an additional nine hundred copies in a special edition of Part I intended for 'propaganda distribution'.

If Orwell had removed Part II from the book and had submitted instead a longer version of Part I, there would never have been any doubt about its acceptability for the club. But Part II's persistent questioning of socialist ideas – as Orwell perceived them – made the book very difficult for Gollancz to accept. The publisher knew that many of the club's members would object to it, but he also realised that Part I was an immensely powerful statement against the exploitation of workers. His solution to the problem was to attach a Foreword to the club edition explaining what was correct in its approach and what was incorrect. It was not enough to say that the book reflected the author's views rather than those of the club's editorial board. Gollancz went beyond that reasonable precaution; he wanted to refute Orwell's controversial points before the members encountered them. If he had wanted to provide only a rejoinder, he could have written an Afterword.

Some of his criticisms are specific, and not without merit but, overall, it is a smug, condescending attack. The most damaging aspect of it is his sweeping attempt to imply that Orwell's book is riddled with misconceptions. 'I had, in point of fact, marked well over a hundred minor passages about which I thought I should like to argue with Mr Orwell in this Foreword; but I find now that if I did so the space that I have set aside would be quickly used up, and I should wear out my readers' patience.' What possible response could be made to such a vague indictment? Even the possibility of a response is pre-empted by the suggestion that a detailed discussion would bore the reader. But as Gollancz well knew, his author was in no position to give a timely response. When the book was published, Orwell – whom Gollancz rebukes for failing to recognise the proper way 'to defeat Fascism' – was in a muddy trench on a remote hilltop in Spain dodging sniper fire from a fascist army.[18]

II

When Orwell went to Spain, he was not certain that he would fight. He lacked neither courage nor conviction, but he doubted whether he had the stamina or the skill to be a good soldier. And because of the chronic weakness of his lungs, he suspected that he would be turned down for health reasons if he tried to enlist. But he did not rule out joining one of the Spanish political militias if it became clear that they could use him. In the meantime he decided that the best way to serve the cause was to observe the war and write about it for the *New Statesman* or for some other English paper sympathetic to the Republican government.

He had been told that he would not be permitted to enter Spain without some supporting documents from a British left-wing organisation. As he learned later, this warning was inaccurate, but he did not want to take the chance that he would be turned away at the frontier, so he sought the assistance of the one left-wing organisation in London whose name would mean something to even the most backward Spanish border guard. He went to the British Communist Party. He managed to put his request directly to its chief, Harry Pollitt. They had never met, but Pollitt seems to have taken an immediate dislike to him. He must have smelled the blood of a 'right-wing deviationist' when Orwell walked into his office because he began to question him very carefully and soon concluded that his visitor was 'politically unreliable'.[19] He refused to help him and ended their interview. It was a distinctly unpleasant meeting, and Pollitt's memory of it may have caused him to launch his highly personal attack on Orwell three months later, in his *Daily Worker* review of *The Road to Wigan Pier*. Not only did he dismiss the writer as a 'disillusioned middle-class boy', but he also ridiculed him for daring to speak out on a 'subject that he does not understand'.[20]

After the hostile reception given him by Pollitt, Orwell tele-phoned the headquarters of the Independent Labour Party, and its officials readily agreed to help him. He was given a letter of introduction to the ILP's Barcelona representative, John McNair. With this matter settled, he was ready to set off for Spain. After saying goodbye to Eileen, he began his journey, travelling first to Paris, where he paid a brief visit to Henry Miller, who told him that the idea of going to Spain was 'sheer stupidity'. Why get involved in someone else's fight? Miller asked. In 1940 Orwell recalled their meeting and the 'forcible' way in which Miller had advocated the merits of selfishness and political indifference. Although he admired Miller's direct, uninhibited style of writing, he was dismayed to find him so shamelessly 'irresponsible'. He was still brooding over the question in 1940, but by that point he would have a striking image to associate with Miller's position, seeing him as a 'willing Jonah' comfortably riding out storms in the warm belly of the whale. 'There you are, in the dark, cushioned space that exactly fits you, with yards of blubber between yourself and reality, able to keep up an attitude of the completest indifference, no matter *what* happens.'[21].

From Paris, Orwell travelled to the Spanish border on a night train packed with men who were going to join the fighting. There were many Frenchmen, but there were also Czechs, Germans, and other nationalities. In the morning, as the train rolled slowly across southern France, Orwell was heartened to see so many workers stopping in the fields to stand at attention and salute the train as it passed. 'They were like a guard of honour,' he recalled in 1944, 'greeting the train mile after mile.'[22] At the border, the Spanish guards seemed pleased with his letter from the ILP, but as he remarked later, the guards were mostly anarchists and ordinarily paid little attention to the documents they were shown. The casual manner of the soldiers and their evident lack of proper equipment and training boosted his opinion of his own qualifications for service. The government was being defended by a disorganised group of political militias, and the quality of the troops varied enormously. Some units were little more than loose gangs of ragged boys in their early teens. 'After one glimpse of the troops in Spain I saw that I had relatively a lot of training as a soldier and decided to join the militia.'[23]

Orwell wanted to join the International Brigade, but after the ILP had gone to the trouble of issuing him a letter of introduction, he felt obliged to go to Barcelona first and meet the party's representative. He found John McNair in an office at the Executive Building of the POUM (the Workers' Party of Marxist Unification). The ILP was affiliated with this independent socialist group, and part of McNair's job was to co-ordinate efforts to give it assistance – financial and otherwise. As the result of an ILP fundraising campaign in England, the POUM had received almost £10,000, as well as an ambulance and a planeload of medical supplies. A contingent of ILP military volunteers was also preparing to go out to Spain to serve in the POUM militia.

'I'm looking for a chap named John McNair,' Orwell said, standing at the door of the office. McNair did not like the sound of the voice addressing him. A Tynesider who had left school at the age of twelve, he was put off by the sudden appearance of this 'great, big, tall chap who spoke with a very pronounced Etonian accent'. Instead of replying nicely, 'I am he', McNair said in his roughest Tyneside accent, 'A 'am yer man.'

Orwell gave him the letter from the ILP, and when McNair realised that his visitor was the author George Orwell, his attitude changed. He had read both *Burmese Days* and *Down and Out in Paris and London*, and had been impressed by them. When he asked what he could do to help, the reply came back, 'I've come to fight against fascism.'

'You're not a Stalinist?' McNair asked.

'No.'

'Then you can join either the CNT or the POUM.'

'I'll join the POUM.'

'You can join the POUM today.'[24]

McNair took him immediately to the Lenin Barracks, which was the military headquarters of the POUM. It was an enormous complex built in an elegant classical style, with wide archways and spacious cobbled courtyards. It had been a cavalry barracks, but the militia had seized it during the July fighting and had mounted a giant portrait of Lenin in the archway over the main gate. Orwell was introduced to the division commander, Jose Rovira, and was told that he would be sent to the Aragon front as soon as more recruits were available to form a fresh *centuria* – a company of a hundred men.

He spent a week at the barracks, but he received no meaningful training while he was there. There were not enough rifles to arm the recruits, so their days were devoted primarily to simple parade-ground drills. Orwell had been through all these routines many times before, beginning with the Cadet Corps at St Cyprian's, and considered them a waste of time. But he was asked to lead some of the drills, and did his best to instil a sense of discipline in the young troops. When McNair came back to check on him the next day, he found him dressed in khaki trousers and a sweater drilling a group of recruits. As he and Rovira watched the tall Englishman patiently trying to instruct the Spanish boys, the division commander declared enthusiastically, 'If we had a hundred men like him we would win the war.'[25]

There was no lack of enthusiasm among the POUM leaders, but their troops were ill-prepared to fight a war against fascist soldiers whose weapons and training were generally superior. Hitler and Mussolini helped Franco by sending 'volunteers' and large shipments of arms and other equipment, but the only major source of supply for the Republic was the Soviet Union, and Stalin was selective in his support of the political militias. He expected absolute obedience in return for his support, and the POUM's brand of Marxism did not conform to his dictates. Consequently, the party's members were branded 'Trotskyists', and Soviet agents in Spain spread rumours that the party was 'Franco's Fifth Column'. Its failure to follow Moscow's lead was used as evidence that it was trying to divide Republican forces so that Franco could take advantage of the weakness.

When he joined the POUM, Orwell had no idea that its credibility was being undermined by Stalin's machinations. He was under the impression that one militia was more or less the same as the next, and that they were united by the common goal of defeating the fascists. If he had stayed in Barcelona for a few weeks, he would have realised how complicated the situation was, but he left for the front at the beginning of January and remained there for almost four months. As far as he could tell from his one week in Barcelona, the future of the Republic looked promising. Walking down the wide avenue of the Ramblás, he was impressed by the egalitarian spirit of Barcelona. A true workers' state seemed to have been established, with even small businesses proudly announcing that they had been 'collectivised'. Nothing impressed him more than the fact that the waiters 'looked you in the face and treated you as an equal'. This was clearly a state of affairs worth fighting for. But his first impressions were misleading. There were tensions at work beneath the surface, and they would be impossible to overlook when he returned to the city in May. The political infighting among the left-wing parties would be out in the open by then, and he would find himself caught in the middle of it.

Although Orwell did not know much about the POUM when he enlisted, McNair made certain that the party and its foreign supporters knew something about their new recruit. *Homage to Catalonia* leaves the impression that Orwell was a relatively anonymous figure in the militia, a man whose presence was little noted beyond the immediate circle of his comrades at the front. But Orwell was being modest. His enlistment was used for propaganda effect in the official weekly English bulletin of the POUM. The paper was called *The Spanish Revolution* and was sold not only in Spain but also in Britain, America, and other countries. It was edited by Charles Orr, of the Socialist Party of the United States, and its offices were located in the POUM Executive Building in Barcelona. Oddly enough, this interesting source of information has not been cited in any previous account of Orwell's time in Spain. The report of his decision to fight with the POUM was given below the headline 'British Author with the Militia', and next to it was an announcement which reminded readers that the party welcomed more foreign volunteers like Orwell. 'FIGHT for the World Revolution. ENLIST in the POUM Militia,' the announcement said. The report itself identifies Eric Blair as a 'well-known British author whose work is so much appreciated in all English-speaking left circles of thought'. It then goes on to explain why he enlisted, and though the statement attributed to him may be more dramatic than the actual words he used, the details are in accord with Orwell's account in *Homage to Catalonia*:

Comrade Blair came to Barcelona, and said he wanted to be of some use to the workers' cause. In view of his literary abilities and intellectual attainments, it appeared that the most useful work he could do in Barcelona would be that of a propaganda journalist in constant communication with socialist organs of opinion in Britain. He said: 'I have decided that I can be of most use to the workers as a fighter at the front.' He spent exactly seven days in

Barcelona, and he is now fighting with the Spanish comrades of the POUM on the Aragon front.[26]

Orwell was part of a *centuria* which was sent to defend a position on a hilltop near Alcubierre. It was a quiet sector, but was not without its occasional moments of danger from random artillery shells or well-aimed rifle fire. The unit was taken to the front by a member of Rovira's General Staff, a Russian-born engineer named Georges Kopp. When they reached the position, which was three thousand feet above sea-level, Kopp placed them under the command of a young captain named Benjamin Lewinski (Orwell uses an alternate spelling – 'Levinski' – in *Homage to Catalonia*). Orwell guessed that his captain was about twenty-five, but in fact Lewinski was only twenty. He was a Pole who had grown up in Paris, where he had been a fur-coat maker before deciding, one day in August 1936, to go to Spain so that he could fight fascism. Kopp had given him the command of this hilltop position in November 1936. The fact that he was so young was outweighed by his ability to speak several European languages – an essential skill on this part of the front where the volunteers included men who spoke French, German, Italian, English, and Catalan. He spoke all of these languages, as well as a few more, though he was not fluent in all of them. Orwell liked him from the moment they met, and affectionately referred to him as 'Ben', but he never ceased to be amused at Lewinski's inventive way of speaking the English language.

After failing to see anything of the opposing army on his first day at the front, he asked his young captain, 'Where are the enemy?' He records the response in *Homage to Catalonia*:

> Benjamin waved his hand expansively. 'Over zere.' (Benjamin spoke English – terrible English.)
> 'But *where?*'
> According to my ideas of trench warfare the Fascists would be fifty or a hundred yards away. I could see nothing – seemingly their trenches were very well concealed. Then with a shock of dismay I saw where Benjamin was pointing; on the opposite hill-top, beyond the ravine, seven hundred metres away at the very

least, the tiny outline of a parapet and a red-and-yellow flag – the Fascist position. I was indescribably disappointed.

When interviewed for this biography in 1990, Lewinski recalled that Orwell's disappointed response was just as the book describes it. And he cheerfully acknowledged that the comment about his English was fair, explaining in a separate letter that it is a language which he had learned on his own, and had never been able to use as much as he would have liked: 'I hope that all what I'm saying in this letter will be very useful to you, excuse my broken english, a language I seldom have the opportunity to use, I wish that will be very well understood.'[27] Lewinski remembered that Orwell's linguistic abilities were excellent. He thought that his friend's French was very good, and he was impressed at how quickly Orwell was able to pick up enough Catalan to communicate effectively with the troops in his unit. It was partly for this reason that Lewinski made him a corporal, or *cabo*, almost as soon as he arrived at the front. Orwell accepted the position, though he confided in a letter to Eileen that he did not want the responsibility. 'Eric has been created a "cabo",' Eileen told Leonard Moore in late January, 'which is I think a kind of corporal & which distresses him because he has to get up early to turn out the guard.'

The lack of discipline among the Spanish youths in his unit was a constant worry for Orwell. The troops received their rifles only hours before taking up their positions at the front, and many of the boys used them carelessly, having no previous experience with firearms of any kind. He saw five militiamen wounded by shooting accidents before he saw any casualties from fascist attacks. One day he rashly decided to photograph a group of machine-gunners with their gun. 'Don't fire,' he said half-jokingly as he stood in front of them focusing his camera. A few seconds later a stream of bullets whizzed past his face. The gun had accidentally been fired, but afterwards the machine-gunners treated the whole incident as a joke.

But the greatest enemy during that first month at the front was the 'unspeakable cold'. Whether they were standing in their

trenches or curled up in their dugouts, the men could not escape
the penetrating chill. Before doing his sentry duty at night, Orwell
tried to pile onto his body as many clothes as he could, but he still
found himself shivering in the frigid air. Icy rains and stiff winds
were common torments, and there was never enough firewood
available to keep everyone warm. It is a miracle that he did not come
down with a fatal case of pneumonia, but somehow he managed to
survive the brutal conditions. His secret weapon in this battle with
the elements was Gerard Manley Hopkins. As he explained to
Stephen Spender in 1938, 'I remember on sentry-go in the
trenches near Alcubierre I used to do Hopkins's poem "Felix
Randal", I expect you know it, over and over to myself to pass the
time away in that bloody cold.' In all of Spain, Orwell must have
been the only man warming himself with words such as these:

This seeing the sick endears them to us, us too it endears.
My tongue had taught thee comfort, touch had quenched thy tears,
The tears that touched my heart, child, Felix, poor Felix Randal . . .[28]

There was only one other British subject in Orwell's unit, a
Welshman named Robert Williams, but on 2 February the ILP
contingent arrived at the front and began fortifying a position at
Monte Trazo, a few miles to the west of Orwell's post. Georges
Kopp decided that all the men from Britain should be together, so
Orwell and Williams made the short trip to Monte Trazo and
became members of the British force, which operated as an
independent unit under the general supervision of Kopp. There
were about thirty men in the group, including Bob Smillie, a
grandson of the miners' leader Robert Smillie. Orwell must have
been struck by the irony that he and Smillie had become
comrades-in-arms; only a few months earlier he had described, in
The Road to Wigan Pier, the kind of hysterical fear which Bob's
grandfather had aroused in middle-class households at the end of
the First World War: 'That was the period of the great coal strikes,
when a miner was thought of as a fiend incarnate and old ladies
looked under their beds every night lest Robert Smillie should be
concealed there.'

The man who had organised the contingent in England, and who had led them out to Spain, was Bob Edwards. He was the Lancashire representative on the National Council of the ILP, and would later become a Labour MP. He was also a regular contributor to the ILP weekly paper in London – the *New Leader*. On 19 February his first report from the front appeared in its pages, and the one member of the contingent whom he praised for battlefield heroics was Orwell. The lack of action on the front had prompted Orwell, Kopp, and Edwards to make some daring patrols under the noses of the enemy. In the description provided by Edwards, Orwell appears to have been a far more effective soldier than *Homage to Catalonia* would lead one to believe: 'Blair . . . is a fine type of Englishman, 6ft. 3in. in height, a good shot, a cool customer, completely without fear. I know this because we have on numerous occasions crept over the parapet and have managed to get very close to the Fascist lines.'

Orwell shared a dugout at Monte Trazo with an Irishman by the name of John 'Paddy' Donovan, who was close to him in age. He thought that Orwell was a brave man, but that he was perhaps too brave for his own good. 'Orwell always wanted to be in action, he never wanted to lie down and take things easy, but wanted always to carry on.' As far as Donovan could tell, his comrade had only a few interests beyond the war itself, one of which was writing. 'Eric was always writing. In the daytime he used to sit outside the dugout writing, and in the evenings he used to write by candlelight.' This was an acceptable pastime – he was keeping a detailed diary of his experiences at the front – but he was fond of another daily activity which made no sense. Despite his lung problems, he insisted on smoking a strong black shag tobacco. He rolled it into cigarettes and kept one going almost constantly. During the evenings their small dugout was full of thick, pungent smoke. Although Donovan generally put up with it, he complained about it to others, and was still complaining many years later: 'Most trying . . . Nearly killed me with his black tobacco.'[29]

The narrow confines of the dugout were a welcome refuge whenever the fascists decided to fire a few artillery shells in the direction of the British volunteers. But Orwell tended to dismiss this threat. The shelling was so infrequent and so inaccurate that he regarded it more as a 'mild diversion' than as a serious danger. Moreover, many of the shells were defective and did not explode. He liked to joke that there were only a few shells used in the war: 'The Fascist guns were of the same make and calibre as our own, and the unexploded shells were often reconditioned and fired back. There was said to be one old shell with a nickname of its own which travelled daily to and fro, never exploding.'[30] But the danger was not as minor as Orwell liked to pretend. As one of Bob Edwards's dispatches to the *New Leader* confirms, the result of the shelling could be lethal even when all the shells failed to explode: 'During the week five shells were fired into this position, but not one of the five exploded . . . A Spanish militia boy was, unfortunately, killed by one of the shells by a direct hit.' Edwards took consolation from the fact that this was a freak occurrence, and 'would not happen again in a hundred years'.[31] But, of course, that thought would not have consoled him if he had been sitting in the same dugout as the Spanish militia boy.

The shelling was worse at the unit's next position. In mid-February Kopp sent them to the outskirts of Huesca, where other POUM forces were besieging the town. They built their sandbag fortifications on a hill only a mile and a half away from the town, and mounted a flag pole over one of the dugouts. Their flag was inscribed with the words, 'ILP, Seccion Inglesa. POUM.', and in one of its corners was the hammer and sickle. The sight of this banner waving in the cold wind may have lifted the spirits of some of the 'lads', but it also provided a good target for the enemy. Bob Edwards proudly described the flag in his report for the *New Leader*, and then went on to describe the latest bombardments:

> Each day at about twelve o'clock the Fascist artillery bombards our post with high explosive shells. On the day of our arrival six shells came whizzing over our parapet. The first one hit the road without exploding, and the other five exploded without doing any great damage to the boys. The following day eight came over at about the same time, causing considerable alarm in the

cook-house, at which they seemed to be directed. This bombardment held up the cooking of our midday meal, much to the annoyance of all the boys.[32]

In *Homage to Catalonia* Orwell refers to these routine attacks as 'a little shell-fire'.

Shortly before the ILP unit moved to their position outside Huesca, Eileen contacted the ILP headquarters in London and applied for a job which had been advertised in the *New Leader*. The paper had asked for a volunteer to serve in John McNair's office in Barcelona. It appears that several people answered the call, but the job was given to Eileen because of her excellent qualifications, not merely because her husband was a member of the party's military contingent in Spain. 'Readers who volunteered to serve as English-French shorthand-typist at Barcelona are thanked for their offer,' the paper announced on 19 February. 'Mrs. Blair, wife of Eric Blair ... has been appointed and left on Monday [15 February].' By the time this report appeared, Eileen was working at her new job and living in an ordinary room at the Hotel Continental. She had closed the village shop, and Nellie Limouzin had moved to the cottage to take care of it and the garden until the couple returned.

It was impossible for Orwell to leave the front, so Eileen went to see him. Georges Kopp had been introduced to her in Barcelona, and she had talked him into taking her out to the front in his staff car. Ordinarily, her request would have been dismissed out of hand, but she was a tenacious woman and Kopp saw that she would not easily be denied. They made the trip in mid-March. A blurred photograph has survived which shows her posing with Orwell and other militiamen beside a machine-gun at their position near Huesca. Everyone looks relaxed, but her visit was not without its dangers. As she reported to Leonard Moore a few weeks later, 'I was allowed to stay in the front line dug-outs all day. The Fascists threw in a small bombardment and quite a lot of machine-gun fire.' This did not frighten her. On the contrary, she boasted to Moore that 'it was quite an interesting visit – indeed I never enjoyed anything more'. She wisely refrained from mentioning the attack when she wrote to her mother about the visit, but she made it clear that she had no regrets: 'I *thoroughly* enjoyed being at the front.'[33]

She found that Orwell was 'very tired' after two and a half months at the front, but that otherwise he was in 'fairly' good health. There was a very small hospital at Monflorite, a short distance behind the front, and the POUM doctor working there had recently examined Orwell. He had pronounced him fit, though he had acknowledged that the Englishman was suffering from 'over-fatigue'. Kopp had given Eileen a tour of this hospital, and she had been appalled by the doctor's slovenliness. In a letter to her mother, she called him 'incredibly dirty' and described the indifference to hygiene in his hospital: 'Used dressings are thrown out the window unless the window happens to be shut when they rebound onto the floor – and the doctor's hands have never been known to be washed.' Until she saw these conditions she had been thinking of volunteering for service as a nurse at the hospital. 'If the doctor had been a good doctor I should have moved heaven and earth to stay,' she told her mother.[34]

Unfortunately, it was to this place that Orwell was sent at the end of March when a cut on his hand became badly infected. He spent ten days there, and during this time the *practicantes* (hospital assistants) stole almost all his valuables, including his camera. To cheer him up, Eileen sent him a box of cigars and a food parcel, and he sent her some of his photographs of the war for safekeeping. He asked her to have reproductions made of them because he had promised copies to various people who had posed for him at the front. 'I shouldn't like to disappoint the Spanish machine-gunner etc.,' he wrote to her. He was not happy with the quality of some of the photographs but, given the circumstances under which they were taken, he was lucky to have captured anything on film. 'Of course some of the photos were a mess. The one which has Buttonshaw looking very blurred in the foreground is a photo of a shell-burst, which you can see rather faintly on the left, just beyond the house.'[35]

The one good thing about his stay at Monflorite was that no one minded if he left his bed and went for long walks. With his arm in a sling, he spent 'several blissful days wandering about the country-side'. Spring had arrived and the air felt 'balmy' after all the time he had spent shivering in the hills. Even though the destructive effects of the civil war were visible everywhere he went, he was delighted to find a few signs of new life in the warm weather. 'Round the drinking-pool that served for the village mules I found exquisite green frogs the size of a penny, so brilliant that the young grass looked dull beside them.'

A few days later he returned to the front and took part in the most serious fighting he would see in the war. Despite the fact that his arm had recently been in a sling, he volunteered to take part in an ambitious night raid on a fascist position at Huesca. Benjamin Lewinski and Jorge Roca, a battalion commander in the division, planned the attack as a two-pronged assault. Orwell's group of volunteers – fifteen Englishmen and fifteen Spaniards – was supposed to creep up to the enemy line, cut the barbed wire, toss hand grenades over the low wall of sandbags, and then storm the position with their rifles firing and bayonets at the ready. At the same time another POUM force would charge the next position on the line, and prevent it from reinforcing the other.

Like most plans in war, this one went awry. Lewinski and Roca led Orwell's group to within a few yards of their objective before the enemy sentry spotted them and sounded the alert. Shots rang out in all directions, and Orwell found that he was caught between the fire of his own troops and that of the fascists. A few hand grenades managed to land among the enemy and, fortunately for Orwell, the firing died down. Lewinski rallied his men and led the charge over the wall, where they found the defenders were either dead or in retreat. Lewinski recalled in 1990 that he had looked round to see if Orwell had managed to survive the assault. To his relief, he found that his comrade was unharmed. 'He was very clever, very logical, and much courage, but I was afraid for him. He was so tall and always standing up. I tell him, "Keep your head down", but he is always standing up.' Paddy Donovan had similar fears for his friend that night: 'The patrol got up close to the barbed wire and Orwell got way in front. Grenades were bursting right, left, and centre. Orwell stood up, very tall, and shouted: "Come on, move up here you bastards".' In response to this call, Donovan had the good sense to yell out, 'For Christ's sake, Eric, get down.'[36] The *New Leader* account of this assault is even more dramatic:

'Charge!' shouted Blair. 'Over to the right and in!' called Paddy Donovan. 'Are we downhearted?' cried the French Captain Benjamin.

In front of the parapet was Eric Blair's tall figure coolly strolling forward through the storm of fire. He leapt at the parapet, then stumbled. Hell, had they got him? No, he was over, closely followed by Gross, of Hammersmith, Frankfort, of Hackney, and Bob Smillie, with the others right after them.

The trench had been hastily evacuated. The last of the retreating Fascists, clothed only in a blanket, was thirty yards away. Blair gave chase, but the men knew the ground and got away. In the corner of the trench was one dead man; in a dugout was another body.[37]

It was not all glory for the volunteers. The assault on the second position had failed completely, leaving those fascist troops free to counterattack. Orwell and the rest of his unit were soon receiving heavy fire and were forced to leave the position which they had overwhelmed only minutes earlier. The path of their retreat took them through rain-soaked fields, and by the time they reached their own lines they were covered in mud. Afterwards Kopp praised the men for their 'audacious raid' and told them that the attack had diverted troops from another part of the front where anarchist militiamen had mounted a large assault against the fascists. 'The action had been a success, as such things go,' Orwell reflected later. When it was all over, and he was safely back in his dugout, he quietly celebrated by smoking the last of the cigars from the box Eileen had sent him.

CHAPTER FOURTEEN

Soldier in Catalonia

I

Orwell served on the Aragon front for a hundred and fifteen days. It was not until the end of April 1937 that he was granted leave and was able to see Barcelona again. He needed a period of rest, and he was badly in need of a hot bath. Lice had been a nuisance for him since his early days in the trenches, and by April they were a constant misery. As he wrote later, 'The lice were multiplying in my trousers far faster than I could massacre them.'[1] The warmer spring weather, however, had made life a little easier, and the bright sun had put some colour in his face. When he arrived in Barcelona, his shabby clothing startled Eileen, but otherwise she thought he was looking healthier. 'He arrived completely ragged,' she wrote to her brother on 1 May, 'almost bare-foot, a little lousy, dark brown, and looking really very well.'[2]

He had applied for his discharge papers, but it was not because he wanted to leave Spain. He wanted to see more action, and was convinced that he would have that chance if he joined the International Brigade and fought with it on the Madrid front. He and Eileen went together to see a representative of the International Brigade, and after much discussion they received conditional approval for George to join one of the front-line units and for Eileen to work in the Madrid office of the Brigade. It was not easy to win this approval because their affiliations with the POUM made them suspect in the eyes of many Republican supporters. The numerous rumours about the POUM being 'Franco's Fifth Column' were so widespread by this time that many people had come to accept them as the truth. It did not help that Eileen worked at the party headquarters. 'Of course we – perhaps particularly I – are politically suspect,' she acknowledged to her brother.

Neither Eileen nor George believed the rumours, but they did not want to become bogged down in political infighting while the fascists grew stronger on the battlefield. At this point Orwell's attitude was that the fight against fascism mattered more than anything else. 'I thought it idiotic that people fighting for their lives should *have* separate parties,' he explains in *Homage to Catalonia*. 'My attitude always was, "Why can't we drop all this political nonsense and get on with the war?"' The rivalries between the various left-wing factions 'exasperated' him, and he found it difficult to sort out the positions of the 'kaleidoscope of political parties and trade unions, with their tiresome names – PSUC, POUM, FAI, CNT, UGT, JCI, JSU, AIT ... It looked at first sight as though Spain were suffering from a plague of initials.'

He had made no secret of his desire to leave the POUM. When he had realised that the action on the Aragon front was relatively light compared with the battles being waged on the Madrid front, he had made it clear to his English comrades that he intended to join the International Brigade as soon as his first leave came up. Bob Edwards had tried to tell him that he was mistaken, that the POUM deserved his support, and that he was looking for more action simply because he wanted more 'material for the book he was writing on Spain'. In one heated argument Edwards called him 'a bloody scribbler', and told him that he had 'no actual experience of the working-class struggle other than as a journalist observer'.[3]

These are serious charges. After Orwell's death, Edwards repeated them on several occasions, and explained them at length in 1970 when he wrote an introduction for a special edition of *Homage to Catalonia*. They have since been used by critics of Orwell who, for one reason or another, want to denigrate the part he played in the Spanish Civil War. Like the rumours against the POUM, Edwards's accusations against Orwell have gained acceptance without being closely examined. It is true that Orwell kept a diary during his time in Spain, and that he intended to use it as the basis for a book on the war. (When Eileen wrote to Leonard Moore in April, after she had visited Orwell at the front, she told him, 'He is keeping quite a good diary, and I have great hopes for the book.')[4] But his main reason for joining the fighting was not to gather 'material' for a book. His reckless courage on the battlefield undercuts that notion. If he had really cared so much about his book, he would have kept his head down and remained in the background as a 'journalist observer'.

He was there to fight fascism, and he did it bravely, as Edwards was well aware. He did not show up at the front, write a few things, and then leave after six weeks. But that is what Edwards did. In his Introduction to *Homage to Catalonia* Edwards says that he and Orwell 'were together for several months' in Spain, but that is not true. Edwards arrived at the Aragon front on 2 February, and he left on 17 March. He visited Barcelona for a few days, and then he went back to Britain, where he attended the ILP's annual conference at Glasgow on 29 March. He never rejoined the contingent in Spain. Britain's non-intervention agreement made it impossible for him to return, but he could not have been unaware of that risk when he left Barcelona.

He continued to write articles about Spain for *The New Leader* – at least seven appeared under his name in the first eight months of 1937. (It is odd that *he* should have called Orwell a 'bloody scribbler'.) He may also have had a hand in the editing of the *New Leader*'s article on the night raid at Huesca. A large photograph of him is featured at the top of the article, which was published on 30 April 1937, and a caption identifies him as the 'Leader of the ILP Contingent'. But he did not take part in this raid. He was in Britain when it occurred. And he was no longer the 'Leader' of the contingent. In his absence the men had elected a new leader – Eric Blair. There can be no doubt that Edwards worked diligently to organise the contingent in London and to bring it out to the front, and that he was a brave soldier; but it is unfortunate that he should have chosen, after leaving Spain, to exaggerate his part in the war, and to cast doubt – without justification – on Orwell's motives.[5]

In any event, Orwell finally decided not to abandon the POUM militia in favour of the International Brigade. His attitude on the question of political infighting changed dramatically in the first week of May when he found himself and his comrades under fire not from the fascist enemy but from their left-wing 'allies'. The trouble began in Barcelona on 3 May. It was precipitated by a government effort to take control of the Telephone Exchange, which was in the hands of the anarchists. Not surprisingly, the anarchists had antagonised the government by running the telephone system according to their own curious notions of efficiency. Telephone calls were arbitrarily cut off, operators were rude, and some eavesdropping may have occurred when the callers were government officials. When the chief of police in Barcelona tried to engineer a quick conquest of the building, the anarchists fought back with gunfire, and in no time rumours spread that one political faction or another was attempting to seize control of the city. Random shooting broke out everywhere. Assault Guards roamed the streets trying to restore order by shooting at practically anything that moved. Communists fired on anarchists, who fired back, and all sides seemed to be taking shots at POUM members.

This chaos lasted for four days, three of which Orwell spent on the roof of a cinema guarding the approach to the POUM Executive Building, directly across the street. From this position he had a wide view of the city and was amazed at the 'folly' of the street fighting raging in all directions. Eileen had taken refuge in the Executive Building, as had Georges Kopp and a small force of POUM militiamen. The great fear was that the government – under pressure from its communist supporters – would blame the POUM for starting the trouble and send the Assault Guards to attack the building. About thirty Assault Guards did take up a position at a café next to the building, but they did not attack. The atmosphere, however, was nerve-racking. As this siege by supposedly friendly forces dragged on hour after hour, Orwell grew furious:

I had been a hundred and fifteen days in the line and had come

back to Barcelona ravenous for a bit of rest and comfort; and instead
I had to spend my time sitting on a roof opposite Assault Guards as
bored as myself, who periodically waved to me and assured me that
they were 'workers' (meaning that they hoped I would not shoot
them), but who would certainly open fire if they got the order to do
so. If this was history it did not feel like it.

After the trouble ended on 7 May and life in the city began to
return to its usual routine, Orwell decided that he would have
nothing to do with the International Brigade because, as he told a
friend, 'I could not join any Communist-controlled unit.'
Suddenly, the complexities of left-wing Spanish politics mattered
very much to him. He was willing to die in a fight against fascism but
not in some pointless squabble over left-wing loyalties. It did not
take him long to realise that a communist bullet might get him
before a fascist one. The communists were looking for ways to
strengthen their power in the Republic and the street fighting gave
them a pretext for intensifying their hate campaign against the
POUM. They began blaming them for all the troubles of the 'May
Days', and distributed a very damaging poster showing a Nazi devil
hiding behind a mask marked 'POUM'. 'Fuera la Careta!' ('Tear
off the mask!') the poster said.

It would have been prudent for the Orwells if they had left Spain
at this point, but after seeing what had happened in Barcelona, they
did not want to abandon their friends in the POUM. Orwell went
back to the front only three days after the street fighting ended, and
Eileen continued to work in John McNair's office. Although Orwell
was sent back to the same general area near Huesca where he had
been in March and April, there were a few things which were
different in May. The government was in the process of bringing all
the militias under its authority, and had been organising a Popular
Army in which militiamen and regular Army troops would serve
together. The Lenin Division, in which Orwell served, was
renamed the 29th Division, and regular Army commissions were
given to its officers. The informal command structure of the militia
gave way to a conventional hierarchy. Kopp was appointed a major,
Benjamin Lewinski was given an official rank of captain and – on

Lewinski's recommendation – Eric Blair's name was put forward for a lieutenant's commission. In the meantime, he held the new rank on a provisional basis.

His period as an officer did not last long. On 20 May, at first light, he awoke and left his dugout to relieve one of his men – an American named Harry Milton – who was standing guard behind a wall of sandbags. Milton recalled that Orwell stood on a sandbag to take a look over the wall. A few seconds later he heard a rifle shot and saw Orwell's long body crash to the ground. A sniper's bullet had hit him while his head was silhouetted against the rising sun. When Milton leaned over him, he saw that the bullet had entered his throat, making a neat hole without causing much bleeding. 'I thought he wouldn't make it,' Milton remembered. 'He had bitten down hard on his lip, and I thought there must be a lot of damage. But he was breathing, and his eyes were moving.'[6] Milton and some of the other men managed to put him on a stretcher and carry him the mile or so to the small hospital at Monflorite. He was conscious the whole time, but was given a shot of morphia to ease his pain, and was then sent to another hospital at Sietamo.

Doctors later told him that the bullet had missed a carotid artery by 'about a millimetre'. He was frequently told how lucky he was to survive a neck wound, but he was not so impressed with his luck. 'I could not help thinking that it would be even luckier not to be hit at all.' But as he later acknowledged, there had been a couple of minutes after the bullet had knocked him down when he had thought that his artery was cut – blood was running from the side of his mouth, and he feared that he had only minutes left to live. Two thoughts had dominated his mind: 'My first thought, conventionally enough, was for my wife. My second was a violent resentment at having to leave this world which, when all is said and done, suits me so well.'

Whether he was willing to admit it or not, he was extremely lucky to be alive. It was later determined that he had been hit by a Mauser bullet fired from a distance of two hundred yards. Yet his recovery was fairly quick. He slowly regained his voice, though it remained no more than a hoarse whisper for some weeks. In less than forty-eight hours he had been moved from the front to a large, rather modern hospital at Lerida, and within a few days he was able to get up and walk in the hospital garden. Kopp brought Eileen there to see him, and arrangements were made to move Orwell to Barcelona as soon as he was fit for the journey. The POUM maintained a well-equipped sanatorium for convalescent troops on the slopes of Mount Tibidabo, outside Barcelona. It consisted of two large villas which had been seized from fascist sympathisers. Orwell arrived there on 29 May and stayed for two weeks.

At Eileen's request Kopp had written to Dr O'Shaughnessy to give him a detailed report of Orwell's condition. Eileen wanted her brother to write a 'colleague's letter' to the specialist in Barcelona who was trying to help Orwell recover his voice. As Kopp explained, they were hoping that the reply to such a letter would contain more information about Orwell's chances for recovery than the Spanish doctor had been willing to divulge to them. Various problems interfered with this plan, but by 10 June Eileen was able to inform her brother that Orwell was 'much better, though he cannot be brought to admit any improvements . . . He is *violently* depressed, which I think encouraging.'[7] His depression was largely the result of his recognition that there was no more that he could do in Spain; his wound had left him unfit for service – his medical discharge included the notation 'declared useless' – and he had no wish to cover the war from Barcelona: 'I had an overwhelming desire to get away from it all; away from the horrible atmosphere of political suspicion and hatred, from streets thronged by armed men, from air-raids, trenches, machine-guns.'

II

The political situation was rapidly worsening. On 28 May the government had banned the POUM's newspaper, *La Batalla*, and on 16 June the POUM party was outlawed. Its leaders were rounded up and thrown into prisons. This action was the direct result of orders given to Colonel Ortega, the director-general of security by the Soviet GPU chief in Spain, Alexander Orlov. The head of the POUM, Andres Nin, was tortured and murdered. But it was not only the leaders who were the targets of this purge. To Orwell's great sorrow, his comrade Bob Smillie was arrested in May, and on 12 June the young man died in prison at Valencia, supposedly of appendicitis. Orwell was unconvinced by the official explanation of Smillie's death, and *Homage to Catalonia* leaves no doubt about the indignation which this death had aroused in Orwell: 'Here was this brave and gifted boy, who had thrown up his career at Glasgow University in order to come and fight against Fascism, and who, as I saw for myself, had done his job at the front with faultless courage and willingness; and all they could find to do with him was to fling him into jail and let him die like a neglected animal.'

Orwell did not learn of Smillie's death, or of the purge launched against the POUM, until it was almost too late for him to escape a fate similar to Smillie's. In 1989 a document came to light in the National Historical Archive in Madrid which leaves no doubt that both Orwell's life and Eileen's were in danger. The document is a security police report to the Tribunal for Espionage and High Treason at Valencia. It details the activities of 'Enric Blair', as he is called, 'and his wife Eileen Blair'. They are described in the report as 'known Trotskyists' and as 'linking agents of the ILP and the POUM'. In the Spanish Republic, in June 1937, these were serious allegations indeed, and if the authorities had managed to get their hands on the couple, they would surely have been arrested. Anything might have happened after that.[8]

Because he had been away from Barcelona between 15 June and 20 June gathering the necessary papers for his medical discharge, he first learned of the purge when he walked into the lounge of the Hotel Continental late at night on the twentieth. Eileen was waiting for him. Before he could greet her she came to him, put her arm round his neck and whispered in his ear: 'Get out!' When they were outside on the pavement, she hurriedly explained to him what had been happening in his absence. Only two nights earlier a group of plain-clothes police had barged into Eileen's room and taken away 'evidence' – books, press-cuttings, letters, all the diaries in which

Orwell had recorded the events and impressions of his stay in Spain, and – rather myteriously – a bundle of his dirty linen. The security police report to the Tribunal for Espionage and High Treason contains information which seems to have been gathered from this raid on their hotel room.

Perhaps the most shocking news for Orwell was that Georges Kopp had been arrested. He had been staying at the Hotel Continental and when he came in on the morning of the twentieth to collect his belongings, before returning to the front, the police took him into custody. They had done this despite the fact that he was preparing to undertake an important military mission authorised by the Ministry of War, and had with him an official letter to prove it. Orwell could not believe that the government was so stupid that it would arrest a loyal soldier such as Kopp. Likewise, he could not imagine that anyone would want to arrest him or his wife. When he asked her, 'Why should anyone want to arrest me? What had I done?', she 'patiently' pointed out that ordinary notions of justice did not apply. 'It did not matter what I had done or not done. This was not a round-up of criminals; it was merely a reign of terror. I was not guilty of any definite act, but I was guilty of "Trotskyism".'

Eileen believed that she had not been arrested because the police were using her as a decoy, not only to help them apprehend her husband, but also John McNair, who was still at large. For the time being the only thing to do was to keep a low profile and prepare for a fast escape from Spain. She went back to her room, but Orwell went into hiding, using his old tramping skills to help him survive on the streets for a few days.

While they waited to make their escape, they met during daylight hours at restaurants and shops, trying to look as much like innocent English visitors as possible. But one day they did something immensely daring. They went to the jail in Barcelona where Kopp was being held and visited him during the normal visiting period, which took place in a large holding cell. Kopp greeted them with the words, 'Well, I suppose we shall all be shot.' Orwell admired Kopp's gallows humour – it was the sort of remark he might have made if the tables had been turned. He wanted to do something to help him; but the only thing that might work would mean putting his own safety at great risk. The police had confiscated Kopp's letter from the Ministry of War, but if he could get it back, it might help to convince other officials that Kopp was needed urgently at the front, and must be released. There was no time to lose. He went off to retrieve the letter, which would mean visiting police headquarters – the one place where he could least afford to be seen. 'I left my wife with Kopp, rushed out and, after a long search, found a taxi.'

His effort proved fruitless. He actually managed to obtain the letter, but it made no difference. The police refused to release Kopp, and kept him in jail for the next eighteen months. All the same, it should not be overlooked that Orwell had been willing to sacrifice his own freedom for Kopp's. As he explains in *Homage to Catalonia*, 'He was my personal friend, I had served under him for months, I had been under fire with him, and I knew his history. He was a man who had sacrificed everything – family, nationality, livelihood – simply to come to Spain and fight against Fascism.' But the truth is that neither he nor anyone else in Spain knew the real Georges Kopp. Much of the personal history which he had given Orwell was untrue. He said that he was a reserve officer in the Belgian Army, a professional engineer, a devoted family man whose wife had died giving birth to the youngest of their four children. And he said that he had been forced to leave his country because the authorities in his native Brussels had discovered that he was making illegal munitions for the Spanish Republic.

The facts tell a different story. He was born in Russia, in Petrograd, on 23 June 1902, and did not go to Belgium until he was ten. He studied at the Free University of Brussels, where his registration form was marked 'Russe', but he did not complete all the requirements for an engineering degree and left the university in 1922. He had five children by his first wife, Germaine Warnotte, whom he divorced in 1934, shortly after the birth of their youngest child. He worked as an engineer in Brussels, but there is no evidence that he was suspected of manufacturing illegal munitions. And there is no evidence that he was ever an officer in the Belgian reserves. As one of his children Pierre Kopp – has recalled, his father simply 'disappeared' in the mid-1930s, and the family did not see him again until after the Second World War. But by then he had married a second time and had started another family in England. (He had three children from this marriage.) Before his father died in 1951, Pierre tried to learn more about him, but discovered that 'he was not keen to talk about the past'. When Pierre read *Homage to Catalonia* later in the 1950s, he was 'surprised' to learn that his father was Belgian. 'During the German occupation of Belgium we were considered by the German police as "apatride d'origine russe", meaning: without nationality but of Russian origin. I don't explain the difference between his supposed-to-be nationality and ours. My mother never told us anything concerning such a change.'⁹

There was one more crucial fact about Kopp which Orwell apparently did not know. Kopp was in love with Eileen. Orwell appears to have trusted Kopp so much that he never raised any question about the close attention which his friend paid to Eileen. Kopp was not a handsome man, but he had enormous charm and made every effort to please Eileen, showing her the kind of flattering attention which Orwell, with his natural reserve and his preoccupation with books and ideas, would not have shown her. Orwell loved his wife, but he was often lost in his own world, unmindful of her needs. And, of course, in this period of the Spanish War they were living apart for almost four months, excluding Eileen's brief visit to the front in March when Kopp drove her there.

If Orwell was not suspicious of Kopp's interest in Eileen, others were. At least two members of the ILP contingent thought that Kopp was trying to seduce Eileen behind Orwell's back, and one remarked privately that he considered it 'a rotten business'.¹⁰ Whether Eileen ever took his advances seriously, or returned his affections, is uncertain. When asked about the relationship, some thirty years later, Eileen's friend – and Orwell's former landlady – Rosalind Obermeyer said, 'Eileen was attractive to men . . . Her eyes always lit up whenever Georges Kopp's name was mentioned, so there may have been some truth in the belief that she and Kopp had an affair.'[11] There is no question, however, that Kopp was in love with Eileen. He kept in touch with her until the end of her life, and his surviving letters to her leave no doubt that he was much closer to her than to Orwell. He wrote to her from prison after she returned to England, asking her – not Orwell – for help in gaining his release. And he sent the letters to her indirectly, addressing them to her brother. On 7 July 1937 he wrote to Dr O'Shaughnessy:

> Will you please transmit to your sister the enclosed copy of a letter I am sending to the chief of Police and tell her that if I have not received a satisfactory reply to same within 48 hours I shall begin a hunger strike . . . In case I am reduced to this measure, I want my friends in England and the ILP people to give this fact the publicity without which it would be useless . . . I have written two letters to Eileen which have been posted [to] your address . . . I am sorry to have to trouble you with all this, but I agreed with your sister to communicate with her through you. Tell her I am intensely thinking of her and give her my love. Shake hands to Eric.

Partly as a result of Eileen's efforts, Kopp's plight was publicised on two successive weeks in the *New Leader*, and the National Council of the ILP sent a deputation to the Spanish Embassy in London to demand his release. The second of the two articles in the paper covered almost an entire page and featured a photograph of Kopp in uniform under the headline 'Soldier of Socialism'. This piece was written by Bob Edwards who included a description of his first meeting with Kopp. They were at the front and Kopp had offered him a cigarette: 'By the flickering light of the match I saw his face, a commanding, almost handsome face with a strong, dimpled chin, laughing lips and blue mischievous eyes surmounted by a broad, smooth brow. My first impression was that it was the face of a German or, maybe, a Dutchman.' Like everyone else who knew Kopp in Spain, Edwards was completely taken in by the Russian's creative explanations of his past. The Englishman recalled one of their conversations during an inspection tour of fortifications along the front:

> 'I'd give a good deal for just one day in Brussels.'
> 'Your native town?' I asked.
> 'Yes,' he replied. 'We Internationals never lose our local patriotism. But, of course, that is quite natural. My home is in Brussels. I left my four children there . . . I wonder . . . if we are ever likely to see our home towns again.'
> . . . .
> 'What about your wife?' I asked. His face saddened.
> 'My wife died at the birth of our youngest baby,' he said, after a short pause.

None of the English efforts to free Kopp was successful, but at the end of 1938, the Spanish communists who had locked him up, and who had periodically tortured him, suddenly decided that there was no point in holding him any longer. He was released just seven weeks before Franco's forces captured Barcelona. He went to England and lived for a time at Greenwich with Laurence and Gwen O'Shaughnessy. When the Second World War began, he joined the French Foreign Legion (they made him a corporal). A year later he sent Eileen a long description of his military adventures, some of which may be true, and he concluded his letter on this affectionate note:

> Well, Eileen dear, perhaps we shall meet again. This is already long enough and I shall not tell you how I feel about French politics, but you must guess. Must I tell you what joy it will be for me to see and hear you, and see everybody in the Family, who I hope are all well? You know all that. You even know what sort of
> pensées choisies
> I am sending you.
> With love,
Georges[12]

Whatever Kopp's 'thoughts' for Eileen may have been, Orwell's thoughts during his last days in Spain were very much concerned with his friend's fate. He visited him in prison more than once, left money with Spanish friends so that they could keep him supplied with cigarettes and extra food, and tried to locate witnesses who would be willing to testify on Kopp's behalf if the case ever came to trial. On Orwell's last day in Barcelona he took advantage of a spare hour to write 'a long letter to the Ministry of War', urging its officials to plead Kopp's case to the police. It was physically painful to write the letter since his right arm was still partly disabled by nerve damage suffered when the sniper's bullet had gone through his neck. 'I wonder if anyone read that letter,' he reflected afterwards, 'written on pages torn out of a note-book in wobbly handwriting . . . and still more wobbly Spanish.' Whether it was read or not, Kopp was fortunate to have such a friend.

III

Orwell and his wife made their escape from Barcelona on the morning of 23 June. They were accompanied by John McNair and Stafford Cottman, one of Orwell's comrades from the ILP contingent. Each of them had obtained proper travel documents from the British consulate and had decided to travel by rail as ordinary tourists. They boarded the train without any trouble, and were not even questioned when two detectives later went through the cars taking the names of foreigners. As a way of making their group look harmless, McNair suggested to Stafford Cottman, who was only nineteen, that he read a book of poetry, as Orwell was already doing (he was reading Wordsworth). McNair handed Cottman a book of John Masefield's poems, and the young man made a valiant attempt to appear interested in it. 'I thought it was a rather silly idea,' Cottman recalled, 'but we did have an easy time of it. No one bothered us.'[13] McNair remembered that when the train crossed the border into France they were so happy that they embraced each other. But as they discovered at the first stop, they had been wise not to delay their escape by another day. The first newspaper they saw at the station contained a report saying that

McNair had been arrested for espionage. 'The Spanish authorities had been a little premature in announcing this,' Orwell dryly observed later. 'Fortunately, "Trotskyism" is not extraditable.'

After he returned to England, Orwell told a friend that Eileen had done a 'wonderful' job of coping with all the hardships which life in Spain had imposed upon her. 'In fact,' he said, she 'actually seemed to enjoy it.'[14] The key word here is 'seemed'. She was brave throughout the four months of her stay, and did not lose her nerve even when the police invaded her room and ransacked it while she was there alone. And in the early days she had shown no signs of fear, and had even boasted that she had enjoyed being under fire at the front. But as the political situation in Barcelona became more dangerous, the strain began to show in her face, her manner and her words. Orwell may have been too absorbed in the dramatic events of May and June to notice the change in his wife, but it was there.

Richard Rees was very much struck by it when he went to Barcelona in the spring and spent an afternoon with Eileen. He had volunteered to serve as an ambulance driver in the Popular Army, and had stopped in Barcelona on his way to the Madrid front. He knew that Eileen was working at the POUM Executive Building and decided to pay her a surprise visit. 'She seemed not so much surprised, as *scared*, to see me, and I accounted for her odd manner by the strain of living in a revolutionary city with a husband at the front. When she said she could not come out to lunch with me, because it would be too dangerous for me to be seen in public with her, I supposed I must have misheard her and made no comment.' Having just arrived in Spain, Rees had only a vague impression of the complex rivalries among the left-wing parties, and he saw no reason why he should not be able to have a simple lunch with a friend. He managed to persuade her to go out with him, but she was obviously uncomfortable, and it was only later – when he knew more about Spain – that he was able to account for her strange behaviour. 'In Eileen Blair I had seen for the first time the symptoms of a human being living under a political Terror.'[15]

When she and Orwell escaped from Spain, she was so anxious to get home that she did not want to waste any time resting in France before making the rest of the journey to England, but Orwell had a different idea. During his long nights on sentry duty in the cold hills along the Aragon front, he had told himself that when his leave came up he and Eileen would go to the seaside to relax. 'Then what a rest we will have,' he had said to her in a letter from the front, adding that they would 'go fishing too if it is in any way possible'.[16] After the troubles in May had ruined his leave in Barcelona, he had become even more determined that they should have their holiday on the coast as soon as it was possible. By early June, when they were preparing to leave Spain, Orwell had devised a plan whereby they would head straight for the seaside as soon as they had crossed into France and have their holiday at last. Eileen agreed, but as she confided in a letter to her brother, she was not enthusiastic about the idea. Her letter hints at the strain she was feeling in the final month of her stay in Spain: 'I have now agreed to spend two or three days on the Mediterranean (in France) on the way home – probably at Port-Vendre . . . I do not altogether like this protracted travel, but . . . he has an overwhelming desire to follow this programme – anyway it has overwhelmed me.'[17]

As it happened, they went to the small fishing town of Banyuls-sur-Mer which is only a few miles north of the Spanish border, parting company from McNair and Cottman, who continued on their way to England. Their holiday was not a success. Orwell found the place 'a bore and a disappointment. It was chilly weather, a persistent wind blew off the sea, the water was dull and choppy, round the harbour's edge a scum of ashes, corks, and fish-guts bobbed against the stones.' The real problem is that neither of them could shake off the traumatic effects of their final days in Spain, and both of them felt guilty about enjoying their freedom in France when Kopp and other friends were unable to do the same. Fishing was a guilty pleasure after what they had seen, and Orwell could not help feeling that his time would be better spent in writing articles which would 'spill the beans' about communist duplicity. He began writing such a piece in Banyuls, and sent a wire to the *New Statesman* asking if they would like to have it when he reached London in a few days. They said yes.

During his time at the front he had received fairly regular deliveries of English papers, forwarded by Eileen, and had concluded that the *New Statesman* was one of the few which was willing to look at the Spanish war objectively. 'It is a credit to the *New Statesman*,' he had written to Cyril Connolly in early June, 'that it is the only paper, apart from a few obscure ones such as the *New Leader*, where any but the communist viewpoint has ever got through.' Orwell worked as quickly as he could to finish his piece for them, which he called 'Eye-witness in Barcelona'.[18] It describes the events of May and June, swiftly summarising material which he would later develop in much more detail in *Homage to Catalonia*. Of course, both this article and the book could have been written much more easily if the police had not confiscated his diaries from the hotel room. He had apparently kept quite a thorough record of his experiences in a manner similar to that of '*The Road to Wigan Pier Diary*'.

Even without the aid of his diary, he was able to explain, in a straightforward and authentic way, the complicated sequence of events which led the Republic to yield to communist pressure and to sanction the brutal suppression of the POUM. But 'Eye-witness in Barcelona' reaches some strong conclusions which were bound to alienate many people on the Left who might otherwise have been inclined to accept the truth of Orwell's report. The most provocative of these conclusions is his statement that the government of the Republic 'has more points of resemblance to Fascism than points of difference'.[19] Left-wing opinion in England was too accustomed to thinking of the Republic as a victim of fascism to accept this, and not many people were prepared to see the element of truth in the broad generalisation, namely, that the Republic was wrong to think that it could use fascist methods to achieve socialist aims.

When Orwell arrived in London at the end of June, he submitted the piece to the *New Statesman*, but Kingsley Martin, the editor, took exception to Orwell's conclusions and refused the article on the grounds that it would 'cause trouble'. At least that was the way Orwell remembered it. The rejection seems to have been made over the telephone, so there is no way to confirm what was said, but a later letter from Martin does confirm Orwell's version of what happened next. According to Orwell, Martin tried 'to sugar the pill' by following the rejection with an offer to review a book on the Spanish war – *The Spanish Cockpit*, by Franz Borkenau. Orwell accepted, but once again he went too far. 'When they saw my review they couldn't print it as it was "against editorial policy", but they actually offered to pay for the review all the same – practically hush-money.' The idea that he was being offered 'hush-money' is far-fetched, but Martin's rejection letter makes it clear that the review was turned down solely because Orwell's opinions were not in line with those of the paper. 'I am sorry that it is not possible for us to use your review of *The Spanish Cockpit*,' the editor said. 'The reason is simply that it too far controverts the political policy of the paper. It is very uncompromisingly said and implies that our Spanish Correspondents are all wrong.'[20] Orwell later published the review in *Time and Tide*, and, assuming that it is the same as the one he submitted to the *New Statesman*, one can see where Orwell must have gone wrong as far as Martin was concerned. 'So far from pushing the Spanish Government further towards the Left,' he declared in the review, 'the Communist influence has pulled it violently towards the Right.' Orwell was restating ideas which had appeared in 'Eye-witness in Barcelona', and Martin was not about to allow his contributor to slip an idea into a review which had been deemed objectionable in an article.

Nevertheless, Orwell could draw only one conclusion from this experience: the *New Statesman* did not want his opinions if they deviated too far from 'policy', and were stated 'uncompromisingly'. The most damaging thing about Martin's rejection is that it does not even try to consider whether Orwell might have been stating the truth. He speaks of maintaining a 'balanced view', and he argues that conclusions must be 'very carefully reached', but he never says that the paper is interested in the truth. Maybe Orwell overstated his case, but it is doubtful that Martin would have approved any attempt to link communism with fascism. During 1937–1938 Orwell tried several different ways of stating the analogy, but perhaps the most succinct version was given in a letter written to a young

305

admirer of his work, Amy Charlesworth. In August 1937 he wrote to her, 'If Fascism means suppression of political liberty and free speech, imprisonment without trial etc., then the present regime in Spain is Fascism ... I don't mean that the rule of the present Government is no better than what Franco would set up if he won, but it is only different in degree, not in kind.'[21]

At this stage in his career, Orwell could always find someone willing to publish his articles and reviews ('Eye-witness in Barcelona' was accepted by the ILP monthly *Controversy*), so Kingsley Martin's rejections were only temporary setbacks. But Martin's response to the first piece must have made Orwell realise that Victor Gollancz would be equally reluctant to publish anything which was critical of the communist movement in Spain. He was so anxious to discover whether his proposed book on the war would receive Gollancz's support that he telephoned the office on a Saturday morning during his first week back in England. Gollancz was at his home in the country, but Orwell was able to speak to Norman Collins. He explained the kind of book he wanted to write, and Collins promised to pass the information along to his employer. On the following Monday, 5 July, Gollancz listened to Collins's account of the call and immediately decided that he did not want anything to do with the book, despite the fact that he had not even talked it over personally with Orwell. He wrote to his author that very day, explaining that he thought the proposed book – as described to him by Collins – would 'harm the fight against fascism'. He did acknowledge, however, that his summary rejection of the book was 'exceedingly presumptuous' since Orwell had actually been fighting fascism while he had been waging his publishing battles from the comfort of his Covent Garden office. One of Gollancz's favourite techniques was to use candour to deflect criticism.[22]

Orwell went to Covent Garden and made his case in person to Norman Collins, but he had no success, and informed his agent that it was 'very unlikely that [Gollancz] would touch a book of that description'.[23] Orwell can hardly be blamed for thinking that there was a 'conspiracy' at work in England 'to prevent the Spanish situation from being understood'. This is what he complained of later that summer in 'Spilling the Spanish Beans', which Philip Mairet published in the *New English Weekly*. No doubt he had Kingsley Martin and Gollancz in mind when he wrote, 'People who ought to know better have lent themselves to the deception on the ground that if you tell the truth about Spain it will be used as Fascist propaganda.'[24]

Fortunately, there were people in English publishing who did know better, and one of them was Fredric Warburg, director of what was at that time a small, obscure publishing house – Secker & Warburg (the publisher himself described it as 'a midget firm, fragile as bone china').[25] In later years Warburg claimed that Orwell had approached him about the book even before he went out to Spain, but it was Warburg who contacted him by letter, and, coincidentally, the letter was written exactly one day after Gollancz wrote his rejection. 'We understand that you are now back from Spain,' Warburg said in his opening sentence, 'and that the wound in your throat is healing. It would appear from a recent issue of the *New Leader* that you have had an exciting escape, and it has been suggested to us that an account of the full story would be of interest to the reading public . . . If you agree, I should like to discuss the matter with you at your convenience. Perhaps you would arrange for an appointment at any time that suits you.'[26] Orwell met Warburg for the first time on 8 July and came away with a good impression. He prepared 'a sort of rough plan' of *Homage to Catalonia* and sent it to Warburg later in the month, explaining that he planned to begin writing it in a few days, and that he hoped to finish it by Christmas.

There were at least a few times in Spain when Orwell thought that he might never get back to his small cottage in Wallington, but in July he and Eileen returned to the village and resumed their quiet life. Aunt Nellie had not taken good care of the place while they were away. There were more mice than usual in the cottage, and the garden was in 'a ghastly mess', according to Orwell. No attempt was made to reopen the shop. Instead the couple began raising chickens, ducks and goats. There was a patch of common ground nearby where the goats were able to graze, and a shed in the back garden where they were stabled. Fanciful names were given to the animals. The cock, for example, was known as 'Henry Ford'. As Orwell explained to Jack Common, this name seemed to fit the bird 'because he had such a brisk, businesslike way of going about his job, in fact, he trod his first hen literally within 5 seconds of being put into the run'.[27] They called their dog – a large, unclipped poodle – 'Marx', who presumably barked a great deal at 'Henry Ford'.

Orwell's voice was growing stronger, though he was still unable to speak loudly. He also discovered that he was unable to sing – 'But people tell me this doesn't matter.'[28] He was feeling well enough to begin asking a few friends to come down for visits. A couple of men from his ILP contingent who had recently returned from Spain paid a visit to give him the latest news about the continuing campaign against the POUM. One former member of his unit, Douglas Moyle, remembered being invited down for a day and taking a long walk with Orwell and Marx. 'It was a nice dog, but of course I was amused by the name, and Eric told me he liked to see how people responded to it. Some guessed that the dog was named after Karl Marx, but others said Groucho Marx, or even Marks and Spencer.'[29]

In his own little village Orwell found that there was some suspicion about his activities in Spain, though it was all from conservatives who had been frightened by stories of Republican mobs looting and burning churches. In a letter to Charlie Doran – a Scottish socialist who had served with him in Spain – Orwell wrote, 'This afternoon Eileen and I had a visit from the vicar, who doesn't at all approve of our having been on the Government side. Of course we had to own up that it was true about the burning of the churches, but he cheered up a lot on hearing they were only Roman Catholic churches.'[30]

'He was reunited with several members of his militia unit when he travelled to Letchworth – only five miles away – for the annual ILP Summer School, which was held in early August. The evening session of 5 August was devoted to a series of short talks by some of the militiamen, who described events both at the front and in Barcelona during the troubles in May. Despite his weak voice, Orwell spoke briefly, sharing the platform with Paddy Donovan and Douglas Moyle. The session began, appropriately enough, with two minutes of silence in memory of Bob Smillie.

Stafford Cottman, who was also present at the summer school, had been in touch with Orwell since their return from Spain. Cottman had come home to Bristol in July to discover that he was the object of a hate campaign being waged by the Young Communist League. Orwell had responded by making a special trip to the town in order to take part in a rally held to protest against the League's treatment of his friend. Before going to Spain, Cottman had been a member of the organisation, but its national council had expelled him after learning that he was fighting with the POUM. 'Comrade Cottman' had been expelled with the words, 'We brand him as an enemy of the working class', and as Orwell later told Charlie Doran, 'The Cottmans' house had been shadowed by members of the YCL who attempt to question everyone who comes in and out.' Orwell was amazed that anyone in England would feel compelled to take such actions against a young man who had bravely risked his life to oppose fascism. 'What a show!' Orwell told Doran. 'To think that we started off as heroic defenders of democracy and only six months later were Trotsky-Fascists sneaking over the border with the police on our heels.'[31]

Near the end of August, Orwell decided that the Communist Party had targeted him for public criticism and was using the pages of the *Daily Worker* to conduct 'a campaign of organised libel' against him. He came to this conclusion after seeing at least three different pieces in the paper condemning him for allegedly saying, in *The Road to Wigan Pier*, that the working classes 'smell'. This was a lie, he told Gollancz, whose help he sought in an effort to put an end to the attacks:

> What I said in Chapter VIII of *Wigan Pier*, as you may perhaps remember, is that middle-class people are brought up to *believe* that the working classes 'smell', which is simply a matter of

observable fact . . . The statement or implication that I think
working people 'smell' is a deliberate lie aimed at people who have
not read this or any other of my books, in order to give them the idea
that I am a vulgar snob and thus indirectly hit at the political parties
with which I have been associated.

On his own Orwell was not in a position to exert any influence
over the *Daily Worker*, but he thought that Gollancz, whose support
for the communist movement was well known, might be willing to
use his influence to help one of his authors. 'I think perhaps it might
be worth your while to intervene and stop attacks of this kind which
will not, of course, do any good to the books you have published for
me or may publish for me in the future.' Gollancz showed this letter
to Harry Pollitt to stop the attacks. Although the campaign against
Orwell did end abruptly, the reason probably had nothing to do with
Gollancz's influence. It is likely, however, that Gollancz pointed out
to Pollitt – as one comrade to another – a threat in Orwell's letter
which could not easily be dismissed: 'I am taking counsel's opinion
. . . If you are speaking to anyone in an authoritative position, you
could tell them that in the case of anything actionable being said
against me, I shall not hesitate to take a libel action immediately.'[32]
If anything was guaranteed to get Gollancz's attention, it was the
word 'libel'. Orwell was only bluffing – he admitted to his agent a
few days later that he did not think there was anything 'legally
libellous' in the paper's 'filthy attack' – but it was a clever ruse.

Orwell was not being overly sensitive to the criticism in the *Daily
Worker*. He understood that their ultimate purpose was to
undermine his credibility as an 'eye-witness in Barcelona'. Why
would anyone take the word of a vulgar snob, an enemy of the
working class who could not stand the smell of them? If it could be
shown that he had no feeling for the ordinary worker, then it would
be easier to dismiss his views on Spain as those of a man 'in Franco's
pay', which was one of the phrases used against Stafford Cottman.
'These people are well aware that I am writing a book about the
Spanish war,' he explained to Leonard Moore, 'and would if they
could, get me written off beforehand as a liar, so as to discredit
anything I say.'[33]

It was against this contentious background in England that Orwell wrote *Homage to Catalonia*, but the meetings, the debates, and the feuds were not so distracting that he fell behind with his work. He finished a rough draft at the beginning of December, and completed the book in mid-January 1938. From a literary stand-point, the weakest parts of his book are those in which he tries to bring out the points of dispute among the left-wing parties. He is frankly apologetic about doing it: 'It is a horrible thing to have to enter into the details of inter-party polemics; it is like diving into a cesspool.' In the 1940s he recalled that a critic whom he respected had told him that it was a big mistake to 'put in all that stuff', and that he had 'turned what might have been a good book into journalism'.[34] The effect is not as bad as that, and in any case the objection is neatly dealt with in the Complete Works edition of 1986, which places Chapters V and XI – the two most political chapters – at the back of the book in two appendices. This was done in accordance with suggestions for revision which Orwell made near the end of his life. As background information, the chapters did indeed make slow reading when placed beside the fast-paced narrative, but his reason for writing them in the first place was that they were needed to counter the lies of the communists, to prove by the careful presentation of facts that certain things had happened, and other things had not. Men and women had been imprisoned because fact had been made subordinate to opinion, and Orwell did not want his readers to forget that innocent people had been harshly punished. 'If I had not been angry about that,' Orwell explained later, 'I should never have written the book.'[35]

Yet even with all its concern for larger political questions, *Homage to Catalonia* is an intensely personal book. Orwell goes to consider-able lengths not to glorify his own story, but to celebrate the simple acts of heroism and decency which he had witnessed in others. All the same, the unmistakable hero of the book is the tall Englishman whose courage and vulnerability make him such a compelling figure in the story of a doomed militia besieged by enemies and friends. The fascination of the tale lies in Orwell's struggle to make sense of a senseless war. With an ancient, rusty rifle he stands guard on a hilltop and contemplates the hopelessness of his position, which is at once tragic and highly comic: 'There were nights when it seemed to me that our position could be stormed by twenty Boy Scouts armed with air-guns, or twenty Girl Guides armed with battledores, for that matter.' With a bullet hole in his throat, he is hauled out of a slippery trench, and while he is being carried down a rocky path, he is thrilled at the touch of a few leaves from an overhanging limb: 'The leaves of the silver poplars which, in places, fringed our trenches brushed against my face; I thought what a good thing it was to be alive in a world where silver poplars grow.' With his previous training in police procedure, he must make a real effort to comprehend the tactics of the communist police, and is genuinely bewildered by the thought that he could be arrested for no apparent reason: 'I kept saying, but why should anyone want to arrest me? What had I done?' And with great compassion, he struggles to come to terms with Bob Smillie's death, insisting on the importance of this one young man's life in a war which had claimed thousands of lives: 'Smillie's death is not a thing I can easily forgive ... What angers one about a death like this is its utter pointlessness. To be killed in battle – yes, that is what one expects; but to be flung into jail, not even for any imaginary offence, but simply owing to dull blind spite, and then left to die in solitude – that is a different matter.'

Homage to Catalonia refuses to accept easy answers. It confronts squarely the ugly, often contradictory facts behind the failure of the socialist revolution in Spain, a failure which so many people refused to acknowledge because it would have 'controverted policy', as Kingsley Martin put it. But the overall mood of the book is not pessimistic or bitter. Quite to the contrary, it is Orwell's most optimistic book. He does not deny that the war was a disaster, but he is careful to note that 'the result is not necessarily disillusionment and cynicism. Curiously enough the whole experience has left me with not less but more belief in the decency of human beings.' The evils done in the name of the revolution do not negate the sacrifices of people such as Smillie, or the bravery of Captain Benjamin Lewinski, or the kindness of John McNair – who risked his life to bring Orwell two packets of Lucky Strikes during the fighting in Barcelona – or the idealism of the Italian militiaman whom Orwell met only briefly – the 'crystal spirit' whose face he never forgot.

Most of all, he would never forget the streets of Barcelona as they were during his first week in Spain. They gave him a glimpse of a different world, a world which he described concisely in a review written for *Time and Tide* in October 1937. The book under consideration was *Red Spanish Notebook*, by Mary Low and Juan Brea. Orwell praised it for its 'intimate day-to-day pictures' of life in the early period of the war, when even the brothels were preaching equality ('Please treat the women as comrades', a notice requested):

> For several months large blocks of people believed that all men are equal and were able to act on their belief. The result was a feeling of liberation and hope . . . No one who was in Spain during the months when people still believed in the revolution will ever forget that strange and moving experience. It has left something behind that no dictatorship, not even Franco's, will be able to efface.[36]

CHAPTER FIFTEEN

The Road to Marrakech

I

Orwell deserved a long rest. He had written six books in six years, and during that period his body had endured two potentially fatal blows – a severe case of pneumonia in 1933, and the bullet wound in 1937. But he would not allow himself the luxury of taking a break – not even a short one. Just as he was finishing *Homage to Catalonia*, a letter arrived offering him a journalist's position in – of all places – Lucknow, India. A polite refusal would have seemed in order, but he wrote back to the editor indicating that he was prepared to take the job, if the Government of India and the India Office would allow it. It was a crazy idea, and he admitted to Jack Common that it was not something he wanted to do. What tempted him to accept it was simply the notion that this was a chance he might later regret passing up. 'It is a frightful bore and I seldom wanted to do anything less, but I feel that it is an opportunity to see interesting things, and that I should afterwards curse myself if I didn't go.'[1]

There was not much money in it. The paper was a liberal one edited by a South African named Desmond Young. He wanted Orwell to be his assistant editor and leader writer, but wrote to him that he could offer only a 'poor salary'. He had read some of his books and was so impressed with his writing that he offered him the position without any prior contact or any effort to collect personal references. The voice in Orwell's work was enough to win him over. But Orwell's doubts about winning permission to enter the country prompted Young to contact a friend in the India Office, A. H. Joyce, and ask for an opinion on the matter. He also asked that Joyce meet with Orwell to discuss the problem and if Joyce did not think that Orwell was serious about taking the job, Young wanted to know. He made it clear that he did not mind if Orwell seemed to be 'a bit difficult', explaining that he was 'prepared to make a good many allowances for anyone who can write as good, clear and forcible English as he can'.

Joyce did meet with Orwell on 18 February and immediately sent a short cable to Young to convey his initial impression of the writer: 'Blair keen for twelve months. Leadering ability undoubted but probably temperamental, unbusinesslike.' He sent a full assessment by airmail that same day, and advised Young that he accept Orwell on a 'trial' basis only. The interview had left him with the feeling that Orwell might prove to be, for Young's purposes at the *Pioneer*, more trouble than he was worth:

> There is no doubt in my mind as to his ability as a leader writer, though I think you may have to be prepared, in view of what I assess to be not merely a determined Left Wing, but probably an extremist, outlook, plus definite strength of character, for difficulties when there is a conflict of views . . . I hope that I have not in any sense been unfair to a man whose intellectual standard is very high, but whose outlook has become soured by circumstances of hardship, though they may have been of his own seeking.

As far as Joyce was able to determine, Orwell had two reasons for wanting the job. He said that he was interested in gaining 'some practical newspaper experience', and that he wanted to 'gather material' for a book on contemporary conditions in India. Although Orwell thought he would stay in the job for an entire year, Joyce needed only one look at the writer's tired, pale face to see that his health might not hold up for that long a time in a place like Lucknow. He was right. Orwell was suffering from overwork, and from his usual winter bronchitis. But there was also a general deterioration of his health, stemming in part from his failure to allow himself a proper period of recovery after he had been shot.

The Government of India was also doubtful about the wisdom of allowing Orwell into the country. It was feared that he would become involved in 'extremist political work' for Indian independence, and that it might not be easy to get him to leave the country once he was in it. This fear appears to have been based entirely on his public career as an author, and not on any evidence of political involvement during his career as a police officer. Because of the slowness with which the bureaucratic wheels turned, Joyce did not receive a formal directive on the subject until April. At that point he was instructed to 'try tactfully to discourage Young from making the appointment and privately convey to him the Government of India's views'.[2]

There was no need to change the editor's mind. By April, Orwell was in no condition to go to India. In early March he had been afflicted with a bad cough, and in a few days his condition had worsened to the point where he was coughing up an alarming amount of blood. 'The bleeding seemed prepared to go on for ever' Eileen later remarked.[3] Her brother examined him and arranged for an ambulance to take him to the Preston Hall Sanatorium in Kent. When he was admitted on 15 March, his condition had stabilised, but he was clearly in a weakened state. Although he was nearly six feet three inches, he weighed only 159 pounds on admission, and X-rays revealed – as one doctor put it – 'irregular and widespread shadows which often occur from aspiration of blood into otherwise healthy areas of lung'.[4]

Yet, right up to the moment when the ambulance came for him, Orwell refused to recognise the seriousness of his condition. On the day before he was taken to the sanatorium, he wrote to Cyril Connolly that he was not going to take the job in India after all – at least not until the autumn. 'The doctors don't think I ought to go.' In an almost casual way, he explained to Connolly that he was writing to him from bed. 'I've been spitting blood again, it always turns out to be not serious.'[5] But it was very serious this time, so serious that he would spend the next five and a half months in the sanatorium. During that time he would be repeatedly tested for tuberculosis, but no conclusive evidence of the disease would be found. His symptoms, however, strongly hinted that he might be tubercular, and therefore he was kept under observation for longer than he had expected on his admission. He expected to be there for only a few days and complained to Eileen that he did not want to spend any more time than was necessary 'in an institution devised for murder' – a reflection of his attitude towards hospitals in general.[6]

One report on his medical condition at Preston Hall indicates very plainly why he was not released earlier, and gives some insight into the overall state of his health:

> In view of the history of recurrent haemoptysis, the condition was considered to be tubercular, and the heavy mottling over the lower lobe of the left lung was thought to be due to a post-haemoptoeic spread of the disease. But as there was also a history of 4 attacks of pneumonia, and since a bronchiectatic dilation could be recognised on the left lower lobe, a primary condition of bronchiectasis (and not tuberculosis) was considered possible. Until Pulmonary Tuberculosis could be definitely excluded, he was treated as suffering from the condition, and was kept strictly at rest, and given a course of colloidal calcium injections intramuscularly, with Vitamin D.

As the consultant surgeon at the sanatorium, Laurence O'Shaughnessy visited Orwell once each week and made every effort to determine whether his brother-in-law was, in fact, suffering from tuberculosis. Dr Arnold Bentley, the physician who preserved Orwell's file at Preston Hall, and who made it available for this biography, believed that 'quite searching and for the time adequate investigations' were made at Preston Hall to detect any sign of tubercle bacilli in Orwell's lungs. If Dr O'Shaughnessy could not make the diagnosis, then it is doubtful that any other lung specialist of the time could have proved otherwise. At the very time that he was attending his brother-in-law, the doctor was in the middle of writing, with two other men, an authoritative textbook on the disease.

In the meantime there was not much that could be done for him. He was given injections of vitamins and minerals and was kept on a healthy diet, which produced a modest weight gain of almost ten pounds. And he was forced to spent a great deal of time resting in bed. When he tried to combine this with long periods of writing, he was rebuked. His medical records contain a notation stating that the doctors had 'warned him duly of the risks of literary research'. He complained to Jack Common, 'The bore is that I can't work . . . I am studying botany in a very elementary way, otherwise mainly doing crossword puzzles.'[7]

Preston Hall was a progressive place with a first-rate staff and pleasant surroundings. The main part of the hospital was housed in an enormous country house built in 1849 by a railway millionaire. The house stands on a hill overlooking the Medway valley, near the little town of Aylesford. In Orwell's time the grounds were spacious and immaculately maintained. There were rose gardens, and a long avenue of tall cedars. The British Legion had purchased the estate in 1925 with the aim of making it a model sanatorium for ex-service men. Orwell was one of the few patients at the institution who had not been in the Army or Navy, but as the brother-in-law of the consultant surgeon, he was fortunate enough to be admitted on a special basis. In addition, he was given a private room. All in all, it was a comfortable arrangement for him, and after he had been there for a week or two, he did admit that it was 'a very nice place'.[8]

Eileen's visits were limited to once a fortnight. It was a long, and expensive, journey from Wallington to Aylesford, and she needed to stay at the cottage in order to care for their animals. Orwell did manage to make a few friends among the patients. One of them was a young man named Victor Stacey, who had worked as an apprentice sign painter before his admission in 1935. In retrospect, Orwell's stay seemed relatively brief to Stacey, who remained a patient for four years. He understood that the patient 'Eric Blair' was the writer 'George Orwell', but that fact was never mentioned by the writer himself. He seemed more interested in non-literary topics, and showed a great deal of curiosity when Stacey talked about some of his colourful Victorian ancestors.

When warmer weather arrived, and Orwell's health began to show real improvement, he was allowed to go for walks outside the grounds. Stacey remembered that Orwell liked to walk to Aylesford and visit the parish church, St Peter's, which stood on a high, breezy hilltop with a good view of the river valley and the town's narrow, medieval bridge. The actress Sybil Thorndike had grown up in the area, and her father had been the vicar in the early 1900s. Orwell noticed the vicar's grave and was much taken by the simple beauty of the inscription, which said that he had 'died at Evensong in his church'. Stacey recalled that Orwell once made a trip, by bus, to see the cathedral at Rochester, and on his return he was proud to inform his friend that he had found a way to save sixpence on the journey:

> It wasn't much, of course, but he must have been anxious about money at the time. He had discovered that if you walked through Aylesford, across the valley, to Blue Bell Hill, and then to the Bell Pub, you could catch a bus to Rochester for only three pence each way, whereas if you caught the bus in Aylesford it was six pence each way, through Maidstone. He was quite pleased with himself for having found this out, and wanted to pass along his knowledge to me, as a friendly gesture, you see.[9]

These extended journeys were not what the doctors had in mind when they told him that he could go for walks beyond the grounds, but it was impossible to make him stick to any regimen for long, except of course to the regimens he chose to impose upon himself.

He could not wait to begin writing another book. The idea for his next novel had come to him at the end of the previous year. 'I have only a vague idea of it as yet, as you may well imagine,' he wrote to Moore on 6 December 1937. 'All I have thought of is this: it will be a novel, it will not be about politics, and it will be about a man who is having a holiday and trying to make a temporary escape from responsibility, public and private. The title I thought of is "Coming Up for Air".'[10] This is as far as Orwell had taken the idea at the time that he entered Preston Hall, but as his health improved he began to think more about the novel, and by June he had 'sketched out' a general plan for it. Eileen reported to Moore that 'the book seethes in his head and he is very anxious to get on with it'.[11] As soon as he was 'completely fit', he intended to begin writing the first chapter. Meanwhile, in April, *Homage to Catalonia* had been published, and he had been carefully reading through all the reviews, hoping that the book would provoke the kind of open analysis of communist tactics which Gollancz and Kingsley Martin had wanted to avoid.

He was surprised at how favourable some of the reviews were. In a piece on four recent Spanish War books, Desmond Flower wrote in the *Observer*, 'The giant of these four, or of any other writers on the Spanish War for that matter, is Mr. Orwell. My admiration for him is enormous and unqualified.' Rarely had Orwell received such praise in a major paper, but part of the reason for it is that Flower did not have a political axe to grind. What appealed to him in the book was its generous spirit of humanity, and its 'objective prose of stately, unhurried, unexaggerated clarity'. He ended the review by declaring that 'Mr. Orwell is a great writer', which was a rather daring assertion to make in a national newspaper in 1938 before *Animal Farm* and *Nineteen Eighty-Four* had made so many other people come to the same conclusion.[12]

Of course, there were also a number of bad reviews. One in the *Listener* barely mentioned the book itself, devoting most of its space to unsubstantiated attacks on the leaders of the POUM, whom the anonymous reviewer vilified as 'traitors'. Orwell felt that it deserved a reply, and he wrote a magnificent letter to the editor shortly after the review appeared. The first part of his reply attempts to refute some of the unfounded assertions about the POUM, but it is in the last paragraph that Orwell scores a direct hit against the critic: 'I do not expect or wish for "good" reviews, and if your reviewer chooses to use most of his space in expressing his own political opinions, that is a matter between him and yourself. But I think I have a right to ask that when a book of mine is discussed at the length of a column there shall be at least some mention of what I have actually said.' The reviewer replied with still more attacks on the POUM, including the condescending remark that the party's ordinary members had been easily misled into becoming 'Franco's fifth column' because they were 'poor and ignorant men', and 'the complexities of the revolutionary situation were beyond them'. In an admirable display of fairness, the editor, J. R. Ackerley, declared that Orwell's objections had not been answered: 'We are bound to say, in printing our reviewer's reply, that we consider it hardly meets the points made by Mr Orwell, to whom we express our regrets.'[13]

Orwell was proud of his book and hoped that it would sell at least three thousand copies. He wanted it to reach four thousand, but thought that very unlikely, and in a letter to Jack Common he complained about the 'financial racket' in the book trade 'which prevents any book from a small publisher getting a proper number of reviews'.[14] But the problem was not that the book failed to receive a fair share of reviews, but that some of the more important pieces were in minor papers or in obscure corners of large papers. Desmond Flower's praise, for example, is not easy to spot in a long column dealing with four books. Whatever the reason, the book did not sell as many copies as Orwell had expected. In fact, its sales were disastrous, and when Orwell first learned of how bad they were, his reaction was disbelief. He heard the bad news from Moore later that year: the book sold only seven hundred copies in its first four months in print. Moore tried to sound upbeat by saying that this figure was 'in all the circumstances . . . very good'. But Orwell knew that there was no way to put this figure in a good light, unless Moore had made a mistake: 'Was it really 700? I ask because it seems to me that 700 would be a terribly bad sale and incidentally would mean a heavy loss for Warburg, and it struck me that it may have been a typist's error.'[15]

The figure was accurate. The first printing had been small – only 1500 copies – so Warburg did not incur a great financial loss. But the book sold so poorly that the publisher still had surplus copies of this edition on hand as late as 1951. The first American edition did not appear until 1952. How could such an important book be neglected for so many years? To a great degree, it was hurt by bad timing. Although Orwell could hardly have worked any faster to bring it out, it was published at a time when the subject had already been examined in several noteworthy books, and the public's attention was moving away from it to other topics. Orwell saw that this was the case and complained of it to Yvonne Davet, one of the French translators of his books. 'The trouble is that as soon as anything like the Spanish civil war happens, hundreds of journalists immediately produce rubbishy books which they put together with scissors and paste, and later when the serious books come along people are sick of the subject.'[16]

The commercial failure of *Homage to Catalonia* made Orwell's low opinion of the book trade sink even lower. He liked to say that it was a 'financial racket' which favoured heavily advertised books, regardless of their quality, and which exerted a certain influence over the reviewers' opinions in the big Sunday papers, as a result of the publishers' large investments in newspaper advertising. Large publishers who spent a great deal of money on such ads were rewarded with favourable, or at least prominent, reviews of their most important titles. Orwell was so convinced that this was the case that he declared, in the summer of 1938:

> When I think of what the book trade is like morally, I wonder why we don't go the whole hog and organise it into a proper racket on American lines. Then if Ralph Straus [the *Sunday Times* critic] failed to deliver the goods, you would just pay so much into the fund and a couple of pineapples would go through his drawing room window.[17]

Ralph Straus was not such a bad critic – in fact, in 1939, he wrote a glowing review of *Coming Up for Air* – but Orwell was often tempted to use well-known figures as convenient symbols of some idea which he wanted to attack. This is a common enough tendency among writers of all political persuasions, but Orwell knew it was unfair, and would not deny it when the point was brought home to him. A good example of this is his expression of regret to Stephen Spender for making 'offensive remarks about "parlour Bolsheviks such as Auden and Spender" or words to that effect'. Connolly had introduced the two men to each other in 1938, bringing Spender along on a visit to Preston Hall. Later, in a letter to Spender, Orwell felt obliged to explain why he had used him 'as a symbol of the parlour Bolshie'. The explanation, even by Orwell's standards, is exceptionally candid:

> *A.* your verse, what I have read of it, did not mean very much to me, *b.* I looked upon you as a sort of fashionable successful person, also a Communist or communist sympathiser, and I have been very hostile to the C.P. since about 1935, and *c.* because not having met you I could regard you as a type and also an abstraction. Even if when I met you I had not happened to like you, I should still have been bound to change my attitude, because when you meet anyone in the flesh you realise immediately that he is a human being and not a sort of caricature embodying certain ideas.[18]

But Orwell believed that caricature was sometimes a necessary weapon in making an argument forceful, and he implied to Spender that he would go on using the weapon against other people when he thought it was justified. His attitude was illogical, but it represented an irresolvable conflict between his feelings as an ordinary human being and his attitudes as a tough-minded critic intent on exposing some error. 'I don't mix much in literary circles, because I know from experience that once I have met and spoken to anyone I shall never again be able to show any intellectual brutality towards him, even when I feel that I ought to, like the Labour MPs who get patted on the back by dukes and are lost forever more.'[19] In using the phrase 'intellectual brutality', he was advocating neither bullying nor lying, but he was admitting that in the heat of intellectual battle he was occasionally guilty of landing some low blows. Connolly recognised his friend's ambivalence towards the use of 'intellectual brutality', and attempted to explain it by saying that Orwell 'suffered from a typically English form of the Oedipus complex, by which, having dealt his father's authority a swingeing blow he would rush up to say, "Have I hurt you?" '[20]

For the sake of Orwell's 'intellectual brutality', it was perhaps a good thing that Connolly did not bring along more literary friends on his visits to Preston Hall. But Orwell did meet one literary figure that year whose help would prove invaluable. Max and Dorothy Plowman came for a visit one day and brought with them the novelist L. H. Myers, who had been wanting to meet Orwell for some time. The two novelists seemed to enjoy each other's company, and they later became friends. But on the strength of his impressions from this one meeting, Myers decided that he wanted to do something to help Orwell, whose books he admired. He had learned that the doctors were advising Orwell to spend six months in a warmer climate, following the stay at Preston Hall. Money was a problem, however, and Orwell was trying to save up enough to rent a 'little cottage' in the South of France. Myers was fortunate to have an independent income, and he thought that he could put some of his money to good use by helping Orwell to go abroad. With admirable generosity, he arranged for the Plowmans to give Orwell £300 as a gift from an anonymous admirer. Orwell never learned the source of the gift, and he accepted it only on the condition that it be considered a loan. Eight years later, when he began making money from the success of *Animal Farm*, he repaid the 'loan', explaining to Dorothy Plowman, 'It's a terribly long time afterwards to start repaying, but until this year I was really unable to.'[21]

II

It was an especially good thing that Myers made his gift when he did because Orwell's doctors informed him, near the end of his period at the sanatorium, that he would need to go some place warmer and drier than the South of France. They suggested Morocco. The cost of living there was not great, but getting there and back by ocean liner did involve significant expense. (For obvious reasons it would not have been wise to make part of the journey overland, through Spain.) Eileen made arrangements for them to sail to Gibraltar on 2 September, but they seem to have been uncertain of their plans for the second stage of the journey. Only a week before they left, Orwell told Jack Common, 'We've booked as far as Gibraltar, then we take another boat to Casa Blanca, and then I'm not sure, but I think we head for the Atlas mountains, wherever they may be. Our geography was so poor that both E. and I thought French Morocco gave on the Mediterranean, whereas it's really the Atlantic.'[22] To help them with their geography, Orwell contacted his former employer at Booklovers' Corner. 'What I particularly want, if you have any second hand, is a Baedeker of French Morocco,' he wrote to Francis Westrope, adding that he would also like to have 'any maps of the country, and a phrase-book or small dictionary of Arabic – nothing elaborate, but something cheap that would help one to pick up a few words of the language.'[23] He knew that he could easily get by in Morocco using only his French, but since he would be living for several months among Arabs, he wanted to make some effort to speak with them in their own language.

Jack Common agreed to take care of the cottage in Wallington, including the animals, while Eileen and Orwell were out of the country. After describing its primitive features to him in detail, Eileen remarked, 'I must say I hope you are strong-minded enough to take Wallington on.'[24] Orwell wrote Common long letters about the care and feeding of the animals, describing such elementary details as the best way of milking Muriel the goat: 'As to the milking you'll probably find it easier by degrees. I did tell you to grease your fingers didn't I? It makes it easier . . . Draw the hand down the teat, being careful not to relax the pressure till you reach the end. When no more milk comes out of this teat, go on to the other.'[25]

Orwell's long stay at Preston Hall did not result in a dramatic improvement in his health, but it did allow him to recover some strength, and to get more rest than he would ever have given himself on his own. He later told Dr J. B. McDougall, the director of the sanatorium, that he was 'extraordinarily happy and comfortable there'. Yet he was eager to get back to a regular routine of writing, and did not want to be under any restrictions. He had been able to do some work at Preston Hall – a few reviews, some notes for his novels – but the only important piece he had managed to complete was a short pamphlet of 5000–6000 words called 'Socialism and War'. He wrote it in May and sent it to Leonard Moore, telling him it was 'just conceivable we might find a publisher for it'. He warned him, however, not to bother sending it to Gollancz, 'as it's right off his line'.[26] What Orwell's 'line' was in this pamphlet is something which will never be known for certain because Moore was unable to find a publisher for it, and Orwell gave up on it, presumably destroying the typescript after instructing his agent, later in the year, not to take 'any more trouble with that wretched pamphlet'. Besides its title, the only other thing which is known about it is that it was 'more or less on the subject of pacificism', according to Orwell.

Some notion of its 'line' may be had from a long letter which Orwell wrote to the *New English Weekly*, responding to criticisms of pacifist thinking in the paper's correspondence columns. He wrote his letter in the same month that he wrote his pamphlet, so some of the phrases and sentences may even be identical. His position on war at this time was fairly simple – there was no use fighting one if the governing classes intended to use it as a way to delay social change. He charged that the English people were being asked to support a 'capitalist-imperialist' war, and that 'flyblown' slogans such as 'in defence of democracy' or 'against Fascism' were being used to hide the fact the capitalists wanted a war. It would allow them to say, 'You can't have a rise in wages *now*, because we have got to prepare for war. Guns before butter.' In Orwell's opinion, the 'left-wing intelligentsia' was also pushing for war, as a way of drawing the European democracies into an alliance with the Soviet Union. His experience in Spain had made him wary of accepting any call to arms. He was still willing to fight fascism, but he had learned to be suspicious of the motives of powerful political leaders who were so willing to accept the possibility of war. He wanted to know what he was fighting for – was it to destroy Hitler? Or was it to preserve capitalist privileges? In Spain he had thought he was fighting fascism, but he had learned the bitter lesson that his communist 'allies' were more interested in expanding and preserving their power than in defeating Franco. He did not want to be cheated in that way again.[27]

This was the way he thought in 1938, but, of course, when war finally came in 1939, and the threat to England's security was suddenly very real, his old-fashioned sense of patriotism – among other things – made him change his mind about fighting. The outbreak of war made him realise that the practical necessity of defeating the Nazis had become so great that there was no choice open to him but to support the war. He never had any doubt, however, that this was an exceedingly imperfect compromise. 'The choice before human beings,' he wrote in 1941, 'is not, as a rule, between good and evil but between two evils. You can let the Nazis rule the world: that is evil; or you can overthrow them by war, which is also evil. There is no other choice before you, and whichever you choose you will not come out with clean hands.'[28]

His anti-war position of 1938 was in keeping with the policies of the Independent Labour Party, and though he had never bothered to join the party while he had been fighting under its banner in Spain, he decided in the summer of 1938 that he needed to make a formal commitment to it. On 24 June he announced in the *New Leader* his reasons for joining the ILP. He explained that he had tried to fight the 'capitalist–imperialist' system as a writer, but that it was no longer enough to work against this system by words alone. 'The tempo of events is quickening: the dangers which once seemed a generation distant are staring us in the face. One has got to be actively a Socialist, not merely sympathetic to Socialism.'

No doubt his relatively quiet period at Preston Hall had given him the time to think about what the future might hold and to reflect on what he had managed to achieve in the past. As far as his political activity was concerned, he seems to have worried that he was in danger of being merely anti-fascist or anti-communist, without being pro-anything. His alliance with the ILP would not last long, but he was obviously looking for some identifiable political position which he could defend and which he could share with a substantial group of other people. Yet the ILP appealed to him, in part, because it was not a large party and was not allied with any powerful special interests. 'It needs all the help it can get,' he said in the *New Leader*, 'including any help I can give it myself.' His need to align himself, at this time, with an organised party is apparent in an important letter which he wrote to the novelist Naomi Mitchison in early June. He was responding to a letter from her about *Homage to Catalonia*:

I am glad you liked the book. As you say, it is harder than ever before to make sure of the right political line. If one allows a free hand to the Communists and their friends he is, I am certain, allowing the whole Socialist movement to be perverted, whereas if one opposes them there is always the chance that one is, objectively if not intentionally, aiding the Fascists ... I have never been much impressed by the C.P. line of talk to the effect, 'People's motives do not matter, the only thing that matters is the objective result of the actions to begin with' – it is much easier to be certain about people's motives than to foresee the result of any course of action, and in practice the C.P. prophecies about the results of this and that have often turned out to be wrong. Secondly, their whole line of thought is based on doing evil that good may come, which in my opinion implies that causes do not have effects. On the other hand there is an ever-present danger of becoming simply anti-Communist, as the Trotskyists do, which is completely sterile even if it isn't harmful.[29]

Joining the ILP was one way to take a positive stand, but Orwell could not behave like a good party man, regardless of the party. A mere year and a half after joining the party he was criticising it for sticking to its anti-war position in the face of Hitler's determined effort to defeat Britain and her allies. In his autobiographical sketch for the American reference work *Twentieth Century Authors*, he stated, 'I was for a while a member of the Independent Labour Party, but left them at the beginning of the present war because I considered that they were talking nonsense and proposing a line of policy that could only make things easier for Hitler.' To this statement, he added another explanation, acknowledging his recognition that, as a writer, he felt obliged to remain free to speak his own line. 'In sentiment I am definitely "left", but I believe that a writer can only remain honest if he keeps free of party labels.' This would remain his position for the rest of his career.

Europe was already beginning to move perilously close to war when Orwell and Eileen left for Morocco in September. The Munich crisis was beginning to take shape, and by the end of the month Hitler's demands for Czech territory would have most of the world worrying that war was imminent. During his six and a half months in Morocco, Orwell followed international events closely, but he was also absorbed in the writing of *Coming Up for Air*, part of which is set in a time far removed from the tumultuous period of the late 1930s. While much of Europe was busy preparing for 'total war', Orwell sat in a small, dusty villa outside Marrakech writing about the luxuriant landscape of the Thames valley and the seemingly stable Edwardian world which he had known in his boyhood.

It was easy to get lost in this world, but he never forgot for a moment that there were threatening noises disturbing the contemporary world. At times he felt almost as though he were in a race to finish the book before a war started. He knew that one could break out at any moment. 'I wonder if the political situation will hold up!' he remarked in the middle of his stay, writing to Jack Common. 'It's getting harder and harder for the English public. I suppose 50 percent of them knew whereabouts Austria was and about 20 percent knew where Czechoslovakia was, but where is the Ukraine? And where are Memel and Eupen Malmedy, not to mention Russian Subcarpathia? The only people who can really keep up with affairs nowadays are philatelists.'[30]

The Orwells arrived in Morocco on 11 September. It was a tiresome journey for both of them, beginning with the voyage from Tilbury to Gibraltar, and then a rough crossing from Gibraltar to Tangier. To fortify himself against seasickness, Orwell brought along a German remedy called Vasano and was happy to discover that it actually worked. He later reported to Dr McDougall that this was the first voyage he had made in which he had not been seasick. He was so proud of this achievement that, according to Eileen, 'he walked round the boat with a seraphic smile watching people being sick'. They took a train from Tangier and arrived in Marrakech on 14 September. The weather was very hot, and the hotel where they stayed on the first night was not exactly what they had expected. 'Lately it has changed hands and is obviously a brothel', Eileen wrote to Ida Blair on the day after their arrival. 'I haven't much direct knowledge of brothels but as they offer a special service they can probably all afford to be dirty and without any other conveniences. However we stayed for one day, partly because Eric didn't notice anything odd about it until he tried to live in it.'[31]

It was not an auspicious beginning, but matters improved quickly when they found more comfortable quarters at the home of a Madame Vellat. They stayed in Marrakech for a month, and then they moved to the Villa Simont, which was a few miles from the town. It stood in the middle of an orange grove, and though it was sparsely furnished, there was more than enough room for two people – two bedrooms, a bathroom, kitchen, large sitting-room and a small observatory on the roof which Orwell was able to use as his study. The couple tried to create a North African version of their life in Wallington, planting a small garden and acquiring some goats and chickens. ('I simply have to have a bit of garden and a few animals,' Orwell told Jack Common.)[32]

From the very beginning Orwell was troubled by the dry, desolate look of the country round Marrakech, and by the dire poverty which existed in the town. After only a few weeks he was already 'pining to be back in England', and after a couple of months he was beginning to think that it had been a waste of time and money to come to Morocco. He did not see that the climate was doing much to improve his health, and he was generally bored by the local sights. He called Morocco 'a beastly dull country, no forests and literally no wild animals, and the people anywhere near a big town utterly debauched by the tourist racket and their poverty combined, which turn them into a race of beggars and curio-sellers'.[33]

The poverty was especially distressing. As far as he could determine, most of the Arab population seemed to be living at the level of about a shilling a day, while their French rulers occupied the best land and exploited its resources 'pretty ruthlessly'. Many of the Arabs were reduced to cultivating tiny patches of dry soil 'with implements which would have been out of date in the days of Moses'. The poor Arabs in the town suffered from appallingly high rates of disease, and when they died, they were buried in miserable little graves. In the diary which he kept during his stay, Orwell recorded his impressions of an Arab burial ground:

The Arab funerals here are the wretchedest I have seen. The
dead man is carried by friends and relatives on a rough wooden
bier, wrapped in a cloth ... A hole not more than two feet deep is
hacked in the ground and the body dumped in it with nothing
over it except a mound of earth and usually either a brick or a
broken pot at one end, presumably the head.[34]

One day during the early weeks of their stay they were sitting at
a restaurant eating their meal when some Arab funeral processions
went by. Eileen later recalled that all the flies had suddenly left the
restaurant 'for a few minutes to sample a passing corpse'.[35]

Eileen was not as unhappy with Marrakech as her husband was,
but she did admit that at first it had seemed 'dreadful to live in'.
Some of her descriptions of the place are almost as good as
Orwell's: 'There are beautiful arches with vile smells coming out of
them and adorable children covered in ringworm and flies. I found
an open space to watch the sunset from and too late realised that
part of the ground to the west of us was a graveyard; I really couldn't
bear Eric's conversation about the view as dominated by invisible
worms and we had to go away without seeing the sunset.'[36]

Several of her letters to friends and relatives have survived from
this period, and they contain more than a few hints of exasperation
with her husband's behaviour, especially his tendency to make a
virtue out of imagining dark possibilities for the future. In a letter to
Marjorie Dakin, which was written in late September, Eileen
reported that Orwell had been talking a great deal about his plans to
construct a dugout at Wallington to protect them from falling
bombs in the coming war: 'But the dugout has generally been by
way of light relief; his specialities are concentration camps and the
famine.' Her letter also indicates that she had come to expect him to
behave unreasonably: 'To my surprise he does intend to stay here
whatever happens. In theory this seems too reasonable and even
comfortable to be in character; in practice perhaps it wouldn't be so
comfortable. Anyway I am thankful we got here.' To some extent,
her criticisms were playful, but there is no mistaking the sense of
frustration underlying them. He made unreasonable demands on

himself, and it is only to be expected that Eileen would have found these demands difficult to live with.

The low point of their stay came in December when both of them became ill, more or less at the same time. The water at their villa was bad, and they were troubled by stomach disorders for a good part of October and November. In this weakened condition they each developed a headache and fever. 'Eric was ill and in bed for more than a week and as soon as he was better I had an illness I'd actually started before his but had necessarily postponed. I enjoyed the illness: I had to do all the cooking as usual but I did it in a dressing-gown and firmly carried my tray back to bed. Now we are both well, or I remember thinking that we were very well last night. This evening we are literally swaying on our feet.'[37] It is interesting to compare this description with his brief comment on his illness. Although he admits in one letter that he was in bed for a week, he dismisses it as a case of being only 'slightly ill'. The one reason he bothers even to mention it is that he was upset at having to lose a week which could have been devoted to his novel.[38]

In January, when they were both in better health, and when a rough draft of *Coming Up for Air* had been completed, they took a brief holiday, going up into the Atlas mountains to see some of the Berber villages. This part of Morocco delighted Orwell. At an elevation of five thousand feet the air was refreshing, and there were deep ravines full of frozen snow. They stayed in a cheap hotel at Taddert, and Orwell appears to have done nothing more taxing than write a couple of letters and make a long entry in his diary. It was a real break, and he returned from the trip feeling refreshed. His most enduring memory of the visit was the fascinating appearance of the village women. He thought that their features were 'exceedingly striking', especially their eyes, though he was amazed at their apparent indifference to dirt. 'You will see exquisitely beautiful women walking about with their necks almost invisible under dirt.'[39]

John Lehmann had written to Orwell in December inviting him to contribute again to *New Writing*, and in this invitation Orwell saw the opportunity to write a sketch based on what he had seen and heard in Marrakech. He drew a lot of his material for the piece from his diary, but Eileen may have suggested to him that he begin it with the scene at the restaurant on the day the funeral processions went by. It is one of his most effective openings: 'As the corpse went past the flies left the restaurant table in a cloud and rushed after it, but they came back a few minutes later.' Like all good openings, this one makes it impossible for the reader *not* to continue reading. The theme of the piece is the 'invisibility' of the poor in Marrakech. On one level, they are, of course, all too visible, with their rags and outstretched hands, their physical afflictions, their corpses. But Orwell knows that these conditions exist because the colonial powers who could improve them have chosen not to see them. As individuals, the poor inhabitants of Marrakech might as well be invisible for all the attention they receive.

The burial grounds illustrate the point more convincingly than anything else. Because the graves are so shallow, and are generally unmarked, it is easy to stumble upon them, quite literally, as Eileen almost did one day. In 'Marrakech' the ragged men and women barely make an impression on their European 'superiors' unless their bones happen to be underfoot:

> They rise out of the earth, they sweat and starve for a few years,
> and then they sink back into the nameless mounds of the
> graveyard and nobody notices that they are gone. And even the
> graves themselves soon fade back into the soil. Sometimes, out
> for a walk, as you break your way through the prickly pear, you
> notice that it is rather bumpy underfoot, and only a certain
> regularity in the bumps tells you that you are walking over
> skeletons.

Orwell does not exempt himself from those who have failed to *see* the humanity in the human forms crowding the streets and the alleyways of the town. He includes in the sketch an expanded version of an incident from his diary which describes a moment when he was feeding bread to gazelles in the public gardens. An Arab worker, hungry for bread, came over to him and asked for some of it. Until the worker approached him, he was invisible – even an animal could command more attention than a hungry man.

Perhaps the most impressive effect in the sketch involves a shift in voice. At the end of the piece a French colonial army made up mostly of black Africans marches along a road, obedient to the commands of their white officers riding beside them on horseback. The long line of soldiers is described in prose which is typically clear but which is more literary than colloquial, employing words such as 'contemptuous' and 'inquisitive'. But then, as the reader is taking in the description of the troops, the voice of the writer makes a startling shift to a voice which asks, in the direct manner of one friend speaking to another, 'How much longer can we go on kidding these people? How long before they turn their guns in the other direction?' Like the opening sentence, these blunt questions are difficult to ignore. They catch the reader off guard and demand at least a moment's consideration of the 'faceless' individuals who make up the great armies and the invisible crowds in the colonial towns. Orwell knows the day will come when those faces will demand to be seen, just as his questions demand to be heard.

CHAPTER SIXTEEN

The Face Behind the Page

After slightly more than six months in Marrakech, Orwell could not wait to get home. He returned on a Japanese liner from Casablanca at the end of March 1939. When the Orwells reached England, Eileen went to visit her family in Greenwich while Orwell went to Southwold, where his father was dying of cancer. Sadly, it was an acutely painful form of intestinal cancer, and there was not much that could be done to help old Mr Blair. Nevertheless, when Orwell arrived, he attempted to be of some use with the household chores, and he spent time reading to his father and telling him stories of life in Marrakech. Yet through no fault of his own Orwell's visit did not go well. He became ill with a high fever, and almost at the same time his mother came down with a bad attack of phlebitis. Eileen had to be summoned from Greenwich to help out. 'I came down all in a rush, as they say,' Eileen later wrote to a friend, 'to do a bit of filial-by-law nursing and was met at the doorstep by Eric with a temperature of about 102. Since then all have been in bed and I have spent the whole day creating confusion in one sickroom after another.'[1]

Orwell did not recover from his illness for almost a week. He treated it as nothing more serious than a bad cold, the result of a change in climate, and as soon as he felt fit to travel, he went with Eileen to stay at their cottage in Wallington. He had finished typing *Coming Up for Air* on the return voyage from Morocco, and was still waiting to hear a reaction from Gollancz, with whom he had left the typescript before going to stay in Southwold. After all the trouble he had experienced from Gollancz, and after the cold treatment which he had been given when *Homage to Catalonia* was rejected, it may seem incredible that he would submit anything else to the publisher. But he had no choice. While he had been away in Spain, a contract had been drawn up by Gollancz which gave him an option on Orwell's next three novels. Eileen had been left in charge of his literary affairs while he was away, and she had signed the contract for him. At the time he probably would have agreed to all its conditions, but it was not a contract which he would find satisfactory in future years, and in 1939 he may well have wanted to try his luck with another publisher. There was always the chance, of course, that Gollancz would not want any of his novels. If the publisher refused to accept the work, he was free to take it elsewhere.

Orwell was fully aware of these conditions during the time that he was working on the book, and there is some reason to believe that he tried to make the novel the kind of book which Gollancz would not want. The strongest evidence for this is the novel's rather harsh treatment of a character who lectures at a meeting of the Left Book Club. The descriptions of the meeting and the speaker are so damaging that Gollancz could not have helped being offended by them. The lecturer is a little middle-aged man in a plain suit who seems harmless enough until he mounts the speakers' platform and begins spouting slogans. He stirs up hatred in the meeting, denouncing the fascists in a 'grating voice', and repeating his slogans over and over. The protagonist of the novel, George Bowling, watches the little man work himself into a frenzy of hate. 'It's a ghastly thing, really, to have a sort of human barrel-organ shooting propaganda at you by the hour. . . . Hate, hate, hate. Let's all get together and have a good hate . . . I saw the vision that he was seeing . . . It's a picture of himself smashing people's faces in with a spanner. Fascist faces, of course.' This is an early version of the Two Minutes' Hate which Orwell would include in *Nineteen Eighty-Four* as an integral part of Big Brother's rule, but even in this milder version it should have been strong enough to make Gollancz reject the novel, and perhaps that was what Orwell was counting on.

In late April he heard from Moore that Gollancz had serious reservations about the book, and was delaying a decision to accept it. He was not surprised. In his reply to Moore he showed little interest in staying with Gollancz, though he took pains not to appear ungrateful for his publisher's help in the early years of his career:

> I thought Gollancz might show fight. The book is, of course, only a novel and more or less unpolitical, so far as it is possible for a book to be that nowadays, but its general tendency is pacifist, and there is one chapter (chapter i. of Part III – I suppose you haven't seen the manuscript) which describes a Left Book Club meeting and which Gollancz no doubt objects to. I also think it perfectly conceivable that some of Gollancz's Communist friends have been at him to drop me and any other politically doubtful writers who are on his list. You know how this political racket works, and of course it is a bit difficult for Gollancz . . . to be publishing books proving that persons like myself are German spies and at the same time to be publishing my own books.[2]

In a postscript to this letter Orwell insisted that even if Gollancz indicated that he might take the book, there could be no question of altering it structurally or, indeed, of making any changes other than minor ones to avoid 'libel actions'. Though he was not trying to appear deliberately intent on subverting his contract, Orwell was making it quite difficult for his publisher to exercise the option. It was Orwell who was showing some fight, after putting up with demands and criticisms from Gollancz in previous years. This was his revenge, and he was going to make Gollancz accept or reject the book as it stood. As he told Jack Common, in no uncertain terms, he was not going to allow Gollancz 'to bugger me [about]'.[3]

Amazingly, the publisher gave in to Orwell and brought out the novel without demanding major changes. It is one of Orwell's best books, a great improvement over some of his early work, and perhaps Gollancz decided that he could not risk spoiling his investment in the writer by turning him away just as he was beginning to come into his own. It was also the case that the book could be excused for being politically suspect since it was 'only a novel', and was thus less of a threat than a more direct polemical attack. Whatever the reason, less than two months later, on 12 June 1939, Gollancz published the novel. It was, however, to be the last Orwell novel to bear the Gollancz imprint. When Orwell turned to fiction again, in 1943, he produced a work which a man of Gollancz's political persuasion could not possibly publish: *Animal Farm*.

It is tempting to consider what might have happened to Orwell's career if he had left Gollancz after *Homage to Catalonia* was rejected. With another publisher, he might have experimented more freely with political fiction and might have written more of it. Instead he wrote only three novels, one of them very short, in the twelve years which followed *Homage to Catalonia*. Probably no other writer in the first half of this century was better prepared than Orwell to make political writing into an art, but one of the great ironies in modern literary history must surely be that such a writer was matched, for so long, with a publisher so ill-prepared to encourage his ambition.

Although Orwell told Moore that *Coming Up for Air* is 'more or less unpolitical', there is a political message in the book, and it is similar to the one which concludes *Homage to Catalonia*. Returning to England from Spain, Orwell describes in his book the scene from his railway carriage as he travels across 'southern England, probably the sleekest landscape in the world', and he marvels at how slight the changes have been in this landscape since the days when he was a boy. It has been spared many of the horrors of the modern world – especially the horrors of modern warfare – and its peaceful aspect makes him think that the troubles in Spain are thousands of miles away, as though they were no more immediate than 'earthquakes in Japan, famines in China'. But the sleepy fields of southern England are not as protected from the outside world as they might seem, and Orwell's vision of the future is one in which this 'deep, deep, sleep of England' is shattered by the sound of bombs.

A large part of *Coming Up for Air* is devoted to a lyrical celebration of the sleepy English countryside, but there is also a powerful sense in the book that the beauty of that landscape may be doomed by the relentless movement of vast, unseen historical forces. George

Bowling returns to that world in memory, and in the flesh, as though he means to take one last look at it before he forgets its appearance or before bombs bury many of its landmarks. When he returns to 'Lower Binfield' in his memory, he sees a golden world frozen in time, immune from modern evils, but the contemporary Lower Binfield is already in the grips of 'progress', with ugly factories and nondescript housing estates. When he visits it in search of familiar sights from his boyhood, he finds that many of them have been changed beyond recognition by new construction and, rather than accept such changes as inevitable, he begins to think that having them wiped out by bombing may not be such a bad fate.

But the novel is not a bitter jeremiad. There is no denying that a gloomy cloud hangs over the world it depicts, but the things in that world which are worth saving are so fondly described that the gloom is pierced by more than a few bright beams of light. The novel has many passages of lyrical beauty, not unbecoming a novelist who once aspired to be a poet, and it is the glow from these passages which lingers in the reader's mind as a reminder of what will be lost in 'total war', and the price which will be paid for ignoring its approach.

The one serious defect in the novel is Orwell's attempt to *be* the voice of his narrator-protagonist. He does not make a convincing middle-aged, overweight, suburban-dwelling, low-brow insurance salesman, and the book is at its best when Orwell is 'out-of-character', speaking in a voice which is recognisably his rather than an imitation of 'Fatty' Bowling's. There are fairly long passages in which Orwell seems to forget that he is supposed to be using Bowling's voice, and it can be irritating when he suddenly switches back into character. It is clear that he wanted to make Bowling's story another experiment in the inside/outside technique which he admired so much in Joyce, but it simply does not work. The good qualities of the book would have been so much better if Orwell had dropped the mask of Fatty Bowling, and used his own voice to provided the proper window pane between Bowling's world and the reader's.

The novel did not face the same dismal response in the

bookshops which had met the publication of *Homage to Catalonia*. It sold three thousand copies, a thousand of which represented a second printing. Again, he was far from bestseller status as a novelist, but the sales figures were respectable, and the reviews were among the best that he had received for a novel. Some critics did, however, point to the first-person narrative as a mistake. 'My only regret,' wrote Margery Allingham in *Time and Tide*, 'is that the story was written in the first person. This device, although it has the important virtue of making the narrative clear and easy to read, tends to falsify the character slightly since [Bowling's] uncanny perception where his own failings are concerned makes him a little less of the ordinary mortal which his behaviour would show him to be.'[4]

On the very day that this review appeared Orwell was on his way back to Southwold where his father was reported to be near death. Contemplating this eventuality earlier in the year, Orwell had written, 'What a hole it seems to leave when someone you have known since childhood goes.'[5] Of course, he had never been as close to his father as he might have hoped to be, but they had got along reasonably well in the latter half of the 1930s, and Orwell had certainly put to rest any notion that he might be a dilettante as a writer. No doubt his father would still have preferred to see him serve out his ordinary term in the Imperial Police, but any lingering resentment over that issue had faded by 1939. On 28 June, at the age of eighty-two, Mr Blair died in his bed at his home in the High Street, Montagu House. His death certificate lists as the primary cause of death 'Carcinoma of Intestines', and a notation reports, 'E. A. Blair, son, present at death.' Orwell was not one to reveal a great deal of emotion over such a sad event, but he did feel the loss deeply. Richard Rees remembered Orwell saying 'with deep satisfaction' that he and his father had reconciled their differences before Mr Blair's death. Rees also recalled Orwell's account of what he had done immediately after his father died. 'He himself had closed his father's eyes in the traditional way by placing pennies upon the eyelids. He further added that after the funeral he had been embarrassed to know what to do with the pennies. "In the end

I walked down to the sea and threw them in. Do you think some people would have put them back in their pocket?" [6]

II

At the time of his father's death he had been working on a new piece of writing which was an extended analysis of a great Victorian figure – a writer who had stood at the top of his profession when Mr Blair was a little boy – Charles Dickens. He and Eileen had spent many hours reading Dickens together in Marrakech. They had taken a copy of *Our Mutual Friend* with them when they had left England, and had spent so much time with it that Eileen boasted they were 'competent to pass the most searching examination on it'. She wrote to Francis Westrope, and asked him to send more Dickens – specifically the early novels *Barnaby Rudge* and *Martin Chuzzlewit*. 'We are desperate for something to read, something *long*,' she explained. [7] But why this outburst of enthusiasm for Dickens? If they had wanted long Victorian novels with which to pass the hours, there was a wide range of choice besides Dickens. It is impossible to know Eileen's reasons, but Orwell spent May, June and July spelling out his reasons in the longest of all his essays, 'Charles Dickens'. The most valuable thing about this piece is that it is unsystematic. Orwell has no box into which he is determined to stuff Dickens, no ideological sledgehammer with which he wants to pound him; he simply wants to talk about why Dickens matters, why – despite all his faults – people still care enough about his works to read them, even though they may have formed distorted impressions of him, or may have been prejudiced against his work in one way or another.

Orwell finds numerous examples in Dickens's work of significant flaws – the cloying sentimentality, the over-reliance on character types, the superficial understanding of commercial and industrial work, the hopelessly unrealistic endings, the avoidance of genuine tragedy. 'No grown-up person can read Dickens without feeling his limitations,' Orwell says, yet he recognises an elementary quality in the works which touches readers and wins their sympathies in a way that a more logical, more realistic, more philosophical writer could never hope to do. 'In his own age and ours he has been popular chiefly because he was able to express in a comic, simplified and therefore memorable form the native decency of the common man.' This seems only another way of admitting that he is not a writer for 'grown-up' readers, but Orwell thinks it is a mistake to under-estimate either the importance or the difficulty of Dickens's achievement. He cannot scoff at the universal appeal of the books because he places a high value on universal appeal. He is fascinated by anything which can stir the hearts of a broad spectrum of humanity, anything, in other words, which can help people to recognise the interests they have in common, the things which unite them rather than those things which reinforce divisions among them:

> All through the Christian ages, and especially since the French Revolution, the western world has been haunted by the idea of freedom and equality; it is only an idea, but it has penetrated to all ranks of society . . . Nearly everyone, whatever his actual conduct may be, responds emotionally to the idea of human brotherhood. Dickens voiced a code which was and on the whole still is believed in, even by people who violate it. It is difficult otherwise to explain why he could be both read by working people (a thing that has happened to no other novelist of his stature) and buried in Westminster Abbey.

In Orwell's view, Dickens's ability to speak to many kinds of people makes him a much more radical writer than he is usually perceived to be in intellectual circles. His 'criticism of society is almost exclusively moral', and is therefore based on general notions of decency, but that is the secret of his success, or as Orwell puts it in one of the many memorable sentences in the essay: 'The vagueness of his discontent is the mark of its permanence.' That may make Dickens suspect intellectually, but Orwell argues that 'a merely moral criticism of society' may prove more revolutionary than some 'politico-economic criticism' which may be fashionable at any given moment. He offers a compelling argument in support of that point: 'Blake was not a politician, but there is more understanding of the nature of capitalist society in a poem like "I wander through each charter'd street" than in three quarters of Socialist literature.'

Of course, in making his arguments for Dickens, Orwell was also making a case for his own efforts to create political art without sacrificing his independence as a writer. In some respects Dickens was a model, an inspiration. In 'Inside the Whale', which was written immediately after 'Charles Dickens', Orwell speaks of literary passages 'in which a writer tells you a great deal about himself while talking about somebody else'. Such passages certainly exist in his essay on Dickens, and nowhere is this dual commentary more apparent than in the final paragraph of the essay where he speaks of Dickens's face. Throughout Orwell's work, he is constantly stressing the importance of the human face – faces speak to him more powerfully than words, a point which is evident not only in his verse tribute to the Italian militiaman, in whose face he saw reflected 'the crystal spirit', but also in the terrifyingly empty face of Big Brother. Many more examples could be given, but in his Dickens essay the face of the writer has a special significance for him. He says that whenever he reads a 'strongly individual piece of writing', he is aware of a face 'somewhere behind the page', which is 'not necessarily the actual face of the writer' but which is 'the face that the writer *ought* to have'. In Dickens's case the face he sees is one which bears unmistakable traces of the face that Orwell also '*ought* to have':

> He is laughing, with a touch of anger in his laughter, but no
> triumph, no malignity. It is the face of a man who is always
> fighting against something, but who fights in the open and is not
> frightened, the face of a man who is *generously angry* . . . a type
> hated with equal hatred by all the smelly little orthodoxies which
> are now contending for our souls.

All that summer of 1939, Orwell was trying to chart the direction of his own talent by examining the directions in which other writers had pushed their talents – not only Dickens, but also the diverse group of contemporary writers whom he discusses in 'Inside the Whale'. He acknowledges that he cannot follow the lead of the great writers of 1920s – 'the Joyce–Eliot group' – because even though he admires their technical innovations in literature, they lack the strong sense of 'purpose' which he seeks: 'Our eyes are directed to Rome, to Byzantium, to Montparnasse, to Mexico, to the Etruscans, to the subconscious, to the solar plexus – to everything except the places where things are actually happening.' And despite his friendship with Spender, he cannot help saying rather bluntly that the Auden generation can exclude him as a potential follower. He criticises them for having too much 'purpose', to the exclusion of almost everything else. 'As early as 1934 or 1935 it was considered eccentric in literary circles not to be more or less "left", and in another year or two there had grown up a left-wing orthodoxy that made a certain set of opinions absolutely *de rigueur* on certain subjects.' The problem for Orwell is how to have 'purpose' and still have 'art', and independence. The conclusion which he reaches in 'Inside the Whale' is very much the same as the one articulated at the end of his Dickens essay: 'Good novels are not written by orthodoxy-sniffers, nor by people who are conscience-stricken about their own unorthodoxy. Good novels are written by people who are *not frightened*.'

The one vital question which Orwell left out of this process of self-analysis was whether he should be spending his time writing in the same literary forms favoured by the Joyce–Eliot group or the Auden–Spender group. He assumed that he should be writing novels or poems, when his talent had never shone as brightly in these forms as it did in his sketches, his essays, his reviews and his non-fiction books. The three brilliant pieces which were published together, in March 1940, under the title *Inside the Whale* – 'Charles Dickens', 'Inside the Whale', and 'Boys' Weeklies' – offer abundant proof of Orwell's strengths, but it did not 'pay', either in terms of money or reputation, to do such work. It was not then, and is not now, afforded the same respect which a good many second-rate novels receive merely because they are fiction. An impressive work like 'Charles Dickens' can easily be dismissed as 'only' a critical essay. And, commercially, there was not much incentive for Orwell to spend half a year working on a book of essays when publishers were reluctant to put up the money for it. Moore sold the book to Gollancz – who had developed an odd interest in it but who was willing to pay an advance of only £30 for it, the lowest of any advance Orwell received in his career. 'I find this kind of semi-sociological literary criticism very interesting', Orwell said near the time of the book's publication, 'and I'd like to do a lot of other writers, but unfortunately there's no money in it'.[8] (Moore does not seem to have bargained very hard with Gollancz over this book, or over any of Orwell's previous books, but his client rarely questioned the deals he made, and remained loyal to him throughout his career.)

Accordingly, Orwell's great ambition for the foreseeable future was to put as much energy as possible into writing not merely another novel but, as he explained to Moore in 1939, 'a long novel, really the first part of an enormous novel, a sort of saga (!) which will have to be published in three parts'.[9] He later gave a name to this project, calling it *The Quick and the Dead*, and he made some notes for it in the early 1940s. But he does not appear to have written any significant part of it, though at least one detail from his notes did find its way into *Animal Farm*. There is a description of a horse being beaten by an Army officer with a whip, and the horse is given the name 'Boxer'. As his excuse for not continuing to work on his saga, Orwell said that he became bogged down in writing reviews, taking on more work than he could adequately handle in order to earn some much-needed money. But he had a better reason than that. In July he warned Moore that the outbreak of war might put all his plans into confusion. Two months later the war was on, and Orwell's attention began to shift from his novel to other, more pressing concerns. It would be almost five more years before he would complete another book-length work of fiction, and that work, *Animal Farm*, would not appear in print until 1945.

Only three weeks before the war began Orwell received a shock. There was a knock at the door of his cottage, and when he opened it, he found himself facing two police detectives who had come to confiscate some of his books. At the post office in nearby Hitchin the authorities had intercepted one of Orwell's letters addressed to Jack Kahane's Obelisk Press in Paris, which had a reputation for publishing 'dirty' books. They were also the publishers of Cyril Connolly's novel – a relatively mild work, as far as sex was concerned – and Henry Miller's books. All of the Obelisk Press books in Orwell's possession were taken away by the detectives, and he was handed a warning from the Public Prosecutor saying that he was 'liable to be prosecuted if importing such things again'. This 'raid' was the sort of thing one might have expected in Spain or Germany, but Orwell was taken aback by the fact that it had happened in Hertfordshire. But because the business was managed politely by the detectives, it seemed less threatening. Afterwards some of the books were even returned to him, with a note from the prosecutor saying that he understood why Orwell, as a writer, 'might have a need for books which it was illegal to possess'. But this show of politeness and understanding could not disguise the basic ugliness of the act – the opening of his mail and the seizure of books from his home. It also led Orwell to wonder whether his mail was being routinely inspected or whether it was merely the Obelisk Press address on his envelope which had prompted the investigation. In any case, after his experience in Spain, he was especially sensitive to any act of surveillance, and this evidence of it in bucolic Hertfordshire did nothing to calm his fears that the spirit of totalitarianism was growing beyond the borders of the fascist and Soviet states. He was not so upset by it, however, that he overlooked the comic absurdity of the prosecutor's willingness to understand his needs as a writer. A few years later, in a review of Miller's *The Cosmological Eye*, he declared:

> It is a pity that some publisher cannot take his courage in his hands and reissue *Tropic of Cancer*. About a year later he could recoup his losses by publishing a book entitled 'What I Saw in Prison', or words to that effect, and meanwhile a few copies of the forbidden text would have reached the public before the entire edition was burned by the public hangman, or whoever it is that has the job of burning banned books in this country.[10]

The one compensation in all this was the fact that Orwell could write these words of ridicule, and have them published without being censored.

If he had been a more consistent person, he might have steadfastly refused to fight for a 'capitalist-imperialist' government which sent detectives to his house to take away his books. He might have continued to argue, as he did in 1937, that 'Fascism after all is only a development of capitalism, and the mildest democracy, so called, is liable to turn into Fascism when the pinch comes.'[11] Instead, when the war started, he discovered that he could not violate his 'traditional loyalties': 'It is all very well to be "advanced" and "enlightened", to snigger at Colonel Blimp and proclaim your emancipation from all traditional loyalties, but a time comes when the sand of the desert is sodden red and what have I done for thee, England, my England.'[12] On 9 September, only six days after war was declared, he voluntarily submitted his name to the Central Register for employment in the war effort. With his bad lungs, he knew that there was little chance of getting into the Army, but he was willing to serve the war effort in any other way possible.

When some of his old friends in the ILP questioned his support of the war, he tried to make it clear that he was not surrendering his left-wing beliefs simply because he wanted to defend his country. He explained his view of this matter in 'My Country Right or Left', which was published in John Lehmann's *Folios of New Writing* near the end of 1940. 'Patriotism has nothing to do with conservatism . . . To be loyal both to Chamberlain's England and to the England of tomorrow might seem an impossibility, if one did not know it to be an everyday phenomenon.' This was not a very convincing answer, but the issue was not one to which he could apply perfectly rational reasons. He loved his country and was willing to fight for it when it was in danger, and that kind of loyalty could not be explained as easily as it could be felt. Ultimately, his best explanation was to say that emotions mattered, and that they could not be neatly expunged in order to hold true to some abstract ideal. In any case, he argued that patriotism could benefit the Left as well as the Right. He spoke of 'the possibility of building a Socialist on the bones of a Blimp, the power of one kind of loyalty to transmute itself into another, the spiritual need for patriotism and the military virtues, for which, however little the boiled rabbits of the Left may like them, no substitute has yet been found'.

Although he was willing to serve, no one asked him to do so. Eileen had more luck. At the beginning of the war she applied for a job in the Censorship Department in Whitehall, and – oddly enough – managed to get it. She went to live at her brother's house in Greenwich, coming back to the cottage only on alternate weekends. Orwell did not want to give up the cottage and held out against the idea of moving to London if there were no offers of wartime work to entice him. But without Eileen in Wallington he was lonely and uncertain about what he should do next. He wrote reviews, finished *Inside the Whale* and followed war news, but for him the first year of the war was a relatively quiet period in which he drifted along waiting for some sign to show him what he should do next. If the war had not come along, he would certainly have jumped into the work of completing the first instalment of his ambitious 'saga', but he could not focus on any long-term work. He was not sure there would even be a long-term period available for working.

Although the military action in the first seven months of the war was light, one could not tell when it might turn very heavy indeed, and the suspense of waiting for some dramatic shift made it difficult for Orwell to work. He became so frustrated that he began to think of ways to prepare himself for a war-related job, and at one point conceived the idea of joining a government training centre at Letchworth, so that he could learn a useful trade – machine draughtsmanship. He thought that the work might prove interesting and would give him 'a trade' to fall back on in peacetime. After the immense productivity and exciting discoveries of the previous three years, the momentum of his career was suddenly gone. He was willing to try just about anything to fill up the time, as long as it did not require a great deal of preparation.

Something of his indecisive mood can be seen in his plans for addressing a group called the 'Women of Today'. In January 1940 he mentioned to Moore that he was scheduled to speak to this organisation in a week, but he admitted that he had not yet decided upon a proper subject for the talk, though two wildly different topics had come to mind. 'How would it be if I spoke on Hitler's *Mein Kampf*, which I've just been reading for the first time with some interest? . . . If they didn't like that, I could speak on Dickens.' In the history of speechmaking Orwell is probably the only person who was ever torn between the choice of speaking on Hitler or Dickens, but these two figures had been much in his thoughts in 1939 – one embodying a hopeful vision of a society based on 'common decency', the other a nightmare of endless strife. Unfortunately, no records have survived to indicate which vision he chose to share with the 'Women of Today'.[13]

CHAPTER SEVENTEEN

Surviving the Blitz

I

In the early spring of 1940 German forces ended the period of relative inactivity which had marked the early months of the war. Hitler sent his troops to invade Norway and by the end of April his conquest of the country was more or less complete. The Royal Navy scored some successes against German destroyers which were supporting the invasion, but otherwise it was an amazingly easy victory for Hitler, and he quickly followed it up with a massive invasion of the Low Countries. These events did not surprise Orwell, who fully expected the war to reach British soil in a matter of months. In April he was busy sowing a huge crop of potatoes as a precaution against the 'famine' which he anticipated in the wake of a long war of attrition. In an earlier season he had experimented with a plan to bury large quantities of potatoes for long-term storage, but on digging them up he had discovered that they were too mouldy to eat. Jack Common's diary for this period includes a description of Orwell hard at work in his garden, seemingly oblivious to the cold winds of early April:

> He was standing with a hoe, looking very frail, deep-furrowed cheeks and pitifully feeble chest. His strong cord trousers gave a massivity to his legs oddly in contrast to his emaciated torso. After tea we talked a great deal, he in that flat dead voice of his, never laughing beyond a sort of wistful chuckle, a weariness in all he said. Again his theme is hardness – curious because his physique

denies that this is his need. Hardness and action! That reiterated when all the while it saddens me to see how obviously he needs love and repose.[1]

Orwell's loneliness during this period in Wallington could not be hidden from an old friend such as Common, but of course he would never have admitted to being lonely, or depressed, or even that he missed having his wife at home. Eileen's decision to work in London was understandable, and no doubt Orwell encouraged her to seek wartime employment, but it was also a convenient way of freeing herself from the isolation of Wallington, and the rather rugged nature of life at the cottage. This was the life which Orwell had created for himself, and he wanted someone to share it with, but it was the kind of demanding existence which few people would willingly accept. Eileen may have found it amusing at first, and she certainly tolerated it longer than most people would have, but various comments in her letters from Morocco show that she was weary of enduring the hardships which her husband was constantly seeking, and when the chance came to take a job in London, she seized it. Her wartime job involved long hours, but it allowed her to return to the kind of working life which she had known in London before her marriage, and it gave her the chance to be close to her family. She enjoyed her brother's comfortable house in Greenwich, sharing it with her mother and her sister-in-law, Gwen, while Laurence O'Shaughnessy was away from home serving as a chest surgeon in the Army Medical Corps.

Eileen's absence from Wallington is noted plaintively at the end of two letters which Orwell wrote to one of their friends, the anthropologist Geoffrey Gorer. Although one was written in January and one in April of 1940, both letters have the same last line: 'Eileen would send love if she were here.' There are more cheerful ways to express this sentiment, but this was Orwell's indirect way of acknowledging how much he was aware of the fact that she was *not* there. He made another revealing remark about Eileen in an autobiographical note which he wrote in mid-April for *Twentieth Century Authors*. The remark follows a list of his likes and dislikes:

351

Outside my work the thing I care most about is gardening,
especially vegetable gardening. I like English cookery and English
beer, French red wines, Spanish white wines, Indian tea, strong
tobacco, coal fires, candle light and comfortable chairs. I dislike
big towns, noise, motor cars, the radio, tinned food, central
heating and 'modern' furniture. My wife's tastes fit in almost
perfectly with my own.

It is difficult to know the extent to which Eileen's tastes
matched his, but it is interesting that he should feel compelled to say
that they were of one mind about these things. When he wrote this
piece, Eileen had been living in Greenwich for almost eight months,
visiting Wallington for only two or three weekends in each month.
Of course, this was wartime, and many couples were forced to lead
separate lives, but in her absence Orwell's remark may reflect a
need to tell himself that Eileen would share his life completely – so
'perfectly' matched were their tastes – if only 'she were here'.

In May he finally decided that he had lived alone long enough
and was ready to move to London to be with Eileen. They found a
top-floor flat at 18 Dorset Chambers, Chagford Street, not far from
Baker Street, and by the middle of the month they had moved in.
Various friends helped to take care of the cottage, and the Orwells
continued to use it for occasional weekend visits. There was still no
war work for him to do, but once he was in London he began
actively searching for a full-time job which would be of some help to
the war effort. He talked boldly about trying to fake his way past a
medical examination in order to join the Army, but when he did
eventually submit to an examination the result was predictable. He
was judged unfit for service on medical grounds. This was
tremendously frustrating for him. 'I hold what half the men in this
country would give their balls to have,' he once remarked to William
Empson, referring to the medical exemption on his National
Service Card, 'but I don't want it.'[2] However, with Nazi troops
sweeping through Holland and Belgium in May, he thought he
might soon see action in London regardless of his medical standing.
If England were invaded, anyone who could hold a rifle might be

pressed into service. Reflecting on this possibility, he told Leonard Moore, 'one may get a chance of a scrap after all.'[3]

In the meantime he chose a far more sedate way of occupying his time in London. He accepted a job writing film and theatre criticism for *Time and Tide*. His first review appeared on 25 May. He did not like the work, and one of the editors at the paper remembered him complaining once that he could not bear to go to another 'bloody play'.[4] He was a bit more tolerant of films, though the preponderance of American productions did not sit well with him because of their tendency to glorify violence for its own sake, and for what he called 'their complete lack of any sense of character or probability to match up with their brilliant technique and snappy dialogue'. One of his reviews of an American film begins, not untypically, 'This fairly amusing piece of rubbish . . .' In another review he condemns American producers for not having more faith in the intelligence of their audience. 'It is always assumed that anything demanding thought, or even suggesting thought, must be avoided like the plague. An American film actor shown reading a book always handles it in the manner of an illiterate person.'[5] He gave one of his most scathing reviews to Raoul Walsh's *High Sierra*. He admitted that the direction was 'competent' and the acting was 'distinctly good', but he could not stomach its attitude towards violence:

> For anyone who wants the *ne plus ultra* of sadism, bully-worship, gun-play, socks on the jaw and gangster atmosphere generally, this film is the goods. Humphrey Bogart is the Big Shot who smashes people in the face with the butt of his pistol and watches fellow gangsters burn to death with the casual comment, 'They were only small-town guys,' but is kind to dogs and is supposed to be deeply touching when he is smitten with a 'pure' affection for a crippled girl who knows nothing of his past. In the end he is killed, but we are evidently expected to sympathise with him and even to admire him.[6]

One film which he did admire enormously, and which he wrote about at considerable length in *Time and Tide*, is Charlie

Chaplin's *The Great Dictator*. He was delighted by Chaplin's satire on Hitler, but he also felt that there was deep emotional power at work in the film which raised it above the level of a merely amusing parody. What he found at work in Chaplin's comic genius was something of the same quality which made Dickens's work so appealing to him. 'What is Chaplin's peculiar gift? It is his power to stand for a sort of concentrated essence of the common man, for the ineradicable belief in decency that exists in the hearts of ordinary people.' Having extended this much praise to the actor-director, Orwell understood that it was the kind of acclaim which could easily be mocked by critics who disliked appeals to such vague qualities as 'decency', and so he included in his review a bit of pre-emptive attack on intellectuals, criticising the 'sleek professors' who attempt to explain away the need for liberty, and other intellectuals who 'can make you out a splendid "case" for smashing the German Trade Unions and torturing the Jews'. Orwell liked *The Great Dictator* so much that he called for the government to subsidise showings of it so that it could be seen by people who could not afford seats in the 'three West End picture houses' where the film had opened. Such a measure would be worthwhile, he argued, because 'the allure of power politics will be a fraction weaker for every human being who sees this film'.[7]

In addition to his work for *Time and Tide*, Orwell also contributed fairly regularly in 1940 to the monthly magazine which Cyril Connolly and Stephen Spender had established shortly after the war began. Orwell was a frequent visitor to the editorial offices of *Horizon*, which were located in two rooms on the ground floor of a narrow Georgian house in Lansdowne Terrace, Bloomsbury. Stephen Spender came to know Orwell much better in this period and used to have long, friendly discussions with him about politics and literature. 'I remember this rather drizzly voice. Listening to one of Orwell's monologues, with all its rambling speculations, was very English in a way. It was like walking through a drizzly street – hearing his very monotonous voice.'[8]

During its ten-year existence *Horizon* published some of Orwell's best pieces, beginning with 'Boys' Weeklies' in March

1940. Other important contributions were 'The Ruling Class' (December 1940); 'Wells, Hitler and the World State' (August 1941); 'The Art of Donald McGill' (September 1941); 'Raffles and Miss Blandish' (October 1944); and 'Politics and the English Language' (April 1946). Serious essays on popular culture are common today, but Orwell was a pioneer in this field, and Connolly was happy to give his old friend the space to express what were then rather novel ideas. Many editors might have dismissed out of hand an essay which subjected something as common as a boys' paper to serious analysis, especially at a time when the dangers of war would have made such work seem trivial, but Connolly was willing to take a chance on it, and to encourage Orwell to do more essays of a similar kind.

Connolly was helpful in other, less obvious ways. A decade before Orwell completed *Nineteen Eighty-Four*, Connolly wrote a short piece about a love affair between a young man and woman in a totalitarian state headed by 'Our Leader', whose face looks down on the people from neon signs high above the streets. The young man is arrested for treason, tortured by officials from the Censor's Department and forced into approving his own death sentence with the words: 'Yes, I have been treated with great kindness.' 'Year Nine', as it is called, was published in the *New Statesman* in January 1938, and was later included in Connolly's essay collection *The Condemned Playground* (1945). Orwell knew the piece, and there can be no doubt that it had an influence on his plans for *Nineteen Eighty-Four*.

II

Although Orwell had enough literary work to keep him busy in 1940 – he wrote dozens of essays and reviews for at least seven different periodicals – he seemed to think that he was wasting time, and that he could accomplish no work of any value as long as the war was casting so much uncertainty over the future. 'I can't write with this sort of business going on,' he declared in the summer, 'and in a few months there is going to be such a severe paper shortage that very few books will be published. In any case I feel that literature as we have known it is coming to an end. Things look rather black at the moment.'⁹ There was good reason for him to be concerned about the future. The Germans defeated France in June, and all the signs seemed to point to an invasion of Britain before the end of the summer. Orwell was expecting the worst, and had taken steps to make sure that he would be ready to fight the Nazi troops if they landed. In June he joined the Home Guard (originally known as the Local Defence Volunteers). These units did not need to be particular about the fitness of their men, and Orwell was welcome in the ranks because of his experience in the Spanish Civil War. He was made a sergeant in the 5th London Battalion. If enemy soldiers had ever reached the leafy streets of St John's Wood – where the 5th had its headquarters – they would have been forced to contend with a dangerous character by the name of Sergeant Blair, who was armed with a variety of homemade explosives and other lethal weapons. ('I can put up with bombs on the mantelpiece,' Eileen announced one day, 'but I will not have a machine gun under the bed.')¹⁰

He spent three years in the Home Guard, and though he never had to fire a shot in anger, he was prepared to put up quite a fight. He wrote articles about the proper way to train the Home Guard and the best tactics to use in street fighting. On 22 June he warned in *Time and Tide* that an invasion might be only days away, and he urged that measures be taken to 'ARM THE PEOPLE'. There was a shortage of rifles, so he advocated that the Home Guard be given immediate access to all the shotguns in gunsmiths' shops, and that hand-grenades be distributed to as many men as possible. It was as though he thought he were back on the streets of Barcelona, and the only hope was to take up positions behind barricades and rooftops, with all the firepower that could be mustered at a moment's notice. 'I had a front-seat view of the street fighting in Barcelona in May 1937, and it convinced me that a few hundred men with machine guns can paralyse the life of a large city.' He was reacting to a real threat, but he was somewhat cavalier about the question of arming a lot of people who might not know one end of a shotgun from the other. His best advice was, 'The powers and limitations of the shotgun (with buckshot, lethal up to about sixty yards) should be explained to the public over the radio.'

He prepared some detailed notes on the techniques of street fighting, and used them as a guide for lectures which he gave not only to men of his own unit but to other Home Guard units as well. Some of his tips were of questionable value. 'Bombs easier to throw downstairs than up,' one note declares. Other points, however, were no doubt useful to men who had never seen any street fighting, and who would not have known the basic dangers: 'Note behaviour of bullets, different from in open country. Except at very obtuse angles, nearly always ricochet. Habit of coming round corners.'[11] He took this kind of instruction very seriously, and was hopeful that the Home Guard would develop into an effective urban guerrilla force – if it were given time to prepare, and if it received the right training and equipment.

From the beginning he was concerned that the effectiveness of the Home Guard would be undermined by elderly, upper-class officers whose notions of fighting were based on obsolete tactics from the First World War. Such men wanted to see a great deal of attention given to marching in open fields, bayonet practice and construction of trenches. He had nothing but contempt for one old general, a veteran of more than forty years' service, who gave a lecture one evening on the Home Guard's mission as 'a static defensive force'. The general told Orwell and the rest of his battalion that they did not need to bother with practising methods of taking cover. Their job, he said solemnly, was to die at their posts.[12]

If the influence of the old conservative officers could be limited, Orwell thought that the Home Guard would make not only a good fighting force against the Germans but would also demonstrate the possibility of achieving 'a democratic People's Army'. In such a force, co-operation among different parts of society would replace the traditional reliance on upper-class leadership, and a large, well-armed popular militia would act as a sort of insurance policy against government tyranny at home. At the end of an article on the

Home Guard in *Tribune*, Orwell wrote: 'THAT RIFLE HANGING ON THE WALL OF THE WORKING-CLASS FLAT OR LABOURER'S COTTAGE IS THE SYMBOL OF DEMOCRACY. IT IS OUR JOB TO SEE THAT IT STAYS THERE.' In wilder moments Orwell became so carried away by his vision of a vast people's army that he imagined it being used to fight a revolution as well as a war, and spoke of a day when blood would run in the gutters and the 'red militias' would be 'billeted in the Ritz'.[13]

One of the volunteers who served in Sergeant Blair's section was Corporal Warburg, otherwise known as Fredric Warburg, the publisher of *Homage to Catalonia*. An army in which a publisher can be subordinate to an author is indeed an ideal one, and many years later Warburg had nothing but praise for the way his sergeant had treated him, recalling affectionately Orwell's pride in serving a democratic force:

> As Sergeant Blair fell in as company marker for my first parade, I discerned the zeal which inflamed his tall skinny body. His uniform was crumpled, but it had been cut to fit him by a good tailor. The tricorn cap, bearing the badge of the King's Royal Rifle Corps, of which technically we were a unit, was perched so jauntily on the side of his head that I feared it might fall off . . . Orwell's expression was Cromwellian in its intensity.[14]

But the only military action Orwell saw in England was a kind which no local defence force armed with shotguns and hand grenades could stop. In August the people of Britain were spared an invasion, and were given instead the Blitz – night after night of bombing from waves of German planes hitting civilian areas with indiscriminate attacks. On the first night of heavy bombing in London, Orwell was at Connolly's flat in Piccadilly, and from the rooftop they could see the burning docks in the East End. With cool objectivity, Orwell silently surveyed the scene and was amazed by 'the size and beauty of the flames'. He was not unmindful of the fact, however, that such destruction was less beautiful if one happened to be close to it. Earlier, on his way to the flat, he had felt the effects of bombs falling near Piccadilly. He had been forced to duck into a doorway to avoid the flying shrapnel, 'just as one might shelter from a cloudburst'.[15] Connolly came to believe that Orwell rather enjoyed this danger. 'He felt enormously at home in the Blitz, among the bombs, the bravery, the rubble, the shortages, the homeless, the signs of revolutionary temper.'[16]

He certainly believed that it was important to face all the terrors which the Blitz could bring, and to make it a point of honour to lead a normal life in the midst of them. Many people felt the same way and exhibited the same courage. He once told Julian Symons that even though he hated living in London, he could not go back to Wallington. 'You've got to stay here while the war's on. You can't leave when people are being bombed to hell.'[17] Early in the Blitz, he was proud to see – during a performance of a play he was assigned to review – that almost no one in the audience took the opportunity to go to shelters at the sound of the air-raid sirens. At one point Eileen suggested that he might want to go to Canada 'if the worst comes to the worst', explaining that he could keep up a propaganda effort for the war against Hitler if Britain were occupied. 'Better to die if necessary,' was Orwell's response. But he added in his 'War-time Diary', 'Not that I want to die; I have so much to live for, in spite of poor health and having no children.'[18]

There were aspects of the Blitz which brought back odd memories from his past. After one raid he saw some mannequins littering the pavement outside a department store which had been bombed, and as he thought about how much they resembled 'a pile of corpses', he was reminded of a similar sight in Barcelona: 'Only there it was plaster saints from desecrated churches.' Listening to the droning sound of bombers crossing the sky in seemingly endless waves reminded him of a quite different sensation which he had felt during his time in Burma: 'The aeroplanes come back and come back, every few minutes. It is just like in an eastern country, when you keep thinking you have killed the last mosquito inside your net, and every time, as soon as you have turned the light out, another starts droning.'[19]

One afternoon Orwell telephoned Eileen at her brother's house, where she had gone to take care of her ailing mother, and during their conversation a great many German bombers appeared over Greenwich. They began dropping their bombs, but Eileen continued talking until there was a sudden loud crash. When she paused at the sound, Orwell asked, 'What's that?' Without any sign of anxiety, Eileen replied, 'Only the windows falling in.'[20] Fortunately, there was no more serious damage to the house than a few broken windows, but the bomb had dropped only a short distance away, in the park, and had cut loose the huge cable holding down a barrage balloon. Like Orwell, Eileen normally refused to go to shelters during raids. 'Neither of them seemed to care about personal safety,' Lydia Jackson recalled. 'Whenever the sirens let out their warning wail, Eileen would put out the lights in their top-floor flat, open the window and watch the happenings in the street.'[21]

The Blitz did not hold many terrors for Eileen because the war had already caused its worst damage as far as she was concerned – it had taken her brother's life, at Dunkirk, in June. The news had left her devastated. They had always been extremely close, and her admiration for him was boundless. He had gone to France with the British Expeditionary Force, serving as a major in the Medical Corps, and had been killed during the final days of the evacuation from the beaches. One reason such an eminent surgeon was at the front lines was that he had volunteered to work in a field hospital so that he could study the effects of chest wounds. He was such a tireless, dedicated researcher that he could not pass up the chance to take advantage of the opportunity to learn more about these wounds, and to use that knowledge to save lives in the future. The sad irony of his death is that he was hit by shrapnel only hours before he was to have been evacuated, and died minutes later, mortally wounded in the chest.

Before she received the bad news, Eileen had been so worried about her brother that she had asked Orwell to go to Waterloo and Victoria stations to see whether he could gain any information about Laurence from the returning troops. Standing tall in the crowds of people, he had studied the soldiers walking past him in the hope of finding someone from the Medical Corps who might have some news. But there were more refugees than soldiers in the stations, and all the soldiers were under orders not to talk about the evacuation from Dunkirk. There were so many people who had come to the stations seeking news about their friends and relatives that the police had been called out to hold them back.

There was nothing anyone could do to comfort Eileen when she learned of her brother's fate. She went into a long period of deep depression which reportedly lasted many months and which led her to the verge of a nervous breakdown. Her friend Margaret Branch recalled that for a time Eileen could barely bring herself to speak to anyone. 'One saw in her the visible signs of depression. Her hair was unbrushed, her face and body thin. Reality was so awful for her that she withdrew – the effects lasted perhaps eighteen months. In her severe depression she was facing the dark night of the soul. Nobody could get through to her.'[22] Lydia Jackson thought that 'Eileen's own grip on life, which had never been firm, loosened considerably after her brother's death.'[23] Tragically, her suffering was made worse in 1941 when her mother died.

There is very little in Orwell's letters or diaries which would indicate that his wife was in such pain. He did not talk about such things to other people, and he would not have agonised over it even in his private diaries. There can be no question that he felt her pain and was moved by it, but he took a stoical attitude towards such things, and was not prepared to deal with them in the open. He was always so careful to keep his emotions under control, at least on the outside, but no one can read very far in his works without realising that the passive expression which he was inclined to present to the outside world masked deeply felt passions. So much of his upbringing had encouraged him to guard his feelings, to keep his thoughts to himself. His powers of observation may have been helped by this conditioning, but it did little to help him deal openly with emotional difficulties of the kind that Eileen's situation presented after her brother's death. It was easier for him to explain her fatigue and depression as a result of the demands of her job. One of his few written comments about her during this period can be found in a letter to Dorothy Plowman, which he wrote in response to the news of Max Plowman's death, in June 1941. The opening sentences of this letter offer a good illustration of Orwell's habit of restraining his emotions. 'I can't say much about Max's death. You know how it is, the seeming uselessness of trying to offer any consolation when somebody is dead.' The sentences which follow these two offer clear evidence of the affection and respect which Orwell felt for Plowman, but, by themselves, his opening words seem cold and distant. His explanation of Eileen's problems is similarly understated. 'For more than a year Eileen was working in the Censorship Department, but I have induced her to drop it for a while, as it was upsetting her health. She is going to have a good rest and then perhaps get some less futile and exasperating work to do.'

Some of Orwell's friends never realised that Eileen was suffering from anything more serious than overwork or the common weariness which people feel in wartime, but others were more perceptive, and more inquisitive. Among these were two new friends, the journalist Tosco Fyvel and his wife Mary. Fyvel was introduced to Orwell in January 1940 by Fredric Warburg, who was trying to form a regular discussion group for writers. Later that summer, Fyvel and his wife shared a house in Berkshire with Fredric and Pamela Warburg, and among the guests who visited Scarlett's Farm, as the place was called, were the Orwells.

> Eileen accompanied him on his visits to us, but we all noticed a profound change in her. She seemed to sit in the garden sunk in unmoving silence while we talked. Mary . . . observed that Eileen not only looked tired and drawn but was drably and untidily dressed. Trying in vain to involve Eileen in conversation, Mary said that she seemed to have become completely withdrawn. Since Orwell and Eileen were reticent to a degree, it was only after her second or third visit that we learned that her brother Laurence . . . had been killed.[24]

Although he could not have anticipated it at the time, Orwell would later have his own personal reasons for regretting Dr O'Shaughnessy's early death. At the end of 1947, when Orwell was first diagnosed as having tuberculosis, he was treated with the latest drug – streptomycin – but there were other drugs in development, and other available treatments, all of which could have been employed to the maximum effect if his brother-in-law had lived and had been able to give him the full benefit of his expertise. This is not to suggest that Orwell was neglected in any way by the doctors who treated him in the late 1940s, but there is just the chance that O'Shaughnessy, who was such an active medical scientist, might have been able to do more for Orwell. By itself, streptomycin was not effective in Orwell's case – some forms of the disease were resistant to it – and the latest drug in 1949 – PAS (para-amino-salicylic acid) – also had mixed results when used on advanced cases like Orwell's. He received PAS, but there is no indication that any of his doctors tried a third treatment, the success of which was reported in the *British Medical Journal* only weeks before he died. This treatment involved a combination of the two leading drugs, and as one expert has noted, the report cited a study which 'demonstrated unequivocally that the combination of PAS and streptomycin prevented the development of streptomycin-resistant strains of the tubercle bacillus'.[25]

Perhaps it is fruitless to speculate on what might have happened if O'Shaughnessy had lived, but rarely does one encounter such a strange working of fate in the interconnected lives of two distinguished men – one brother-in-law a writer who would die of tuberculosis, the other a leading chest specialist who died young on a battlefield where he had gone to learn more about his speciality. But, given the way that Orwell neglected his health, even Dr O'Shaughnessy might not have been able to save him.

III

While Eileen grieved, Orwell did what he did best – he buried himself in great mounds of work. As the war dragged on, and its hardships and danger came to seem almost routine, his attention shifted from the problems of fighting Germans in the streets of London to the old familiar challenges of writing articles and reviews. He was getting better at this business, and one day in the summer of 1940 he suddenly became aware of a major change in the way he worked. 'Nowadays, when I write a review, I sit down at the typewriter and type it straight out. Till recently, indeed till six months ago, I never did this and would have said that I could not do it. Virtually all that I wrote was written at least twice, and my books as a whole three times – individual passages as many as five or ten times.' Orwell refused to believe that this change reflected an improvement in his talent, crediting it instead to the fact that he 'ceased to care' about reviews, 'so long as the work will pass inspection and bring in a little money'.[26] The error of this judgement can be seen by glancing at any of Orwell's reviews from this period. In every one of them there is at least one distinctive phrase, one uncommon touch, and quite a few of them are enjoyable to read from beginning to end, as well as enlightening, which is saying a lot for anyone's review work. No one who had ceased to care about his writing could ever craft a sentence as perfect, and as perceptive, as this one from Orwell's review of the unabridged translation of *Mein Kampf*: 'The Socialist who finds his children playing with soldiers is usually upset, but he is never able to think of a substitute for the tin soldiers; tin pacifists somehow won't do.'[27]

Orwell never had enough confidence in his abilities, but his impressive talent was beginning to attract notice in some unexpected places. He had not had one of his books published in America since *A Clergyman's Daughter* in 1936, but in December 1940 he received an invitation to write for one of the most influential magazines in America – the *Partisan Review*. One of the editors, Clement Greenberg, asked him to write a 'London Letter' for the magazine, one which would give American readers some idea of what was happening 'under the surface' in English political and cultural affairs. 'You can be as gossipy as you please and refer to as many personalities as you like,' Greenberg told him. 'The more the better.'[28] Why was Orwell, who was not that well known in America, chosen for this job? The answer is that he may not have been well known to Americans in general, but the *Partisan Review* editors were very much aware of his work, and admired it. Greenberg, in particular, was in a position to appreciate Orwell's growing importance as a literary figure in London. He had published a piece in *Horizon*, and had seen some of Orwell's work in its pages, but he had also learned a good deal about the writer from Cyril Connolly's American wife. Jean Connolly, whom Orwell knew and liked, had separated from her husband in May 1940 and had returned to America. She settled in New York and made new friends in the literary world, one of whom was Clement Greenberg, whose lover she became. She was able to tell Greenberg everything he wanted to know about George Orwell.

Orwell accepted the offer and his first 'London Letter' appeared in *Partisan Review* in the spring of 1941. He contributed several more of these informal reports, submitting his last one in 1946, and he also sent the magazine other pieces, including a brief but important statement on Ezra Pound's antisemitism and the Bollingen Prize: 'He *may* be a good writer (I must admit that I personally have always regarded him as an entirely spurious writer), but the opinions that he has tried to disseminate by means of his works are evil ones, and I think the judges should have said so more firmly when awarding him the prize.'[29]

During the war Orwell's London Letters were subject to censorship by the Ministry of Information, and in April 1941, after he had submitted his second Letter, he received a note from the Senior Press Censor informing him that a deletion had been made in his text before it was sent to New York: 'I am directed to inform you that it was not possible to pass for publication the passage referring to the possible lynching of German airmen, who had baled out of their planes and come down by parachute. The passage was excised and the article has been sent on.' This kind of work was not too far removed from the work which Winston Smith does in the Ministry of Truth (or Minitrue in Newspeak – interestingly, the telegraphic code for the Ministry of Information was MINIFORM). Orwell should not have been surprised, however, by the censor's actions. At a time when enormous efforts were being made to increase American support for the British war effort, it would not have done much good to let Orwell speculate on whether downed enemy pilots were being lynched by the good yeomen of England.

But a few months later, after this particular London Letter had appeared in print, new information cast a different light on this episode, increasing Orwell's suspicions about government methods. When he received the new information, he pulled the Press Censor's letter from his files and made this notation on it: 'This letter, probably sent to me by an error, contains proof that the censorship altered my articles in some way (probably by re-typing a whole page) that concealed the fact that they had been altered. The editor of P.R. wrote to me, & also mentioned in a footnote to the article, that there had been *no* excisions from this letter.'[30] It was bad enough to have to submit to censorship, but what worried Orwell was the way in which the elimination of certain material could be carried out without anyone else being the wiser. The editor in New York had thought it admirable that Orwell's copy had escaped any trace of the censor's pen, but he had obviously been duped by the successful concealment of the alteration.

It is perfectly conceivable that Orwell included the detail about lynched airmen in his London Letter simply to test the censorship rules. How far would they let him go? If they cut the reference, he would have some idea. He liked creating tests of this kind. It is the sort of thing he did in *Coming Up for Air* when he tested Gollancz's willingness to accept the novel by including in it an attack on the publisher's own book club. But he could not have anticipated just how clever the Ministry of Information would be in trying to implement their rules without tarnishing Britain's image in America.

One good thing about the war is that it temporarily brought Orwell back into the good graces of his old adversary Gollancz. When Stalin agreed to the Non-Aggression Pact with Germany in August 1939, Gollancz had a change of heart about communism, regarding Stalin's act as a betrayal of the Left. Gollancz suddenly began preaching 'respect for what are called the Christian virtues – justice, mercy, forgiveness, charity, kindness and tolerance'.[31] It was a most remarkable shift. Orwell was stunned. 'Gollancz has grown a beard & fallen out with his Communist pals,' he told Geoffrey Gorer in April 1940. He had not seen him for three years, but after the 'betrayal', Gollancz was eager to learn of other acts of Soviet treachery which he had overlooked in the past. 'He asked me whether it was really true that the GPU had been active in Spain during the civil war . . . It's frightful that people who are so ignorant should have so much influence.'³²

Gollancz would once again be a friend of the Soviet Union later in the war, but in 1940–1941 he could not hear enough bad things about the communists, and he published a collection of several critical pieces by diverse hands under the title *The Betrayal of the Left: An Examination and Refutation of Communist Policy*. When this appeared in March 1941, it included two essays by Orwell, one of which was 'Fascism and Democracy'. In that essay he declares, 'Communism was from the first a lost cause in western Europe, and the Communist parties of the various countries early degenerated into mere publicity agents for the Russian regime . . . Instead of pointing out that Russia was a backward country which we might learn from but could not be expected to imitate, the Communists were obliged to pretend that the purges, "liquidations", etc. were healthy symptoms which any right-minded person would like to see transferred to England.' Orwell's repudiation of communism could not be stated any more bluntly than this, yet only three years earlier Gollancz would not have dreamed of allowing such a thing to be said under his imprint.

Gollancz was not fortunate enough to publish Orwell's most important work of 1941, *The Lion and the Unicorn*. This appeared in February as the first in a new series called *Searchlight Books*, which were published by Secker and Warburg, and edited by Orwell and Tosco Fyvel. The short volumes were advertised as 'popular but serious' works which would 'serve as an arsenal for the manufacture of mental and spiritual weapons needed for the crusade against Nazism'. There were supposed to be at least seventeen volumes in the series but it ended after only ten had appeared, and none of them was as good as the first. Orwell wrote it with considerable speed in the autumn of 1940, and when it was published, it enjoyed a large sale, surpassing that of any previous book by Orwell, except for *The Road to Wigan Pier*. Slightly more than twelve thousand copies were sold in two editions.

The Lion and the Unicorn is both a fond tribute to the good sense of the English people and a stirring indictment of their traditional rulers. The England that Orwell declares his loyalty to is a place where tyranny cannot easily establish a foothold because of the deep commitment to what he calls 'private liberty', by which he means 'the liberty to have a home of your own, to do what you like in your spare time, to choose your own amusements instead of having them chosen for you from above'. This liberty is threatened by the pressures of modern life, but as long as it is respected, the general tendency of the people will be against authoritarianism and its symbols. He takes comfort in the knowledge that goose-stepping Storm Troopers would not find favour among the common people. 'There are, heaven knows, plenty of army officers who would be only too glad to introduce some such thing. It is not used because the people in the street would laugh.'

Above all, what he admires in the English character is a strain of gentleness, an unwillingness to worship brute power for its own sake. He likes the fact that the ordinary policeman does not carry a gun and that open disrespect for the law is relatively uncommon. A thousand exceptions can be raised to any one of his points because they are all generalities, but he is not interested in proving anything by hard facts or sharp definitions – he is talking about impressions, and the importance of using them to shape some common sense of the national character, an ideal which will never be realised in all its aspects but which will provide a general sense of purpose and direction.

Ultimately, he sees the country as one large family which should be working together but which has suffered because, in his memorable phrase, it is 'a family with the wrong members in control'. What he advocates is a new order arising from the establishment of a 'specifically *English* Socialist movement, one that appeals to the English character, and is not tainted by Marxism, which was a German theory interpreted by Russians and un-successfully transplanted to England'. His socialism would not be 'doctrinaire, nor even logical', and would 'leave anachronisms and loose ends everywhere' – the lion and the unicorn will still be resplendent on the soldiers' cap buttons, the old judge will still wear his 'ridiculous horsehair wig'. But the essential order of society would change by instituting radical reforms – major industries and land would be nationalised; incomes would be limited so that the difference between the income of the wealthiest person and that of the poorest is no greater than ten to one; the educational system would be operated on democratic lines; and the Empire would be reformed to give India its freedom and the other colonies more representation. Perhaps the most important element of this English socialism lies in one sentence: 'It will never lose touch with the tradition of compromise and the belief in a law that is above the State.' Some of Orwell's ideas may be unappealing or unworkable, but there is a great deal to be said for any system which would respect the limits of its power. Orwell wanted all this to come to pass within a year or two. He wanted real change as the reward for the common man's loyalty to England during the war. If ever there was a rousing conclusion to a social tract, the last, long paragraph of *The Lion and the Unicorn* has it. The middle part sounds like the spirit of Thomas Jefferson or Tom Paine speaking in a modern voice:

England has got to be true to herself . . . It is goodbye to the *Tatler* and the *Bystander*, and farewell to the lady in the Rolls-Royce car. The heirs of Nelson and of Cromwell are not in the House of Lords. They are in the fields and the streets, in the factories and the armed forces, in the four-ale bar and the suburban back garden; and at present they are still kept under by a generation of ghosts.

369

CHAPTER EIGHTEEN

Talking to India

I

The Lion and the Unicorn helped to spread Orwell's fame as an eloquent spokesman for democratic socialism, and one indication of his growing popularity was an invitation he received to speak at a joint meeting of the Oxford University English Club and the Democratic Socialist Club. He agreed to address these two groups and chose as his topic, 'Literature and Totalitarianism'. The lecture took place on the evening of 23 May 1941, and afterwards an anonymous student offered an appraisal of the speaker in the *Cherwell* magazine:

> Some celebrities who write well are apt to be rather disappointing
> to meet. George Orwell was an exception, as he looked just as
> one had always hoped and expected him to look. He talked in
> vague generalisations, which to students of logic are perhaps
> upsetting; but in answering questions which varied from socialist
> boys' weeklies to Marxian melodies for the masses, he showed
> that his position as a leading Left Wing critic is clearly justified.
> One final word: must the Chairman address us as 'Comrades and
> Friends'? He would do well to read *The Road to Wigan Pier*!¹

Not only was Orwell receiving the respect of young admirers, but he also seems to have exerted some influence on their thinking, as the objection to 'comrade' makes clear. His words must have thoroughly captivated the audience since there is no mention of

Orwell's poor speaking voice, which has been described in various ways, but no one has ever been so bold as to say that he spoke forcefully and resonantly. Usually, descriptions of his voice use some variation of the phrase 'thin and high'.

With such a voice, Orwell would not seem to be a likely candidate for a career in broadcasting. Of all the wartime jobs available, he would surely have been more at home – and more useful – in something like cryptography or spying, but no one at the BBC seems to have minded the sound of his voice, and there were no objections when he was offered a position as a Talks Assistant in 1941. His previous experience in broadcasting was limited to a few talks given in the previous nine months. His first time on the radio was as a guest of Desmond Hawkins in the BBC Home Service Programme 'Writer in the Witness Box'. He and Hawkins discussed the subject of 'Proletarian Literature' on 6 December 1940, and a transcript of their discussion was later published in the *Listener*. This was followed by five more broadcasts – one featuring Hawkins, Orwell and V. S. Pritchett, in a programme devoted to the question 'What's Wrong with the Modern Short Story?', and four which featured talks by Orwell, reading from his own scripts, on the general subject of literary criticism. All five of these broadcasts were done for the Indian Section of the Empire Service, and were produced by Z. A. Bokhari, the head of the section. He must have been pleased with the work because he recommended Orwell for a full-time job in the Indian Section, and a subsequent offer from the Empire Service was made. Orwell accepted it on 18 August, agreeing to work at the grand salary – for him – of £640 a year.

This was Orwell's war work, his contribution to the fight against Nazism. India had an army of over two million men, a fact of great psychological importance to the overall war effort, and British authorities in India were anxious to keep the country loyal, and to encourage the view that Britain's security was of vital importance to Indians. The Germans were well aware of this situation and were constantly broadcasting propaganda to the subcontinent in an effort to undermine support for British rule. It was effective, to some extent, and there was some worry at the India Office that the BBC was not doing enough to counteract the propaganda offensive from the Germans. The purpose of the Indian Section of the Eastern Service was to make the voice of Britain heard in India. It was a propaganda effort which was meant to reinforce – as subtly as possible – the ties between the two countries, and to provide a favourable view of England in the face of enemy efforts to damn everything English. It was a way of reminding the Indian people that their support mattered, and was appreciated in Britain.

What it amounted to was a kind of cultural imperialism. So many of the programmes broadcast to India had nothing to do with Indian culture or Indian affairs. There were some distinguished Indians who delivered talks for the service, and subjects of immediate concern to people in India were dealt with, but there was also an enormous amount of attention given to programmes on English politics, English history, English literature, English science, English customs, etc. And the news broadcasts, and commentaries on public events, inevitably carried an English bias. Nothing could be said over the air which had not been carefully screened by BBC censors who were trying to maintain a certain slant on the news and a certain image of the British conduct of the war.

This was not the job for Orwell. He must have known from his experience in Burma that he was not one who could work well within any large organisation. He had never been employed in a large office before, where the schedule was fixed and rules were numerous. At the BBC his workday began at nine-thirty and ended at six-fifteen, with an additional three hours on Saturdays. His first office was in Portland Place, but in 1942 the Eastern Service moved to 200 Oxford Street, where a former department store building had been renovated to provide basic office space, recording studios, and a canteen. His own office was no more than a cubicle with walls which reached only half way to the ceiling. He shared this space with a secretary, and much of his day was spent dictating letters and scripts against the noisy backdrop of the surrounding offices. When he could manage it, he liked to go out for lunch to a nearby pub, but sometimes he went to the canteen. The food was not good, and Orwell derived some pleasure from exaggerating the poor quality.

As he went past the menu board one day, he joked to a colleague standing in front of him: 'A year from now you'll see "Rat Soup" on that board, and in 1943 it will be "Mock Rat Soup".'[2]

Hundreds of letters by Orwell have survived in the BBC archives, and they tell a dismal story of office drudgery. They are the kinds of letters which every bureaucrat has to write, letters confirming appointments, requesting information, extending invitations, acknowledging material received, and correcting errors. These letters begin with such lines as 'I am sending herewith . . .'; 'I wonder if it would be possible . . .'; 'Many thanks for your letter of . . .'; and 'I am just writing to confirm . . .'. It was Orwell's responsibility to find the right speaker for the right topic and then to make sure that the speaker had something to say, and said it at the appointed time. It must have been fun at first to write to distinguished speakers such as T. S. Eliot, E. M. Forster, and G. B. Shaw. But after a while it was just part of the job, and sometimes the famous men were nasty. When Orwell wrote to Shaw seeking permission to broadcast an excerpt from *The Doctor's Dilemma*, the reply was 'I veto it ruthlessly.'[3]

Regardless of the response, this routine correspondence was an enormous waste of Orwell's energy, energy which should have been going into more meaningful work. The job did give him the opportunity to write imaginative pieces from time to time, but they are inferior to his best journalism. Some of them were dictated at great speed, and all of them exhibit a simplistic style. In general Orwell seems to have set his sights too low in his broadcast writing. This was partly because he realised that spoken words needed to be kept simple, but it was also because he was often writing at such great speed, and under the pressure of deadlines. This is especially evident in his talks on literary or social questions. The following sentence from 'Money and Guns' has a bloated appearance which one would not ordinarily find in Orwell's prose: 'You can see from this the way in which the mere necessity of war is bringing about in the English people a more creative attitude towards their amusements.'[4]

He did make valiant efforts to enliven the programmes for which he was responsible. One of his innovations was a radio 'magazine' called *Voice*. The first instalment was broadcast on 11 August 1942 and featured poetry readings by Herbert Read, William Empson, and a discussion of one modern poet by a forum which included Orwell. He also had the idea of telling a story on the air in five parts, each one written by a different author. Orwell began the tale, and he gave E. M. Forster the job of finishing it. One other success of his time at the BBC is his excellent radio adaptation of *The Fox* by Ignazio Silone. There is a hint in it of his future work in *Animal Farm*. The adaptation begins in a pig-sty, and one newborn pig is christened Benito Mussolini.

Occasionally, the censors caused some real trouble, and he fought back. Overall responsibility for censorship lay in the hands of the Ministry of Information, which delegated authority to censors within the BBC. One of these cautious gentlemen took exception to a talk on the Spanish Civil War by Orwell's friend Mulk Raj Anand and prevented it from going on the air. Anand had been commissioned to do the talk by Orwell, who steadfastly supported him in the affair, and who insisted that payment be made for the cancelled broadcast. He also came to the defence of someone who had once tried to censor him. Kingsley Martin spoke on education, giving a left-wing view which BBC officials objected to. Orwell had invited Martin to give the talk, and was later accused of neglecting proper procedures for supervision of the speaker. When he was reprimanded by one of his superiors, he was accused of showing 'scant respect for the normal courtesy and discipline appropriate to an organisation such as ours'.[5]

He could not help rubbing some people up the wrong way. As luck would have it, one of his superiors was Norman Collins, Gollancz's erstwhile assistant ('squirt' was Orwell's name for him). No doubt justifiably, Collins felt that Orwell was not properly deferential towards his authority, and complained about it to others in the organisation. As Orwell went about the business of trying to make his job less monotonous, dreaming up new topics for talks and contacting the best speakers he could find, Collins kept a close watch on him and decided to warn the Eastern Service Director –

L. F. Rushbrook-Williams – that matters were getting out of hand. He charged that, in the matter of issuing invitations to speakers, Orwell was failing to follow the proper chain of authority, and that he was generally behaving 'too independently of the existing organisation'.[6] Orwell was told to mend his ways, which meant – in practical terms – that he had to spend more time writing memos to people like Collins explaining what he was up to.

Some people thrive on the minor details of bureaucratic life, but Orwell was always wanting to get on with his work without becoming bogged down in tiresome discussions about policy. It does not matter that he was perhaps allowed more freedom than other Talks Assistants – he was never going to be comfortable working in a system as hierarchical, and as memo-ridden, as the Eastern Service. He meant it when he said that his work made him feel like 'an orange that's been trodden on by a very dirty boot'.[7] It was dirty not because it was necessarily corrupt – Orwell later complimented the BBC for being 'relatively truthful' – but because it was what it was – a large organisation full of people pushing endless pieces of paper from the bottom ranks to the top, and back down again. He never ceased to be amazed at the waste of paper, especially since it contrasted so sharply with the scarcity in the book trade during the war. In 1944 he wrote in *Tribune*, 'Would you credit, for instance, that of every radio programme that goes out on the air, even the inconceivable rubbish of cross-talk comedians, at least six copies are typed – sometimes as many as fifteen copies? For years past all this trash has been filed somewhere or other in enormous archives.'[8]

One person who knew him well at the BBC was his secretary, Elisabeth Knight. She was assigned to his office in the later months of his employment, and found him a considerate, even-tempered person. 'He couldn't have been better to work for,' she recalled. 'He was very organised, but relaxed. He never told me off and never put pressure on me, no last minute demands. He was quiet, but not withdrawn. His eyes were lively and watchful.' She often used to find him in the office when she arrived; he would be sitting quietly at his desk – dressed in a tweed jacket, a brown shirt, and corduroy trousers – rolling a cigarette. He dictated to her as she typed, and they were soon able to work at a rapid pace. 'He dictated so well that after I'd been doing it for several weeks, he never had to dictate punctuation because it was so obvious where to punctuate. I was typing flat out, and he rarely paused. After he started on a topic there was little hesitation. He knew how many pages would fill up a fifteen-minute talk or whatever, so he knew when to stop dictating.' One aspect of his behaviour did cause some confusion, however. He was known to her, and to most people in the building, as Eric Blair, but in contacting potential speakers for his broadcasts, he often used his pseudonym. 'If I answered the phone, I always said, "Mr Blair's office", and then people sometimes said, "Oh, sorry, I wanted George Orwell", and then you had to tell them quickly that they had reached the right number.'[9]

During his early days as a writer of news commentaries Orwell did not use his pseudonym to identify himself as the author of the scripts when they were read on the air. In some cases these scripts were broadcast by him, but it was more often the case that they were broadcast by others, with the implication that they were the work of the speaker. After his first year in the Eastern Service the suggestion was made by one of his superiors that he might think of lending his name to the broadcasts on the chance that it might attract more listeners. Orwell was reluctant to do this unless he could be sure that the integrity of his pseudonym would not be compromised. 'George Orwell' was his creation – a figure to which he had given an identifiable voice as a result of a long and difficult process – and he was quite naturally protective of it. He did not want it compromised by too close an association with BBC broadcasts which might be subject to increasingly strict control as the war progressed. In other words, he was not willing to risk the good name of George Orwell, if he could avoid it. 'If I broadcast as George Orwell,' he told the director of the Eastern Service, 'I am as it were selling my literary reputation.'[10] He did eventually use the pseudonym on the air, but this made him all the more determined to say what he really thought. It was impossible, however, to be as blunt as he would have wanted because the censors would never have allowed it. All he could do was be as honest as possible within the limitations, avoiding any traps which might lead him into making false statements. But any use of his name in the service of a propaganda effort – however mild it might have been – was a compromise of sorts, and he could not ignore that fact.

There were occasions when he wrote things for broadcast which did not reflect his real sentiments. One of his news commentaries from February 1942 gives a charitable view of 'Premier Stalin' which is at odds with everything he wrote about the dictator in his own articles and letters: 'Considering the atrocious manner in which the Germans have behaved in their invasion of Russia, [Stalin's] speech was notable for its lack of vindictiveness and for the wise and large-minded way in which it distinguished between the German people and their rulers.' Strictly speaking, this was not a false statement – especially with its qualifying phrase at the beginning – but 'wise' and 'large-minded' are terms which Orwell would not have granted Stalin outside the walls of the BBC, where the official policy was to portray the Russian allies in a favourable light.

Orwell was willing to write such things because he believed, in the beginning, that his job allowed him to make at least a small contribution to the war effort. Of course, he would have preferred a military position of any kind to this civilian work, but he went along with it until he realised that his service was more or less pointless. After more than a year on the job he learned from an intelligence officer named Laurence Brander, who worked for the BBC in the East, that there were in fact very few Indians listening to the broadcasts aimed at them from London. As Brander confirmed, the Indians had relatively few shortwave sets. He estimated that in a country of nearly three hundred million people, there were probably only 150,000 sets. Though it was small, this potential audience was an influential section of the population, but surveys conducted by Brander revealed that not many of these listeners were bothering to tune into the BBC Eastern Service, except for news broadcasts. Orwell tried to give a positive interpretation of this situation in the introduction he wrote for *Talking to India*, a volume of selected talks from the Eastern Service broadcasts. (Allen and Unwin published the book in 1943, and Orwell was its editor.) 'Obviously the listening public for such programmes must be a small one,' he wrote, 'but it is also a public well worth reaching, since it is likely to be composed largely of University students.'

His private view was much different. Orwell confided in his diary that Brander's report was so depressing that he could hardly bring himself to acknowledge the facts. He was faced with the realisation that all of his efforts to put high quality programmes on the air were serving no practical purpose. Too few people were paying any attention to them. What was the point of recruiting top-notch speakers and devising grand topics for them to discuss when perhaps only a few hundred Indians throughout the huge sub-continent would be listening?

Within his first year on the job Orwell seems to have guessed that this dreary reality was facing him, but he went ahead with his work anyway, and tried – as far as possible – to get into the spirit of the undertaking. But from the start it was unrealistic for anyone at the BBC to imagine that a significant number of Indians would be flocking round the shortwave to hear Stephen Spender speak on 'Poetry and Traditionalism', or Professor Egerton on 'Experimental and Applied Science', or George Orwell on 'British Rations and the Submarine War'. The whole undertaking was marred by an assumption that the subjects which interested a small group of English intellectuals would also interest large numbers of people living thousands of miles away, who would be hearing these highbrow topics addressed to the accompaniment of crackling sounds from the static of a small shortwave radio. Orwell knew what conditions were like in the East, and perhaps should have been among the first to suggest that the Eastern Service forget about all its plans for talks and forums, and concentrate instead on providing first-rate news broadcasts and music. This was the conclusion supported by Laurence Brander's reports, but by the time it was available, Orwell may not have had the energy left to fight for a change. Most likely, he understood that no one would listen, that the engines of the BBC were relentlessly grinding away according to a predetermined pace, and that a minor producer in one section of the organisation could not hope to slow it down.

For Orwell personally, the most discouraging news came from the results of a survey which Brander distributed to various listeners in India. The purpose of this survey was to determine what programmes were favoured by people who were trying to pick up the broadcasts on a regular basis. This group was also asked to name their favourite 'Personalities' on the Eastern Service. Orwell's name was included on a list of possible choices, along with E. M. Forster, J. B. Priestley, and Professor Joad. Priestley received a very high approval rating of sixty-eight per cent, and not far behind were Joad (56%) and Forster (52%). Orwell was disheartened to learn that his rating was among the very lowest of all the names on the list – only 18%.[11]

Orwell's many BBC letters and scripts contain interesting information about the way his section functioned in relation to the larger bureaucracy, and they shed light on his working methods within the constraints imposed upon him. So much material is available – huge amounts of paper, including not only correspondence and scripts but also internal memos and reports, and booking slips for broadcasts which Orwell supervised or participated in – but simply because all this paper was preserved does not mean it should be taken too seriously. Orwell, quite rightly, considered most of it 'trash' – he also called it 'bilge' – and there is no point in trying to make substantial claims for the merits of his many news commentaries or his talks on literary and political subjects. Long before he left the BBC, he was fully aware of the fact that the volume of paper he was producing was not worth the considerable effort which he put into it. Moreover, this work wasted so much of his energy that it was difficult for him to find the strength to do anything else. He was very clear about all this in his diary, which indicates that a deepening sense of despair was overtaking him even before he had finished his first year on the job. In the entry for 23 July 1942, he writes:

I am doing nothing that is not futility and have less and less to show for the time I waste. It seems to be the same with everyone—the most fearful feeling of frustration, of just footling round doing imbecile things, not imbecile because they are a part of the war and war is inherently foolish, but things which in fact *don't* help or in any way affect the war effort, but are considered necessary by the huge bureaucratic machine in which we are all caught up. Much of the stuff that goes out from the BBC is just shot into the stratosphere, not listened to by anybody, and *known* to those responsible for it, not to be listened to by anybody.

Some things which he experienced at the BBC did eventually prove useful to him when he was able to draw on them for inspiration in the creation of the nightmare bureaucracy of the Ministry of Truth. Compared to this fictional monstrosity, the BBC was as harmless as Orwell implied when he joked that 'its atmosphere is something halfway between a girls' school and a lunatic asylum'.[12] But in his time as one of its employees he learned enough about the workings of large organisations to understand how they can create justifications for meaningless activity, and how they can persuade so many of their workers to take this work seriously. And he was reminded of how stultifying it can be to work in an atmosphere where the threat of censorship is ever present. He felt that way in Burma, of course, where a kind of unofficial censorship was imposed by pressure from the empire builders straining under the loads of their white men's burdens. But it was the routine, institutionalised nature of the censorship at the BBC which Orwell found intriguing, and depressing.

The effect of working in such a place was that eventually it became impossible to think of putting any words on paper without considering the response of the censors. Censorship does not have to be strict to induce this thought, it needs only to be present in some form, and to be applied with regularity. At the BBC the one method of censorship which was most unnerving involved the use of a 'switch censor' during a broadcast. This simply meant putting some trusted bureaucrat in front of a switch so that he or she could cut off the broadcast of any speaker who might be tempted to say something unsanctioned by official policy. The exigencies of wartime perhaps justified this technique in the cases of some live broadcasts, but it was of doubtful necessity to employ a switch censor to monitor Orwell's use of the air waves. As he sat at the microphone delivering his remarks, there would sometimes be a switch censor sitting nearby, ready to silence him at any moment so that the security of the British Isles would not be threatened by any seditious comments aimed at a few thousand listeners in India.

Orwell had his revenge against this sort of thing in *Nineteen Eighty-Four*, but he also had other ways of striking back. He seems to have had occasional confrontations with his immediate superior – Bokhari – who could be high-handed in his dealings with subordinates. When one of Bokhari's friends – Lionel Fielden – wrote a pompous treatise on India, Orwell asked to review it for *Horizon* and was given an inordinate amount of space for the piece, which he used to demolish the book's pretensions, calling its tone 'nagging', condemning its praise of India as 'tourist-like gush', and declaring its overall argument 'irrelevant'.[13] The book was dedicated to Bokhari.

II

Appearing in September 1943, the review was a parting shot. On the twenty-fourth of that month Orwell submitted his resignation. He wrote a restrained letter to the Eastern Service Director carefully explaining his reasons for leaving, and thanking him for his 'understanding and generous attitude'. But he was forthright about his dissatisfaction with the job, saying that he had felt for some time that he was 'wasting' his time on 'work that produces no result'. He made it equally clear that the service needed to take a different view of its mission, but he was not prepared to use up any more of his time waiting for some change to occur. 'Whether these broadcasts should be continued at all is for others to judge, but I myself prefer not to spend my time on them when I could be occupying myself with journalism which does produce some measurable effect.'[14] This was the second time he had given up a well-paid government position, but it would be the last. If the war had not come along, he would never have been tempted to take it in the first place; at least his sense of loyalty did not keep him at it until the end of the war, which would have involved two more wasted years.

He found better patrons, one of whom was David Astor at the *Observer*. The two men were introduced by Cyril Connolly, who worked as the literary editor of the *Observer* in 1942–1943. Their first meeting took place at a restaurant near the Oxford Street offices of the Eastern Service, and despite the fact that one man was the son of a lord and the other the son of a minor civil servant, they established an easy intimacy with each other very early on, and would be strong friends for the rest of Orwell's life. Astor had read and enjoyed *The Lion and the Unicorn* before meeting Orwell, but he did not know much about his personal history, his other books nor even what he looked like:

> I remember that on that first meeting when I walked into the restaurant, I noticed this tall figure standing to one side, looking a bit detached, and as I walked towards him, he came up in a very friendly way and asked, 'Are you David Astor?' We got on very well, almost as though we had known each other before. But he was something of a familiar type to me. He was dressed in grey flannel trousers and looked a little like a prep school master – he wore the modest comfortable dress of a teacher or librarian. He was not as neat as a soldier, but there was a military air to him.[15]

Astor invited Orwell to contribute articles and reviews to the paper, and his first pieces appeared anonymously in the late winter of 1942. On 8 March 1942 one piece came out under the heading 'Mood of the Moment' and advanced the view that the 'mood' among the British people was one of frustration because of the lack of progress in the war and the lack of reform at home. There was no sign that the people were any closer to achieving the goals set forward in *The Lion and the Unicorn*, but Orwell still thought that they would welcome 'sweeping changes' if the chance to make them presented itself. The reasons for making such changes were more compelling than ever: 'Britain is too much tied to the past and to an outworn social system . . . There is more waste, more inequality of wealth, more thwarting of intelligence, more nepotism, more privilege, than a nation which has been two years at war can afford.'

Orwell's hopes were the same as they had been at the time when *The Lion and the Unicorn* was published, but he was beginning to see that the exciting period in 1940, when England had been preparing to make a last stand against an invading army, was a time which had already come and gone. By early 1942 the threat of invasion seemed much less likely – Hitler had already turned his attention elsewhere, breaking his pact with Stalin and sending his armies into Russia – so the sense of urgency, the feeling that some dramatic event was going to plunge the country into chaos or bring into being a new dispensation, had faded, leaving behind a sense of frustrated expectation. One compensation for Orwell, however, was that, thanks to his new friendship with David Astor, he had access to the pages of a large national paper in which he could share his thoughts with not merely thousands of readers but hundreds of thousands.

But not everything went smoothly for him at the *Observer*, in part because David Astor had not yet assumed full control of the paper and was not able to guarantee that everything Orwell wanted to say would be printed. A problem developed in September 1942 when he was asked to review a book by O. D. Gallagher called *Retreat in the East*. He turned in his piece on time, completing it in the spare hours allowed to him after a full week of work at the BBC, and was not at all pleased when he discovered several days later that the editor of the paper – Ivor Brown – had rejected it after seeing it in proof. The problem, he was told, was that the review contained criticism of the Empire which went too far and might 'play into the hands of a few ill-disposed Americans', reinforcing prejudice against Britain among isolationists. Orwell's review did nothing more than point out the relevant information in the book about the shocking way in which the Empire's defences had collapsed in Singapore and Burma, but this was enough to cause Brown to pull it at the last minute. He apologised for the decision, but it was the sort of thing which Orwell was bound to resent, and which he could not easily excuse. As literary editor, Connolly had commissioned the review, but there was nothing he could do if Brown refused to print it. Nevertheless, Connolly received the heat of Orwell's anger. It may be that Orwell believed he had been misled about the intentions of the *Observer*, but his reaction was uncommonly strong: 'I don't write for papers which do not allow for at least a minimum of honesty. There is no point in reviewing a book unless one can say what is in it. The author of *Retreat in the East* got in some good cracks at the civilian community in Malaya etc. and I merely quoted a typical one. I had no idea that silly owl Brown had anything to do with the literary page of the Observer.'[16] Astor and Connolly managed to smooth Orwell's ruffled feathers, but this episode illustrates how pervasive the problem of censorship was in his career, and how bitter he felt about attempts to keep him from saying what he thought.

Brown must have made an extra effort to win back his angry contributor because by the time Orwell left the BBC the two men were involved in friendly discussions about a possible journalistic assignment in North Africa and Italy. It was one more chance for Orwell to take a closer look at the effects of the war, and he was eager to accept the position – provided the War Office would issue him the proper credentials. In his letter of resignation from the BBC he made note of the fact that he was thinking of going to North Africa for the *Observer*, but he understood that his plan was dependent on, among other things, the results of a medical exam required by the War Office. And once again his chest condition held him back. His credentials were denied, and he had to pass up the offer from Brown.

In the wake of this development he fell back on another plan, which was less exciting but which would prove in the end much more productive. For the past few years he had been writing reviews and other pieces for the left-wing weekly *Tribune* and, just at the time when he was leaving the BBC, the literary editorship of the paper was offered to him. He accepted it and remained in the job for the next fifteen months. As he later admitted, editorial work was not one of his strengths. He was slow to make decisions and was always behind with his correspondence. He also suffered from, in his words, 'a fatal tendency to accept manuscripts which I know very well are too bad to be printed'. But he attributed this flaw to the fact that he had spent too many years getting rejection slips and did not like the notion of giving them out himself. 'It is questionable whether anyone who has had long experience as a free-lance journalist ought to become an editor. It is too like taking a convict out of his cell and making him governor of the prison.'[17] A good example of his soft treatment of contributors can be seen in a letter which he wrote to a reviewer who had sent him an unsatisfactory piece of work. Orwell was almost apologetic in pointing out to the man that his review had failed to say anything about the book under consideration: 'I am sorry to make further trouble, but could you just add to this review a line or two about the book itself, i.e. about Nevill's book. What you say about Harriet Martineau is interesting and in a review of this kind it is all right to devote most of the space to exposition, but I think we ought to just mention whether the author has done his work well or badly.'[18]

Orwell had his disagreements with the editorial board, which was headed by Aneurin Bevan, but in general he enjoyed a remarkable degree of freedom at the paper, and was appreciative of its place as an independent voice within the socialist movement. 'It is the only existing weekly paper,' he wrote in 1947, 'that makes a genuine effort to be both progressive and humane – that is, to combine a radical Socialist policy with a respect for freedom of speech and a civilised attitude towards literature and the arts.'[19] His greatest contribution to the paper was not as literary editor but as columnist. In that capacity he was in his proper element. The idea for the title of his column has often been attributed to Orwell, but 'As I Please' was not his invention. The idea was recommended to him by Jon Kimche, his former co-worker at Booklovers' Corner. When Orwell came to work at *Tribune*, Kimche had already been working there for nearly two years, serving as chief assistant to Bevan. According to Kimche, the orginator of the 'As I Please' idea was Raymond Postgate, a former editor of the paper, who had used it first, in 1939, when he wrote a column in *Controversy* under the title 'I Write As I Please'. It was described at that time as a feature in which the writer could discuss anything which appealed to him, including 'shoes and ships and sealing-wax and cabbages and kings'.[20] The range of subjects which Orwell addressed in his column was every bit as wide as this original plan suggested.

Although the credit for inventing the 'As I Please' format must go to Raymond Postgate, Orwell developed it to its greatest potential, using it skilfully to bring together wayward strands of thought. He had never had the opportunity before to make use of such an unrestricted format. For once he was able to enjoy a high level of freedom to say what he wanted to say in whatever way he wanted to say it. It was a format for which his talent was especially well-suited, one in which it could shine with apparent ease. It must also have been a relief to him to be writing as he pleased, after spending two years grinding out material according to the dictates of the BBC. He was lucky to have the support of Aneurin Bevan. As Michael Foot later commented, Bevan 'was the only editor in Fleet Street who, in those days before Orwell's reputation was sure, would have given him complete freedom to offend all readers and lash all hypocrisies, including Socialist hypocrisies.'[21]

He wrote four 'As I Please' columns during his first full month on the staff. One can detect a palpable sense of relief in these pieces, a feeling on Orwell's part that he has finally been set free from the restrictions and inhibitions of the previous two years. The format seems to have emerged in perfect order from the very beginning, Orwell shows no signs of needing to experiment with it. He knows exactly what he wants to do, striking the right note of confidence and unassuming grace in the first column. The secret to his ability to make these pieces seem so effortless is his knack of discussing several subjects without appearing to be wandering from one to the other. He does not always try to provide a proper transition between subjects, but the transition is there all the same because it is implicit in the confidence of his tone as he drops one topic and turns to look at the next. He avoids the appearance of abruptness in a way that few writers could match.

Even in his first pieces the diversity of his interests is amazing. At one moment his thoughts are engaged with the sad fate of a long-forgotten Victorian novelist, at another he muses on the usefulness of political pamphlets and proudly notes the large size of his collection of these works. One moment he might sketch a scene in the back streets of London, and then discuss some incredibly beautiful flower growing beside a fence in a small village. In one piece he takes his readers on a brief architectural tour, beginning with St John's church, across the road from Lord's, complaining from his vantage point on the upper deck of the number 53 bus that the war memorial in front of the pretty little church has ruined the view. He then goes without explanation to the top of the hill at Greenwich Park, and speaks with pleasure about the 'mild thrill of standing exactly on longitude o'. But the real point of taking his readers there is to inform them that it is the site of the 'ugliest building in the world' – the Greenwich Observatory.

He revels in his latest discovery of a rare book which practically no one else would care to have. It is called *The Chronological Tablets, Exhibiting Every Remarkable Occurrence Since the Creation of the World Down to the Present Time*. Published in 1801, it confidently gives the date of creation not merely as autumn 4004 BC, but as September 4004 BC. This was the kind of absolutely useless, wrong-headed information which Orwell loved, and 'loved' is not too strong a word for it. But there are more serious questions taken up in 'As I Please', and he is capable of shifting quickly from a funny anecdote to a solemn reflection. One paragraph may be concerned with something as trivial as the price of tea, and then the next may plunge into the difficulties of making a case for war crimes trials against Hitler and his henchmen after the war is over.

One serious question to which he devoted a good deal of attention in his early columns was the growing problem of anti-Americanism in Britain, fuelled in large part by the increasing number of GIs arriving in the country to prepare for the eventual invasion of the Continent. The first column, in fact, begins with Orwell setting a scene in a tobacconist's shop where two drunken American soldiers are making a nuisance of themselves. The scene is written out in the manner of a radio play, complete with cue for the narrator to join the action: 'Enter Orwell' the passage says, and then Orwell exchanges lines of dialogue with the soldiers who, in their drunkenness, express a desire to knock his head off. The scene is short but effective and original, within the essay format, and it makes a good introduction to the more serious, extended arguments which Orwell wants to express on the issue of anti-American feeling. His main concern is that the government has done too much to suppress any public discussion of anti-American feeling, out of the fear that it will only make the situation worse. Of course, Orwell wants it to be brought out into the open, and he chides the government for wanting to 'soft soap' the issue. Later, a good many readers wrote to *Tribune* to criticise his position and to accuse him of being anti-American. He neatly evaded the point by declaring, 'I am much less anti-American than most English people are at this moment.'[22]

The very use of the phrase 'soft soap' to explain the government's treatment of a sensitive problem brings out one of the special charms of Orwell's prose style in 'As I Please'. He is able to use very informal language in such a way that it does not seem sloppy or loose. For most writers the use of slang or other informal expressions creates dangerous pitfalls, tempting them to be too casual in the construction of sentences. Orwell had a talent for fitting loose expressions into tight sentences. For example, the phrase 'block it up' is, by itself, an awkward phrase and can easily damage the balance of any sentence which includes it, but not when Orwell uses it. He knows how to make it sound smooth and sharp, as in this sentence on an English tendency to spoil the view of pleasant landscapes: 'Whenever you do by some chance have a decent vista, block it up with the ugliest statue you can find.'[23]

Before 'As I Please' came along, any one of these stray thoughts of his could have been the beginning of a long essay, but only so many long essays can be turned out in an average year, and during that time a lot of stray thoughts can come and go without ever being captured on paper. 'As I Please' allowed him to increase his annual catch in a dramatic way, and as a whole, the many columns which he wrote for *Tribune* in the 1940s form a splendid monument to his literary powers and his dynamic character.

So strong was the autobiographical impulse in Orwell that there is some reflection of his character in almost everything he wrote, and one essay which he produced in the early 1940s gives a particularly good insight into his fundamental outlook on life. Published in February 1942, 'The Art of Donald McGill' is ostensibly an apology for the ordinary, unsophisticated art forms of that favourite creature of Orwell's – the common man. But his argument in favour of the seaside postcards is, more importantly, an argument in favour of those claims on our attention which we are tempted to dismiss as useless, trivial, and even faintly absurd. Such clutter is part of the richness of life, and Orwell is suspicious of any desire to sweep it away. Winston Smith's attachment to his glass paperweight is a revolutionary act because it is an expression of an individual mind which is capable of being sentimental, unpredictable and wilful. The same can be said of Orwell's large collection of cards, with their ridiculous exaggerations and lame jokes. 'The corner of the human heart that they speak for might easily manifest itself in worse forms,' he writes of the cards, 'and I for one should be sorry to see them vanish.'

They belong to a view of life which Orwell associates with Sancho Panza. 'There is one part of you that wishes to be a hero or a saint, but another part of you is a little fat man who sees very clearly the advantages of staying alive with a whole skin. He is your unofficial self . . . His tastes lie towards safety, soft beds, no work, pots of beer and women with "voluptuous" figures.' Orwell is often portrayed as a Don Quixote figure, a crazy idealist who was willing to sacrifice everything – his health, his security, his career, his happiness, his life – for his dreams. He was every bit of that, but it is important to remember that he identified with Sancho too. Outwardly, there were few signs in his lean body that a Sancho was lurking within, but he was there, and Orwell respected his presence. One can hear Sancho's voice emerging again and again in the writer's books, essays, letters, diaries. It comes through clearly in, for example, this account of a conversation with Osbert Sitwell, as given in Orwell's diary for 21 September 1942: 'He said that in Cornwall in case of invasion the Home Guard have orders to shoot all artists. I said that in Cornwall this might be all for the best.'

There is a great appreciation in 'The Art of Donald McGill' for the fact that special consideration must be given to the side of human life which Sancho represents, and that no understanding of society can be valid if it fails to take into account the importance of the 'unofficial self'. Theorists and social planners go astray when they try to factor out this unreliable element in the average person. Orwell's answer to those who want to create more rules for men and women to live by is this simple reminder: 'On the whole, human beings want to be good, but not too good, and not quite all the time.'

CHAPTER NINETEEN

Animal Story

I

For a time in the early 1940s both Orwell and Eileen were involved in broadcasting. In the spring of 1942 she took a job at the Ministry of Food in Portman Square, where her chief responsibility was to oversee the daily broadcast of a Home Service programme called *The Kitchen Front*. Every morning listeners could tune in and receive five minutes of helpful hints on how to prepare good meals within the limits of wartime scarcities and restrictions. Countless recipes were offered, talks on diet and nutrition were given by respected doctors and scientists, reports on food preparation in other countries were delivered, and various cooking techniques were explained. Like her husband, Eileen wrote scripts for broadcast, and contacted speakers. She also spent many hours answering correspondence from all the listeners who submitted favourite recipes or cooking tips.

The Kitchen Front was a propaganda programme which tried to make people think that food rationing was not such a bad thing. Listeners were told of the virtues of eating a lot of potatoes, and the Ministry of Food was proud to have discovered one hundred delicious ways to prepare them. *The Kitchen Front* spread the good word on the latest recipe discoveries. Perhaps the most outrageous was something called 'murkey', which was a turkey dinner with only one thing missing – the turkey. The dish included vegetables, a potato, stuffing and gravy but no serving of meat. The dish was supposedly so good that it did not need meat.

Eileen did not mind doing this kind of promotional work. She liked to cook, for one thing, but she also enjoyed the broadcasting part of her work. She was good at it, and at one point she was recruited by her husband to do a broadcast for him on the Eastern Service. He asked her to organise a series of programmes called *In Your Kitchen*, and she introduced the first of these on the air. A script of her broadcast to India is in the BBC Archives, and gives some notion of her speaking style. It also reveals that her husband had made her aware of the fact that there were probably only a small number of people who might be listening in India. In the final part of her introduction she said, 'That is the story of "The Kitchen Front Broadcast", and now once a week you are going to hear one or two of our recipes, at least I hope you are going to hear them. Miss Panthaki is going to broadcast them anyway.' As a preview of this series, Eileen was interviewed on the Eastern Service by one of Orwell's colleagues, Venu Chitale, who described 'Mrs Blair' as a woman with a 'reservoir of quiet humour . . . Again and again some of it seems to come out in between an amused smile and a penetrating remark.'[1]

Although Orwell would certainly have been driven mad by the sort of work required for *The Kitchen Front*, it was work which seemed to have the opposite effect on Eileen, helping to bring her out of the depression which had nearly overwhelmed her after Laurence O'Shaughnessy's death. She was never the same woman after she lost her brother, but her spirits did revive, and she began to go out more often. She enjoyed the company of several friends at the Ministry of Food, one of whom was Lettice Cooper. 'Eileen's mind was a mill that ground all the time slowly but independently,' Lettice remembered. 'Diffident and unassuming in manner, she had a quiet integrity that I never saw shaken.' Eileen's appearance left a strong impression on her friend. 'She was of medium height, a little high-shouldered. She was very pretty, and had what George called a "cat's face", blue eyes and near-black hair. She moved slowly. She always looked as if she were drifting into a room with no particular purpose. She had small very shapely hands and feet. I never saw her in a hurry, but her work was always finished up to time.'[2]

When Eileen began working at the Ministry of Food, she and her husband were living at a large block of flats just off the Abbey Road. It was a sturdy, modern building – a good place to be during the Blitz – but it was a little too modern for Orwell's tastes, and when the worst phase of the bombing raids had passed, he looked for a place whose atmosphere was more suitable. They found such a place at 10a Mortimer Crescent. They occupied the lower half of a large, semi-detached Victorian house which was well-built but slightly shabby. Orwell liked its old-fashioned charm. 'It conjured up those middle-to-lower-middle class nineteenth century households on which his mind loved to dwell,' Anthony Powell recalled, 'particularly enthroned in the works of his favourite novelist, Gissing.'[3]

After moving to Mortimer Crescent, the Orwells had plenty of room for entertaining, though the level of comfort which they offered their guests was basic. Orwell liked to show off his small workshop in the basement, where he did carpentry as a hobby, and in the back garden he reportedly kept a few chickens, which was apparently not illegal in London at that time. David Astor recalled Orwell's earnest advice on raising chickens. 'It's not a good idea to give the chickens names,' he confided, 'because then you can't eat them.'[4]

Orwell enjoyed a relatively active social life during this period. Most of it took place in the daytime, when he would go to lunch with friends or spend an hour with one or two of them at a pub on the way home from the *Tribune* office in the Strand. Some of the new friends he made in the war years were several years younger; one of these was Michael Meyer, who was only twenty-two at the time they met. He had been a pupil at Wellington when Orwell's old schoolfriend Bobbie Longden was its headmaster. Meyer was serving in the RAF at Bomber Command Headquarters when he was introduced to Orwell on a visit to London in 1943. He had edited *Cherwell* at Oxford, and had managed to make friends with such distinguished older writers as Graham Greene and Herbert Read. On 11 June 1944 he celebrated his twenty-third birthday by inviting both Orwell and Greene to join him for lunch at the

Hungarian Czarda in Dean Street. It was the first meeting between the two famous novelists, and according to Meyer, 'they got on extremely well' – so well, in fact, that they stayed in the restaurant until it closed, and then went to a nearby pub where they continued talking for a while longer. The three men shared two more meals during the next few weeks, but Orwell seemed to lose interest in Greene after reading more of his work. He did not care for Greene's Catholic theology, and later subjected it to strong criticism in a review of *The Heart of the Matter*. 'This cult of the sanctified sinner seems to me frivolous,' he commented in the review, 'and underneath it there probably lies a weakening of belief, for when people really believed in Hell, they were not so fond of striking graceful attitudes on its brink.'[5]

Orwell's friendship with Meyer did not fade. They saw a good deal of each other in the mid-1940s. On one memorable day they went to a West End production of both parts of *Henry IV*, starring Laurence Olivier and Ralph Richardson. They spent seven hours in the theatre, and then went to a Chinese restaurant for dinner. As Meyer later recalled, their day at the theatre left them exhausted. This was particularly true of Orwell, who had tried to keep up with his younger friend as they had rushed through the streets to reach the theatre in time for the opening curtain. The fast pace of their walk had left him almost breathless. 'I remember the dreadful whistling heaviness of his breathing for fully five minutes after we had taken our seats, and my shame at having forgotten the state of his lungs.'[6]

Another young friend of this period was Julian Symons, who met Orwell at the *Tribune* office in 1944. According to Symons, he 'was not predisposed to like [Orwell]', and he had good reason to feel that way. In 1942 Orwell had somehow reached the conclusion that there was 'a vaguely Fascist strain' in a piece which Symons had contributed to George Woodcock's *Now* magazine, and this bogus idea had found its way into one of his London Letters to *Partisan Review*. Naturally enough, Symons resented the slur, but when they finally met, Orwell had the good sense to admit he was wrong and to apologise. 'Shouldn't have said you were a Fascist,' he told him.

'Very sorry about that.' Symons was impressed, especially when the apology was made in print. In the London Letter which he contributed at the end of 1944, he declared, 'I particularly regret having said in one letter that Julian Symons "writes in a vaguely Fascist strain" – a quite unjustified statement based on a single article which I probably misunderstood.' As Symons later said of this incident, 'It is not uncommon for journalists to make wild assertions, but only those of great integrity admit, rather than bury, their mistakes.'[7]

The two men became friends and saw each other regularly in London. There was a period in 1945–1946 when he and Symons had lunch every week with Anthony Powell and Malcolm Muggeridge at the Bodega in Bedford Street, near the Strand. He was a little self-conscious about his friendship with a writer as politically conservative as Powell (not to mention Muggeridge, who was a relatively new friend). He once confided to Symons, 'Tony is the only Tory I have ever liked.' Symons observed how much amusement Powell and Muggeridge derived from Orwell's tendency to make unreasonable generalisations about politics. Many years later Muggeridge wrote of one outrageous example: Orwell suddenly announced, 'All tobacconists are Fascists,' and began to expand on the point as though its truth were self-evident. 'Momentarily, one was swept along,' Muggeridge recalled. 'Yes, there was something in it; those little men in their kiosks handing out fags and tobacco all day long – wouldn't they have followed a Hitler or a Mussolini if one had come along? Then the sheer craziness of it took hold of one, and one began to laugh helplessly, until – such was his persuasiveness – one reflected inside one's laughter: after all, they are rather rum birds, those tobacconists.'[8]

Powell recalled that Orwell 'was one of the most enjoyable people to talk with about books'. His conversations about his favourite authors were 'full of parallels and quotations', and Powell was of the opinion that literature, not politics, was 'his true love'. Powell was intrigued by the contradictions in Orwell's character, and recognised that politics 'both attracted and repelled him', and that literature, though it was 'close to his heart, was at the same time tainted with the odour of escape'. On a visit to Orwell's flat Powell discovered that his friend's love of carpentry was connected to a deep desire to do something practical and straightforward, something untainted by contradictions. 'Don't you ever feel the need to do something with your hands?' Orwell asked him. 'I'm surprised you don't . . . I've installed a lathe in the basement. I don't think I could exist without my lathe.'[9]

Based on what he saw of Eileen during the later years of the war, Powell concluded that she was 'a little overwhelmed by the strain of keeping the household going, which could not have been easy'. It was indeed difficult for her to do her job at the Ministry of Food and also manage the domestic chores at a time when so many food products and other basic goods were rationed. She received a little help on evenings and weekends after Ida Blair and Avril moved to London in 1942. They lived in a flat not far from Mortimer Crescent, and both women had wartime jobs. Avril worked in a sheet-metal factory, and Ida – despite being in her late sixties – found work as a shop assistant at Selfridge's.

Unfortunately, Ida was not in good health. She insisted on going to her job every day even though it required her to work long hours each week. She was able to keep up with its demands until one week in early March 1943 when she began having breathing difficulties. She was taken to hospital, but her condition quickly worsened. On 19 March – only one week after she had been admitted – she died. Orwell was with her at the time, and witnessed the death certificate, just as he had done when his father died in 1939. The primary cause of Ida's death was heart failure, but two secondary causes are listed on her certificate, and these are of some significance since they suggest that it may have been from his mother that Orwell inherited his weak lungs. The two causes were listed as acute bronchitis and emphysema of the lungs.

Orwell never commented on his mother's death, and there is a remarkable lack of information about her in his written work. One of the few places she is mentioned is in his essay 'Why I Write'. She is spoken of there with some fondness as an indulgent mother who proudly listened to her young son recite some of the poetry he had made up. But there is no attempt to draw a vivid portrait of her or to reveal any personal details about her, not even her name. The piece was written only a few years after her death, but one would never know it from reading it. She is just part of a childhood memory, a kind of disembodied figure out of the past. There is no hint in any material by or about him that he felt anything but love and respect for his mother, but the depth of those feelings cannot be gauged because he chose to keep so much to himself. Despite his remarkable candour on many personal subjects, there were simply some details of his life which he could not, or would not, discuss openly.

It is significant, however, that in the months which followed his mother's death, he began to yearn more than ever before to have a child of his own. He never made any secret of his desire to have a child, but his life had been filled with so many hardships that the idea of raising a family had never seemed more than a distant dream. It was a somewhat more practical possibility in the 1940s because Orwell was better able to earn a living, and because he was more or less willing to stay in one spot for an extended period. But there was another problem. If he wanted a child, he would have to adopt one. He was sterile, or at least he seems to have convinced himself of that fact. He disclosed this information to more than one friend, but whether it was true or not is impossible to say.

Whatever the case may have been for Orwell, Eileen believed that she was not infertile. She made that clear to Lettice Cooper after Orwell had first raised the possibility that they might try to adopt a baby. 'It isn't anything to do with me,' she said to Lettice when she was asked why they had not had a child of their own.[10] One of Orwell's young friends in the Forties, the Canadian poet Paul Potts, remembered that when the question of adoption was raised he had said to Orwell: 'Why not get Eileen to bear a child by somebody else? At least it would be Eileen's child.'[11] But Orwell had been shocked by this suggestion and had refused to consider it. In the beginning the idea of starting a family was Orwell's alone. Eileen was reluctant to go along with it because she was worried that she would not be able to give enough of herself to a child, and that

397

her health – which was fragile – would not hold up under the strain of caring for an infant. But Orwell had his heart set on the idea, especially in the months following his mother's death, and it was difficult for anyone to talk him out of a plan once he had decided to pursue it.

The difficulty of adopting a baby was not great for them because they could rely on the good offices of Gwen O'Shaughnessy. In her medical practice she routinely dealt with young women who had become pregnant as a result of a brief wartime affair, and who were looking for a way to give up their unwanted babies to deserving couples. Gwen encountered so many of these cases that she adopted one of the babies herself – a girl – despite the fact that she was a working widow. Orwell wanted a boy, and in May one was born to a patient of Gwen's who wanted to give him up for adoption. Gwen made the necessary arrangements, and in June the Orwells became the parents of a fine, healthy baby whom they named Richard Horatio Blair.

Although Eileen was doubtful about the wisdom of their decision, she soon became convinced that it was the right thing to do. It seemed to bring new life to their marriage. Orwell wanted to take part in all aspects of the baby's care, and the attention which he paid to the child brought the couple closer together than they had been since their first year of marriage. David Astor, for one, had the impression that George and Eileen were 'renewing their marriage round their new child'.[12] Eileen became devoted to Richard. She had planned to continue working in the Ministry of Food, but she left the job after she realised how much she enjoyed motherhood. Both parents were excessively indulgent, and a little overawed by the new responsibility. Nothing concerning Richard was too trivial to contemplate. When Rayner Heppenstall wrote one day to offer his congratulations, he extended an offer to do the child's horoscope. Orwell did not dismiss the idea as superstitious nonsense, which is what one might have expected him to do. Instead he replied, 'I would like you very much to draw little Richard's horoscope. He was born on May 14th. I thought I had told you, however, that he is an adopted child. Does that make any difference to the horoscope?'[13]

Lettice remembered how nervous Eileen was before going to the legal hearing which, if all went well, would finalise the adoption. She saw her on the day of the court appearance and was struck by how impressively neat Eileen looked. She was wearing a round-brimmed yellow felt hat, and a well-cut tweed suit. 'I had never seen her in such respectable clothes before,' Lettice recalled. The two women met again on the next day, and Eileen was delighted to report that all had gone well. 'The baby even smiled at the judge,' she said with evident pride.[14]

II

Only two months before Richard was born, Orwell completed work on a short book which would change the shape of his career beyond all recognition. *Animal Farm* would make him a bestselling author not only in Britain but also in America and other parts of the world. It was the last thing he suspected would happen to him. He never dreamed that his book would have such a strong impact, and he was unprepared for the sudden fame which came to him as a result of its success. What he had set out to do was simply to make a forceful attack, in an imaginative way, on the sustaining myths of Soviet communism. Put that way, it hardly sounds like a potential bestseller, and there was no reason for him to assume that it would attract many more readers than his books usually attracted – a sale of five thousand copies would have delighted him.

The idea for the book had been in the back of his mind since his return from Spain. Having barely escaped from the long reach of Stalin's agents, he began to reflect on how a genuine revolutionary movement in Spain could have allowed itself to come so completely under the control of a dictator living thousands of miles away. Of course, the fact that Stalin was able to supply the Republic with arms was important, but the influence went beyond the ordinary level of bartering arms for political influence. Stalin enjoyed a god-like status, and the Soviets had expounded a mythology of the Russian Revolution which had given their activities a sacred aura. The Revolution was glorious, and everything done in its name was automatically part of that glory. Orwell saw how this powerful image had seduced not only the Spanish revolutionaries – who wanted to think of themselves as comrades following the pattern of Soviet success – but also well-meaning socialists everywhere. In his Preface to the Ukrainian edition of *Animal Farm* (which was distributed by a Ukrainian Displaced Persons Organisation in Munich), Orwell speaks of his desire to combat 'the negative influence of the Soviet myth upon the western Socialist movement'. What better way to fight that myth than to create a mythical story of animals whose successful revolt against tyranny degenerates into a greedy struggle for power?

As Orwell made clear in *The Lion and the Unicorn*, he wanted to see the triumph of an English socialism untainted by the Soviet model. Yet he continued to be amazed during the Second World War at how obstinate socialists were in supporting that obviously alien model – at least it was obvious to Orwell that such a system was alien, that it could not possibly be transplanted to England. And what was worse, any criticism of the Soviets was difficult to make because the myth of the revolution blinded its supporters to the ugly aftermath of that revolution. The evil of Stalin's purges could not be admitted because true believers could not afford to admit it – they would cease to be true believers if they did. The enemy, however, was not really Stalin and his agents, but the power of myths to suppress rational thought, and to substitute high-sounding slogans for real debate. It is too narrow to say that *Animal Farm* is anti-communist. 'The enemy is the gramophone mind,' Orwell wrote in a preface for the English edition, pointing out that any ideology – communist or otherwise – could encourage such a state of mind. It was important to take exception to it 'whether or not one agrees with the record that is being played at the moment'.[15]

But when Orwell wrote his book the gramophone minds were playing their tunes so loudly that his message almost failed to get a proper hearing. After he had finished it, he discovered that no one seemed interested in publishing it. This did not come as a complete surprise. By 1944 Stalin's reputation in Britain had made a dramatic recovery from its low standing after the 1939 pact with

Hitler. He was an ally of Britain again, and his soldiers were keeping large numbers of German forces occupied in the defence of the Eastern Front. This fact caused Gollancz, and many others like him, to go back to supporting the Soviet Union, and this support tended to be unquestioning. Orwell knew of Gollancz's position, and told Leonard Moore that there was no point in submitting the book to the firm. But under the provisions of the contract drawn up in 1937, he was obliged to give Gollancz the right of first refusal on his fictional works. Although Orwell tried to dissuade Gollancz from exercising this option, the latter insisted on seeing the book, and then promptly returned it with a curt note stating that his firm could not possibly publish such a work. 'We couldn't have published it then,' Gollancz later said. 'Those people [the Soviets] were fighting for us and had just saved our necks at Stalingrad.'[16]

This kind of reasoning held that any criticism of the Soviets was 'playing into the hands' of the Nazis. Orwell was astounded to see how often he was told that he could not address all the aspects of a question because doing so might 'play into the hands' of one enemy or another. He thought that this phrase was 'a sort of charm or incantation to silence uncomfortable truths'.[17] And all sorts of people used it – at the *Observer* Ivor Brown had cited it as his excuse for rejecting Orwell's review of *Retreat from the East*; and in the very month that Gollancz was using it to reject *Animal Farm*, Orwell was hearing the same excuse from another large newspaper which had recently invited him to become a contributor – the *Manchester Evening News*. He had reviewed a book for them called *Faith, Reason and Civilisation*, by Harold Laski, and had been moderately critical of its pro-Soviet bias, but that was going too far in the opinion of the editor, who rejected the review on the grounds that it put the Soviet Union in a bad light. In a letter to Dwight Macdonald, the editor of the New York magazine *Politics*, Orwell complained that he had tried to avoid being too critical of Laski's book: 'I have gone about as far as was consistent with ordinary honesty *not* to say what pernicious tripe the book is, and yet my remarks were too strong even for the *Manchester Evening News*. That will give you an idea of the kind of thing you can't print in England nowadays.'[18]

Many influential people in Britain did not want to risk giving serious offence to the Soviet dictator at this crucial period in the war, and Orwell found that his book was unacceptable at more than one publishing house. It was, in fact, rejected by four in England. Nicholson and Watson saw the book after Gollancz, but they, too, were quick to turn it down for political reasons, despite strong support for it from one of their young editors – André Deutsch, who had encouraged Orwell to send it to the firm in the first place. The typescript was next dispatched to Jonathan Cape, where it initially received a favourable reception. Acting on a recommendation from one of his editors – Veronica Wedgwood – Jonathan Cape met Orwell and told him of his willingness to publish *Animal Farm*. Complications soon arose, however, over Orwell's long-standing contract with Gollancz, and after several weeks of negotiation, Cape finally decided not to take a risk on Orwell as long as his future works were tied up elsewhere. Gollancz insisted that he still had an option on Orwell's next two novels – exercising his option on *Animal Farm* did not count, he argued, because it was not a 'full-length' work. This splitting of hairs served little purpose except to undermine Orwell's position with other publishers, forcing him to honour debatable contractual obligations in order to complicate his bargaining position. It was a senseless and petty game.

For his part, Cape seems to have been looking for excuses to reject the book. His talks with Gollancz may have convinced him that *Animal Farm* would involve him in too much controversy. The prospect worried him enough to cause him to seek the advice of an acquaintance at the Ministry of Information, who warned him not to take the book. This was purely an unofficial response to a question which Cape had raised about the book, and there was never any actual threat of censorship from the government, but when Orwell was told about Cape's conversation with the official, he recognised immediately that the book could be stopped merely by a campaign of whispers against it. The right hints in the right places could do the trick without anyone ever having to make an official case against it. He made his most scathing comment on this subtle form of censorship when he wrote in *Tribune*, 'Circus dogs jump when the trainer cracks his whip, but the really well-trained dog is the one that turns his somersault when there is no whip.'[19]

After Cape turned it down, the typescript of *Animal Farm* was nearly destroyed by Hitler's forces. Every day in June 1944 the enemy sent about fifty V-1 flying bombs – the so-called 'doodle bugs' – to the general vicinity of London where they landed randomly, causing widespread damage. Near the end of the month one landed in Mortimer Crescent and the force of the explosion caused the ceilings to collapse in Orwell's flat. No one was hurt, but the flat was ruined beyond repair. Orwell located the typescript of his book in the rubble, finding it 'crumpled' but still readable. He and Eileen were able to find temporary lodgings elsewhere in London for the next couple of months, and then they moved to a top-floor flat in Islington, at 27b Canonbury Square.

Apologising for the 'blitzed' condition of his typescript, Orwell sent it to a third publisher – T. S. Eliot at Faber and Faber. Unfortunately, he had no better luck with Eliot this time than he had experienced thirteen years earlier, when he had sent him a version of *Down and Out in Paris and London*. Eliot took only a couple of weeks to give Orwell the firm's decision. His letter of rejection was as stiff and cold as the one he had written for *Down and Out*. It also completely missed the point of the book: 'Your pigs are far more intelligent than the other animals, and therefore the best qualified to run the farm . . . What was needed (someone might argue) was not more communism but more public-spirited pigs.'[20]

In late July Orwell tried one more publisher. He sent *Animal Farm* to Fredric Warburg, who wasted little time before deciding to accept it. The odd thing is that Orwell and Moore waited so long to take it to him. Even though Warburg had published *Homage to Catalonia* and *The Lion and the Unicorn*, Orwell seems to have convinced himself that the publisher would not want to risk scarce paper supplies on *Animal Farm*, and therefore he held off taking the book to him until it was clear that no one else was likely to accept it. In fact, at one stage Orwell seriously thought about having the book privately printed, and he discussed with David Astor the possibility of borrowing £200 to pay the costs. Astor agreed to the request, though it was such a tentative notion that Orwell did not bother to explain what the book was about or why established publishers were uninterested in it – and Astor did not ask.

Paper rationing was a problem for Warburg – more so for a small firm such as his than for the bigger houses which had entered the war era with significant stocks of paper on hand. So he did make it clear to Orwell that the book would have to wait for publication until his supplies of paper were adequate. On 29 August he met with Orwell and made a verbal commitment to publish the book in the coming year, and to pay an advance of £100 for it. Although his concerns about paper were real, he was able to delay publication for such a long period that it did not appear until after Hitler had been defeated, and Stalin's usefulness as Britain's ally was at an end. That delay, whether deliberate or not, took some of the sting out of the book's effect on its first readers. If it had appeared in the summer of 1944, there might have been a much greater outcry over its publication, which would have pleased Orwell.

As it happened, he had little reason for complaint. Published in Britain on 17 August 1945, the book sold more than 25,000 hardcover copies in the first five years – about ten times the normal sale for one of his books. The greatest surprise came, however, when the American edition appeared in 1946. Its sales reached 590,000 in four years. In the *New Yorker* Edmund Wilson was uncommonly lavish in his praise, calling *Animal Farm* 'absolutely first-rate' and drawing favourable comparisons with Voltaire and Swift. He declared that it was time to begin thinking of Orwell as a major author, and that readers should take another look at his earlier, neglected books. It was the kind of review that every writer dreams of, but it was only the prelude to an even greater success, when *Nineteen Eighty-Four* appeared, just three years later.

As a clever satire on Stalin's betrayal of the Russian revolution, *Animal Farm* caught the popular imagination just when the Cold War was beginning to make itself felt. For many years 'anti-Communists' enjoyed using it as a propaganda weapon in that war, but this was a gross misrepresentation of the book and a violation of the spirit in which Orwell wrote it. He was not a fanatical opponent of the Soviet Union. Indeed, given the fact that

Stalin's agents had almost managed to imprison him in Spain, his view of the Soviet system was most enlightened. In September 1944 he explained his position to Dwight Macdonald:

> I think that if the USSR were conquered by some foreign country the working class everywhere would lose heart, for the time being at least, and the ordinary stupid capitalists who have never lost their suspicion of Russia would be encouraged ... I wouldn't want to see the USSR destroyed and think it ought to be defended if necessary. But I want people to become disillusioned about it and to realise that they must build their own Socialist movement without Russian interference, and I want the existence of democratic Socialism in the West to exert a regenerative influence upon Russia.[21]

In *Animal Farm* the fat capitalist Mr Pilkington has no more feeling for the 'lower classes' he exploits than the pigs have for the 'lower animals'. As a model arrangement for exploitation, *Animal Farm* excites Pilkington's interest and prompts him to praise the pigs for their stern measures, and to declare a common bond: 'Between pigs and human beings there was not and there need not be any clash of interests whatever.' In any case, *Animal Farm* is much more than a gloss on the failings of the Russian Revolution. It should also be seen in an earlier context. As Orwell noted, the 'central idea' for the book came to him on his return from Spain, when his anger towards Stalin was balanced by his admiration for the early days of the workers' revolution in Barcelona. Simply because Stalin betrayed those Spanish workers does not mean that their revolution itself was wrong. Orwell knew what the real evil was. Five months after he finished writing *Animal Farm*, he gave readers of the *Observer* a succinct explanation of the 'object-lesson' offered by the Spanish Civil War: 'The Spanish war [should] be kept always in mind as an object-lesson in the folly and meanness of Power Politics.'[22]

Animal Farm affirms the values of Orwell's ideal version of socialism, making it clear that before the barnyard revolt was subjected to the treachery of the pigs 'the animals were happy as they had never conceived it possible to be'. But he also makes it clear that there is no future for socialist revolutions if they look to the Soviet model for inspiration or spawn Soviet-style leaders. The book provides a powerful illustration of the consequences which must follow if such leaders are accepted. The animals allow themselves to become fairly easy prey for Napoleon, who relentlessly accumulates power by playing on the weaknesses of his comrades. However much Orwell may have wanted it to be otherwise, he was realistic enough to see that revolutions create reactionary elements within themselves, and that sooner or later the bright promise of early successes is obscured by attacks from those elements. The promise was still worth believing in, and fighting for, but there was nothing to be gained from denying the hard realities. Writing in the *Observer* in September 1944, he remarked, 'A moment always comes when the party which has seized power crushes its own Left Wing and then proceeds to disappoint the hopes with which the revolution started out.'[23]

A few months later he took another look at *The Lion and the Unicorn*, and went out of his way to admit that his hopes for major social changes in 1940 had been unrealistic. He admits all this in a London Letter to *Partisan Review*, dated December 1944: 'I wanted to think that we would not be defeated, and I wanted to think that the class distinctions and imperialist exploitation of which I am ashamed would not return. I over-emphasised the anti-Fascist character of the war, exaggerated the social changes that were actually occuring, and underrated the enormous strength of the forces of reaction.' He is so hard on himself in this statement that it almost sounds like a forced confession at a show trial. The Grand Inquisitor in this case, however, was his own conscience, which would not allow him to sweep aside unpleasant facts.

Orwell's realism is too easily mistaken for despair. One of his remarkable qualities was his ability to face grim possibilities without losing all hope. He could admit that the odds were against him and still insist that victory was possible. This can be seen in an important letter about *Animal Farm* which he sent to Dwight Macdonald in America. In it he argues against a pessimistic view of the book. It is worth quoting at length because he is so specific about his intentions:

Re. your query about 'Animal Farm'. Of course I intended it
primarily as a satire on the Russian revolution. But I did mean it
to have a wider application in so much that I meant that *that kind*
of revolution (violent conspiratorial revolution, led by
unconsciously power-hungry people) can only lead to a change of
masters. I meant the moral to be that revolutions only effect a
radical improvement when the masses are alert and know how to
chuck out their leaders as soon as the latter have done their job.
The turning-point of the story was supposed to be when the pigs
kept the milk and apples for themselves. (Kronstadt). If the other
animals had had the sense to put their foot down then, it would
have been all right. If people think I am defending the status quo,
that is, I think, because they have grown pessimistic and assume
that there is no alternative except dictatorship or laissez-faire
capitalism . . . What I was trying to say was, 'You can't have a
revolution unless you make it for yourself; there is no such thing
as a benevolent dictatorship.'[24]

What is surprising in *Animal Farm* is that its great seriousness
about the nature of political change is balanced by a great comic
sense – a willingness to laugh at human failings in a way which is
untinged with bitterness or despair. His other major books have so
little humour in them that it is amazing to find so much in the pages
of this one small book. At times, in the early chapters, the light
touch of his satire makes one almost forget that it has a political
point. It can be enjoyed solely for its art. The fact that the ridicule is
gentle is important because it does not undercut sympathy for the
animals as their initial victories slowly turn into defeat, and their
idealism becomes soured.

Some of the best thrusts of satire are directed against the earnest
activities of Snowball, the pig counterpart of Trotsky. As his name
suggests, it is not enough for Snowball to let the revolution develop
according to its own momentum. He must speed it along, and
increase its efficiency, by organising Animal Committees, such as
the Clean Tails League for the cows, and the Wild Comrades' Re-
education Committee, the object of which is to tame rats and
rabbits. Snowball's absurd officiousness is brilliantly captured
when he mounts the ladder 'with some difficulty (for it is not easy

for a pig to balance himself on a ladder)' and writes the seven commandments of the revolution on the barn, using a brush between the two knuckles of his trotter. Snowball's bravery in the great Battle of the Cowshed is recognised by the award of 'Animal Hero, First Class'. But this mockery of Soviet awards is made even funnier by the explanation that the honour of 'Animal Hero, Second Class' was also created after the battle, and 'was conferred posthumously on the dead sheep'.

Some of Eileen's friends were quite convinced that this sudden outpouring of humour in Orwell's work was the result of her influence. She did follow its progress as Orwell worked on it in the winter of 1943–1944, sitting up in bed at night to read what he had produced during each day. Orwell later acknowledged that she had helped in the planning of the book, and her friends recalled that she used to refer to it approvingly even while it was being written, making it clear that her hopes for its success were high. It is probably the case that some of the wry bits of humour in the book were either her inventions or were inspired by her comments. Indeed, at least a few passages in the book have a rhythm and tone which call to mind certain passages in her letters. But her greatest contribution to the book may simply have been her encouragement. Because it was such a daring thing to write the book at that time in the war, Orwell must have been relieved to have Eileen's support and approval for his efforts, especially during the long period after its completion when publishers were turning it down.

At the end of 1944, with *Animal Farm* in Warburg's hands awaiting publication, Orwell could sit back and take some time to contemplate the next step in his career. He had more than enough work to occupy him in the short-term while he thought about the shape of his future. The responsibility of serving as literary editor of *Tribune* would have provided sufficient work for most people, but he was also writing his 'As I Please' columns, his London Letters, reviews for the *Observer* and the *Manchester Evening News*, and he was busy putting together another book of his essays. On top of all this, he had a young baby at home to occupy his attention.

But another one of his obsessions intervened to take him away from all this. As the war began to draw to a close, he wanted desperately to see some of the remaining military operations, and to examine with his own eyes the ruins of Hitler's empire. When the chance came to serve as a war correspondent for the *Observer* in France, he managed to get the job in spite of his poor health, and was determined to leave for the front lines as soon as possible. In February 1945 he gave up his job at *Tribune*, put on a war correspondent's uniform, and set off to report on the last gasps of Nazism. He promised to come back in two months' time, and Eileen and Richard waited for his return at a house near Newcastle belonging to Gwen O'Shaughnessy. He was putting his life in danger once again, not least because his health was so questionable that any illness might cause dire consequences without proper medical care. Of course, this was in addition to the ordinary risks of reporting the movements of the war. All that Eileen could do was hope that his luck held, and that he returned at the time he promised. She seemed to have faith that he would make it back on time. While he was away, she received a letter from a woman at the BBC asking Orwell to do some freelance broadcasting work, and in her reply, Eileen promised that he would get in touch as soon as possible. 'He is a curiously reliable man,' she wrote.[25]

CHAPTER TWENTY

Lost Chances

I

The Hotel Scribe, in Paris, was a favourite with journalists in the final months of the war, providing a comfortable base for correspondents from all over the world as they reported on the movements of the Allied forces in the West. Orwell stayed there, off and on, for a month, and sent an article each week to the *Observer*, as well as a few pieces to the *Manchester Evening News*. It was the first time he had been in Paris since 1937, when he had passed through on his way home from Spain. The war had not caused much physical damage in the city, but basic goods and services were limited, and the cold, wet streets in the early months of 1945 looked dismal after four years of German occupation. (One attraction of the Hotel Scribe was the fact that its central heating was in full operation, whereas many parts of the city had neither heat nor electricity.) Orwell lamented that Paris was 'horribly depressing compared with what it used to be'.[1]

One bright moment came on the day when he made the acquaintance of another famous author staying at the hotel. Having seen the name of Ernest Hemingway on the register, he found the room number, went upstairs and knocked. He discovered Hemingway busily packing his bags, and he shyly introduced himself as 'Eric Blair'. This brought the rude reply, 'Well, what the fucking hell do you want?'

'I'm George Orwell.'

'Why the fucking hell didn't you say so?' Hemingway responded and reached into one of his bags for a bottle. 'Have a drink. Have a double. Straight or with water, there's no soda.'[2]

They had a drink together and talked briefly, but Hemingway had to leave in a few minutes, and there was no chance for them to have a serious discussion. As short as this encounter was, Hemingway did not forget it, and spoke with admiration of Orwell when he recalled their meeting three years later in a letter to Cyril Connolly.[3] For his part, Orwell seems to have been amused by Hemingway's rough manner, as though it pleased him to see the American behaving so predictably.

He met one other famous visitor to the city in March, the philosopher A. J. Ayer, with whom he established a lasting friendship. They shared a few meals together during that month, talking mostly about politics and the London intellectual scene. Orwell showed nothing more than a polite interest in Ayer's work. He had too much faith in common sense to make any philosophical system the object of serious study. This did not disappoint Ayer, who found that it was quite enough to enjoy Orwell's company without bringing logical positivism into it. 'He was no enemy of pleasure. He appreciated good food and drink, enjoyed gossip, and when not oppressed by ill-health was very good company.'[4]

Eileen wrote to her husband regularly and gave him the latest news on Richard's development, which she knew he was anxious to have. The couple's pride in their new son is clearly evident from a letter which she wrote to Leonard Moore shortly after Orwell went to Paris. Moore was eager to know how Orwell was getting along, and Eileen wrote to tell him that she had received one letter from her husband and was expecting another soon, though she warned him not to expect much information, explaining that the letter would probably be dominated by talk of Richard – 'in whom Eric is passionately interested'. Eileen's own affection is apparent in the remainder of the letter: 'The baby is nine months old and according to his new father very highly gifted – "a very thoughtful little boy" as well as very beautiful. He really is a very nice baby. You must see him sometime. His name is Richard Horatio.'[5]

A few days after writing this letter Eileen went to see a doctor in Newcastle and came away from the visit with bad news. She was told that several tumours had been found in her uterus, and that a hysterectomy would have to be performed before the end of the month. She was assured that the operation would be relatively simple. For some months her health had been weak. She had suffered from anaemia and dizziness, but had tried to ignore these problems. She had done her best not to alarm Orwell, keeping her suspicions about her condition to herself so that he would not delay his trip to France. But her doctor – Harvey Evers – made it clear that she could not afford to postpone her operation beyond a few weeks, and she reluctantly accepted his advice.

She did not write to Orwell immediately to explain the situation, but instead made a brief trip to London to confer with Gwen O'Shaughnessy. After reviewing the diagnosis, Gwen gave her approval and telephoned Dr Evers to set an exact date for the operation. Arrangements were also made for Richard's care during the period of several weeks when Eileen would be unable to look after him. In the meantime Eileen attended to some last-minute business, which included checking on their flat in Canonbury Square to make sure that it was still in good condition. To her surprise, she discovered that none of Orwell's mail had been forwarded to him. It was all lying in a great pile on the floor. Eileen tried to answer some of the more important letters, and in one to Cyril Connolly she explained why a reply had been delayed. 'George arranged with a man in London to forward his mail . . . But he picked a good businessman who thought he should not forward anything until he had the address in writing from George. George of course has never written to him at all, & I thought myself pretty admirable because I gave him [the businessman] the address by telephone as soon as I had it.'[6]

The identity of this mysterious businessman would rate no more than a brief mention if it were not for the fact that he was a familiar figure from Orwell's past who had reappeared after a long absence. Eileen was making an excuse for his negligence by referring to him as a 'good businessman', because she did not want to speak ill of her old friend Georges Kopp, who was living in London after making a daring escape from behind enemy lines. Orwell had asked him to look after the flat and to forward mail, but despite the fact that Eileen had given him an address, he had not bothered to send anything along.

Over the past few years Eileen had often feared that Kopp had disappeared for ever, but periodically letters would arrive from him describing his latest adventures, reassuring her that he was still very much alive. In 1943 he wrote to her from France where he had been working as a British agent. That letter reached her only because Kopp had taken the risk of having it smuggled out of enemy territory by a secret courier. At the end of 1943, when his identity as a spy was in danger of being revealed, an RAF plane flew him out of France under the cover of darkness and brought him to safety in England, where he was allowed to settle permanently. He sought help from the Orwells immediately, and Eileen arranged for him to stay with Gwen, as he had done five years earlier when he left the Spanish prison where he had been locked up for many months. In 1944 his charms won the heart of Gwen's sister, Doreen, who quickly married him, and who had three children by him in the next five years.

When Eileen was ready to leave London after consulting with Gwen, it was Kopp who took her to King's Cross Station late one evening and saw her off. The only clue to her feelings for him at this point is a comment which she made a few days later about his young son, who was several months younger than Richard. She wrote to Lettice Cooper that she had 'expected to be jealous' when Doreen had shown her the child, and that the baby was indeed unusually handsome – 'with the hair & hands of a talented musician'. As much as she loved Richard, she admitted that Kopp's baby was the more attractive of the two. There is the implication in her letter that she was contemplating what life might have been like for her if she had been in Doreen's place. Although she was too realistic to make a fuss over lost opportunities, she could not help feeling some ambivalence about her choices, as she revealed when she wrote of Kopp's child, 'I didn't prefer him to Richard, preferable though he is.'[7]

It is doubtful that she said much to Kopp about her impending operation, but she could not keep the news from her husband any longer. On 21 and 22 March she wrote a letter to Orwell which took up eight typed pages. She decided to tell him what she knew. She explained that she had 'several rapidly growing tumours' which would have to be removed, and that she had chosen to have the operation performed in Newcastle rather than in London because it was less expensive. The charge was fifty pounds – no minor sum in those days – and she was worried that he would object to the cost. 'The absurd thing is that we are too well off for really cheap rates – you'd have to make less than £500 a year. It comes as a shock to me in a way because while you were being ill I got used to paying doctors nothing . . . What worries me is that I really don't think I'm worth the money. On the other hand of course this thing will take a longish time to kill me if left alone and it will be costing some money the whole time.'[8]

If Orwell had been in Eileen's position, he would have been equally apologetic about the expense, and would have taken the same tough attitude towards the possibility of death, but neither one of them would have hesitated to spend their last penny on a necessary operation for the other. (*Animal Farm* had not yet been published, and there is no way that they could have anticipated the large financial gain which it would bring.) Eileen's letter did not reach Orwell before the operation took place, but the *Observer* arranged for a cable to be sent to him in which Eileen asked for his consent. She gave him only a day's notice, but he promptly sent back a cable stating his agreement. She had decided that it was best not to have him rush back for the event, and had told him as much. In her long letter she explained her reasoning, 'By the time you get home I'll be convalescent at last and you won't have the hospital nightmare you would so much dislike.' She put the matter more directly to Lettice, 'It's a mercy George is away . . . George visiting the sick is a sight infinitely sadder than any disease-ridden wretch in the world.'[9]

Although she was worried about money, Eileen kept her sense of humour about the ordeal facing her. When she made a typing error in a letter to Lettice, she quickly turned it into a joke: 'As Richard's adoption was through I thought I might now deal with the grwoth (no one could object to a grwoth) I knew I had.' To Cyril Connolly, she recalled her amused reaction when she opened an envelope addressed to her husband and discovered 'an extract from some kind of Who's Who in which George is described as having married me before I was born & some years before he went to Eton'. She also retained her inventive way of expressing difficult ideas. She wanted her husband to give up journalism and concentrate on writing another book, but since she knew that it would not be easy to get him to take this advice, she used the example of someone else's conduct to show him the wisdom of it:

> I should like to see you stop living a literary life and start writing again and it would be much better for Richard too, so you need have no conflicts about it. Richard sends you this message. He has no conflicts. If he gets a black eye he cries while it hurts but with the tears wet on his cheeks he laughs heartily at a new blue cat who says miaow to him and embraces it with loving words. Faced with any new situation he is sure that it will be an exciting and desirable situation for him, and he knows so well that everyone in the world is his good friend that even if someone hurts him he understands that it was by accident and loses none of his confidence.[10]

After nearly nine years of marriage, Eileen – the woman who had once aspired to be an educational psychologist – had come to appreciate only too well the importance of 'conflicts' in her husband's character, and she was trying to use his love for Richard to make him see how easily he could change his ways if he chose to do so. She must also have realised, however, that no matter how much she urged him to change, he would never be able to resist accepting more challenges, that his 'conflicts' were so much a part of him that they would go on driving his behaviour as long as his health permitted.

Even though he did not learn of Eileen's operation until the last minute, he knew enough about her health to understand that she might suffer some sort of trouble while he was away, and yet he did not take steps to keep in closer contact with her, relying only on the slow postal service to bring him news of her and Richard, and at best such news was ten days old when it reached him. He was too caught up in his fascination with the last days of the Third Reich to give proper attention to the situation at home, and he was accustomed to thinking that Eileen could manage without him. He had his work to do, she had hers, and that was that. Neither would accomplish anything if they spent too much time worrying about the other. His own health was so poor that he was, in fact, forced to seek medical care in Cologne shortly after he filed his first report from the city in late March. When Eileen's cable was sent to him from her hospital in Newcastle, he had just recently been released from a hospital in Cologne, where he had been treated for some unspecified chest complaint.

On 29 March 1945 Eileen began a letter to Orwell. She was in her hospital bed waiting to be taken away to the operating theatre, and was in a hopeful mood: 'Dearest I'm just going to have the operation, already enema'd, injected (with morphia in the *right* arm, which is a nuisance), cleaned and packed up like precious image in cotton wool and bandages. When it's over I'll add a note to this and it can get off quickly.' The drug began to take effect after she had completed only a few more sentences, and the last lines are written in a faint, progressively unsteady hand until they come to an abrupt end: 'This is a nice room – ground floor so one can see the garden. Not much in it except daffodils and I think arabis but a nice little lawn. My bed isn't next the window but it faces the right way. I also see the fire the clock . . .'[11] A short time later the operation began. But within minutes something went wrong. Eileen's body reacted adversely to the anaesthetic, and she suffered a heart attack. She was too weak to withstand the shock and all attempts to revive her failed. She died on the operating table. She was only thirty-nine.

II

The doctors who operated on her were not held responsible for the circumstances which caused her heart attack. The statement on her death certificate was clearly meant to absolve them of any blame: 'Cardiac failure whilst under anaesthetic of ether and chloroform skilfully and properly administered for operation for removal of uterus.' Gwen O'Shaughnessy was in Greenwich at the time of the operation, but she was the first to be notified of the death, and she in turn sent a cable to Orwell. When the message reached him, he was stunned. As he explained later, 'No one had anticipated anything going wrong, and I did not even hear she was to have the operation then till the last moment ... I telegraphed my consent to the operation, only to get another telegram next day telling me she was dead. It was a horrible shock.'[12] Although he was still recovering from his illness, he decided to return to England right away, and was able to find a military aircraft which would fly him back.

When he reached London, he paused briefly to convey the news of Eileen's death to the writer Inez Holden, who had been a good friend of the Orwells since the beginning of the war. Fortunately, Inez kept a detailed diary – she and Orwell had once planned to publish a joint 'War Diary' – and on 30 March, which was Good Friday, she recorded her impressions of her friend's visit. When he appeared at her door, she barely recognised him. He looked tired and sickly, and was dressed in unfamiliar clothing. 'He wore a long Guardsman-like coat. He was in the uniform of a war correspondent. A Captain. He had taken eight M and B tablets and left the hospital and flown over.' He talked openly about Eileen's death and did not try to hide his grief. 'He thought it was especially sad for Eileen because things were getting better, the war ending, Richard adopted and that she believed that her health would be all right after this operation. George was terribly sad.' Because Orwell was so good at hiding his feelings, other friends who saw him or heard from him in the next few weeks were struck by his calm attitude towards Eileen's death, and mistakenly interpreted this as evidence of a lack of feeling. When he saw Inez, he had not yet had time to regain his usual composure, and her diary captures something of the desolate mood of the moment: 'I went with George to the station. First having a drink with him. There was all this sadness in our minds and at the gloomy station a man was playing a hurdy gurdy, dim crowds waited by the barrier and in the bar a man shouted "Time" almost as soon as we had begun our drinks.'[13]

When he arrived in Newcastle, he was met by Gwen, and together they made the arrangements for Eileen's funeral. After a simple ceremony she was buried in St Andrew's and Jesmond Cemetery, Newcastle. When he went through her effects, Orwell found the unfinished letter which she had been writing just before her death, and he took some comfort from the fact that it showed no evidence of apprehensiveness on her part. 'The only consolation,' he wrote to Lydia Jackson on 1 April, 'is that I don't think she suffered, because she went to the operation, apparently, not expecting anything to go wrong, and never recovered consciousness.' He confided that her death was especially 'cruel . . . because she had become so devoted to Richard'. He had no intention of giving Richard up, but it was obviously going to be a great burden for him to take care of an infant son and earn his living as a writer. And, of course, he could not replace the love that Eileen had been able to give the child. 'It is a shame Eileen should have died just when he is becoming so charming,' he reflected; 'however, she did enjoy very much being with him during her last months of life.'[14]

Because Doreen Kopp was staying at home with a young son, it occurred to Orwell that she might also be willing to take care of Richard until he could make arrangements to employ a full-time nurse. She agreed. He may have had his suspicions about Georges Kopp's interest in Eileen, but there is no evidence that he ever said anything about it. He did later confess that his marriage had been a troubled one at times, though he took most of the blame on himself, and admitted that he had occasionally been unfaithful to Eileen – though he did not say with whom. He made these candid admissions in a letter to a young woman named Anne Popham, to whom he rashly proposed only a year after Eileen's death. She refused him – they barely knew each other – and he apologised for having been so forward with her, implying that he had been driven to it by loneliness ('I wonder if I committed a sort of crime in approaching you. In a way it's scandalous that a person like me

should make advances to a person like you.') To explain his motives
in more detail, he told her about his marriage:

> I have very little physical jealousy. I don't much care who sleeps
> with whom, it seems to me what matters is being faithful in an
> emotional and intellectual sense. I was sometimes unfaithful to
> Eileen, and I also treated her very badly, and I think she treated
> me badly too at times, but it was a real marriage in the sense that
> we had been through awful struggles together, and she
> understood all about my work, etc.[15]

With whom did Orwell have his affairs? He did not have much
faith in his attractiveness to women, and lacked the smooth manner
which might have given him the confidence to enter into affairs with
ease. It should also be kept in mind that his bad health and
staggering workload did not leave him a great deal of time or energy
for romance – with Eileen or anyone else. As he made clear in his
letter to Anne Popham, he was loyal to Eileen in an emotional and
intellectual sense, but he probably had at least a few casual affairs,
one of which reportedly involved a young woman at the BBC, and
another involved his secretary at *Tribune*, Sally McEwan. Paul
Potts, and others, have mentioned the relationship with the woman
at the BBC, but Potts was quite convinced that there was never any
danger of Orwell abandoning his wife. 'George would never have
left Eileen. They were man and wife.'[16] The relationship with Sally
McEwan may have been more serious. Orwell later told Celia
Paget, Arthur Koestler's sister-in-law, that both he and Eileen had
been unfaithful, but that his affair with Sally had caused Eileen
much distress, and that she had made a 'fiendish row' over it.[17] He
had agreed to break off the affair, and evidently the last months of
the marriage had been relatively good ones, especially since
Richard's presence had drawn them closer together.

So many of the facts are shadowy, but there is not much to be
gained by apportioning blame for the problems in the marriage. In
the end it is enough to say, as Orwell did, that it was 'a real
marriage', and that after all they had been through together, a real
bond of love had developed between them. There can also be no

doubt that her death was a great blow to him, but he accepted it – as
he would have expected her to accept his death if she had survived
him – and he went on with his life, determined to give Richard a
good home, and to continue building the career to which Eileen had
contributed so much support. Almost a year after his wife's death,
he wrote to Dorothy Plowman, 'It was a terrible shame that Eileen
didn't live to see the publication of *Animal Farm*, which she was
particularly fond of and even helped in the planning of. I suppose
you know I was in France when she died. It was a terribly cruel and
stupid thing to happen.' To another friend, Orwell lamented, 'If
only one hadn't left so much unsaid.'[18]

He was so upset in the days following her death that he could not
bear to go about his ordinary business at their flat in London. He
wanted to escape from everything for a few weeks, and he thought
that the best thing for him to do was to return to the Continent. On
4 April he explained his plans in a letter to Dwight Macdonald.
Eileen's death, he wrote, 'has upset me so that I cannot settle to
anything for the time being . . . I want to go back and do some more
reporting, and perhaps after a few weeks of bumping about in jeeps
etc. I shall feel better.'[19] He began this odd form of therapy a few
days later, and did not return to London until the end of May.

The stark images of destruction which he witnessed in Germany
in April and May were certainly powerful enough to take his mind
off his own troubles. He saw the ruins of once-beautiful German
cities, the tired, hungry refugees fleeing from the destruction, and
the dead soldiers of the defeated German Army lying along
roadsides or in city streets. In one town his attention was caught by
the sight of an enemy soldier's body stretched out at the foot of a
bridge. The man had died defending his retreating comrades, and
after the fighting was over some citizen of the town had placed on
his breast 'a bunch of the lilac which was blossoming everywhere'.[20]
In a camp for German soldiers he watched a young Jewish man
from Vienna, who was temporarily serving in the American Army,
give a solid, swift kick to a captured SS officer. He could not blame
the man for taking out his frustrations on the prisoner – 'Heaven
knows what scores this particular man may have had to wipe out;

very likely his whole family had been murdered' – but he was fascinated by the shabby, wretched appearance of the officer and found that he had little desire to see such men pay for their crimes. He understood the enormity of their crimes, but a harsh campaign of revenge did not appeal to him. Once these 'monsters' were defeated, they seemed less monstrous to him, and he could not help feeling sorry for their human condition. 'So the Nazi torturer of one's imagination, the monstrous figure against whom one had struggled for so many years dwindled to this pitiful wretch, whose obvious need was not for punishment, but for some kind of psychological treatment.'[21]

No one was more opposed to fascism than Orwell, but he argued that it was important not to engage in wholesale retribution against Germans because it could not change what had already happened in the war, and it would be demeaning to the victors. 'Who would not have jumped for joy, in 1940, at the thought of seeing SS officers kicked and humiliated? But when the thing becomes possible, it is merely pathetic and disgusting.'[22] As an abstract idea, revenge had a certain appeal, but it was always important to Orwell to look beyond abstract notions and find the concrete reality. 'There is often the need of some concrete incident before one can discover the real state of one's feelings,' he wrote in his essay on the SS prisoner, which was appropriately titled 'Revenge is Sour'.

After the German surrender was signed in early May, he observed the contest of power and influence which broke out between the Russians and the Western allies, and he astutely observed that this might soon lead to a situation in which the political divisions would become fixed for the long term. He hoped that this could be avoided, and that both sides could establish joint rule over the country, instead of dividing it into 'watertight zones'. He knew that the Soviets were trying to 'elbow' their way into a stronger position, but he thought that quick action from Britain and America could thwart the Soviet plans. 'We are unlikely to come to a good understanding with the Russians unless we take up their challenge boldly. The present piecemeal occupation of Germany and Austria is exhausting and unsatisfactory to them as much as to us, but they may hope to elbow us out of these countries altogether if they oppose clear policies to feeble or divided ones.'[23]

Although Hitler's defeat had brought dramatic changes to the Continent, Orwell had the impression that after almost six years of war the basic conditions in British life had changed very little. There had been no social or political revolutions. In June he observed, 'If I had to say what had most struck me about the behaviour of the British people during the war, I should point to the *lack* of reaction of any kind. In the face of terrifying dangers and golden political opportunities, people just keep on keeping on, in a sort of twilight sleep in which they are conscious of nothing except the daily round of work, family life, darts at the pub, exercising the dog, mowing the lawn, bringing home the supper beer, etc. etc.' In *Homage to Catalonia* and *Coming Up for Air*, he had imagined that Hitler's bombs might finally disrupt England's deep sleep, causing it to change radically or die. But neither had happened, and his reaction was a mixture of disappointment, disbelief, and grudging respect: 'Never would I have prophesied that we could go through nearly six years of war without arriving at either Socialism or Fascism, and with our civil liberties almost intact. I don't know whether this semi-anaesthesia in which the British people contrive to live is a sign of decadence, as many observers believe, or whether on the other hand it is a kind of instinctive wisdom.'[24]

III

In June Orwell began looking in earnest for a nurse-housekeeper who could help him care for Richard, and who could live with them at the flat in Canonbury Square. He found such a person in July. Susan Watson was twenty-eight and had spent the war years working at a day nursery in Hampstead. At nineteen she had married a Cambridge don – a mathematician at King's College – but the marriage had not worked out, and they had lived apart since the early days of the war. They had one child – a daughter – whose fees at boarding school were paid by her father, but otherwise Susan received very little financial support from her husband and needed to work in order to make ends meet. Mutual friends recommended her to Orwell, and he offered her a job at five pounds a week, with room and board as an extra. She considered that arrangement a generous one for the times, and was pleased to have a nice place where her daughter could come to stay during school holidays.

Susan was intrigued by the fact that Orwell asked her almost nothing about her background or experience. His one test for her employment seems to have been asking her to help him give Richard a bath. She proved satisfactory in this task and gave the correct answer when he suddenly asked, 'You will let him play with his thingummy, won't you?' She calmly replied, 'Yes, of course.'[25] She was also surprised that he made no comment about the fact that she walked with difficulty. One of her legs had been impaired by cerebral palsy. But throughout the time that she worked for him, he never made any remark about this disability except to say that he would be happy to carry Richard up and down the stairs leading to the flat if she wanted him to.

She found him to be an easy person to work for, but she could not help being amazed at how hard he worked. He began at eight or nine in the morning, and usually did not stop until lunch, when he would go out to a nearby pub or meet friends for a meal elsewhere. He took another break for high tea, which Susan prepared for him, and which included such things as kippers, Gentleman's Relish on toast, homemade scones with jam, and tea so strong that – when rationing allowed – ten or eleven teaspoons were allowed to stew in the pot before being served with fresh milk, but no sugar. After taking part in this ritual, he would go back to work, and sometimes continue until early in the morning. Susan became so used to sleeping at night with the sound of the typewriter in the background that she would wake up when it stopped.

She learned that he was a man with many peculiar interests and habits. He sometimes woke up in the mornings with a shout, suffering from nightmares, and later explained to Susan that in Burma his manservant had helped him awaken peacefully by gently tickling his toes. She taught Richard to do this and was delighted to find that it worked. In the mornings, while she made breakfast, she would hear him giggling after Richard had gone in to wake him. He liked Victorian clutter and bought an old 'scrap screen' to keep out draughts in the sitting-room. He decorated it with cards featuring paintings of, among other things, pretty girls carrying baskets of fruit. He seemed to be fond of a cosy domestic atmosphere, yet he once remarked to Susan that if it were not for Richard he would like to live in a lighthouse.

It was not difficult to see that he enjoyed creating for himself the impression that he could live a simple, self-reliant existence if he wanted to. One evening when she went into his room to tell him that his tea was ready, she found him making gunpowder, presumably practising his skills in preparation for the day when bullets would be scarce or illegal. In an effort to keep his life simple he once asked her to dye all his shirts navy blue. And she discovered one night when he was ill that he had no use for proper pyjamas but wore woollen combinations in bed. Proper, shop-bought toys for Richard were also unnecessary. When the boy took an interest in one of his carpentry tools – a small leather hammer – he let him take it to bed, and the child slept with it as though it were a cuddly toy. 'I suggested to George one morning at breakfast that I should buy Richard a teddy bear to cuddle. George answered in genuine surprise, "What does he need that for when he has my small hammer to take to bed?"' Susan remembered that he had a special fondness for objects which were adapted to serve some use for which they were not intended or were put together in a way which was flawed in some respect. Her grandmother once knitted a pair of socks for him, and though one came out a lot shorter than the other, Orwell wore them and even insisted that he liked them.

Eileen's presence was something which could still be felt in the flat. A photograph of her holding Richard was prominently displayed on the mantelpiece, and her clothes were still hanging in one closet. One day Susan gently asked whether she should send them to a charity, but Orwell simply waved this idea aside and said, 'No, Susan, you can have them.' At a time when clothing was still rationed this was not an insignificant gift. On one occasion when

Susan's eight-year-old daughter Sally was staying at the flat, Orwell brought out Eileen's box of jewellery and told the little girl that she could play with its contents.

'Oh, why do you have them?' the child asked, admiring the collection.

'I'm saving them for a rainy day,' he answered.

'And what will you do with them on a rainy day?'

Orwell thought about this question for a moment, and then said, 'Why, I think I'll give them to you, Sally.'[26] And he did.

While Susan was working for Orwell, *Animal Farm* was published. It became clear very quickly that the book was going to be a great success, but during the first few weeks following publication one problem did bother Orwell. Susan recalled that he came home one afternoon mumbling something about bookshops. As it happened, he had found *Animal Farm* placed among the children's books in a couple of shops, and he had taken it upon himself to move them. He had already discovered that the book was easily misunderstood by people who gave it only a cursory glance. Dial Press in America had rejected it because, Orwell was told, there was no market for animal stories.

The money from the book's large sales did not begin to flow into Orwell's account right away. The American edition, which sold in such vast quantities, did not even appear until August 1946. But the book's popularity brought Orwell many offers to write articles and reviews, and for a period of several months in 1945–1946 he was a regular contributor to four papers – the *Evening Standard*, the *Manchester Evening News*, the *Observer*, and *Tribune*. The sheer volume of his journalism at this time is incredible. Week after week, the words flowed from his typewriter, and many of the pieces which were done so swiftly, and with such apparent ease, have since become classics.

The best work appeared in the *Evening Standard* and *Tribune*. In one ten-week period the latter paper published 'Decline of the English Murder'; 'In Front of Your Nose'; 'Some Thoughts on the Common Toad'; 'A Good Word for the Vicar of Bray'; and 'Confessions of a Book Reviewer'. The last of these pieces is an honest appraisal of the drudgery involved in regular reviewing, an activity which consumed so much of Orwell's energy in the 1940s, but which he could not resist coming back to year after year. He knew that it was a great waste of his time to review so many mediocre books, and understood that doing so forced him to invent reactions towards books for which he had 'no spontaneous feelings whatever'. If a reviewer was really honest, he said, nine out of ten reviews would have to begin with the words, 'This book does not interest me in any way, and I would not write about it unless I were paid to.' He knew that the price of doing otherwise was high. The regular reviewer, he remarked, 'is pouring his immortal soul down the drain, half a pint at a time'. About the only good thing he could find to say about book reviewing was that it did not corrupt the soul as much as reviewing films. 'Everyone in this world has someone else whom he can look down on, and I must say, from experience of both trades, that the book reviewer is better off than the film critic, who cannot even do his work at home, but has to attend trade shows at eleven in the morning and, with one or two notable exceptions, is expected to sell his honour for a glass of inferior sherry.'[27]

For the *Evening Standard* he wrote a short series of weekly articles about ordinary aspects of English life. They exhibit some of his most engaging qualities as a writer and as a human being. The outstanding pieces are 'A Nice Cup of Tea' ('How can you call yourself a tea-lover if you destroy the flavour of your tea by putting sugar in it?'); 'But Are We Really Ruder? No' ('I do not think I have ever been in a country where a blind man or a foreigner gets more attention than he does in England, or where fewer quarters of big towns are unsafe at night, or where people are less inclined to shove you off the pavement or grab your place on a bus or train.'); 'The Case for the Open Fire' ('Some people, obsessed by "functionalism", would make every room in the house as bare, clean and labour-saving as a prison cell.'); 'Just Junk' ('Which is the most attractive junk shop in London is a matter of taste, or for debate; but I could lead you to some first-rate ones in the dingier areas of Greenwich, in Islington, near the Angel, in Holloway, in Paddington, and in the hinterland of the Edgware Road.'); 'Banish

This Uniform' ('If we can't design a new and agreeable form of evening dress at least let us see to it that the old one, with its vulgarity, its expensiveness and its attendant misery of hunting for lost collar studs under the chest of drawers does not come back.'); ' "Bad" Climates Are Best' ('The time was when I used to say that what the English climate needed was a minor operation, comparable to the removal of tonsils in a human being. Just cut out January and February, and we should have nothing to complain about.')

This was such a fertile period for Orwell that he could afford to send some excellent pieces to such small magazines as George Woodcock's *Now*. It was in the pages of this magazine that his 'How the Poor Die' appeared. Woodcock was a friend and was well aware that Orwell could make a great deal more money sending his work elsewhere. 'But Orwell never cut away the literary ladders by which he himself had climbed,' Woodcock wrote later, 'and he was always willing, when he had the time, to write for impecunious little magazines.'[28] Because so much of his work was spread over a wide variety of papers and magazines, the overall quality of his journalism was obscured. Indeed, it was not until the publication of the four-volume *Collected Essays, Journalism and Letters*, in 1968, that the average reader could begin to appreciate the scope of his achievement as a master of the essay form. Besides *Inside the Whale*, the only collection of Orwell's essays to appear in his lifetime was the Secker and Warburg volume, *Critical Essays*, published in February 1946 (it came out two months later in America under the title *Dickens, Dali and Others*). But this book contained only ten pieces, and two of them had already been published in *Inside the Whale*.

The most important of the remaining essays in this volume was one which had not been previously published – 'Benefit of Clergy: Some Notes on Salvador Dali'. This was written in 1944 and was supposed to have appeared in an annual anthology called *The Saturday Book*, but it was pulled from the volume because the publishers – Hutchinson – were afraid that it might be considered obscene. Orwell had already been paid and had received a proof copy when he learned that his essay had been cut during the final stages of production. In fact, it was done at such a late date that Orwell's name and the title of his contribution remained on the Contents page. At the page where his piece was to have begun, a tiny footnote said, 'The Editor regrets that a contribution by Mr George Orwell, entitled "Benefit of Clergy: Some Notes on Salvador Dali", has been unavoidably omitted.' This was, of course, disappointing, but Orwell derived some amusement from the fact that he later received a number of press cuttings about the book, and in every one he was mentioned as a contributor. Not a single reviewer had noticed that his essay had been removed.[29]

It was not really Orwell's fault that his piece was considered too risky to print. He was merely trying to convey a clear sense of Dali's sexual experiences and fantasies as they were given in the autobiography *The Secret Life of Salvador Dali*. Among the various things which Orwell discusses are Dali's fond recollections of painting the image of a woman's 'drawers bespattered with excrement', and of watching a woman urinate while standing up (Dali is especially pleased by the fact that the woman 'misses her aim and dirties her shoes', as Orwell puts it). There is also some attention given to the painter's interest in torture, murder and necrophilia. Orwell describes all this in a quiet, dispassionate way, and then he offers a simple assessment of the book. He says it stinks. What interests him, however, is not Dali or his book but the response which the 'perverse' subject matter of the painter's art brings out in people. Orwell admits that Dali's work has merit from a purely artistic standpoint, and that the artist 'has fifty times more talent than most of the people who would denounce his morals and jeer at his paintings'. He knows that if he showed the book to a typical 'art-hating English person', he could predict the response. 'They would flatly refuse to see any merit in Dali whatever. Such people are not only unable to admit that what is morally degraded can be aesthetically right, but their real demand of every artist is that he shall pat them on the back and tell them that thought is unnecessary.' But it is equally discouraging to him to think that many of those who would argue in favour of Dali's work would take a similarly narrow view. 'If you say that Dali, though a brilliant draughtsman, is a dirty little scoundrel, you are looked upon as a savage. If you say that you don't like rotting corpses, and that people who do like rotting corpses are mentally diseased, it is assumed that you lack the aesthetic sense.'

In matters of art Orwell finds that orthodoxy is as important as it is in politics. The philistines are determined to deny the independence of artistic vision, while its defenders are just as determined to exalt it beyond the reach of criticism. Neither side wants to admit exceptions to their rules, and both sides like to assume that people must either be for them or against them. 'Between these two fallacies there is no middle position; or, rather, there is a middle position, but we seldom hear about it.' One reason that this 'middle position' is rarely given much attention is that it is *not* simplistic. It is easy to say that Dali is a good artist or a miserable specimen of humanity, but what Orwell advocates is a response which refuses to pretend that issues are so easily defined. 'One ought to be able to hold in one's head simultaneously the two facts that Dali is a good draughtsman and a disgusting human being.'

He wants Dali to be free to paint whatever he likes, declaring that 'it is doubtful policy to suppress anything', but Orwell also wants to be free to say that artists are not 'exempt from the moral laws that are binding on ordinary people'. He does not want to see artists enjoying 'a kind of benefit of clergy' which says that because they are artists they can say or do anything they want. 'Just pronounce the magic word "art", and everything is OK. Rotting corpses with snails crawling over them are OK; kicking little girls on the head is OK.' The price of saying things like this is that extremists on either side of the question will denounce you, but as Orwell implies in his essay on Dickens, he was prepared to be 'hated with equal hatred by all the smelly little orthodoxies which are now contending for our souls'.

It is not surprising that Orwell would apply moral standards to his consideration of a painter's work – he had been applying such standards in his literary criticism for years. 'Responsibility' is a key word in his critical vocabulary because he could not separate art from society. 'An artist is also a citizen and a human being,' he reminds the readers of his essay on Dali. So deep was his belief in this notion that he applied it not only to a writer's subject and argument but also to the writing process itself. In his most influential essay, 'Politics and the English Language', which was published in *Horizon* in April 1946, he makes the case that bad writing is morally wrong as well as politically and aesthetically wrong.

The essay repeatedly uses moral terms to describe weak habits of writing. Bad writers, Orwell says, suffer from 'mental vices' and their stylistic faults are termed 'swindles and perversions'. In his view they are 'dishonest' because they have failed to communicate in an authentic voice, relying on a convenient stock of stale words and phrases rather than working to achieve fresh, personal expressions of thought. The chief attraction of writing such empty prose is that it is easy. The mind does not have to be fully awake to stay at it. Instead of bothering with the tedious business of searching for just the right expression, one can simply press into service the first words which come to mind. After commenting on the hard work which good prose requires, Orwell says, 'But you are not obliged to go to all this trouble. You can shirk it by simply throwing your mind open and letting the ready-made phrases come crowding in. They will construct your sentences for you – even think your thoughts for you, to a certain extent – and at need they will perform the important service of partially concealing your meaning even from yourself.'

If no one is truly 'obliged' to bother with the demands of writing good English, then why not take the easy way out and let the 'ready-made' language do the job? Good writers do otherwise, Orwell suggests, because they recognise a moral obligation to avoid such writing. One is perfectly free to 'shirk' this obligation, but the word 'shirk' is itself carefully chosen by Orwell to indicate the failure of responsibility which bad writing entails. He is willing to admit that he has not always been able to practise what he preaches. The temptation to pad a phrase or slip in an overworked metaphor is so great that no writer can resist it entirely, and Orwell confesses that even in writing 'Politics and the English Language' he has occasionally succumbed to the temptation. 'Look back through this essay', he says near the end of it, 'and for certain you will find that I have again and again committed the very faults I'm protesting against.' Because the process of writing presents an endless range of choices with every sentence, a writer can quickly become overwhelmed at any stage and choose the easiest solutions, though they may not be the best ones. However scrupulous a writer may try to be, these easy solutions remain a 'constant temptation' like 'a packet of aspirins always at one's elbow'. Swallowing one of these pills now and then will do little harm, but Orwell obviously wants to warn against the danger of taking an overdose.

The damaging effects of a complete surrender to bad English are made clear in the essay when he shows what a modern writer of the worst kind might do to a beautiful passage from the Book of Ecclesiastes. Instead of 'I returned and saw under the sun that the race is not to the swift, nor the battle to the strong', the modern writer might say, 'Objective consideration of contemporary phenomena compels the conclusion that success or failure in competitive activities exhibits no tendency to be commensurate with innate capacity.' There are several reasons why this translation is so dreadful, but what really sets it in motion is the elimination of the pronoun 'I'. The cold, impersonal passive voice does wonders for anyone inclined to write bad English. By shifting the emphasis away from the writer, the passive helps to obscure the troublesome question of responsibility. No one seems responsible for the construction 'objective consideration . . . compels' because no one in particular seems to be saying those words.

In Ecclesiastes the verse which directly precedes the one quoted by Orwell reads, 'Whatsoever thy hand findeth to do, do it with thy might.' This is roughly the same advice which Orwell's essay offers. Its purpose is not to make its readers think of themselves as potentially brilliant, faultless writers but as plainspoken, conscientious ones determined to put forth all the effort that good writing requires. Orwell's emphasis, therefore, is on that moral effort, not on the artistic considerations. Although great writers will always be rare, even a writer without much talent can at least escape being bad in the sense that Orwell uses that term, that is to say, in the sense that a bad writer is an irresponsible and careless stylist.

Interestingly, the ideas in this essay have an important connection to *Nineteen Eighty-Four*. Newspeak is a perfect language for a society of bad writers because it reduces the number of choices available to them. Orwell describes it as 'the only language in the world whose vocabulary gets smaller every year'. Of course, Big Brother likes it because it deprives people of their freedom to make choices. Before it corrupts politically, Newspeak corrupts morally, since it allows writers to cheat themselves and their readers with ready-made prose.

Orwell could have made his life easier by writing in a prose style which was less demanding. But in all his work he drove himself relentlessly to resist the weaknesses which he describes in 'Politics and the English Language'. Although writing did not have to be so exhausting, he chose to make it so because he felt that he was bound to give as much of himself to his writing as he could. This was an old-fashioned notion, and perhaps a few years of psychiatric therapy could have cured him of it. Instead he created an enormous body of prose which, at its best, sings. And in large part he achieved this because – quite simply – he thought it was the right thing to do.

An Island Far Away

I

Orwell's reaction to Eileen's death can be gauged in one crude, quantifiable way. In the year which followed the tragedy he wrote more than 130 articles and reviews. He kept himself so busy that there were not many spare hours when he could reflect on the fact that she was gone. He could not blot out all his memories of her – nor did he want to try – but work was one practical refuge from depressing thoughts about the past. None of these many pieces give any hint of the tragedy except 'A Good Word for the Vicar of Bray', which appeared in *Tribune* on 26 April 1946. Only sixteen days earlier he had visited the cottage at Wallington for the first time since Eileen's death, and had been faced with the sad job of sorting through some of the letters and other personal effects which she had left behind. In the essay he refers to this visit ('Recently, I spent a day at the cottage where I used to live'), and though there is no mention of Eileen, the short piece is a poignant meditation on death, guilt, and immortality.

The main idea for it was suggested by a small detail about the life of the Vicar of Bray, the subject of the popular old song who was determined to keep his job at all costs. ('I am sure I have kept true to my principle,' he is reported to have said, 'which is to live and die the Vicar of Bray.') On a visit to the little church at Bray, in Berkshire, Orwell had once been shown a 'magnificent yew tree' supposedly planted in the eighteenth century by the famous parson, and this led him to reflect that the selfish man had become 'a public benefactor after all' since his 'beautiful tree . . . has rested the eyes of generation after generation'. Orwell liked this simple notion of doing good beyond the grave, and it prompted him to recall the plantings which he had made at his cottage. During his visit to Wallington he had 'noted with a pleased surprise' that his rose bushes and fruit trees were flourishing, and he had taken satisfaction from the thought that they might go on giving pleasure to others long after he was gone. There was even the possibility that they might help to atone for some of his failings in life: 'The planting of a tree, especially one of the long-living hardwood trees, is a gift which you can make to posterity at almost no cost and with almost no trouble, and if the tree takes root it will far outlive the visible effect of any of your other actions, good or evil.' What he did not tell the *Tribune* readers was that most of his trees and bushes had been planted in the first year of his marriage, and that they were living reminders of the hopes he and Eileen had shared for their new life together. Those plantings had prospered, though the hopes had died. The essay gives the impression that Orwell is engaged in casual, abstract speculation, but sorrow and regret over his wife's death lie at the heart of the piece.

Only old friends such as Richard Rees might have recognised the connection between Eileen's death and 'A Good Word for the Vicar of Bray', but it would have been easy for his friends to overlook the piece. He was writing so much at the time that it must have been difficult to keep up with all his work. His essay was one of ten pieces which appeared under his name in the month of April, some in *Tribune*, some in the *Manchester Evening News*, a couple in the *Observer*, and one in *Horizon*. Such a pace of writing was too demanding, and could not be sustained. Moreover, there were further demands on his time from several different directions – besides attending to Richard and taking care of various duties at home, he was subjected to requests from political and literary groups who wanted him to speak to their meetings, and from the BBC which wanted him to write more scripts. Publishers and editors gave him all the work he could handle – and more – so that finally he saw the impossibility of keeping up with all the demands on his time, and began turning down their requests more often. By April he was complaining to one friend, 'Everyone keeps coming at me wanting me to lecture, to write commissioned booklets, to join this and that, etc. – you don't know how I pine to get free of it all and have time to think again.'[1]

Given his burdens, it is surprising that he accepted an invitation, in the summer of 1945, to serve as the vice-chairman of an organisation called the Freedom Defence Committee. Its goals were sufficiently broad for Orwell to identify with them, and the work of the group was aimed at specific abuses which could easily arouse the sympathy of any lover of liberty. It had been formed in response to various government efforts to restrict freedom of expression in wartime, but its general aim was to oppose all such restrictions, whether related to national security or not. Herbert Read was chairman, and other active supporters included Bertrand Russell and E. M. Forster. After his *Animal Farm* royalties began to come in, Orwell gave generous donations of money to the organisation, spoke on its behalf at a public meeting and wrote a powerful essay in support of its principles – 'Freedom of the Park', which was published in *Tribune* in December. This piece was provoked by the arrest outside Hyde Park of five people who had been selling pacifist and anarchist papers. For this simple act, four of the five were sentenced to six months' imprisonment. They were convicted on grounds of obstruction, which simply meant that they had failed to 'move on' when the police had asked them to. Orwell was scathing in his criticism of this arbitrary use of a technicality in the law. 'As far as I can discover, selling newspapers in the streets *is* technically obstruction, at any rate if you fail to move on when the police tell you to ... If they had also arrested someone who was selling *Truth*, or the *Tablet*, or the *Spectator*, or even the *Church Times*, their impartiality would be easier to believe in.'[2]

Orwell made the point that freedom of speech is always at risk, even in democratic countries, because 'the law is no protection'. No matter what laws exist the only real protection is the force of public opinion. 'If large numbers of people are interested in freedom of speech, there will be freedom of speech, even if the law forbids it; if public opinion is sluggish, inconvenient minorities will be persecuted, even if laws exist to protect them.' As Orwell saw it, the special value of such organisations as the Freedom Defence Committee was that they could help to mobilise public opinion when abuses were discovered.

Orwell was especially troubled by the fact that the five men were arrested and convicted under the new Labour government, which had swept to power after defeating Churchill and the Conservatives in the summer election. He was genuinely perplexed by this circumstance. 'A thing I would like to know – it is a thing we hear very little about – is what changes are made in the administrative personnel when there has been a change of government. Does the police officer who has a vague notion that "Socialism" means something against the law carry on just the same when the government itself is Socialist?' Of course, the Labour government could not change everything overnight, but Orwell saw in this minor incident that much more was needed than a mere change from a Conservative government to a Labour one. Labour could pass all the new laws it wanted, but they would mean little if the changes were not accepted wholeheartedly at the bottom of the system – with the policeman on the street, for example – as well as at the top.

As a correspondent for the *Observer*, Orwell had spent a fortnight covering the summer election ('Most of my waking hours were spent in the streets or in pubs, buses and teashops, with my ears pricked all the time').[3] That experience itself had shown him that the Labour victory did not necessarily mean the beginning of fundamental changes in British society. He saw the victory as reflecting merely a 'drift towards the Left, not accompanied by any strong revolutionary yearnings or any sudden break-up of [the] class system'.[4] He was convinced that the majority of people who voted for Labour were not ready for real change, but wanted only the adoption of certain specific improvements. 'In the popular regard the Labour party is the party that stands for shorter working hours, a free health service, day nurseries, free milk for school children, and the like, rather than the party that stands for Socialism.'[5]

Although he was capable of sternly criticising Labour policy, he did have hopes that greater social changes might eventually occur under a Labour government. In 1948 he wrote, 'With Labour securely in power, perhaps for several successive terms, we have at least the chance of effecting the necessary changes peacefully.'[6] The great challenge was to do it 'peacefully'. The party's leaders needed to go on working for change without giving in to the temptation to impose it summarily. It was a difficult balancing act requiring both restraint and boldness. Orwell worried that too much restraint would make a Labour government more or less indistinguishable from a Conservative one, and that too much boldness would result in dictatorship. Cautious gentlemen in bowler hats were a fixture of British government, and could be counted on to behave in a certain way, but what could be expected of true revolutionaries who were committed to a radical agenda? Would they be tempted to achieve their ends at any price? In a perceptive essay called 'Catastrophic Gradualism', which was published a few months after Labour came to power, Orwell warned of the dangers of accepting either the aimless leadership of 'practical men' or the dictatorial rule of power-hungry ideologues. 'The practical men have led us to the edge of the abyss, and the intellectuals in whom acceptance of power politics has killed first the moral sense, and then the sense of reality, are urging us to march rapidly forward without changing direction.'[7]

Much of 'Catastrophic Gradualism' is concerned with Arthur Koestler's ideas about the use of political power as they were put forward in the influential *Horizon* essay, 'The Yogi and the Commissar' (1942). Orwell disagreed with Koestler on many points, but he was intrigued by the writer's emphasis on the ways in which the desire for power, in and of itself, distorts the ideals of revolutionary struggle. Orwell was a much better writer than Koestler, and was able to sum up the important concept in one precise sentence: 'In the minds of active revolutionaries, at any rate the ones who "got there", the longing for a just society has always been fatally mixed up with the intention to secure power for themselves.' Orwell was not inclined to follow Koestler's drift into

437

the vague realm of 'contemplation' – the Yogi's mystical 'conquest of the desire for power' – but he did see the value of using Koestler's ideas as a way of attacking the dangerous appeal of the Commissar mentality among certain left-wing thinkers.

Although Orwell's political writings earned him many enemies, they also helped him to make a number of important friends. Koestler was one such friend. They met at the beginning of the 1940s, and by the end of the war their friendship was close. They liked to argue about ideas, but Koestler was taken aback by the rigorous criticism applied to him whenever his friend reviewed one of his books. Of Koestler's *Arrival and Departure*, Orwell once remarked – quite accurately – that it was 'not a satisfactory book', and added, 'The pretence that it is a novel is very thin; in effect it is a tract . . . With all too neat a symmetry, the book begins and ends with the same action – a leap into a foreign country.'[8] Koestler did not expect Orwell to be all praise, but it was difficult to be friends with someone who spoke so plainly about his shortcomings. It was the case, however, that Orwell devoted an entire essay to analysing all of Koestler's works up to the early 1940s, and of course this was a compliment since he would not have given up so much time to it if he had thought the author unworthy of sustained attention. Koestler concluded that Orwell was only applying the same strict standards to his friends that he always applied to himself, and that he did not see his comments as being harsh or unfriendly. The phrase 'uncompromising honesty' was not a cliché for Orwell, Koestler once observed; it was an idea he took seriously. But so great was his commitment to it that it obscured his view of other realities: 'I don't think George ever knew what makes other people tick,' Koestler once said, 'because what made him tick was very different from what made most other people tick.'[9]

II

Almost a year after Eileen's death, Orwell gave renewed consideration to a plan which he had shared with her in the last months of her life. He wanted to find a special retreat where he could escape the pressures of London for long periods at a time, and in 1944 David Astor had recommended the remote Scottish island of Jura. Astor's family had an estate on the island, and he thought Orwell might like to spend a brief holiday there. He never dreamed that his friend would want to *live* on the island. But when Orwell learned that a large farmhouse – 'Barnhill' – was available at a spot overlooking a beautiful green bay, he could not wait to move to Jura. One of the last letters Eileen wrote to her husband concerns their plans to give up their lease on the cottage at Wallington and to sign a new lease for Barnhill. She had written to the landlady, Margaret Fletcher, and had obtained a good deal of information about the place. She was ready to move there if Orwell insisted on taking it, but she was not enthusiastic about the idea. She had every reason to doubt the wisdom of going there for any extended period. The house itself was enormous compared with The Stores – there were five spacious bedrooms, a large sitting-room and dining-room, and a big kitchen. But like the cottage, it had no electricity. This might have been easier for Eileen to bear if the place were not so isolated. Barnhill stands near the northern tip of the island, and in Orwell's day the nearest neighbour was more than a mile away; the road leading to the place was nothing more than a primitive track which connected it to Margaret Fletcher's house several miles away, and the nearest shop was twenty-five miles to the south. It was the only one on the island. The population of about three hundred was scattered over an area of 160 square miles.

The work involved in maintaining a household in such a spot would have been too much for Eileen, and she knew it. Her sudden death made Orwell abandon the idea, at least for a few months, but in early 1946 he began to give it renewed attention. He wanted Richard to be able to grow up in the country, and thought that the wild environment of Jura would be a young boy's paradise. The child could learn to fish and hunt and would have miles of uninhabited countryside to explore. It had the makings of a paradise, for Orwell at any rate. And there was the particular advantage of being so far removed from London that people could not easily get in contact with him. Barnhill had no telephone and mail came only once or twice a week, so there would be ample opportunity to live as one pleased without the constant interruptions of a successful literary life in London. Despite the fact that the rent was 'almost nothing', as Orwell put it, no one else had tried living in the house since 1934.

He had no intention of becoming a hermit. He simply wanted to have more time to spend on writing something more substantial than short pieces for papers and magazines. He wanted people to come and visit him. He liked the idea of having a steady stream of friends coming and going. There was enough room in the house to allow him to work quietly even with a few guests under his roof, and their presence would give him the chance to continue engaging in the kind of friendly debates which he so much enjoyed in London. Barnhill would be not only his farmhouse but his office, his restaurant, his pub, his inn, and there would be few reminders of the outside world of wars, dirty streets, modern factories, and power politics.

His idea was that Susan Watson would continue to serve as a nurse-housekeeper in Jura, but he also wanted another woman in the house. He wanted to go off to his island with a wife. In the early months of 1946 he proposed to at least three women. He was lonely, and anxious to find someone who would be a good mother to Richard, but he was also looking for someone who would share his dream with him, someone young and strong who might enjoy the challenge of living far away from the ordinary conveniences of civilisation. He approached Anne Popham, who was staying in his building in Canonbury Square, because he thought she was lonely and would be glad to have a chance for a new life with someone who could give her an instant family. 'I do so want someone who will share what is left of my life,' he told her. He was able to make a good case for a marriage based on the idea that Richard needed a mother, but he was not at all convincing on his own behalf. In a long letter to her, he dismissed himself as unattractive, unhealthy and old. It was a generally bleak self-portrait, with only a slight touch of humour: 'There is no knowing how long I shall live, but I am supposed to be a "bad life". I have a disease called bronchiectasis which is always

liable to develop into pneumonia, and also a "non-progressive"
tuberculous lesion in one lung, and several times in the past I have
been supposed to be about to die, but I always lived on just to spite
them.'

One point in his favour, he said, was that he might indeed die in
the next few years, and leave behind an estate which would be worth
having. Convinced that he was physically unappealing, he was quite
blunt about the bargain he was offering:

> What I am really asking you is whether you would like to be the
> widow of a literary man. If things remain more or less as they are
> there is a certain amount of fun in this, as you would probably get
> royalties coming in and you might find it interesting to edit
> unpublished stuff etc. . . . You are young and healthy, and
> deserve somebody better than me: on the other hand if you don't
> find such a person, and if you think of yourself as essentially a
> widow, then you might do worse – i.e. supposing I am not actually
> disgusting to you. If I can live another ten years I think I have
> another three worth-while books in me, besides a lot of odds and
> ends, but I want peace and quiet and someone to be fond of
> me.[10]

He was doing his best to win her sympathy, but the result was
that he made himself seem impossibly dreary to anyone whose
motives were not mercenary. Anne's were not, and she had no
desire to accept his proposal. He had made his intentions very clear
while she was visiting him in his flat one day. It was an awkward
scene. He had asked her to come to his bedroom, and when she had
sat down on the edge of his bed, he had embraced her. She was
embarrassed by the abrupt manner in which he had then confronted her with the question of marriage, and had made her exit as
soon as possible without giving him any encouragement. Orwell
knew that he had made a fool of himself and was sincere in the
lengthy apologies which he offered her afterwards. 'I fully realise
that I'm not suited to someone like you who is young and pretty and
can still expect to get something out of life. There isn't really
anything left in my life except my work and seeing that Richard gets
a good start. It is only that I feel so desperately alone sometimes.'[11]

Less awkward, but hardly more successful, was his proposal to another young woman – Celia Paget. He met her when he was with Richard. The three of them shared a railway compartment on a journey to Wales. They were travelling to Arthur Koestler's cottage, where each had been invited to spend several days at Christmas 1945. Koestler's wife, Mamaine, was Celia's twin, and it had occurred to Koestler that his sister-in-law might be just the woman for his friend Orwell. He reasoned that if he brought them together, they might find that they liked each other. For his part Orwell was drawn to Celia right away. She was a slender, attractive woman with a confident manner. She had been a fashion model in the late 1930s, and had worked informally for *Horizon* magazine during the last years of the war. She knew who Orwell was and found him interesting, and Koestler did what he could to persuade her that his friend would make a good husband.

Their Christmas holiday in Wales was a success. She was delighted with Richard, and was impressed by Orwell's great affection for the child. A short time later he asked her to his flat for dinner. She was happy to be invited, and was prepared to be his friend, but he wanted more than that and was as quick to propose to her as he had been to Anne. Celia was attracted to him and took her time before giving him a definite answer, but when it came, it was the same as Anne's. Her refusal, however, was very gently and thoughtfully expressed, and did not cause them to drift apart afterwards. They became friends and remained on good terms until the end of his life.

It was also in this general period that Orwell met Sonia Brownell, who was a friend of Celia's. Both women had worked at *Horizon*. In 1945, Sonia became an editorial assistant to Cyril Connolly at the magazine, but in rather a short time she established herself as an indispensable force in the office who kept things running when Connolly was away, which was increasingly the case after 1945, when he decided that he had grown tired of editing and wanted to spend more time writing. By the end of the 1940s many people were under the impression that the magazine was being run more or less by Sonia alone. That was an exaggeration, but it was true that she was remarkably efficient and thorough, and that she managed to establish a significant degree of control over Connolly and the magazine. He was in love with her at one point, but she was somehow able to keep him at a reasonably safe distance, flattering him with attention and expressions of admiration but frustrating all his attempts to make love to her. Connolly enjoyed romantic complications, so he continued to play her game for months, though it became increasingly frustrating, and he began to think that she was afraid of sex.

It would be more accurate to say that sex made her uneasy. She had been educated at the Convent of the Sacred Heart in Roehampton, and the nuns who taught her were not inclined to make her think well of her body. In fact, she was not supposed to think of it at all. Part of the normal routine at the convent was for the girls to take their baths wearing long white gowns so that they would not have to confront their nakedness. To keep them from taking any undue interest in their bodies, they were forbidden to have mirrors. And to make certain that they kept their minds on the hereafter, each girl was required to sleep on her back with her arms folded on her chest, so that she would be prepared to receive God if He came to take her in the night. The result of this morbid, repressed upbringing was that Sonia became determined to rebel against it in every way possible. She rejected Catholicism completely as soon as she left the convent, and in later life made a point of spitting on the pavement whenever she saw a nun. Sex had its fascinations for her as something previously forbidden, but she also seems to have been burdened by guilt as a result of her education, and her relations with men were always difficult.

She did not lack lovers. When she was only twenty, in 1938, she was involved with a much older man – a respected scholar of medieval poetry for whom she worked as a secretary. One year later she fell in love with the painter William Coldstream, who met her at the Euston Road School of Painting and Drawing in 1939. She lived near the school and was invited by the staff to serve as a model for some portrait studies. She agreed, and her presence at the school was quickly noted by the painters, who admired her beauty and who fondly referred to her as the 'Euston Road Venus'. She was indeed attractive – she had light brown hair, large eyes and a bright complexion. After Coldstream became her lover, he introduced her to his friend and fellow student at the school Stephen Spender, who in turn introduced her to Connolly.

Sonia met Orwell at the end of 1945. She was invited to a dinner party at Connolly's house and Orwell was one of the guests. She did not like his abrupt ways or his tendency to hold himself apart from others. As one who was forthright and exuberant, she felt that Orwell was a cold Englishman. She was fond of all things French, including French men, and one of her strongest terms of disapproval was to say that something was 'so English' or to refer to a man as 'typically English'. But gradually she developed an interest in Orwell as a character who was not so easy to define as she had originally thought. She liked his literary essays, and came to respect him as an astute critic, but was less impressed by his passion for political issues, which she regarded as largely a waste of his time. She thought that he should be more 'artistic', but she did like the fact that he was not so involved with art and ideas that he was incapable of taking an interest in the ordinary things of life. She later praised him as 'the only intellectual who could mend a fuse or an iron'.[12]

Sonia's beauty and her energetic ways attracted Orwell, but he was also drawn to her because of her toughness. She always spoke her mind and was not afraid of sternly reprimanding people who tried to cross her or who failed to do as she expected. As an editor she was not especially imaginative, but she was consistent and decisive. Her opinions were not always well informed, but they were never weak. 'I met Joseph Cotten at Cyril's the other night,' she wrote to a friend in the 1940s, 'and thought him the stupidest man I'd ever met.' In Orwell's eyes her brashness was heartening. To some people, this same quality came across as a sign of arrogance or pretentiousness, but Orwell thought she was brave, and he became convinced that she would be a good person to help him manage his career, especially if he were seriously weakened by illness and needed a strong voice to speak out for him. He saw her as someone who would fight aggressively for his rights with publishers and editors, and in that respect he was absolutely correct in his judgement of her.

Sonia's tough exterior was convincing, but, like many people who take care to appear tough, she was trying to conceal some deep feelings of insecurity. She said very little about her family, but the facts about them were not in keeping with her image of herself as a sophisticated woman of the world. Her father was a man of modest means who worked as a freight broker in Calcutta, where she was born in August 1918. He died of a heart attack not long after she was born, and more misfortune for the family followed this event. Her mother remarried, but this second husband proved to be an impossible alcoholic who eventually went bankrupt. Her mother was forced to leave India and to return to London, where she borrowed some money from old family friends and established a boarding house in South Kensington. This business supported her for the rest of her life and gave her enough money to send Sonia and an older sister, Bay, to the Convent of the Sacred Heart.

When Sonia completed her Catholic schooling at the age of seventeen, her mother dipped deeper into the family's limited funds to send her to a finishing school in Switzerland. Even as a young girl Sonia was able to write and speak French with impressive ease, and it was thought that a year of additional education at the school in Neuchâtel would help her to perfect her French. She did indeed make good progress at the school, and had decided to remain there for another year when she experienced a tragedy which would cast a shadow over the rest of her life.

One day in the summer of 1936 she went canoeing on Lake Neuchâtel with another girl and two boys. The lake was calm when they began paddling across it, but when they were far from shore, a squall hit the lake and the canoe capsized. Sonia was a good swimmer and began immediately to make her way towards the shore, but when she turned to see whether her friends were following she realised that they were all struggling in the water and were crying out for help. She swam back to them, but by the time she reached one of the boys, the other two friends had disappeared under water. She put out her arm to rescue the boy, who was thrashing the water violently, and he grabbed it. Like many drowning people, however, he began to panic, and he pulled Sonia towards him. She tried to release her arm from his grip, but he would not let go. As he began to go under, she was in danger of being dragged down with him.

Sonia was not one to take half-measures, and in this unfortunate incident, her own strong instincts for survival took over and made her overreact. She managed to free her arm, but when the drowning boy continued to struggle with her, she decided that she would not let him get the better of her. She grabbed him by the hair and pushed his head under water. She was able to hold him down for several seconds, and then she let go, thinking that he would stop trying to fight her and would come to the surface. But he did not come up. She looked round for any sign of him, and then realised that he must have lost consciousness. By this point she was exhausted and frightened, and rather than risk another encounter with the boy, she turned away and began swimming as fast as she could.

She reached a rock which was sticking out of the lake and pulled herself from the water. When a pleasure steamer came along a short time later, she stood up on the rock and waved for help. She was rescued, but she later learned that all three of her companions had drowned. She felt that one of those deaths was her doing. 'Mother had to go out to get her and bring her back to England,' her older sister, Bay, remembered. 'Sonia was terribly shaken, and I don't think she ever got over it. She certainly didn't want to stay out there any longer.' The authorities in Switzerland assumed that each of the drownings was entirely accidental, but Sonia told her mother and sister the truth. She later told the story to her half-brother, Michael, to whom she was very close, and she left no doubt in his mind that she considered herself responsible for the one boy's death. 'I held him under,' she said.[13]

A few of Sonia's close friends knew about the incident in Switzerland, but they were generally led to believe that the tragedy for her was simply that she was the lone survivor. She seems to have left out the details about her struggle with the drowning boy. She definitely had a need to talk about the incident, and brought it up from time to time with her family and with certain friends. 'I think she always had it very much in her mind,' her friend Diana Witherby recalled.[14] Whether Orwell knew of it is not clear, though she may well have told him the more innocent version at some point.

Sonia fascinated him, perhaps more than any other woman in his life, and he seems to have had a good insight into her character almost from the beginning. Although he had no luck with his proposal of marriage when he first approached her in 1945–1946, she did allow him to take her to dinner, and she did come to visit him at Canonbury Square on at least one occasion. According to her friend at the time – Janetta Woolley – she also allowed Orwell to sleep with her. From Sonia's point of view it was a disaster. She felt sorry for him and gave in to his 'clumsy' efforts at lovemaking, as she called them. Afterwards she told Janetta that he had made love to her quickly and without any great show of passion. 'He seemed pleased,' she said, 'but I don't think he was aware that there was not any pleasure in it for me.'[15]

She was probably right about his not being aware of his failure to please her. Certainly his image of her did not lose any of its lustre over the next few years. She rarely saw him between spring 1947 and spring 1949, but he thought about her a lot, and after he went to live in Jura, he made a valiant effort to entice her to visit him there. 'I do so want you here,' he wrote to her from Barnhill, sending her elaborate directions for the two-day journey from London. She had no interest in roughing it on some distant island, and did not encourage him to repeat the invitation after she politely excused herself the first time. But he did not give up his interest in her. A mutual friend – Lys Lubbock, who was Cyril Connolly's companion during most of the Forties – believed that there was a special quality to Sonia's beauty which had an almost magical effect on Orwell's imagination:

In those days there was a lovely glow of health in her appearance. She had a pink-and-white complexion and golden blonde hair

447

that she was quite proud of, washing it every night and doing it up herself. In the sunshine it glowed and was the crown to her beauty. I think it was this radiance of health that so attracted Orwell, who perhaps saw her as a kind of life force to compensate for his own poor health.[16]

Her outspokenness, her vigour, her beauty, her apparent toughness, all held enormous appeal for him, and he was able to bring some of it to life in the novel which he began writing on Jura. In *Nineteen Eighty-Four*, Julia talks and acts like Sonia, and even has a job which is the futuristic equivalent of editorial assistant at *Horizon* – she works on the novel-writing machines in the Fiction Department, 'running and servicing a powerful but tricky electric motor'. Like Sonia, Julia enjoys showing her disapproval of things by exclaiming, 'Oh, rubbish!'

The most appealing thing about Julia is her refreshingly straightforward manner. 'Girls are always supposed to be so pure,' she tells Winston. 'Here's one who isn't, anyway.' When Winston makes love to her for the first time, he tells her, 'I hate purity, I hate goodness. I don't want any virtue to exist anywhere. I want everyone to be corrupt to the bones.' To this earnest expression of desire, Julia confidently replies, 'Well, then, I ought to suit you, dear. I'm corrupt to the bones.' But she is so intent on always giving the toughest response to any situation that she appears to be willing to do anything to get what she wants. After describing his loveless marriage with Katherine, Winston tells Julia of a time when he was standing near the edge of a cliff with his wife and was tempted to push her. 'Why didn't you give her a good shove?' Julia asks. 'I would have.' To which Winston says, 'Yes, dear, you would have.'

III

When Orwell went north to Jura to occupy Barnhill for the first time, he did so without any hope that he would be sharing it with a new wife any time soon. It is impossible to say whether he proposed to only three women, or whether it was more, but no one was on the verge of accepting him, and for all he knew, no one would marry him in the foreseeable future. He extended invitations to visit him to Celia, Sonia and a few other women friends, and there was always the chance that one of the women would accept the invitation, arrive in Jura and fall in love with the place. Brenda Salkeld, Inez Holden, and Sally McEwan were among the women who braved the long journey to share a week or two with him in his island paradise, but it was not the kind of life which the average person would want to experience for anything longer than a few weeks. That much is clear from a letter which Orwell wrote to Sally McEwan, his former secretary at *Tribune*, explaining to her the challenge of reaching Barnhill. 'So looking forward to seeing you . . . But I'm very sorry to say you'll have to walk the last 8 miles because we've no conveyance. However it isn't such a terrible walk if you can make do with rucksack luggage – for instance a rucksack and a couple of haversacks. I can tote that much on the back of my motor bike (only conveyance I have), but not heavy suitcases.'[17] Despite such difficulties, Sally enjoyed her stay with him as much as anyone, and nearly forty years later she still had vivid memories of walking over the hills above Barnhill and watching the rough seas in the distance, and of waking up in the mornings to large breakfasts of potato cakes and porridge. But either Sally was not proposed to, or she was not prepared for a longer stay, because she returned to London in a fortnight.

Orwell relished the complications involved in travelling to his retreat. Living on Jura was one long adventure, and the hardships were an indispensable part of the island's appeal. Although Inez Holden was one of the friends who took the trouble to visit him, she thought his adventure was too wild. 'George had a fantastically silly Robinson Crusoe mind,' she remarked many years later. She recalled one example from her stay on Jura. 'He took pieces of wood and said if you put sulphur on them and let them be for a time, you would have matches.' She was unimpressed by this ingenuity. 'But you can buy a box for twopence on the mainland,' she told him.[18]

Susan Watson was one who did not have any second thoughts about joining Orwell in his adventure. She took Richard there and cared for him on the island during the summer of 1946, coping with the difficult conditions of the place to the best of her ability, and managing rather well despite her bad leg. But the terrain was against her, as she discovered one day when she and Orwell went to Margaret Fletcher's house to meet a car bringing Brenda Salkeld for a visit. 'She stepped out looking very handsome indeed,' Susan recalled, 'and extremely smart in a grey flannel suit, polished brogue shoes with her beautifully done hair controlled by an invisible net. I stretched out my hand to greet her, did not notice the adjacent bog and sank into it up to my waist.'¹⁹

Susan did not have the chance to prove that she could live on the island for a long period because she gave up her job only two months after going up to Barnhill. According to her, she was pressured into making this decision by Orwell's sister Avril. When she first arrived at the house, she was surprised to find that Avril was already there. Orwell had said nothing about it, despite the fact that his sister had come with the intention of staying the entire summer. Moreover, Avril had the idea that she would be her brother's housekeeper, and that she would take care of his child. She had never married, and since her mother's death in 1943, her life had been rather aimless and lonely. Without really saying much about her plans to her brother, she had made up her mind to help him, to devote her time to his needs. He was in the odd position of being able, at last, to provide for her. Most of his life he had been so poor that she would never have imagined relying on him for support, but she had little to lose at this stage in their lives. There was not much else for her to turn to, and there was no question that he could afford to give her a decent life at his side. The problem was that Susan already had the job which Avril wanted.

That problem was quickly taken care of. In Susan's opinion, Avril never took the time to get to know her, and as soon as they were both together at Barnhill, a kind of running battle over domestic matters broke out. Because of her disability, Susan was – not surprisingly – slow in performing such routine tasks as making breakfast or washing up. And as Richard became faster on his feet, she had more and more trouble keeping up with him. Avril began almost immediately to criticise her slowness, and to make cutting remarks about her difficulty in performing certain heavy tasks in the kitchen. She told her that she really did not have any business working as a housekeeper, and made it clear that all her work could be done much more effectively by someone else, and by that, of course, Avril meant herself. She was right. By all accounts, Orwell's sister was an excellent cook and housekeeper, and was the natural choice for the job in her brother's household, but she treated Susan unfairly. It was a petty kind of treatment. One day she reprimanded her for calling the master of the house 'George'. She explained, 'His proper name is *Eric.*' On another occasion she criticised her when she noticed her struggling to darn a sock. 'You call yourself a nurse,' Susan remembered being told, 'but you can't darn a sock.' Because of her cerebral palsy she sometimes had difficulty with her co-ordination when performing such simple tasks.

Susan tried to discuss her situation with Orwell, explaining that his sister was making life miserable for her, and that either this would have to stop or she would have to leave. Orwell failed her in this instance. His unwillingness to become involved in a messy domestic battle caused him to tell her to work the problem out on her own. He was sympathetic, up to a point, and made it plain that he did not want to see her go, but he also preferred not to make life difficult for his sister, and he certainly did not want to be put in the position of taking the side against her. No doubt he must have felt trapped on both sides, but when faced with having to choose between Avril and Susan, he could not turn his back on his sister. This was a particularly delicate problem at the time because it came so close to a sad event in the Blair family, the death of Marjorie Blair. On 3 May 1946, just twelve days after her forty-eighth birthday, Orwell's older sister had died in hospital, suffering from kidney disease. He and Avril had attended her funeral only a few weeks before they went up to Barnhill. In fairly quick succession – within a period of just seven years – they had lost their father, mother, and sister. As the only surviving members of their immediate family, they were naturally drawing closer to each other, and perhaps Avril's treatment of Susan can be explained by the fact that she was feeling overly protective towards her brother.

In any case, Susan tried to make things work, but in the end the constant criticism from Avril proved too much for her. She explained her feelings to Orwell one more time, and he gave her the choice of either accepting a small sum of money and leaving the job for ever, or staying on and trying to work things out with his sister. She chose to take the money and leave, but she did so with great reluctance. She bore Orwell no ill will over the incident. By this point in her time with him, she knew him well enough to understand that he wanted to help her, and was willing to stick by her, but that he was not inclined to go against his sister, or to assert himself in a way that might cause an upheaval in the house. It was clear from the beginning of her stay in Jura that one of the two women would have to go, and perhaps Susan should have accepted right away that it would not be Avril. In any case she packed her belongings and returned to London, feeling not only hurt by the way in which Avril had treated her, but also genuine sorrow at having to leave Richard and George, to whom she had become deeply attached in the year that she was with them.

She may have felt overly sensitive to any criticism from Avril, and in her own mind the comments about her disability may have taken on more importance than Avril had intended. But she could not have been mistaken about the feeling that Avril wanted her job, and that her presence was an inconvenience. The sad thing is that no matter how seriously Avril may have been determined to persuade her to leave, the critical remarks which were made about her were ones which stung deeply. In fact, they remained so strong in Susan's mind afterwards that she became convinced that people like Avril would never accept her as long as she was so obviously at a disadvantage physically. A friend had written to her about an operation which was supposed to be effective in improving the particular problem which caused her lameness. It involved severing a tendon in her foot. This was supposed to make it possible for her to improve her balance, but it turned out to be a piece of quackery which, after the operation was performed, left her more disabled than she had been previously. This terrible mistake plagued her for the rest of her life, and understandably she was later tempted to lay some of the blame for this unfortunate problem on Avril, telling herself that she would not have been so desperate to seek a remedy for her condition if Avril had not made her feel so self-conscious about her limitations on Jura. Orwell seems never to have understood how deeply Susan felt about these things, and though she remained in contact with him after her unsuccessful operation, she did not reveal to him the part that Avril's comments had played in her decision to seek some kind of medical cure. Her relations with Orwell were good to the very end, though she could not help regretting his inability to deal in a more forthright way with the awkward situation Avril's presence had created.

Whatever she may have said to Susan, Avril was indeed intent on establishing herself as her brother's helper, and she remained in that position until the end of his life. Her intentions were no doubt good, but her treatment of Susan was regrettable. In her memoir of her brother, which was published in 1961, she said nothing about Susan, and made it appear as though the job of helping him with Richard had been hers without question. 'He had previously asked me if I'd like to go up during the summer and give him a hand with helping in the house and helping with young Richard and so on. I was only too pleased. I'd just managed to escape from an essential works order – I'd been working in a factory all during the war and felt that really a spot of country air would just be about the thing I wanted.'[20]

She did become attached to Barnhill, and continued living there for at least a year after her brother's death. She was clearly more help to Orwell than Susan might have been because she was stronger, and life on the island required strength. It was not a place for people who were, for whatever reason, physically weak. Avril took to the rugged life with great determination and came to appreciate its isolation and natural beauty almost as much as her brother did. Her enthusiasm for the place is evident in a letter to Humphrey Dakin which she wrote one month after arriving on the island:

The house faces south & we have a lovely view over the Sound of

Jura with little islands dotted here & there. Eric has bought a little
boat & we go fishing in the evening which is the time the fish rise.
They are simply delicious fresh from the sea. In fact, on the whole
we live on the fat of the land. Plenty of eggs & milk & ½ lb butter extra
weekly on to our rations. Our landlord gave us a large hunk of
venison a short while ago which was extremely good. Then there are
local lobsters & crabs . . . I am really enjoying it all immensely.[21]

In the autumn of 1946 Orwell returned to London – accompanied by Avril and Richard – and spent the next seven
months at Canonbury Square. He was tempted to make Barnhill his
permanent home, and was intent on going back in the spring,
perhaps to try the experiment of living there for a full year. The
climate is not as harsh as might be imagined. Jura is warmed by the
Gulf Stream, and in several ways Orwell found its climate
agreeable. 'These islands are one of the most beautiful parts of the
British Isles,' he told one correspondent, and then added, 'Of
course, it rains all the time, but if one takes that for granted it
doesn't seem to matter.'[22] What he really needed was good medical
care and a long rest, neither of which was possible for him on Jura.
Although there was a doctor on the island, his office was twenty-five
miles from Barnhill. To make matters worse, Orwell did not take
advantage of the quiet environment to give himself a long rest.
Instead he kept busy doing minor repairs round the house, working
in his garden, fishing, hunting, and – of course – writing. In terms of
work it had not made much difference that he had escaped from the
demands of journalism. When he had put that burden behind him,
he had taken on a much more difficult task, though potentially a far
more rewarding one. In August 1946 he had begun writing a long
novel.

It was a work which had been taking shape in his imagination over
the past few years. The tentative title for it was 'The Last Man in
Europe', but, eventually, he would alter it to *Nineteen Eighty-Four*.
Almost all of it was written on Jura, an island far removed from the
kind of world described in the book. But Orwell was not merely
writing about a future totalitarian state. His book was a deeply
personal statement as well, and with the wild landscape of Jura

surrounding him, he turned his mind back to the past to find the models for various incidents and characters described in a remote world of the future. The past to which he returned was largely his own past, drawing on experiences which stretched back to his early youth in Henley, and which also touched upon more recent experiences, such as his service at the BBC and his brief but memorable love affair with Sonia Brownell.

IV

When he went back to London in early October 1946, he had about fifty pages of the novel in rough draft, but he did not add much to this until he returned to Jura in the spring. As long as he was in London, he was resigned to getting 'back on the journalistic treadmill'. Fortunately, however, he was successful at suppressing his temptation to do a lot of reviewing. Instead he resumed his 'As I Please' column for *Tribune*, and this provided the bulk of his journalistic work. His very first column in this new series began with a long examination of an unnamed American fashion magazine. It is not surprising that Orwell would subject such a common periodical to serious analysis, in the manner of his essay 'Boys' Weeklies', but he had a personal reason for looking at the magazine in the first place. It was a copy of *Vogue*, and in addition to its many photographs of glamorous women, it contained a photograph of Orwell. The magazine had decided that the author of *Animal Farm* was a rising literary star worthy of a brief report, which was featured above an advertisement for something called Djer-Kiss Perfume ('Expensive? Yes. An orchid costs more than a marigold'). Orwell must have felt a mixture of pride and embarrassment to see his personal life described in the breezy style of the *Vogue* correspondent: 'Nowadays, Orwell lives in a top-floor flat in London, with his twenty-odd-months-old son. The stuff around his rooms – a Burmese sword, a Spanish peasant lamp, the Staffordshire figures, show something of his foreign life and his strong English solidity. Educated at Eton, Orwell has since then had the kind of picaresque life that is so superb in English autobiographies.'[23]

Orwell said nothing about this piece to his *Tribune* readers, entertaining them instead with a delightful commentary on the odd combination of innocence and sophistication reflected in the fashion sections. He was fascinated by the exaggerated claims of the advertising, citing such lines as 'Supple and tissue-light, yet wonderfully curve-holding' and 'Moulds your bosom into proud feminine lines'. Living in a country which was still struggling with the hardships imposed by rationing, he was shocked by the luxury of the world presented in the magazine's 325 pages, with its seemingly endless 'pictures of ball dresses, mink coats, step-ins, panties, brassières, silk stockings, slippers, perfumes, lipsticks, nail varnish – and, of course, of the women, unrelievedly beautiful, who wear them or make use of them'. It was such an unreal world that he felt compelled to make 'a fairly diligent search through the magazine' for evidence that women were anything other than creatures endowed with eternal youth and beauty. He found 'two discreet allusions to grey hair', but not much else. 'If there is anywhere a direct mention of fatness or middle age I have not found it. Birth and death are not mentioned either: nor is work except that a few recipes for breakfast dishes are given.' The truth is that his own photograph – a typical portrait showing him in an old, tattered tweed jacket with a dark shirt and tie – is the one thing which is definitely out of place in this otherwise elegant world. That fact must have pleased him almost as much as the final sentence in the magazine's description of him: 'Fairly much a leftist, George Orwell is a defender of freedom, even though most of the time he violently disagrees with the people beside whom he is fighting.'

The difference between the rich life portrayed in *Vogue* and the reality of life in postwar Britain became even more striking later in the year when the nation was hit by a severe fuel shortage during the worst winter in more than fifty years. In December and January there were heavy snows, strong winds, and ice-covered roads. By early February 1947 the fuel crisis had become so severe that the government was forced to impose drastic reductions on the use of power for both industrial and private consumers. The cuts even affected such things as the BBC's Third Programme, which was shut down for a fortnight, as were all weekly papers – including *Tribune*. On 27 February Orwell's 'As I Please' column was printed in the *Daily Herald* with a note explaining that the paper was giving 'space to *Tribune*, the Socialist weekly, which has had to suspend publication because of the power cuts'.

In Canonbury Square Orwell ran out of coal and for a time was burning peat in his small fireplace. In his column he praised it as an attractive alternative to coal and wood. 'It gives out less heat than coal, but is cleaner and easier to handle, and, unlike wood, it is suitable for small fireplaces. A few million tons of it a year would make a lot of difference if, as seems likely, we are never going to have quite enough coal again.' As much as Orwell liked the idea of everyone burning peat, his own supply soon ran out and he was forced to take desperate measures. Near the end of the crisis he wrote in *Tribune* that people were burning all sorts of things in their fireplaces, 'not despising the furniture as a last resort', which led him to confess: 'I kept going for a day myself on a blitzed bedstead, and wrote an article by its grateful warmth.'

His own situation was even worse than he was willing to admit at the time. In addition to the ordinary pains caused by the frigid weather, he was suffering from lung problems again. He finally confessed to Fredric Warburg, later that spring, that his health had been 'wretched . . . ever since about January (my chest as usual)'. He blamed it on the 'beastly cold' of the winter. He had tried to ignore his health problems during the long cold spell, but it was impossible. Just keeping warm was a struggle. Avril remembered how difficult life was for her brother: 'We had no fuel, and Eric had been ill on and off during the winter with one thing and another. We even got to the point of chopping up young Richard's toys and putting them on the fire in Eric's room to try and keep him warm while he was writing.'[24]

After such a miserable winter, they were only too happy to escape London at the first sign of spring. In a letter to Brenda Salkeld he gave some indication of his mood at the end of the winter, and spelled out his plans for the spring. On 20 March he wrote to her from Canonbury Square:

I have now literally no fuel whatever. However it isn't quite so stinkingly cold, in fact we've distinctly seen the sun on more than one occasion, and I heard some birds trying to sing the other morning . . . I've only one more job to do and hope to get that out of the way before we leave for Barnhill, as I do so want not to have to take any bits and pieces of work with me. We have arranged to leave on April 10th, and if I can fix the tickets are going to fly from Glasgow to Islay, which ought to cut out about 6 hours of that dismal journey . . . I think after this stinking winter the weather ought to be better this year.

They did leave London on 10 April – making part of the journey by aeroplane – and two days later Orwell was enjoying 'beautiful spring weather' at Barnhill. 'There are daffodils all over the place,' he wrote to Sonia Brownell.[25] He was still feeling weak, but was ready to resume work on his novel, and was convinced that he would be more comfortable on Jura than in London. 'One is better off for fuel here,' he explained in a letter to Anthony Powell, 'and on the whole better off for food.'[26]

Just before leaving London, Orwell had received some good news. Victor Gollancz had written to him that he was releasing him from any further contractual obligations. This was not a decision which the publisher had initiated. He had done it only after Orwell had insisted upon it. When the time arrived for *Nineteen Eighty-Four* to be published, Orwell wanted it to go to Secker and Warburg, and did not want to take the slightest risk of Gollancz publishing it. Although it was doubtful that Gollancz would accept the book, Orwell did not want to waste time submitting it to him first, which his contract with the publisher would have required him to do. The worst case was that Gollancz might try to delay giving Orwell a decision on the novel, or that he might warn others against it, as he had with *Animal Farm*. Orwell was polite but honest in his written request for release from the contract, telling Gollancz that 'it would be better if you are willing to bring the whole thing to an end'. He specifically mentioned the problem with *Animal Farm* as something which he did not want to encounter again, and he said that he felt he owed Secker and Warburg an option on all of his future work because the firm had demonstrated the courage to back him in a controversial situation. 'The crucial case was *Animal Farm*. At the time when this book was finished, it was very hard indeed to get it published, and I determined then that if possible I would take all my future output to the publisher who would produce it, because I knew that anyone who would risk this book would risk anything.'[27]

Gollancz tried to resist his author's request, but Orwell was steadfast in his determination to side with Fredric Warburg, and he was forced to make his request a second time when his first letter failed to work. His experience had taught him that Gollancz was unreliable, and he more or less told him so in his second letter:

> I am afraid of further differences arising, as in the past. You know what the difficulty is, i.e. Russia. For quite 15 years I have regarded that regime with plain horror, and though, of course, I would change my opinion if I saw reason, I don't think my feelings are likely to change so long as the Communist Party remains in power. I know that your position in recent years has not been far from mine, but I don't know what it would be if, for instance, there is another seeming rapprochement between Russia and the West, which is a possible development in the next few years. Or again in an actual war situation . . . I know Warburg and his opinions well enough to know that he is very unlikely ever to refuse anything of mine on political grounds.[28]

Gollancz finally realised that there was no point in continuing his strained relationship with Orwell. He wrote to him at the end of March 1947 with the news that he had decided to terminate their contract, in accordance with Orwell's wishes. He received a short reply on the day before Orwell left for Jura. It was only two sentences long. In the first Orwell explained that he was a little slow in replying because he had been ill. In the second he made the only comment which was necessary: 'Very many thanks for your generous action.'

Love and Death

I

Near the end of 1947, while he was living on Jura, Orwell was able to complete the first draft of *Nineteen Eighty-Four*, though he considered it 'a most dreadful mess' and thought that 'about two thirds of it will have to be rewritten entirely besides the usual touching up'.[1] A large part of the manuscript has survived, and it reveals that this book did in fact go through a long and apparently painful period of revision. Much of it was written in longhand and then typed, and then revised extensively by hand, and then typed again. He was clearly attempting to create a work which was more advanced in every way than anything he had written before. The pains he took with the book are obvious after even a cursory glance at the manuscript. Some pages are so heavily revised that it takes quite an effort to follow Orwell's complicated series of additions and subtractions in his draft. By and large, the changes were for stylistic purposes, not structural or thematic ones. He wanted to establish just the right tone for the novel, and he wanted to show in the very style of his own prose how much would be lost in a future world dominated by the impoverished vocabulary of Newspeak. Readers of the novel have been so absorbed by its riveting story that they have not paid enough attention to the excellence of so many of its passages of prose.

The process of writing the book would have been painful for Orwell even if his health had remained good throughout its composition, but in fact he experienced a steady decline in his ability to cope with the lung problems which had affected him for so long. He had tried to ignore those problems or to overcome them by sheer force of will. He did not want his weak condition to prevent him from doing whatever he wanted. During the summer of 1947 the weather on Jura was so clear and dry – six weeks without any rain – that he made the mistake of overexerting himself on long expeditions to various parts of the island, taking little care to guard his health. He was full of enthusiasm for these adventures, and his spirits were still high in the early autumn when he described his 'marvellous summer' in a letter to Celia Paget: 'We went for some wonderful picnics on the other side of the island, which is quite uninhabited but where there is an empty shepherd's cottage one can sleep in. It is a beautiful coast, green water and white sand, and a few miles inland lochs full of trout which never get fished because they're too far from anywhere.'[2]

His enthusiasm for this wild region caused him to make a frightening mistake one day in August. It began with an uneventful boat trip to Glengarrisdale Bay, on the uninhabited side of the island. He was accompanied by Avril and Richard, and by Marjorie's three children, who had come to Jura for a summer holiday. The oldest of these three was Henry Dakin, a young Army officer. Jane Dakin was in her early twenties, and her sister, Lucy, was still in her teens. The entire party went in Orwell's small fishing boat, which was powered by an outboard motor, and they all stayed in the shepherd's cottage near the bay, sleeping on blankets and piles of bracken. After two days of hiking, swimming and fishing, they were ready to make the return journey to Barnhill. Avril and Jane decided to go back to the house on foot – it was a rugged walk of about six miles from one side of the island to the other – while Orwell and the others went in the boat, going back the way they had come, round the northern tip of the island. The return would have been as uneventful as the voyage out if Orwell had not misjudged the tides. As the boat entered the Gulf of Corryvreckan, which separates Jura from the island of Scarba, they ran into trouble. Writing to Brenda Salkeld several days later, he explained how they had just barely escaped death:

Four of us including Richard were nearly drowned. We got into the whirlpool, owing to trying to go through the gulf at the wrong state of the tide, and the outboard motor was sucked off the boat. We managed to get out of it with the oars and then got to one of the little islands, just rocks covered with sea birds, which are dotted about there. The sea was pretty bad and the boat turned over as we were getting ashore, so that we lost everything we had including the oars and including 12 blankets. We might normally have expected to be there till next day, but luckily a boat came past some hours later and took us off. Luckily, also, it was a hot day and we managed to get a fire going and dry our clothes. Richard loved every moment of it except when he went into the water. The boat which picked us up put us off at the bay we used to call the W bay, and then we had to walk home over the hill, barefooted because most of our boots had gone with the other wreckage. Our boat luckily wasn't damaged apart from the loss of the engine, but I'm trying to get hold of a bigger one as these trips are really a bit too unsafe in a little rowing boat.[3]

'A bit too unsafe' was putting it mildly. He was extremely lucky to have manoeuvred his little boat out of danger in the notoriously treacherous waters of the Gulf of Corryvreckan. He managed it only because Henry Dakin was strong enough to row the boat away from the edge of the whirlpool after the engine had been lost. Orwell's casual disregard for danger was typical, but this time it almost cost not only his own life but also those of Henry, Lucy and Richard. Although Richard was too young to realise how frightening the situation had been, Lucy and Henry were well aware of it, and were surprised at how calmly 'Uncle Eric' had reacted to the situation. Lucy later recalled that while they had been struggling to escape from the whirlpool, Orwell had noticed a seal watching them as it swam along in the distance, and he had observed in a matter-of-fact way, 'Curious thing about seals, very inquisitive creatures.' Lucy thought that it was hardly the right moment to be pondering the habits of seals. Long after this episode, she remarked of her uncle, 'He was sweet and kind, but in another world.'[4]

He was so happy on Jura that he intended to spend the winter there. The decision to stay on was made easier by the fact that he and Avril had some extra help at the house. In September a young Scotsman named Bill Dunn had come to live at Barnhill as part of an arrangement which allowed him to farm the adjoining land. Richard Rees, who had been staying with Orwell during the summer, had entered into a partnership with Dunn, putting up £1000 to pay for livestock and equipment. Orwell liked the idea, and occasionally reported on the progress of the farm to friends. One letter to David Astor, written in 1948, gives some notion of how quickly the plan developed. 'The farm is building up. [Bill Dunn] has now got about 50 sheep and about 10 head of cattle, some of which are my property.' There was one fat pig on the farm whose time was quickly running out. He was 'to be baconed shortly', Orwell said, and would not be replaced. Perhaps understandably, the pig and the author of *Animal Farm* had not got along. 'I had never kept one before and shan't be sorry to see the last of this one. They are most annoying destructive animals, and hard to keep out of anywhere because they are so strong and cunning.'[5]

As much as Orwell was looking forward to staying on his island, he found that his health would not permit it. His active life during the summer and early autumn had taken its toll. In November – just as he was completing the first draft of *Nineteen Eighty-Four* – he suffered a bad coughing attack similar to other ones earlier in his life, and he experienced the dreadfully disturbing symptom of spitting up blood. He was taken to a small town near Glasgow – East Kilbride – where he was admitted to Hairmyres Hospital, an institution specialising in lung problems. Up to this point, he had never been diagnosed as having tuberculosis, though the presence of the disease in his lungs had long been suspected. If the condition had been active earlier, it had simply managed to escape detection for one reason or another. But this time the doctors were able to make a positive diagnosis of tuberculosis. Writing to John Middleton Murry from Hairmyres, Orwell explained that he had 'T.B.' and referred to it as 'the disease which was bound to claim me sooner or later'.[6]

He was given a new treatment for the disease, so new in fact that it was generally unavailable in England. It involved the use of the drug streptomycin, which had been invented in America in 1944. The doctors advised that it might help to curb the growth of the disease, and perhaps even cure it. To his great credit, David Astor came to the rescue, and arranged through family connections in America to have a special shipment of the drug sent to Orwell's hospital. Various tuberculosis patients in America had experienced dramatic improvements in their conditions after using the drug, and Orwell was hopeful that it would work for him. He was so sick this time that even he was willing to admit that he could no longer ignore the seriousness of his condition. In early 1948 the drug arrived from America and Orwell was given regular doses of it. David Astor was willing to help pay the costs of the treatment if they got out of hand. As a letter to Orwell's doctor – Bruce Dick – shows, Astor was not only a generous friend, but a tactful one as well. In February 1948 he wrote:

> As regards the cash situation, I am in communication with Blair on this and am trying to convince him that I would be very glad to help him in this matter. I would rather you did not mention to him that I had told you of my offer, as I think the only possibility of persuading him to be reasonable is that it should be a very private matter between him and me. But I mention it so that you will not hesitate to request me to get other stuff from over there which may be useful to him.[7]

At first, the effects of the drug were too strong for him. (It appears that he was given dosages which were far greater than he could tolerate.) His hair started falling out and his skin turned a frightening shade of red, though the condition of his lungs did improve. 'I am a lot better,' he wrote to Julian Symons in April 1948, 'but I had a bad fortnight with the secondary effects of the streptomycin. I suppose with all these drugs it's rather a case of sinking the ship to get rid of the rats.'[8] He was a brave patient. In early May he told Astor, 'My skin is still peeling off in places and my hair is coming out, but otherwise . . . I am a lot better. They let me up for an hour a day now and let me put a few clothes on, and I think they might let me out if only it was a bit warmer. I suppose it's too early to say whether the streptomycin has done its stuff, but any way they've had 4 negative reactions running, so the germs must have taken a pretty good knock.'9

During the rest of the spring his lungs continued to get better, and by July he was finally able to go home. His general condition, however, was still very weak from the powerful effects of the drug, and he would have been well advised not to return to the rough environment of Jura, but of course he went there anyway. And he did not bother to rest. Instead he picked up where he had left off with *Nineteen Eighty-Four* and began feverishly working on it, trying to finish it before the end of the year.

No one was able to make him slow down. Avril continued to look after him in the best way that she could, but she knew him too well to think that anything she said would stop him from trying to finish the book in the time he had set for himself. Richard Rees was staying at Barnhill during part of this period, and he also was unable to make his friend slow down. Orwell went to his bedroom and stayed for hours at a time writing the book. It was his last great obsession. Day after day he worked on the manuscript, without a break. In a way, it would have been better for him if he had gone back to London because at least there he would have been interrupted more often by visitors, by telephone calls and by the daily problems of life in a large city. But on Jura there were no interruptions, only the sound of the sea in the distance. He could work as though he were writing the book on another planet.

By November 1948 he had finished the novel, though it was in such a disorganised state that a fair version needed to be typed before it could be submitted to the printers. Orwell tried to arrange for a typist to do the work, but it was almost impossible to make such arrangements from Barnhill, especially since he preferred to have a typist come to the island to do the work. When a typist could not be found, he decided to do the entire job himself. 'I am on the grisly job of typing out my book,' he wrote to Astor on 19 November. He could easily have waited a few more weeks, or he could have moved to Glasgow and supervised the final preparation of the typescript there before sending it to Leonard Moore in London. But he was in no mood to wait. He wanted to make certain that it was finished as soon as possible, and the only way to get it done before the end of the year was simply to type all of it himself.

To make matters worse, his health began to decline rapidly. The good effects of the American drug had faded, and he was once again coughing and wheezing in an alarming way. All the same, he struggled to type the book sitting up at a desk or – when he became too tired – on a sofa with the typewriter balanced on his lap. He worked at amazing speed, and in about three weeks he had completely finished typing the book. In early December he sent it to London. By that stage he was coughing up blood again, and once more he was obliged to seek serious medical help. On 18 December he wrote to Tosco Fyvel, 'Everything is going well here except me.'[10]

This time Gwen O'Shaughnessy helped by finding him a place at a sanatorium high up in the Cotswolds at a village called Cranham in Gloucestershire. With Richard Rees to help him travel part of the way, he left Barnhill at the beginning of 1949 and made the long train journey to the sanatorium. Rees recalled that his friend was 'very weak, though mentally as active as ever and full of ideas for future work – a novel, and essays on Conrad, Gissing and Evelyn Waugh'.[11] On 6 January, Orwell arrived at the sanatorium. Within a week of his arrival, he was given a new drug – PAS (para-amino-salicylic acid). He joked to Astor that it sounded 'rather as if it was just aspirin in disguise'. Sadly, it did not work in his case. It simply made him feel 'sick all the time', as he put it. He was then given more streptomycin, but as he told Gwen O'Shaughnessy the results were 'dreadful', and the treatment had to be stopped after only a single dose.[12]

These drugs were so new that no doctor had enough experience with them to understand the best way to use them in treating advanced cases such as Orwell's. He may have benefited from smaller doses, or from a combination of drugs and other forms of treatment. Unfortunately, the most potent drug – isoniazid – was not developed for use in tuberculosis cases until 1952, which was two years too late for Orwell.[13] But the fact that he was given PAS at the sanatorium in Cranham shows that he was receiving the very latest treatment for the disease. The doctors there seem to have made every effort to achieve an improvement in his condition. He was expected to rest as much as possible, and though he did not like the idea of forsaking work, he wanted to be co-operative. As he explained to Jack Common, 'I've got to do damn-all, including not trying to work, for a long time, possibly as long as a year or two, though I trust it won't be quite as bad as that. It's an awful bore, but I am obeying orders, as I do want to stay alive at least 10 years, I've got such a lot of work to do besides Richard to look after.'[14]

To keep up his spirits, he liked to dream of the day when he would be allowed to fish again. 'I have discovered that there is a stream just near here with trout in it,' he wrote to Richard Rees, 'so when I am somewhere near the point of getting up I'll ask Avril to send me my fishing things.'[15] Although he was not supposed to do any serious writing, he did keep a notebook at Cranham and jotted down some random observations. One day in March he set himself the task of composing a precise description of his surroundings:

> I live in a so-called chalet, one of a row of continuous wooden huts, with glass doors, each chalet measuring abt 15' by 12'. There are hot water pipes, a washing basin, a chest of drawers & wardrobe, besides the usual bed-tables etc. Outside is a glass-roofed verandah. Everything is brought by hand – none of those abominable rattling trolleys which one is never out of the sound of in a hospital. Not much noise of radios either – all the patients have headphones ... The most persistent sound is the song of birds.[16]

While he was at Cranham he may have made some additions to another notebook which he had been keeping for a couple of years. It contained his private list of people in the West whom he suspected of being 'crypto'-communists. He was fearful that 'enormous mischief' could be done by 'apologists of the Stalin regime' who pretended to be politically independent, and in 1947 he had publicly quarrelled with one Labour MP – Konni Zilliacus – over the issue. He had accused Zilliacus of being one of several 'crypto-communists' in Parliament, and when this statement was vehemently denied by the politician, Orwell refused to withdraw his charge. In *Tribune* he wrote, 'What I believe, and will go on believing until I see evidence to the contrary, is that [Zilliacus] and others like him are pursuing a policy barely distinguishable from that of the C. P., in that they are in effect the publicity agents of the USSR in this country, and that when Soviet and British interests appear to them to clash, they will support the Soviet interest.'[17] Orwell wanted to know where prominent people stood politically, and he was suspicious of those who were evasive about it. For him, it was a question of basic honesty, and he expected Stalin's British supporters to be forthright about their views if they were willing to make their case fairly. But he had no sympathy for conservatives who wanted to outlaw any open political activity by communists. 'To suppress the Communist Party *now*, or at any time when it did not unmistakably endanger national survival, would be calamitous,' he wrote in the *New Leader* in 1947. 'One has only to think of the people who would approve!'[18]

His notebook lists over a hundred names of possible 'cryptos', many belonging to people he did not know personally. It is a random list which mixes very famous personalities with obscure writers, and much of it is based on pure speculation. In compiling it, he seems to have had the assistance of Richard Rees, who later spoke of their collection of names as 'a sort of game we played – discussing who was a paid agent of what and estimating to what lengths of treachery our favourite betes noires would be prepared to go'.[19] The notebook includes such names as Nancy Cunard, C. Day Lewis, the Indian writer Cedric Dover, the Labour politician Tom Driberg, the *Picture Post* editor Tom Hopkinson, Kingsley Martin, Sean O'Casey, J. B. Priestley, Michael Redgrave, Paul Robeson, G. B. Shaw, John Steinbeck, and Orson Welles. Beside many of the names are personal comments. The scientist Solly Zuckerman is described as being a 'strong sympathiser only', with the added comments, 'Could change. Politically ignorant.' Next to Sean O'Casey's name is the annotation, 'Very stupid', and next to Kingsley Martin's name is the observation, 'Decayed liberal. Very dishonest.'[20]

Orwell was doubtful that some of the names on his list really belonged there, but he included them anyway because he was engaged in a continuous exercise of determining who was sincere and who was not. It was primarily to satisfy his own curiosity. Some names have a question mark beside them, some names have been crossed out, and ample space has been left for additions. What he was up to is explained in an indirect way in his *New Leader* comments on the 'cryptos':

> The important thing to do with these people – and it is extremely difficult, since one has only inferential evidence – is to sort them out and determine which of them is honest and which is not . . . They have undoubtedly done a great deal of mischief, especially in confusing public opinion about the nature of the puppet regimes in eastern Europe; but one ought not hurriedly to assume that they all hold the same opinions. Probably some of them are actuated by nothing worse than stupidity.[21]

II

During Orwell's first month at Cranham, Fredric Warburg came to see him about his novel. Warburg had already written to say how much he liked the book. He recognised what an important novel *Nineteen Eighty-Four* is, and was willing to make every effort to publish it in a way which would please his author. He planned to have proofs of the book ready in March, and to publish it in June. In the meantime there was the matter of the title. As late as January 1949 the choice was still in doubt. But when Warburg visited Orwell on the 21st, the two men agreed that 'Nineteen Eighty-Four' was better than 'The Last Man in Europe', and the question was settled then and there, though only with regard to the British edition. As Orwell said in a letter to Leonard Moore the next day, he did not mind if the American edition bore a different title. Earlier in the month Moore had sold the American rights to Harcourt Brace, and apparently the firm had expressed some reservations about using 'Nineteen Eighty-Four' for the title. In response to this news, Orwell told his agent, 'I doubt whether it hurts a book to be published under different names in Britain and the USA – certainly it is often done – and I would like Harcourt Brace to follow their own wishes in the matter of the title.'[22]

In the matter of the text itself he was not willing to accept any alterations, and he was adamant on this point when cuts in the novel were suggested by the Book-of-the-Month Club in America. He was led to believe that the Club would take the novel only if he cut the appendix on Newspeak and the long section devoted to Emmanuel Goldstein's 'The Theory and Practice of Oligarchical Collectivism'. Warburg later wrote that Orwell risked the loss of 'a minimum of £40,000' by refusing to make these cuts, but the integrity of the book meant more to him than even this enormous sum. On 17 March he wrote to Moore, 'A book is built up as a balanced structure and one cannot simply remove large chunks here and there unless one is ready to recast the whole thing ... I really cannot allow my work to be mucked about beyond a certain point, and I doubt whether it even pays in the long run.' He was right, of course, and fortunately for him, the Club decided to see things his way. Three weeks later he announced to Richard Rees, 'I have just had a cable saying that the Book-of-the-Month Club have accepted my novel after all, in spite of my refusing to make the changes they demanded. So that shows that virtue is its own reward, or honesty, is the best policy, I forget which.'[23]

Both the American and the British publishers brought out the novel in June, and the acclaim was immediate on both sides of the Atlantic. In the *New Statesman* V. S. Pritchett wrote that it was 'impossible to put the book down', and in the *New Yorker* Lionel Trilling called the book 'profound, terrifying, and wholly fascinating'. The *Evening Standard* called it 'the most important book published since the war'. In July the *New York Times Book Review* reported that the novel had received sixty reviews in American publications, and that ninety per cent were 'overwhelmingly admiring, with cries of terror rising above the applause'.[24]

It is Orwell's most compelling work, and its enormous success over the years is well deserved, but it is also his most misunderstood work. Endless theories have been put forward to explain its vision of the future, but not many critics have been willing to see how firmly rooted it is in Orwell's past. Almost every aspect of Orwell's life is in some way represented in the book. Winston Smith's yearning for the green wilderness of the 'Golden Country' is very much connected to Orwell's long-standing affection for the lost Edwardian world of his childhood in Henley. The objects of that older world have been discarded as 'junk' in Big Brother's world, but Winston tries to hold onto a few pieces of this 'junk' as a way of maintaining his links with the past. In a similar way Orwell spent a good deal of time in the 1940s, while he was living in London, haunting junk shops with mountains of old, apparently useless items from another age. Just as Winston finds a beautiful paperweight in an old shop and clings to it as though it were a kind of life preserver, so Orwell praised junk shops in the *Evening Standard* in 1946 – celebrating the joys of 'useless' relics from a time long before Hitler and Stalin and atom bombs. He specifically mentioned his delight at discovering 'glass paperweights with pictures at the bottom. There are others that have a piece of coral enclosed in the glass.'[25] Winston's, of course, has a piece of coral embedded in it, and he examines it intently, surprised that anything so delicate could survive in a brutal age.

Orwell's experience of bullying at St Cyprian's cannot be discounted as an influence on *Nineteen Eighty-Four*. He was working on 'Such, Such Were the Joys' when he was in the early stages of writing the novel, and there is an overlapping of theme between the two works. Both are concerned with the ways in which people can be manipulated to look up to their tormentors as superior beings who should be respected – even loved – rather than as the objects of the hate which they have earned. Young Eric Blair was made to feel guilty because he did not love Mrs Wilkes, and he took comfort in knowing that, in his heart of hearts, he felt only hatred for her. Likewise, Winston must struggle against the temptation to love Big Brother, fighting back the desire to surrender his hatred in the face of overwhelming power. He feels just as helpless against such power as young Eric felt in the face of Mrs Wilkes's authority.

For models of authoritarian power at work Orwell could look to incidents from his life in the Indian Imperial Police, his experiences in Barcelona when the government was trying to suppress the POUM, and his encounters with the absurdities of wartime censorship – at the BBC as well as in his ordinary work as a journalist. It is not the case, by any means, that these relatively mild forms of tyranny are worthy of any close comparison with Big Brother's nightmarish rule, but all of these elements helped to give Orwell a certain feel for the life which he describes in the novel, a life which is ultimately the work of his imagination, but which is based on real experience. When he describes torture in the novel, for example, he is able to draw on his memories of milder forms of torture – both mental and physical – at St Cyprian's, and in Burma. And when he describes the mindless, never-ending warfare, with bombs exploding randomly every day, he had only to recall the sensations he felt during the Blitz, and later during the attacks from Hitler's V-1 flying bombs and V-2 rockets. The cold, drab environment – with its scarcities and bad food – is partly a reflection of conditions in Britain during much of the 1940s.

It is easy to forget that *Nineteen Eighty-Four* is a love story, but the oppressive gloom of the State's control is briefly lifted when Winston and Julia are able to enjoy their secret moments together. For them sex becomes a form of liberation, a way not only of rebelling against the dictates of the Party, but also a means by which they can enjoy the sense of freedom in the release of passion. Julia's uninhibited approach to sex is portrayed as a hopeful sign of the ordinary person's determination to be free of outside restrictions, no matter how beneficial they may be in the abstract. The Party is eager to control the sex instinct because it is the one area in each person's life which is so resistant to outside restrictions. If the Party can kill the sex instinct, it can strengthen its control over everyone, but Winston and Julia show that destroying such a powerful urge is impossible, and that the mere expression of that urge can be a valid form of protest against Big Brother. It is a reaffirmation of life in the face of Big Brother's attempt to eliminate all signs of a vital existence among his subjects.

After the novel's publication Orwell insisted that he had not tried to be a prophet, that he was trying only to warn the world against the threat of totalitarianism, whether from the Right or the Left. His vision, however, is so realistic and compelling that readers from his day onwards have come away from the novel feeling that they have been given a prediction. Big Brother's power is regarded as a force which will rise up at some point in the future and crush humanity. The fact that this vision is so believable is a tribute to Orwell's imaginative use of so many strands of his experience to create a plausible version of an all-powerful state. But it is still an imaginative act, and it was not the work of a man who wanted to overwhelm his readers with pessimism. He wanted to shock them into resisting forces which might some day impose more and more controls over their lives, and if they heeded his warning, the terrors of '1984' could be avoided. The year was an arbitrary choice, and despite the fact that many people in the Fifties, Sixties, Seventies and early Eighties took it seriously as a 'dreaded year', Orwell did not mean for it to represent anything other than a general date in the future, conveniently switching the last two digits of the year in which he completed the book – 1948. The fact that he was willing to allow his American publishers to use another title is one indication that he did not regard the year as a crucial feature of his book. His alternative title, 'The Last Man in Europe', is less striking, but it does convey the notion of a long struggle against tyranny which might come down to the last free man having to decide whether he will love Big Brother or die fighting him. The implication is that many more must make that decision before it falls to the last man, and it will come to him only if those countless others have made the wrong decision first.

Orwell's concern that someone like Big Brother might gain power in Europe was real enough, and in Stalin's Russia there was a sobering example of what such a mighty figure could do. Orwell was wary of the communist threat to the rest of Europe, and his fears multiplied after the war, when the expansionist policies of the Soviet Union were a distinct danger. But it was not only the Soviets who worried him – it was any powerful state which might be tempted to bully its own citizens, as well as those of other countries. In the novel the former British subjects of Airstrip One are part of an empire which includes America. This does not necessarily mean that Big Brother is American – simply that his empire is dominated by his largest possession, and its standards have been imposed on smaller places. The currency of his realm is the dollar. But Big Brother is neither a capitalist nor a communist. His ambition lies in the brute exercise of power, and his only real allies are fear and hate.

In a letter to Francis A. Henson, of the United Automobile Workers in America, Orwell made it clear that *Nineteen Eighty-Four* is a warning against totalitarian methods in general, regardless of time or place: 'The scene of the book is laid in Britain in order to emphasise that the English-speaking races are not innately better than anyone else and that totalitarianism, *if not fought against*, could triumph anywhere.' (The italics are Orwell's.) He also made it clear that he did not see his book as a specific assault on socialism. He had grave doubts about its future, but he never stopped being a socialist. 'My recent novel is NOT intended as an attack on Socialism or on the British Labour Party (of which I am a supporter) but as a show-up of the perversions to which a centralised economy is liable and which have already been partly realised in Communism and Fascism.'[26]

For years Orwell had been moving towards the conclusion that dictators such as Hitler and Stalin used ideology to provide a smokescreen for their naked abuse of power. It was simplistic to think of Hitler as a fascist, or of Stalin as a communist. In both their cases the one true purpose, which came before all else, was the establishment of totalitarian rule. And, unfortunately, the worship of power for its own sake is not limited to any particular group of people. Its appeal is widespread, and once a leader begins to exploit it effectively, it can grow by great leaps until it encounters another force which can meet its power with equal power. As a correspondent in Occupied Germany at the end of the war, Orwell had a brief glimpse of what life might be like in a world divided by large powers into 'zones of influence'. He reported on the pressures being exerted by the Soviet Zone on the other powers, and suspected that at some point – if these pressures were not resisted – they might lead to a war, or perhaps even a condition of more or less permanent warfare among the various zones. He suggests such a possibility in his novel, in which the big powers who have divided the world into zones of influence wage constant war with each other.

Arthur Koestler's interest in power politics – in *Darkness at Noon*, 'The Yogi and the Commissar', and other works – helped to influence Orwell's thinking in *Nineteen Eighty-Four*, but the entire range of influences is enormous because the novel is a kind of summing up for Orwell, a representation of ideas and influences which had been at work in his mind for two decades and more. Some influences went back many years – such as Jack London's *The Iron Heel* (1909) and Aldous Huxley's *Brave New World* (1930) – and some were fairly recent in their impact on Orwell, such as Zamyatin's *We* (1923), which Orwell read for the first time in the mid-1940s, and James Burnham's *The Managerial Revolution*, which was written in 1940 and discussed at length by Orwell in 1946 in an article for *Polemic* magazine. Occasionally, a critic will come forward and announce that Orwell's novel is 'unoriginal' because certain aspects of its plot resemble elements in one of these books, or in some other work. But such thinking assumes that the quality of Orwell's prose is not a vital part of his novel's originality. His distinctive style places his novel on a plane high above his various 'models'. Certainly no one is likely to find in Zamyatin or Burnham a paragraph which can match the resonant power of Winston's effort to explain his fondness for the glass paperweight: 'I don't think it was ever put to any use. That's what I like about it. It's a little chunk of history that they've forgotten to alter. It's a message from a hundred years ago, if one knew how to read it.'

Of all the writers who influenced Orwell's thinking in his novel, Burnham is one who deserves a close examination, not because he inspired Orwell in a positive fashion, but because he gave him an identifiable position to react against in a very specific way. Orwell was always at his best when he was on the attack, and his *Polemic* essay on Burnham is a brilliant criticism of the whole concept of power worship. More important, Orwell does not simply react to

Burnham. He uses the rubble of Burnham's argument to construct his own positive view, and this view has great relevance to *Nineteen Eighty-Four*.

In his essay Orwell rejects Burnham's idea that great men and great powers control the destiny of the world. Burnham sees raw force at work in the world making things happen in sudden, dramatic ways, and he discounts the power of ordinary people to resist these giant powers. Orwell, however, says that Burnham and others who share his fondness for power have misunderstood the nature of historical change. 'Power worship blurs political judgement because it leads, almost unavoidably, to the belief that present trends will continue. Whoever is winning at the moment will always seem to be invincible.' Orwell points out that the great power that is feared one year is often destroyed by its own overreaching ambition within a few years and inevitably loses its aura of invincibility, if not its actual force. He argues that there is good reason to believe that this fate will overtake Stalin's Russia, just as it overtook Hitler's Germany. 'The Russian regime will either democratize itself, or it will perish.' He is hopeful that one way or another the regime will die because he thinks that the common man will triumph in the end. Winston Smith may fail, but the proles have it within their power to destroy Big Brother at any minute if they desire it. The key thing is to bring the restraining force of public opinion into play. As long as it has a chance to make itself heard, the State will have to curb its appetite for power. He makes this point well in a comment on Hitler's fall:

> The immediate cause of the German defeat was the unheard-of folly of attacking the USSR, while Britain was still undefeated and America was manifestly getting ready to fight. Mistakes of this magnitude can only be made, or at any rate they are most likely to be made, in countries where public opinion has no power. So long as the common man can get a hearing, such elementary rules as not fighting all your enemies simultaneously are less likely to be violated.[27]

Under Big Brother's rule it is certainly true that public opinion has no power, but that is because the common people have not awakened to the fact that they have always had the power to make their voices heard. 'If there was hope, it lay in the proles,' the novel declares. 'You had to cling on to that.' Whether the proles will rise up and refuse to be a part of a slave system is something which Orwell cannot be sure of, but he does not abandon that hope.

It is true that Orwell was a sick and dying man when he wrote *Nineteen Eighty-Four*, and to some extent the pain of his illness cast a gloom over the book. It is likely, however, that the novel would have been just as gloomy if he had been healthy. He never meant to make the conclusion of his story sweet and pleasant. The conclusion to his previous full-length novel, *Coming Up for Air*, is nearly as dark as the end of the later book. War is coming, George Bowling sees, and the bombs will fall no matter what anyone does, but perhaps some good will come of the destruction. Winston Smith confesses his crime before the ultimate managerial type – O'Brien – who is happy to make all kinds of specious apologies for the State, and who enjoys breaking Winston's will because its stubborn quality is such a challenge.

But the reader is not a passive figure who sees George Bowling's depressing view of the future – or *Nineteen Eighty-Four*'s even more depressing view of the future – and concludes that such things must come to pass. In both novels there is a powerful subtext at work. While readers follow the main text to its final, dark vision, there is a subtext keeping before the reader many reminders of the price which will have to be paid if the dark vision becomes a reality. In *Coming Up for Air* Hitler's bombs must not destroy all vestiges of the Golden World of Lower Binfield as it was before the last war. Something of that world must be preserved. Not just its relics, but something of its sensibility. There must be a place in the modern world for things which have no power associated with them, things which are not meant to advance someone's cause, nor to make someone's fortune, nor to assert someone's will over someone else. There must be room, in other words, for paperweights and fishing rods and penny sweets and leather hammers used as children's toys.

And there must be time for wandering among old churchyards and making the perfect cup of tea and balancing caterpillars on a stick and falling in love. All these things are derided as sentimental and trivial by intellectuals who have no time for them, but they are the things which form the real texture of a life. *Nineteen Eighty-Four* makes it clear what life would be like without them, and it is that subtext which makes Orwell's strongest point for something hopeful in the future. Readers see Winston fail, but they also see how a whole society failed years before '1984' when the people of that society allowed the State to strip them systematically of their right to be sentimental and trivial, taking away their rich language and replacing it with an ugly, utilitarian one, and denying them the ordinary pleasures of a private life. Big Brother is a powerful image in the novel, but so is Winston's paperweight and his Golden Country. If people are willing to fight for such things, and are willing to see that the freedom to enjoy them means more than any '-ism' or any leader, then there will be hope for the future.

III

It is sometimes said that Orwell had a death-wish. It would be better to say that his life-wish was too extreme. He ruined his health writing his last novel, but he did not make this sacrifice because he wanted to die. He wanted to affirm a hope and project a warning to a world which he wanted to save from catastrophe. He drove himself so hard because there were too many things which he wanted to accomplish, and he could not stop himself from pursuing goals once he had set them. His behaviour was irrational and extreme, but it was not part of some death-wish. As he said in *Homage to Catalonia* when he described his feelings after being shot, he did not want to leave this world which he had come to love so well. And in the aftermath of finishing *Nineteen Eighty-Four*, he did not slowly sink towards death without putting up a terrific struggle. 'Don't think I am making up my mind to peg out,' he told Fredric Warburg. 'On the contrary, I have the strongest reason for wanting to stay alive.'[28] He fought with all his strength to cling to life, planning new articles and books to write, dreaming of returning to his island, and hoping for one last chance at marriage.

In the spring of 1949 he received a visit from Sonia Brownell at the sanatorium in the Cotswolds where he was staying. She came to see how he was progressing, and to see what she could do to help him. She felt genuinely sorry for him, but she was also more interested in him as a result of the continuing success of *Animal Farm*, and the brilliant début of *Nineteen Eighty-Four*. It was clear that his reputation was rising faster than that of any other writer in his generation, and she wanted to have a part in that. She had always been attracted to men who seemed to have potential for achieving greatness in some branch of culture, and she wanted to encourage and promote that potential. She had tried to devote her consider-able energies to promoting William Coldstream and Lucian Freud, both of whom were lovers of hers in the Forties, and just before she visited Orwell in 1949 she had been having an affair with Maurice Merleau-Ponty, the French philosopher. She admired him enor-mously, and had hoped he would leave his wife and marry her, but he broke off the affair that summer. She could never get him to say that he loved her without qualification. Like a good philosopher, he used to say to her, 'I love you, I think.'[29] Finally, he decided that he did not love her at all and told her so. The news hurt her a great deal, and when she went to see Orwell she was feeling rejected and vulnerable, so much so that she did not say no when Orwell reminded her of his earlier marriage proposal. She did not say yes right away either, but she was interested in the idea, and gave herself some time to think it over.

She did not love Orwell and had doubts about the merits of his work,but she knew that if they married she would have money and a good cause to fight for – Orwell was the cause and his growing royalties represented the money. Moreover, her job at *Horizon* was in doubt because Connolly was threatening to close the magazine at the end of the year, and she was anxious to make some arrangement for securing her future after her editorial job was finished. But quite apart from any financial considerations, she did have a sincere desire to help Orwell in his struggle to stay alive, and she thought that he might live for at least a few more years with her assistance. 'She could see that she made him very happy,' her friend Diana Witherby recalled, 'and making him happy made her happy. She liked that, though it was never a case of actually being in love with him. That's the part that surprised me. I knew she wanted a real romance in her life, and I didn't think she would accept a loveless marriage.'[30]

Orwell wanted so much to stay alive that he thought his marriage to Sonia might provide the extra inspiration he needed to continue fighting for his life. She had been the object of his fantasies, and marrying her would be a dream come true. He presented to her a case not unlike that which he had given to Anne Popham and Celia Paget. He was much older, his health was bad, and he might die at any time. On the other hand he wanted someone to take care of him and to help him stay alive, and the reward would be the income from his books. There was a good chance that he might live for several years longer, but if he died he wanted Sonia to manage his estate for him. He knew that she was well qualified to deal with publishers and agents, given her experience at *Horizon*, and he knew that she would be tough about it, which is what he wanted. By July she had given him her answer. Yes, she would marry him. Orwell was delighted, but he wanted to keep their intentions a secret for a little while, though he did share the news with Astor in mid-July. 'I intend getting married again. I suppose everyone will be horrified, but it seems to me a good idea.'[31]

At the beginning of September he was moved to University College Hospital, London, where a chest specialist – Dr Andrew Morland – had agreed to treat him. (In 1930, when Morland was a young doctor, he treated D. H. Lawrence for tuberculosis, but had been unable to prevent the disease from taking the life of his famous patient.) Morland was a friend of Warburg's and had examined Orwell at Cranham a few months earlier, at which time he had concluded, 'With further rest I do not anticipate a cure but he might well reach a stage at which he could do several hours writing a day combined with physical rest. He would then reach the stage which we call the "good chronic", i.e. able to potter about and do a few hours sedentary work.'[32] Orwell had wanted Dr Morland to be frank about the number of years which might be left to him. 'I know doctors hate committing themselves on that,' he had said to Warburg, 'but I won't hold it against him if he's wrong.' All that Morland would tell him was that he had 'quite a good chance of staying alive for some years'.[33] The doctor had visited him again at Cranham in August and had made the suggestion at that time that he come to his hospital in London for further treatment. By that stage Orwell felt that any change might be an improvement. To David Astor, he wrote:

> I feel so ghastly, I can't write more than a scrawl to thank you for sending those nice vases & the flowers ... I have these ghastly temps. every day, sometimes up to 103. Morland nevertheless thinks I am not doing badly & says he doesn't notice any deterioration in me between his two visits. He wants me to move to his own hospital, University College Hospital. It's doubtful whether there's any other treatment they can try on me, but he thinks, & the other people here seem to agree, that a change might do me good. So I shall probably be moving there soon ... I can't write more, I'm really too shaky, as you can see from my handwriting perhaps.[34]

One advantage of being at University College Hospital was that Sonia lived only a short distance away – in Percy Street – and could visit him regularly. The basic plan for his treatment in London was not complicated. It involved primarily keeping him at rest as much as possible. He was too ill to be subjected to more vigorous treatment, but the notion was that as soon as he showed some definite signs of improvement, he could be moved to another sanatorium in the Swiss Alps, where presumably the mountain air would help his lungs. In the 1920s Dr Morland had been medical superintendent of the Palace Sanatorium at Montana, in the Valais, and he recommended the place to Orwell, who approved the choice. In the meantime he could do nothing more strenuous than write short notes to people and take satisfaction from studying the wide press coverage which accompanied the publication of his novel. Thanks to the large sale to the Book-of-the-Month Club, he had all the money he needed to pay his hospital bills, and to support Richard and Avril, and a good deal more to spare. In September, Sonia took some of what he had to spare and used it to buy an expensive engagement ring for herself. It was described by a reporter for one London newspaper as having a design made up of rubies, diamonds and an emerald. According to the paper, the 'blue-eyed thirty-year-old' had chosen it herself 'because she thought it pretty'.[35]

On 13 October the couple married in a brief ceremony held at Orwell's bedside in the hospital. David Astor acted as best man, and Sonia was accompanied by her friends Janetta Woolley and Robert Kee, who was Janetta's husband at the time. The hospital chaplain, a Reverend Braine, conducted the ceremony. The scene was still sharply etched in Janetta's memory nearly forty years later:

> His room was very small, and it felt crowded even though there were just a few of us. In the corner was a hospital trolley with a bottle of champagne brought by Sonia. Robert stood beside her, and David Astor and I stood on the other side of Orwell's bed. I don't think he ever got out of his bed. He sat up during the wedding, and I remember him smiling. He was beaming with pleasure. It obviously made him very happy, and I must say that I found the whole ceremony extremely moving.[36]

Afterwards they went to the Ritz for a wedding dinner, with Orwell remaining behind in his bed.

For the next three months Sonia visited him each day, and took care of his business affairs, answering his correspondence and making arrangements for his move to Switzerland. His condition became progressively worse, and by the end of the year he was shrunken and his complexion looked like wax. He had so little fat on him that the hospital staff had difficulty finding places on his body where they could give him injections. Stephen Spender visited him and later gave a painful description of Sonia's tendency to play the part of 'a bossy hospital nurse'. One day she came into Orwell's room while he was talking to Spender about D. H. Lawrence's death from tuberculosis:

> 'Oh, do let's stop talking about this. Let's talk about something cheerful,' said Sonia, suddenly like a bossy hospital nurse. Then she explained that she had to go to a cocktail party, and would not be back that evening. Orwell protested faintly, but she put him off, in her bustling way.[37]

He had many visitors, but perhaps the saddest thing about his long stay at University College Hospital was that he saw very little of Richard while he was there. He was very fearful that his son might pick up the tubercular infection as a result of being near him, and so Avril kept him away except for a few brief visits. This forced separation from Richard was heart-rending. 'I am so afraid of his growing away from me,' he had written earlier in the year, 'or getting to think of me as just a person who is always lying down & can't play. Of course children can't understand illness. He used to come to me & say, "Where have you hurt yourself?" – I suppose the only reason he could see for always being in bed.'[38]

Despite the decline in his health, he wanted to go on to the Swiss sanatorium at the beginning of the year, and his doctors agreed. A special plane was chartered to take him there. So hopeful was he about the chances of eventually recovering that he persuaded one of his friends to buy him a new fishing rod so that he could use it in the mountain streams after the sanatorium had worked its magic on him. Then he would return to England, he hoped, and resume life somewhere in the country with Richard and Sonia at his side. Referring to Sonia, he told Humphrey Dakin, 'I've got someone who will love me now.'[39]

He was due to leave on Wednesday, 25 January 1950, and Sonia had found a friend who was willing to help her take him to Switzerland. He was her former lover Lucian Freud. Everything was set for the journey, and on the Friday before they were to leave, Sonia and Lucian were in a good mood. They went to a nightclub in Soho with their friend Anne Dunn, and stayed late into the evening. And then Sonia was called to the telephone. The hospital had managed to find her, and they were calling to tell her about her husband. Shortly after midnight Eric Blair had died. His lungs had finally given out, and there was nothing that could be done to save him. The date was 21 January 1950. He was forty-six.

Among the papers he left behind was a notebook with an entry which is headed, 'Death Dreams'. It describes the dreams which had troubled him for almost two years. He wanted to know what they meant:

> Sometimes of the sea or the sea shore – more often of enormous, splendid buildings or streets or ships, in which I often lose my way, but always with a peculiar feeling of happiness & of waking in sunlight. Unquestionably all these buildings etc. mean death – I am almost aware of this even in the dream, & these dreams always become more frequent when my health gets worse & I begin to despair of ever recovering. What I can never understand is *why*, since I am not afraid of death (afraid of pain, & of the moment of dying, but not of *extinction*), this thought has to appear in my dreams under these various disguises.[40]

He was always analysing, always standing to one side and observing, trying to make some sense of this life. Perhaps, before the end, there was time for one last analysis, one brief thought about the final adventure. Whatever it was, it does not matter that it was lost. The voice remains. I can hear it. It begins, 'Curiously enough . . .'

Epilogue

Orwell stated in his will that he wanted to be buried 'according to the rites of the Church of England', and though he did not belong to any parish church, his request was honoured. Anthony Powell and Malcolm Muggeridge arranged for the funeral service to be held at Christ Church, near Regent's Park. The vicar – the Reverend W. V. C. Rose – had never heard of Orwell, but Muggeridge was able to persuade him that the deceased was 'a writer of distinction' who deserved special consideration. An announcement of the funeral appeared in *The Times* on 25 January, the day that Orwell was supposed to have gone to Switzerland: 'BLAIR – on Jan. 21, 1950, in hospital, ERIC ARTHUR BLAIR (George Orwell). Funeral Service at Christ Church, Albany Street, N.W.1, to-morrow (Thursday), at 11 a.m. Flowers may be sent to Leverton & Sons, Ltd. [Funeral Directors], 212, Eversholt Street, Euston, N.W.1.' The day of the funeral was cold, and the church was unheated. Fredric Warburg greeted the mourners at the door. Inez Holden remembered him saying over and over, 'How good of you to come.'[1] Powell chose the lesson from the last chapter of Ecclesiastes, and Muggeridge later noted in his diary the poignant effect of listening to such lines as 'Man goeth to his long home, and the mourners go about the streets.'[2]

This traditional ceremony was followed by another at the graveside. Orwell had wanted to be buried in a country churchyard, and David Astor found a place for him in the village of Sutton Courteney, Oxfordshire, where the Astors had an estate. The vicar

485

of the village church – the Reverend Gordon Dunstan – happened to be an admirer of Orwell's work and was quick to give his consent to the burial. The church, part of which was built in the thirteenth century, stands near the Thames and is called All Saints. Orwell is not the only famous person buried in the churchyard. His grave lies very close to the imposing tomb of Herbert Asquith, the man who was Prime Minister when Eric Blair was a boy. Orwell did not know that he would be buried at All Saints – Astor approached Reverend Gordon Dunstan with the request after his friend's death – but he would have appreciated the fact that the Thames Valley, which he loved so much, has become his final resting place. There is nothing on his headstone to indicate that he achieved fame as a writer. He is buried under his own name, in accordance with his wish, and the inscription follows the simple form given in his will:

HERE LIES
ERIC ARTHUR BLAIR
BORN JUNE 25TH 1903
DIED JANUARY 21ST 1950

The settlement of his estate was a straightforward business. There was a large insurance policy to benefit young Richard Blair, but the rest of his money – including future royalties on all his books – went to his wife. Orwell may have believed that Sonia would bring up Richard, but she did not have any desire to be a mother and left the five-year-old boy in the care of Avril, who was happy to continue looking after him. 'Sonia obviously didn't want Rick,' Jane Dakin recalled.[3] But Avril made a good home for him. She married Bill Dunn in February 1951 and moved from Barnhill to a farm on the mainland of Scotland, and there Richard grew up. Avril outlived Orwell by many years, surviving to the age of seventy.

In the meantime Sonia tried to make a new life for herself, with the help of Orwell's money. Her period of mourning was short. Two months after her husband's death she went to the South of France for a long holiday, and invited Merleau-Ponty to join her. She was still in love with him, and was hopeful that he would want to revive their affair. Something went wrong, however, and they parted in anger. She gave Cyril Connolly a general account of what happened when she met him in St Tropez. In April 1950 Connolly mentioned their meeting in a letter to Lys Lubbock, who had worked with Sonia at *Horizon* (the magazine published its last issue in January 1950.) 'Had very nice lunch with Sonia,' Connolly wrote, 'who seemed well . . . She made it up with Merleau P. who came down south & went to Les Baux & Saint Tropez with her, but then they had a frightful row and parted, she says now for ever.'[4]

Although she was legally 'Mrs Blair', Sonia began using 'Orwell' as her surname, and as the popularity of her late husband's work increased in the 1950s and 1960s, she achieved a certain measure of fame as the widow of the famous author.[5] She was an active figure in the literary world. In the 1950s she worked as an editor at the publishing house of Weidenfeld and Nicolson, and in the 1960s she was co-editor of a small magazine called *Art and Literature*, which was based in Paris. (One of her fellow editors was the poet John Ashbery.)

She used her influence and editorial skills to promote Orwell's reputation in two major projects. With the assistance of David Astor and Richard Rees, she established the George Orwell Archive in the Library of University College, London. The collection was opened in 1960, and its large number of manuscripts, letters, books, and articles have made it an invaluable centre for research on Orwell's life, his works, and his era in history. A few years later Sonia gave inspiration and direction to a second project – the publication of a four-volume edition of Orwell's essays, journalism and letters. Much of the difficult work of establishing dates and tracking down obscure materials and references was done by Ian Angus, who was in charge of the Orwell Archive at the time. He and Sonia shared the editorial credit for the volumes.

When the edition came out in 1968, it created a strong resurgence of interest in Orwell, and gave abundant evidence of the wide range of his talents and interests. Sonia also hoped that it would eliminate the need for a biography, and in her brief introduction she claimed, 'With these present volumes the picture [of Orwell's life] is as complete as it can be.' Although the volumes themselves were full of fascinating information, Sonia made the mistake of insisting that they were the work of a relatively uncomplicated character. She seems to have been sincere in her belief that Orwell was a plain man who 'was not secretive or inhibited'. On the other hand, she may have wanted to promote this impression as a way of discouraging biographical investigations. In any case it was quite misleading for her to declare: 'He left very few of those "papers" which writers always seem to leave, providing such marvellous hunting-grounds for critics or biographers. He left no personal papers: there is nothing either concealed or spectacularly revealed in his letters.'

In his memoir of her, David Plante called Sonia a 'difficult woman', but it should also be noted that she had a wide circle of friends, many of whom were devoted to her. They held her in high regard, praising her vivacity, her loyalty, and her generosity. After Plante's book was reviewed in the *Listener*, Diana Witherby wrote a letter to the editor in an effort to remind readers that Sonia was not always so 'difficult': 'In earlier youthful days not only was she generous, but as a friend in no way was she difficult. On the contrary, she was predictable in her responses. She was always happy to hear of success or good news concerning her friends, and immediately warmly helpful to them if they were troubled or distressed.'[6]

In the 1970s – the last decade of Sonia's life – there was one clear reason why others regarded her as 'difficult'. She was a heavy drinker, and in her later years she could be very unpredictable and cruel after she had been drinking. She tried the patience of her best friends, and her habit helped to rob her of both her health and her good looks. In the late 1970s she became gravely ill with cancer. She struggled to overcome it, but lost her battle on 11 December 1980, dying in London at the age of sixty-two.

After her death the income from the Orwell estate went to Richard. By the time this inheritance finally came to him, he was in his mid-thirties, was married and was the father of two boys. He was living modestly on his salary as an employee of a company which manufactured agricultural equipment. Unlike Sonia, he had never attempted to publicise the fact that he was related to Orwell. He had led a quiet life as Richard Blair, not as 'Richard Orwell'. He has not changed his attitude since he became the sole beneficiary of the estate. He has continued to stay out of the spotlight, dividing his time between his home in the Midlands and a small resort business which he operates on the western coast of Scotland.

He retains only one major document from his father's papers. It is his adoption certificate. There is no startling information recorded on it, but it does have one notable alteration. At some point Orwell put a burning cigarette against the line containing the names of Richard's true parents and created a ragged hole where the names used to be. There are burn marks at the edges. It was a pointless act – other copies of the document exist in government files – but perhaps he took this action in a lonely moment after Eileen's death, vaguely thinking that he was creating a stronger tie with his son by eliminating the reminder of the boy's other parents.

Many adopted children might resent such tampering, but Richard has said he does not mind it. He does not even want to know the identities of the missing names. He is content to be Richard Horatio Blair, the son of Eric Arthur Blair and Eileen O'Shaughnessy. He is a part of them. The book belongs to all of us.

In the years since the first edition of this biography appeared, several discoveries have added to our understanding of Orwell's life. Among the most important are two sets of papers from the National Archives in Kew: the Special Branch file on Orwell's activities as a journalist and broadcaster; and some Foreign Office papers relating to his list of 'crypto-communists'. Released in 2005, the first set is especially revealing, for it demonstrates that Orwell had good reason to worry about the problem of surveillance from faceless bureaucratic organisations. Concerned by what they called the 'bohemian' writer's 'advanced Communist views', the security services kept a close eye on him over a period of several years.

Scotland Yard's interest was first aroused in 1936, while Orwell was on his famous trip to Wigan. The town's chief constable found the author's visit suspicious and, within a fortnight of his arrival, sent an official request for more information about him. As the request makes clear, local officers had not only followed Orwell but also monitored his correspondence. In response, Special Branch detectives prepared a very detailed – and mostly accurate – report on the man identified to them by Wigan police as 'ERIC A. BLAIR or GEORGE ORWELL, about 35yrs., 6', slim build, long pale face'. The finished report was so thorough that it included such minor information as the exact dates of his school terms at St Cyprian's.

A copy was sent to Wigan, and another to MI5, along with a passport photograph taken at the time Orwell left Burma in 1927. Though there was no evidence that he was a danger to anyone, the report characterises him as an eccentric intellectual with a strong interest in revolutionary movements and, therefore, as someone worth watching. And so, additional reports were filed over the years, including one in response to his wartime broadcasts to India. Apparently, informants were only too happy to feed the suspicion that he was some sort of communist agent. 'Several of his Indian friends say they have often seen him at communist meetings,' the Special Branch noted in 1942.

Enough energy was spent on tracking Orwell's activities that – as a former policeman himself – he may well have picked up clues he was under investigation. At any rate, if he became more than a little paranoid about Big Brother watching him, we now know why.

Such paranoia may also have played a part in his decision to keep his own list of 'crypto-communists'. That list is discussed here in chapter twenty-two, but Foreign Office papers released after publication of the first edition reveal that among the friends to whom Orwell showed the list was Celia Paget, who worked after the war at the Information Research Department—a shadowy government office responsible for anti-communist propaganda. At some point in the late 1940s, Celia made it clear to Orwell that his vast political knowledge might be of some use to her bosses. If she had not been such a good friend, it is doubtful that the author would have agreed to give the IRD his views in general, and his list in particular. But he did indeed hand over a partial version of the list, and some critics have seized on that fact as evidence he was a 'snitch'.

The truth is that his list had no impact on anyone's career. It may have interested Celia and a few other officials at the IRD, but they had no power to 'blacklist' people or spy on anyone. A dying man gave it to them because he wanted to leave something behind to set the record straight. It was proof not simply of his own opposition to Soviet-style communism, but also of his anger with evasive 'fellow-travellers' who worked behind the scenes to undermine any criticism of Stalin. One of these people was Peter Smollett, who was the official at the Ministry of Information who advised Jonathan Cape not to publish *Animal Farm*.

A former correspondent of *The Times* and chief of the Russian section at the Ministry of Information, Smollett not only appears on Orwell's list, but is also labelled as 'very dishonest' and 'almost certainly [an] agent of some kind'. As Professor Peter Davison has shown, Smollett was a Soviet agent who used his trusted position at *The Times* to spy on the West and spread subversion. His real name was Peter Smolka, and he came to London from his native Austria in the 1930s, when an English friend invited him to London. That friend's name was Kim Philby and, for a short time in the mid-1930s, Smolka/Smollett and Philby were partners in a small news service used as a front for gathering confidential information for Stalin.

It is doubtful that Orwell knew much about Smolka/Smollett, but his instincts told him to be wary of the man. He would not have been surprised to learn that this Austrian communist was among the enemies of *Animal Farm*. The advantage that such foes enjoyed was anonymity, and one purpose of Orwell's list was to take some of that protection away from them. Sadly, in Smolka/Smollett's case no one paid much attention to the warnings against him. He served *The Times* for many years as their man in Vienna and died with his reputation unsullied in 1980.

When he gave Celia his list, Orwell said it was not 'very sensational'; but he made a point of claiming that it might do some good here and there. Specifically, he mentioned that it might serve as a warning against 'people like Peter Smollett worming their way into important propaganda jobs where they were probably able to do us a lot of harm'. Orwell was not out to suppress communists, but merely to level the playing field by identifying the sympathies of those who tried to hide theirs. He betrayed no one by compiling his list. The betrayal had already occurred from his supposed friends on the Left, such as Victor Gollancz and Kingsley Martin, who tried to stop him doing what he did so well – namely, facing unpleasant facts and discussing them freely.

He felt this betrayal most keenly when he tried to report the truth about Soviet treachery during the Spanish Civil War. Time and again, British colleagues tried to censor him, and the efforts to discredit him had disastrous effects. His powerful account of the events in Spain, and his important warnings about the Stalinists, went unheeded. But in the aftermath of his experience in Spain, he found a mission – to save British socialism from the danger of following the Soviet model, and to fight for the right to speak his mind.

In *Animal Farm* and *Nineteen Eighty-Four*, he made his struggle universal by giving the world powerful tales that expose duplicity and betrayal in timeless ways. Winston Smith's desperate effort to save the truth from being destroyed or perverted by his enemies is a reflection of Orwell's own experience. But it has also come to mirror the struggles of ordinary people everywhere who have been inspired by the author's work and have tried, in their own ways, to resist the lies and 'smelly orthodoxy' that continue to corrupt so much of political life.

Select Bibliography

Bryder, Linda. *Below the Magic Mountain: A Social History of Tuberculosis in Twentieth-Century Britain.* Oxford: Clarendon, 1988.

Buddicom, Jacintha. *Eric and Us: A Remembrance of George Orwell.* London: Frewin, 1974.

Burgess, Anthony. *1985.* London: Hutchinson, 1978; Boston: Little, Brown, 1978.

Caldwell, Mark. *The Last Crusade: The War on Consumption.* New York: Atheneum, 1988.

Connolly, Cyril. *Enemies of Promise.* London: Routledge, 1938; Boston: Little, Brown, 1939.

—. *The Evening Colonnade.* London: David Bruce and Watson, 1973; New York: Harcourt, 1975.

—. *A Romantic Friendship: Cyril Connolly's Letters to Noel Blakiston.* Ed. Noel Blakiston. London: Constable, 1975.

Crick, Bernard. *George Orwell: A Life.* London: Secker and Warburg, 1980; Boston: Little, Brown, 1980; Rev. ed. Harmondsworth: Penguin Books, 1982.

—. *Essays on Politics and Literature.* Edinburgh: Edinburgh University Press, 1989.

Critical Essays on George Orwell. Ed. Bernard Oldsey and Joseph Browne. Boston: G. K. Hall, 1986.

Cunningham, Valentine. *British Writers of the Thirties.* Oxford and New York: Oxford University Press, 1988.

Danziger, Danny. *Eton Voices.* London: Viking, 1988.

Edwards, Ruth Dudley. *Victor Gollancz: A Biography.* London: Gollancz, 1987.

Fussell, Paul. *Thank God for the Atom Bomb and Other Essays.* 1988. New York: Ballantine, 1990.

Fyvel, T. J. *George Orwell: A Personal Memoir.* London: Weidenfeld and Nicolson, 1982; New York: Macmillan, 1982.

George Orwell: A Collection of Critical Essays. Ed. Raymond Williams. Englewood Cliffs, New Jersey: Prentice-Hall, 1974.

George Orwell: The Critical Heritage. Ed. Jeffrey Meyers. London and Boston: Routledge, 1975.

Heppenstall, Rayner. *Four Absentees.* 1960. Harmondsworth: Cardinal, 1988.

Hewison, Robert. *Under Siege: Literary Life in London, 1939–1945.* London: Weidenfeld and Nicolson, 1977.

Hitchens, Christopher. *Prepared for the Worst: Selected Essays and Minority Reports.* New York: Hill and Wang, 1988; London: Chatto, 1988.

Hodges, Sheila. *Gollancz: The Story of a Publishing House.* London: Gollancz, 1978.

Hollis, Christopher. *A Study of George Orwell: The Man and His Works.* London: Hollis and Carter, 1956; Chicago: Regnery, 1956.

Inside the Myth: Orwell, Views from the Left. Ed. Christopher Norris. London: Lawrence and Wishart, 1984.

Longhurst, Henry. *My Life and Soft Times.* London: Cassell, 1971.

Maxwell, Gavin. *The House of Elrig.* London: Longman, 1965; New York: Dutton, 1965.

Meyer, Michael. *Not Prince Hamlet: Literary and Theatrical Memoirs.* London: Secker and Warburg, 1989.

Meyers, Jeffrey. *A Reader's Guide to George Orwell.* London: Thames and Hudson, 1975.

Ogilvy, David. *Blood, Brains and Beer.* New York: Atheneum, 1978.

Orwell Remembered. Ed. Audrey Coppard and Bernard Crick. London: Ariel Books (BBC), 1984; New York: Facts on File, 1984.

Orwell: The War Broadcasts. Ed. W. J. West. London: Duckworth and BBC, 1985. US edition: *Orwell: The Lost Writings.* New York: Arbor House, 1985.

Orwell: The War Commentaries. Ed. W. J. West. London: Duckworth and BBC, 1985; New York: Pantheon, 1985.

Orwell's Nineteen Eighty-Four: Texts, Sources, Criticism. Ed. Irving Howe. 1963. New York: Harcourt, 1982.

Parker, Eric. *College at Eton.* London: Macmillan, 1933.

Patai, Daphne. *The Orwell Mystique: A Study in Male Ideology.* Amherst: University of Massachusetts Press, 1984.

Plante, David. *Difficult Women: A Memoir of Three.* London: Gollancz, 1983. New York: Atheneum, 1983.

Powell, Anthony. *To Keep the Ball Rolling: The Memoirs of Anthony Powell.* Harmondsworth: Penguin Books, 1983.

Pryce-Jones, David. *Cyril Connolly: Journal and Memoir.* London: Collins, 1983; New York: Ticknor and Fields, 1984.

Rai, Alok. *Orwell and the Politics of Despair.* Cambridge: Cambridge University Press, 1988.

Rees, Richard. *George Orwell: Fugitive from the Camp of Victory.* London: Secker and Warburg, 1961; Carbondale: Southern Illinois University Press, 1962.

—. *A Theory of My Time.* London: Secker and Warburg, 1963.

Reilly, Patrick. *George Orwell: The Age's Adversary.* London: Macmillan, 1986; New York: St Martin's, 1986.

Rivett-Carnac, Charles. *Pursuit in the Wilderness.* Boston: Little, Brown, 1965.

Rodden, John. *The Politics of Literary Reputation: The Making and Claiming of 'St George' Orwell.* New York: Oxford University Press, 1989.

Spender, Stephen. *Journals: 1939–1983.* Ed. John Goldsmith. London: Faber, 1985.

Stansky, Peter, and William Abrahams. *The Unknown Orwell.* London: Constable, 1972. New York: Knopf, 1972.

—. *Orwell: The Transformation.* London: Constable, 1979. New York: Knopf, 1980.

Steinhoff, William. *George Orwell and the Origins of 1984.* Ann Arbor: University of Michigan Press, 1975. British edition: *The Road to '1984'.* London: Weidenfeld and Nicolson, 1975.

Thomas, Hugh. *The Spanish Civil War.* London: Eyre and Spottiswoode, 1961; Rev. ed. Harmondsworth: Penguin Books, 1986.

Thompson, John. *Orwell's London.* London: Fourth Estate, 1984. New York: Schocken Books, 1985.

Wadhams, Stephen. *Remembering Orwell.* Markham, Ontario: Penguin Books Canada, 1984.

Warburg, Fredric. *All Authors Are Equal.* London: Hutchinson, 1973; New York: St Martin's Press, 1974.

White, Antonia, *Frost in May*. London: Desmond Harmsworth, 1933.

Williams, Raymond. *Orwell*. New York: Viking Press, 1971; London: Fontana Books, 1971.

Woodcock, George. *The Cystal Spirit: A Study of George Orwell*. 1966. New York: Schocken Books, 1984.

The World of George Orwell. Ed. Miriam Gross. London: Weidenfeld and Nicolson, 1971. New York: Simon and Schuster, 1971.

Zwerdling, Alex. *Orwell and the Left*. New Haven: Yale University Press, 1974.

Books by George Orwell

Down and Out in Paris and London. London: Gollancz, 1933; New York: Harper, 1933.

Burmese Days. New York: Harper, 1934; London: Gollancz, 1935.

A Clergyman's Daughter. London: Gollancz, 1935; New York: Harper, 1936.

Keep the Aspidistra Flying. London: Gollancz, 1936; New York: Harcourt, 1956.

The Road to Wigan Pier. London: Gollancz, 1937; New York: Harcourt, 1958.

Homage to Catalonia. London: Secker and Warburg, 1938; New York: Harcourt, 1952.

Coming Up for Air. London: Gollancz, 1939; New York: Harcourt, 1950.

Inside the Whale. London: Gollancz, 1940.

The Lion and the Unicorn. London: Secker and Warburg, 1941.

Animal Farm. London: Secker and Warburg, 1945; New York: Harcourt, 1946.

Critical Essays. London: Secker and Warburg, 1946. US edition: *Dickens, Dali and Others*. New York: Reynal and Hitchcock, 1946.

The English People. London: Collins, 1947.

Nineteen Eighty-Four. London: Secker and Warburg, 1949; New York: Harcourt, 1949.

Sources, Abbreviations and Notes

The George Orwell Archive, University College, London, is the most important source of information on Orwell. Its collection of material includes a large body of Orwell's manuscripts, personal papers and correspondence. Unless otherwise indicated, unpublished letters and other unpublished documents cited in my notes can be found in the Orwell Archive.

Nine volumes of *The Complete Works of George Orwell*, edited by Professor Peter Davison, appeared in 1986–7, and the final volumes are scheduled for publication in 1993. The nine published volumes contain authoritative texts for *Down and Out in Paris and London*, *Burmese Days*, *A Clergyman's Daughter*, *Keep the Aspidistra Flying*, *The Road to Wigan Pier*, *Homage to Catalonia*, *Coming Up for Air*, *Animal Farm* and *Nineteen Eighty-Four*. My notes cite these texts in the Penguin edition, which was published in 1989–90.

I am grateful to Professor Davison for allowing me to consult typescripts of other texts that he is preparing for the remaining eleven volumes in *The Complete Works of George Orwell*. These include his important discoveries of letters from Orwell to Yvonne Davet, material in the files of the publishing firm of Victor Gollancz and many documents from the BBC Written Archives Centre, Caversham. I have shared with him my discoveries, and therefore all unpublished works by Orwell that I have cited in my biography will be included in his edition of Orwell's letters, essays and journalism.

Since the four-volume *Collected Essays, Journalism and Letters*, edited by Sonia Orwell and Ian Angus, will be superseded by Peter Davison's edition, I have not given full citations to the 'old' edition in my notes. I provide dates for all references to Orwell's essays, journalism and letters,

497

and if the piece has also been published in the four-volume *CEJL*, I
indicate that fact by using the abbreviation in parenthesis, along with
the appropriate volume number.

On the first citation of a book, my notes give information on the
place of publication, publisher and date of publication. A shortened
form is used for subsequent references. The Select Bibliography has a
list of sources consulted in the writing of this biography.

The following shortened terms are used in the Notes:

Berg	Berg Collection, New York Public Library.
Caversham	BBC Written Archives Centre.
CEJL	*Collected Essays, Journalism and Letters of George Orwell.* Ed. Sonia Orwell and Ian Angus. Four Volumes. London: Secker and Warburg, 1968. New York: Harcourt, 1968.
CH	*George Orwell: The Critical Heritage.* Ed. Jeffrey Meyers. London and Boston: Routledge, 1975.
Colindale	British Newspaper Library, Colindale.
Eastbourne	Eastbourne Central Library, Sussex.
Eton	School Library, Eton.
IA	Ian Angus. Formerly the Deputy Librarian, University College, London, Ian Angus was in charge of the Orwell Archive in the 1960s. His interviews with Orwell's friends and family are an invaluable source.
IOL	India Office Library, London.
Life	*George Orwell: A Life*, by Bernard Crick. Revised edition. Harmondsworth: Penguin Books, 1982.
Lilly	Lilly Library, Indiana University. For information on the library's large collection of letters by George Orwell, see my article in the *Times Literary Supplement*, 6 January 1984.
Texas	Harry Ransom Humanities Research Center, University of Texas.
Tulsa	McFarlin Library, University of Tulsa.
WB	*Orwell: The War Broadcasts.* Ed. W. J. West. 1985. Harmondsworth: Penguin Books, 1987.
Yale	Sterling Library, Yale University.

Introduction

1. George Orwell, letter to Geoffrey Trease, 7 May 1940 (Texas).
2. *Twentieth Century Authors*, ed. Stanley Kunitz and H. Haycraft (New York: Wilson, 1942).
3. George Orwell, letter to Julian Symons, 10 May 1948 (*CEJL*, IV).
4. Lionel Trilling, Introduction, *Homage to Catalonia*, by George Orwell (New York: Harcourt, 1952), xi.
5. Quoted in Peter Lewis, *George Orwell: The Road to 1984* (New York: Harcourt Brace, 1981), 115.
6. George Orwell, 'Benefit of Clergy: Some Notes on Salvador Dali', *Critical Essays* (London: Secker and Warburg, 1946) and *CEJL*, III.
7. George Orwell, 'Poet in Darkness', *Observer*, 31 December 1944. In several reviews, Orwell took the position that literary biography should not avoid discussion of intimate matters. In the last year of his life, he complained that a recent biography of Dickens had failed to provide enough information about Dickens's 'treatment of his children and of that unobtrusive, almost invisible figure, his wife' ('Mr Dickens Sits for His Portrait', *New York Times Book Review*, 15 May 1949). In 1945 Orwell called for a new biography of Arthur Conan Doyle, 'a biography which would be neither patronising nor ... simply a labour of piety' ('My Dear Watson', *Manchester Evening News*, 15 November 1945). His approval of a forthright approach to literary biography can also be found in a review of Una Pope-Hennessy's *Charles Dickens* ('Charles the Great', *Observer*, 2 September 1945). In that piece he objected to John Forster's 'official' biography of Dickens because it 'suppressed or slurred over various incidents which must have been known to a fairly large circle of people at the time'.
8. Susan Watson to author, interview, August 1989.
9. Sonia Orwell, letter to *Times Literary Supplement*, 13 October 1972.
10. Bernard Crick, *Essays on Politics and Literature* (Edinburgh: Edinburgh University Press, 1989), 215.
11. Bernard Crick, *Life*, 151. In *Orwell and the Politics of Despair* (Cambridge University Press, 1988), 61 and 174, Alok Rai – an Indian scholar – challenges the accuracy of the figures in Crick's list.

Chapter One: First Impressions

1. George Orwell, letter to Leonard Moore, 14 July 1939 (Lilly). The *Sunday Times* review of *Coming Up for Air*, written by Ralph Straus, was published on 25 June 1939.
2. George Orwell, 'Such, Such Were the Joys', *Partisan Review*, September–October 1952 (*CEJL*, IV).
3. Humphrey Dakin to IA, interview, April 1965.
4. George Orwell's Preface to the Ukrainian edition of *Animal Farm*, reprinted in *CEJL*, III, and in Peter Davison's edition of *Animal Farm* (London: Secker and Warburg, 1987; Harmondsworth: Penguin Books, 1989).
5. Richard Hughes, 'The Opium War', in *The Horizon History of the British Empire*, ed. Stephen W. Sears. (New York: American Heritage, 1973), 159. Other sources of information about India and the Opium Department include David Edward Owen, *British Opium Policy in China and India* (New Haven: Yale University Press, 1934); and *The Imperial Gazetteer of India* (Oxford: Clarendon, 1909).
6. Stephen Wadhams, *Remembering Orwell* (Markham, Ontario: Penguin Books Canada, 1984), 43. This excellent book includes lengthy excerpts from interviews recorded for the Canadian Broadcasting Corporation's 'George Orwell: A Radio Biography' (January 1984). Wadhams conceived the project and conducted the interviews. The book's Introduction was written by George Woodcock, who was also the narrator of the radio broadcast.
7. Ibid. 31, and Jane Morgan to author, interview, July 1990.
8. Jacintha Buddicom, *Eric and Us* (London: Frewin, 1974), 22. Ida Blair's diary of 1905 clearly indicates that she and her family moved to Ermadale on 27 September 1905 ('Ermadale – we moved in here today').
9. George Orwell, Unpublished Notebook, [1948].
10. George Orwell, 'English Poetry Since 1900', BBC broadcast on the Eastern Service, 13 June 1943. See *WB*, ed. W. J. West, 128.
11. Orwell remembers the plumber's children in 'Such, Such Were the Joys'; *The Road to Wigan Pier*; and Unpublished Notebook [1948].
12. George Orwell to Arthur Koestler, letter, 10 January 1946 (*CEJL*, IV).
13. Humphrey Dakin to IA, interview, April 1965.
14. Orwell mentions his birthday gift in 'Politics vs Literature: An

Examination of *Gulliver's Travels*', *Polemic*, No. 5 (1946). Reprinted in
CEJL, IV. His comment on Swift is taken from a script broadcast on
the BBC, 'Jonathan Swift, an Imaginary Interview'; 2
November 1942. See *WB*, ed. W. J. West, 112–113.
15. George Orwell, 'Why I Write', *Gangrel*, No. 4 [Summer 1946]
(*CEJL*, I).
16. Ida Blair's diary, 1905.
17. Humphrey Dakin to IA, interview, April 1965.
18. Unpublished Notebook, [1949].

Chapter Two: Cold Lessons

1. Unless otherwise indicated in the notes, all quotations from
Orwell in this chapter are taken from 'Such, Such Were the Joys'.
2. George Orwell, letter to Cyril Connolly, 14 December 1938
(*CEJL*, I).
3. David Pryce-Jones, *Cyril Connolly: Journal and Memoir* (London:
Collins, 1983), 34.
4. George Orwell, letter to F. J. Warburg, 31 May 1947 (*CEJL*, IV).
5. Mrs Wilkes's memorial service was held in Eastbourne on 17
August 1967. A printed card from that service was among Connolly's
papers at his death. It reads, in part, 'Cicely Ellen Philadelphia
Vaughan Wilkes, 1 December 1875 to 11 August 1967' (Tulsa).
Connolly attended the service. 'No one spoke to me', he reported
afterwards.
6. Cyril Connolly, *The Evening Colonnade* (New York: Harcourt,
1975), 332 and 340.
7. For general background information on St Cyprian's, I am
indebted to Marie Lewis of the Eastbourne Central Library. I have
also received invaluable help from four old St Cyprianites: Douglas
and William Blackwood; Major-General H. R. B. Foote, VC; and
Lieutenant Colonel J. B. M. Horner.
8. W. H. J. Christie, 'St Cyprian's Days', *Blackwood's Magazine*, May
1971. I am grateful to Mrs Christie for giving me additional
information about her husband and his years at the school.
9. Gavin Maxwell, *The House of Elrig* (New York: Dutton, 1965), 81.
10. Charles Rivett-Carnac, *Pursuit in the Wilderness* (Boston: Little,
Brown, 1965), 11.

11. General Foote to author, interview, November 1988.

12. David Ogilvy, *Blood, Brains and Beer* (New York: Atheneum, 1978), 15.

13. Henry Longhurst, *My Life and Soft Times* (London: Cassell, 1971), 30.

14. Connolly, *The Evening Colonnade*, 340.

15. Copies of the *St Cyprian's Chronicle* have been preserved at the Eastbourne Central Library in a collection donated by Walter Christie, at the request of local historian Michael Ockenden.

16. Quoted in Peter Stansky and William Abrahams, *The Unknown Orwell* (1974; London: Granada, 1982), 50.

17. Quoted in Cyril Connolly, *Enemies of Promise* (1938; Harmondsworth: Penguin Books, 1979), 187–188.

18. *St Cyprian's Chronicle*, July 1915 (Eastbourne).

19. George Orwell, *Keep the Aspidistra Flying*, ed. Peter Davison (1936; Harmondsworth: Penguin Books, 1989), 44.

20. Christie attached the note to the photograph, which he donated to the Eastbourne Central Library.

21. Orwell had no fond memories of Charles Loseby. In 'Such, Such Were the Joys', he is described, without being named, as a 'solemn, blackhaired imbecile of an assistant master, who was later to be a Member of Parliament'. After the war, Loseby was in the House of Commons for four years (1918–1922), serving as National Democratic and Labour MP for East Bradford.

22. *St Cyprian's Chronicle*, July 1915 (Eastbourne).

23. *St Cyprian's Chronicle*, January 1917 (Eastbourne). Also see Pryce-Jones, *Journal and Memoir*, 29.

Chapter Three: Consolation Prizes

1. Unless otherwise indicated, all quotations from Orwell in this chapter are taken from 'Such, Such Were the Joys'.

2. W. H. J. Christie, 'St Cyprian's Days'.

3. Ibid.

4. *St Cyprian's Chronicle*, January 1918 (Eastbourne).

5. Gavin Maxwell, *The House of Elrig*, 92.

6. Cyril Connolly, *Enemies of Promise*, 176. Mr Sillar's name is given as 'Mr Potter' in Connolly's book.

7.   See George Orwell, letter to Julian Symons, 10 May 1948 (*CEJL*, IV). After his memorable experience with *Sinister Street*, Orwell must have been pleased to find, many years later, that his own writing had won the admiration of Compton Mackenzie, who wrote an enthusiastic appreciation of Orwell's first three novels, declaring in the *Daily Mail*: 'I have no hesitation in asserting that no realistic writer during the last five years has produced three volumes which can compare in directness, vigour, courage and vitality with these volumes from the pen of Mr Orwell.' See Andro Linklater, *Compton Mackenzie: A Life* (London: Chatto, 1987), 258–259.

8.   Cyril Connolly, *Enemies of Promise*, 179.

9.   For the best account of this episode, see Pryce-Jones, *Journal and Memoir*, 28–29.

10.   Cyril Connolly, *The Evening Colonnade*, 333.

11.   George Orwell, 'As I Please', *Tribune*, 24 November 1944 (*CEJL*, III).

12.   Cyril Connolly, *Enemies of Promise*, 175.

13.   Pryce-Jones, *Journal and Memoir*, 29.

14.   Cyril Connolly to Maud Connolly, n.d. [1916?] (Tulsa).

15.   Eric Blair, letter to Ida Blair, n.d. [mid-July 1916?]. Blair's use of such difficult words as 'presentiment' and 'Savonarola' suggests that this letter dates from an advanced stage in his education at St Cyprian's.

16.   Avril Dunn, 'My Brother, George Orwell'. *Twentieth Century*, March 1961.

17.   George Orwell, *The Road to Wigan Pier*, ed. Peter Davison (1937; Harmondsworth: Penguin Books, 1989), 117.

18.   Jacintha Buddicom, *Eric and Us*, 11.

19.   Ibid., 13.

20.   George Orwell, 'Bare Christmas for the Children', *Evening Standard*, 1 December 1945.

21.   Ibid.

22.   Ibid.

23.   Jacintha Buddicom, *Eric and Us*, 39.

24.   Ibid., 32.

25.   Ibid., 23.

26.   This quotation and other details concerning this episode are taken from articles in the *Henley Standard*, 6 January 1984 and 25 November 1988. A version of this story in Stansky and Abrahams (*The Unknown*

Orwell, 75) gives the date as Christmas 1914, but the files of the *Henley Standard* show that the performances took place in December 1915 and January 1916.

27. *St Cyprian's Chronicle*, January 1917 (Eastbourne).

28. Cyril Connolly, letter to Maud Connolly, 16 July [1916]. Details about the Harrow History Prize of 1916 are taken from documents in the Cyril Connolly collection at the McFarlin Library, University of Tulsa.

29. Harrow History Examination, 1916 (Tulsa).

30. *St Cyprian's Chronicle*, January 1917 (Eastbourne).

31. Ibid.

32. W. H. J. Christie describes Mrs Wilkes's style of teaching English in 'St Cyprian's Days'.

33. Jack Common, 'Orwell at Wallington', *Stand*, Volume 22, no. 3 (1980–1981).

34. Victor Stacey to author, interview, August 1989.

35. The fire at the school is described in 'Cold Bath before Breakfast', *Eastbourne Herald*, 7 March 1981. This article is partly based on information about the fire in *Herald* reports from May 1939.

Chapter Four: King's Scholar

1. Richard Rees, *George Orwell: A Fugitive from the Camp of Victory* (London: Secker and Warburg, 1961), 142.

2. Christopher Hollis, *A Study of George Orwell: The Man and His Works* (London: Hollis and Carter, 1956), 13–14.

3. 'Such, Such Were the Joys'.

4. See Andrew Gow papers (Eton). For permission to examine these papers, and for kindly answering my various questions about Eton, I am indebted to Dr Eric Anderson, the Head Master, and Michael Meredith, the School Librarian.

5. George Orwell, 'Wells, Hitler, and the World State', *Horizon*, August 1941 (*CEJL*, II).

6. George Orwell, Theatre Review of George Bernard Shaw's *The Devil's Disciple*, in *Time and Tide*, 3 August 1940.

7. George Orwell, 'War-Time Diary', 27 March 1942 (*CEJL*, II). Wells also resented Orwell's remarks in 'The Rediscovery of Europe', *Listener*, 19 March 1942.

8. Eric Parker, *College at Eton* (London: Macmillan, 1933), 260.

9. Lord Home quoted in Danny Danziger's *Eton Voices* (London: Viking, 1988), 139.

10. George Orwell, 'My Country Right or Left', *Folios of New Writing*, Autumn 1940 (*CEJL*, I).

11. Ibid.

12. *Eton College Chronicle*, 17 November 1921 (Eton).

13. Richard Steele to author, interview, June 1989.

14. Sir Steven Runciman, quoted in Stephen Wadhams, *Remembering Orwell*, 20.

15. George Orwell, 'Inside the Whale', *Inside the Whale* (London: Secker and Warburg, 1940) and *CEJL*, I.

16. 'Such, Such Were the Joys'.

17. Eric Blair's poem is quoted in Jacintha Buddicom's *Eric and Us*, 71.

18. Jacintha Buddicom to author, interview, November 1988.

19. Eric Blair's sonnet is quoted in Jacintha Buddicom, *Eric and Us*, 87.

20. Army Records Centre, letter to IA, 23 April 1968.

21. Ida Blair, letter to Laura Buddicom, 14 November 1917, quoted in Jacintha Buddicom's *Eric and Us*, 68–69.

22. Cyril Connolly to T. E. Beddard, n.d. (Tulsa). 'NHB' was Connolly's good friend Noel Blakiston, who later edited a volume of Connolly's letters to him, *A Romantic Friendship* (London: Constable, 1975). See also Pryce-Jones, *Journal and Memoir*, 44–45.

23. Christopher Eastwood quoted in Stephen Wadhams, *Remembering Orwell*, 17. Eastwood's brief tenure as Crown Commissioner of Lands was marked by controversy. He was criticised during the Crichel Down affair of 1953–1954, which began as a dispute over the government's power to dispose of surplus agricultural land, but which ended in a classic debate over the question of ministerial responsibility. Eastwood died on 14 October 1983.

24. In an interview with Ian Angus, Cyril Connolly discussed the Eastwood affair and also remembered Blair 'having a crush on Godfrey Meynell', who was later killed on the North-West Frontier and posthumously awarded a Victoria Cross. (Cyril Connolly to IA, 17 August 1966.) Orwell's sense of guilt was perhaps a factor in his strong criticism of Connolly's novel, *The Rock Pool*. Though he praises Connolly's literary abilities, he objects to the novel's subject matter. 'Even to want to write about so-called artists who spend on sodomy

what they have gained by sponging betrays a kind of spiritual inadequacy . . . The fact to which we have got to cling, as to a life-belt, is that it *is* possible to be a normal decent person and yet to be fully alive.' Orwell's protest seems overstated, and the image of the 'life-belt' betrays a sense of insecurity on his part. See *New English Weekly*, 23 July 1936 (*CEJL*, I).

25. Richard Steele to author, interview, June 1989.

26. Denys King-Farlow to BBC, interview for 'George Orwell: A Programme of Recorded Reminiscences', produced by Rayner Heppenstall, 2 November 1960; King-Farlow ms., Orwell Archive.

27. Denys King-Farlow to BBC, interview, 1960.

28. King-Farlow to IA and Sonia Orwell, interview, April 1967.

29. Sir Roger Mynors quoted in Stephen Wadhams, *Remembering Orwell*, 19.

30. Eric Blair, letter to Steven Runciman, [August 1920] (*CEJL*, I).

31. Quoted in Jacintha Buddicom, *Eric and Us*, 106.

32. Eric Blair, letter to Prosper Buddicom, January 1921, quoted in Jacintha Buddicom, *Eric and Us*, 111.

33. Lilian Holland (Jacintha Buddicom's aunt), letter to Laura Buddicom, 29 August 1917, quoted in *Eric and Us*, 59.

34. John Chandos, *Boys Together: English Public Schools, 1800–1864* (London: Hutchinson, 1984), 353.

35. *Eton College Chronicle*, 27 Oct 1921 (Eton).

36. *Eton College Chronicle*, 13 Oct 1921 (Eton). The date of Blair's speech is incorrect in Bernard Crick, *Life*, and in Peter Stansky and William Abrahams, *The Unknown Orwell*. In both books it is given as 4 June 1921.

37. Christopher Hollis, *A Study of George Orwell*, 18. Orwell used the phrase 'medieval chaos' in conversation with David Astor (David Astor to author, interview, July 1988).

38. George Orwell, 'For Ever Eton', *Observer*, 1 August 1948.

Chapter Five: Lost in Mandalay

1. R. W. G. Willis to author, interview, June 1989.

2. Andrew Gow quoted in *CH*, ed. Jeffrey Meyers, 378.

3. Sir Steven Runciman quoted in Stephen Wadhams, *Remembering Orwell*, 21.

4.   Blair's recruitment papers for the Indian Imperial Police are in the India Office Library, London.

5.   I am in debt to several experienced 'Burma hands' for information about the country in the 1920s, in general, and the Indian Imperial Police, in particular. Among those who gave me interviews were two men who served with Orwell in the Imperial Police – Cyril Hampton and J. C. de Vine. I also received information from William Tydd, formerly of the Imperial Police, and F. S. V. Donnison, formerly of the Indian Civil Service, and author of a volume on Burma in the series 'Nations of the Modern World' (New York: Praeger, 1970). For information about crime in Burma, see J. S. Furnivall, *Colonial Policy and Practice* (Cambridge: Cambridge University Press, 1948), 138–139; and the annual *Report on the Police Administration of Burma*, copies of which are in the IOL.

6.   George Orwell, letter to Jacintha Buddicom, 15 February 1949. See *Eric and Us*, 151.

7.   Jacintha Buddicom, *Eric and Us*, 143–144.

8.   Ibid., 117.

9.   George Orwell, 'As I Please', *Tribune*, 20 October 1944 (*CEJL*, III).

10.   George Orwell, 'Notes on the Way', *Time and Tide*, 30 March 1940.

11.   William Tydd, *Peacock Dreams* (London: BACSA, 1986), 15. BACSA is a private group that issues periodic publications about South Asia and supports the maintenance and registration of British Cemeteries in South Asia. The secretary is Theon Wilkinson, and the headquarters is in Chartfield Avenue, Putney.

12.   Ibid., 7.

13.   Roger Beadon to BBC, interview for a radio broadcast 'Memories of George Orwell', 1969. Part of this interview was printed in 'Roger Beadon Talks to Pamela Howe', *The Listener*, 29 May 1969. Beadon calls the *pongyi kyaung* a Burmese temple, but this is, in fact, the term for a monastery.

14.   *On Honourable Terms: The Memoirs of Some Indian Police Officers, 1915–1948*, ed. Martin Wynne (London: BACSA, 1985), 20.

15.   George Orwell, 'Portrait of an Addict', *Observer*, 13 September 1942. As Orwell says in this review, Robinson 'was axed' from the military police in 1923 'and settled down for a couple of years in

Mandalay, where he devoted himself almost exclusively to smoking opium.'

16. Dennis Collings to author, interview, November 1988. For a contemporary description of the custom of leaving calling cards, see 'Life in Burma: How It Strikes a Newcomer', *Rangoon Gazette Weekly Budget*, 5 July 1926 (Colindale).

17. George Orwell, *Road to Wigan Pier*, 135.

Chapter Six: Servant of the Empire

1. Bernard Crick (*Life*, 144) argues that Blair 'got poor and lonely postings' because he was, in part, 'unclubbable'. Without giving any specific names, he suggests that more than one of Blair's superiors bullied him and generally made life unpleasant, with the result that he enjoyed little professional success in the police service. Again, without naming names, Stansky and Abrahams make much the same argument, *The Unknown Orwell*, 163.

2. I am grateful to Andrew Griffin of the IOL for helping me find useful documents and official volumes of service records. Much of the information in this chapter is based on my research at the IOL, and is drawn largely from the following: The annual *Report on the Police Administration of Burma* for the years 1922–1927 (Rangoon: Government Printing Office); the *Burma Police Manual*, 4th ed., (Rangoon: Government Printing Office, 1926); the annual *Report on the Prison Administration of Burma* for the years 1923–1927 (Rangoon: Government Printing Office); the Civil Lists, Burma, Pay & Allowances of Officers; the History of Services of Gazetted and Other Officers, corrected up to 1928. By checking the records of all police officers in this last volume, I was able to determine the names of Blair's various superiors. Also, of particular help were the many volumes of the *Imperial Gazetteer of India*, and the more specialised *Burma Gazetteer*, both of which were published by the Government of India. Blair's postings, and the names of his superiors, are as follows:

1) 29 November 1922 to 25 January 1924: Mandalay Police Training School (including one month of training with a military unit at Maymyo), Superintendent Clyne G. Stewart.

2) 26 January 1924 to 30 May 1924: Myaungmya, Superintendent Peter Burke, and Superintendent U Ba Thin.

3) 31 May 1924 to 15 December 1924: Twante, Hanthawaddy District, Superintendent Henry Lanktree.

4) 16 December 1924 to 25 September 1925: Syriam, Hanthawaddy District, Superintendent Henry Lanktree.

5) 26 September 1925 to 18 April 1926: Insein, Superintendent U Ba.

6) 19 April 1926 to 22 December 1926: Moulmein, Amherst District, Superintendent Geoffrey Waterworth, and Superintendent H. C. Mills.

7) 23 December 1926 to 30 June 1927: Katha, Superintendent U Maung Maung.

3. Bernard Crick (*Life*, 156) quotes the story about 'De Vine', using information provided to him by an American oil worker named L. W. Marrison. Crick then concludes that De Vine was probably a bully.

4. J. C. de Vine to author, interview, March 1989.

5. George Orwell, *The Road to Wigan Pier*, 132.

6. George Orwell, 'As I Please', *Tribune*, 21 July 1944 (*CEJL*, III).

7. Harold Acton, *More Memoirs of an Aesthete* (London: Methuen, 1970), 152.

8. Quoted in W. H. J. Christie, 'St Cyprian's Days'.

9. Roger Beadon to BBC, interview. Beadon's BBC interview with Pamela Howe has been used to support the idea that Blair was bullied by his superiors, but his comments on this matter are not convincing. He knew little about Blair after their time in Mandalay – his visit at Insein was their only other time together – and he admitted to the BBC that he had only a 'feeling' that one superintendent had treated Blair badly.

10. George Orwell, letter to F. Tennyson Jesse, 14 March 1946 (*CEJL*, IV).

11. Frank G. Carpenter, *From Bangkok to Bombay*, (Garden City: Doubleday, 1924), 78–79.

12. I am very much in debt to Maung Htin Aung's little-known essay 'Orwell of the Burma Police', *Asian Affairs*, 60 (1973); also helpful was Htin Aung's 'Orwell and Burma', in *The World of George Orwell*, ed. Miriam Gross (London: Weidenfeld and Nicolson, 1971), 19–30. For a good analysis of Orwell's ideas about Burma, see John Gross, 'Imperial Attitudes', *The World of George Orwell*, 32–38.

13. George Orwell, *The Road to Wigan Pier*, 137.

14. Ibid.

15. Orwell's medical records are in the possession of Dr Arnold Bentley, Preston Hall Hospital, Kent. Bernard Crick implies that Blair became ill from some unknown cause in Moulmein and was sent to Katha for reasons of health. 'His one good posting to Katha could have been for its mild, dry climate' (*Life*, 171). It is true that the climate in Katha is milder than that in Lower Burma, but the word 'dry' is misleading. As the *Imperial Gazetteer* states, 'The annual rainfall averages 58 inches at Katha.'

16. See the *Indian Year Book*, 1922, published by *The Times of India.*

17. See Orwell's contribution to *Twentieth Century Authors.*

18. Orwell apparently took the name U Po Kyin from a Burmese officer in the Imperial Police. See Htin Aung, 'Orwell of the Burma Police'.

19. Information from passenger list, *Rangoon Gazette Weekly Budget*, 18 July 1927, cited in Alok Rai's *Orwell and the Politics of Despair*, 61.

20. George Orwell, 'My Country Right or Left' (*CEJL*, I).

21. George Orwell, *The Road to Wigan Pier*, 101.

22. George Orwell, Film Review, *Time and Tide*, 5 July 1941.

23. George Orwell, 'Inside the Whale' (*CEJL*, I).

24. George Orwell, *The Road to Wigan Pier*, 137.

Chapter Seven: London and Paris

1. See Blair's review of E. R. Curtius's *The Civilisation of France* in the *Adelphi*, May 1932.

2. George Orwell, *The Road to Wigan Pier*, 137–138.

3. Avril Blair, 'My Brother, George Orwell', *Twentieth Century*, March 1961.

4. Mabel Fierz to BBC, interview for Melvyn Bragg's television programme, 'The Road to the Left' (1970). See transcript in *Orwell Remembered*, ed. Audrey Coppard and Bernard Crick (London: Ariel Books, 1984), 94–98.

5. Mabel Fierz to IA, interview, October 1967.

6. Blair's Leave and Deputation Pay Account, in IOL, notes that he retired with effect from 1 January 1928 and was paid only to 31 December 1927, even though he was on authorised leave to 11 March 1928. I am indebted to Andrew Griffin, of the IOL, for this

information, and for the telegram which states the Government of India's acceptance of Blair's resignation.

7. Brenda Salkeld to BBC, interview for 'George Orwell: A Programme of Recorded Reminiscences', 1960.

8. Orwell's pay is given in his BBC contract, dated 18 August 1941.

9. George Orwell, *The Road to Wigan Pier*, 138.

10. All quotations in this paragraph are taken from 'Such, Such Were the Joys'.

11. George Orwell, *The Road to Wigan Pier*, 138.

12. Ruth Pitter to BBC, interview for 'Ruth Pitter's Personal Memories of George Orwell', broadcast January 1956.

13. Ibid.

14. Orwell recalls this story in 'As I Please', 26 May 1944, *Tribune* (*CEJL*, III).

15. George Orwell, *The Road to Wigan Pier*, 141–142.

16. Jack London's descent into the 'abyss' took place in the summer of 1902, the *The People of the Abyss* was published in 1903.

17. George Orwell, *The Road to Wigan Pier*, 138.

18. Introduction to the French edition, *La Vache Enragée*, published by Gallimard, May 1935, (*CEJL*, I).

19. George Orwell, letter to Celia Paget Kirwan (later Celia Goodman), 27 May 1948 (*CEJL*, IV).

20. George Orwell, 'Inside the Whale'.

21. George Orwell, 'As I Please', 28 January 1944, *Tribune* (*CEJL*, III).

22. For detailed information on Eugene Adam, or 'Lanti', see Peter G. Forster's excellent *The Esperanto Movement* (The Hague: Mouton, 1982), 188–211.

23. George Orwell, 'As I Please', 28 January 1944, *Tribune*.

24. Avril Blair to IA, interview, April 1964.

25. Nellie Limouzin, letter to Eric Blair, 3 June 1933.

26. Humphrey Dakin to IA, interview, April 1965.

27. Mabel Fierz first recalled this story for IA in October 1967, giving the name of the girl-friend as Suzanne and mentioning the fight with an Arab rival. She later provided more information to the BBC in 1970.

28. L. I. Bailey, letter to Eric Blair, 28 March 1929. In his first letter, 19 February 1929, Bailey says, 'Would you please thank your aunt for

her kind letter.' This sentence is deleted, without any marks to indicate the deletion, in Crick, *Life*, 193.

29. The first quotation is taken from the Author's Preface to the Ukrainian edition of *Animal Farm*; the second comes from George Orwell, letter to Jacintha Buddicom, 15 February 1949.

30. Information about the dates of Blair's stay comes from J. Alvernhe, letter to Sonia Orwell, 25 November 1971. Some circumstances of his illness and treatment are given in his Preston Hall medical history, compiled in 1938.

31. George Orwell, 'How the Poor Die', *Now*, No. 6 [November 1946] (*CEJL*, IV).

32. Eric Blair, '*Comment on Exploite un Peuple: L'Empire Britannique en Birmanie*', *Le Progrès Civique*, 4 May 1929.

33. Eric Blair, letter to Max Plowman, 22 September 1929 (*CEJL*, I).

34. For interview comments from Brenda Salkeld, and for further information about my discovery of the annotated copy of *Down and Out*, see Nicholas Shakespeare, 'Jilting Mr Blair', *Daily Telegraph*, 16 September 1989.

35. There is some evidence that the 'Hotel X' may have been the Hotel Lotti. See the incident described in *Grace and Favour: The Memoirs of Loelia, Duchess of Westminster*, (London: Weidenfeld, 1961), 225.

36. Orwell's approach is reasonable enough, but he caused unnecessary confusion when he later told the readers of the French edition that 'everything I have described did take place at one time or another', which is not really true. Probably as a way of avoiding libel suits, he also said, 'I have refrained, as far as possible, from drawing individual portraits of particular people.'

37. This postcard has no date, but is postmarked 12 December 1929.

Chapter Eight: A Provincial Life

1. See Orwell's review of *Bridge into the Future: Letters of Max Plowman*, *Manchester Evening News*, 7 December 1944. See also, Orwell, letter to Dorothy Plowman, 20 June 1941 (*CEJL*, II).

2. Richard Rees, *George Orwell: Fugitive from the Camp of Victory*, 143.

3. Jack Common, 'Orwell at Wallington', *Stand*.

4. George Orwell, Review of *Herman Melville*, by Lewis Mumford, *New Adelphi*, March–May 1930 (*CEJL*, I).
5. George Orwell, 'In Front of Your Nose', *Tribune*, 22 March 1946 (*CEJL*, IV). 'The Spike' was published in the *Adelphi*, April 1931 (*CEJL*, I).
6. Avril Blair to Ian Angus, interview, April 1964.
7. Blair described the 'ghost' incident in a letter to Dennis Collings, 16 August 1931 (*CEJL*, I).
8. Orwell to Sir Sachaverell Sitwell, 6 July 1940. Orwell had written a review of Sitwell's *Poltergeists*, and the purpose of this letter was to share with the author some further thoughts on the subject of unexplained events. The review did not appear until September 1940, in *Horizon*. Letter in possession of Daniel J. Leab.
9. R. S. Peters, 'A Boy's View of George Orwell', *Psychology and Ethical Development* (London: Allen & Unwin, 1974), 460–463.
10. Dennis Collings to author, interview, November 1988.
11. Brenda Salkeld to author, June 1989. All comments by her are taken from this interview.
12. Orwell, letter to Brenda Salkeld, [10? December 1933], and Orwell to Salkeld [10? March 1933] (*CEJL*, I).
13. Orwell, letter to Brenda Salkeld, 27 July 1934 (*CEJL*, I).,
14. Mabel Fierz to BBC, interview, 1970.
15. Mabel Fierz quoted in Stephen Wadhams, *Remembering Orwell*, 44.
16. Mabel Fierz to Ian Angus, interview, October 1967.
17. Eric Blair, letter to Dennis Collings, 16 August 1931 (*CEJL*, I).
18. Eric Blair, letter to Brenda Salkeld, [July 1931].
19. Eric Blair, letter to Dennis Collings [27 August 1931].
20. George Orwell, *The Road to Wigan Pier*, 144.
21. Blair's experiences as a hop-picker are described in his 'Hop-Picking Diary', 25 August to 8 October 1931 (*CEJL*, I).
22. Ibid., 28 August 1931.
23. Eric Blair, letter to Dennis Collings [27 August 1931].
24. Eric Blair, letter to Dennis Collings, 4 September 1931. The return address for this letter is given as 'Mereworth, Kent'.
25. 'Hop-Picking Diary', 2 to 19 September 1931.
26. Eric Blair, letter to Dennis Collings, 4 September 1931.
27. 'Hop-Picking Diary', 19 September 1931.
28. In a letter to Leonard Moore, 26 April 1932 (*CEJL*, I), Blair gives

the history of his efforts to find a publisher for the book that eventually became *Down and Out in Paris and London.*

29. See Eric Blair, letters to T. S. Eliot, 30 October 1931 and 4 November 1931 (*CEJL*, I).

30. Eric Blair, letter to Brenda Salkeld, [November 1931].

31. Eric Blair, letter to Leonard Moore, [November 1931] (Berg).

32. Eric Blair, letter to Leonard Moore, 6 January 1932 (Berg).

33. Excerpt from Eric Blair, letter to Brenda Salkeld [October 1931], quoted by Salkeld in letter to IA, 4 April 1963.

34. Blair describes his tramping experiment in 'Clink', written in August 1932 (*CEJL*, I).

35. Eric Blair, letter to T. S. Eliot, 17 February 1932.

36. T. S. Eliot, letter to Eric Blair, 19 February 1932. Eliot told Blair that the book was rejected because it was 'too short' and 'too loosely constructed'.

37. Mabel Fierz to IA, interview, October 1967.

Chapter Nine: Writer and Teacher

1. Mabel Fierz quoted in Stephen Wadhams, *Remembering Orwell*, 46.

2. Eric Blair, letter to Leonard Moore, 26 April 1932 (*CEJL*, I).

3. Ibid.

4. Eric Blair, letter to Eleanor Jaques, Tuesday [14? June 1932] (*CEJL*, I).

5. Ibid.

6. Geoffrey Stevens to author, interview, June 1989.

7. Ibid.

8. Eric Blair, letter to Leonard Moore, Friday [23 December 1932] (*CEJL*, I).

9. Eric Blair, letter to Leonard Moore, 1 July 1932 (*CEJL*, I).

10. Quoted in Ruth Dudley Edwards, *Victor Gollancz: A Biography* (London: Gollancz, 1987), 188.

11. Ibid., 175.

12. Ibid., 188.

13. Avril Blair, 'My Brother, George Orwell', *Twentieth Century*.

14. Eric Blair to Eleanor Jacques, Tuesday [14? June 1932]. Passage

deleted from *CEJL*, I. I am grateful to Dennis Collings for information about Eleanor Jaques.
15. Eric Blair to Eleanor Jaques, Monday [19 September 1932]. Passage deleted from *CEJL*, I.
16. Eric Blair to Eleanor Jaques, Wed. night [19 October 1932]. Passage deleted from *CEJL*, I.
17. Ibid.
18. Eric Blair, letter to Eleanor Jaques, Wed. [30 November 1932]. Passage deleted from *CEJL*.
19. Eric Blair, letter to Eleanor Jaques, 18 November 1932 (*CEJL*, I).
20. Eric Blair, letter to Eleanor Jaques, Wed. [19 October 1932], and Thursday [25 May 1933] (*CEJL*, I).
21. Eric Blair, letter to Eleanor Jaques, Wed. [30 November 1932] (*CEJL*, I).
22. Eric Blair, letter to Eleanor Jaques, Tue. [13 December 1932] (*CEJL*, I).
23. Anthony Powell, 'George Orwell: A Memoir', *Atlantic Monthly*, October 1967.
24. See 'A Note on the Text', *Down and Out in Paris and London*, ed. Peter Davison (Harmondsworth: Penguin Books, 1989).
25. Eric Blair, letter to Leonard Moore, 12 August 1932 (Berg).
26. Eric Blair, to Leonard Moore, Sat. [19 November 1932] (*CEJL*, I).
27. Eric Blair, letter to Leonard Moore, 12 August 1932 (Berg).
28. Eric Blair, letter to Brenda Salkeld, Sunday night [July 1931].
29. George Orwell, letter to Rayner Heppenstall, 16 April 1940 (*CEJL*, II).
30. George Orwell, letter to Leonard Moore, 17 January 1933 (Berg).
31. See *CH*, ed. Jeffrey Meyers, and *Time and Tide*, 11 February 1933.
32. George Orwell, letter to Brenda Salkeld, Tuesday night [late August? 1934] (*CEJL*, I).

Chapter Ten: George Orwell, Novelist

1. Avril Blair, 'My Brother, George Orwell', *Twentieth Century*.
2. George Orwell, letter to Leonard Moore, 1 February 1933 (*CEJL*, I). Possenti's letter appeared in *The Times* on 31 January 1933.

3. George Orwell, letter to Eleanor Jaques, Sunday [26 February 1933 (*CEJL*, I).

4. George Orwell, letter to Leonard Moore, 21 February 1933 (Berg).

5. George Orwell, letter to Leonard Moore, Saturday [25 March 1933] (Berg).

6. *Nation*, 6 September 1933 (see also *CH*, ed. Jeffrey Meyers, 45).

7. James T. Farrell, *New Republic*, 11 October 1933 (see also *CH*, ed. Jeffrey Meyers, 46).

8. George Orwell, letter to Leonard Moore, 1 February 1933 (*CEJL*, I).

9. George Orwell, letter to Eleanor Jaques, 18 February 1933.

10. George Orwell, letter to Leonard Moore, 21 February 1933 (*CEJL*, I).

11. George Orwell, letter to Brenda Salkeld, Saturday [June ? 1933 (*CEJL*, I).

12. George Orwell, letter to Eleanor Jaques, Thursday [25 May 1933] (*CEJL*, I).

13. George Orwell, letter to Eleanor Jaques, Tuesday [6 June 1933].

14. George Orwell, letter to Eleanor Jaques, 7 July 1933 (*CEJL*, I).

15. George Orwell, letter to Eleanor Jaques, Thursday [20 July 1933] (*CEJL*, I).

16. Dennis Collings to author, interview, November 1988.

17. George Orwell, letter to Eleanor Jacques, 7 July 1933 (*CEJL*, I).

18. George Orwell, letter to Eleanor Jaques, Thursday [20 July 1933] (*CEJL*, I).

19. George Orwell, letter to Leonard Moore, 17 October 1933 (Berg).

20. George Orwell, letter to Leonard Moore, Sunday [26 November 1933] (*CEJL*, I).

21. George Orwell, 'Why I Write'.

22. George Orwell, letter to Julian Symons, 20 April 1948 (*CEJL*, I).

23. George Orwell, letter to Brenda Salkeld, Sunday [10? December 1933] (*CEJL*, I).

24. Avril Blair, 'My Brother, George Orwell', *Twentieth Century*.

25. See George Orwell, letter to Leonard Moore, Thursday [28 December 1933] (*CEJL*, I); and Orwell, letter to Moore, 4 January 1934 (Berg).

26. George Orwell, 'Why I Write'.

27. Sheila Hodges, *Gollancz: The Story of a Publishing House* (London: Gollancz, 1978), 59.

28. George Orwell, letter to Henry Miller, 26 August 1936 (*CEJL*, I).

29. George Orwell, letter to Dr W. M. C. Harrowes, 15 November 1946.

30. Ibid.

31. George Orwell, letter to Leonard Moore, Thursday [8 February 1934] (*CEJL*, I).

32. George Orwell, letter to Leonard Moore, 12 March 1934 (Berg).

33. I am grateful to William Tydd and J. C. de Vine for helping to confirm that U Po Kyin is the Burmese officer in Roger Beadon's group photograph at the Police Training School, Mandalay. See also, Maung Htin Aung, 'Orwell of the Burma Police'.

34. Roger Beadon to BBC, interview, 1969.

35. George Orwell, letter to Leonard Moore, 2 February 1934 (Berg).

36. George Orwell, letter to Brenda Salkeld, 7 March 1935 (*CEJL*, I); and Brenda Selkeld to author, interview, July 1989.

37. George Orwell, letter to Brenda Selkeld, Tuesday night [18 September 1934].

38. George Orwell, letter to Brenda Salkeld, Tuesday night [late August ? 1934]. Passage deleted from *CEJL*.

39. Ibid.

40. Ibid.

41. George Orwell, letter to Brenda Salkeld, Wednesday night [early September ? 1934] (*CEJL*, I).

42. George Orwell, letter to Julian Symons, 10 May 1948 (*CEJL*, IV).

43. George Orwell, letter to Fredric Warburg, 31 May 1947 (*CEJL*, IV).

44. George Orwell, letter to Brenda Salkeld, Tuesday night [18? September 1934].

45. George Orwell, letter to Brenda Salkeld, Wednesday night [early September ? 1934] (*CEJL*, I).

46. Elaine (Nellie) Limouzin, letter to Myfanwy Westrope, 23 September 1934, (Eton).

47. See Orwell, letter to Leonard Moore, Saturday [20 October 1934] (Berg).

Chapter Eleven: Booklovers' Corner

1. George Orwell, letter to Brenda Salkeld, 16 February 1935. Passage delted from *CEJL*.
2. Jon Kimche to author, interview, June 1989.
3. George Orwell, 'Bookshop Memories'. *Fortnightly*, November 1936 (*CEJL*, I).
4. George Orwell, 'As I Please', *Tribune*, 14 January 1944 (*CEJL*, III).
5. George Orwell, letter to Brenda Salkeld, 7 May 1935.
6. George Orwell, letter to Brenda Salkeld, Tuesday [15? January 1935]. Also see Orwell's use of the 'Bedworthy' character in his essay 'In Defence of the Novel', *New English Weekly*, 12 and 19 November 1936 (*CEJL*, I).
7. George Orwell, 'Bookshop Memories'.
8. Kay Ekevall quoted in Stephen Wadhams, *Remembering Orwell*, 56.
9. Kay Ekevall, letter to IA, 28 March 1968.
10. Orwell's phrase 'the joy of mere words' is found in 'Why I Write'. His published poems in the *Adelphi* include ['Sometimes'], March 1933; ['Summer-like'], May 1933; ['A Dressed Man'], October 1933; 'On a Ruined Farm Near the His Master's Voice Gramophone Factory', April 1934; 'St Andrew's Day, 1935', November 1935; 'A Happy Vicar', December 1936.
11. George Orwell, letter to Brenda Salkeld, Tuesday night [late August ? 1934] (*CEJL*, I).
12. George Orwell, 'Looking Back on the Spanish War'. First published in 1943 (*CEJL*, II).
13. For the American sales figures of *Burmese Days* see 'A Note on the Text', by Peter Davison, in the Penguin edition (1989) of the novel.
14. George Orwell, letter to Leonard Moore, 14 November 1934 (*CEJL*, I).
15. Orwell repeated Rubinstein's objections in the list of alterations accompanying his letter to Gollancz, 17 December 1934.
16. George Orwell, letter to Leonard Moore, 22 January 1935 (*CEJL*, I).
17. Ibid.
18. George Orwell to Gollancz, 2 February 1935.
19. George Orwell, letter to Leonard Moore, 22 February 1935 (Lilly).

20. The list of alterations is attached to Orwell's letter to Gollancz, 28 February 1935.

21. George Orwell, letter to Brenda Salkeld, 16 February 1935. Passage deleted from *CEJL*.

22. Rosalind Obermeyer to IA, interview, January 1967.

23. Richard Rees, *A Theory of My Time* (London: Secker, 1963), 64.

24. Rayner Heppenstall, *Four Absentees* (1960; Harmondsworth: Cardinal, 1988), 30. Unless otherwise indicated, information about Heppenstall's relationship with Orwell is taken from *Four Absentees*.

25. George Orwell, letter to Brenda Salkeld, 7 March 1935. Passage deleted from *CEJL*.

26. George Orwell, letter to Brenda Salkeld, 16 February 1935 (*CEJL*, I).

27. George Orwell, letter to Leonard Moore, 22 February 1935 (Lilly).

28. *Spectator*, 22 March 1935. Reprinted in *CH*, 59–60.

29. *New Statesman*, 23 March 1935. Reprinted in *CH*, 61.

30. *Observer*, 10 March 1935. Reprinted in *CH*, 58.

31. George Orwell, 'Notes for My Literary Executor', 31 March 1945, unpublished.

32. Rosalind Obermeyer to IA, interview January 1967.

33. Edna Bussey, letter to IA, 19 September 1968.

34. I am very grateful to Catherine O'Shaughnessy Moncure for information about her family. She is the daughter of Dr Gwen O'Shaughnessy, Laurence's wife. Sources on Laurence's distinguished medical career include the following obituary notices: *The Times*, 8 June 1940; *The Lancet*, 15 June 1940; *The British Medical Journal*, 15 June 1940.

35. Elisaveta Fen (Lydia Jackson), 'George Orwell's First Wife', *Twentieth Century*, August 1960.

36. Ibid.

37. George Orwell, letter to Rayner Heppenstall, Tuesday night [September ? 1935])*CEJL*, I).

38. *New Statesman*, 6 July 1935.

39. See 'Some Letters of George Orwell', *Encounter*, January 1962.

40. *Woodford Times*, 25 October 1935 (Colindale).

41. George Orwell, letter to Rayner Heppenstall, Friday [18 October 1935].

42. George Orwell, letter to Leonard Moore, Saturday [26 October 1935] (Lilly).
43. George Orwell, letter to Leonard Moore, 30 September 1935 (Lilly).
44. Mabel Fierz to IA, interview, October 1967.

Chapter Twelve: A Window on Wigan

1. George Orwell, letter to Rayner Heppenstall, 5 October 1935 (*CEJL*, I).
2. George Orwell, letter to Brenda Salkeld, Wed. night [early September ? 1934] (*CEJL*, I).
3. George Orwell, *The Road to Wigan Pier*, 199–200.
4. George Orwell, letter to Geoffrey Gorer, 15 September 1937 (*CEJL*, I).
5. Jack Common, 'Orwell at Wallington', *Stand*.
6. George Orwell, letter to Brenda Salkeld, 7 May 1935.
7. George Orwell, 'Why I Write'.
8. George Orwell, letter to Leonard Moore, 8 November 1935 (Lilly). In September Orwell wrote the first instalment of a fiction serial for the *News Chronicle*, but it was rejected in November. An editor named Miss Gosse then suggested that he might want to write 'something on unemployment'.
9. George Orwell, letter to Cyril Connolly, 14 February 1936 (*CEJL*, I).
10. Joe 'Jerry' Kennan to BBC, interview for Melvyn Bragg's 'The Road to the Left', 1970. See *Orwell Remembered*, 130–133.
11. George Orwell, '*The Road to Wigan Pier* Diary', 21 February 1936 (*CEJL*, I).
12. 'Your Questions Answered', BBC, 2 December 1943 (*CEJL*, I).
13. Norman Collins, letter to George Orwell, 17 February 1936.
14. George Orwell, letter to Collins, 18 February 1936.
15. George Orwell, letter to Jack Common, 17 March 1936 (*CEJL*, I).
16. George Orwell, letter to Leonard Moore, 24 February 1936 (Lilly).
17. George Orwell, letter to Richard Rees, 29 February 1936 (*CEJL*, I).

18. *'The Road to Wigan Pier* Diary', 24 February 1936.
19. Ibid.
20. Ibid., 13 February 1936.
21. George Orwell, Unpublished 'Notes for *The Road to Wigan Pier*'. Orwell took this quotation from *The Coal Scuttle*, by Joseph Jones.
22. George Orwell, *The Road to Wigan Pier*, 56–57.
23. George Orwell, 'Notes for *The Road to Wigan Pier*'. Some of this information appears in the finished book in a different form.
24. George Orwell, *'The Road to Wigan Pier* Diary', 22 March 1936.
25. Ibid., 16 March 1936.
26. Tommy Degnan to BBC, interview, for Melvyn Bragg's 'The Road to the Left', 1970.
27. Cited in Valentine Cunningham's valuable study, *British Writers of the Thirties* (Oxford: OUP, 1989), 330.
28. *Daily Worker*, 17 March 1937.
29. *Left News*, March 1937.
30. George Orwell, *'The Road to Wigan Pier* Diary', 15 February 1936.
31. George Orwell, *The Road to Wigan Pier*, 145.
32. Foreword to the Left Book Club edition of *The Road to Wigan Pier*.
33. George Orwell, 'The Freedom of the Press', published posthumously in the *Times Literary Supplement*, 15 September 1972, and reprinted in Peter Davison's edition of *Animal Farm* (Harmondsworth: Penguin Books, 1989).
34. Richard Rees, *George Orwell: Fugitive from the Camp of Victory*, 48–49.
35. George Orwell, *'The Road to Wigan Pier* Diary', 7 March and 9 March 1936.
36. Background details on The Stores, Manor Farm, and Agrar Ltd., have been pieced together from several sources. See the privately printed pamphlet by Esther M. Brookes, *Monk's Fitchett: The Road to George Orwell* (Letchworth, Hertfordshire: David's Bookshop, n.d.). Ms Brookes bought The Stores in 1948 and gives some of its history in her pamphlet. Also see her brother's letter to the *Cambridge Weekly News*, 22 December 1988. John Brookes points out that The Stores and Manor Farm were once owned by Agrar. Both Ms Brookes and her brother call the company 'Agar', but a photograph of The Stores, dated 1928, in Ms Brookes's own pamphlet clearly shows a sign over

the door with the words, 'Wallington, Cash Stores, Agrar Ltd'. For
Orwell's knowledge of the model farm scheme at Manor Farm see his
letter to Jack Common, 3 April 1936 (*CEJL*, I).

37. George Orwell, letter to Jack Common, 12 October 1938 (*CEJL*,
I).

38. George Orwell, letter to Geoffrey Gorer, Sat. [May ? 1936]
(*CEJL*, I).

39. Cyril Connolly to BBC, interview for Melvyn Bragg's 'The Road
to the Left', 1970.

40. *New Statesman*, 25 April 1936.

41. Cyril Connolly, letter to Orwell, [early May 1936], (Tulsa).

42. *New English Weekly*, 23 July 1936 (*CEJL*, I).

43. Cyril Connolly, *The Evening Colonnade*, 341.

44. See Orwell's 'Notes for My Literary Executor', 31 March 1945.

45. George Orwell, letter to Anthony Powell, 8 June 1936. Also see
To Keep the Ball Rolling: The Memoirs of Anthony Powell
(Harmondsworth: Penguin Books, 1983), 66. I am indebted to
Anthony Powell for discussing Orwell with me in November 1989.

Chapter Thirteen: Foreign and Domestic

1. Harper & Brothers, letter to George Orwell, 23 April 1936 (Lilly).

2. George Orwell, letter to Leonard Moore, 2 May 1936 (Lilly).

3. George Orwell, letter to Denys King-Farlow, 9 June 1936 (*CEJL*,
I).

4. George Orwell, letter to Geoffrey Gorer, Sat. [May ? 1936]
(*CEJL*, I).

5. Quoted in T. R. Fyvel, *George Orwell: A Personal Memoir* (New
York: Macmillan, 1982), 135.

6. Lettice Cooper to author, interview, March 1989.

7. George Orwell, letter to Denys King-Farlow, 9 June 1936 (*CEJL*,
I).

8. Denys King-Farlow to BBC, interview for 'George Orwell: A
Programme of Recorded Reminiscences', 1960.

9. George Orwell, letter to John Lehmann, 27 May 1936 (*CEJL*, I).

10. See George Orwell, 'As I Please', *Tribune* 21 January 1944
(*CEJL*, III), and 'A Good Word for the Vicar of Bray', *Tribune*, 26
April 1946 (*CEJL*, IV).

11. Elisaveta Fen (Lydia Jackson), 'George Orwell's First Wife', *Twentieth Century*, August 1960.
12. I am indebted to Clive Fleay for this information. See his scrupulously researched 'Voices in the Gallery – George Orwell & Jack Hilton', *Middlesex Polytechnic History Journal*, Spring 1985.
13. Richard Rees, *George Orwell: Fugitive From the Camp of Victory*, 147.
14. George Orwell, *Homage to Catalonia*, ed. Peter Davison (1938; Harmondsworth: Penguin Books, 1989), 189.
15. See Sheila Hodges, *Gollancz: The Story of a Publishing House*, 126–127.
16. George Orwell, letter to Leonard Moore, 15 December 1936 (*CEJL*, I).
17. Eileen Blair, letter to Leonard Moore, 11 February 1937 (Lilly).
18. Orwell wrote a polite letter to Gollancz on 9 May 1937 to 'thank' him for the Foreword. He says that he 'liked the introduction very much', but as Sonia Brownell pointed out much later, Orwell actually disliked the Foreword and wrote his polite response 'because to do so would have been a question of good manners with him'. He was also hoping that Gollancz would publish his book on Spain, and it would not have done him any good to antagonise Gollancz over something which had happened two months earlier, and to which he could not give a satisfactory response, from his post in Spain. Interestingly, the letter was written immediately after the street fighting in Barcelona. Orwell had nearly been killed, and the most important thing to him at this time was to survive to tell the world the truth about what he had seen. As he explained in his letter to Gollancz, 'I greatly hope I come out of this alive if only to write a book about it . . . I hope I shall get a chance to write the truth about what I have seen.'
19. George Orwell, 'Notes on the Spanish Militias', written in 1939 (*CEJL*, I).
20. *Daily Worker*, 17 March 1937.
21. George Orwell, 'Inside the Whale.'
22. George Orwell, 'As I Please', *Tribune*, 15 September 1944 (*CEJL*, III).
23. George Orwell, 'Notes on the Spanish Militias'.
24. John McNair to IA, interview, April 1964.
25. Ibid.

26. 'British Author with the Militia', *The Spanish Revolution*, 3 February 1937.

27. Benjamin Lewinski to author, interview, November 1990.

28. See George Orwell, letter to Stephen Spender, 2 April 1938 (*CEJL*, I).

29. John Donovan to IA. April 1967.

30. George Orwell, *Homage to Catalonia*. Unless otherwise indicated, Orwell's comments on Spain are taken from this source.

31. Bob Edwards, 'Trenches on the Black Mountain', *New Leader*, 19 February 1937.

32. Bob Edwards, 'On the Aragon Front', *New Leader*, 5 March 1937.

33. Eileen Blair, letter to Leonard Moore, 12 April 1937 (Lilly); and letter to her mother, 22 March 1937.

34. Eileen Blair, letter to her mother, 22 March 1937.

35. George Orwell, letter to Eileen Blair, Monday [5? April 1937] (*CEJL*, I).

36. Benjamin Lewinski, letter to author, December 1990, and John Donovan to IA, April 1967.

37. 'Night Attack on the Aragon Front', *New Leader*, 30 April 1937.

Chapter Fourteen: Soldier in Catalonia

1. George Orwell, *Homage to Catalonia*. Unless otherwise indicated, Orwell's comments on Spain are taken from this source.

2. Eileen Blair, letter to her brother, 1 May 1937.

3. Bob Edwards, Introduction, *Homage to Catalonia*, Folio Society ed., 1970.

4. Eileen Blair, letter to Leonard Moore, 12 April 1937 (Lilly).

5. Details of Bob Edwards's service in Spain are taken from information in his contributions to the *New Leader*, and from John McNair's 'On the Spanish Front', *New Leader*, 12 February 1937. Although the ILP contingent reached Barcelona in mid-January, they did not take their positions at the front until 2 February.

6. Harry Milton to author, interview, March 1989.

7. Eileen Blair, letter to Laurence O'Shaughnessy, n.d. [10 June 1937].

8. See Robert Low, 'Archives Show How Orwell's 1937 Held More

Terrors Than His 1984', *Observer* 5 November 1989. Karen
Hatherley, a British student, discovered the document in Madrid.
9.   Pierre Kopp, letter to author, 24 September 1990. See also Bert
Govaerts, 'Georges Kopp', *Vrig Nederland*, 24 August 1985. I am also
grateful to Mary Kopp Wheeler for information about her father.
10. Jock Braithwaite, an ILP militiaman, said this to another man in
the unit, Stafford Cottman. Information from Cottman to author,
interview, June 1989, and from Cottman to IA, interview, July 1965.
11. Rosalind Obermeyer to IA, interview, January 1967.
12. Georges Kopp, letter to Eileen Blair, 8 September 1940.
13. Stafford Cottman to author, interview, June 1989.
14. George Orwell, letter to Rayner Heppenstall, 31 July 1937
(*CEJL*, I).
15. Richard Rees, *For Love or Money* (Carbondale: Southern Illinois
University Press, 1960), 153.
16. George Orwell, letter to Eileen Blair, Monday [5? April 1937]
(*CEJL*, I).
17. Eileen Blair, letter to Laurence O'Shaughnessy, n.d. [10 June
1937].
18. George Orwell, letter to Cyril Connolly, 8 June 1937 (*CEJL*, I).
19. In a letter to his French translator, Yvonne Davet, 19 August
1937, Orwell explains that the rejected piece for the *New Statesman*
was later published as 'Eye-witness in Barcelona', *Controversy*, August
1937. The rejected piece was not 'Spilling the Spanish Beans', as
Crick suggests (*Life*, 340).
20. Kingsley Martin, letter to Orwell, 29 July 1937.
21. George Orwell, letter to Amy Charlesworth, 30 August 1937.
22. Victor Gollancz, letter to Orwell, 5 July 1937 (Lilly).
23. George Orwell, letter to Leonard Moore, 8 July 1937 (Lilly).
24. George Orwell, 'Spilling the Spanish Beans', *New English
Weekly*, 29 July and 2 September 1937 (*CEJL*, I).
25. Fredric Warburg, *All Authors Are Equal* (London: Hutchinson,
1973), 1.
26. Fredric Warburg, letter to Orwell, 6 July 1937 (Lilly).
27. George Orwell, letter to Jack Common, 25 August 1938.
28. George Orwell, letter to Rayner Heppenstall, 31 July 1937
(*CEJL*, I).
29. Douglas Moyle to author, interview, June 1989.

30. George Orwell to Charlie Doran, 2 August 1937. Mrs Doran donated this letter to the Waverley Secondary School, Drumchapel, Glasgow.
31. Ibid.
32. George Orwell, letter to Victor Gollancz, 20 August 1937.
33. George Orwell, letter to Leonard Moore, 27 August 1937 (Lilly).
34. George Orwell, 'Why I Write'.
35. Ibid.
36. George Orwell, *Time and Tide*, 9 October 1937 (*CEJL*, I).

Chapter Fifteen: The Road to Marrakech

1. George Orwell, letter to Jack Common, 16 February 1938 (*CEJL*, I).
2. I am indebted to Barry Bloomfield, of the British Library, for using his good offices to obtain for me the relevant materials in the India Office Library concerning the *Pioneer's* job offer to Orwell.
3. Eileen Blair, letter to Jack Common, Monday, [March 1938].
4. Dr Arnold Bentley to author, letter, 19 October 1989. Unless otherwise indicated, all information about Orwell's illness in 1938 is taken from his medical files at Preston Hall Sanatorium, which are now in the care of Dr Bentley.
5. George Orwell, letter to Cyril Connolly, 14 March 1938 (*CEJL*, I).
6. Eileen Blair, letter to Jack Common, Monday [March 1938].
7. George Orwell, letter to Jack Common, Wed. [March 1938] (*CEJL*, I).
8. Ibid.
9. Victor Stacey to author, interview, June 1989.
10. George Orwell, letter to Leonard Moore, 6 December 1937 (Lilly).
11. Eileen Blair, letter to Leonard Moore, 30 May 1938 (Lilly).
12. *Observer*, 29 May 1938.
13. *Listener*, 16 June 1938.
14. George Orwell, letter to Jack Common, Tuesday [July 1938].
15. George Orwell, letter to Leonard Moore, 11 October 1938 (Lilly).
16. George Orwell, letter to Yvonne Davet, 18 August 1938.

17. George Orwell, letter to Jack Common, Tuesday [July 1938].

18. George Orwell, letter to Stephen Spender, Friday [15? April 1938] (*CEJL*, I).

19. Ibid.

20. Cyril Connolly, *The Evening Colonnade*, 337.

21. George Orwell, letter to Dorothy Plowman, 19 February 1946 (*CEJL*, IV).

22. George Orwell, letter to Jack Common, 25 August 1938.

23. George Orwell, letter to Frank (Francis) Westrope, 25 August 1938 (Eton).

24. Eileen Blair, letter to Jack Common, 20 July 1938.

25. George Orwell, letter to Jack Common, 25 August 1938.

26. George Orwell, letter to Leonard Moore, 28 June 1938 (Lilly).

27. See George Orwell, letter to *New English Weekly*, 26 May 1938 (*CEJL*, I).

28. George Orwell, 'No, Not One', *Adelphi*, October 1941 (*CEJL*, II).

29. George Orwell, letter to Naomi Mitchinson, 7 June 1938 (Texas).

30. George Orwell, letter to Jack Common, 12 January 1939.

31. Eileen Blair, letter to Ida Blair, 15 September 1938.

32. George Orwell, letter to Jack Common, 29 September 1938 (*CEJL*, I).

33. George Orwell, letter to Cyril Connolly, 14 December 1938 (*CEJL*, I).

34. George Orwell, unpublished 'Diary', 22 December 1938.

35. Eileen Blair, letter to Geoffrey Gorer, 4 October 1938.

36. Eileen Blair, letter to Marjorie Dakin, 27 September 1938.

37. Eileen Blair, letter to Mary Common, 5 December 1938.

38. George Orwell, letter to John Sceats, 24 November 1938 (*CEJL*, I).

39. George Orwell, letter to Geoffrey Gorer, 20 January 1939 (*CEJL*, I).

Chapter Sixteen: The Face Behind the Page

1. Eileen Blair, letter to Mary Common, [April 1939].

2. George Orwell, letter to Leonard Moore, 25 April 1939 (Lilly).

3. George Orwell, letter to Jack Common, Sunday [9 April 1939] (*CEJL*, I).

4. *Time and Tide*, 24 June 1939 (reprinted in *CH*, ed. Jeffrey Meyers, 154).
5. George Orwell, letter to Jack Common, 19 March 1939.
6. Richard Rees, *George Orwell: Fugitive from the Camp of Victory*, 145.
7. Eileen Blair, letter to Frank (Francis) Westrope, 29 November 1938 (Eton).
8. George Orwell, letter to Geoffrey Gorer, 3 April 1940 (*CEJL*, I).
9. George Orwell, letter to Leonard Moore, 14 July 1939 (Lilly).
10. *Tribune*, 22 February 1946. See also George Orwell to Victor Gollancz, 8 January 1940, and Orwell's unpublished 'Diary', 12 August 1939.
11. George Orwell, letter to Geoffrey Gorer, 15 September 1937 (*CEJL*, I).
12. George Orwell, 'The Limit to Pessimism', *New English Weekly*, 25 April 1940 (*CEJL*, I).
13. George Orwell, letter to Leonard Moore, 25 January 1940 (Lilly).

Chapter Seventeen: Surviving the Blitz

1. Jack Common, 'Orwell at Wallington', *Stand*.
2. Quoted in William Empson, 'Orwell at the BBC', *The World of George Orwell*.
3. George Orwell, letter to Leonard Moore, 7 May 1940 (Lilly).
4. Lettice Cooper to author, interview, March 1989.
5. See *Time and Tide*, 15 February 1941, and 30 November 1940.
6. *Time and Tide*, 9 August 1941.
7. *Time and Tide*, 21 December 1940.
8. Sir Stephen Spender to author, interview, March 1989.
9. George Orwell, letter to James Laughlin, 16 July 1940 (*CEJL*, II).
10. Quoted by Patricia Donahue to author, interview, March 1990.
11. George Orwell, unpublished lecture notes, 'Street Fighting'.
12. George Orwell, 'War-time Diary', 23 August 1940 (*CEJL*, II).
13. See George Orwell, 'The Home Guard and You', *Tribune*, 20 December 1940; and George Orwell, 'My Country Right or Left', (*CEJL*, I).
14. Fredric Warburg, *All Authors Are Equal*, 36.
15. George Orwell, 'War-time Diary', 8 April 1941 (*CEJL*, II).
16. Cyril Connolly, *The Evening Colonnade*, 345.

17. Quoted in John Thompson, *Orwell's London* (London: Fourth Estate, 1984), 49.
18. George Orwell, 'War-time Diary', 24 June 1940 (*CEJL*, II).
19. George Orwell, 'War-time Diary', 24 September 1940 (*CEJL*, II).
20. George Orwell, 'War-time Diary', 20 March 1941 (*CEJL*, II).
21. Elisaveta Fen (Lydia Jackson), *Twentieth Century*, August 1960.
22. Quoted in T. J. Fyvel, *George Orwell: A Personal Memoir* (New York: Macmillan, 1982), 135.
23. Elisaveta Fen, *Twentieth Century*.
24. T. J. Fyvel, *George Orwell: A Personal Memoir*, 105.
25. Linda Bryder, *Below the Magic Mountain: A Social History of Tuberculosis in Twentieth Century Britain* (Oxford: Clarendon, 1988), 256. See also *British Medical Journal*, 31 December 1949.
26. George Orwell, 'War-time Diary', 17 June 1940 (*CEJL*, II).
27. *New English Weekly*, 21 March 1940.
28. Clement Greenberg, letter to George Orwell, 9 December 1940.
29. *Partisan Review*, May 1949. For a close analysis of Orwell's complex attitude towards antisemitism, see David Walton's 'George Orwell and Antisemitism', *Patterns of Prejudice*, vol. 16, no. 1 (1982), 19–34. As Walton points out, Orwell's early works – especially *Down and Out in Paris and London* – contain some unkind portraits of Jews. But as Orwell became more aware of the dangers of fascism, he realised that antisemitism was a terrible evil which had no place in any civilised society, and he denounced it on many occasions. In February 1939, as Hitler's persecution of the Jews was accelerating, Orwell declared in the *Adelphi*: 'This is the worst possible moment for airing theories about the "Jews" as a mysterious and, from a western point of view, sinister entity. Even more at this moment than at most times it is important to remind people that the Jews are human beings before they are Jews.' He made his most memorable remark on the subject in *Tribune* on 28 January 1944 (*CEJL*, III): 'Antisemitism . . . is simply not the doctrine of a grown-up person.'
30. Press and Censorship Bureau, letter to George Orwell, 21 April 1941.
31. Quoted in Ruth Dudley Edwards, *Victor Gollancz: A Biography*, 307.
32. George Orwell, letter to Geoffrey Gorer, 3 April 1940 (*CEJL*, I).

Chapter Eighteen: Talking to India

1. *The Cherwell*, 5 June 1941.
2. George Orwell, 'As I Please', *Tribune*, 31 December 1943. Passage deleted in *CEJL*, III.
3. George Bernard Shaw, letter to Orwell, 26 October 1943.
4. George Orwell, 'Money and Guns', BBC broadcast, 20 January 1942. See text of broadcast in *WB*, ed. W. J. West, 71–73.
5. J. B. Clark, memo to L. F. Rushbrook-Williams, Eastern Service Director, 5 August 1943. See *WB*, ed. W. J. West, 297.
6. Norman Collins, memo to L. F. Rushbrook-Willians, Eastern Service Director, 8 December 1942. See *WB*, ed. W. J. West, 46.
7. George Orwell, letter to Rayner Heppenstall, 24 August 1943 (*CEJL*, II).
8. George Orwell, 'As I Please', *Tribune*, 20 October 1944 (*CEJL*, III).
9. Elisabeth Knight to author, interview, March 1989.
10. George Orwell, memo to L. F. Rushbrook-Williams, Eastern Service Director, 15 October 1942 (*CEJL*, II).
11. These figures are given in Laurence Brander, memo to L. F. Rushbrook-Williams, Eastern Service Director, 22 September 1943 (Caversham).
12. George Orwell, 'War-time Diary', 14 March 1942 (*CEJL*, II).
13. *Horizon*, September 1943 (*CEJL*, II).
14. George Orwell, letter to Eastern Service Director, 24 September 1943 (*CEJL*, II).
15. David Astor to author, interview, July 1988.
16. George Orwell, letter to Cyril Connolly, Saturday [1942].
17. George Orwell, 'As I Please', *Tribune*, 31 January 1947 (*CEJL*, IV).
18. George Orwell, letter to R. S. R. Fitter, 17 February 1944.
19. George Orwell, 'As I Please', *Tribune*, 31 January 1947 (*CEJL*, IV).
20. Jon Kimche to author, interview, June 1989. See also, Raymond Postgate, 'I Write As I Please', *Controversy*, March 1939.
21. Michael Foot, *Aneurin Bevan, Volume One: 1897–1945* (New York: Atheneum, 1963), 349.
22. George Orwell, 'As I Please', *Tribune*, 3 December 1943 (*CEJL*, III).

23. George Orwell, 'As I Please', *Tribune*, 31 December 1943 (*CEJL*, III).

Chapter Nineteen: Animal Story

1. Eileen's broadcast took place on 23 December 1942, on the Eastern Service. Venu Chitale's preview was broadcast on 22 December 1942. (Information from Caversham.)
2. Lettice Cooper, 'Eileen Blair', *PEN Broadsheet*, Autumn 1984.
3. Anthony Powell, *To Keep the Ball Rolling*, 71.
4. David Astor to author, interview, July 1988.
5. *New Yorker*, 17 July 1948 (*CEJL*, IV).
6. Michael Meyer, *Not Prince Hamlet* (London: Secker and Warburg, 1989), 72.
7. Julian Symons, 'Orwell: A Reminiscence', *London Magazine*, September 1963. I am grateful to Julian Symons for discussing this article with me in June 1991.
8. Malcolm Muggeridge, 'A Knight of the Woeful Countenance', *The World of George Orwell*, 169.
9. Anthony Powell, *To Keep the Ball Rolling*, 71.
10. Lettice Cooper to author, interview, March 1989.
11. Paul Potts to IA, interview, April 1963.
12. David Astor to author, interview, July 1988.
13. George Orwell, letter to Rayner Heppenstall, 21 July 1944.
14. Lettice Cooper to author, interview, March 1989.
15. 'The Freedom of the Press', *Times Literary Supplement*, 15 September 1972, and Penguin ed. of *Animal Farm* (1989).
16. Quoted in Paul O'Flinn's 'Orwell and *Tribune*', *Literature and History* (6), 1980.
17. George Orwell, 'As I Please', *Tribune*, 9 June 1944 (*CEJL*, III).
18. George Orwell, letter to Dwight Macdonald, 23 July 1944 (Yale).
19. George Orwell, 'As I Please', *Tribune*, 7 July 1944 (*CEJL*, III).
20. T. S. Eliot, letter to Orwell, 13 July 1944. For more information about Orwell's efforts to find a publisher, see my 'Orwell and His Publishers: New Letters', *Times Literary Supplement*, 6 January 1984.
21. George Orwell, letter to Dwight Macdonald, 5 September 1944 (Yale).

22. George Orwell, 'The Eight Years of War: Spanish Memories', *Observer*, 16 July 1944.

23. George Orwell, 'Back to the Land', *Observer*, 3 September 1944.

24. George Orwell, letter to Dwight Macdonald, 5 December 1946 (Yale).

25. Eileen Blair, letter to Mrs Cocking, 25 March 1945 (Caversham).

Chapter Twenty: Lost Chances

1. George Orwell, letter to Roger Senhouse, 28 February 1945.

2. Paul Potts, *Dante Called You Beatrice* (London: Eyre and Spottiswoode, 1960). Excerpt in *Orwell Remembered*, ed. Coppard and Crick, 248–260.

3. See Ernest Hemingway, letter to Cyril Connolly, 15 March 1948 (Tulsa).

4. A. J. Ayer, *Part of My Life* (London: Collins, 1977). Excerpt in *Orwell Remembered*, 210–212.

5. Eileen Blair, letter to Leonard Moore, 2 March 1945 (Berg).

6. Eileen Blair, letter to Cyril Connolly, 25 March 1945.

7. Eileen Blair, letter to Lettice Cooper, 23 March 1945.

8. Eileen Blair, letter to Orwell, 21–22 March 1945.

9. Eileen Blair, letter to Lettice Cooper, 23 March 1945.

10. Eileen Blair, letter to Orwell, 21–22 March 1945.

11. Eileen Blair, letter to Orwell, 29 March 1945.

12. George Orwell, letter to Mr Byrne, 28 June 1945.

13. Inez Holden, diary in possession of Celia Paget Goodman.

14. George Orwell, letter to Lydia Jackson, 1 April 1945.

15. George Orwell, letter to Anne Popham, 18 April 1946.

16. Paul Potts to IA, interview, April 1963.

17. Celia Paget Goodman to author, interview, June 1989.

18. George Orwell, letter to Dorothy Plowman, 19 February 1946 (*CEJL*, IV); and Arthur Koestler, letter to David Astor, January 1950.

19. George Orwell, letter to Dwight Macdonald, 4 April 1945 (Yale).

20. George Orwell, 'Revenge Is Sour', *Tribune*, 9 November 1945 (*CEJL*, IV).

21. Ibid.

22. Ibid.

23. George Orwell, 'Obstacles to Joint Rule in Germany', *Observer*, 27 May 1945.

24. George Orwell, 'London Letter', *Partisan Review*, Summer 1945 (*CEJL*, III).

25. Susan Watson to author, interview, August 1989.

26. Sally Watson to author, interview, March 1990.

27. George Orwell, 'Confessions of a Book Reviewer', *Tribune*, 3 May 1946 (*CEJL*, IV).

28. George Woodcock, *The Crystal Spirit: A Study of George Orwell* (1966; New York: Schocken Books, 1984), 28.

29. George Orwell, 'As I Please', *Tribune*, 9 February 1945 (*CEJL*, III).

Chapter Twenty-One: An Island Far Away

1. George Orwell, letter to Arthur Koestler, 13 April 1946.

2. George Orwell, 'Freedom of the Park', *Tribune*, 7 December 1945 (*CEJL*, IV).

3. George Orwell, 'British General Election', *Commentary*, November 1945.

4. Ibid.

5. George Orwell, 'Britain's Struggle for Survival', *Commentary*, October 1948.

6. Ibid.

7. George Orwell, 'Catastrophic Gradualism', *Commonwealth Review*, November 1945 (*CEJL*, IV).

8. George Orwell, 'Arthur Koestler', *Critical Essays* (London: Secker and Warburg, 1946). See also reprint in *CEJL*, IV.

9. Arthur Koestler to BBC, interview for 'George Orwell: A Programme of Recorded Reminiscences', 1960. See *Orwell Remembered*, 169–170.

10. George Orwell, letter to Anne Popham, 18 April 1946.

11. George Orwell, letter to Anne Popham, 15 March 1946.

12. *Bronda* interview with Sonia Brownell, 20 May 1963.

13. Bay Brett (Sonia Brownell's sister) to author, interview, June 1989, and Dr Michael Dixon (Sonia Brownell's half-brother) to author, interview, June 1989.

14. Diana Witherby to author, interview, March 1990.

15. Janetta Woolley to author, interview, March 1990.
16. Lys Lubbock to author, interview, November 1988.
17. George Orwell, letter to Sally McEwan, 5 July 1946.
18. Inez Holden to Ian Angus, interview, n.d.
19. Susan Watson to author, interview, August 1989.
20. Avril Blair, 'My Brother, George Orwell', *Twentieth Century*, March 1961.
21. Avril Blair, letter to Humphrey Dakin, 1 July 1946.
22. George Orwell, letter to Frank Barber, 15 April 1947.
23. See George Orwell, 'As I Please', *Tribune*, 8 November 1946; and see 'Vogue Spotlight', *Vogue* (US ed.), 15 September 1946. Orwell was also the subject of an article in *Time*, which described him as 'tall, pale, chronically ailing' (4 February 1946).
24. Avril Blair, 'My Brother, George Orwell'.
25. George Orwell, letter to Sonia Brownell, 12 April 1947 (*CEJL*, IV).
26. George Orwell, letter to Anthony Powell, 8 September 1947 (*CEJL*, IV).
27. George Orwell, letter to Victor Gollancz, 14 March 1947 (*CEJL*, IV).
28. George Orwell, letter to Victor Gollancz, 25 March 1947 (*CEJL*, IV).

Chapter Twenty-Two: Love and Death

1. George Orwell, letter to Roger Senhouse, 22 October 1947.
2. George Orwell, letter to Celia Paget, 27 October 1947.
3. George Orwell, letter to Brenda Salkeld, 1 September 1947
4. Lucy Dakin quoted in Stephen Wadhams, *Remembering Orwell*, 190–192.
5. George Orwell, letter to David Astor, 9 October 1948.
6. George Orwell, letter to Middleton Murry, 20 February 1948.
7. David Astor to Dr Dick, letter, 19 February 1948.
8. George Orwell, letter to Julian Symons, 20 April 1948 (*CEJL*, IV).
9. George Orwell, letter to David Astor, 4 May 1948.
10. George Orwell, letter to Tosco Fyvel, 18 December 1948.

11. Richard Rees, *George Orwell: Fugitive from the Camp of Victory*, 150.

12. George Orwell, letter to David Astor, 12 January 1949, and to Gwen O'Shaughnessy, 17 April 1949.

13. For a very readable account of the development of drugs in the treatment of tuberculosis, see Mark Caldwell's *The Last Crusade: The War on Consumption* (New York: Atheneum, 1988).

14. George Orwell, letter to Jack Common, 27 July 1949.

15. George Orwell, letter to Richard Rees, 17 April 1949.

16. George Orwell, Unpublished Notebook, [1949].

17. George Orwell, letter to *Tribune*, 17 January 1947.

18. George Orwell, 'Burnham's View of the Contemporary World Struggle', *New Leader*, 29 March 1947 (*CEJL*, IV).

19. Richard Rees, letter to IA, 10 June 1967.

20. George Orwell, Unpublished Notebook, [1948].

21. George Orwell, 'Burnham's View of the Contemporary World Struggle', *New Leader*, 29 March 1947 (*CEJL*, IV).

22. George Orwell, letters to Leonard Moore, 20 January 1949 and 22 January 1949 (Berg).

23. George Orwell, letter to Richard Rees, 8 April 1949 (*CEJL*, IV).

24. *New Statesman*, 18 June 1949; *New Yorker*, 18 June 1949; *Evening Standard*, 7 June 1949; and *New York Times Book Review*, 31 July 1949.

25. George Orwell, 'Just Junk', *Evening Standard*, 5 January 1946.

26. George Orwell, letter to Francis Henson, 16 June 1949 (CEJL, IV).

27. George Orwell, 'James Burnham and the Managerial Revolution', *Polemic*, May 1946 (*CEJL*, IV).

28. George Orwell, letter to Fredric Warburg, 16 May 1949 (*CEJL*, IV).

29. Quoted by Diana Witherby to author, interview, March 1990.

30. Ibid.

31. George Orwell, letter to David Astor, 18 July 1949.

32. Dr Morland, letter to Fredric Warburg, 25 May 1949.

33. George Orwell, letters to Fredric Warburg, 20 May, and Friday [27 May 1949].

34. George Orwell, letter to David Astor, 25 August 1949.

35. *Star* (London), 17 September 1949 (Colindale).

36. Janetta Woolley to author, interview, July 1988.

37. Stephen Spender, *Journals: 1939–1983* (London: Faber, 1985), 109.
38. George Orwell, letter to Richard Rees, 3 March 1949 (*CEJL*, IV).
39. Humphrey Dakin to IA, interview, April 1965.
40. George Orwell. Unpublished Notebook, [1949].

Epilogue

1. Inez Holden to Ian Angus, n.d.
2. Malcolm Muggeridge, *Like It Was* (New York: Morrow, 1982), 369.
3. Jane Dakin to author, interview, July 1990.
4. Cyril Connolly to Lys Lubbock, Tuesday [April 1950]. This letter can be found in Special Collections, Mugar Memorial Library, Boston University.
5. For a period of seven years, Sonia was Mrs Michael Pitt-Rivers. She married Pitt-Rivers in 1958, four years after the infamous trial in which he was accused of commiting an act of 'indecency' with two RAF men. He was convicted and sentenced to eighteen months. Writing to Cyril Connolly on 15 July 1958, Sonia offered one explanation for her decision to marry again: 'We Virgos find ourselves compelled to make alliances with others (in this case Gemini!).' Sonia and Michael Pitt-Rivers divorced in 1965.
6. Diana Witherby, letter to the editor, *Listener*, 17 February 1983. David Plante's book concerned three 'difficult' women – Jean Rhys, Sonia Orwell and Germaine Greer. *Difficult Women: A Memoir of Three* (London: Gollancz, 1983; New York: Atheneum, 1983).

Acknowledgements

I owe my primary debt of gratitude to Mark Hamilton, the literary executor of the Orwell estate. At every stage in the writing of this book, his support was steadfast and his counsel was wise.

Anyone who is a serious student of Orwell's work must be grateful to Ian Angus for his diligent efforts, over many years, to collect and preserve important documents. A great deal of valuable information about Orwell is available because Ian Angus took the trouble to track it down. He is a resourceful literary detective, a scrupulous editor, and a generous friend.

Many people who knew Orwell have given me assistance, patiently submitting to interviews in person or over the telephone. For taking time to answer my questions, I am happy to thank David Astor, Richard Blair, Guinever Buddicom, Jacintha Buddicom, Dennis Collings, Lettice Cooper, Stafford Cottman, John Craxton, André Deutsch, Patricia Donahue, Anne Dunn, Bill Dunn, J. C. de Vine, Major-General H. R. B. Foote, Celia Paget Goodman, the late Sir Lawrence Gowing, Cyril Hampton, Waldemar Hansen, Sir Frederick Harmer, Monica Hunton, Robert Kee, Jon Kimche, Elisabeth Knight, the late Lys Lubbock Koch, the late John Lehmann, Benjamin Lewinski, Donald Macnabb, Harry Milton, Catherine Moncure, A. B. Money-Coutts, Jane Dakin Morgan, Douglas Moyle, the late Roderigo Moynihan, Peter Quennell, Janetta Woolley Parladé, Paul Potts, Anthony Powell, Brenda Salkeld, Sir Stephen Spender, Lady Spender, Victor Stacey, Richard Steele, Geoffrey Stevens, Mary Struve, David Sylvester,

Julian Symons, Sally Watson, Susan Watson, R. W. G. Willis, Diana Witherby.

For additional information relevant to Orwell's biography, I am happy to thank Dr Eric Anderson, Reverend George Appleton, Dr Arnold Bentley, Douglas Blackwood, William Blackwood, the late Bay Brett, Lady Brewis, Elizabeth Christie, Peter Davison, Dr Michael Dixon, F. S. V. Donnison, Clive Fleay, Miriam Gross, J. B. M. Horner, K. Martin Horswell, Jessica Ingleby, Pierre Kopp, W. H. Tydd, Mary Kopp Wheeler, G. E. D. Walker, W. J. West, Rosemarie Wilkinson, Theon Wilkinson.

Among librarians I owe a special debt to Gillian Furlong and her assistants at the George Orwell Archive, University College, London. They were unfailingly helpful, prompt and friendly. I want also to thank Sid Huttner of the McFarlin Library, University of Tulsa; William Cagle and Saundra Taylor of the Lilly Library, Indiana University; Michael Meredith of the School Library, Eton; Andrew Griffin of the India Office Library, London; Barry Bloomfield of the British Library; Marie Lewis of the Eastbourne Central Library.

For encouragement and assistance I am grateful to Ann Angus, Ronald Baker, Leslie Barratt, Eleanor Blair, John Coldstream, Tom Derrick, Mary Ann Duncan, Lisa Glass, Bill Hamilton, Lady Selina Hastings, Terry Karten, Phoebe Koehler, Peter and Deirdre Levi, Cecil Nelson, Ed Pease, John Rodden, Jack Rollins, Nicholas Shakespeare, June Shelden, Stuart and Sophie Sperry, Dorothy Stowe, D. J. Taylor, Stephen Wadhams, Tom Weldon.

For their love and support, I am deeply grateful to Sue, Sarah, and Vanessa.

Index

Initials EB and GO refer to Eric Blair and George Orwell, both being
used where appropriate – see author's note on page ix